THE POCKET DICTIONARY OF AMERICAN SLANG is compiled from the first full-sized dictionary of American slang ever published—a pioneering work devoted to establishing a comprehensive reference book of the substandard level of American language. A work ten years in preparation, the *Dictionary of American Slang* is the combined effort of the late Harold Wentworth, editor of the *American Dialect Dictionary,* and Stuart Berg Flexner, a senior editor of *The Random House Dictionary of the English Language.*

Contained here are definitions of almost all of the slang words in common use today, providing an inexpensive working dictionary based on the entries of the most authoritative work in the field and its supplement of new terms and phrases.

THE POCKET DICTIONARY OF AMERICAN SLANG is an abridgment of the *Dictionary of American Slang,* published by the Thomas Y. Crowell Company, and available in a hardcover edition at $7.95.

THE POCKET
DICTIONARY OF
AMERICAN
SLANG

A popular abridgment of the *Dictionary of American Slang*

Compiled and Edited by

HAROLD WENTWORTH
and STUART BERG FLEXNER

PUBLISHED BY POCKET BOOKS NEW YORK

THE POCKET DICTIONARY OF AMERICAN SLANG

Thomas Y. Crowell edition published June, 1960

A *Pocket Book* edition
1st printing........January, 1968

CONTENTS

EDITOR'S NOTE

This abridgment of the DICTIONARY OF AMERI-
CAN SLANG contains approximately 50 percent of the
original hardcover book and its supplement, including
almost all of the most common slang words in use today.
The publisher has omitted the least common entries,
those no longer popular or highly restricted in their use.
All words designated in the original edition as of taboo
usage have also been omitted.

To reduce the size of the original book further, much of
the scholarly apparatus has been omitted from this edition, such as literary citations, some cross-reference material, and various features of the Appendix. The
scholar or reader who wants the examples that date and
illustrate usage, more extensive commentary, the qualified
usages, and discussions of the sociocultural factors influencing the creation of slang words and the linguistic
processes involved in their formation will, of course,
still find the complete hardcover volume and its supplement available.

I am very pleased that the DICTIONARY OF AMERI-
CAN SLANG is now available to all in this inexpensive
paperback edition, and hope that this abridgment will
serve as an up-to-date working slang dictionary for many
general readers and those with an interest in and
curiosity about the American language.

STUART BERG FLEXNER
March, 1967

EXPLANATORY NOTES

A BRIEF EXPLANATION of the kind of information found in a typically full entry in the text will make this dictionary more useful. But first a note on the selection of the words themselves: In addition to including as large and representative a body of American slang as possible, some colloquialisms, cant, jargon, argot, and idioms frequently used in popular novels and movies appear because the user is likely to encounter them and want to know what they mean. Moreover, in a few instances standard words are also listed because many readers still consider them slang and will expect to find them here. Naturally, priority has been given to popular and historically valuable slang words over words having but little or routine use. Entries come from every period of American history, but the emphasis is placed on modern slang. Certain categories have, by and large, been minimized: popular nicknames, abbreviations, and affectionate names for regions, states, and cities, and their inhabitants. All but the most popular neologisms and recurring nonce words have been rejected. Many words referring to the particular maneuvers and plays in sports have been excluded, but some true slang deriving from sports has been included. Many words referring to specific styles of dress, coiffure, food, etc., have been omitted; but the more popular, such as *black cow, crew cut, dagwood* are included. Finally, words coined and popularized for a season or two by the fashion industry or by advertising are largely excluded. Trade names are, for the most part, ignored.

The entries themselves conform to the following pattern:

Entry words. Each entry word appears in boldface type. The absolute system of alphabetization is used: multiple-word entries are listed in alphabetical order as if they were spelled as one word. Phrases and clauses which are solely and completely slang are normally entered under their first word; phrases and clauses which are slang only because a key word is used in a slang sense are listed under that slang word in almost all instances.

Since many slang words are seldom found in print, confusion exists about exact spelling and the use of hyphens. Where several variants exist, they are listed in decreasing order of popularity. When a phrase or clause may have alternate wording, the alternate words are given in parentheses, in decreasing order of popularity. When a phrase or clause includes a direct or indirect object (depending on who is being spoken to, or whether the object is animate or inanimate), the possible variant noun or pronoun uses are bracketed.

Parts of speech. Single-word entries are labeled with their usual basic part of speech in italics before the definition. Many entries may be commonly used as several parts of speech and are so marked before the appropriate definition. One of the characteristics of modern slang is the blurring of parts of speech, the converting of a word historically used as one part of speech into another part of speech. Many words used historically as nouns are now used as verbs, as the standard "*to orbit* a satellite." Adding all such functional shifts would have unnecessarily lengthened this dictionary; but some of the most frequent are included.

Definitions. If a word is commonly used as more than one part of speech, definitions for other forms are given. When a word has more than one meaning for any part of speech, each is numbered in boldface type. When simple definite histories of the various meanings are known, the definitions are given in chronological order of origin.

When etymologies and original usage dates are not well established or easy to follow, the various meanings are listed in decreasing order of popularity or interest. When it may not be obvious that one meaning has evolved from a previous one, an arrow ($\rightarrow$) is placed before the dependent meaning. Quotes around slang words are used only to show that a word having both slang and standard meanings is used in its slang sense when this might not be obvious or to indicate that a word is referred to as a word rather than for its meaning.

Etymologies and comments. Etymologies are given only when they are valuable and of interest. Many etymologies are omitted as being obvious from glancing at the word; others are unknown; still others are so complex or so fully given in the standard etymological works[1] that they are only summarized or hinted at here. In any case, only the slang etymologies are included; if a slang word originated from a standard English or a foreign word, further etymologies of these origins are not given.

Italicized comments are added to many definitions and entries. These usually refer to possible origins, primary group users, approximate dates of origin or peak popularity, or to the spirit with which the word is uttered.

A lower case *c* before a date means *approximately.*

Some words are labeled as being colloquial *(colloq.),* primarily associated with World War II *(W.W.II),* or used primarily by major subgroups, as *railroaders' use, hobo use,* etc. Such comments are general: *railroaders' use* may refer to words used only by engineers, brakemen, or conductors; *hobo use* covers all uses by hoboes, tramps, and vagabonds, who actually differ greatly in their way of life and attitudes; *underworld use* covers many specific groups, most words being further restricted to pickpockets, counterfeiters, confidence men, etc.

Words marked *W.W.II use* may have originated before the war or late in the war; the label only indicates that the use is associated with or was very popular during W.W.II. *Army use* and *Navy use* are comments referring to the regular Army and Navy, meaning that the word has seen continuing use in those branches of the Armed Forces, as opposed to words made popular by the large number of men in uniform during wartime.

The comments *cool use, swing use,* etc. are also general, making no distinction between East and West Coast origins or between use by actual musicians and fans. The comment *jive use* primarily refers to Harlem jive use *c*1935, though some jive terms originated outside of Harlem and before and after this approximate date of the peak of jive term popularity. The comment *Negro use* primarily refers to the slang of Negroes living in large, industrial, Northern cities; *lunch-counter use* refers to all types of small restaurants, coffee shops, etc., and most frequently to waiter and waitress uses coined *c*1935; *teenage use* refers to those words first popularized by that group; *prison use* refers only to convict use, but prison guards eventually pick up many of these terms. Words marked *archaic* in general use may still be quite popular among certain older and regional groups.

Cross references. When a word is a less popular slang synonym for another word an $=$ sign tells the reader to turn to the major word where a more complete definition is given.

---

[1] Interested readers would enjoy browsing in Skeat's or Weekley's etymological dictionaries, the many volumes of the *Oxford English Dictionary,* or the volumes of *A Dictionary of American English.*

Abbreviations

abbr. abbreviation, abbreviated
adj. adjective, attributive adjective
adv. adverb, -ial, -ially
advt. advertisement, advertising
Am., Amer. American
anon. anonymous
ant. antonym
appar. apparently
approx. approximately
art. article
attrib. attributive, -ly, attributed

bk. book
Brit. British, Briton

c. *circa*, about
cap. capitalized
colloq. colloquial, -ly, -ism
conj. conjunction

def. definition; definite
derog. derogatory, derogatory use
dial. dialect, -ical
dict. dictionary

E. east, eastern
ed. edition; editor
e.g. *exempli gratia*, for example
Eng., Engl. England, English
equiv. equivalent
esp. especially
est. established
ety. etymology, etymological
euphem. euphemism, euphemistic, -ally
exclam. exclamation, exclamatory
expl. expletive

f. and the following page
fem. feminine
ff. and the following pages
fig. figurative, figuratively
fn. footnote
Fr. French

freq. frequent, -ly; frequent use

gen. generally
Ger. German

Hebr. Hebrew
hist. history

i. intransitive
i.e. *id est,* that is
indef. indefinite
inf. infinitive
interj. interjection
intr. intransitive

l. line
lit. literal, literally
ll. lines

mag., Mag. magazine
masc. masculine
ms. manuscript
n. noun; nominative
N. north, northern
naut. nautical, nautical use
newsp. newspaper
no. number
N.W. U.S. Northwest U.S.
N.Y.C. New York City

obj. object; objective
obs. obsolete
occas. occasional, -ly, occasional use
orig. original, -ly

p. page
partic. participle
perh. perhaps
pl., plur. plural
pop. popular, -ly
pp. pages
pred. predicate
prep. preposition
pret. preterit (past tense)
prob. probably
pron. pronoun
prop. proper
ptc. participle
pub. published; publication

ref. refer; reference

S.   south, southern

s.   section

sing.   singular

sl.   slang

Sp.   Spanish

specif.   specifically

stand.   standard; standard usage

subj.   subject; subjunctive

suf.   suffix

Sup.   Supplement

SW   southwest, southwestern

syl.   syllable

syn.   synonym, -ous

synd.   syndicated

t., tr.   transitive

univ.   university

usu.   usually

v.   verb

var.   variant

v.i.   verb intransitive

vol.   volume

v.t.   verb transitive

W.   west, western

W.W.I   World War I

W.W.II   World War II

&   and

=   equivalent in meaning to; means, denotes

+   and; combined with, added to (in etymologies)

→   from which is derived, whence

[ ]   encloses words not in the slang expression (as direct and indirect objects)

( )   encloses variant words which may or may not be used as part of a slang expression

THE POCKET
DICTIONARY OF
AMERICAN
SLANG

A. *n.* Fig., a high or the best grade; success; ability.

a —. 1. Lit. and fig., a portion, share, or order of something. 2. Sometimes used as a sing. possessive pronoun = my, your, his or her. Thus "I didn't get a share of the profits" often = I didn't get my (rightful or expected) share. 3. Always used before certain sl. words or phrases, often when "the" is expected, often to give a colorful or underworld connotation. 4. Often used to mean "an order of—" when said before a specific dish. Thus "a cup" = an order of a cup of coffee and "a bowl" = an order of a bowl of soup. *In this dictionary such expressions are listed under the second or main word of the phrase.*

AA. *n.* Antiaircraft gun; antiaircraft fire. *W.W.I and W.W.II use.*

ABC's. *n.* 1. The alphabet. 2. The basic facts or skills of any job or field of endeavor.

Abe's cabe. *n.* A five-dollar bill. *Orig. jive use, c1935; rock-and-roll use since c1955.*

Able. *n.* The first of the three squads in an Army platoon.

A-bomb. *n.* 1. Any exceptionally fast hot rod; a car with a powerful or souped-up motor. *Hot-rod use since c1955.* 2. An atomic bomb. *Colloq. since c1945.*

abortion. *n.* 1. Any plan or act that is so unusual as to be a travesty; something that is a complete failure or does not succeed as planned or expected; any entertainment or performance that is so dull or inferior that it seems a travesty. 2. Any cheap or inferior item or object; esp. an item of poor design or quality when compared to a superior one. *Some student and young adult use since c1945.*

accidentally-on-purpose. Describing a wilful action so carried out as to appear accidental or adventitious; maliciously; slyly. *First used c1885; in vogue at frequent intervals since. Pop. student use c1940.*

ac-dc; ac/dc. *adj.* Bisexual. *Some jocular use since c1940.*

ace. *n.* 1. A one-dollar bill. 2. Any person of proved and outstanding skill in a given field of endeavor. 3. Any agreeable, generous, kind male person. 4. The first item in order of importance. 5. = ace in the hole. 6. A person skilled in any specific work. *Colloq.* 7. Specif., an Air Force fighter pilot who has shot down at least five enemy planes. *Air Force use since W.W.I.* 8. = prince. *adj.* Excellent; diligent; proficient; skilled; experienced. —s. *adj.* Agreeable; first rate; generous; pleasing; kind; the best. *Use. Since c1950; from ace. adv.* O.K., all right.

ace-deuce. *n.* Three, esp. a three or trey of playing cards. —y. —y. *adj.* 1. High and low; containing extremes of high and low numbers or positions; both right and wrong, or embodying contradictory elements. *Orig. sports use. From card games in which the ace is the highest and the deuce the lowest card.* 2. Containing a variety of ideas or materials; general in appeal; so vague, generalized, or inclusive as to offend no one; satisfactory; O.K. *Prob. reinforced by confusion with okey-dokey.*

ace-high. *n.* In the card game of poker, a hand containing an ace but no pair, or a straight having an ace as the highest card. *adj.* Successful, respected. *Since c1880.*

ace in the hole. 1. Any important fact, plan, argument, person, or thing held in reserve until needed, esp. until needed to turn failure into success. *From stud poker.* 2. An ace faced down on the table so other players are not aware of it. *Since c1920, colloq.*

ace up [one's] sleeve. A surprise; an ace in the hole. *Colloq. From the cardsharp's trick of hiding needed cards in his sleeve.*

ack-ack. *n.* An antiaircraft gun;

antiaircraft fire. *W.W.I and W. W.II use.*

across, get. 1. To explain successfully; to be understood, comprehended, or accepted. *Colloq.* **2.** = get away with.

across, put. *v.i., v.t.* **1.** To perform or execute deceitfully; to swindle or cheat. **2.** To present an idea or plan so that another comprehends it. *Colloq.*

across the board. 1. A type of horseracing wager in which equal amounts of money are bet on the same horse to win, place, and show. *Sporting use since c1935.* **2.** Inclusive; pertaining in the same ratio to all members of a group. Thus an "across the board" raise to the employees of a factory is a raise given to each employee at the same time and in the same percentage of increase. *Mainly labor union and political use; since c1940.*

action. *n.* **1.** Gambling activity, esp. fast play for high stakes. **2.** Activity; excitement. **3.** A plan, proposition, proposal, esp. for a business or social project.

ad lib; ad-lib. *v.t., v.i., n., adj.* **1.** To speak extemporaneously; to deviate from a written script; to improvise in music. **2.** To make a spontaneous, short, witty remark. *Colloq.* **3.** To contribute new elements to a discussion or other undertaking, whether or not they are desirable. **4.** A remark or passage that a performer interpolates in an established script or musical score.

adobe dollar. A Mexican peso. *S.W. dial. use.*

A for effort. A phrase applied, sometimes disparagingly, to those who have blundered or failed in spite of great earnestness.

African dominoes. Dice. *Usu. jocular. Game of "coups" was first introduced from France in New Orleans, where large Negro and Creole population quickly accepted it. Since c1920.*

African golf = African dominoes.

air. *v.i., v.t.* **1.** To jilt. **2.** To broadcast by radio or television. *Colloq.*

air, get the. To be jilted; to be fired from one's job; to be dismissed, as by a lover or friend.

air, give [someone] the. To dismiss an employee, lover, or friend; to reject or jilt; to throw out; to snub someone. *First common c1920; still in wide use.*

air, go up in the. 1. To miss a cue or forget one's lines; said of an actor. *Theater use.* **2.** To lose self control through vexation; to become angry, confused, or excited.

air, take the. To go away. *imp.* Go away!

air [one's] belly. To vomit. *Dial.*

air-breather. *n.* **1.** A jet airplane whose fuel is burned by being mixed with air taken into the engine during flight. *Air Force and pilot use.* **2.** A guided missile whose fuel is burned by being mixed with air taken into its engine during flight. *Air Force and rocketry use.*

airing, take [someone] out for an = take for a ride.

air out. To stroll; to saunter. *Orig. Negro use.*

airs, put on. 1. To assume manners, refinement, or prestige which one does not have. **2.** To act or be snobbish or aloof.

air strip. A single concrete, asphalt, or hard-packed earth strip used as an airplane runway in takeoffs and landings.

aisles, in the. Fig., so humorous or entertaining that the audience falls out of their seats for freer expression of their exuberance. Said of an audience wowed by a superlative stage show.

akey-okey. *interj.* & *adj.* O.K.; all right; satisfactory.

alfalfa. *n.* **1.** Whiskers; a beard. *Dial.* **2.** Money; esp. a small insignificant sum of money. Lettuce.

Alibi Ike. One who habitually makes excuses or offers alibis for his actions.

alkied; alkeid; alkeyed. *adj.* Drunk.

alky; alki; alchy. *n.* 1. Alcohol; specif. liquor. *"Alky" is now the only common form.* 2. Methanol as used for engine fuel. 3. Commercial alcohol. 4. A drunkard, esp. a jobless, homeless alcoholic.

all. *n.* Everything or everyone; anything or anyone. *Often added to a stand. or sl. v.t. after "it," esp. in utterances of exasperation, anger, or desperation; e.g., "Damn it all," etc. adv.* Completely; thoroughly. *Often used before sl. verbs and phrases for emphasis, thus: "All balled up," "all burned up," "all dolled up," etc.*

alley apple; alley-apple. 1. A piece of horse manure. 2. A rock or stone.

alligator. *n.* 1. A jive or swing music enthusiast; a hep person. *Mainly swing use. Usu. shortened to "gator" or "gate." Common in the rhyming "See you later, alligator" = Good-by, which saw wide swing use and still has some general use.* 2. A white jazz musician. *A mildly disparaging term used by Negro jazzmen in New Orleans, c1915 and later.* 3. A jitterbug. *c1935.*

alligator, make like an = drag ass. *Because an alligator's tail drags on the ground. Some teenage use since c1955.*

alligator bait. [derog.] A Negro, esp. one from Florida or Louisiana. *Dial.*

all in. Exhausted; tired. *Colloq. since c1910.*

all-out. *adj.* Complete, thorough, exhaustive. *E.g., "He made an all-out effort." Colloq.*

all-right. *adj.* Dependable, trustworthy, friendly; also hep. *Usu. attrib. use.*

all right already. "That's enough, my patience is at an end; stop talking, teasing, criticizing, or nagging." *The most common "already" phrase*

all shook; all shook up. Excited, stimulated, disturbed, upset. *Orig. rock and roll use, c1955; at present the only major rock and roll contribution to general sl.*

all six, hit on. To do well; to do all that one is capable of doing. *Orig. in ref. to the smooth-running automobile engines when all six cylinders were working well.*

all the way. 1. Completely; for all time; without reservation. *Usu. used to indicate agreement or support for a person or venture.* 2. Chiefly in phrase "to go all the way" = sexual intercourse, or complete sexual satisfaction as opposed to necking or a feel. *Mainly student use.*

all wasted. 1. Wrong, inappropriate; not adequate. *Cool, far out, and beat use since c1955.* 2. Not hip. *Mainly beat use.*

all wet. Mistaken, misguided, wrong; esp. convinced of, portraying, or loudly arguing a mistaken idea or belief. *Colloq. since c1930.*

along, get. To make a living; to exist; to continue living one's life regardless of adversity or disappointment.

along with, go. To agree with a suggestion, idea, or person; to accept another's idea, plan, or deduction.

already. *adv.* Sometimes used at the end of a phrase or sentence to indicate emphasis, immediacy, impatience, or exasperation. Thus "Let's go already," or "Shut up already." *Sometimes jocular use,* implying Yiddish speech patterns.

also-ran. *n.* One who fails to achieve a specific goal; in general, a person whose talent or luck is only moderate. *From the horse-racing term = a horse that has finished no better than fourth in a race.*

alter kocker; alter cocker. An elderly but active man, usu. one who is stubborn or shrewd.

altogether, in the. Naked. *Colloq.*

alum; alumn. *n.* An alumnus or alumna.

alvin; Alvin. *n.* A rustic; an unsophisticated or inexperienced person; one who can be hoaxed easily. *Some carnival, circus, and underworld use.*

alyo. *n.* 1. Any routine task; a state of calm or safety; a person who is not easily excited or confused. *Mainly underworld and sports use.* 2. An agreement between criminals and police, leading to protection and safety for the criminals; the fix.

am. *n.* An amateur performer or actor; a ham.

amateur night. 1. Fig., any time or place in which professional workers or athletes perform ineffectively. 2. Any occasion in which many children or youths participate. 3. Any occasion of sexual intercourse between a male and a chance acquaintance who is not a professional prostitute.

ambish. *n.* Ambition; aggressiveness. *Theater use.*

ambulance chaser. Lit., a lawyer who follows an ambulance to the scene of an automobile accident or other disaster to offer his professional services to the injured; an unethical or overly aggressive lawyer. *Since c1920.* Fig., a shyster.

Ameche. *n.* A telephone. *From Don Ameche, an actor who played the film role of Alexander Graham Bell, founder of the Bell Telephone Company. Usu. jocular use.*

Americano. *n.* American; specif. a person from the United States.

ammo. *n.* 1. Ammunition of all kinds. *Since c1930; common W. W.II use by Armed Forces.* 2. Any information or other material that can be used as evidence in an exposé, argument, defense, or the like. 3. Money.

ammonia. *n.* Carbonated water. *From its resemblance to ammonia water, possibly reinforced by spirits of ammonia, also added to nonalcoholic drinks during Prohibition era.*

amp. *n.* An ampere. *Colloq.*

amscray. *v.i.* To scram; to beat it. *The most common word carried over from Pig Latin to sl.*

anchor. *n.* A pickax. *Hobo, railroad, and labor use since c1915.*

anchor man. In sports, the player who defends his team's goal or goal line.

—— and. *conj.* → *n.* Conventional lunch-counter usage to signify the second of two items that always go together; e.g., "coffee and" = coffee and doughnuts, "ham and" = ham and eggs, "pork and" = pork and beans, etc.

And how! = You said it!—an emphatic affirmative. *Colloq. since c1920.*

and such. "And similar items."

angel. *n.* 1. One who donates money to a politician's campaign fund. *Since c1920.* 2. One who finances any undertaking, esp. a stage show or play. *Theater use since c1925.* 3. A thief's or confidence man's victim. *Underworld use since c1935.* 4. A homosexual, esp. one who plays the male role and supports or frequently buys gifts for his partner. *Since c1935. v.t.* To finance an enterprise, esp. a stage play or show. *Theater use since c1935.*

angel teat. 1. Any mellow whisky with a rich bouquet. 2. Any pleasant or easy task.

angle. *n.* 1. One's selfish motive; any unethical way of profiting or benefiting. 2. That part of a plan, action, or scheme from which a person hopes to profit or benefit. 3. The profit or benefit a person expects to gain from a seemingly altruistic or profitless plan, action, or scheme.

animal. *n.* 1. = pony: a literal translation of a foreign text used unfairly. *Some student use since c1920.* 2. Any ugly, vulgar, or sexually aggressive person. *Student and Army use c1940–c1950.* Cf. beast.

ankle. *v.i.* To walk; to amble. *Orig. c1935.*

answers, [one who] knows all the.
1. A wise guy; a person who has a
brash or audacious answer to
everything. 2. A cynic; one who
claims to have seen and done
everything and cannot feel enthusiasm.

ante. *v.t., v.i.* 1. In poker, to contribute one's share to the pot before a hand is played. 2. To put
up money for any wager. 3. To
contribute to any undertaking. *n.*
In poker, each player's initial
wager, or his share of the pool or
pot established before a hand
dealt.

ante up. *v.t., v.i.* = ante.

anti. *n.* One who is not in favor of,
or who is against, any specific
plan or action. *From the stand.*
prefix.

ants. *n.pl.* Anxiety; concern; eagerness; lust; anger. *From* ants in
[one's] pants.

ants in [one's] pants, to have. Fig.,
to fidget with anxiety, anger, lust,
or eagerness.

A-number-1; A-number-one = A-1.
A more emphatic form. Colloq.
since c1835. From the way in
which ships were once classified,
Class A, Number 1 being the
newest, fastest type of ship.

any, get. To have sexual intercourse; lit. to "get" sex. *Often in*
the male greeting, "Getting any?"
= "How is your sex life?"

anyhoo. *adv.* Anyhow. *A jocular*
mispronunciation considered so-
phisticated c1945–c1950.

any old. Any; typical, a typical
example of; unspecified; e.g.,
"any old house," "any old woman," etc. *Since c1910.*

A-1; A-one. *n.* Any excellent or
first-rate person or thing; the
best; the most agreeable. *Often*
used attrib.; colloq. adj. Superior; likable.

ape. *n.* 1. The apex; the climax;
the ultimate. *Far out, beat, and*
rock and roll use c1958. 2. A
hoodlum or strong-arm man; a
gorilla. *adv. & adj.* Good; well;
the best; completely; thoroughly

exciting or satisfying. *Far out,*
beat, and rock and roll use.

apple. *n.* 1. A fellow, a guy. *Usu.*
preceded by an adj., e.g., "smooth
apple," one who is or thinks he
is suave or charming; "wise ap-
ple," an impertinent youth. Col-
loq. 2. The earth; the globe. 3.
Any large town or city. 4. A street
or district in which activity or
excitement may be found. 5. A
ball, esp. a baseball. *Since c1925.*
6. A bomb or hand grenade; a
"pineapple." 7. = alley apple. 8.
= square.

applebutter. *n.* Smooth talk; idle
conversation. *Dial.*

apple knocker; appleknocker. *n.*
A farmer; a rustic; an experienced or unsophisticated person.

apple-pie. *adj.* Neat; perfect; orderly; easy. *Usu. attrib. or pred.*
adj. use. Colloq.

apple-polish; apple polish. *v.i. &*
v.t. To curry favor; to bestow
flattery in order to gain personal
advantage. *Not as old as apple-*
polisher. —er. *n.* One who curries
favor with a superior, specif. a
student who truckles to his teacher. *Student use since c1925. Com-*
mon since c1935. From the tra-
ditional figure of the student who
gives his teacher an apple as a
gift.

apple-shiner; apple shiner. *n.* =
apple-polisher.

appropriate. *v.t.* 1. To steal or take
something, usu. an item of small
value. 2. To obtain something by
pilferage. *W.W.II Army use.*

apron. *n.* A bartender. *From the*
white apron bartenders wear.

aqua. *n.* Water. *Some student and*
jocular use since c1915; from the
Latin.

aquarium. *n.* A Roman Catholic
rectory, priest's house, or chaplain's quarters. *Some student and*
Army use. Because the fish live
there.

Arab; arab. *n.* 1. Any wild-looking
person; an excitable or passionate
person. *Since c1850.* 2. Any dark-
complexioned person, esp. if belonging to a group traditionally

considered to be somewhat excitable or primitive in emotional matters; specif. a Jew or a Turk. **3.** A huckster or street vendor, esp. those who possess a Central European or Middle Eastern cast of countenance.

Arkansas toothpick. Any hunting knife when used for fighting, esp. a Bowie knife; a bayonet. *Since c1840; now dial.*

Arky; Arkie. *n.* **1.** A migratory worker from Arkansas. **2.** Any poor Southern farmer, esp. a sharecropper. **3.** A farmer who fled the dust-storm region of the West, specif. Oklahoma, during the 1930's. *From confusion of "Arkie" and "Okie."*

arm, on the. 1. On credit; credit; often implying that no payment will be made. *Based on "on the cuff."* **2.** Free of charge.

armchair general. Fig., one who freely gives his opinions on technical matters with which he is not personally concerned and on which he may be ill informed; a kibitzer; a Monday morning quarterback. *Orig. W.W.II use.*

arm on [someone], put the. 1. To detain or restrain by physical force, specif. to arrest. **2.** To hit with the fist; to beat up. **3.** To ask for, demand, or borrow money from.

armored cow. *n.* Canned milk; powdered milk. *Ex. of term supposedly common in the Armed Forces but actually synthetic.*

armored heifer = armored cow. *Synthetic.*

Armstrong; armstrong. *n.* A high note or series of notes played on a trumpet, esp. in jazz. *From Louis Armstrong, jazz musician who first exploited the instrument's upper register.*

arm-waver. *n.* One whose enthusiasm, self-righteousness, patriotism, etc., leads to wild arguments or inopportune speeches.

army banjo = banjo.

around the bend; around-the-bend. Having completed the longest, most difficult, or crucial part of a task.

arrive. *v.i.* **1.** To attain success; to become accepted in a profession or social group. *Colloq.* **2.** To become or be hip. *Orig. jive use c1935.*

art. *n.* **1.** Photographs of wanted criminals. **2.** Newspaper photographs of celebrities. **3.** = pinup. —*y adj.* Pretentiously artistic; ostentatiously bohemian in speech or manner. *Since c1900, colloq. since c1930.*

article. *n.* **1.** A person. Usu. modified by an adjective of quality; e.g., a "smart article," a "slick article," etc. **2.** A fellow, a guy; esp. a person considered shrewd or quick to advance his own interests.

artillery. *n.* **1.** A revolver, pistol, shotgun, knife, or other hand weapon. *Since c1920; associated with underworld use.* **2.** A hypodermic needle. *Drug addict use since c1935.*

ash can; ashcan. *n.* A high-explosive depth charge used by surface ships to destroy submarines. *USN use since W.W.I. From their appearance.*

Asiatic. *adj.* Crazy; wild; eccentric; *W.W.II USN use.*

ask for it. Lit. and fig., to ask for trouble; to act in a way that invites trouble. *Since c1900.*

asleep at the switch. Off one's guard; unaware or unwary; derelict in one's duty. *From railroad use.*

ass. *n.* A fool; a stupid or foolish person. *Colloq.* —*y adj.* **1.** Mean; malicious; stubborn; impolite; debased. **2.** Shiny, said of the seat of a pair of trousers or a skirt.

at liberty. Unemployed.

attaboy! *exclam.* = That's the boy! An expression of approval for deserving behavior or a successful performance. Also "attagirl!" *Since c1910.*

aunt; Aunt. *n.* **1.** A brothel madam; an old prostitute. **2.** An elderly male homosexual. —*ie n.*

1. = aunt. 2. An antimissile missile. *Air Force use.*

Aussie. *n.* An Australian. *Since W. W.I.* **adj.** Australian. *Not derog.*

author. *v.t.* To write or compose, as a book, play, or the like.

auto. *n.* An automobile. —**mobile.** *n.* A fast worker; a fast-moving, fast-talking, or fast-thinking person. *Orig. Amer. Yiddish sl.*

Auzzie. *n.* = Aussie.

aw. *interj.* A speech sound signifying disapproval, disappointment, disbelief, etc.; often followed by an additional sl. word or phrase, as "Aw, gee!" "Aw, heck!" "Aw, nuts!" etc. *Colloq. Exceedingly common in speech but seldom adopted in literature, even in vernacular writing.*

away. *adv.* 1. In prison. *Underworld use.* 2. In baseball, out; used only in phrase "There is one away," "There are two away," etc., meaning there is one out, two are out, etc.

away, put. 1. To commit to an asylum or jail. *Colloq.* 2. To knock unconscious, usu. by a blow from a blunt instrument. 3. to kill. 4. To eat or drink. 5. To classify; to categorize.

away, put it. To eat large quantities of food; to eat voraciously.

away with [something], get. 1. To win or capture; to succeed. 2. To do something that is illegal or forbidden without getting caught or punished. Often in the phrase "get away with it." *Since c1920, the most common use.* 3. To steal or take something; to make a getaway with something. 4. To finish eating or drinking something.

awful. *adj.* Very unpleasant; very sad; exceedingly disagreeable, ugly, unskillful, or otherwise objectionable. *Colloq.* —**ly.** *adv.* 1. Very; very much; a general intensive. *Colloq.* 2. Very badly. *Colloq.*

A.W.O.L.; a.w.o.l; awol. Absent without leave. *Armed Forces use since W.W.I. Used to designate a soldier who does not answer roll-*call but has not been away long enough to be classified as a deserter. *Since c1935 the letters have been pronounced and written as one word. Also occasionally used in nonmilitary establishments, e.g., schools.*

ax; axe. *n.* A musical instrument, esp. in a modern jazz context. *Far out and beat use.*

ax, get the. To be fired or dismissed; lit., to be severed from one's employment or school, or from a relationship.

ax, give [someone] the. To fire or dismiss someone; to fire an employee; to dismiss a student from school; to dismiss one's boy friend or girl friend.

ax, the. *n.* 1. Fig., a sudden separation from one's job; a firing or discharge. → 2. A dismissal from school. → 3. Rejection by one's fiancé, lover, etc. *All uses colloq.*

axle grease. Butter.

ax to grind. 1. A grievance, esp. one that the complainant wishes to discuss. *Colloq.* 2. An idea, cause, argument, etc., to which one continually reverts; an obsession.

B

B. *n.* Benzedrine. *Orig. narcotic addict use; some student use since c1950.*

Babbitt. *n.* A smug, self-satisfied conformist; specif., a middle-class, successful, small-town businessman who does not question society or the prevailing ethics, politics, homey virtues, religion, etc. *From the chief character in the novel* Babbitt, *by S. Lewis.*

babbling brook. A talkative woman; a chronic talker, esp., a gossip.

babe. *n.* A girl, a woman of any age; specif., a sexually attractive girl or young woman. *Implies familiarity, or that the girl or young woman is spirited.* **Babe.** *n.* A large, fat man; esp., a large, fat baseball player;—used as a nickname. *As irony, and because many fat men have baby faces.*

Reinforced by Babe Ruth, the baseball star of the 1920s who was a heavy-set man. —s. *n. sing.* = babe.

Babe-Ruth. *n.* In baseball, a home run. *From Babe Ruth, the famous home-run hitter.*

baby. *n.* 1. = babe, esp. one's sweetheart or a babe who is the object of one's special attention. *Since at least c1900. "Babe" is more common = a girl; but "baby" alone may have the connotation of "sweetheart."* 2. A man, a fellow, a guy; esp., a mean or intimidating man; a tough guy. 3. Anything which, like a baby or a "baby," is the object of one's special attention, interest, or masculine admiration or affection; anything that gives a man pride or a feeling of power to possess, create, or build; that with which familiarity or association gives a man a feeling of masculine pride or power.

baby doll. A pretty girl.

baby kisser. A politician, esp. one campaigning for public office. *Because the traditional politician is supposed to shake the hands of adults and kiss babies in an attempt to seem friendly and win votes.*

baby-sit; baby sit. *v.i.* To stay with a child or with children while the parents are away; to be responsible for a child or children in the absence of the parents. *The person who baby sits may be either a professional, as a nurse or a teenager who works for a fee, or a friend or relative who assumes the responsibility as a favor.* —ter. *n.* One who baby-sits. *Orig. teenage use c1945; now very common among all age groups.*

baby-skull. *n.* An apple dumpling. *Archaic and dial.*

bach; batch. *n.* bachelor; an unmarried man. *Since c1850. v.i.* To live alone; to live as a bachelor. *Since c1870; often used in "to bach it."*

bachelor girl. An unmarried, self-sufficient young woman who lives alone or with another woman. *A euphem., the term often implies that the woman is unmarried by choice, usu. because of her devotion to a career.*

back. *v.t.* To give one's support to a person, project, or plan; lit., to wager one's money on the success of someone or something.

back, get off [someone's]. To stop harassing, teasing, criticizing, or otherwise molesting someone; usu. a command or entreaty. *Lit.* = "stop riding me." *Very common during and since W.W.II.*

back, on [someone's]. 1. A phrase used with the verb "to be" to signify the action of criticism, teasing, or harassment. 2. A phrase used with the verb "to be" to signify a moral, emotional, financial, or physical dependency. 3. Teasing, criticizing, nagging, or annoying a person acutely or constantly.

back alley. 1. Any alley, street, or part of a cheap, disreputable section of a city or town; a slum area; a section of a city or town where vice abounds. 2. A slow, sensuous type of jazz, played in a rhythm as if accompanying a strip-tease dance or even coitus and often with the instruments imitating human sounds.

Back Bay. *adj.* Fashionable, wealthy.

backbone. *n.* Courage; perseverance; honesty.

back-cap. *v.t.* To disparage. *Some use since c1890.*

back-gate (-door) parole. The death of a prisoner, from a natural cause. *Underworld and prison use.*

back number. A thing that or, esp., a person who is old-fashioned, out of date, or behind the times; a has-been. *Still in use. From the term as applied to old magazines no longer on current sale at magazine stands.*

back off. 1. To stop teasing, annoying, or riding someone. *Usu. an imperative or an entreaty.* →

2. To slow down; to speak slower or explain in more detail; to ease one's foot off the gas pedal of a car in order to slow its speed. *Teenage use since c1950.*

backroom. *adj.* Of, by, for, or from political expediency; associated with the people or opinions concerned with current politics.

backroom, boys in the. Those politically wise; politicians, their staffs, and friends.

back talk. Impudent talk; an impertinent retort. *Colloq.*

back up. *v.t.* To support, verify, testify in favor of, or back a person, statement, or plan. *v.i.* To talk slower, to explain more fully, to restate or repeat.

back up, to have one's. To be angry, to be in an angry or critical mood.

back yard. Collectively, the performers in a circus, as opposed to the administrative staff. *Circus use.*

bad. *adj.* Eminently appropriate or suitable; excellent, wonderful; orig., adroitly played or arranged. *Cool and far out use. In order to be cool and to demonstrate a lack of emotion, cool and far out sl. and jargon sometimes relies on understatement. Saying that something one likes or considers good is "bad" is, of course, the ultimate understatement.* —**die.** *n.* **1.** The villain in a movie, play, or other entertainment; an actor who plays the role of a villain, a heavy; specif., a movie bad man. **2.** A criminal, hoodlum, or tough guy; a mischievous person. **3.** An unsuccessful attempt.

bad actor. 1. A mean, vicious, or poorly trained animal. **2.** A mean, malicious, or deceitful person. **3.** A confirmed criminal.

badge bandit. 1. A motorcycle policeman. *Hot rod use.* → **2.** A policeman. *Some general teenage use since c1955.*

badger; badger game, the. *n.* **1.** A method of blackmailing a man whereby a female accomplice of the blackmailer entices the victim into a compromising sexual situation, at which point the blackmailer enters and theatens exposure of the man unless money is paid. *Since c1920.* → **2.** Fig., any blackmail, extortion, or intimidation; any deception for personal or political gain.

bad man. Orig., in the cowboy days of the old West, a villainous robber and psychopathic murderer; now, in movies about the old West, a robber or gunman; the villain.

bad news. A bill for money owed, esp., as given personally to the customer by a waiter in a nightclub.

bad time. 1. = hard time. **2.** A situation that is dangerous, frightening, or uncomfortable. **3.** time that has been spent in the guardhouse and is not credited toward one's required period of military service. *Some Army use during and since W.W.II.*

Baedeker. *n.* A guide book. *From Karl Baedeker, of Leipzig, Ger., publisher who issued a series of travel guide books.*

baffle-gab. *n.* The ambiguous, verbose, and sometimes incomprehensible talk or writing often done by bureaucrats; officialese.

bag. 1. An unattractive or ugly girl or young woman; an old woman, esp. a gossipy old shrew. *Since c1925. Orig. and still derisive, but now freq. used as a term of jocular familiarity or even affection, as by a man in talking or referring to his wife or sweetheart, or by a woman talking in a jocular mood about a friend or herself; the "old" connotation thus may become "old friend," or a humorous ref. to one the same age as the speaker.* **2.** In baseball, a base. *Since before 1930. v.t.* **1.** To dismiss an employee from his job. **2.** To arrest a person. *From the now stand. to bag = to seize.* **3.** To be unnecessarily absent from school; to skip school. *May be regional use.* —**gage.** *n.* A girl or woman, esp. one's wife, sweetheart, or date. —ger. *n.* In baseball, a hit that enables the batter to reach the specified base. *Thus two bagger = a double; three bagger = a triple; four bagger = a home run.* —ging. *n. =* bagplay. —man. *n.* One who is assigned to collect bribe, extortion, or kidnaping money.

bag, in the. 1. Certain; sure; safe; secure; cinched. 2. Rigged or fixed in advance, as a crooked sporting event. 3. Completed successfully.

baggage smasher. One whose work is handling baggage. *Since c1850; still used, mainly railroad, airplane, and trucker use.*

bag of wind. = windbag.

bag on, have (get, tie) a. To go on a drinking spree; to be on a drunken spree; to be drunk.

bag-play. *n.* Currying favor; an act or instance of attempting to curry favor; an attempt to impress a superior with one's ability or importance.

bag-puncher. *n.* A boxer.

bags of. Much or many. *Fig., possessing bags full of something.*

bail out. 1. To help another who has met with failure; to relieve someone of debt, embarrassment, or the like; to come to another's aid. *From "bail."* 2. To abandon a project, task, or relationship that is unsuccessful before losing further time and/or money; specif., to rid oneself of a girl friend or fiancé. *From the term = to parachute from an airplane.* 3. To make a parachute jump from a crippled airplane. *Colloq.* 4. To avoid work; to goof off. *W.W. II. Air Force and some Army use.*

bait. *n.* A man who is pretty or seems effeminate, or a woman who is handsome and seems masculine, and thus is attractive to or receives the unwanted attentions of homosexuals.

baked wind. = hot air.

Baker. *n.* Used instead of any intended word beginning with the letter "b," esp. as a euphem. for "bitch" in "son of a bitch" or for "bastard." *From the Army use as the second letter in the spoken alphabet. Some use during and since W.W.II.*

Baker flying. 1. Danger; keep off; keep out. *From USN use; a red Quartermaster B or Baker flag is flown to indicate danger, as when a ship's loading ammunition or fuel.* 2. = have the rag on.

baker's dozen. Thirteen of anything. *From the bakers' traditional custom of giving 13 when a dozen is asked for, to ensure full measure and as a bonus to the customer.*

bald. *adj.* 1. Not wrapped; usu. said of a handout lunch. *Hobo use. Usu. in "bald lump."* 2. Fig., bald-faced.

bald face(d). *adj.* Obvious; bare; fig., unmasked; usu. in "bald-faced lie."

bald-headed row. Orig. and mainly the front row of seats in a burlesque theater where wealthy, elderly men sit to have the best view; fig., men or a group of men, esp. if old, who stare at women; fig., the front row or rows of seats in any theater where wealthy, elderly men and their companions sit.

baldy; baldie. *n.* A bald man.

ball. *n.* 1. Lit., a party, esp. a wild, unrestrained, uninhibited, boisterous, or noisy party. Fig., any good time or way of life; any place in which or period during which one enjoys oneself thoroughly, and any thing or person that adds to one's pleasure or is pleasing or enjoyable; specif., that which or one who contributes to complete, unrestricted, exciting, or thrilling good times or enjoyment. *Some early c1935 Negro jive use. Orig. pop. by bop and cool use, and assoc. with jazz and avant-garde groups. Now common student and teenage use, with less emphasis on being unrestricted and exciting, and some general use. Of multiple orig.: from ball = dollar and prison allowance; of course, from ball =*

formal dance or masquerade; and at least reinforced by obs. **ball off** = *to treat or be generous, and* **goof ball** = *narcotic pill.* 2. Specif., a pill or portion of a narcotic drug, orig. marijuana. *Addict use.* 3. Specif., a passionate, uninhibited session of necking or petting; an evening or period of sexual abandonment, a sex orgy. *v.i.* To have a good time, esp. an exciting one; to play cool or far out music pleasingly; to enjoy oneself or have a good time within the cool, far out, or beat milieu; to have an uninhibited, personally satisfying, unique, cool, or beat good time. —**ing.** *n.* Having fun, esp. uninhibited, wild, or exciting fun; orig. having fun by dancing; specif., having fun by dancing, drinking, necking, in coitus, or at an exciting, wild party. *Jive and some Negro use since c1935.*

ball, get on the. To become alert, adroit, knowledgeable, or hep. *Usu. said as a command or as an urgent request.*

ball, have [oneself] a. To enjoy oneself thoroughly and without reservations, restrictions, or inhibitions; to have a good time. *Orig., c1945, bop talk; c1955 common with teenagers, college students, and others. From "ball"* = *formal dance party and "ball"* = *marijuana.*

ball, keep [one's] eye on the. To be alert.

ball, on the. 1. To be alert and have vitality and ability; to be in the know, to be hep. *First pop. assoc. with bop and cool use; some student use since c1935; common since c1940; very popular during W.W.II.* 2. Alert; active; diligent, efficient; prompt; clear-thinking. 3. In baseball, to pitch effective curves, or to have a wide variety of effective pitches, said of a pitcher. *There is no indication that this baseball use is older than the general sl. use.*

ball and chain; ball-and-chain. One's wife.

balled up; balled-up. Confused; disorganized; perplexed; abounding with mistakes or blunders. *Colloq. Orig. ref. to the accumulation of snow in the curve of a horse's hoof or shoe in winter. This could cause a horse to slip or fall and had to be removed.*

ball of fire. A brilliant, energetic person; an energetic person who strives hard for rapid success; a go-getter or dazzling performer of any kind.

balloon. *v.i., v.t.* To forget one's lines entirely during a theatrical performance; to go up in one's lines. *Some theater use.*

balloon-head. *n.* A stupid person. —**ed.** *adj.* Stupid.

balloon juice. 1. Empty, noisy talk; lit., hot air. *Some use since c1900.* 2. Gas as used in a balloon, specif. helium. *Some use during and since W.W.I.*

balloon room. A room where marijuana is smoked; a marijuana pad. *Some addict use.*

balls on [something], put. To make more emphatic, colorful, attractive, or the like.

ball the jack. 1. To go, move, or work very rapidly or fast. *Orig. logger use, from highballing.* → 2. To gamble or risk everything on one attempt or effort.

ball up. 1. To fail at recitation or on an examination. *Regional student use.* → 2. To confuse, mix up; to ruin or spoil by confusion or blundering. **ball-up.** *n.* Confusion; a mess. *Some use since c1900.*

bally. *v.i.* To attract a crowd to a side-show by describing the show loudly and sensationally, usu. on a platform in front of it, as by a barker; to advertise vocally a side-show and urge people to come and see it. *Carnival and cirus use. From "ballyhoo."* *v.t.* To urge one's wares on a crowd which one has attracted by a spiel. *Pitchmen's use.* *n.* 1. = **bally stand.** *Carnival and circus use.* 2. = **ballyhoo;** publicity. —**hoo; bally-hoo.** *n.* 1. A short, free exhibition or sample of a side-show, accompanied by a barker's spiel, given on a platform or bally stand in front of the side-show tent in order to attract spectators and lure them inside as paying customers. *Carnival and circus use since at least c1910.* → 2. Lit. and fig., advertising, favorable publicity; esp., loud, colorful advertising; lit. and fig., boisterous, happy noise created to give an impression that one's customers are satisfied, or an impression that a good or attractive performance, entertainment, product, or plan is available. 1949: "Working without benefit of ballyhoo to date, tiny Haiti has outdone itself in building a world's fair." King Features Synd., Oct. 18. *Since c1925.*

bally show. A carnival side-show; esp., one having continuous or regularly scheduled performances. *Carnival and circus use.*

bally stand. The platform in front of a side-show tent on which the barker stands, and on which a free exhibition or a sample of the show may be performed in order to lure spectators inside. *Carnival and circus use; also used by pitchmen.*

bam. *v.t.* To strike or hit. *Of imitative orig.*

bambino. *n.* 1. A baby; a young child. *From the Italian.* 2. A man, esp. a strong or tough man; a fellow, a guy. *Since c1920.*

bamboozle. *v.t.* To hoax; to deceive, trick, or swindle.

bamboula. *n.* A primitive, often erotic dance as performed by New Orleans Creoles since c1900.

banana. *n.* 1. A comedian, specif. in a burlesque show. *The most important, best, or senior comedian is the "top banana," the next is "second banana," and so on. At least reinforced by the soft, water- or air-filled banana-shaped bladder club carried as a stand. item by such comedians and usu. used to hit other come-*

dians over the head. Orig. theatrical use, but fairly well known generally. 2. A sexually attractive mulatto or light-skinned Negro woman; a trim high-yellow girl. *Some Negro use.*

banana-head. *n.* A stupid person.

banana oil. 1. = **bananas!** 2. Nonsense; insincere talk, exaggeration; bunk, apple sauce.

bananas! *interj.* Nonsense! *An expression of refutation or incredulity, usu. addressed to someone who has told a small exaggeration or lie.*

banana stick. A baseball bat made of inferior wood. *Some baseball use.*

band. *n.* A woman. *Some Negro use. Prob. from "bantam."*

bandbox. *n.* A small or rural workhouse or jail; a county jail, esp. one from which it seems easy to escape. *Some convict use. Reinforced by "bandhouse."*

bandit. *n.* An enemy aircraft. *W. W.II Air Force and Army use, orig. in combat communications.*

bandwagon. *n.* Extreme nationwide popularity of a politician, entertainer, plan, or endeavor which pays that person or persons associated with him or it well in money or prestige.

bandwagon, hop (get, jump, climb, leap) on the. To join the majority or most popular faction after withholding one's opinion or vote until the majority or relative popularity is known; to like, praise, accept, or show enthusiasm for a person, idea, or product only after popularity and general acceptance are assured; specif., to vote for or campaign for a political party or candidate after one is assured of the party's or candidate's popularity and relatively sure chances of winning an election, so as to be sure of being with the winning party or candidate.

bang. *n.* 1. An injection of a narcotic drug. *Addict use.* → 2. A thrill; excitement or pleasure. *Almost always in "to get a bang* *out of." v.t.* **1.** To have coitus (with); to fornicate. **2.** To take narcotic drugs, esp. heroin, intravenously. *Common addict use. adv.* Exactly; smack. *Colloq.*

bang-bang. *n.* A Western movie; a horse opera. *From the high incidence of gunshots in such films.*

bang out of, get a. To enjoy; to be pleasantly excited by; to get a thrill or a kick from.

bang to rights. In the act of committing a crime; dead to rights.

bang-up. *adj.* Excellent, first-rate; exciting proficient; modern, stylish; elegant;—said of both people and things.

banjo; Irish (Army) banjo. *n.* A shovel, esp. a short-handled shovel, as used to dig potatoes or dig a fox hole. *Hobo and railroad use since c1920; railroad and Army use since c1940.*

banjo hit. In baseball, a hit between the infield and outfield. *Some baseball use.*

bank on. To depend or rely on.

bankroll. *v.t.* To finance, esp. to finance a theatrical production or nightclub.

bantam. *n.* = **chick.** *Primarily Negro use.*

barbecue. *n.* **1.** A sexually attractive girl or young woman. *Negro use.* **2.** A gathering, esp. an informal social or business gathering.

barber. *n.* **1.** A talkative baseball player. *Some baseball use since c1925. Because barbers traditionally are talkative.* **2.** A baseball pitcher who is willing and able to force batters away from the plate by pitching fast balls close to their heads. *From close shave, reinforced by the famous pitcher Sal Maglie, who was nicknamed "the Barber" and was known for this type of pitch.*

barber-shop. *n.* Close-harmony singing, esp. of songs pop. *c1875–c1910. From the traditional style of barber-shop (employees') quartets.*

bareface(d); bare-face(d). *adj.* **1.** Undisguised; bold; impertinent;

obvious; said of a speech or act. *Usu. in "a bare-faced lie."* → **2.** Impertinent; bold; obvious; specif., flaunting lies, exaggerations, or unsuitable, unbecoming, unacceptable words or acts; said of a person.

barf. *v.i., v.t.* To vomit. *Some student use.*

bar-fly. *n.* **1.** A person of either sex who often and protractedly drinks at a bar; a heavy drinker of whisky; a souse, a tippler. → **2.** Specif., an alcoholic who frequents bars in order to beg or mooch free drinks from others.

barge in. 1. To walk into or enter a place without hesitation or ceremony; to intrude. → **2.** To interrupt, esp. to interrupt a conversation in order to add one's own opinion or advice; to offer or give one's advice or aid when not requested to do so; to butt in.

bar-girl = **B-girl.**

bark. *n.* **1.** Money. **2.** Human skin. **3.** Fur pelts, as used in fur coats. *v.i., v.t.* To give orders, criticize, or talk in a loud, curt, angry voice. *Colloq.* —**er** *n.* **1.** One who draws a crowd of potential customers to a sideshow tent by describing the show and introducing the performers in sensational terms; a sideshow spieler or ballyhoo man. *General use. Carnival and circus people prefer "spieler" or "talker."* **2.** A pistol; an artillery cannon. *Some continued Army and underworld use.* **3.** A funny joke or saying. **4.** a first-base coach in baseball.

bar-keep. *n.* A barkeeper or bartender.

barking dogs. Tired or sore feet.

barn-burner. *n.* Anything remarkable or sensational. *Dial.*

barn door. *n.* Any large object. *Usu. used in the colloq. phrase "big as a barn door."* —**s.** Prominent front teeth, esp. the two upper center incisors.

barney. *n.* Something done dishonestly, as a fixed prizefight or race.

barn-storm. *v.i.* To travel as an entertainer, making short or one-night stands in rural towns. —**er.** **1.** One who barn-storms; orig. an actor, now often a traveling carnival act or stunt man. → **2.** Specif., an inferior actor.

barnyard golf. The game of pitching horseshoes. *Jocular.*

barracks lawyer. A soldier who is free with unwanted advice, is argumentative, habitually complains, or pretends to a knowledge of military rules and regulations. *W.W.II Army use.*

barrel. *v.i.* To speed, to go fast; specif., to drive a car rapidly. *Since c1930, mainly student use; now general use and common hot rod use, where technically barrel = an engine cylinder.*

barrel, in the. Without money; broke. *Negro use. Fig., having no clothing and wearing a barrel.*

barrel, over a. **1.** Fig., to be helpless; specif., to be helpless before one's creditors; to be in dire need of money, to be broke and in debt, to owe a debt which one cannot pay, esp., to have too little money to continue operating a business; fig., to be in another's power, so that one has to accept business, personal, or social conditions set by another, or bear his insults and malicious words or deeds. *In allusion to the state of a person put over a barrel to clear his lungs of water after a water mishap.*

barrel-house; barrelhouse. *n.* **1.** A brothel; orig. a combination cheap saloon, brothel, and rooming house. → **2.** A tail-gate form or style of jazz; a rough and ready manner of performing, usu. associated with ensemble improvisations and a driving rhythm. *The term is a hark-back to the early days of the century in New Orleans, but whether or not it was actually used then, or only later, is uncertain.*

base, get to first. To achieve the first step toward one's objective, often intimacy with the opposite sex. *Almost invariably in the negative, "He won't get to first base with her." From the baseball term.*

base, off. **1.** A place or situation in which one is an intruder. **2.** Descriptive of an unfounded statement or a person who utters such a statement; intrusive; interfering. *From the baseball use.*

bash. *n.* **1.** Any exciting, memorable party; an exciting, or violently exciting, good time; a "ball." **2.** = jam session. *v.t.* To hit; to strike. *Colloq.*

basket. *n.* **1.** The pit of the stomach; the solar plexus.

bastard. [derog.] *n.* A despicable man; an untrustworthy, selfish, unethical man; a thoroughly disliked person of either sex; a son of a bitch. *The stand. but taboo meaning of "illegitimate" is present only as a fig. implication reinforcing "despicable." One of the most common derog. sl. terms. As many other such derog. words, this may be used between friends as a familiar, jocular, even affectionate term of address. The word is so common that virtually all children learn the sl. meaning long before they know the stand. meaning.*

bastile; bastille. *n.* A jail. *Still some use. Common in rural journalism and facetious speech.*

bat. *n.* **1.** A prostitute, orig. one who walks the streets; a promiscuous woman. *Used mainly by youths and students.* → **2.** A girl or young woman; esp., an unattractive or ugly girl. *Mainly used by youths and students. Since c1910. Not necessarily uncomplimentary.* → **3.** A gossipy or mean old woman; a shrew or termagant. *Colloq.* **4.** A spree; specif., a drinking spree, a binge. **5.** A jockey's whip. *Common horse-racing use. v.i.* To go on a spree or binge; to carouse.

bat, go to. To be sentenced to prison.

bat, on a. On a drunken spree.

bat against [someone], go to. To testify against someone.

bat around. To loaf or idle; to move, seek entertainment, or live aimlessly.

batch. *v.* = bach.

batch out. To start and accelerate a hot rod from a standing start. *Hot rod use since c1955.*

bateau. *n.* A boat. *From the Fr. Dial. and some jocular use since c1700.*

bat for [someone], go to. To come to the aid of someone; to stand up for; to stick up for; to defend someone. *Common.*

bat [one's] gums. To converse; to talk idly but volubly; to chat. *W.W.II Army use.*

bath, take a. To go into bankruptcy.

bat hides. *n.pl.* Paper money.

bathtub; bath-tub. *n.* 1. A motorcycle sidecar. *The most common use.* 2. A very large car, as a limousine or an old touring car. 3. A small ship.

baton. *n.* A club, esp. a policeman's club or nightstick.

bat [something] out. To create or make something quickly; specif., to create and write something, as an article, quickly on a typewriter.

bats. *adj.* Crazy; nuts. *From bats in [one's] belfry.*

bats in [one's] belfry, have. To be crazy, very eccentric, or odd.

batter. *v.t.* To solicit a person for a gift, as of money, food, or the like; to beg of passers-by in the street; to knock on a door with intent to beg. *Hobo use. v.i.* To beg food, money, or the like; to beg.

battery acid. Coffee. *W.W.II Army use.*

bat the breeze. To gossip; to talk, esp. to talk idly. *W.W.II Army use.*

battle-ax. *n.* A stout, sharp-tempered, mean, and/or belligerent woman, usu. an old woman.

battlewagon. *n.* 1. A battleship. *Orig. USN use; now generally known.*

batty. *adj.* Crazy; nuts. *Colloq. From "bats in [one's] belfry."*

bawl. *v.i., v.t.* To weep. *Common use.*

bawling out. A loud angry reprimand. *Since before c1915.*

bawl out; ball out. To scold someone angrily and usu. loudly; to reprimand. *Colloq. Since before c1910.*

bayou blue. Inferior or bootleg whisky. *Dial and archaic.*

bay window. A person's, esp. a man's, protuberant stomach or abdomen. *Colloq.*

bazoo. *n.* A person's mouth, esp. regarded as an organ of speech. *Since c1860. From the Dutch "bazuin" = trumpet.*

bazooka. *n.* A small, antitank rocket launcher. *W.W.II Army use. From the musical instrument of comedian Bob Burns, which resembled a length of 2-inch pipe.*

B-boy. *n.* A mess sergeant. *Some W.W.II Army use reported. From "busboy," based on "B-girl."*

beach, on the. Out of work; unemployed. *Radio employee use; from nautical use.*

beagle. *n.* A sausage. *From "dog."*

beak. *n.* 1. A lawyer. *Some archaic underworld use.* 2. A person's nose.

beam, off the. Incorrect, wrong, mistaken; not pertinent or applicable; functioning poorly. *Popular c1940–c1945.*

beam, on the. Correct, right; fig., on the right track or course; functioning well; on the ball; said of people. *Since c1940; from aviation use. Popular during W.W.II.*

bean. *n.* 1. The head; specif., the human head. *By far the most common use. If not orig., at least pop. by baseball players and announcers.* 2. A commissary or mess sergeant; a cook or cook's helper; usu. as a nickname. *Some Army use since W.W.I. v.t.* To hit a person on the head with a stone, club, or other weapon. specif., to hit a baseball batter on the head with a pitched ball. **—s.**

n.pl. money —ery. *n.* 1. A restaurant, specif. a cheap one. *Still used. From "bean wagon."* 2. A jail. *Some dial. use. Because beans are a traditional staple of the prison diet.* —ie. *n.* Specif., a skull cap which covers only the crown of the head; any cap or beret. *Since c1945, mainly children and student use. From "bean"* = head.

bean ball. A pitched baseball that intentionally or unintentionally comes near or hits the batter's head.

bean-eater. *n.* 1. A resident of Boston, Mass. *Because Boston baked beans are the traditional favorite of Bostonians.* 2. A Mexican, esp. a poor Mexican. *Dial.*

bean pole; bean-pole; beanpole. *n.* Any tall, skinny person. *Fig.,* one as tall and slim as a bean pole.

bean rag. A red pennant flown from a ship to indicate that only a minimum crew is on duty because it is mealtime; a red pennant raised at mealtime. *USN use.*

beans. *n.* Nothing. *interj.* An expression of disbelief.

beans, know [one's]. To know the facts of or be skilled in one's chosen field of endeavor.

bean-shooter. *n.* 1. = bean, *n.sing.* 2. A small-caliber pistol.

bean wagon. Any small restaurant, often having only a lunch counter and stools, with no tables and chairs, that serves inexpensive meals and snacks quickly and with a minimum of ceremony.

bear. *n.* A remarkable, first-rate person or thing; a humdinger. = beast, an ugly girl. *Some teenage use since c1955. adj.* Tending to favor low or stable values and prices of corporate stocks; favorable to the holding of, or long-term investment dealing in, corporate stocks. *Stock market use, common.* —ish. *adj.*

bearcat. *n.* A powerful, aggressive person; an excellent or fervent fighter.

beard. *n.* An intellectual person;

an egghead; a cool, far out, or beat person; a member of the avant-garde. *Bop musicians introduced beards, usu. goatees, into fashionable hip society. Since the early 1950s beards have become somewhat common, as a mask of nonconformity, with various avant-garde, cool, far out, beat, and intellectual groups.*

beast. *n.* 1. A cheap prostitute or B-girl; fig., one who preys on men. *Orig. pop. by W.W.II USN use.* → 2. An ugly girl; a disliked girl. *Student and teenage use since c1945.* → 3. Any girl, whether ugly and stupid or beautiful and passionate, but esp. the latter. *Modern jazz use.* 4. A fast, experimental airplane; a fast airplane that is difficult or dangerous to handle. *W.W.II Air Force Use.* 5. A high-powered car, esp. a hot rod that has been souped up with great success. *Hot rod use since c1950.* → 6. A rocket or guided missile. *Some Armed Forces use since c1950.* —ly *adj. & adv.* Awful; unpleasant; awfully; very. *Universally known.*

beat. *n.* 1. A loafer; a moocher. *Since c1860. From "deadbeat."* 2. Lit. and fig., a neighborhood, area, or field of endeavor in which an employee is assigned to work. *Orig. the area assigned to a foot policeman, and which he walked and guarded; specif., the area or field of endeavor from which a reporter gathers news. Colloq.* 3. News published first in a given newspaper; the reporting and publishing of a news item by a newspaper before its competitors; a scoop; the news item so reported. *Newspaper use since c1870.* 4. The rhythm of a piece of music; specif., the basic rhythm of a jazz performance as accented by the drums, bass viol, and other rhythm instruments. *Mainly jazz use; has been adopted more and more by classical musicians.* 5. = hipster; the world and time of the hipster; fig., the generation of the hipster;

any attitude, belief, fashion, fad, or manner characteristic of hipster life. *Common since c1955.* adj. 1. Physically exhausted, tired, completely weary. *Since c1930; wide student and teenage use since c1945.* → 2. Emotionally exhausted; exhausted by emotional or nervous strain or concentration; discouraged. *A logical growth from the previous meaning; pop. by bop use c1946;* → 3. = beat up; dilapidated or disheveled; ugly. *Negro jive use since c1935.* 4. Intensely believing in and protecting one's own true nonemotional, nonintellectual, nonsocial, amoral identity, to the exclusion of any commercial, material, and social interests or desires; cool; in rapport with, believing in, or appreciative of hipsters and their attitudes, beliefs, fashions, and fads; of, by, for, or pertaining to the hipster or hipsters' attitudes, beliefs, fashions, or fads. *v.t.* 1. Orig., to ride free of charge, or, specif., to avoid paying one's fare on a train; to avoid paying, as a bill owed to a merchant; to see an entertainment without buying a ticket of admission. *Orig. hobo use. Now general use. From "deadbeat."* → 2. To escape or avoid punishment or a reprimand.

beat around. To wander aimlessly, as a pastime or in search of fun; to loaf or idle.

beat around the bush. To talk around a subject, to avoid being frank and direct in talking, esp. in telling someone bad news or expressing one's opinion or conclusion.

beat [one's] brains out. To work hard in an attempt to solve a problem; to attempt to solve a tedious, difficult, or complex problem.

beaten down to the ankles. Completely exhausted or beat.

beaten-up. *adj.* = beat-up.

beat [one's] gums (chops). To talk, esp. to talk volubly but

without point. *Assoc. with hip use, but pop. by W.W.II Armed Forces use. Often in the negative as "now you're not just beating your gums"* = now you are talking sensibly.

beating, *a. n.* 1. A defeat or loss that one has suffered. 2. A massage; a facial.

beat it. To go or go away; to leave or depart; to scram; —often as an imperative, as to children or inferiors. *Common since c1905, when it replaced "skedaddle."*

beatnik. *n.* A beat person; one who lives a beat life; specif. any atypical member of the beat generation. *Orig. synthetic newsp. use, now becoming common.*

beat out [something]. 1. To play a piece of jazz emphasizing the rhythm or tempo. 2. In baseball, to reach first base safely on a bunt or a weakly hit ball by running fast enough to arrive at the base before the ball thrown by the fielding player. 3. To compose on a typewriter or to typewrite rapidly. 4. To talk about or discuss something. *c1935 jive use.*

beat pad. A marijuana joint, esp. one which sells inferior reefers.

beat the band, to. To do anything excessively, intently, or remarkably. *Since c1900.*

beat the drum. 1. To talk too much. → 2. To brag, advertise, or seek attention or appreciation.

beat the rap. To be acquitted of a legal charge in court; to escape punishment.

beat [someone's] time. To court or pay too much attention to another's girl or boy friend; to become a competitor for a girl someone else is courting; esp. to win the girl someone else has been courting; to win out over a rival. *Student use since c1930.*

beat to the ground. Completely beat or exhausted.

beat-up. *adj.* 1. Dilapidated, worn out, shabby, damaged; said of things. 2. Ugly, disheveled; said of people.

beat up [one's] gums (chops) = beat [one's] gums (chops).

beat [one's] way. To travel without paying; to travel in the cheapest possible manner.

beaujeeful; beaugeeful. adj. Ugly; garish; in bad taste, loud, corny. From the Jewish immigrant mispronunciation of "beautiful." To turn a word into its antonym by mispronouncing it is common, but such corruptions are usually nonce words.

beaut. n. An unusually beautiful or remarkable person, thing, or situation; specif., a beautiful woman. Often used ironically when applied to things or situations. Since c1850. From "beauty."

beaver. n. 1. A full beard. 2. A person wearing a beard. 3. One who works diligently; a hardworking, diligent, active man. Since c1850; colloq.

bed, go to. To go to press; to be printed.

bedbug. n. A Pullman porter, traditionally Negro. Railroad and Negro use.

beddie-weddie. n. A bed. One of the more common baby-talk terms used by adults in talking to young children.

bed house. A brothel. Some Negro use.

bedrock. n. The basic facts; the the underlying facts. adj. Basic.

bedstead = flying bedstead.

bed with [someone], go to. To have sexual intercourse with someone.

bee. n. An obsession; any unusual or unfounded idea or belief which another cherishes. From "bee in one's bonnet."

beef. n. 1. A complaint, esp. a complaint to the police; the cause of a complaint; an argument, a quarrel. Since c 1900; from the older "cut a beef." 2. A fat or husky person. 3. A customer's bill or check. Some hotel, night club, and restaurant use. v.i. To complain, find fault, protest or object; specif., to complain to the police, to inform; to argue or quarrel. —er. n. 1. One who complains; esp. an habitual complainer. Since c1915. 2. A football player. —ing. n. Complaining; arguing; quarreling.

beefeater. n. 1. An Englishman. 2. A strong, muscular person.

beef-squad. n. A gang of tough men or hoodlums organized or employed for any specif. violent purpose.

beefsteak. v.t. To saddle or ride a horse so poorly that his back becomes raw, as a beefsteak. Some cowboy use.

Beefsteak and Onions. The Baltimore and Ohio railroad. Hobo use, with some jocular use by those otherwise acquainted with the term.

beef trust. n. Any group of stout or fat people; specif., a chorus of large, stout, or fat girls or women, or a baseball or football team composed of exceptionally large, stout, or fat players.

beef up. 1. To slaughter a cow for beef. Lit. = to store up on beef by slaughtering a cow. Rural use. 2. To kill deliberately, as troops in battle.

bee in [one's] bonnet, a. An idea, exp. an eccentric or obsessive idea or an unfounded conviction. Colloq.

beekie. n. 1. Any nosy person. From "beak." 2. A company spy.

been = has-been.

been had; been taken; been took. To have been taken advantage of, deceived, cheated, or tricked; overcharged, sold misrepresented merchandise; swindled.

bee on [someone], put the. 1. To ask a person for a loan or gift of money. The more common use, equally as common as "put the bite on [someone]." 2. To make a request of a person. 3. To harass; to annoy. All uses since c1920.

beer belly. 1. A greatly protruding abdomen; lit. and fig., assumed to be caused by excessive drinking. *Since c1920.* → 2. Any man with a protruding abdomen.

beer-jerker. *n.* One whose work is drawing beer from a bar tap into glasses or growlers; a waiter or waitress who serves beer.

beer-joint = **joint.**

beer up. To drink a lot of beer.

bees and honey. Money.

beeswax. *n.* Business. *Usu. in* "Mind your own beeswax" = "Mind your own business" and "none of your beeswax" = "none of your business." *Common in child speech since c1920; also some adult euphem. use.*

beetle. *n.* 1. A girl. → 2. *Specif.,* an independent, ultramodern, somewhat tomboyish girl, typically one with a short hair style, a preference for wearing slacks, a good education, and an interest in jazz, bullfighting, and motorcycles. *Though not as common, the beetle is to the post-W.W.II period what the flapper was to the post-W.W.I period. Intellectually, she is close to the "lost generation" and has contributed much to the "beat generation."* 3. A race horse. *cf.* roach. 4. A Volkswagen automobile, made in Germany. *From its appearance.*

beeveedees. *n.* = **B.V.D.'s.**

beewy. *n.* Money, esp. coins or small change. *USN use, from pronouncing "B.W.I.", the abbr. for British West Indies. All traders in the Caribbean area understand the question, "How much beewy?"*

beezer. *n.* 1. A person's nose. *Orig. hobo and prize fight use.* 2. The face; the head. *Various ety. have been suggested.*

Be good. *interj.* Good-by; so long. *Fairly common valediction since c1930.*

behind. *n.* The buttocks, rump. *Colloq.*

behind the eight ball. In a troublesome, unfortunate, or losing position. *From the term in the game of pool.*

beige. *n.* A light-complexioned Negro. *Negro use.*

be into [someone] for [a certain amount of money]. To owe a person a certain amount of money.

bejesus, the; be-Jesus, the. *Fig.,* the stuffing or insides of a person. *Always in such expressions as* "knock [hit, kick, beat] the bejesus out of him."

belch. *n.* A complaint; a beef. *Circus, hobo, and underworld use.* *v.i., v.t.* To complain; to 'beef'; to inform; to squeal. *Circus, hobo, and underworld use.*

belfry. *n.* The head. *Not common in U.S. except in* "bats in [one's] belfry."

bell, hit the = ring the bell.

bell, [that, it] rings a (the). To recall something to one's mind, to be remembered or recognized; to bring forth a response of recognition.

bellhop; bell-hop. *n.* 1. In a hotel, any employee, usu. a youth who carries suitcases to one's room and does other such errands; a bellboy. *Because he comes hopping in response to a bell signal.* → 2. A Marine. *In allusion to the fancy uniform. Some W.W.II use.* *v.i.* To work as a bellhop.

bell-ringer. *n.* 1. A door-to-door salesman or canvasser. → 2. A local politician. 3. A fact or bit of information that enables one to remember or comprehend something. 4. A tobacco chewer. *From the joke, common in vaudeville, of causing a bell to ring at the instant a chewer scores a bull's-eye on a cuspidor.*

bells. *n.pl.* 1. In non-nautical use, equivalent to "o'clock" in phrases telling the time of day. *This sense is derived from but is very different from the nautical sense.* 2. A vibraphone, specif., when used as a jazz instrument. *Some cool and far-out use.*

bells (knobs) on, be there with. 1. To be, fig., dressed in one's best, present in a given place; always used in the future tense, indicating enthusiasm or a definite promise to be present. 2. Emphatically; definitely. *Often used after a criticism or oath. E.g.,* "He is a jughead with bells on."

belly. *n.* 1. = belly laugh. *Mainly theatrical use.* —ache. *v.i.* To complain, esp. to complain either loudly or for a long time. *Common since c1915. n.* A complaint; a session of nagging. —r. *n.* One who complains frequently.

belly brass. *n.* Fraternity, fraternal, honorary, or civic insignia, keys, seals, decorative emblems, usu. gold, worn as charms dangling from a watchchain across the belly or chest of a vest, esp. by college youths. *c1920.*

belly-burglar. *n.* = belly-robber.

belly-buster. *n.* = belly-whopper.

belly button. The navel. *Colloq.*

belly fiddle. A guitar. *Some synthetic jazz use.*

belly-flopper. *n.* = belly-whopper.

bellyful. *n.* Fig., as much as or more than one can stand of something unpleasant; a surfeit.

belly gun. A pistol; a short-barreled revolver of any caliber, inaccurate at a distance, but effective at very close range, as at the belly of a person being held up.

belly laugh. A deep, loud, long, uninhibited laugh, esp. a convulsion powered chiefly by action of abdominal muscles. *Colloq.*

belly-robber. *n.* Any person whose work is to buy and/or prepare food, esp. a USN commissary steward, an Army mess sergeant, or a logging camp cook. *Orig. USN and Army use c1915.*

belly-rub. *n.* A dance or dancing party, esp. a student dance or dancing at a dance hall or meeting place where one may dance with strangers.

belly-smacker. *n.* = belly-whopper.

belly up to. To approach something straight on, to move straight ahead; fig., to push one's belly toward or up to something.

belly-wash. *n.* Almost any commercially prepared beverage or other drinkable liquid; whisky, beer, coffee, tea, soft drinks, or soup.

belly-whopper; belly-buster; belly-smacker; belly-flopper. *n.* In diving, the act of striking the water stomach first; in sledding, the act of striking one's stomach against the sled; in riding, to fall on one's stomach; such a dive, sled ride, or fall. *Mainly children's use. Dial. variations include belly-bump, belly-bumper, belly-bust, belly-whop, belly-flop, etc.*

belt. *n.* 1. A blow with the fist. 2. In baseball, a hit. 3. A marijuana cigarette; the effect of smoking a marijuana cigarette. 4. A swallow or swig of a drink, specif. of whisky. *v.t.* 1. To hit a blow with the fist. *Colloq.* 2. To swallow; fig., to put a swallow of something under one's belt. 3. To drink any specif. beverage, usu. a variety of whisky, habitually; to drink a lot, esp. of whisky; to drink greedily or quickly.

belt in, pull [someone's]. To prepare for hard times, a difficult job, or the like. *Colloq.*

belt the grape. To drink heavily.

bench warmer. An athlete who is not good enough to play as a regular performer with his team and hence spends most of his time sitting on the players' bench, a substitute or idle athlete. *Since c1925.*

bend. *v.t.* 1. To slur a note in playing jazz. 2. To steal. *Underworld use.* 3. To "break" a law; to violate common ethics or principles of behavior, but not break any existing law. *v.i.* To fight; to have a fight. *Some teenage street gang use. n.* Lit. and fig., a bow made, usu. by a performer in acknowledgment of applause. *Theater use.* —er. *n.* 1. A spree of whisky-drinking; often in on a bender. → 2. A spree involving something other than drinking. 3. A stolen car.

bend [someone's] ear. 1. To talk to an interested listener; to talk on an important, secret, or interesting subject. → 2. To talk too much, to bore another with talk;

to gossip or tell all of one's personal plans.

bend (crook, tip) [one's, the] elbow. To drink or tipple; to have a drink. **—s.** To drink whisky with a person, as at a bar; esp. to drink to excess.

bender, on a. On a drunken spree. *Colloq.*

bends, the. *n.* The acute pains caused by too rapid depressurization, as when a deep-sea diver returns too quickly to the surface. *Colloq.*

bend the throttle. To drive very rapidly. *Some teenage use since c1945.*

Benjamin. An overcoat. *Orig. Eng. use.*

benny; bennie; Benny; Bennie. *n.* 1. = Benjamin. *Usu. "Benny."* 2. Any amphetamine pill, esp. Benzedrine. *Addict and student use since c1945.* 3. A break in a military formation, as caused by an inexperienced soldier. *W.W. II Army use.*

bent. *adj.* 1. Drunk. *Fairly common; most pop. c1925.* 2. Having very little money; nearly broke. 3. Stolen, said esp. of a stolen car. *Underworld use.*

bent eight. A car with an eight-cylinder engine; an eight-cylinder engine. *Orig. and mainly hotrod use.*

Bermudas. *n. sing. & pl.* 1. A species of large, sweet onion; onions. 2. A species of lawn grass; grasses. 3. Knee-length shorts; walking shorts. *Pop. since c1953. The most common use of this word. All three of the above items supposedly orig. on the island of Bermuda.*

berry. *n.* A dollar. *Most common c1920–c1930. Still in use.*

best fellow. A girl's sweetheart; one's beau. *Colloq.*

best girl. A boy's sweetheart. *Colloq.*

Betsy; Betsey. *n.* 1. A gun, whether a pistol, revolver, rifle, or shotgun. 2. The sun. *Some farmer and dial. use.*

better half. One's wife. *Usu. jocular use. The most common use.*

betwixt and between. Undecided; uncertain.

bewitched. *adj.* Drunk. *Dial.*

B-girl. *n.* 1. Lit., a nonprofessional prostitute who sits in bars in order to meet prospective clients, esp. soldiers. *W.W.II use. An abbr. for "bar girl," reinforced by the connotation of "grade B."* → 2. A girl employed by a bar or cheap nightclub, either as an entertainer or as a shill, i.e., as a customer who allows male patrons to buy her drinks. *The girl may receive a commission on each such drink sold, and often the drinks given to her are only tea or colored water instead of the whisky that the male patron has paid for.* → 3. Any promiscuous girl or woman. V-girl. *Since c1938. Orig. "bar-girl."*

bialystok. *n.* A semihard, round onion roll with a hole in the center. *From the town of orig., Bialystok, Russia.*

bibble-babble. *n.* Babble.

bibful. *n.* A lot of talk, esp. by one person, and specif. gossip or talk about personal subjects.

bible. *n.* 1. Any authoritative book, listing, reference, guide, catalog, compilation of data, or set of rules; specif. the Sears Roebuck mail order catalog [rural use], the program of a circus, stage show, or movie [circus and theater use], the various Armed Forces regulations and the articles of war. [W.W.II Armed Forces use], salesman's catalog and price list, or an employee's bills or receipts which must tally with the money in the cash register. *All uses since c1930.* 2. At a circus, the hinged platform of planks that the reserved seats stand on. *So called because it opens like a book and closes with a slap.* 3. The truth.

bicycle, on [one's]. Retreating from opposing fighter, fighting a defensive fight, dodging and stepping back from blows. *Prize fight use since c1920.*

bid. *n.* An invitation, esp. to a major student social affair, as a prom, or to join a college fraternity or sorority. *Common student use since c1900; colloq.*

biddle = bindle.

biddy. *n.* 1. A woman, esp. an old, gossipy woman; a termagant or shrew. **chick.** *From "biddy" = hen, prob. reinforced by earlier meanings of "biddy."*

biff. *n.* 1. An unsuccessfully played high note on a brass instrument. *Musician use.* 2. = biffer. *Some Negro use.* *v.t.* To strike, as with the fist. *Fairly common since c1900.* —er. *n.* A homely girl who compensates for her lack of attractiveness by being promiscuous; a homely but promiscuous girl. *Some Negro use.*

big. *n.* = Mister Big. *Underworld and teenage street gang use since c1950.* *adj.* 1. Important, the most important. *Colloq.* → 2. Successful; celebrated; influential; famous; popularly accepted, esp. said of entertainers or entertainment. *adv.* Successfully. —gie. *n.* A big shot; a prominent person.

big, go over. To become a popular success, esp. as an entertainer or entertainment; said of an entertainer, song, book, or the like.

big, make. To succeed, esp. in one's chosen career.

Big Apple, the; big apple, the. 1. Any large city; specif., New York City. → 2. The main business and entertainment section or street of a city. 3. = big time, the.

big-band. *adj.* Pert. to swing or jazz music played by a large band, usu. composed of 14 to 20 men, as opposed to smaller or pick-up groups. **big band.** *n.* A large jazz band; specif., a swing band.

Big Bertha; big Bertha. 1. A type of very large, long-distance cannon used by the German forces in W.W.I; any large cannon. → 2. A fat woman.

big boy. 1. Any tall youth or man, usu. in direct address. 2. An im-

portant person, a big shot. 3. Any recognizably large or important item, specif. a hundred-dollar bill [underworld use] or a hamburger sandwich with two hamburgers on it [lunch-counter use].

big brother. Specif., a police or welfare state; any society or any aspect of any society, national organization, or accepted political belief that originates, enforces, or encourages group welfare and group values over individual freedom, thought, or emotion. *From the term as used in George Orwell's 1949 novel,* 1984.

big browneyes. The female breasts.

big cheese. 1. An important person, a big shot. 2. A stupid or rude male; a lout. *Both uses since c1925.*

Big D. Dallas, Texas.

Big Daddy; big daddy. 1. One's father. 2. = daddy. 3. An affectionate nickname, usu. used in direct address, for any male, esp. a large, active, extroverted male. *Exclusive female use. Far-out and beat use.*

big deal. 1. Anything important, exciting, satisfying, interesting, lavish, or highly publicized, be it a business deal or a social or athletic function. → 2. An important, influential, interesting, or well-known person. *Wide student use since c1940.* → 3. Sarcastically, anything or anyone believed to be unimportant, uninteresting, or unimpressive. *Wide student use since c1940. Often used as a belittling exclamation to deflate another's enthusiasm, as in reply to a suggestion or an eager proposal.*

Big Dick. In crap-shooting, the point 10.

Big Ditch, the. 1. The Atlantic Ocean. *Since c1900.* 2. The Panama Canal.

big drink. 1. The Atlantic Ocean. *Since c1915.* → 2. Either the Atlantic or the Pacific Ocean. *Since c1940.*

big drink of water. A youth or

man, esp. if tall, who is uninteresting, dull, or boring.

big eights. Long woolen winter underwear. *Some Negro use.*

big George. A quarter; the sum of 25¢. *From the face of George Washington which appears on the U.S. 25¢ piece.*

big gun. An important or influential person; a high official. *Since c1840.*

big head; big-head. *n.* 1. A hangover; any or all of the physical, mental, and psychological reactions to having consumed too much whisky on the previous night. 2. Conceit. *Colloq.* → 3. A conceited person. *Colloq.* —**ed.** *adj.* Conceited. *Colloq.*

big house, the; Big House, the. Any state or federal penitentiary. *Underworld use; universally known.*

big idea. *n.* An unwelcome suggestion, proposal, or action.

big-league. *adj.* Professional; on a large scale.

big lie, the. A major political misrepresentation or complex of misrepresentations freq. repeated by political leaders in the hope that it will eventually be believed. *A cold war term, since 1948.*

big man. 1. An important or influential man; one who is in authority. *Since c1885; colloq.* 2. = big man on campus.

big man on campus. Lit., a popular, important student, usu. a leader in social, athletic, and extracurricular activities. *Traditionally the big man on campus is much sought after by female students.*

big moment. One's sweetheart or lover. *Some student use since c1935.*

big mouth. A person who talks often and/or loudly; a person who always has an opinion to state; one who talks about the personal life of others or says things better left unsaid.

big name. A prominent, famous, or celebrated person, usu. in the field of entertainment. **big-name.** *adj.* Famous; celebrated.

big noise. 1. An important, sensational, or highly publicized statement or deed. 2. An influential person.

big number = big man.

big one. 1. A thousand-dollar bill; a thousand dollars. 2. A bowel movement. *Part of the euphem. bathroom vocabulary taught to young children.*

big one, the. An important entertainment.

big picture, the = picture, the. *Some use since c1955. From the large movie screens accommodating exceptionally wide pictures; several trade-name processes such as "Vista-Vision," "Cinerama," and "Cinemascope" were widely advertised by film makers and distributors as giving "the big picture," c1955.*

big pipe. A baritone saxophone. *Some cool and far-out use.*

big pond, the. The Atlantic Ocean. *Fairly common.*

big pot = big shot.

big rag = big top. The main tent of a circus. *Circus use.*

big red apple = Big Apple, the.

big school. A state or federal penitentiary. *Hobo and underworld use since c1920.*

big shit. [taboo] = big deal.

big shot; bigshot. *n.* A very important person, usu. one who is highly successful and famous in a specif. field, or one who is an executive or person in authority; esp. a very influential person in politics, crime, business, society, or the like. *The one-word form is not common; c1930. The term often implies dislike or distrust, and that the person has gained his importance through unethical or aggressive practices, motivated by a love of power.* **bigshot.** *adj.* 1. Very important, influential, successful, or wealthy. → 2. Ostentatious, garish, expensive; suitable for a big shot.

big stink. 1. A loud, sustained complaint, harangue, or angry commotion. 2. A scandal.

big-talk; big talk. *n.* Boastful or exaggerated talk. *v.t.* To talk boastfully to another, to talk to another as if one is superior in authority.

big time, the. Any endeavor from which large salaries or profits are obtained; the higher strata of business, crime, entertainment, sports, or the like. **big-time.** *adj.* 1. Of, part of, or pert. to the big time. → 2. Highly remunerative, highly remunerated; famous. → 3. Important; major.

big-time operator. 1. One who figures in many exchanges of favors; one who plays petty politics to achieve minor goals. *W.W.II Army use.* → 2. A student who is prominent in school and social activities; a student who is a leader in extracurricular activities and is quick to accept current fads of student dress, speech, and belief; a male student who is adroit in establishing relationships with female students. *Very common student use c1940–c1945, and has retained some popularity.*

big-timer. *n.* 1. = big shot. → 2. Esp., a professional gambler.

big-top. Specif., the main tent of a circus; generally, the circus, circusses, or circus life. *Orig. circus use; colloq. since c1890.*

big trouble, the. The depression of the 1930's. *Hobo use.*

big wheel. 1. An important, influential person; a person in authority; a big shot. *Common since W.W.II. A logical metaphor from mechanics' "to roll a big wheel" = to be important or influential, was in use before 1850. Influenced by "wheel horse."* → 2. A student important in school and social activities; a big-time operator.

bike. *n.* 1. A bicycle. *Colloq. since c1880.* → 2. A motorcycle. *Common since c1945.* → 3. A motorcycle policeman.

bikini. *n.* 1. An abbreviated wom-

en's two-piece bathing suit consisting of just enough material to cover the crotch and breasts. *Introduced c1950, this revealing style orig. in Europe; it has become somewhat modified and is now less daring than it was.* → 2. Any short, revealing bathing suit, men's swimming trunks, shorts, or other sports clothes.

bilge. *n.* Worthless talk or writing; tripe; blah. *From the seafaring term. Orig. maritime use; universally known by c1920. v.t.* To fail a student; to expel a student.

bilge out = bilge.

bill. *n.* 1. The human nose. *Colloq.* 2. A $100 bill; the sum of $100.

Bill Daley. A long lead in a race, esp. a long lead early in the race. *After "Father" Bill Daley, the famous jockey instructor, who always advised his pupils to take the lead and keep it.*

billy. *n.* 1. A policeman's club. *Since at least 1850. Colloq.* 2. A bucket or large can used for heating wash water or for cooking. *Some hobo use. From Australian use.*

billy can = billy, 2.

bim. —bo. *n.* 1. A man, esp. a strong or tough man; a fellow, a guy. *Although this meaning of "bimbo" is usu. said to be derived from "bambino," it seems to have derived from the earlier meaning of a kind of punch or blow.* 2. A prostitute; a girl or woman who is promiscuous. *Since c1930 the most common use.* 3. An insignificant, unimportant person. *Since c1840.*

bind. *n.* A predicament, as caused by conflicting obligations, an overfull work schedule, or the like; a tight spot; a jam.

bindle. *n.* 1. A blanket rolled up so that it may be carried easily across one's back, often with one's clothes and other possessions rolled up inside it; a bedroll. *Hobo use since before c1880.* → 2. Any package or bundle. *Hobo use since c1900.* → 3. Specif., a packet of narcotics, esp. when folded as an envelope. *Underworld use since c1920.*

bindle man = bindle stiff.

bindle stiff; bindlestiff. *n.* 1. A migratory harvest worker; esp. a hobo who carries a bundle of blankets or a bedroll, usu. containing all his possessions. *Since c1890.* 2. Any poor, homeless, jobless, unskilled tramp, beggar, or wanderer. *Since c1900.*

bing. *n.* A prison cell used for solitary confinement of prisoners; the hole. *Prison use.*

binge. *n.* 1. A drunken spree. → 2. A spree of any kind; a period of self-indulgence.

bingle. *n.* 1. In baseball, a hit, usu. a single. *Still common baseball use.* 2. A large supply or cache of narcotics. *Addict use.*

bingo! *exclam.* An exclamation denoting sudden action, success, or comprehension. *From the game of bingo, in which the winner shouts "Bingo!" to signify that he has won. The usage very much resembles the classical "Eureka!" = "I have found it!"*

bingo-boy. *n.* A drunkard.

binnacle list. A list of sailors too sick to report for duty; a sick list. *Some USN use.*

binny. *n.* An extra large or concealed pocket in a shoplifter's overcoat where stolen items are secreted. *Underworld use.*

bird. *n.* 1. Any man; a fellow, a guy. *The most common use.* 2. A girl or woman. *Some use since c1900; in the U.S. the word has never meant "prostitute," as it does in Brit. sl.* 3. = Bronx cheer; raspberry. *Universally known.* 4. The eagle used as an insigne of rank (U.S. Army colonel, U.S. Navy captain). *Armed Forces use since W.W.I.* 5. A rocket; a guided missile. *Military use since c1947.* 6. = yardbird. —ie; —y. *n.* A bird;—a child's word also used by adults. *adj.* Unusual, eccentric, weird. *Said of a disliked person. Common*

student use since c1955. —ies. *n.-pl.* = bird legs; —seed. *n.* Any dry, packaged breakfast cereal. —seye. *n.* A small packet or portion of a narcotic drug. *Addict use.* —wood. *n.* Marijuana cigarettes. *Addict use.*

bird-brain. *n.* A person of slight intelligence; a stupid or foolish person. *Since c1940; wide student, children, and teenage use c1945, esp. in semijocular direct address or as epithet.* —ed. *adj.* Stupid.

birdcage. *n.* 1. A prison cell. *Underworld use.* 2. A sleeping area in a flophouse. *Often the beds are separated by chicken wire to reduce the incidence of robbery.*

bird colonel = chicken colonel.

bird dog. 1. Anyone whose job is to hunt or find objects or people; specif., an antique dealer or art dealer commissioned to find a specif. object, a detective who specializes in finding missing persons, a business agent who hunts for prospective customers, a talent scout who looks for promising young entertainers, or a baseball, football, or basketball scout who searches for promising athletes. *Since c1930; because bird dogs are raised for hunting* 2. A chaperon at a school dance. *Some prep-school and college use since c1935.*

bird-dog. *v.i.* 1. To dance with or become overly friendly with a superior's girl or wife. *Mainly Army use; since W.W.II.* 2. To attempt to or to steal another's girl; to beat [someone's] time. *Student use since c1945.*

birdie. *adj.* = nuts. *A fairly new teenage use.*

bird legs. Skinny legs.

birds and the bees, the. The basic facts of sex, conception, and birth, esp. as explained to children. *Colloq.*

bird's-eye maple. *n.* A light mulatto girl, esp. if sexually attractive. *Since c1925.*

birthday suit. *n.* One's completely bare skin; a state of nakedness;

usu. in "one's birthday suit." *Because the bare skin is fig. the "suit" which one was given when one was born. Colloq.*

biscuit. *n.* 1. The face or head. *Mainly prize fight use; since c1920.* 2. Any coin; any banknote of comparatively low denomination. 3. A woman, esp. a worldly or cruel woman. *A biscuit is harder and less sweet than a cookie.*

biscuit hooks. The hands.

bistro. *n.* A restaurant; a café.

bit. *n.* 1. A prison sentence, not necessarily a short one. 2. A small part in a play or entertainment. *Theatrical use since c1920. Now colloq.* → 3. Any expected or well-defined action, plan, series of events, or attitudes, usu., but not necessarily, of short duration; one's attitude, personality, or way of life; fig., the role which one assumes in a specif. situation or in life. *Orig. bop and cool use.*

bitch. *n.* 1. A woman, usu., but not necessarily, a mean, selfish, malicious, deceiving, cruel, or promiscuous woman. *Very old. Since past studies usu. have omitted such "vulgar" words, the history of this one is hard to trace.* → 2. Any difficult or unpleasant task; anything unpleasant. *Common by c1900. Very common.* 3. = bitch lamp. *v.t.* To cheat someone. *v.i.* To complain, to gripe; to criticize; to nag. *Common since W.W.II. adj.* Substitute; makeshift; homemade; not of usual quality or value. *Like many such "vulgar" words "bitch" has a definite taboo connotation; during W.W.I this connotation became acceptable in the speech of rough or socially unacceptable people, and during and since W.W.II many such formerly taboo words have become common in the speech of many, esp. of young adults.* —y; —ey. *adj.* 1. Having the attributes of a bitch. 2. Sexually provocative; having sex appeal.

bitch box. A public-address loudspeaker. *W.W.II Army and USN use.*

bitch kitty. 1. An obstinate, disagreeable, or bad-tempered girl or woman. → 2. A difficult or disagreeable task. *Both uses since c1930.*

bitch lamp. A makeshift lamp, usu. a container of grease or oil with a rag for a wick; an oil lantern. *Orig. hobo use, c1920.*

bitch session. 1. = bull session. 2. A meeting for the presentation of grievances, as when union representatives present employees' complaints to their employer.

bitch up [something]; bitch [something] up. To ruin or spoil something.

bite. *v.i.* To be gullible; to believe a deception; to allow oneself to be tricked. *v.t.* To borrow money from a person; to ask a person for money. *Cf. put the bite on.*

bite, the. *n.* 1. A request for money; the act or instance of borrowing money. See **put the bite on.** → 2. Expense; cost. 3. One's proportion or share of the cost; the price, the money one has to pay; specif., money demanded of one, as for a bribe or extortion.

bite on [someone], put the. 1. To ask for a loan or gift of money; to put the bee on [someone]. *The most common use.* 2. To blackmail; to extort money from; to shake down. → 3. To request, borrow, or try to obtain an item from someone known to possess it. *All uses since c1935.*

bite the dust. 1. To die. *Since c1870.* → 2. To meet with disaster; to fail.

biz. *n.* Business. Now specif. theatrical or show business. *Mainly theater use.*

blabbermouth. *n.* One who talks too much or reveals secrets. *Colloq.*

blab off. 1. To reveal a secret; to say what is better left unsaid. 2. To talk too much.

black. *n.* A Negro. *Not necessarily derog. adj.* 1. Shameful; discouraging. *Colloq.* 2. Without cream; said of a cup of coffee.

black, in the. 1. To run a business at a profit; operating at a profit. 2. To be solvent. *From the black ink commonly used on the credit side of business ledgers, as opposed to red ink.*

black and tan. 1. A mulatto; mulatto. *Since c1880.* 2. Catering to an audience of both Negroes and white persons

black and white. An ice-cream soda made with vanilla ice cream and chocolate sauce. *Mainly Eastern use.*

blackbaiter. *n.* A person with an intolerant attitude toward Negroes. *Dial.*

Black Betsy. A baseball bat. *Baseball use. Orig. the name of Babe Ruth's bat.*

black-coat. *n.* 1. An undertaker. 2. A clergyman.

black cow. 1. A soda made with root beer and vanilla ice cream. *The most common Eastern use.* 2. Chocolate milk. *Some use since c1940.* 3. = black and white. *The most common Western use.*

black eye. Fig., a lowered status or reputation; something that will injure one's prestige. *Since c1900.*

black gang. The engine-room workers on a ship. *From the days when Negroes were usu. employed as stokers on coal and wood-burning vessels.*

Black Maria. 1. A police wagon or truck used to take arrested persons to jail. 2. A hearse.

black market; black-market. *n.* Fig., the market where contraband is sold or bought; illegal or unethical sales, usu. of contraband or stolen or government-rationed items. *Orig. W.W.II sl., applied to the obtaining, often by theft, selling, and buying of scarce or rationed items that were in scant civilian supply owing to their military use. Now*

stand. adj. Illegal, unethical; pert. to contraband or stolen merchandise.

Black Mike. A meat and vegetable stew. *Hobo and logger use.*

black out. 1. To faint, to lose consciousness. *Colloq.* 2. To lose one's memory of a specif. happening. *Colloq.*

black-strap. *n.* Coffee. *Implying that it is as thick as black-strap molasses. Logger use and some Armed Forces use.*

black stuff. Opium. *Narcotic addict use.*

bladder. *n.* A newspaper. *Orig. underworld use. From the Ger. "blatt" = newspaper.*

blade. *n.* A young man, esp. one who believes himself socially adroit, sophisticated, and witty. *Almost always used in a jocular sense.*

blah. *n.* Senseless or exaggerated talk; useless talk; bunk, boloney. *adj.* 1. Nonsensical; worthless. 2. Bland; unexciting, unappetizing, or unappealing.

blah-blah; blah blah; blahblah. *n.* = blah.

blame(d). *adj.* = blast(ed). *Since c1825.*

blanket. *n.* 1. A pancake; a hotcake. 2. A cigarette paper. —s. *n.pl.* Pancakes; a stack of pancakes.

blanket drill. *n.* Sleep. *Army use since before c1930.*

blast. *n.* 1. A blow, as with the fist. *Colloq.* → 2. In baseball, a powerful hit, esp. a home run. → 3. Fig., any attack, as a verbal assault or speech. → 4. Fig., any violence, as a robbery. 5. A thrill; a feeling of great satisfaction; a kick, a charge. → 6. That which gives a thrill, esp. a drink or narcotics. → 7. A party, esp. a wild or abandoned one; a period of excitement. 8. = gasser. 9. A complete or conspicuous failure. From "bomb." *v.t.* 1. In baseball, to hit. 2. In sports, to defeat a team or opponent, esp. by a decisive score. 3. To shoot someone. 4. To attack another verbally. *v.i.*

1. To criticize publically; to complain; to broadcast; to advertise; to proclaim the merits of a product extravagantly. 2. To take injections of narcotic drugs, as an addict; to smoke a marijuana cigarette.

blasted. *adj.* 1. Without funds, completely broke. 2. Exceeding; damned.

blaster. *n.* 1. A gunman. *Underworld use.* → 2. A gun.

blast off. To leave a place or gathering, esp. quickly, without ceremony, or at the request of another; often used as a request or command; to beat it.

blast on [someone], put (lay) the. 1. To criticize a person severely, either in speech or in print; to take someone to task. 2. To hit with the fist.

blast party. *n.* A party of narcotic addicts, esp. marijuana smokers.

blat. *n.* A newspaper.

bleed. *v.t.* To obtain money from a person, esp. to obtain an exorbitant amount or to obtain it by extortion. *Colloq.* *v.i.* To complain; to nag. *Some c1940 use.* —**er.** *n.* In baseball, a one-base hit, a lucky hit, or a weakly hit ball.

bleenie. *n.* A frankfurter or weenie. *Dial.*

blimp. *n.* An obese person.

blind. *adj.* Drunk. *n.* 1. = blind baggage. 2. = blind date. 3. A fine, as imposed by a court. 4. A letter bearing an illegible or incomplete address; a nixie. *Post office use.* *v.i. & adj.* To know or do something perfectly; fig., to know or be able to do something so well that one need not use one's eyes; to answer all questions asked by an examiner. *Since c1900; mainly student use.* —**ed.** *adj.* Drunk.

blind baggage. A railroad baggage or mail car with no door or a locked door at the front end; the space between such cars where hobos may hide and ride. *Hobo use.*

blind date. A social engagement at which one's partner is a previously unknown person of the opposite sex, usu. the friend of a friend; also, such a partner. *Student use since c1920. Colloq.*

blind drag = blind date.

blind pig. A speakeasy; an unlicensed saloon.

blind-pigger. *n.* The proprietor of a blind pig.

blind tiger. Cheap or inferior whisky.

Blind Tom. A baseball umpire. *In allusion to the traditional allegation that umpires cannot see the pitches, etc., that they judge. Baseball use.*

blinger. *n.* An extreme instance or example of anything.

blink, on the. 1. Not in working order; not functioning or not functioning properly; not in good condition, in disrepair; said of tools, machines, and the like. *Since c1920.* → 2. Not feeling well; without vigor; said of people. → 3. Dead; said of people.

blinkers. *n.pl.* The eyes.

blinkie. *n.* A beggar who feigns blindness. *Orig. hobo use*

blip. *n.* A nickel; sum of 5¢. *adj.* 1. Excellent; very good. *Jive use since c1935.* → 2. = hip. *Cool use since c1950.*

blip jockey. A human monitor of electronic equipment, especially warning or detecting equipment, giving off visual responses.

blip off. To kill; to murder, esp. by shooting.

blister. *n.* 1. An annoying person; one whose presence detracts from the peace or gaiety of a gathering. *Still some use.* 2. A promiscuous girl or woman; a prostitute. *Dial.* 3. A woman hobo. 4. A semispherical glass or transparent plastic covering, as for an airplane cockpit or gun turret.

blitz. *v.t.* To polish the buttons and buckles of one's uniform; to polish and clean a barracks in preparation for inspection. *W.W. II Army use. After the commercial "Blitz Cloth," a polishing cloth. n.* 1. = blitzkrieg. 2. An important conference; a major flap. *W.W.II use.*

blitzkrieg; Blitzkrieg. *n.* A quick line used to gain sympathy from an attractive girl or someone who has money that can be borrowed; the rush act. *W.W.II Army use.*

blizzard head. In telecasting, a very blonde actress from whom the lighting must be subdued.

blob. *v.i.* To make a mistake.

block. *n.* 1. The head. *Common since before 1900. Not now generally used absolutely, but common in such colloq. expressions as "knock [one's] block off."* 2. = blockhead.

block and tackle. One's wife, boss, or superior; anyone who can or does restrain one's actions. *Colloq.*

blockhead. *n.* A stupid person. *Still in freq. use.*

bloke. *n.* A man, a fellow, a guy.

blood. *n.* 1. A socially active male college student, a leader of student activities, a big man on campus. 2. Ketchup. *Since c1910.*

bloody murder. 1. A decisive defeat; complete ruin or failure; an exhausting task. 2. Loud or emotional anger. *Almost always in "to yell (scream, etc.) bloody murder."*

blooey, go; blooie, go; flooey, go; flooie, go. To cease operating properly; to collapse or fall apart; to fail suddenly. *Lit. = to explode.*

bloom. *n.* In television, a televised glare from some white object, as a shirt front, within range of the camera lens; a womp.

bloomer. *n.* 1. A location where, or a day when, business is bad; a poorly attended show or place of business; a business failure. *Orig. circus use.* 2. A blunder; a mistake; a boner.

bloomer boy. *n.* A paratrooper. *Some W.W.II use. From the cut of his jump-uniform trousers.*

bloop. *n.* 1. An extraneous dull sound in a record, caused by im-

proper splicing of two sections of a tape recording. *Since c1945.* 2. A fluke; a blunder. *v.i.* To make a howling sound; said of a radio receiver. *Radio amateur use since c1925. v.t.* To hit someone, esp. to hit someone with a long, slow punch. —er. *n.* 1. A blow with the fist, esp. a long, slow punch. 2. In baseball, a slow, high-arching pitch; a weakly hit, high-arching ball, a fluke hit, a Texas leaguer. 3. = bloomer, a blunder.

blot out. To kill. *Underworld use.*

blotter. *n.* 1. The ledger of arrests and arrested persons kept at a police station. 2. A drunkard.

blotto. *adj.* Drunk; esp. unconscious from drink. *Of Brit. orig. Usu. a pred. adj., but used attrib.*

blow. *n.* 1. A storm. *Orig. maritime use. Colloq.* → 2. Any loud or angry confusion. 3. A gun. *Some underworld use.* 4. A greeting or other sign of recognition; a tumble. *v.t.* 1. To inform against someone; to squeal on someone; to betray someone. *Underworld use.* → 2. To expose a scandal to the public; to unearth and broadcast illegal or unethical dealings. 3. To treat someone to something, as to a drink, meal, or entertainment. 4. To play a musical instrument, esp. in jazz style, whether a wind instrument or not. *Musician use before c1920. Some c1935 jive use; jazz use; very common cool and way out use.* → 5. To perform any act, esp. to perform any act well. 6. To lose something, as a prize, in defeat; to lose one's chance of success or of winning; to fail to use one's opportunity to advance or succeed, esp. by one's own blunder or apathy. *Common since c1920.* 7. To spend or lose money, usu; quickly or on unnecessary items. 8. To eliminate or cancel part of an agreement or business. 9. To forget or blunder one's lines in a stage show. *Theater use.* 10. To throw a baseball fast and hard. *v.i.* 1. To brag; to exaggerate. *Since c1850.* 2. To become angry, to lose one's temper. 3. To take a narcotic by inhalation. *Addict use.* → 4. To smoke tobacco. *Some prison use. v.i. & v.t.* To go away, to depart; to leave a place, esp. rapidly or secretly; to escape, as from prison; to desert an enterprise. *The most common use. interj.* A command or entreaty, usu. in anger, to leave, to scram.

blow a fuse. To lose one's temper, to become violently angry, to blow one's top. *Colloq.*

blow a gasket = blow a fuse.

blow away. To depart; to blow.

blow-boy. *n.* A bugler. *Some Army use.*

blow [one's] cap = blow [one's] top.

blow [one's] cork = blow [one's] top.

blowed-in-the-glass. Genuine; first-rate; refined; of the highest order. *Hobo use. From liquor bottles with the brand name blown in the glass.*

blowen. *n.* Any woman, but esp. a prostitute or promiscuous woman. *Underworld use since c1850.*

blower. *n.* A handkerchief.

blow for canines. To play in the very highest register of a trumpet. *Cool and far-out use; prob. synthetic. In allusion to the ability of dogs to hear notes at a pitch above the range of the human ear.*

blowhard. *n.* 1. A braggart. *Since c1860.* 2. A loud, freq. emotionally upset or fault-finding talker.

blow in. 1. To spend money, usu. foolishly and quickly. 2. To arrive at or enter a place, esp. suddenly, unexpectedly, and from a distant place. Usu. in past tense.

blow-in. *n.* A new arrival at a place or gathering. *Hobo use.*

blowing. *n.* Playing jazz music; the act or an instance of playing jazz music.

blowing cat. A jazz musician.

Blow Joe. An enlisted man. *Some Army use since c1940. An inversion of "Joe Blow."*

blown up. Drunk. *Dial.*

blow-off; blowoff. *n.* 1. A climax; the end, the conclusion; esp. the final or climactic insult or indignity which precipitates a fight. → 2. A quarrel; the cause of a quarrel. 3. A pitchman's first customer who often is given a free item in order to induce further sales. *Carnival use.*

blow off steam = let off steam.

blow one. An order to draw a glass of beer. *Used in relaying orders to a bartender. In allusion to the foam on top of a glass of beer, which can be blown off.*

blow one up. To light a cigarette; to begin smoking a fresh cigarette. *Some prison use.*

blow-out; blowout. *n.* 1. A celebration or spree, esp. a festive, noisy, or extravagant one. 2. A large outdoor crowd. *Pitchman use.* 3. An unsuccessful robbery attempt. *Underworld use.* **blow out.** To spend money, usu. quickly and foolishly. See **blow.**

blowpipe. *n.* A rifle.

blow smoke. To boast, to brag, to exaggerate. *Implying that the speaker is having a pleasant dream, as induced by smoking opium.*

blow [one's] stack = blow [one's] top.

blow the lid off. To expose a scandal to the public; to expose illegal or unethical practices.

blow the whistle. 1. To inform, to sing. 2. To expose a scandal; to threaten to expose a scandal.

blow [one's] top (stack, wig, topper, cork, noggin,' roof, lump, etc.). 1. To commit suicide. *Some underworld use.* 2. Fig., to become insane with excitement or enthusiasm. *Orig. jive use, now cool use.* 3. To lose one's temper; to become violently angry; lit. and fig., to have a tantrum as a result of uncontrollable rage. *The most common use.* "Blow [one's] top" is the orig. and most *freq. term.* 4. To talk too much. *Underworld use.* 5. To do something exceedingly well, esp. to play a musical passage with skill and enthusiasm. *Cool use.* 6. To become insane or sick from narcotics, esp. marijuana. *Addict use.*

blowtop. *n.* A person who angers easily; one who often blows his top.

blowtorch. *n.* A jet fighter plane. *Air Force use since c1950.*

blow-up; blowup. *n.* 1. A fit of anger. → 2. Fig., an explosion; an uproar; a quarrel; a fight. 3. An enlarged photograph. *v.t.* To enlarge a photograph. *v.i.* 1. = **blow [one's top].** 2. blow, to forget or blunder one's lines in a stage performance.

blow up a storm. To play jazz with spirit and skill.

b. l. t. An order of a bacon, lettuce, and tomato sandwich. *Common lunchcounter use in relaying an order.*

blubber. *v.i.* To cry.

blubberhead. *n.* A stupid person; a fathead.

blue. *adj.* 1. Lewd, lascivious, obscene, erotic. *Colloq. by c1900; perhaps because the color of blue is associated with burning brimstone.* 2. Drunk. 3. Risqué; vulgar; suggesting the obscene. 4. Melancholy; sad; depressed. *Colloq.* *n.* 1. A conscientious, law-abiding student. 2. [derog.] A very dark complexioned Negro. 3. The sky. → 4. Heaven. *Jive use.* *v.t.* To perform music in blues manner.

blue balls. [taboo]. A case of venereal disease, esp. gonorrhea.

blue-book; Blue Book; bluebook. *n.* 1. A test or examination. *Student and college use since c1890. From the thin, blue-covered notebook of blank pages commonly provided by colleges for students to use in writing answers to examination questions.* 2. Any list or directory.

blue-eyed. *adj.* Innocent, gullible; idealistic; unworldly.

blue-eyed boy = fair-haired boy.

blue funk. A state of emotional depression, esp. when caused by romantic disillusionment, losing a lover, or confusion. A state of loneliness, aimlessness, or confusion.

bluejeans; blue jeans. *n.* Blue denim pants, worn by teenagers and adults of both sexes. *Originally "jeans" or "Levis," now rarely called "slacks." Accent first syllable.*

blue loco. 1. Loco weed. → 2. = loco.

blue man. A uniformed policeman.

blue murder = bloody murder.

blue nose. *n.* A person with strongly puritanical moral convictions; one who believes that having a good time is immoral; an ultraconservative. *Orig. in Colonial times = an aristocrat.*

blue note. A flatted note characteristic of the blues.

blue ruin. 1. Inferior liquor, esp. gin. *Archaic and dial. since c1920.* 2. A catastrophe; complete ruin, failure, or disgrace.

blues, the. *n. sing.* 1. Despondency; a sad, melancholy, depressed mood. 2. Specif., a fundamental part, specific form, and mood of jazz music. *One of the main origins of jazz was the sad or melancholy Negro work, prison, and funeral songs of slavery and oppression. In general use = any slowly played jazz or popular musical piece with sad lyrics of lost or rejected love.*

blurb. *n.* 1. A short laudatory essay or review of a new book, printed on its jacket to entice prospective readers to buy it. *Since c1915.* → 2. Any laudatory article, advertisement, short sales talk, or the like, whether given freely or as part of a paid advertising campaign, which increases the sales appeal of an item, performance, or entertainment; the mention of a commercial product, firm, or performer of entertainment in a published source. *The word was coined by Gelett Burgess.*

blushing bunny. Welsh rabbit with tomato soup as one of the ingredients.

BMOC; B.M.O.C. = big man on campus. *A very common student abbr. since c1940.*

BO; B.O. 1. Abbr. for "body odor," esp. underarm perspiration odor. *Popularized c1940 by heavy Lifebuoy Soap advertising campaign.* **2.** Theatrical business conditions; specif., the "box office" receipts for the sale of tickets to a play or other entertainment. *Theater use.* → **3.** The appeal or ability of an entertainer that attracts audiences to buy tickets to his performances. *Theater use.*

bo; 'bo. *n.* **1.** A hobo. **2.** A boy or youth; orig. a catamite. *Prison use.* **3.** A man; used only in direct address, usu. to a stranger. *Prob. from the Sp. "vos" = you.*

board. *n.* A ticket to an entertainment. —**s.** *n.pl.* Playing cards; a deck of playing cards.

boat. *n.* An automobile. *Since c1920.*

boat race. A dishonest race; specif., a horse race in which one entry is allowed to win by the others.

bob. *n.* **1.** Money. *From the Brit. "bob" = a shilling, reinforced by the nickname "Bob" suggested by the synonym "Jack."* → **2.** A dollar; the sum of $1.

bobble. *n.* A mistake; an error. *Since c1900. Colloq. v.i. & v.t.* To make a mistake; esp., in sports, to fumble.

bobby-socker; bobby-soxer. *n.* **1.** An adolescent girl. *From the bobby socks which most such girls wore as part of the fashionable high school costume during the early 1940's.* → **2.** A young teenager of either sex, esp. one whose interests, dress, and personality conform to adolescent fashions.

bobby socks; bobby sox. *n.* Long white cotton socks worn to a

length just below the knee or as anklets with thick cuffs. *Orig. pop. with teenage girls c1940.*

bob tail; bobtail. *n.* A dishonorable discharge from military service. *Armed Forces use since W.W.I. From the former custom of cutting out the phrase "... service honorable and faithful" from the bottom of the discharge certificate.*

bodega. *n.* **1.** A liquor store, a store that sells whisky by the bottle. *Some S.W. dial. use since c1850. From the Sp. In Spanish-speaking countries a "bodega" is a grocery store, which also sells liquor.* **2.** A grocery store. *Some N.Y. City dial. use, through Puerto Rican immigrant use.*

body. *n.* A sexually attractive girl or young woman with a good figure. *Starting in the middle 1940's, a succession of actresses, singers, and movie stars were nicknamed "The Body," and referred to as such by columnists, newsmen, and the public*

body and soul. A lover; a member of the opposite sex with whom one is sexually, emotionally, and mentally compatible. *Probably orig. with the pop. song "Body and Soul."*

body-snatcher. *n.* **1.** An undertaker. **2.** A kidnaper. **3.** A stretcher-bearer. *Some W.W.II use.*

boff. *v.t. & v.i.* To hit; to cuff, to slap; to treat roughly. *v.i.* To vomit. *n.* **1.** A blow, with the fist or open hand. **2.** A laugh elicited from an audience, or the joke causing the laugh. *Although probably used by show-business people much earlier, the word begins to appear in mass media c1945.* **3.** Any television, radio, movie, or stage show, or any book, piece of music, or other entertainment, that pleases the audience. *Most often used to refer to a popular play or musical comedy.*

boffo. *n.* **1.** A dollar. *Note plural is either "—s" or "—es."* **2.** A year; esp. a one-year prison sentence. *Some underworld use since c1930.* 3. A loud laugh or a joke; a boff. 4. A very successful or popular movie, stage show, story, or other entertainment. *adj.* 1. Loud; said of a laugh 2. Very favorable; enthusiastic; said of a critical comment or review. *Theater use.* 3. Highly successful and popular;—said of a performer or an entertainment. 4. Slapstickish, funny, uproarious.

boffola; buffola. *n.* 1. A laugh, esp. a deep, loud laugh; a belly laugh. *Since c1945.* 2. A joke that should or does elicit loud laughter.

boff out. To lose one's money; to be without funds.

bog-hopper. *n.* An Irishman; a person of Irish descent.

bogie; bogy. *n.* 1. An enemy airplane, specif. an attacking fighter plane. *W.W.II Air Force use; more commonly = a Japanese fighter plane than a German one.* 2. In golf, a score of one point over par.

bog-pocket. *n.* A stingy or thrifty person.

bog-trotter. *n.* = bog-hopper.

bogue. *adj.* Bogus; false; fake. *Far out use.*

bohunk; Bohunk. *n.* 1. A clumsy or stupid person. 2. [derog.] Any uneducated, unskilled immigrant from central Europe. *From "Bohemian" plus "Hungarian" reinforced by "Hunk."*

boiled. *adj.* Drunk. *With "stewed" and "fried," one of the common cooking terms = drunk.*

boiled rag = boiled shirt.

boiled shirt. Any person or activity which is formal or lacking in human warmth.

boiler. *n.* A still. *Dial.*

boiler-maker; boilermaker. *n.* A drink consisting of a jigger of whisky in a glass of beer. *The most common meaning. Colloq.* → 2. Any strong alcoholic drink.

boilermaker's delight. Fig., an alcoholic drink only suitable for the strongest of men; moonshine; inferior whisky. *Since c1910.*

boke. *n.* The nose. *Underworld use.*

bolexed up = bollixed up.

Bolivar. *n.* A pistol or revolver. *Some underworld use since c1935.*

bollixed; bolaxed. *adj.* = bollixed up.

bollixed up; bolaxed up; bolexed up. Confused; mixed up; balled up.

boll weevil; boll-weevil. *n.* 1. A nonunion worker; a scab. → 2. Any unwanted fellow worker; a worker who threatens the job security of an older employee; a new worker.

bolo. *n.* 1. An unskilled rifleman. *Army use since c1930. Implying that, like a "bolo," a bullet fired by an unskilled rifleman may return to harm the shooter or those near him.* 2. In boxing, a slow, high overhand or sidearm punch, as opposed to a short, fast direct jab.

boloney; baloney; bologny. *n.* Nonsense; false information or talk, even if believed by the speaker; worthless or pretentious talk; tripe, bunk, hokum, hot air, blah. *Also used as a one-word comment or interj. From the colloq. pronunciation of "bologna," the sausage. adj.* Spurious; phoney.

bolus. *n.* A physician. *Underworld use since c1850. From "bolus" = a large pill, usu. for a horse.*

bomb. *n.* 1. An inflammatory or startling statement. → 2. An unbelievable or unreal object or action. → 3. A conspicuous failure, esp. a performance or entertainment which receives bad reviews and public disapproval. Fig., a dud. 4. A car. *Hot-rod use since c1950.*

bomber. *n.* A marijuana cigarette; a stick. *Addict use, esp. among young and teenage addicts. Since c1945.*

bomb-shell; bombshell. *n.* 1. A stunningly attractive, energetic, or sexy girl or woman [or person] whose appearance or actions attract immediate attention or enthusiasm. *Orig. the term implied wildness, audacity, and lust for life; but soon it was used by columnists, press agents, and the like to refer to any physically attractive female.* → 2. A young woman, esp. a showgirl, with a reputation for being promiscuous.

bone. *n.* 1. A dollar. → 2. Specif., a silver dollar. *Dial. only.* 3. An argument or disagreement; a task that is not carried out according to instructions and thus brings on criticism and ill feeling. *From the colloq. phrase, "I have a bone to pick with you."* *v.i.* 1. To work hard. → 2. To study diligently, esp. to concentrate on studying during a brief period prior to an examination. *Since c1850. The most common use.* *v.t.* 1. To annoy, bother, or nag a person; to dun a person for payment of a debt. 2. To beg or solicit from a person; to offer a person an illegal or unethical business proposition. *Underworld use.*

bone-bender. *n.* A physician.

bone-breaker. *n.* 1. A physician. 2. A task, job, or goal that is extremely difficult. 3. A wrestler.

bone-cracker. *n.* A wrestler; a bone-breaker.

bone-crusher. *n.* A wrestler.

bone-eater. *n.* A dog.

bone-factory. *n.* 1. A hospital. 2. A cemetery. *Primarily Eastern use.*

bone-head; bonehead. *n.* 1. A stupid person. *Colloq.* → 2. A stubborn person. → 3. An error committed through stupidity. —ed. *adj.* Stupid. *Since c1860.*

bonehead play. In sports, an error caused by bad judgment.

bone orchard. A cemetery. *Primarily Western use.*

boner. *n.* A mistake; an error or blunder. *Has seldom, if ever, been used in U.S. with the Eng. sl. meaning, i.e., a blow with the fist on the lowest vertebra. c1830. Colloq.*

boner, pull a. To make an error or blunder.

bones. *n.pl.* 1. Dice. *According to Farmer & Henley, this word was used by Chaucer in 1386. In allusion to the fact that dice were orig. made of bone.* 2. Any thin person. 3. Traditionally, the end man in a minstrel show; a nickname for any blackface comedian. *From the fact that such an entertainer often played the bones.* 4. Two short rods, such as two rib bones, used to keep a clacking rhythm as an accompaniment to music or dancing. *The bones are held loosely between adjacent fingers of one hand and clacked together by rapidly agitating the hand.* 5. Money. *From "bone" = a dollar.*

bone-shaker. *n.* Any unstable or dilapidated vehicle, specif. an early model bicycle, an early model Ford automobile.

bone-top. *n.* A stupid person.

bone up. 1. To study. See **bone, bohn.** 2. To pay a debt. See **bone.**

bone up on. To study or review a specific subject intensively during a short period.

bone-yard; boneyard. *n.* A cemetery. *Since c1870.*

bonfire. *n.* A cigarette, esp. a stub of a cigarette smoked by another.

bong. *adj.* Excellent. *In allusion to the colloq. "to ring the bell."*

bonzer. *adj.* Good; excellent; admirable. *n.* An object or action that is so well constructed or accomplished as to fit its use perfectly. *Orig. Australian sl., intro. into U.S. during W.W.II.*

boo. *n.* = **bo.** *adj.* Excellent; remarkable; satisfying.

boob. *n.* 1. A stupid person; a simpleton, a sap, one easily victimized. *Since c1910.* → 2. A person who is extremely innocent or too trusting for his own good. → 3. Specif., a person who is innocent politically and culturally. 4. A jail. *Some underworld use. From "booby hatch." In the U.S. never used in the sense of the*

35 · **boondock**

Eng. sl. verb = *to make a mistake.* **5.** = **Babbitt.**

boobie; bubie. *n.* A term of endearment or affection. *Pop. by comedian Jerry Lewis c1950–1955. Seems to be, but is not, a Yiddish word. The "—ie" is the usu. affectionate diminutive ending.*

boobies. *n.pl.* = **boobs.**

boo-boo. *n.* **1.** A minor flesh wound; an accident causing such a wound. *Limited to children's use in ref. to a scratch, etc. Prominent among Jewish children in N.Y.C. Seems to be, but is not, a child's word.* → **2.** A faux pas; an embarrassing mistake; in sports, a blunder or error. *Popularized by comedian Jerry Lewis. c1950.*

booboos. *n.pl.* The testicles.

boobs. *n.pl.* The breasts. *Usu. to refer to the prominent breasts of a well-developed young woman (appreciatively) or to the sagging breasts of an elderly woman (depreciatively). The word is almost always used by a male in talking about a woman to another male, but is not taboo.*

boob trap. A nightclub. *From "boob" plus "trap," reinforced by "booby trap."*

booby hatch. *n.* An insane asylum. *The only meaning in use now. Universally known.*

booby trap. 1. A hidden explosive device triggered to a common object, in order to kill or injure a person who is expected to touch or handle the object. *Wide use during W.W.II* → **2.** Any plot, plan, or situation that may lead to death, injury, distress, embarrassment, or financial disaster.

boodle. *n.* **1.** An entire lot; a large number or amount of anything. **2.** Bribe money; money stolen from public funds; esp. graft. → **3.** A petty, grafting jail official; a corrupt politician. → **4.** Money. **5.** Cake, candy, ice cream, or similar food. *Usu. delicacies sent to prisoners, students, or soldiers by* friends or relatives. —r. *n.* A hobo who lives at the public expense by spending the winter in jail. *Hobo use.*

boogerboo. *v.i., v.t.* To pretend; to fake. *n.* An insincere person, a phoney. *Some Negro use.*

boogie-woogie. *n.* **1.** In jazz, a fast blues with an iterative bass figure played in double time, i.e., eight beats to the measure, associated with the Kansas City mode of jazz. **2.** Loosely, any jazz, jive, swing. *Since c1935. v.i.* To enjoy oneself thoroughly. *Some Negro use.*

book. *n.* **1.** A life sentence in prison. *Most freq. underworld use since c1930. Usu. "the book."* → **2.** Any maximum or extreme punishment, penalty, or criticism. **3.** = **bookie;** a bookie's establishment.

bookie. *n.* A horse-racing bookmaker.

books, hit the. To study, esp. to study hard. *A colloq. among students.*

boom-boom. *n.* **1.** A bowel movement. *Part of young children's euphem. bathroom vocabulary.* **2.** A pistol or small-caliber rifle. *Some W.W.II Army use.*

boomer. *n.* **1.** A migratory, itinerant, or transient worker. → **2.** A railroad worker, logger, construction crew member, or other worker who changes jobs often; a worker who works steadily for one employer but on projects far removed from his own home.

boom stick. *n.* **1.** An itinerant railroad worker, a railroad worker who often moves from job to job or from one region to another. *Hobo use.* **2.** A gun. —s. *n.pl.* A pair of drumsticks, esp. as used by a jazz or rock-and-roll musician. *Some synthetic jazz use; some teenage rock-and-roll use since c1955.*

boondock. *adj.* Used or suitable for rough outdoor use, such as hiking. —er. *n.* One who likes to live in, or who is stationed in, a jungle or tropical swamp. *W.W.*

II USN and U.S. Marine use. —ers. *n.pl.* Shoes suitable for rough outdoor use, specif. heavy-duty G.I. shoes. *W.W.II Marine use.* —s. *n.pl.* An isolated forest, swamp, mountain, or jungle region; uncivilized country; wild terrain. *W.W.II Armed Forces use. From the Tagalog "bundok" = mountain.*

boost. *v.i. & v.t.* 1. To steal, esp. by shoplifting; to pilfer. *Since c1915.* 2. To make a false bid over a real one, as is sometimes done by an auctioneer's accomplice to raise the bidding on an auctioned item. 3. To compliment, praise, recommend, endorse, or encourage someone or something. *Colloq.* —er. *n.* 1. A shoplifter or thief, often female. 2. A pitchman's assistant who pretends to buy in order to start real buying; a shill. 3. An enthusiast; one who admires and habitually praises a person, place, or thing.

boot. *v.t.* 1. To kick someone or something. *Colloq.* 2. To discharge; to fire; to sack. 3. To criticize or give a person a bad recommendation. 4. To make a specific error or blunder; to ruin something. 5. To lose an opportunity. *From the image of kicking away one's chances of success, reinforced by the specif. baseball use = to kick a baseball while attempting to pick it up.* 6. To introduce one person to another. → 7. To introduce a person to the facts concerning a specif. situation; to explain something. *n.* 1. A USN or Marine recruit; a newly enlisted sailor. *Colloq. Orig. USN use. In ref. to the leggings once worn during training; the word has remained pop. through W.W.I and W.W. II.* 2. In baseball, an error. 3. A discharge or dismissal. 4. An introduction. *adj.* Newly recruited, new on a job; inexperienced.

boot, get the. To be fired from one's job. *Fig. = to be kicked out.*

boot, the. *n.* An act or instance of

dismissal, either by an employer or a friend; the termination of a relationship.

boot camp. The first training center to which naval recruits go for their initial training. *Colloq.*

boot it. 1. To walk or march. *Since c1900.* 2. To make a mistake or blunder.

bootleg. *n.* Coffee, esp. inferior coffee. *Since c1915. A little Armed Forces and prison use. v.t.* To carry the ball deceptively, as in football and other sports. —ger. *n.* A dealer in or seller of illicit liquors. *Colloq.*

boot one. To make a mistake or blunder, esp. in baseball.

booze. *n.* Any type of liquor. *Colloq. Said to have been popularized in U.S. by Philadelphia distiller, E. G. Booze, c1840.*

boozed up. *adj.* Drunk. *Common 19th cent. sl. expression; still used.*

booze-fighter. *n.* One who habitually drinks large quantities of whisky; a drunkard. *Since c1910.*

booze hound = booze-fighter.

booze up. To drink liquor; to fill up on liquor.

bop. *v.t.* To strike, esp. with the fist. *Common since c1930. n.* 1. A blow; a hit. *Since c1930.* 2. A form and style of jazz music characterized by triadal chords with the first and third notes played an octave below the second and a little after it. The last two notes of a phrase thus often resemble the vocal sound "re-bop" or "be-bop," from which the word "bop" is commonly thought to have evolved. *Prob. from the Sp. "arriba" = up, which Afro-Cuban musicians shout to each other while playing, by way of encouragement. Often shortened to "riba," its use is directly equivalent to the U.S. "go" and "go man go." Thus Sp. "arriba" → Sp. "riba" → U.S. sl. "rebop" → "bop."* 3. A fight between members of rival teenage street gangs, a rumble. *adj.* Of, by, for, or pertaining to devotees of bop, their attitudes, modes, fashions and fads. *v.i. & v.t.* To fight, esp. to fight as a member of a teenage street gang, against a rival gang; to fight a rival teenage street gang. *Teenage street gang use.*

bop glasses. *n.* Horn-rimmed spectacles. *The dress of the bop musician often included heavy horn-rimmed glasses, esp. glasses with tinted lenses.*

borax. *n.* **1.** Cheap or inferior material or merchandise. *Orig. used by Jewish immigrants.* → **2.** Lies; exaggeration; misrepresentation; horse shit. **3.** Any gaudy object, colorful knickknack, souvenir, or small cheap item. *adj.* **1.** Cheaply made; of inferior quality. **2.** Gaudy; showing bad taste.

border, the. *n.* The U.S.–Mexican border.

borscht circuit, the. Summer vacation hotels in the Catskill Mountains. *Theater use. Many of these hotels have a predominantly Jewish clientele, and borscht (beet and potato soup) is associated with their European ancestry. The hotels constitute a circuit in which many well-known entertainers perform. Since c1935.*

bosh. *n.* Nonsense; blah. *Colloq.*

bossy; Bossy. *n.* A cow. *From the affectionate name traditionally given cows by farmers. adj.* Dominating; autocratic. *Colloq.*

bot. *n.* A bottle

botch = potch.

both hands. Ten.

bottle. *n.* A bottle of whisky. *The most common use. In the U.S. the word is never used in the Eng. sl. sense = a lecture or reprimand.*

bottle, hit the; sauce, hit the; booze, hit the; redeye, hit the; hit the [etc.]. To drink alcoholic beverages frequently or habitually, usu. to excess; to take one or more large drinks; to drink from or of whisky or wine; to become drunk. *"Hit the bottle" is very common.*

bottle baby. **1.** An infant fed from a bottle rather than suckled. *Colloq.* **2.** An alcoholic.

bottle club. A private drinking club; specif., an association of people, often unknown to one another, for the sole purpose of providing themselves with liquor and a place to drink it after the legal closing hours of public bars or in a city or county where the public sale of alcoholic beverages is prohibited.

bottle-man. *n.* A drunkard or habitual drinker.

bottom. *n.* The buttocks. *Since c1790.*

bottom man. The person with the least seniority, skill, experience, authority, or importance in a specif. group. *Almost always as part of the phrase "bottom man on the totem pole."*

bounce. *v.i.* To fail of payment by a bank;—said of a check. *Generally speaking, a check bounces because there are not enough funds in the payer's account to cover it. v.t., v.i.* **1.** Lit and fig., to throw or kick out of a place; to expel, as from college or a classroom; to eject or expel forcibly, or to be ejected or expelled. *A prime example of a sl. word derived from the standard image of an inanimate object and applied to a person, in this case the image of a ball that bounces when thrown.* **2.** To discharge; to fire from a job; to be so discharged or fired. *Still fairly common.* **3.** To pay [a bill]. *n.* **1.** Pep; energy; vitality. **2.** In jazz, a lively tempo; a tune customarily played in such a tempo. —**r.** *n.* **1.** A tough, burly man employed to throw unwelcome people out of a public place, as a theater, hotel, saloon, or dance hall; occasionally the one who is thrown out. *From the standard image of "bounce," perhaps reinforced by the Eng. sl. "bounce" = a remarkable specimen.* **2.** A check written against a bank account that does not contain enough funds to pay the amount. 3. A forged check. *Underworld use.*

bounce, the. *n.* 1. An act or instance of dismissal, esp. from a public place; any forcible ejection of a person from a public place. 2. Expulsion; a discharge.

bouncy-bouncy. *n.* [taboo]. The act or an instance of coitus. *Some jocular use.*

bovine extract. Milk. *Prob. synthetic.*

bowl. *n.* 1. An outdoor stadium or arena, esp. a football stadium. *From the shape, often like a bowl. Colloq.* 2. An order of a bowl of soup. *Very common lunch-counter use.*

bow-wow; bowwow. *n.* 1. A dog. *Baby talk; very old.* 2. A sausage, a frankfurter, a "dog." *Since c1900. Jocular use.* 3. A gun. *From the common use in sensational fiction of the word "bark" to describe a gun's report.* —s. *n.pl.* The feet; the dogs. *adj.* Beautiful; perfect; remarkable.

box. *n.* 1. A coffin. *Colloq.* 2. A safe; a vault. *Common underworld use.* 3. Any stringed instrument, specif. a guitar, c1930, or a piano, c1955; an accordion. *Jive and cool use.* 4. The mouth; the mouth and larynx; the voice "box." 5. A camera; specif. a simple camera in the shape of a box with a preset lens opening and exposure time. 6. An ice box; a refrigerator. *Colloq.* 7. A phonograph. 8. = pad. *Some cool and far-out use.* 9. A police telephone operator.

box, go home in a. To die or be killed.

box, in a. In difficulty or trouble; in a dilemma.

boxcar; box-car. *adj.* Long, high, as in "long odds," "high odds." *Mainly racetrack use; from the high numbers freq. seen on the sides of railroad freight cars.* —s. *n.pl.* 1. In craps, a throw of double-6, i.e., a throw in which each dice turns up a 6; the highest number in craps, a 12. 2. Shoes, esp. large shoes.

box man. 1. A specialist in opening locked safes; a safe-cracker. 2. A professional dealer in the game of blackjack or 21. *Because orig. the cards were drawn from a box.* → 3. A gambling-house employee, as a cashier or croupier, directly involved with a gambling game.

box of teeth. An accordion.

boy. *n.* 1. [derog.]. A male Negro of any age. → 2. Any menial servant, regardless of age, working in a public place; a porter, elevator operator, or the like. 3. A male who plays the female role in a homosexual relationship; a catamite; any effeminate man.

boy friend. A girl's or young woman's sweetheart. *Colloq.*

boyo. *n.* A fellow, a youth or adult male. *Almost always in direct address to a friend, but not a close friend, and usu. in "me boyo."*

boys, the. *n. pl.* 1. Men, esp. the drinking and poker companions of the speaker and the like. 2. A gang of hoodlums or organized criminals.

boys uptown, the. 1. The organized political bosses of a city or district. *From Tammany Hall, the N.Y.C. Democratic organization, which has its headquarters in uptown Manhattan.* → 2. Any group of influential or notorious criminals; influential criminals.

bozo. *n.* A man; fellow; guy; esp. a large, rough man or one with more brawn than brains. *From Sp. dial. "boso" (from "vosotros") = you (pl.), which resembles a direct address.*

bra. *n.* A brassière. *Since c1920. Colloq.*

brace. *v.t.* 1. To accost a person and beg or solicit money from him; to ask for or borrow money from a person. → 2. To accost or meet a person in order to accuse him of a misdeed, to challenge him, or to arrest him; to find and confront someone. *n.* An extremely exaggerated posture of standing to attention. *Some*

Armed Forces and military academy use. —r. *n.* A drink of liquor.

brace, take a. To improve; usu. said of an athlete or gambler.

bracelets. *n. pl.* A pair of handcuffs. *Since before 1900.*

brag-rags. *n.pl.* Ribbons representing military decorations and campaign medals.

brain. *n.* 1. A good student; an intelligent or intellectual person; a thinker or scholar. 2. An electronic computer; any complex navigational unit, usu. containing an electronic computer. 3. A detective. *Some underworld use.* *v.t.* To hit someone on the top of the head, as with a club. —ery. *n.* A university. —s. *n. sing.* Anyone in authority, a boss; an official. —y. *adj.* Intelligent; intellectual. *Colloq.*

brain-box. *n.* 1. The head. 2. The pilot house on a river towboat.

brain child. Any product of one's intellect or imagination, as a plan, invention, work of art, or the like. *Colloq.*

brain picker. One who develops, exploits, or profits from the ideas or artistic concepts of others. *Colloq.*

brain storm. A sudden idea, usu. one that leads to action or the solution of a problem; a brilliant and spontaneous insight; a good idea.

brain tablet. A cigarette. *Some Western use.*

brainwash; brain wash. *v.t.* 1. To induce an attitudinal change in a person, usu. a captive, by means of psycho-educational methods, sometimes supplemented by drugs and physical coercion. *This form of psycho-educative conditioning developed in the USSR, based upon the original work of Pavlov with conditioned reflexes of dogs.* → 2. To change another's opinion; to convince someone of something. *n.* A conversion from one belief to another; persuasion.

brain wave = brain storm.

brannigan; branigan. *n.* 1. A

spree. → 2. A loud quarrel, row, or fracas; a fight; noisy and violent confusion.

brass. *n.* 1. Impudence; effrontery. *Since Elizabethan times. Colloq.* 2. Cheap, imitation, or fake jewelry. *Hobo, circus, pitchman, and underworld use.* 3. Military officers, esp. high-ranking military officers; a military officer. *Often preceded by a sl. adj.* = high-ranking, such as "heavy," "top," "big," etc. Common during and since W.W.II. From the officers' brass insignia, but see brass collar, brass hat. → 4. Military authority. → 5. High-ranking civilian police officials. → 6. An official; officials; influential people; persons in authority; executives.

brass hat. An official; any important or influential person; one in authority, a boss.

brass tacks. The essential facts; the practical realities. *Colloq.*

brawl. *n.* 1. A dancing or social party that develops into a rough, drunken, or wild party. 2. A fight.

bread. *n.* 1. Money. *Orig. c1935 jive use. Now associated with cool and hip use.* 2. One's employer, manager, or boss. *From the worker's dependency on him for wages with which to buy the necessities. Often introduced into conversation to warn other employees that the boss is watching or listening.*

breadbasket. *n.* The stomach. *Mainly child, prize fight, and sports announcer use.*

break. *v.t.* 1. To subdue or, fig., "break" the spirit of a wild horse so that he may be trained and ridden; to train a horse to be ridden. *c1847. Orig. Western use. Universally known.* 2. To separate, as two boxers. 3. To take a short rest period from work, as for refreshment. 4. To escape from prison. 5. To bankrupt someone. → 6. To ruin another's chance for success; to impugn someones' reputation. *n.* 1. = lick. In jazz, an improvised interpolation between two passages of music, usu. played by a solo instrument while the other instruments of the ensemble, including the rhythm instruments, rest; the improvisation itself. 2. An escape from prison or from any confining or disagreeable situation. 3. A social error or blunder; a faux pas. 4. Luck; opportunity; a stroke of fate, either good or bad. *Since c1925; colloq.* 5. Specif., a reduction in a prison sentence by a parole board. *Underworld use.* 6. A short rest period from work, usu. 10 or 15 minutes, often used for refreshments, esp. coffee. *Colloq. since c1945.*

break-away. *adj.* Pertaining to an object made to collapse easily at the pull of a string, press of a concealed button, or the like. *Thus a break-away dress is made to fall off the wearer, a striptease dancer, at the pull of a string; a break-away knife has a blade which recoils into the hilt at the push of a button, etc.*

breaker-upper. *n.* One who or that which breaks up.

break in. 1. To gain entry, specif. to enter a prison by any means other than violence; to surrender voluntarily for imprisonment. 2. To tame or train, as a horse; to attune, adapt, or adjust a new article of merchandise by using it, as a new pair of shoes or a new automobile.

break-in. *n.* A burglary.

break it up. 1. To stop fighting or quarreling;—usu. a command. *Colloq.* 2. To win a lot of money, fig., to win so much money in a gambling game that the game must end because the other players are broke.

break over. To make an exception to one's usu. rule or practice. *Dial.*

break the ice. 1. To accomplish a specific deed for the first time. → 2. To become initiated; to begin an apprenticeship. → 3. To become friendly or intimate with another or others; to overcome

strangeness, shyness, aloofness, or formality with another person, persons, or esp. with an entire group of people, as at a social gathering. *Most common use.*

break the news. To beat up someone.

breakthrough. *n.* An important or critical advance toward completion or the success of a project or endeavor. *From the freq. W.W. II military aim of breaking the enemy's defenses.*

break up. To cause lovers, friends, or relatives to separate or become angry with one another. *Colloq.*

break-up. *n.* A separation, as between lovers.

break wind. To eruct.

breathe easy. To be relieved of worry; to be assured of success; to escape from danger. *Colloq.*

breeze. *n.* An easy task; a cinch. *v.i.* 1. To depart; to leave; to go away, esp. quickly. 2. To travel or move, either rapidly or easily. 3. Specif., to flee, to escape from jail.

breeze in. To arrive or enter as though, with, or on a breeze; to saunter in; hence to win a race without great effort.

breeze off. 1. To be quiet; to shut up. 2. To leave; to depart.

breezy. *adj.* Affable; nonchalant; supercilious.

briar. *n.* A file or hacksaw. *Underworld use since c1830.*

briar-hopper. *n.* A farmer. *Dial.*

brick. *n.* 1. A happy, carefree person. *From the Celtic "brigh" = energy, spirit, and the superlative "brigheil" = high spirits.* → 2. A pleasant, thoughtful, trustworthy, generous person; an admirable person. *Since c1910; colloq. —yard.*

bricks, hit the. 1. To go on the street on foot; to start walking on a sidewalk or pavement. → 2. To leave a public place; to withdraw to the street. → 3. To be released from prison. *Underworld use.* → 4. To go on strike; to stage a walkout. 5. Specif., to walk the streets all night because one does not have a place to sleep; to beg on the streets; to walk a beat; to march on a picket line. *Hobo, police, and union use; some general use.*

bricks, the. *n. sing.* 1. The pavement or sidewalk; the street. → 2. The world outside prison walls. *Prison use.*

bricks and mortar. School notes and books. *From the notion of a school as nothing but a brick and mortar building; reinforced by "mortarboard." Rock and roll use, c1955.*

bricktop. *n.* A red-haired person; —often used as a nickname; a head of red hair. *Since at least 1850.*

briefs. *n. sing.* A pair of men's cotton undershorts with an elastic waist. *They are usu. white and are legless, as opposed to the skivvy, which has short legs. Colloq.*

brig. *n.* A naval prison or cell; a guardhouse; any prison.

bright. *n.* Day; the daytime. *Orig. c1935 jive use; bop and cool use since c1946.*

brig rat. A prisoner. *Some Armed Forces use.*

bringdown. *n.* 1. A disappointing, unsatisfactory, or depressing performance or job. 2. A habitually sad, gloomy person. *adj.* 1. Unsatisfying; incompetent; inexperienced. 2. Depressing; gloomy. *All uses cool and far-out; since c1953.*

bring down the house. To elicit a big ovation from an audience, as in a theater.

bring home the bacon = bring home the groceries.

bring home the groceries. 1. Fig., to earn money with which to buy the necessities of life. → 2. To succeed in a job or task; to produce tangible results; to accomplish what one has set out to do.

briny, the. *n.* The ocean. *Since c1900.*

broad. *n.* 1. A young woman or girl; a woman. 2. A promiscuous woman; a prostitute; a woman

whom the speaker does not respect.

Broadway boy. A loud, garishly dressed, small-time gambler or ladies' man.

brodie; Brodie. *n.* A failure, mistake, or blunder; a mixup. *After Steve Brodie who claimed to have jumped from the Brooklyn Bridge on July 23, 1886. Although he was found in the water under the bridge, his feat was never proved, and thus if he didn't jump he received much mistaken acclaim; if he did jump he made the mistake of having no accredited witnesses to attest the validity of his claim and thus jumped in vain. v.i.* 1. To fail; to make a mistake. 2. To commit suicide, esp. by jumping off a bridge or building.

broke. *adj..* Without money; penniless. *Usu. pred. adj., occasionally attrib. adj.*

broken arm. Food that has been uneaten or only partially eaten after being served at a meal; a plate of such food; leftovers; table scraps.

broken-striper. *n.* A warrant officer. *USN use.*

bromide. *n.* 1. An old joke or saying. 2. A trite saying; a trite homily; a dull person. *Coined by Gelett Burgess.*

bronc; bronk. *n.* 1. = bronco. 2. A bad-tempered horse. *Dial.* 3. A catamite. *Some c1925 hobo use.*

bronco. *n.* A wild, untrained horse; a horse not yet broken for riding. *Orig. western use = a bad-tempered wild horse.*

bronco buster. A cowboy; lit., one who breaks or tames broncos. *Colloq.*

bronco peeler = bronco buster.
bronco snapper = bronco buster.
bronco twister = bronco buster.
bronk. *n.* = bronco.
Bronx cheer. *n.* 1. Any loud, derisive noise, such as a hiss, a boo, or a raspberry. → 2. An adverse criticism or remark; any written or spoken statement of ridicule or derision.

brookie. *n.* A brook trout.

broom. *v.i.* To run or walk away, esp. to flee. *Negro use.* —**stick.** *n.* 1. One's wife. *In allusion to "witch," the traditional rider of broomsticks. Dial.* 2. Any thin person.

broom in (up) [one's] tail (ass), get (have) a. [taboo]. To have or show enthusiasm over a job or task; to work hard; to become or be a diligent honest worker. *From a pop. joke about an employee whose hands are busy but whose boss gives him the additional task of sweeping the floor; hence he must hold the broom in this unorthodox manner.*

brother. *n.* 1. A man, fellow, guy. *Some use in direct address to strangers, as in the street beggar's traditional, "Brother can you spare a dime?" From the freq. religious use of the word.* 2. In direct address, a man who has aroused the speaker's resentment, often leading to quarrelsome or threatening talk or blows.

brown. *n.* Butterscotch sauce. *Some student use.*

brown Abe. *n.* A penny. *Orig. c1935 jive use; cool use, some rock and roll use.*

browned off. *adj.* Angry, esp. angry with disappointment, as at another's mistake, slight, or tardiness.

Brownie. *n.* 1. An apple polisher. *Some W.W.II. use.* 2. A penny.

brown off. To make a mistake or blunder; to ruin or spoil something.

Brown Top. The main tent at a chautauqua; a chautauqua big top.

brud. *n.* A brother. *From dial.* "brudder."

bruiser. *n.* A big, strong male, esp. one with a rough appearance or manner. *Usu. in "big bruiser." Colloq.*

brunch. *n.* A late morning meal eaten in lieu of both breakfast and luncheon, a combined breakfast and luncheon. *Since c1900. From telescoping "breakfast" and "lunch."*

brush. *n.* 1. = brush-off. Usu. in give [someone] the (or a) brush. 2. A beard; whiskers. 3. An encounter, esp. one involving a fight, quarrel, or unpleasantness; a skirmish. *v.i., v.t.* To fight; to defeat by fighting; to beat up. *adj.* 1. Bearded; bewhiskered. *Not common, but used in such combinations as "brush-face."* 2. Rural, rustic. *In such combinations as "brush-show" = a rural nonprofessional show; "brush-canary" = female singer of hillbilly songs; "brush-whisky" = illegal whisky, as made in rural or mountain districts.*

brush, give [someone] the. To ignore or snub someone; to dismiss someone curtly and without much concern.

brush, the. *n.* 1. The jungle; forested country; uncivilized regions of any kind. *Colloq.* 2. = brush-off.

brush cut. A mode of hair cut in which all the hair (front, top, and sides) is cut to the same short length, usu. less than an inch. *c1910. A male haircut, forerunner of the crew cut. c1950, a fashionable women's hair style. Orig. because the short, straight hair resembles the bristles of a brush.*

brush-down. *n.* The act of brushing clothes.

brushes. *n.pl.* A pair of thin drumsticks with flat soft brushes of wires or plastic on the ends. They are used to give the drums a soft, smooth, muted sound. *Orig. jazz use; now the most common word for these items in all forms of jazz and popular music.*

brush off; brush-off. 1. To ignore, snub, or get rid of a person or thing; fig., to brush aside. 2. To go away, to leave. *Usu. as an entreaty or command.* **brush-off.** *n.* The act of brushing off a person or thing, esp. the act of jilting a suitor; an instance of ignoring a friendship or a friend's request; a rejection.

brush up. 1. To brush clothes or the like. → **2.** To clean up; to dress up; to spruce up. **3.** To review, relearn, or acquire additional information about a specific subject. *Colloq.*

bruss. *n.* An extremely exaggerated position of attention. *Army use.*

BS; B.S.; b.s. 1. A Bachelor of Science degree; one who holds such a degree. *Stand.*

BTO; B.T.O.; b.t.o. = big-time operator. *This abbr. is at least as common as the full expression.*

bub. *n.* **1.** A boy or youth. *Used in direct address. Colloq.* → **2.** *A derog. or humorous form of direct address to an adult male, implying that the person is insignificant. Very common since c1940.*

bubble-chaser. *n.* A U.S. Air Force bombardier. *Some W.W.II use.*

bubble dancer; bubble-dancer. *n.* A person who washes dishes. *Lunch-counter use and W.W.II Army use. Common and one of the more successful sl. terms based on a humorous image.*

bubble-head; bubblehead. *n.* A stupid person. *Often used as a term of address or as a nickname.*

bubble queen. A girl worker in a laundry.

bubbly. *n.* Champagne. *Orig. Eng. use, introduced into U.S. sl. during W.W.I. Common with newsp. columnists and writers, some facetious general use.*

bubie = **boobie.**

buck. *n.* **1.** A dollar; the sum of $1. *In wide colloq. use since at least c1850. The true origin is not definitely known.* **2.** A young male Indian → **3.** Any young male, esp. a muscular or spirited one. *Colloq.* **4.** Specif., a young male Negro. *v.t.* To resist; to defeat. *Usu. in the negative, as in such phrases as "you can't buck the system"; "it's fate, don't buck it," etc. Colloq. v.i.* **1.** To strive in any way for personal advance-

ment, as by dressing neatly, studying hard, or competing for favors or promotion. *Wide W.W. II use; perh. from "buck private," the lowest Army rank and hence the one in which one must work most for promotion.* → **2.** To side with or seek favor with those in authority. —**er.** *n.* **1.** One who curries favor with his superiors; an aspirant to promotion. **2.** A cowboy. —**o.** *n.* **1.** A fellow; guy. *Since c1900. Used by old sailors and cowboys. Connotation of an independent, outdoor person.* **2.** A bully. *Orig. seaman use. adj.* Strong, rough, tough, self-reliant.

buck, pass the. To pass on to someone else a problem, responsibility, or a person having a problem requiring attention. *Since c1910; colloq.*

buckayro. *n.* = **bucker.**

buckeroo. *n.* = **bucker.**

bucket. *n.* **1.** An automobile, esp. a large, old automobile. **2.** A ship, esp. an old or slow ship; in the Navy, esp. a destroyer. *Often used as a term of familiarity or affection rather than derision.* **3.** Any ugly or unpleasant girl or woman. *In the U.S. the word is never used as a v.* = to travel fast, *as it is in Eng. sl.* **4.** The rump, the buttocks. **5.** A disliked, objectionable, dull person. *Some student use since c1945.* **6.** A toilet.

bucket-head [derog.]. *n.* **1.** A German soldier. *Some W.W.I and W.W.II use. Orig. in allusion to the shape of the German field helmet, which resembled a "bucket"* = toilet or chamber pot. **2.** A stupid person.

bucket of bolts. A car, esp. an old, dilapidated car that rattles when in motion.

bucket-shop; bucket shop. *n.* An office where illegal, worthless, or highly speculative stocks are sold, often by telephone and with unethical sales talks; posing as a legitimate stockbroker's office, but using aggressive means and misrepresentation bordering on swindling.

buck general. A brigadier general in the U.S. Army.

buckhara. n. = bucker.

buckle down. To replace frivolity or apathy with a serious attitude and hard work, in order to succeed.

buck naked. Completely naked.

buck private. An Army private, esp. a new recruit.

bucks, in the. In funds; having money.

buckshee. adj. 1. Spare; extra; loose. 2. Free. Some maritime use since W.W.I, from Brit. sailor sl. Prob. of Arabic orig., from "buckshes" = tip.

buck slip. Any written paper which passes a given problem on to another person or office.

buck up. To cheer up. Since c1840.

bud. n. Friend; fellow. Always used in direct address, often to a stranger, usu. in the vocative at the end of a sentence, and always to a male. Since c1850. Colloq. From "brother." —dy. n. 1. = bud. Equally as common as "bud" and used in exactly the same way. Also since c1850. 2. A partner. 3. A man's male friend; a chum; a comrade, esp. a close friend whom one will aid or protect. Colloq. v.i. = buddy up. To be a close friend to someone; to move about with another; to share living quarters. Often in the phrase, "They buddy together." —dyroo. n. = buddy.

buddy-buddy. n. 1. A close friend. W.W.II Army and USN use. → 2. One who is not a friend; an enemy; a disliked person. This sarcastic use is by far the most common since c1945. The reduplication has been used to strengthen the word "buddy" and also to reverse its meaning. → 3. An overly friendly person; one who tries too hard to make friends, join a group, or be hep. v.i. To be overly friendly; to

curry favor. adj. Too friendly; insincere; presuming.

Buddy poppy. A paper replica of a Flanders poppy sold by W.W.I veterans on Memorial Day.

buddy seat. 1. A motorcycle sidecar. c1940. Because the two riders are close together. 2. A position of authority; c1950. Because others must now try to be friendly or curry favor.

buddy up. 1. To share living quarters; to combine resources. Male student use. 2. To seek out, court, or ingratiate oneself with another for personal advancement or gain; to form a friendship for ulterior motives; to apple-polish.

buddy [someone] up; buddy up to [someone]. To curry favor with someone, usu. someone in authority. From "butter up" with the mispronunciation reinforced by "buddy."

buff. n. A devotee, a fan, a bug; one whose hobby or passion is collecting specific items, going to specific events, or associating with a specific occupational group.

buffalo. v.t. 1. To confuse another purposely. Since c1870. → 2. To cheat or take advantage of another, usu. by confusing him. → 3. To intimidate, frighten, or bluff someone; to cow someone. Since c1900. → 4. To control a situation. n. A girl or woman, esp. if she is extremely fat.

buffaloed. adj. Deceived; tricked; cheated.

buffalo head. A nickel.

buffer. n. A chief boatswain's mate. U.S.N. use.

bug. n. 1. An enthusiast; one who is obsessed by an idea or pursuit. Colloq. → 2. An obsession; an idea or belief with which one is obsessed. → 3. An irrational mood; a grouch or bad mood. Since c1930. Mainly prison use. → 4. An angry mood. Usu. in "to have a bug on." → 5. A psychologist. Some prison use. 6. Any defect or cause of trouble in a machine, equipment, or plan; specif. a defect in a new machine that becomes apparent only when the machine is put into operation. *Colloq.* 7. An asterisk. *Printing and publishing use.* → 8. Specif., an asterisk appearing next to the weight a horse is carrying in a horse race, as on a program, to indicate that a 5-pound weight decrease has been granted because the horse is being ridden by an apprentice jockey. *Race-track use.* → 9. In horse-racing, the 5-pound allowance in weight given to a horse being ridden by an apprentice jockey. → 10. An apprentice jockey who has ridden his first race within the present year or who has not won his 40th race. → 11. A race horse that has never won a race. *Also from the asterisk that used to be placed next to the name of such a horse, as on a program.* Cf. maiden. 12. A small, usu. printed, label or trademark; specif., the union label printed on publications to show they have been printed in a union workshop. *From the shape.* 13. Specif., a hot-rod; the driver of a hot-rod. *Hot-rod use since c1950.* → 14. Specif., a Volkswagen, the small German car; any small, inexpensive foreign car. *From their appearance.* 15. A semiautomatic telegraph key, operating from side to side instead of up and down, which sends "dashes" automatically, speeding message sending. *Telegrapher, radio amateur, railroad, and USN use since c1920.* 16. A burglar alarm. *Underworld use. Here "bug" may be a shortened form of "burglar alarm."* 17. A dictaphone or other such recording device concealed to record conversations without the speakers' knowledge; any device allowing a third person to overhear a conversation, esp. a telephone conversation, without the speakers' knowledge; any wire-tapping device. 18. A bacterium;

a germ or microbe or virus; any micro-organism. *Colloq.* → 19. Any virus disease or infection; a cold; dysentery. *Common during and since W.W.II.* 20. Any small, cheap item of merchandise, as sold by a novelty vendor or pitchman. *Circus use since c1800.* 21. A large industrial ladle, as used in pouring molten steel, baker's dough, or the like. *v.t.* 1. To examine a person psychiatrically or psychologically; to pronounce a person mentally irresponsible for his actions; to pronounce a person insane. *Mainly prison use, since c1930.* 2. To install a burglar alarm in a specif. location. *Underworld use.* 3. To conceal a microphone-recording device in a room or other location in order to record conversation surreptitiously; to listen to a recorded telephone conversation without the speakers' knowledge. *v.i., v.t.* To be angry or irritated (at someone); to bother, irritate or anger someone; to confuse or bewilder someone.

bugaboo. *n.* A nemesis; a real or imagined obstacle that cannot be overcome; something that always causes failure or bad luck; ungrounded or unnecessary fear or dislike of a real or imagined thing, as a child's fear of the dark. *Colloq.*

bug doctor. A psychiatrist or psychologist, as one employed by a penal institution. *Since c1930.*

bug-eyed. *adj.* 1. Having protruding eyeballs. 2. Astonished, surprised; struck with wonder or amazement.

bugger. *n.* A fellow; a chap; a thing. *Esp. applied to small or cute persons or things, as a small boy.*

buggy. *n.* 1. A caboose of a train, esp. of a freight train. *Railroad use since c1895.* 2. An automobile; esp. an old dilapidated automobile. *Since c1925; has been very common, esp. in jocular use.* 3. Any vehicle. 4. = bus. *adj.* 1.

Foolish; silly. *Some use since c1920.* → 2. Crazy. *Very common since c1930.*

bughouse. *n.* An insane asylum.

bug-hunter. *n.* An entomologist; a naturalist. *Since c1890.*

bug in [one's] ear. 1. An obsession; a cherished concept, idea, or plan. 2. A rumor, gossip, or secret or private information which one believes to be true.

bug in [one's] ear, put a. To warn someone by implanting an idea in his mind, to forewarn; to insinuate, imply, or suggest something to a person, esp. so that he may reach his own conclusion or not remember from whom he received an impression or idea.

bug-juice. *n.* 1. Liquor, esp. inferior whisky. *Since c1875.* 2. Any beverage, esp. a synthetic or artificially colored beverage; any soft drink. 3. Gasoline. 4. The residue of tobacco in the bowl of a frequently used pipe. *All uses orig. from the tobacco-colored secretion of grasshoppers.*

bug man. *n.* A circus concessionaire who sells chameleons and turtles.

bugologist. *n.* An entomologist. *Since c1875.*

bugology. *n.* 1. Entomology. *Since c1850.* → 2. Biology. *Some student use since c1900.*

bug out. 1. To protrude. *Since c1870. Now usu. in ref. to naturally protruding, staring eyes.* 2. To withdraw, retreat, lose one's enthusiasm, or compromise, owing to exhaustion, cowardice, or fear; to turn chicken. → 3. To leave or drive away rapidly. *Hot-rod and teenager use since c1950.* *n.* 1. One who habitually withdraws or compromises; one who cannot be depended upon. → 2. A military retreat. *Korean War Army use.*

bugs. *n.* Biology. *Student use. adj.* Insane; crazy; eccentric; obsessed. *Very common.*

bug test. A psychological test. *c1945.*

bug up. To become or be excited; to become or be confused or bewildered.

build. *v.t.* 1. To prepare a person for victimizing; to build up. *Orig. underworld use.* 2. To exaggerate, project, or predict something. *v.i.* To increase, to grow in complexity, quantity, or intensity; may be said of a jazz performance. *n.* 1. A show whose earnings continue to increase. *Theater use.* 2. A person's physique, shape, or figure, specif., of an attractive young woman. *Colloq.* —er = stew-builder.

builder-upper. *n.* One who or that which builds up, esp. one who or that which increases physical stamina or morale in a person.

build-up; buildup. *n.* 1. Preparations, esp. advance publicity, to make a person, product, or plan of action acceptable, well known, or desirable; the art of creating a demand, usu. for an entertainer or a product. *Usu. in "to give [someone or something] the build-up."* 2. Anything said or done to win the confidence of a prospective victim of a confidence man; anything said or done to win the confidence of a customer. *Orig. underworld use.*

build up. *v.t.* To create self-confidence or determination in another by compliments or flattery; lit., to build up another's ego.

bulge. *n.* 1. An advantage; a lead. 2. Any part of the body that easily shows signs of obesity; esp. the buttocks, stomach, or breasts. *After W.W.II the name of the last major German offensive, "The Battle of the Bulge," was humorously applied to woman's constant fight for a trim figure.*

bull. *v.t., v.i.* 1. To talk, discuss, or converse; esp. to talk at great length; to pass the time by talking. 2. To talk insincerely; to exaggerate; to talk with more intensity or at a greater length than one's knowledge warrants.

Since c1850. **3.** To bluff; to accomplish a task crudely or without knowledge owing to one's aggressiveness, energy, or enthusiasm. *Colloq. n.* **1.** A policeman; a law enforcement officer of any kind, as a uniformed policeman, detective, plain-clothes man, F.B.I. agent, prison guard, railroad policeman, or the like. *Prob. earlier than c1800. Orig. hobo and underworld use; since c1920 very common with all ranks of the underworld. Prob. of gypsy orig. from Sp. sl. "bul" = policeman, reinforced by the image of a bull as big and aggressive. Often used in combinations to designate the type of law enforcement officer.* **2.** Stupidity; insincerity; idle talk; exaggeration; lies; cant; esp. stupid, insincere, exaggerated, or untruthful talk, attitudes, or deeds; nonsense, hokum, boloney; conceit; bluff. *Often used as a one-word reply or opinion. Has now been in universal sl. use for many years. Prob. euphem. for "bullshit."* **3.** An elephant of either sex. *Circus use since c1920.* **4.** An ace playing card. *From "bullet."* Any smoking tobacco. *adj.* **1.** Causing or favoring high prices, esp. in the stock market. *Stock market use.* **2.** Large; largest; strong; most powerful.

bull cook. One who does menial tasks around a ranch, lumber camp, or the like; a camp flunky, kitchen helper, or errand boy. *Since c1920. Hobo, logger, and rancher use.*

bulldog. *n.* The earliest daily edition of a newspaper. *Newspaperman use. v.t.* **1.** To exaggerate or lie for personal gain about one's past or success; to attempt to increase demand for a product or service by exaggeration of merit. **2.** To wrestle a steer or calf to the ground by its horns, head, or neck. —**ging.** *n.* **1.** The act of wrestling a steer or calf to the ground, so that it may be branded. *Colloq.* **2.** Exagger-

ating or lying about one's success for personal gain; trying to increase the demand for a product or service by blatantly exaggerating its merits. **3.** A short or snubnosed revolver. *Mainly police and underworld use.*

bulldoze. *v.t.* To cow; to coerce.

bullet. *n.* **1.** In card-playing, an ace. *Usu. used in poker in the plural, e.g., "two bullets beat a pair of kings." Since c1930. Because, like bullets, no player can argue with aces.* **2.** A rivet. *Airplane factory use during W.W.II.* —**s.** *n.pl.* **1.** Any beans other than green or string beans. *Since c1900, orig. prison and USN use. Because such beans traditionally cause explosive stomach rumblings and eructations.* → **2.** Peas, esp. the hard varieties such as chickpeas or cowpeas. *Since c1920, orig. USN use.*

bullet bait. Soldiers, sailors, or marines, esp. when young or untrained, who are likely to be exposed to enemy fire; esp. marines. *Some use during and after W.W. II.*

bull fiddle. The double-bass viol. *Colloq.*

bull-fighter. An empty railroad freight car. *Railroad and hobo use.*

bull head; bull-head. *n.* **1.** A stupid or stubborn person. *Since c1850.* **2.** A nickel; five cents. *Archaic. From the figure of a buffalo on the nickel.*

bullheaded. *adj.* Stubborn. *Colloq.*

bullish. *adj.* Tending to favor high values and prices of corporate stocks; favorable to the selling of or short-term dealings in corporate stocks. *Stock-market use.*

bull of the woods, the. Any important person; one who acts with or assumes authority. *Since c1940.*

bullpen; bull pen. *n.* **1.** A small prison room used to confine convicts awaiting transfer, interrogation, or punishment. *Orig. prison use.* **2.** A prison; any enclosure serving as a temporary cell or prison for those awaiting official judgment. *Orig. prison and underworld use, c1900.* → **3.** An [enclosed] area near a baseball diamond where pitchers practice throwing and limber up as they wait to be called upon to enter the game. *Baseball use since c1920.* **4.** A men's college dormitory. *Some student use.* **5.** A living room or other room of a house or sorority house where a male student waits for his date while he is judged by the girl's family or sorority sisters. *Student use, c1940.*

bull session. *n.* **1.** An informal and often lengthy conversation or series of discussions, freq. idle or boastful, on a variety of topical or personal subjects, esp. among a group of male students. *Universally used by male students since c1920. Also common W.W. II Army use.* → **2.** Any discussion, short or long, either serious or for the purpose of passing idle time. *Since c1940.*

bullseye, hit the. 1. To succeed. **2.** To satisfy a specific taste or desire.

bullstaller. *n.* One whose inefficiency impedes the progress of a specific task.

bull's wool. *n.* Stolen clothes.

bully. *adj.* Fine, excellent, first-rate. *Associated with students c1850–1920. No longer common; now considered affected or pseudo-Brit.*

bum. *n.* **1.** Generally, a beggar, tramp, hobo, vagrant, or loafer; also, any jobless man or youth having little or no income; a poor, poorly dressed, and unkempt frequenter of saloons; a down-and-outer; sometimes, a hoodlum. *Common since c1880, the word has degenerated. Orig. = a vagabond or wandering hobo, by 1900 had taken on the connotation of beggar, one who has not the romantic wanderlust or pride of some early vagabonds. Later = a moneyless, prideless,* filthy, hopeless derelict and habitual drunkard. *During the Depression the word took on a little more status owing to the vast number of unemployed and tramps. During times of prosperity, however, the connotation of drunken derelict is the main one. No self-respecting vagabond or hobo would allow anyone to call him a bum today. From the German "Bummler," a good natured vagabond, an idler, a stroller + the British word "bum" = the buttocks.* → **2.** A drifter; a grifter. **3.** Any male without a professional occupation, goal in life, or social prestige; any disreputable or disliked youth. *Since c1920.* → **4.** A prize fighter, esp. one who is not a successful or good fighter. *Prize fight use since c1920.* → **5.** Any well-known athlete of country-club sports, such as tennis or golf, who lives on the hospitality of socially prominent sports fans. *Since c1920.* → **6.** Any sports enthusiast, usu. of skiing, tennis, or golf, who changes his job location frequently in order to be near ski slopes, golf courses, or the like; any sports fan who follows a sport, athlete, or team to various cities or locales, to the complete disruption of jobs and home life. *Since c1920.* → **7.** Any unskilled worker or athlete. *Since c1925.* → **8.** A promiscuous woman, esp. if uneducated and unsophisticated; a cheap prostitute. *Very common since c1940.* → **9.** An inferior racehorse; a slow-running racehorse. **10.** A fellow, a guy. *Used jocularly or affectionately since c1945.* **11.** Fig., anything considered as useless or unsatisfactory or as having the traits of a bum. **12.** Any person less successful than others think he should be; any person with but little money or status; a person without energy or ambition. **13.** The human posterior. *Colloq.* *v.i.* **1.** To live as a tramp or bum. *Since c1870.* → **2.** To beg; to go begging. *Since c1880. v.t.* **1.** To beg food, drink, money, a smoke, a ride, or the like. *Since c1865; in common use by c1900.* → **2.** To beg from a person. → **3.** To borrow something, esp. to borrow an item so insignificant that its return or replacement is not expected, such as a cigarette, match, or pencil. *Since c1940; very common. Colloq. adj.* **1.** Of inferior quality; inferior; unsatisfactory; not serving an intended purpose. → **2.** False, untrue; inaccurate; unreliable. **3.** Sickly; without energy. **4.** Spoiled; overripe. *Said of food.* —mer. *n.* A worthless youth or man, esp. one given to habitual borrowing. —my. *adj.* **1.** Slightly ill. **2.** Spoiled or overripe. *Said of food.*

bum, on the. 1. Living as a beggar or hobo; living and wandering as a tramp; begging. *Colloq. since c1900.* → **2.** Living any disreputable, disorderly life. **3.** In bad condition. *Said of a sick or indisposed person or a nonfunctioning or improperly functioning thing. Since c1900.*

bum around. 1. To loaf; to wander idly; to do nothing. *Since c1860.* → **2.** To associate with as a friend; to pass the time loafing, idling, or wandering with another.

bumblepuppy. *n.* **1.** In the card game of bridge, a game played without a plan or thought. → **2.** A card player who plays without much thought or interest. *Both uses since c1935. From the fictional and satirical game of "bumblepuppy," a highly organized, rule-ridden game described in Aldous Huxley's "Brave New World." Also a 19th-century children's tennis game in which the ball was hit so as to arc as high as possible over the net.*

bum-out. *n.* An assignment to easy work. *Some prison and Army use. c1950.*

bump. *v.t.* **1.** To dismiss an employee; to fine a person. *Since c1915.* → **2.** To reassign work

from an employee of lesser seniority to one of great seniority in order to retain the older employee and dismiss the younger. *Railroad and general union worker use since 1860.* → **3.** In U.S. federal government agencies, to replace another employee who is less retainable. *Since cW.W. II.* **4.** To defeat an opponent or opposing team. *Fig., to bump a person or team off a list of victors.* **5.** To make pregnant; to knock up. **6.** To give an employee an increase in salary or responsibility; to promote someone. *Since c1935.* **7.** In the card game of poker, to raise or increase the amount each player must bet to stay in the game. *Since c1935. Note the opposite meanings of* 1, 2, 3, *and* 7. *v.i.* **1.** To die. *Some use since c1940.* **2.** In dancing or during a striptease, to thrust the pelvis forward suddenly. *n.* **1.** A murder. **2.** A promotion; an increase in salary. *Since c1940.* —er. *n.* A striptease performer or erotic dancer; one who does bumps.

bump off; bump-off; bumpoff. *v.t.* To kill; to murder. *Underworld use since c1915. Freq. W.W.I. Army use. v.i.* To die. *Since c1920. Orig. hobo use.* bump-off; bumpoff. *n.* A murder. *Since c1920.*

bum-rush. *v.t.* To give someone the bum's rush.

bum's rush, the. 1. The ejection of a person from a room or public place by physical force. **2.** *Fig.,* any discourteous treatment used in getting rid of a person.

bum steer. A false clue; advice or information that proves to be wrong. *Common since c1925.*

bun. *n.* **1.** A state of drunkenness; a jag. *Perhaps from "bungey." Since c1920.* **2.** The human posterior.

bunch. *v.i.* To leave, depart, or withdraw. *n.* **1.** = mob. *Underworld use.* **2.** Money, esp. a large sum of money; a bankroll.

bunco artist; bunko artist. A professional swindler; a confidence man. *Newsp. and police use. Synthetic underworld use.*

bundle. *n.* 1. An amount of money; esp. a large amount of money. *Since c1900. Common since 1920 with the connotation of money illegally or unethically obtained; since c1935 such a connotation is not necessarily implied.* 2. A sexually desirable girl or young woman, esp. if small and cute. *Since c1930.*

bunk. *n.* Boloney; exaggeration; lies; cant. *Colloq.* *v.t.* To cheat.

bunk fatigue. *n.* A period of sleep or rest in bed; sleep. *Wide W.W. II Armed Forces use. This meaning orig. C.C.C. and Army use c1935.*

bunk flying. Talking about flying; exaggerated recounting of stories of flying. *W.W.II Air Force use.*

bunk habit = bunk fatigue.

bunkie. *n.* A roommate or bunkmate; a buddy. *More common than "buddy" during W.W.I. Army use. Mainly student use since W.W.I. Colloq.*

bunny. *n.* 1. A person; a guy or girl; a bewildered, confused, or habitually perplexed person. *Usu. in a phrase such as "tough bunny," "cuddle bunny," or "dumb bunny." Usu. preceded by an adj. such as "poor," "helpless," or "lost," the term implies affection or sympathy more often than criticism. Since c1925.* 2. A male prostitute to male homosexuals.

bun on, have a. 1. To be drunk. *Fairly common since c1925.* → 2. To be under the influence of a narcotic.

burg. *n.* A town; a city. *Since c1850. From "burgh." The word is assuming a connotation of a city or town that is disliked, because it is either too small and quiet or too big and noisy.*

burglar. *n.* Anyone who swindles, cheats, or takes advantage of another; any unethical businessman.

burgle. *v.t.* To burglarize. *Since c1850. Now considered jocular.*

buried. *adj.* Serving a life or a very long prison sentence. *Underworld and prison use. v.i., v.t.* To be in prison; to be put in prison, esp. if held incommunicado or in solitary confinement. *Since c1930; underworld use.*

burlap, the. *n.* = the sack. *Jocular.*

burleycue; burlecue; burlicue. *n.* A burlesque show.

burly. *n.* Burlesque.

burn. *v.t. & v.i.* 1. To cheat a partner out of his business profits or criminal loot. *Since 1800.* → 2. To rob, swindle, cheat, or take advantage of another. *Since c1800.* → 3. To be disappointed bitterly in business or love; to lose confidence or faith in others owing to past disappointments. *Since c1940.* 4. To electrocute a person, as legal punishment, in the electric chair. → 5. To kill; esp. by shooting. *Since c1935.* 6. To anger a person; to burn up. 7. To fight or assault a rival gang or member of a rival gang, esp. with clubs or knives. *Teenage street gang use since c1955.* 8. To apply pressure, mistreatment, or "heat" to a person to induce his resignation or to break down his morale. 9. [taboo] To become infected with, or to infect another with, a venereal disease. *v.i.* 1. To die by penal electrocution. 2. To become angry; to show one's anger; to burn up. *Since c1930.* 3. To move with great speed. *Colloq.*

burn down. 1. To shoot a person. 2. To refuse or reject another, or to deflate another's ego, or another's optimism, work, or plan, by severe criticism, sarcasm, or angry remarks.

burned-out. *adj.* 1. Tired, exhausted; specif., exhausted and depressed after the effects of a drug have worn off. *Drug addict use.* 2. Bored.

burnie. *n.* A partially smoked marijuana cigarette; a marijuana cigarette shared between two or more addicts. *Drug addict use.*

burn off = burn up. *Some use since late W.W.II; later popularized by freq. use in Walt Kelly's synd. newsp. comic, "Pogo." Reinforced by "browned off."*

burn one over. In baseball, to pitch a fast ball.

burn the breeze. To run at full speed; to drive a car at full speed. *Mainly Southwestern use, since c1930.*

burn the road. To drive a car fast. *Since c1930.*

burn [someone] up. 1. To make [a person] angry; to enrage; to irritate. *Very common.* **2.** To electrocute a criminal in the electric chair. **3.** To do one's job or to perform sensationally; to better previous records. *Common in sports since c1940.* **4.** To search a place thoroughly. **5.** To do anything intensely, rapidly, or thoroughly. *Colloq.*

burn with a low blue flame. To be in the most extreme stage of intoxication.

burp. *v.i., v.t.* To belch. *n.* A belch. *Of echoic origin. "Burp" has largely replaced "belch" in popular U.S. speech. Colloq.*

burp gun. 1. A small automatic gun used by the German Army during W.W.II. *Wide Army use during W.W.II. So called from its sound in firing.* → **2.** Any machine gun.

burr. *n.* = cold shoulder.

burr cut = crew cut.

burrole. *n.* **1.** The human ear. → **2.** An eavesdropper; one who seeks information; a stool pigeon. *Some underworld use since c1930. From Eng. underworld use.* **3.** Begging.

burrole (burrola), on the. To live the wandering life of a criminal, person wanted by the police, confidence man, or even of a hobo or beggar; to live the life of a drifter.

bury. *v.t.* To betray a friend or co-worker.

bury yourself! *interj.* = drop dead!

bus. *n.* **1.** A car, esp. one's own. *Since c1915; often implies that car is old; always said affectionately.* → **2.** An airplane. *Some W.W.I and W.W.II use. Some commercial aviation use. v.t.* To clear used dishes and silver from tables, esp. in a restaurant or cafeteria, and take them to the dishwasher. *Common since c1925. Prob. from the four-wheeled cart used in many public eating places. Colloq.* —**boy; bus-boy; bus boy.** *n.* One who busses dishes. *Common since c1925.*

buscar. *n.* **1.** Unexpected or forbidden pleasure; boodle; that which provides unexpected pleasure. *Thus "buscar" can be a woman or provided by a woman, the unexpected arrival of money, or a box of sweets, etc. Some W.W.II use.* → **2.** A close friend, esp. one from whom one can borrow money or with whom one shares a pleasurable experience. *A new slang word, still gaining popularity.*

bush. *n.* **1.** = bush league. *Fairly common since c1930.* **2.** A list of students whose scholastic standing or conduct is unsatisfactory. *Since c1925, student use.* **3.** A beard. *adj.* Pertaining to or reminiscent of small towns or rural areas; unsophisticated, nonprofessional, amateurish, *v.t.* To tire a person out; said of a task or action; to exhaust someone physically, mentally, or emotionally; to sap someone's energy. *From "bushed."* —**ed.** *adj.* Tired, fatigued, exhausted, as if from being lost or walking in circles. *Since c1870. Common since W.W.II.* —**er.** *n.* **1.** A baseball player in or from a minor league. → **2.** An inept, inexperienced, unsophisticated person; esp. an athlete. → **3.** A hick; one with hick concepts or manners.

bushes, the. Small towns or rural communities; the sticks. Cf. **bush league.**

bush league; bush-league. *n.* In baseball, a minor league of professional or semiprofessional teams, usu. composed of players lacking the experience or ability, or players who are too old, to be able to compete in the major leagues. *Common since c1925; colloq. adj.* Fig., small-timer; second-rate; amateurish, nonprofessional, unsophisticated.

bush parole. An escape from prison; one who has escaped from prison. *Prison and underworld use since c1920.*

bush patrol. 1. = necking. *Usu. jocular use, implying that one is going to take one's date into the seclusion of a clump of bushes or a park.* → 2. Sexual intercourse.

bushwa(h); booshwa(h); boushwa(h). Bunk; boloney; blah. *Often used as a one-word comment and as an exclam. Common since c1920; not now heard from young people.*

business, know [one's] = know [one's] onions.

business, the. *n.* 1. Rough treatment; murder; a beating; a bawling out; planned rudeness. 2. The equipment necessary for giving oneself an injection of a narcotic drug — hypodermic needle, cotton, etc.—or the substitutes often used, i.e., a pin, an eye-dropper, a bent spoon, etc. *Drug addict use.*

business end of [something]. The dangerous, critical, or most important part of something; the front section or end of a piece of machinery. Thus, "the business end of a gun" = a gun's muzzle; "the business end of a truck" = a truck's engine.

businessman's bounce. Dance music or a popular song played in fast tempo, satisfying to those with little knowledge of dancing or of jazz. *Derisive use by musicians.*

bus ride! = subway!

buss = bus.

bust. *n.* 1. A failure of any kind; one who cannot complete a specif. task successfully or who has failed to attain a specif. goal; an inferior or worthless thing; an item which does not serve its intended purpose. → 2. A notice of failure, as a note dismissing a student from a school or an order demoting a soldier in rank. *Since c1890.* 3. A drunkard; a bum or hobo. *Dial.* 4. A punch with the fist. *Since c1915.* 5. A raid by the police. *v.t.* 1. To break something. *Colloq.* 2. To fail an examination, recitation, or course of study; to fail a student. *Common student use by c1900.* → 3. To demote a military man in rank; specif., to demote a noncommissioned officer to the rank of private. *Common Army use since W.W.I.* 4. To tame a wild horse, fig. to break the spirit of a wild horse. 5. To hit, as a person. *Since c1920.* 6. To break open or crack a safe or strong box; to enter or break into a place in order to rob it. *Underworld use.* 7. To ruin something; to make a mistake. 8. To catch another in the act of doing something illegal or unethical. *Rock-and-roll and some general teenage use since c1955.* 9. To disperse a gang or group; to force a gang or group to leave a specific public place, street corner, or the like. *Teenage gang use since c1955. adj.* Broke; penniless. *Fairly common.* —ed. *adj.* 1. Reduced in rank. *Army use since cW.W.I.* 2. Without money; broke. 3. Arrested. —er. *n.* 1. An unusually large person. *Since c1850. Dial.* 2. A fellow, a guy, esp. a wise guy. *Almost always in direct address to a stranger, usu. one who has aroused the speaker's anger.* 3. A square, a Babbitt. *Some far-out use since c1955.*

bust a gut. To use all one's strength in attempting to accomplish a specif. task, either a manual or other task, successfully; to try to the best of one's ability; fig., to try so hard that one ruptures oneself. *Since c1945.*

bust [one's] conk. To work hard; to apply oneself diligently.

busthead; bust-head. *n.* 1. Inferior or cheap whisky, liquor, or wine; fig., whisky so raw that one's head will burst from drinking it. → 2. A drunkard, esp. a hobo or derelict who is a drunkard.

bust out. *v.i.* To be dismissed from a college or university because of failing grades. **bust-out.** *n.* The conclusion of a swindle, when the victim surrenders his money; the trick or swindle that causes a victim to lose money. *Police use; synthetic underworld use. v.i., v.t.* To lose all one's money gambling, specif. at dice; to win all of someone's money at gambling, specif. at dice, and specif. by crooked means. **—s.** Crooked or loaded dice.

bust-out joint. A notoriously crooked gambling house.

bus up = bus.

but. *conj.* And. *adv.* Very; definitely. *Often used only to emphasize the word following; sometimes used to signal a coming repetition of the preceding word. Typically, it joins a monosyllabic, flat adverb (such as "good," "loud," "quick," "soon," "bad," etc.) to a preceding predicate or other verbal construction. Occasionally it precedes an adj.*

Butch; butch. *n.* 1. The youngest male child of a family. *Dial. and archaic.* 2. A tough or rough youth or man; a tough or rough-looking man. 3. A type of men's haircut. *Cf.* crew cut. 4. A vendor, a butcher. 5. A mistake. 6. A female homosexual who plays the male role. *v.t.* To spoil or ruin something. **—er.** *n.* 1. A vendor of small items, as newspapers or candy, as in a train or at a circus. *Colloq.* 2. An inferior surgeon. 3. An inferior barber. 4. Any person who is particularly clumsy at work requiring manual dexterity.

butcher shop. A hospital.

butcher wagon. An ambulance.

butt. *n.* 1. The rump. *Colloq.* 2. The remainder, esp. the last year or few months of a military enlistment or prison sentence. *Since c1915.* → 3. A short time; a short enlistment or prison sentence. 4. A whole cigarette, an unsmoked cigarette. *From stand.* "butt" = *the stub of a partially smoked cigarette or cigar.*

butter. *n.* Flattery. *Colloq.* *v.t.* = butter up.

butter-and-egg man. A wealthy, unsophisticated, small-town businessman who tries to become a playboy, esp. one when visiting a large city; a wealthy Western farmer or businessman visiting in a big Eastern city. *Common since c1920. Popularized by nightclub entertainer Texas Guinan.*

butter-ball. *n.* Any plump person, esp. a young woman.

buttercup. *n.* A girl, esp. an attractive, innocent girl.

butterfingers. *n. sing.* A clumsy person, esp. a person who habitually drops things; specif., a baseball player who drops the ball when attempting to catch it. *Since c1900; colloq.*

butterflies; butterflys. *n. pl.* Fluttery sensations in one's stomach, caused by anxiety or nervous tension. *n. sing.* Nervousness; apprehension. *From the expression "to have butterflies in one's stomach," descriptive of nervous tension.*

butterfly ball; butterfly pitch. In baseball, a slow, floating pitch; a knuckleball.

butterfly kiss. A caress given by winking one eye so that the lashes brush against the face of the receiver.

butterfly pitch = butterfly ball.

butter up. To flatter someone; to flatter or court someone so that person will be receptive to a request for aid or a favor.

butt in (on). To interfere; to intrude; to give one's advice or opinion when one has not been asked to do so; orig., to interrupt a person who is speaking, in order to talk or give one's own opinion. **butt-in.** *n.* An unwelcome intruder; one who butts in.

buttinsky; buttinski. *n.* One who habitually interrupts a speaker, interferes, or tries to give advice or opinions to others; lit., one who butts in. *One of the few U.S. words with a "—sky" suffix denoting "one who," rather than the usual "—er" suffix. Based on the Central European "—sky," "—ski" suffix.*

button. *n.* 1. The chin, the point of the jaw. *Prize fight use. Colloq.* 2. A baby. *Dial.* 3. [taboo]. The clitoris.

button, on the. 1. On the point of the chin, said of a perfectly aimed blow. → 2. Exactly; completely right or correct; comprehending basic issues, revealing; satisfying. 3. Exactly on time, on the dot.

button down; button-down. *v.t.* 1. To classify, recognize, or peg someone. 2. To finish or complete a task, to be confident that one will complete or finish a task successfully. *Not as common as "button up."* 3. To lock up or make secure a room or building; to clean or straighten up a room or building. *n., adj.* A men's style of shirt collar, in which the points of the collar button to the shirt front. *Colloq.*

buttons, have all [one's]. To be of normal mentality or behavior.

button(s) missing, have a (few). To be crazy; to be eccentric. *Colloq. Also common in Eng.*

button up. 1. = button up [one's] lip. 2. To accomplish a task successfully. *During and since W.W. II.* 3. To lock up, close up, or make secure an item, room, or building.

button up [one's] lip. To stop talking; to shut up; to keep a secret.

butt out. To stop interrupting; to stop giving unwanted advice or opinion. *Usu. a command. Antonym of "butt in."*

buy. *v.t.* 1. To agree to something or with someone; to believe; to acquiesce; to accept as true; to approve. 2. To accomplish or effect. 3. To hire; to engage the services of.

buzz. *n.* 1. A telephone call; a ring, usu. in "give [someone] a buzz." *Colloq.* 2. A thrill, a kick, a charge, a feeling of excitement, pleasure, satisfaction, or the like. *Since c1935.* 3. A police squad car. *Rock-and-roll and some general teenage use since c1955. From the siren's sound.* 4. A kiss, esp. a quick compassionate kiss, as on the cheek. *v.t.* 1. To telephone a person. 2. To give information to someone in confidence, to whisper to someone. 3. To announce one's arrival to another, as by ringing a doorbell; to call for someone by ringing a buzzer. 4. To beg from someone or at a place. *Hobo use since c1920.* → 5. To pilfer from a place; to rob a person. *Underworld use since c1925.* 6. While flying, to swoop low and fast over a place with a great noise of engines; said of an airplane or pilot. → 7. To go on a spree in a specif. town or bar. *W.W.II Air Force and Army use.* 8. To intoxicate. *From "buzz" = a thrill, reinforced by previous meaning of "to go on a spree."*

buzz along. To leave, to depart, esp. from a social visit. *Since c1935.*

buzzard. *n.* 1. A contemptible man; specif., an old, unkempt man. *Since c1800.* 2. Chicken served at a meal; turkey served at a meal. *Army, prison, and student use.* 3. An eagle insigne, as worn by an Army or USN officer. *Since c1920; Armed Forces use.*

buzzard colonel. A full colonel in the U.S. Army, as opposed to a lieutenant colonel. *Some W.W. II use.*

buzz around the barrel. To get something to eat; to eat, esp. a snack. *Rock-and-roll use since c1955.*

buzz-buzz. *n.* Buzz; noise; specif., the noise of a crowd, as at an athletic contest.

buzzer. *n.* A policeman's badge; a badge worn or carried by any officer of the law.

buzz off. To go away; to leave; specif., to beat it. *Usu. a command.*

B.V.D.'s. *sing.* A suit of men's underwear. *From the trade-mark "B.V.D." a well-known brand.*

by. For phrases beginning with "by," see under principal word of phrase.

by. *prep.* 1. With; e.g., "Five skins is jake by me." 2. From; at; e.g., "I'll buy you a drink by Antek." *This use resembles the Fr. "chez," but derives from Yiddish usage.*

bylow. *n.* A Barlow knife; usu. a single-bladed folding knife with a bone handle; any knife with a large, flat blade. *A corruption of "Barlow."*

byway. *n.* A sidewalk; a road; an aisle.

by with [something], get. 1. = get away with [something]. 2. To be mildly successful; to be adequate, but not ambitious enough to be truly successful. 3. To be almost caught or punished, but to escape.

C

C. *n.* 1. A hundred dollars; orig. a hundred-dollar bill. *From "century" or the Roman numeral "C" which at one time was printed on all $100 bills.* 2. Cocaine; sometimes, heroin. *Drug addict use.* 3. A bookmaker's commission. *Racing use.*

cab. *n.* The cockpit of an airplane.

cabbage. *n.* 1. Money; banknotes; paper money. *Colloq.* 2. Tobacco. *Dial.*

cabbage-head. *n.* 1. A person's head;—used disparagingly. → 2. A stupid person. *Colloq.*

cabbage leaves. Paper currency.

cabbie; cabby. *n.* A cab-driver; now specif. a taxi-driver.

cabin girl. A chambermaid, esp. a girl or woman whose job it is to make the beds and straighten up the rooms each day on a ship, at a motel, or the like.

caboodle. *n.* An entity, group, or lot; the entire lot of people or things.

cack-broad. *n.* = cackle-broad. Cf. kack.

cackleberries and grunts. Bacon and eggs.

cackle-broad; cack-broad. *n.* A fashionable, wealthy, or society woman; lit., a woman who talks a lot in a hifalutin manner.

cad. *n.* = Caddy.

Caddy; Caddie. *n.* A Cadillac automobile. *Some use since c1925. Most common use since c1945.*

Cadillac. *n.* An ounce of heroin; heroin; sometimes, cocaine. *Addict use. From "C"; as is true with much argot, once "C" becomes known to those outside the addict groups, and can be classified as sl., the addicts need a new word and build it on "C." Once "Cadillac" is somewhat familiar to those outside the group, it will be replaced by another word. Reinforced by the fact that an ounce of heroin, or any drug, seems just as expensive and desirable to an addict as a Cadillac automobile might be to someone else.*

Caesar. *n.* A type of men's haircut. *Because it resembles the hair style seen on typical busts of Julius Caesar and was first popularized by actor Marlon Brando, who wore such a hair style while playing Mark Antony in the movie "Julius Caesar."*

cage. *n.* The human body; the human skeleton. *v.t.* To imprison.

cager. *n.* 1. A basketball player. *Some use since c1925.* 2. A drunkard. *Dial.*

cagey; cagy. *adj.* Crafty; cunning; wary; sly. *Colloq.*

cake, take the. Of an action, person, thing, or concept, to be so unusual as to be unbelievable; to be extremely audacious; to have unusual behavior or characteristics; fig. to win a cake as being the most unusual freak ever encountered. *Orig. to win the prize in a cakewalk (dancing) contest. Usu. in "You take (or "that takes") the cake." Colloq. and very popular since c1890.*

cake-cutter. *n.* One who shortchanges the public. *Circus use.*

cake-eater. *n.* A ladies' man, a dude; a male flirt; a playboy. *Lit., prob. a young man who often attends ladies' tea parties, where cake may be served.*

calaboodle. *n.* = caboodle.

callaboose. *n.* A prison or prison cell; a jail. *From the Sp. "calabozo."*

calf love. *n.* = puppy love.

calf-slobber. *n.* Meringue, as on pies.

California. *n.* A type of men's haircut, similar to the Detroit.

California blanket. *n.* Newspaper used as bedding. *Hobo use.*

California kiss (-off) = kiss-off. *East Coast use.*

calk off = caulk off.

call. *n.* 1. The act of or an instance of one's name being called, as over a public address system. 2. A telephone call, specif. for the purpose of waking a person. 3. A meeting; an interview; a period or session during which a director or producer of a play or movie interviews and tries out prospective actors, dancers, singers, etc., for jobs; a rehearsal. *Theater use.* 4. A desire to urinate or, usu., to have a bowel movement. *Because one must answer "Nature's call."*

call-back. *n.* A request to return; an instance of being called back, in person, on the phone, etc.

call down. *v.t.* To rebuke, scold, bawl out, etc. *Colloq.*

call girl. 1. A prostitute; lit., a prostitute who works in a call house. → 2. By confusion and popular misconception = a prostitute who visits a known or recommended customer at his hotel room or apartment when called on the telephone to do so, as opposed to a prostitute who solicits customers in a public place or works in a brothel; a prostitute whose known or recommended clients visit her apartment after making an appointment by telephone. *Use of the telephone makes the call girl less conspicuous, and less apt to arrest, than the average prostitute. The arrangement usu. insures her of a wealthy, socially prominent clientele. Call girls have been in business since c1935, and their existence known to the general public since c1950.*

call house. 1. A brothel; lit., a brothel in which the clients may call upon the prostitutes to do anything at any time. → 2. By confusion and popular misconception = a house, apartment, or room where telephone messages are received and relayed to call girls; a place where call girls live; a brothel where appointments are made by telephone.

call it quits. To give up one's attempt to do something; specif., to become divorced, separate, break one's engagement, or the like.

call joint = call house.

campus. *v.t.* 1. To discipline or punish a student by confining him to the campus. *Some student use since c1920.* 2. To discipline a student by withdrawing a privilege, not necessarily the privilege of leaving campus.

campus butcher. In college, a ladies' man; one who slays the girls.

can. *n.* 1. A toilet; a rest room. *Since c1900. Though still considered vulgar, became common during W.W.II.* 2. The human rump; usu. used of men only to indicate that part of the body which bears the brunt of a fall, or in "fat can," indicating obesity or that the man sits too much and is lazy; usu. used of women only to indicate the rump as contributing to or detracting from sexual appearance. 3. A jail, a prison; a police station. 4. A safe or strongbox. *Underworld use since at least c1910.* 5. The human head. *Some use since c1915.* 6. A boat, specif., a destroyer. *USN use during and since W.W. I, wide W.W.II USN use.* 7. Specif., a hot rod, a car redesigned by the, usu. teenage, owner to give it greater speed or acceleration. *Hot-rod use since c1950.* 8. A storage battery. *Orig. W.W.II USN use. v.t.* 1. To expel a student from school. *Student use.* → 2. To discharge or fire an employee. *Colloq.* → 3. To eject a person from a place; to forbid a person entrance to a place, almost always a public place, as a bar, restaurant, night club, or the like. 4. To stop, cease, or put an end to something, usu. to cease talking, or talking about a specif. subject or with a specif. attitude, at least temporarily. 5. To complete successfully; to clean thoroughly. 6. To imprison.

can, (put) in the. To approve the final sequences or shots of a movie; lit., to put a reel of finished film in a metal container, or can, ready for distribution to movie houses. *Movie use.*

canary. *n.* 1. A girl or young woman. → 2. Specif., a woman singer, a professional female vocalist, almost always one who sings popular songs or jazz music with a band. *Orig. radio and jazz use.* 3. An informer; lit., one who "sings." 4. A compliment; praise; critical acclaim. *From the Yiddish "kein nahurra" (Yiddish sl. "canurra") = no evil eye or no bad luck. v.i.* To sing, usu. professionally

candy. *n.* Cocaine. *Drug addict use. adj.* Stylish or garish—said of dress; frivolous; facetious.

cane corn. Lit., corn whisky, as made from corn and cane sugar; moonshine; home-made or bootleg whisky.

can-house; canhouse; can house. *n.* A brothel.

canned. *adj.* 1. Drunk. 2. Recorded, as on a phonograph recording; said of music or talk. *Since c1925.* → 3. Photographed on movie film; filmed. *Movie use.* 4. To be a prisoner.

canned goods. *sing.* A virgin; a male or female without sexual experience.

canned up. Drunk. See **canned**.

cannery. *n.* A jail. *From "can."*

cannon. *n.* 1. A pistol; a revolver; any gun. 2. A professional thief or robber. *Contrary to pop. belief, this use did not evolve because a thief carries a cannon = gun. This use grew out of the Yiddish "gonif" = a thief, shortened to Amer. sl. "gon" or gun. Thus "gun" = thief, and "cannon" = a big or important thief. Orig. underworld use. Since c1910.* → 3. Specif., a pickpocket; in a team or gang of pickpockets, the one who actually removes the wallet from the victim's pocket. *Since c1920. Orig. underworld use. v.t.* To rob a person or a place, esp. by picking pockets.

cannon ball. 1. A fast express train; orig., a fast freight train. *Since c1915. Orig. hobo use. From its speed.* 2. A message sent from one prisoner to another, as via a trusty or known guard; a message surreptitiously sent from prison by a prisoner, as to his underworld friends.

cannon fodder. Infantry troops, esp. young, inexperienced troops, who are likely to suffer many casualties; troops, sent to attack the enemy, who have little chance to win the battle, owing to bad planning, inexperience, poor equipment, or the like. *Wide W.W.I use, some W.W.II use.*

can of corn. 1. In baseball, a high, slow fly ball. *Baseball use.* 2. A man, a fellow, or a guy, esp. one who has done something audacious.

can on, get a. To be or become drunk.

can-opener. *n.* Any tool used to open a safe in order to rob it. *Underworld use.*

cans. *n. pl.* Radio earphones; any radio or telephone earphones worn on the head. *Orig. radio amateur use.*

cantaloupe. *n.* A baseball.

canto. *n.* A regular division of any sports contest; a round of a prize fight; an inning of baseball; a quarter of a football game; etc.

cap. *n.* 1. A captain. → 2. A man, esp. in direct address to a stranger who commands respect. *Used by beggars, porters, and servants who wish to practice concealed flattery upon their clients.* See **captain.** 3. A capsule, esp. of a narcotic, such as heroin. *v.t.* To do better than another; to overbid another person, tell a better joke, or the like.

cap, go-to-hell. *n.* = overseas cap, Army or Marine. *Esp. when worn at a rakish angle. W.W.II Army and Marine use.*

Cape Cod turkey. Codfish. *Some jocular use.*

caper. *n.* 1. A whisky-drinking spree. *Some use since c1875.* → 2. Any spree; a period or instance of fun, excitement, or exhilaration. *Common student use since c1945.* → 3. A prank. → 4. Specif., an instance of a crime, esp. a robbery; a job. *Since c1925, orig. underworld use.*

capon. *n.* An effeminate man, usu. a homosexual. *From "capon."*

captain. *n.* A generous person; a free spender. *Hobo use.*

captain of the head. Lit., one in charge of the latrine aboard ship; fig., a novice or stupid person, a useless or blundering person, who cannot be assigned to important work. *W.W.II Armed Forces jocular use, orig. USN use.*

card. *n.* A portion of a drug used by an addict. **—er.** *n.* A profes-

sional gambler, esp. a card player. *Some use since c1850.*

cards, in the. Expected; impending. *Often negative, as "It's not in the cards."*

car-hop; carhop. *n.* A waiter or, usu., a waitress who serves food to patrons in parked cars. *Based on "bell-hop." v.i.* To work as a car-hop.

carny; carney; carnie. *n.* 1. A carnival. → 2. A carnival worker. → 3. The special idiom or argot spoken by carnival workers.

carpet, on the. 1. Summoned to appear before one's employer, administrative superior, or the like, as in his office, for a reprimand. *Since c1900; colloq. Freq., the one summoned walks in onto a carpeted floor from his uncarpeted workroom, and stands on the carpet while being adversely criticized.* → 2. Reprimanded, scolded, severely criticized, by anyone. *Always used with the past tense.*

carps. *n. sing.* A stage carpenter; often as a nickname. *Theater use.*

carrot-top. *n.* A red-haired person; often as a nickname.

carry. *n.* A sick, wounded, or injured person who must be taken to a hospital by stretcher or ambulance.

carry a (heavy) load. To be drunk. *Has been gaining in pop. since c1940.*

carry a lot of weight. To be very influential.

carrying weight. The blues.

carry the banner. To walk the streets all night for want of a place to sleep.

carry the difference. To go, or be, armed; to carry a gun.

carry the load. To be depended upon by others to do most of the work; to have much work to do; to be responsible for the successful accomplishment of a specif. task.

carry the mail. To be depended upon to do the most work; to accomplish a task successfully, esp. a task that is necessary to others.

carry the torch (for [someone]). To suffer or be sad, melancholy, or self-pitying from unrequited love.

carve. *v.t.* To give one a thrill; to send. *Swing use c1935–c1945.*

Casanova; casanova. *n.* A man who is charming to, courts, and is sexually successful and adroit with a variety of women. *Colloq; from the name of the famous lover.*

case. *n.* **1.** An odd, unusual, or eccentric person; a precocious child. **2.** The act or an instance of being romantically attached to one of the opposite sex; an obsession for one of the opposite sex; a crush. *Colloq.* **3.** The act of inspecting a place to be robbed in order to gain useful information; an inspection. *Orig. underworld use.* → **4.** The last of any item; mainly card-playing use. Thus in the game of poker the case ace is the last or fourth ace in the deck. *v.t.* **1.** To look something over carefully with the view of dealing with it later, esp. the scene, as a bank, of a prospective robbery. *Orig. underworld use.* **2.** To scrutinize a person; orig. to scrutinize a prospective victim to ascertain how much money he is carrying.

case-ace. *n.* In card games, esp. poker, the fourth ace after three aces have already been dealt. *From the game of faro.*

case-dough. *n.* A small amount of money, specif., as saved for use in emergencies.

case note. A dollar; a one-dollar bill.

case out. To follow or befriend another so as to help earn and share in profits, earnings, winnings, or loot; to bet with or on another.

cash in [one's] chips. 1. To terminate a business transaction, sell one's share of, or stock in, a business, or the like, in order to realize one's cash profits. *From the*

gambling term. → **2.** To die. *The most common use.*

cash in on[something]. To obtain a profit or an advantage, esp. due to one's having superior or confidential knowledge; to take full advantage of any opportunity; to realize the maximum profit, publicity, promotion, or advantage of a specific situation.

cast a kitten = have kittens. To express one's anger, anxiety, fear, excitement, amusement, or the like, esp. violently; to have a fit.

castle. *n.* Any dwelling. *Jocular use.*

cat. *adj.* Drunk. *n.* **1.** A spiteful woman; a malicious gossip. *Colloq.* **2.** A lion, tiger, leopard, or any other animal of the cat family. *Circus use.* **3.** A man who dresses in the latest style and pursues women; a dude, a sport; one who tomcats; one who is worldly, wise, or hep. *Prob. from* "alligator" → "gator" → "gate" *and then corrupted to* "cat," *reinforced by* "tomcat." *Mainly Negro use.* **4.** A jazz musician. *Associated with and pop. by swing use, but has much older and more general jazz meaning. Wide bop use, but cool and far-out musicians are not referred to as cats by their devotees. Fairly well known general use since c1940.* **5.** A devotee of jive or swing, a hepcat. *Jive and swing use c1935–c1942.* **6.** A devotee of, or a member of, a group that is, or anyone that understands or appreciates, bop, cool, far-out, or beat; anyone who is a member of the avant garde of music, art, or literature; any nonconformist; specif., a hipster. *Used by members of these groups since c1950; fairly common general use since c1955, mainly owing to the sensational newspaper articles about hipsters and the beat generation.* **7.** A man, a fellow, a guy; since c1950, any human being. *Some c1938 jive and swing use. Wide bop, cool, far-out, and beat use since c1950. v.i.* **1.** To court or seek women for sexual reasons; to consort with prostitutes or promiscuous women. *Some use, mainly Negro, since c1900.* 2. To gossip; to make disparaging remarks. 3. To loaf or idle; to spend one's time idling on street corners. *Some teenage street gang use since c1950.* —ty. *adj.* Spiteful; prone to malicious gossip. *Colloq.; in ref. to a cat's sharp claws, reinforced by a cat's spitting.*

catch. *v.t.* 1. In "to catch a smoke" = to smoke a cigarette. *Since c1925.* 2. To attend, see, or hear any entertainment, performance, or performer. 3. To receive a complaint, strong criticism, a bawling out, punishment, or the like. *Usu. in "to catch it" or "to catch hell." Colloq. n.* A person highly desirable for a specif. job or relationship; esp. a worthwhile, attractive, popular, or wealthy person of the opposite sex who will make a highly desirable husband or wife. *Colloq. v.i.* To receive a complaint or bawling out.

catch, the. *n.* The flaw, the part of an otherwise good plan or easy task that may cause difficulty or be difficult; a trick.

catch flies. 1. To distract an audience's attention from another performer on the stage by making an unnecessary motion or motions. *Theater use.* 2. To yawn, esp. in boredom.

catfit. *n.* A fit of anger; any emotional outburst due to extreme anger, disappointment, or the like.

cat-haul; cat haul; cathaul. *v.t.* To subject a person to prolonged, severe questioning. *From the earlier lit. sense of dragging a clawing cat down the bare back of a person tied prone.*

catholic. *n.* A pickpocket.

cat house; cathouse; cat-house. *n.* 1. A brothel, esp. a cheap brothel. 2. = barrelhouse, style of jazz music.

cat lick. A Catholic. *A jocular and derog. corruption.*

cat out of the bag, let the. To disclose a secret, often, though not always, inadvertently. *Colloq.*

cat plant. An oil or gasoline refinery.

cats and dogs. 1. Low-priced stocks, as those yielding no revenue or being of dubious value. *Financial use since c1900.* 2. Odds and ends, bits and pieces.

cat's eye. A type of boy's playing marble, of any color, having a crescent-shaped area of a second color in the center. *Young boy use.* —s. *n. sing.* Tapioca pudding.

cat's-paw. *n.* A pawn; a dupe.

cattle train. A Cadillac automobile. *Negro use.*

caulk off. To sleep; to go to sleep. *USN use since c1925.*

cavalier. *n.* In prize fighting, a skilled boxer, as opposed to a strong slugger. *Some use since c1920.*

cave. *n.* 1. A room; a pad. *Some use since c1935. Orig. jive use, now far-out use.* → 2. A small or windowless office. —man. *n.* 1. A strong, virile, rough, or rude man; esp. one who is sexually attractive. 2. In prize fighting, a strong slugger, as opposed to a skillful boxer. *Some use since c1920.*

cayuse. *n.* A horse, esp. a small, hardy animal descended from the wild horses of the Northwest. *Western colloq. use.*

c c pills. Laxative pills of any kind. *From the laxative pills dispensed by the Armed Forces Medical Corps. W.W. II use.*

Cecil. *n.* Cocaine. *Addict use.*

Cee. *n.* = C.

ceiling, hit the. To become greatly excited or violently angry; to go up in the air; blow one's top.

celeb. *n.* A celebrity. *Since c1910; orig. theatrical and newsp. columnist use.*

cellar. *n.* The lowest standing in a baseball league.

cement-mixer. *n.* Any act, as dancing, that includes a vertical rotation of the pelvis; a person who performs such movements, but usu. a strip-tease dancer or prostitute. *From the rotary motion of a cement-mixing machine.*

century. *n.* A hundred dollars; a $100 bill.

chain-gang; chaingang. *n.* A gang of prison laborers, usu. Negroes, chained together or wearing shackles and working at hard manual labor, as roadbuilding. *Colloq. Chain-gangs are still common in the South.*

chain lightning. Inferior liquor. *Dial.*

chain-smoke. *v.i.*, *v.t.* To smoke cigarettes continuously, lighting the second from the first, the third from the second, and so on. **—r.** *n.* One who chain-smokes.

chair, the. *n.* 1. A chairman or mediator of a meeting or organization. *Stand. parliamentary use.* 2. The electric chair; death in the electric chair.

chair-warmer. *n.* An idle person.

chalk. *n.* 1. A horse favored to win a race; a betting favorite. 2. Milk; esp. powered milk. *Prison use; W.W. II Armed Forces use. adj.* Favored to win;—said of a race horse; playing favored race horses or short odds;—said of a bettor.

chalk-eater; chalk eater. *n.* One who bets only on favorites. *Common horse-racing use.*

Chamber of Commerce. A toilet. *From "chamber pot."*

champ. *n.* 1. A sports champion, esp. in boxing. *Colloq.* 2. A bum; an unsuccessful person. *Owing to the popular image of prize fighters as men of more brawn than brain, and to various scandals in modern ring history, the word is as often used sarcastically or condescendingly as to convey honor or respect.*

change. *n.* Money.

change [one's] luck. To have sexual intercourse, esp., in the South, with a Negress; used only by white males.

change the channel. To change the topic of conversation. *Teenage use since c1955. From the television use.*

change-up; changeup. *n.*, *v.t.*, *adj.* In baseball, a pitch delivered with an impressive windup but little speed, used to confuse the batter and destroy his timing. *Since c1940.*

chank; chanck; shank. *n.* A chancroid or chancre; a case of venereal disease, esp. syphilis.

channel. *n.* A vein, usually in the crook of the elbow or the instep, into which narcotics addicts inject drugs. See main line.

chappie. *n.* A fellow, a chap.

chaps. *n.pl.* Leather or fur leggings worn by cowboys to protect their legs from cactus and brush while riding. *Since c1820. Orig. Sp. "chaparajos," used by Sp. cowboys [Mexico and S. A.] as a protection against the chaparral bush.*

chapter. *n.* 1. An inning of baseball. 2. Any complete action or episode, such as a particular sequence of experiences in the life of a person.

chapter and verse. Rules; a list of rules, taboos, commands, etc. *Orig. ref. to ability to quote exact chapters and verses from the Bible.*

character. *n.* 1. An eccentric; a person whose mental or behavioral processes are unusual. *Common since c1940. The term is used to show either deprecation of a person's eccentricity or affection for a person's individuality.* 2. A person; a man; esp. one who is not personally known to or respected by the speaker.

charge. *n.* 1. An injection of a narcotic. *Underworld and addict use since before c1925.* → 2. Marijuana. *Addict use.* 3. An extreme sensual or psychological response. 4. Sexual excitement, esp. from merely visual contact with the opposite sex. *Orig.*

from the popular image of activation through an electric charge and/or the sensation of electric shock. v.t. To rob. May derive from psy. excitement thieves experience in their work.

chariot. *n.* Any vehicle; esp. an automobile or a train caboose.

charity girl. A sexually promiscuous young woman. *Applied only to young unmarried, seemingly respectable females. Became somewhat common during W.W. II.*

Charley. *n.* 1. Any minor stiffness or pain of the joints or muscles. *Orig. Charley horse.* 2. A stupid or blundering soldier. *c1945, Army use.* **charley.** *n.* A watchman.

Charley Coke. A cocaine addict. **Charley coke.** *n.* Cocaine. *Addict use.*

Charley horse. A soreness and stiffness in arm or leg muscles induced by strain or excessive exercise.

Charlie. *n.* = Charley coke.

Charlie Brown! *exclam.* An exclamation indicating surprise. *From the character in the synd. comic strip "Peanuts," whose behavior freq. elicits from other characters the expression, "Good grief, Charlie Brown!"*

charm. *v.t.* To court, flatter, or attempt to impress a person, usu. one of the opposite sex or a superior, esp. with a line.

chart. *n.* 1. Specif., published information showing the past performances of race horses so that bettors may compare the merits of horses in a race. 2. A musical score or written arrangement. *Some cool and far-out use since c1950.*

chase. *v.t.* 1. To court a girl; to seek sexual contact with a particular woman. 2. To pursue a business opportunity. 3. To look for a job, a rare item, etc. *n.* Any rapid, confusing activity. —*r.* *n.* 1. An order, glass, or drink of water, soda, beer, or other mild liquid, taken immediately after

a drink of neat liquor. *Colloq.* 2. A woman chaser. 3. An employee whose assignment is to hurry other manual workers in their work. 4. An exit march; music played as an audience leaves a theater; the finale in an entertainment. *Circus and theater use.*

chase [oneself], (go). Lit., to depart; to beat it; fig., to stop annoying or bothering. *Often used absolutely.*

chassis. *n.* The human body, esp. the female torso.

Chattanooga. *n.* A railroad train. *An example of literary sl., used only in fiction and newsp. Derived from pop. song of 1940's, "Chattanooga Choo-Choo."*

chatterbox. *n.* 1. An anti-aircraft machine gun. *W.W.II.* 2. An announcing or intercommunication system. *W.W.II.*

chaw. *n.* A bite or portion of chewing tobacco. *Colloq.*

cheap. *adj.* 1. Stingy. *Colloq.* 2. Unrefined; open to accusations of being promiscuous (said of a girl or woman). 3. Having a bad reputation, as of one who gives and withdraws affection, loyalty, or sexual favors easily. —ie. *n.* Any cheaply made, dilapidated, or secondhand item.

Cheap John. *adj.* Inferior; unknown; unimportant; said of people and places. *n.* A flophouse, cheap brothel, or esp. a dirty, dilapidated saloon.

cheapskate. *n.* A stingy, niggardly person; a person who seeks cheap goods or pleasures; a person who attempts to avoid his share of expenses. *Now stand.*

cheat. *v.i., v.t.* To be sexually unfaithful to one's spouse or permanent sexual partner. —er. *n.* An unfaithful person. —ers. *n.pl.* 1. Spectacles. 2. Marked cards. —ing. *n.* The act or an instance of being sexually unfaithful to one's spouse.

cheat stick. 1. A slide rule or other such calculating device that can be used instead of manual calculation. 2. A wage-rate scale by which any employee's pay is determined.

check. *interj.* O.K.; definitely; "I understand"; "I'll do it"; and the like. *Usu. a one-word reply. n.* 1. A dollar. 2. A certain quantity, a small package, esp. of contraband or narcotics.

check bouncer. One who writes checks against nonexistent bank accounts or against accounts containing insufficient funds to cover the check.

check crew (gang, mob, team, etc.). Working groups composed of both Negro and white members.

checkerboard. *n.* A town, neighborhood, public gathering place, factory, etc., which contains both Negro and white elements.

checkeroo. *n.* A name applied to any item, such as a shirt, dress, etc., made of checked cloth.

checks, cash in [one's] = cash in [one's] chips.

checks (chips), pass in [one's]. To die. *Since c1870.*

cheek. *n.* Impudence; audacity; nerve. *Colloq.* —**y.** *adj.* Audacious; having a lot of nerve; rude.

cheerio; cheero; cheery. *interj.* 1. Good-by. *Colloq. An Eng. sl. term; in the U.S. it is almost invariably a humorous colloq., often implying that the meeting has been cheerless or dull. Also, further corrupted to mean* → 2. Hello.

cheers. *interj.* 1. A common informal toast, meaning "To your health," "To our health," etc. 2. A one-word compliment signifying approval; = "Well done!" → 3. A one-word comment to signify disapproval or defeat; used sarcastically.

cheese. *n.* 1. Any important person or object, usu. in such phrases as the big piece of cheese, the big cheese, the real cheese, etc. 2. An insignificant person, esp. an unworthy person in a position of authority. 3. A lie, nonsense, cant, exaggeration. *A good example of sl. degeneration.*

4. Money. *v.t.* To stop; to leave off. —**cake.** *adj.* Sensual; provocative; said of pictures or photographs of girls. *n.* 1. Published photographs of young women in clothes and poses that emphasize their sex appeal; also, one such photograph. *Much popularized during W.W.II. See pin-up. Term orig. from photographers' asking subjects to say "cheese" in order to simulate a smile. One of many sl. terms relating food and sex.* → 2. A sexually attractive young woman.

cheese bun. An informer.

cheesed off. *adj.* Bored; disgusted; angry.

cheesehead. *n.* A stupid person.

cheese it; cheeze it. *exclam.* 1. A warning or command to cease an improper activity in order to avoid detection. 2. To run away or disperse. *c1810 to present. Orig. "cheese it, the cops."*

cheesy. *adj.* 1. Lacking in style; worthless; of cheap or inferior material, design, or workmanship; unsatisfactory for any reason. 2. Stylish.

chef. *n.* One who prepares opium for smoking. *Addict use.*

cherry. *n.* 1. Other than sexually, one who has not been initiated. 2. Lack of experience, savoir faire, or confidence. *Another of the sl. words relating food and sex. adj.* Virginal; new; in good condition; specif. as good as new; said of merchandise, esp. used or secondhand merchandise.

cherry pie. 1. Something easily attainable, easy or pleasant to accomplish. 2. Money readily obtained; money acquired unexpectedly or from work other than one's usual occupation. *Circus use.*

chest hardware. Military medals. *W.W.II Armed Forces use.*

chestnut. *n.* An old, often repeated joke, story, musical composition, etc. *Colloq. since c1885.*

chew. *v.i., v.t.* 1. To eat; to be able to obtain food. 2. To talk, converse, gossip. *n.* An overbearing, disliked person. *Orig. "a big chew of tobacco."* —ed. *adj.* Angry, tired, defeated. —ings. *n.pl.* Food.

chewallop; chewalloper. *n.* A fall or a dive that makes a big splash or flopping noise. *Onomatopoeia.*

chew a lone [something]. To do something by oneself that is usu. done with others; e.g., "to chew a lone drink," "to chew a lone song," "to chew a lone summer." *Used by young people, students, etc., in moods of self-pity.*

chew [someone's] ear off. To deliver a long monologue; to talk tediously.

chewed up. *adj.* 1. Thoroughly beaten or defeated. → 2. Depressed.

chewing gum. Double talk; cant; utterance garbled as if the speaker were chewing gum; information that is incomplete or mixed up.

chew out. *v.t.* To reprimand a person severely; to bawl out. *Very common during W.W.II; still in frequent use among civilians as well as servicemen. Orig. to chew or bite someone's ear, nose, finger, etc., in a frontier fight; hence, angry enough "to chew him up" = demolish, vanquish.*

chew over. To discuss, talk over.

chew the fat. To talk; to gossip; to chat at length, esp. about trivial matters.

chew the rag. To argue.

chew [one's] tobacco. To make a statement; esp. to deliver a homily or a rustically philosophical opinion. Usu. in the cliché: "I don't chew my tobacco but once." *Archaic and dial.*

chib. *n.* = shiv.

Chicago. *adj.* Resembling a gangster; giving a tough appearance, hinting of illegality or brutality. Often used in phrase, "that Chicago look," to signify the dark, closely tailored clothing popularly associated with gangsters.

Chicago pineapple. A small bomb or grenade. *Because such items were associated with Chicago* hoodlums during the Prohibition era.

chi-chi; chichi. *n.* Something or someone stylish or fancy; fanciness; stylishness. *adj.* Smart, stylish; pretentious, affected; fancy.

chick. *n.* 1. Prison food. *Underworld use.* 2. A girl or young woman, esp. if attractive, pert, and lively; a hip girl or woman. *c1935, jive use, esp. in Harlem. Orig. "chicken"; ref. to a live, perky chicken with secondary connotation of food, another ex. of relation between food and sex. Also ex. of sl. word used only by males. Associated with jazz, now common.* —en. *n.* 1. An attractive young woman. *Since c1900.* 2. A young and puny or innocent Army or USN inductee. 3. A victim of a robbery, kidnaping, confidence game, etc. 4. Insignia of a U.S. Army colonel or a USN captain, used disparagingly. *W.W.II. Often used in term "chicken colonel" to distinguish a full colonel from a lieutenant colonel.* 5. An excessive show of authority; unnecessary discipline or regimentation, in either military or civilian life. 6. Cant; boloney, bunk; testiness in discourse or behavior. 7. Small tasks or duties that are boring or perhaps unnecessary. *adj.* 1. Afraid; cowardly; yellow. 2. Underhanded; sneaky; thoughtless or inconsiderate. 3. Strictly conventional in conduct; following (esp. Army) rules too closely; misusing authority; petty, mean.

chicken colonel. *n.* A U.S. Army colonel.

chicken feed. Small change; any small amount of money, esp. compared to what one expects to have in the future.

chicken-head. *n.* A stupid person.

chickenheart. *n.* A coward. —ed. *adj.* Cowardly; lacking persistence.

chicken-livered. *adj.* Cowardly.

chicken out. To withdraw from a plan, task, or endeavor because of fear; to quit.

chicken tracks. *pl.* Illegible handwriting.

chickie. *imp.* A warning or command to cease an improper activity in order to avoid detection; an imperative warning to run or disperse. *Very pop. among N.Y.C. adolescents and juvenile delinquents since c1945.*

Chic Sale. An outdoor toilet; an outhouse. *From humorist Chic Sales, who wrote a widely circulated catalogue of outhouses, a satirical booklet; archaic.*

chief. *n.* 1. One's boss or superior. 2. A fellow or guy; usu. used in direct address to strangers.

chief itch and rub. The most important person; the head of any group, e.g., school principal, Army officer, office overseer, etc.

chili-bowl. *n.* A haircut that leaves the hair too short and untapered, as if the barber had placed a bowl over the head and shaved around it.

chill. *v.t.* 1. To effect a permanent solution, esp. in an emotionless and hypereffective manner. 2. To resolve a complaint or awkward situation; to square a complaint. 3. To render (someone) unconscious, either in the boxing ring or elsewhere. *Underworld use.* 4. To kill. 5. To cause another to become angry; to elicit anger. *v.i.* 1. To submit willingly to another's domination, to let oneself be taken advantage of. → 2. To submit to arrest without resisting. 3. To become suspicious or cold toward a plan or person. 4. To become discouraged, to lose enthusiasm (also *v.t.*). —off. *v.i., v.t.* = chill.

chill, put on the. To act coldly toward a person; to snub.

chiller. *n.* 1. A melodrama; a horror story or thriller. 2. A gun.

chiller-diller. *n.* A book, movie, or play, esp. a movie, which fascinates its audience by suspense, mystery, or scenes of fear and horror. *Based on "chiller" plus "dilly."*

chill on [someone], **put the.** To kill someone.

chime in. To interrupt and intrude in a conversation or discussion; to give unasked-for advice or an opinion; to butt in.

chimney. *n.* The human head. *Negro use.*

chin. *v.i., v.t.* To talk; converse. *Replaced the older "chin music."*

chin, take it on the. To suffer a severe failure; to undergo complete defeat or frustration. *Now common.*

china. *n.* The teeth.

china chin = glass jaw.

china-clipper. *n.* A person whose job is washing dishes. *Pop. among servicemen, W.W.II.*

Chinaman. *n.* A sailor who works in a ship's laundry.

Chinaman's chance. An extremely poor chance. Only used in phrase "hasn't got a Chinaman's chance" = no chance at all. *Orig. from Calif. gold rush, 1849, when Chinese worked old claims, streams, and even wash abandoned by white prospectors, in hope of finding gold; reinforced by poor lot of Chinese in a segregated society.*

chinch. *n.* A bedbug. *Some hobo, ranch, logger, and Army use.* —pad. *n.* A cheap hotel or rooming house.

Chinee. *n.* 1. A Chinese. *Since c1870.* 2. A complimentary ticket of admission to an entertainment, esp. a sporting event.

Chinese ace. A pilot who lands a plane with one wing low. *From the pun "one wing low" = Wun Wing Lo.*

Chinese landing. A plane landing made by a "Chinese ace." *Orig. aviator use; common in Army Air Force, W.W.II.*

Chinese three-point landing. An airplane crash, esp. an airplane crash caused by a pilot's error while attempting a landing. *W.W.II Air Force use.*

Chinese tobacco. Opium.

chin fest. A session of idle talk

and gossip; a discussion; a bull session.

chin music. Talk; esp. unnecessary conversation, small talk, gossip. *Since c1835.*

chino. *n.* 1. A variety of cotton twill cloth. *Orig. the cheap cotton worn by Chinese coolies, applied by U.S. soldiers stationed in China (pre-W.W.II) to their own cotton summer uniforms, transferred to civilian use by post-W.W.II Army surplus clothing stores, and now applied to* → 2. A style of trousers having tapered legs, a belt in the back, and made of a cotton twill cloth. *Such garments have now become associated with the Ivy League style of dress; an outstanding example of word upgrading.*

Chinook wind. Warm spring winds; the beginning of spring. *Alaskan and northwest U.S. use.*

chintzy. *adj.* Unfashionable; unsophisticated; unenlightened; corny or cheap.

chip. *v.t.* To steal. —s. *n.* 1. Money. *Since c1860.* 2. French fried potatoes. *Eng. sl., used by U.S. troops during W.W.II.*

chip in. 1. To pay one's share of an expense; to contribute money toward a group undertaking. *Colloq. From the game of poker. Since c1860.* → 2. To contribute to a discussion.

chippie; chippy. *n.* A promiscuous woman or delinquent girl, orig. a prostitute, dance-hall girl, female bartender, or the like. *Now usu. jocular, as sounding archaic. Although this word prob. does not come from "chip," it once was used in the same sense as "piece."* *adj.* Amateurish; small.

chippie joint. A brothel.

chips, cash in [one's]. To die. *Since c1875; from the gambling usage.*

chips (checks), hand in [one's]. To die. *From gambling use, where one actually hands one's chips or checks to a cashier or the dealer on leaving the game.*

chips, in the. Affluent; having money. In reference to poker chips.

chips are down, the. Signifying a situation of urgency or ultimacy, sometimes portending failure or disaster; signifying a situation in which the consequences of any action will be irrevocable.

chirp. *v.i., v.t.* 1. To sing; said of a female singer, usu. professional. *c1930.* 2. To inform, to give information to the police; to "sing." —er. *n.* 1. A female singer. 2. An informer. *Orig., British use, "chirp" = mouth.*

chisel. *v.i., v.t.* 1. To cheat (someone); to take advantage of (someone); to obtain (something) by unfair or niggling means. *Since c1830.* 2. To borrow with little expectation of repaying, esp. something of insignificant value. *Ex.: one chisels a cigarette or a few cents but borrows $50 or a cup of replaceable sugar.* —er. *n.* A petty crook; a schemer associated with trivial enterprises.

chit. *n.* 1. An insignificant person; a rude, vulgar, audacious, or obnoxious person;—always a young person. 2. A paper, card, or ticket entitling the bearer to merchandise, usu. food or service; private "script" issued by a business firm.

chitchat. *n.* Chat; amiable or idle conversation.

chiv. *n.* = shiv. —ey; chivvy. *v.i., v.t.* To badger (someone); to nag (someone).

chocolate. *adj.* Negro; pertaining to Negroes.

choke; choke in; choke up. *imp.* An order or command to stop talking. *v.i.* 1. To stop talking; to stop doing whatever one is doing. 2. To slow down; to take it easy. 3. To be on the verge of tears; to be unable to speak as the result of emotional stress. —r; chocker *n.* 1. Anything worn closely around the throat, esp. a tie, stiff collar, or necklace. *As a necklace, a definite and popular fashion, no longer sl.* 2. A cheese, large pie, or any other big, solid article of food.

chop. *n.* 1. Quality. 1950: "Imported champagne of the very first chop." *Orig. Hind. "chāp" = a seal or stamp, such as would indicate official clearance or approval.* 2. The mouth or jaws. 3. A very critical or insulting remark, a dig; lit., a cutting remark. *Some use since c1950.* —s. *n.sing.* 1. The mouth; the lips. 2. The legs, esp. the thighs; the hips. *Negro use. n.pl.* 1. The teeth, natural or false. 2. The chin, mouth, jaws, or cheeks.

chop-chop. *imp.* & *adv.* Hurry up; to do [something] promptly, correctly, and in a satisfactory manner. *W.W.II. A pidgin Eng. term used by Chinese and Armed Forces; used humorously by U.S. civilians. Orig. may be reduplication of Hind. "chāp" = a seal or stamp, hence in India or China official approval or a mark of high quality. n.* Food, eating, or anything related to either. *Used by U.S. soldiers in Korean War. Orig. may be reduplication of stand. Eng. "chop" or from the Hind.; note most common use by U.S. Armed Forces via Korea.*

chopper. *n.* 1. A ticket taker or conductor; one who tears a ticket into two parts to show that it has been used. 2. A machine gun (usu. the Thompson submachine gun); a machine gunner. *Mainly mobster use; seldom adopted in Armed Forces.* 3. A helicopter.

chop [one's] teeth. To talk idly; to interject unnecessary remarks into a conversation. Often in phrase "now you're just chopping your teeth" = you're saying something worthless.

chow. *n.* Food; mealtime. *Very common during and after W.W. II. Var. attributed. Said to have been used by Chinese railroad workers in West, which may indicate orig. directly from Chinese "chow" = food. v.i.* To eat. *W.W.I and W.W.II.*

chowderhead. *n.* A stupid person;

one who uses poor judgment. —ed. *adj.* Stupid. *Since c1835.*

chow down. *v.* To eat a meal. *n.* A meal. *W.W.II.*

chow hall. An eating place; esp. an Army mess hall, school dining room, etc., where members of a group are required to eat and where mass-produced, usu. bland, food is served. *adj.* Unimaginatively prepared food; sloppy serving.

chow hound. A hearty eater; a glutton; one whose table manners leave something to be desired. *W.W.II use by all branches of the Armed Forces. Orig. one who, like a hound dog, scents food before the signal is given to begin feeding, and hence is able to obtain bigger helpings and the best food by being first in the chow line. Now frequently used in civilian speech.*

chow line. 1. A line, as of soldiers, students, etc., waiting to be admitted to an eating place or waiting to be served (cafeteria-style) inside. *Very common W.W.I and W.W.II use.* 2. Any clique of soldiers found usu. together, as in a chow line. 3. The row of counters from which food is dispensed in a cafeteria; also the employees who tend the counters and steam tables.

chow time. Mealtime.

Christer. *n.* 1. A pious, sanctimonious college student; a prude. 2. A person who shuns drinking, dancing, or other group activities; a wet blanket.

Christmas. *n.* 1. Any ostentatious display, as of clothing, jewelry, etc. 2. A garish article of clothing or jewelry, or one that sparkles. 3. A shower of metallic foil dropped by an airplane or artillery shell to jam enemy radar or communications systems. *W.W.II use. Orig. "all lighted up like a Christmas tree."*

Christmas tree. *n.* The piping constituting and controlling an oil or gas well; the derrick of an oil or gas well.

chromosome. *n.* An insignificant or small person. *c1945; student use.*

chronicker. *n.* 1. A watch or clock. 2. A newspaper.

chuck. *n.* 1. Food; a meal. 2. Money. *v.t.* 1. To have done with. 2. To eat. *v.i.* 1. To pitch for a baseball team; to throw a ball. *Colloq.* 2. To be quiet; to "shut up." 3. To vomit. *c1940; student use.* —**er.** *n.* 1. A baseball pitcher. 2. A baseball inning. *Orig. a polo term.*

chuck a dummy. To feign a fainting fit in order to win sympathy. *Hobo use.*

chuck-a-lug = chug-a-lug.

chuck habit; chuck horrors. 1. The craving for food experienced by a dope addict whose supply of narcotic is suddenly discontinued. 2. A fear of not having enough to eat; therefore the compulsion to eat as much as possible whenever food is available. *Hobo use.* 3. A fear of, obsession for, or horror of food, esp. one kind of food, as a reformed drug addict for sweets. 4. A psychotic fear or obsession with prison; insanity resulting from confinement in prison.

chuck it. *imp.* A command to "shut up" or cease whatever one is doing.

chucklehead. *n.* A stupid person. —**ed.** *adj.* Stupid.

chuck wagon. 1. A wagon carrying food and a cookstove, used to feed cowboys and other outdoor workers on the job. 2. Any small roadside or neighborhood lunch counter. *c1940.* 3. A buffet meal of unlimited servings for a nominal, prefixed price. *c1950.*

chug-a-lug. *v.i., v.t.* To drink a glassful of a beverage, or the amount of a beverage remaining in a glass, in one gulp or in a series of uninterrupted swallows without pausing for breath. *Common student use c1940–c1950. The beverage was usu. beer and was chug-a-lugged in haste, on a dare, or to demonstrate one's*

capacity for alcoholic drink. *Onomatopoetic from sounds of swallowing and imbibing.*

chum. *n.* 1. A close personal friend. Still used by preteenagers, but elsewhere almost invariably replaced by "buddy." 2. Now used sarcastically for "chump." *v.i.* 1. To occupy a room with another. 2. To curry favor with someone, esp. a teacher. —**my.** *adj.* Friendly.

chum-buddy. *n.* A particularly close friend; more than a chum.

chump. *n.* 1. A dupe, one who is easily deluded; a stupid person. 2. A paying customer, esp. a patron of a carnival, circus, burlesque show, etc.

chump, off [one's]. Insane.

cider barrel. An ocean-going tug.

cig. *n.* A cigarette.

cigar. *n.* A compliment. *From the carnival barker's "give the man a big cigar," a prize for winning at a game.*

cigaroot. *n.* A cigarette. *Used facetiously. Orig. cigarette + cheroot.*

cinch. *n.* A certainty; someone assured of success or something easily accomplished. *Colloq. Since before 1875. From the cinch of a saddle, which secures it. v.t.* 1. To make sure of anything. 2. to bring someone else into difficulty; to spoil another's schemes.

cinder. Of or pertaining to the railroad. Thus "cinder bo" = a hobo long experienced with hopping freight trains; "cinder-shark" = a cardshark or gambler who fleeces railroad travelers; and the like.

cinder bull. A private policeman or detective employed by a railroad. *Hobo use.*

cinder dick. A railroad detective.

circuit blow (clout) (wallop). A home run in baseball.

circuit slugger. A baseball player who hits frequent home runs.

circular file. A waste basket. *Fairly common in business offices.*

circus. *n.* 1. An obscene show; a naked dance or naked dancing.

2. Any large, colorful spectacle. 3. Excitement. 4. A feigned fainting spell. *Hobo use.*

cit. *adj.* Civilian clothes, as opposed to a uniform.

city slicker. A city dweller, specif. a shrewd, worldly, stylishly dressed one, regarded by rural people as a swindler; almost always disparaging use by rural people.

civvies. *n.pl.* 1. Civilian clothes; mufti. *Used during W.W.I but very common during and after W.W.II.* 2. Clothes other than work clothes; whatever one wears off the job. *Primarily referring to clothes other than Armed Forces uniforms but also used by any uniformed workers; used by convicts to mean clothes other than prison uniforms.* 3. Civilians.

clacker. *n.* A dollar.

claim agent. A bettor who "claims" to have placed a winning bet, though there is no proof of this, in hopes of collecting winnings.

clam. *n.* 1. A dollar. 2. A mistake; a boner.

clambake. *n.* 1. A party or gathering, usu. for the purpose of entertainment; a loud or raucous party or gathering. 2. A session of swing music; a jam session. 3. Any discordant or lively gathering, such as a political convention, business meeting, or the like. 4. An insufficient radio rehearsal; hence an unsuccessful radio program. → 5. A showy failure. 6. A private gathering for official or business purposes, the public disclosure of which might harm the participants; a confused or fruitless official meeting.

clamp down. 1. To become stricter, as in the enforcement of regulations; to strengthen authority; to increase supervision. 2. To clean up a room, house, office, ship, etc. *Orig. USN use.*

clamps on, put the. To steal.

clam shovel. A shovel, esp. a short-handled shovel, used to dig trenches, truck gardens, etc.

clam up. To refrain from talking or to stop talking; to refuse to disclose information, esp. to the police or a judge.

clanks, the. *n.* Delirium tremens; the shakes.

claptrap. *n.* Nonsense; lies; exaggerated talk; bull.

claret. *n.* Blood. *Since c1860; prize fighter use.*

class. *n.* High quality; élan; tone; stylishness; savoir faire; dignity. *Since c1890; now colloq.* —**y.** *adj.* Highly fashionable; stylish.

classis chassis; classy chassis. *n.* A sexually attractive or healthy-looking physique, specif. of a girl or young woman. *Assoc. with swing use.*

claw. *n.* A policeman. *v.t.* To arrest.

claw on [someone], put the. 1. To arrest, detain, or esp. to identify another for arrest or detention. *Underworld use.* 2. To ask another for a loan of money.

clay eater. 1. A native of the South Carolina or Georgia low country. *Orig. from clay-eating habit common among Negroes and poor whites.* → 2. Any Southern farmer or local rustic.

clay pigeon. 1. A vulnerable person or thing; a person easy to victimize, cheat, or take advantage of; a job that is a cinch. *From the "clay pigeon" targets used in trapshooting.* 2. An airplane catapulted from a ship. 3. An easy task.

clean. *adj.* 1. Innocent of carrying illegal goods, usu. arms, contraband, or narcotics; esp. used in ref. to those searched by police. *Underworld use.* → 2. Innocent in general; not guilty of a supposed crime. 3. Free of dangerous radioactive contamination. *Since c1955.* 4. Without money; broke. 5. Inoffensive; not obscene or lewd; not dirty; free of sexual or sinful connotations. *Colloq.* 6. Technically proficient, without mistakes; free of distracting or inharmonious elements, esp. as applied to art or design. —er; —ers. *n. & n.pl.* Used in phrase "taken to the cleaners" to signify having lost one's money or possessions through gambling, theft, natural disaster, etc.

cleaners, go to the. To have all one's money taken away through gambling or being robbed or cheated. *Fig. to have one's pockets "cleaned" of money.*

clean out. *v.t.* To win all someone's money.

clean up. To make a large profit quickly; to win a large bet. "That show must be cleaning up."

clean-up; cleanup. *n.* Police or vice squad activity to eradicate crime and immorality in a particular area.

clear sailing. Easy to accomplish successfully; easy; without worry or strain; enjoyable.

clef. *v.t.* To compose a song. —fer. *n.* A songwriter. *Synthetic.*

Clem; clem. *n.* 1. A small-town resident; a rustic; one who can be hoaxed easily; esp., to circus people, the members of the local community in which the circus is playing temporarily. → 2. A fight between carnival or circus employees and local townspeople. → 3. A rallying call for help from circus people when a fight with townspeople seems imminent. *v.t.* To disperse rioting townspeople at a circus.

clemo. *n.* 1. Executive clemency; a parole or commutation of a prison sentence. → 2. An escape from prison.

click. *v.i.* 1. To be a success; to be received favorably by an audience. 2. To fall into recognizable or apprehendable patterns of thought or feeling; to be classified or remembered; to fit together exactly, to match in color, size, shape, or value. *n.* 1. A commercial success in the entertainment field. 2. A clique.

cliffdweller. *n.* A resident of a large apartment house.

cliffhanger; cliff hanger. *n.* A

melodramatic story, play, book, or movie. *From early movie serials when each installment ended in suspense, as with the heroine hanging precariously over a cliff.*

climb. *v.t.* To reprimand, scold, or criticize (someone) severely. *W.W.II Army use.*

clinch. *n.* An embrace. *v.t., v.i.* 1. To embrace. 2. To determine conclusively; to complete. —er. *n.* A deciding factor; the crux of an argument.

clink. *n.* 1. A jail, prison cell, or guardhouse. *Orig. the proper name of a famous prison in Southwark, London. Reinforced onomatopoetically from sound of jail door closing.* 2. A Negro. *Negro use.* —er. *n.* 1. A jail. 2. An unwanted noise heard on a long distance telephonic transmission line. 3. A squeak or unwanted reed sound produced by a clarinet or saxophone player. Hence, any mistake, error, or boner, esp. a sour note in music or an error in baseball. *Orig. from the clinker, or unburnable cinder, in a coal fire.*

clinks. *n.pl.* 1. Money. 2. Ice cubes; small pieces of ice. *Orig. onomatopoetic.*

clip. *n.* 1. A sharp blow. *Since c1830.* 2. A thief or robber. *Underworld use.* 3. A clever person; a trickster. *v.t.* 1. To hit a person sharply, usu. with the fist or a heavy object. *Colloq. Since c1860.* 2. To cheat, swindle, or rob someone. 3. To kill, usu. by shooting. 4. To steal. 5. To arrest. —per. *n.* 1. An attractive girl. *c1835.* 2. A killer; a thug. —ping. *n.* A sharp blow; esp. a foul blow, or an illegal block in football.

clip-artist. *n.* A professional swindler, cheater, or robber.

clip-joint; clip joint. *n.* A place of public entertainment where one is likely to be overcharged, swindled, cheated, or robbed.

clobber. *v.t.* 1. To defeat decisively, thoroughly; to beat up; to attack aggressively and with concentrated power. *Colloq.* → 2. To berate; to criticize or reprimand severely. —ed. *adj.* Drunk.

clock. *v.t.* 1. To hit. 2. To time, to keep time. —er. *n.* One who times the workouts of race horses in order to rate their performances.

clock watcher. 1. A person who takes little interest in his work; lit., one who watches the office or factory clock in expectation of quitting time. → 2. One who will not do a favor; an ungenerous person.

clodhopper. *n.* 1. A sturdy or cumbersome shoe; esp. a man's work shoe. → 2. An awkward, unsophisticated person; esp. a farmer. 3. An old, dilapidated car, bus, train, or plane that is only useful for short trips; transportation used in local areas.

clonk. *v.t.* To hit or strike.

close. *adj.* 1. Warm and humid; said of the weather. *Colloq.* 2. Stingy. *Colloq.* 3. In complete control, in complete mastery, as of one's life, creativity, musical instrument, or the like. *Far-out use since c1955. Prob. from the gambling phrase "to play close to one's vest" = to keep one's cards out of the sight of others and thus to play skillfully or to take no unnecessary risks.*

closed; closed down; closed up. *adj.* Out of business, usu. owing to official prohibition; said esp. of a town or region in which gambling houses, brothels, etc., have been closed by police action.

close shave. Lit. and fig., avoidance of or rescue from imminent danger, destruction, or failure; a narrow escape.

close up. To stop talking.

close-up. *n.* 1. A near view. *Orig. the picture made by a camera set close to the object; popularized by pioneer movie producer D. W. Griffith, c1920.* → 2. A close scrutiny. → 3. A biography.

clotheshorse; clothes horse. *n.* An extremely well-dressed or fashionable person; usu. implies that sartorial elegance is the subject's only merit.

clothesline. *n.* 1. Personal problems; family disagreements. 2. In baseball, a line drive, i.e., a ball hit so sharply that its flight appears virtually level.

cloud, on a. 1. Extremely happy; fig., so elated as to be unaware of mundane obligations or occurrences. 2. Under the influence of narcotics; in a dream state induced by drugs. *Some narcotic addict use.*

cloud buster. 1. In baseball, a high fly ball. 2. A skyscraper. 3. A fast, new airplane.

cloud seven, on. 1. Completely happy, perfectly satisfied; in a euphoric state. 2. = on a cloud.

clout. *v.t.* 1. To hit or strike a person or object with force. *Colloq.* 2. To steal; esp. to shoplift or to steal an automobile or from an automobile. 3. In baseball, to hit a pitched ball with great force. *n.* 1. A hit or blow. 2. In baseball, a hit. —er. *n.* 1. An automobile-stealing gang, esp. the member who actually does the stealing. 2. One who looks over an establishment to see how it may best be robbed. 3. In baseball, a heavy hitter.

clover, in; clover, in the. Wealthy; successful; in a position in which one can enjoy wealth or the results of success.

clover-kicker. *n.* A farmer; a country boy.

clown. *n.* 1. An ebullient, ineffectual, boastful, or purposeless person whose words or actions cannot be taken seriously; hence an incompetent or unreliable person. *Oral; common.* 2. Any rustic. 3. A rural police officer, esp. a sheriff, constable, or deputy. 4. = square. *Cool and far-out use since c1955. v.i.* To tease; to scuffle; to refuse to act or talk seriously.

Clown Alley. Lit., the aisle of tents or wagons where circus clowns live and prepare for their performances; fig., circus life in general.

clown around = clown, *v.i.*

clown-wagon. *n.* A freight train's caboose.

clubhouse lawyer. A member of a sports team, social group, etc., who freely offers his personal opinions to fellow members. *Baseball use.*

club-winder. *n.* A railroad brakeman.

cluck; kluck. *n.* 1. A stupid, dull, or incompetent person; a dunce; a dope. 2. [derog.] A very dark Negro. *Negro use. v.t.* To do well; esp. to make a high grade in an examination. *adj.* Stupid.

cluck and grunt. Eggs and ham.

clue. *v.t.* To inform someone of a fact or opinion; to reveal a fact or opinion; to reveal a confidence or a secret. *Pop. c1945–c1955. n.* A piece of news; a pertinent fact; a personal opinion.

clunk. *v.t.* 1. To hit or strike, esp. on the head. 2. To throw down; to plunk down; esp. money; to pay cash. *n.* 1. A stupid person, a cluck. 2. A hit; a blow. 3. Any cumbersome object; esp. a heavy shoe. 4. A person's foot. —**er.** *n.* 1. Something that is inferior or worthless. 2. A dilapidated, worn out car, bus, or other machine. 3. An awkward person; esp. an inferior golfer, tennis player; etc.; a duffer.

clunkhead. *n.* A stupid person. *Increased in pop. after frequent use by Arthur Godfrey on radio and television.*

clutch. *n.* 1. An embrace. 2. An emergency, predicament, or exigency; in sports, a decisive or critical play in a close contest; the decisive moment in any sequence of events or operations. *Very common sportswriter use.* —**ed.** *adj.* Angry.

clutch the gummy. To fail; to be left to take the blame; to be cheated. *Orig. on model of "hold the bag" = to clutch the gunny bag or sack; reinforced by "gummy" = sticky.*

C-note. *n.* = C, specif. a $100 bill. *More recent than C-speck.*

coal-pot. *n.* A stove; a tobacco pipe.

coast. *n.* 1. To inhabitants of the Atlantic seaboard, the Pacific coast; to inhabitants of the Pacific seaboard, the Atlantic coast. 2. A sensation of utter relaxation, buoyancy, or satisfaction, esp. as the result of drugs or listening to jazz. *v.i.* 1. To do or obtain something without great effort; to rely on one's reputation or past achievements in order to succeed or gain fame without making further effort. *Colloq.* 2. To pass a school examination or course easily. *Student use.* 3. To experience a sensation of utter relaxation, buoyancy, or satisfaction, esp. as the result of drugs or listening to jazz music. *Drug addict and jazz musician use.*

coattail, on [someone's]. 1. Dependent upon someone for success, usu. said of an unknown or unpopular candidate in a political election who wins on the strength of the popularity of another candidate on the same ticket. → 2. Dependent upon someone, usu. a friend or relative, for success in business, sports, or any enterprise.

cob. *n.* A farmer or small-town local.

cob, off the = corn, corny. *Orig. teenage use, c1940.*

cob-roller. *n.* Any small or very young farm animal, esp. a small pig. *Implies that the animal is too small to eat properly and merely pushes the corn cobs with its nose when trying to take a normal bite.*

cock-and-bull; cock-and-bull story. An exaggerated account; a story recounted with embellishment or lies. *Colloq.*

cock-eyed; cockeyed. *adj.* 1. Eccentric; confused or chaotic; crazy, screwball. 2. Drunk. 3. Unconscious. *Colloq.* → 4. Crazy; insane. *Colloq.* → 5. Wrong; mistaken; misstated. *Colloq.* 6. Askew; crooked. *Colloq. adv.* Very.

cockroach. *n.* 1. A person interested in small schemes, esp. a small businessman. 2. A person who is exceptionally busy, esp. with many small projects.

coco. *n.* The head. *From coconut.* **—nut.** *n.* 1. The head. 2. A dollar.

co-ed; coed. *n.* A girl or woman student at a coeducational college or university. *A prime example of a word once sl. and now universally accepted as stand.; since c1900. adj.* 1. Coeducational; appropriate to both sexes. *Colloq. since c1900.* 2. Dovetailed; fitting together perfectly, as a joint.

coffee and. 1. The cheapest meal obtainable. → 2. The necessities of life. *Used by gamblers, small-time con men, vagabonds, etc.*

coffee and cake(s). A small salary, a small amount of money; lit., just enough money for the necessities of life; chicken-feed.

coffee-and-cake-job; (—joint; —layout; —place; —spot, etc.). A job or place of business that is very limited in scope and financial remuneration.

coffee-and-cake-time. 1. The point at which one's funds are exhausted and it is necessary to earn more money. → 2. A time or place that seems well suited to the obtaining of money; esp. by a robber, con man, etc.

coffee cooler. One who seeks easy work; a shirker.

coffee grinder. 1. A strip teaser or other female performer who makes suggestive grinding motions with her hips and abdomen. 2. A prostitute. 3. A professional movie-studio cameraman. 4. An aircraft engine. *Air Force use since c1940. All four meanings allude to the grinding movement of a coffee grinder; the first two meanings also imply that one needs to perform such movements to earn one's coffee and.*

coffee-pot; coffee pot. *n.* A lunch counter or small restaurant.

coffin. *n.* 1. A safe for valuables. 2. Any car, bus, plane, etc., considered to be unsafe. 3. An armored car or tank. *Some W.W.II use.*

coffin corner. In football, any of the four corners of the playing field. *So called because a ball-carrier trapped in these corners may be easily tackled.*

coffin nail. 1. A cigarette. *Since c1890. From the saying that each cigarette one smokes drives one more nail into one's coffin.* → 2. One who smokes a lot. → 3. Anything regarded as likely to shorten one's life.

coffin tack = coffin nail.

coil. *n.* 1. Life. *Some jocular use, from the literary "mortal coil."* 2. Any electrical device or gadget, esp. a condenser or generator.

coin. *n.* Money. *Extremely pop. c1900–c1935. Later use usu. restricted to small amounts of money. v.t.* To earn something, as money or praise.

coke. *n.* 1. Cocaine. *Orig. addict use.* 2. Coke, a popular shortened form of Coca-Cola, a carbonated beverage. *The makers of Coca-Cola have registered as trademarks both the full and shortened name and insist that they be printed with initial capitals.* **—d.** *adj.* Under the influence of a narcotic, orig. of cocaine.

coked up = coked.

coke head. 1. A cocaine addict. 2. Any stupid, dull, slow-reacting person.

cokie; cokey. *n.* 1. A narcotic addict; esp. a cocaine addict. 2. A boy; anyone who lacks experience.

cold. *adj.* 1. Basic; ungarnished; without frills. 2. Disinterested; lacking in ambition, skill, energy, or luck. 3. Dead. → 4. Unconscious; completely unconscious. 5. Sexually frigid. 6. Without, or without showing, emotion or interest, esp. love or sexual passion. *The above meanings ref. to a lack of motion or life, as if one were actually frozen. The following meanings ref. to something frozen while at the peak of perfection.* 7. Without error; excellent. 8. Well performed, esp. without practice or forewarning. *adv.* Certainly, really.

cold biscuit. 1. An unattractive or dull girl. → 2. A person of either sex who lacks sex appeal.

coldcock; cold-cock. *v.t.* 1. To knock someone unconscious, with the fist, a club, etc. 2. A specif. way of hitting someone over the head with a blackjack or strangling someone with a piece of wire, always without warning, in order to render the person completely incapable of action.

cold deck; cold-deck. *n.* A stacked or marked deck of playing cards. *adj.* Unfair; with planned or pre-arranged results in another's favor. *v.t.* To take advantage of; to make unable to succeed owing to some previous and unalterable condition; to plan or prejudice against some result or person.

cold feet, to have. To lose courage; to be afraid.

cold fish. A person of reserved temperament; one who is unfriendly, reserved, withdrawn, dull, unemotional, or lacking in vivacity or sex appeal; dispassionate, one who displays no love, passion, or affection.

cold haul. *v.t.* 1. To take advantage of; to victimize. 2. To accomplish a task or obtain a goal easily and without effort. → 3. To accomplish a task or attain a goal in a slipshod manner, without enthusiasm or the necessary effort that would have made the accomplishing or attaining worthwhile; to fail to take full advantage of an opportunity. *v.i.* 1. To expend no more effort than necessary. 2. To depart rapidly; to flee.

cold in hand. Without money; broke. *Negro use.*

cold meat. A dead person; a cadaver. *Still in use. May have orig. meant a person killed or knocked unconscious in the boxing ring.*

cold-meat box. A coffin. *Some use since c1890.*

cold-meat cart. A hearse. *Since c1820.*

cold-meat party. A wake; a funeral.

cold pack. A knockout or knockout blow. *Prize fight use.*

cold shoulder. A coldness of manner; the obvious and conscious ignoring of a person or plan. *v.t.* To obviously and consciously ignore (someone).

cold storage. 1. A grave; a cemetery. 2. The imaginary place where an idea or project is stored until one is ready to act upon it.

cold turkey; cold-turkey. 1. The act of being suddenly and completely deprived of the use of narcotics, usually during a medical cure of narcotics addiction. *Addict use.* 2. At an auction, to stop the bidding and sell an item at a previously set price. 3. On the spur of the moment; without preparation or forewarning. 4. To know a subject or to be able to perform so well that no practice or research is necessary. 5. Objective; frank; blunt; unemotional.

collar. *n.* 1. A policeman. → 2. An arrest. *v.t.* 1. To arrest. → 2. To comprehend; to understand thoroughly.

collar a nod. To sleep.

collateral. *n.* Money.

collision mat. A waffle. *Some USN use since c1920.*

colly. *v.t.* To understand, to comprehend. *Primarily Negro use, used in the rural areas of the South as much as in Harlem and in jive circles; it seems to predate "collar."*

color blind. Unable to tell the difference between one's own money and someone else's; in other words, not averse to stealing or cheating. *Jocular use.*

combo. *n.* **1.** A combination of things; esp. of foods in a sandwich or salad or of beverages in a mixed drink. **2.** A combination of people; esp. a professional dancing team, a dance orchestra, and, since c1940, specif. a small jazz band, usu. of three or four members. *Pop. by bop and cool use. Progressive music is usu. played by such small bands, as opposed to large swing bands.* **3.** The combination of a lock on a safe or vault. *All meanings from "combination."*

come a cropper. To fall, esp. on one's posterior.

come across. 1. To pay money owed; to produce what is expected of one. **2.** To pay a bribe; to bribe. **3.** To surrender information or allegiance to another. **4.** [taboo]. To surrender sexually; to grant sexual favors when expected or asked to; said only of the female.

come again. To repeat what one has just said, because the listener has not heard or because the matter in question needs further clarification.

come apart at the seams. To lose one's composure; to lose one's confidence.

come around. To agree or acquiesce, after initially disagreeing or refusing; to be persuaded or convinced. *Common use.*

comeback. *n.* **1.** A recovery of health, prosperity, success, public acceptance, or the like. *Colloq.* **2.** A retort; a riposte. *Colloq.* **3.** A complaint or exposure of one's previous actions; imposed retribution for an act committed in one's past.

come clean. To tell the complete truth; to confess, as to the police.

comedown. *n.* **1.** A drop in one's social or business status. *Since c1840. Colloq.* **2.** A project giving less satisfaction, esteem, monetary gain, etc., than expected; a disappointment. *Colloq.* **3.** An intended victim who grabs a pickpocket's hand in the act of stealing. *Underworld use.*

come-in. *n.* **1.** Spectators waiting in line to buy tickets or waiting for a performance to begin. *c1920.* → **2.** The time between the opening of the main tent and the beginning of the grand entry at a circus. *Circus use.*

come off it. To stop doing or saying what one is doing or saying; esp. because one's actions or words are meaningless or offensive; usu. a command.

come off [one's] perch. To stop acting in a superior or snobbish manner.

come-on; come on. *n.* **1.** Lit. and fig., an invitation. **2.** That which is appealing, attractive, or enticing about any thing or person; that which attracts. **3.** Specif., sex appeal. **4.** Act of enticing someone to spend money, do a favor, or esp. to enter into a situation in which he will be victimized. **5.** A dupe; the person who succumbs to a confidence game. **6.** An employee who buys the first ticket to a circus or a carnival side-show, who buys the first item a huckster offers, or who gambles, pretending to be a customer, in order to entice real customers to buy or gamble; a shill. *adj.* Enticing; made desirable for the purpose of gaining money, esteem, etc. *v.i.* To arrive; to enter or present oneself; to begin, as to begin talking or playing music; to participate; to perform; to do these things with a purpose or specif. attitude or skill, as if one were on a stage; always followed by an adj. telling the purpose, attitude, or skill of the one who has come on, or esp. of the initial impression made by that person on those present. *Orig. cool use, c1950. From theater and radio use; reinforced by the older "come on like gangbusters."*

come on like gangbusters. To enter, arrive, begin, participate, or perform in a sensational, loud, active, or striking manner. *From the radio program "Gangbusters" which always began or came on (the airwaves) with sound effects of police sirens and machine-gun fire. Since before c1945.*

comer. *n.* One who or that which shows great promise of being a success; one who is making a rapid advance in a specif. field of endeavor.

come through. 1. To confess; to admit one's guilt. 2. To pay or give money, encouragement, or other support as expected. 3. To be as successful as expected; to deliver the desired results; to excel; to please.

come to school. To give up one's vices, unruliness, or eccentricities; to conform; to compromise.

comeuppance. *n.* A deserved rebuke or punishment; esp. a rebuke that deflates the sufferer's ego or allows him to see an idea or plan in a realistic perspective.

comfortable. *adj.* Drunk. *Some use since c1950.*

comma-counter. *n.* One who overemphasizes the importance of minor details; one who demands perfection in small things, but who lacks imagination or a comprehensive understanding of his subject or job; a pedant.

commercial. *n.* 1. Any laudatory statement; praise; a good reference. 2. A musical piece played by an orchestra or band at a spectator's or dancer's request.

commie; Commie; Commy. *n.* A member of the Communist party or the international Communist movement; a Communist; a Communist sympathizer. *Colloq. adj.* Communist; Communistic.

commo. *n.* Candy, tobacco, cigarettes, etc., obtained by a prisoner through a penal institution's inmates' commissary. *From "commissary."*

comp. *n.* 1. A nonpaying guest or spectator, as at a hotel, restaurant, or place of entertainment. 2. A complimentary or free ticket. *The above two meanings*

from *"complimentary."* 3. An abbr. for "composition." 4. An abbr. for "compositor." *v.t.* An abbr. for "compose." —*o. n.* 1. A cheap dress shoe that is pasted or nailed together instead of being sewn. *From "composition."* 2. A "comprehensive examination." *Student use.*

company man. An employee, usu. a white-collar worker, whose loyalty to his employer is greater than his loyalty to his fellow employees.

company monkey. In the Army, a company clerk.

con. *n.* 1. A convict; an ex-convict; one who is serving or has served a prison term. *Colloq.* → 2. A criminal; a hoodlum. 3. A confidence game, a swindle; the world of the confidence game. 4. Tuberculosis. *Mainly dial. From "consumption."* → 5. A consumptive person. *Mainly prison use.* *v.t.* 1. To swindle; to persuade, convince, or victimize another to accept or believe a deception by or as by a confidence game; to cheat. → 2. To trick; to fool; to persuade another to do something not in his best interests; to persuade.

conchie; conchy. *n.* A conscientious objector to military service. *W.W.I use in Eng.; W.W.II use in both Eng. and U.S. From "conscientious" with common sl. suffix of "—ie" or "—y."*

Coney Island. 1. A lunch wagon; a quick lunch, esp. one consisting of a hot dog with lots of condiments. 2. A large hot dog, served on a roll and covered with relish, sauerkraut, etc. 3. Any large sandwich filled with hot or cold meat, vegetables, relishes, etc. *The above three meanings are from the assoc. of such sandwiches with the food concessions at Coney Island amusement park in N.Y.C., esp. with "Nathan's" lunch-counter and restaurant, known for its large hot dogs, served with sauerkraut.* 4. A glass of beer that contains much foam and little beer. *Orig.* "*Coney Island head.*" See head. *adj.* Gaudy; showy; loud.

Coney Island head = Coney Island.

confab. *n.* A talk, conversation, or conference. *v.i.* To talk or confer. *Before c1925 used as carnival sl.; now general; abbr. from "confer" and the artificial jocular word "confabulation."*

confetti. *n.* Bricks. *An example of sl. exaggeration.*

confisticate. *v.t.* To confiscate. *W.W.II maritime use. Maritime sl.; a prime example of group sl., known to outsiders, but after almost 200 years still used almost exclusively by the orig. group. A synthetic, humorous word formed by infixing a hard consonant to a stand. word.*

con game. 1. A confidence game; a swindle. 2. Any enticement. 3. Anything against the law; anything unethical. 4. Any way of earning money easily; an easy life.

con job = con game.

conk. *n.* 1. The head. → 2. The face. → 3. The nose. *From "conch."* *v.t.* 1. To hit a person on the head. → 2. To defeat thoroughly, esp. in sports.

conk-buster. *n.* 1. Cheap liquor. *Negro use.* 2. Any difficult problem, task, or the like; fig., anything so complex that one breaks one's head in thinking about it. *Primarily Negro use.* → 3. An intellectual Negro.

conk off. 1. To stop work; to rest when one should be working. 2. To go to sleep; to sleep.

conk out. 1. To break down and stop running; said of an engine or machine, esp. an airplane engine. 2. To tire suddenly; to stop work and rest or sleep; to become exhausted; said of a person. → 3. To die.

con man. 1. A confidence man; a swindler. *Colloq.* 2. Anyone who earns money easily; a person who has an easy life. 3. Any handsome, charming male; one with

a beguiling smile and a persuasive way of talking.

conn. *n.* The command of a naval vessel.

connection. *n.* A dope peddler or seller; one who can obtain narcotics. *Addict use.*

constructed. *adj.* = stacked, a more emphatic form; e.g. "She ain't stacked; man, she's constructed." *A new use.*

contact. *v.t.* To call, phone, or write a person for a business or social reason; to communicate with. *Colloq.* *n.* A person who can provide one with an introduction to a group or with whom one can conduct negotiations. *Colloq.*

Continental. *n.* A type of men's haircut.

contract. *n.* A political or business favor; a bribe; the fix.

convertible. *n.* A corporate security that can be converted to a security of another corporation. *Common stock-market use.*

convict. *n.* 1. A zebra. *Circus use.* 2. A schemer; one who is unethical or untrustworthy.

cooch. *n.* 1. Any lascivious dance; the hootchy-kootchy. *Orig. carnival and circus use.* 2. An unethical scheme; an unfair enticement; an obvious deceit.

coo-coo. *adj.* 1. Insane, crazy; extremely unconventional. 2. Stupid; unrealistic in one's views. *n.* An insane person; one who is crazy, stupid, or unconventional. *From "cuckoo," a bird whose cry sounds somewhat demoniac to some ears.*

cook. *v.t.* 1. To die by electrocution, as in the electric chair. *Fairly well known.* 2. To ruin, to make a failure of. *v.i.* 1. To fail; to suffer the consequences of failure, stupidity, audacity, or the like. *Colloq.* 2. To happen, develop, evolve, take place, transpire, etc. *Used chiefly in phrases* "what's cooking?" "what cooks?" *Orig. from "what's cooking on the front burner?"* = *what's the main item of news or interest?*

c1940. Heavy W.W.II use, student use. Orig. jive use. **3.** To do or think the right or desired thing; to enter into the spirit or mood of jive, swing, or of a group of people; to agree; to be in the know, to be hep. Usu. in "Now you're cooking," said approvingly. Orig. jive and swing use. Pop. c1940 and still some use. **4.** To be excited, stimulated, or filled with enthusiasm. n. One who plans a course of action; a leader. —book. n. A chemistry laboratory manual. Student use. —ed. adj. **1.** Knocked out; unconscious. → **2.** Exhausted; finished without having attained one's goal. → **3.** Inadequate; defeated. **4.** Drunk. —er. n. A sexually attractive girl. Some c1940 student use. From "cook," reinforced by "looker." —ie; —ey; —ee. n. **1.** One who cooks or prepares opium for smoking; an opium addict. Addict use. **2.** A girl or young woman, esp. an attractive, vivacious one. **3.** A man; usually a man who is self-confident, clever, or brusque; usu. in "tough cookie" or "smart cookie." **4.** Any person, esp. a clever, brash, or energetic one. **5.** [taboo]. The female genitalia. Negro use.

cookie-cutter; cooky-cutter. n. **1.** A policeman's badge. Circus use. → **2.** A policeman. **3.** Anyone who is supposed to be tough but isn't; a weakling. Most common use. **4.** An inadequate weapon, esp. a knife.

cookie pusher; cooky pusher. 1. A man, usu. a young man, who prefers group feminine society, as tea parties, easy tasks, and nonmasculine sports; an effeminate, weak, or cowardly man; a man deeply concerned with the social graces. → **2.** A man who does little hard work and tries to obtain promotion by courting his superiors; an apple polisher. **3.** A government career man, esp. a State Department official. Orig. ref. to the many teas that State Department workers need to at-

tend. During the 1952 presidential campaign, Republican politicians and editorialists used the term with double-entendre to imply that members of the Democratic administration were effeminate and that homosexuals were employed by the State Department.

cook-out; cookout. n. **1.** A meal cooked out of doors, as over a back yard home grill, by camping groups, etc. → **2.** A gathering, hiking trip, camping trip, or the like, during which an outdoor meal is cooked. Used freq. by Boy and Girl Scout groups, suburbanites, etc.

Cook's tour; Cook's Tour. A trip, a sightseeing excursion; any tour; traveling; a ride. From Thomas Cook and Son, a prominent firm of travel agents, known for organizing European tours, esp. in the 19C.

cook up. 1. To fabricate, as a story, alibi, or the like. **2.** To plan or scheme; to concoct an idea or plan of action; to invent. Colloq. May be the base for the jive and swing use of "cook."

cook with gas. To do, think, or feel the right or desired action, thought, or emotion; to enter into or appreciate the spirit, modes, fashions, and fads of swing; to be in the know, to be hep. An emphatic variation of "cook" = to do the right thing. Orig. swing use. Fairly well known c1940, still some use.

cool. v.t. **1.** To postpone; to wait for. Associated with and most common as cool, far out, and beat use, but in use much earlier, as in the expression "to cool one's heels" = to wait. **2.** To kill someone. Some use since c1920. **3.** To fail, esp. to fail an examination; to ruin a chance for success; to fail to take advantage of an opportunity. Some student use since c1935. n. A form and style of jazz characterized by soft tones, improvisations based on advanced chord extensions, the use of harmonic and rhythmic devices adapted from "classical" music, etc. *Cool or progressive jazz was first developed by West Coast musicians and by the early 1950's had supplanted bop as the major jazz movement. The originators of cool jazz were chiefly white musicians with university training and a highly sophisticated knowledge of musical techniques, both jazz and classical. As a result the cool movement has been characterized as an "intellectual" approach to music and life in general.* adj. 1. In complete control of one's emotions; hip but having a quiet, objective, aloof attitude; indifferent to those things considered nonessential to one's individual beliefs, likes, and desires; pertaining to cool or progressive jazz; similar to or sharing the taste, dress, and attitudes of cool musicians. *Orig. used by those who played and appreciated cool or progressive jazz; since c1948, common since c1955.* → 2. Aloof; unconcerned; disdainful; emotionless and amoral. *Beat use since c1950.* 3. Thrilling; played in an exciting, satisfying, expert way; said of any jazz music; stimulating; hot, jivy, groovy. *Some use since c1950, a logical mistake by devotees of earlier, more emotional forms of jazz and by nonlisteners.* 4. Satisfying; pleasant; in good taste; attractive. 5. Played in the style of cool music. 6. Eliciting an intellectual, psychological, and/or spiritual response; intellectually, psychologically, and/or spiritually exciting and satisfying; on a higher intellectual level than, and removed from, mere physical, sensual excitement or satisfaction; unemotional, without obvious excitement, disaffiliated. *Orig. bop use, c1946. Now the most common bop word, with frequent far out, and beat use. Fairly well known, and fairly common student and teenage use. Some older adult*

use. *All uses and meanings of "cool" have the basic connotation of intellectual, psychological, and/or spiritual excitement and satisfaction, negation of mere obvious, physical, sensual excitement. In this basic meaning "cool" is, of course, the direct antithesis of "hot."* —er. n. 1. Any of various cooling drinks made with liquor. *Colloq.* 2. A prison. *Colloq. since c1900.* → 3. A solitary confinement cell or block of cells. *Prison use.* 4. A certainty; a cinch.

cool it. To relax, calm down; to work less strenuously, slow down; to stop annoying, insulting, threatening, or being angry; to take a vacation. *Cool and far out use since c1955.*

cool off. 1. To become calmer; to lose one's enthusiasm or anger. 2. To kill.

cool out. 1. To calm someone; to appease. 2. To beat up someone so that his anger or enthusiasm will be stopped. 3. To kill. 4. To investigate another's intentions; to find out if someone is angry. *Above four meanings primarily underworld and sports use.* 5. To reduce exercise slowly so that one does not become suddenly chilly; esp., to walk a horse after a race so that he will calm down slowly.

cool [something] over. To think about something; to consider all the aspects of a plan, idea, or the like; to view from all angles objectively and carefully.

coon. n. A stupid person; one who can be swayed easily; a strong or brutal man with little brains. *From mispronunciation of "goon."* v.t. To steal.

coop; co-op. n. 1. A co-operative store, enterprise, or society; a building in which each resident owns his own apartment; such an individually owned apartment. *From stand. abbr. for "co-operative," "co-op"; now often pronounced as one syllable and sp. without hyphen.* 2. Any small dilapidated shelter, residence, room, store, etc.; lit., a place resembling a chicken coop. 3. A jail. 4. A coupe. *Orig. humorous; now common.*

coop-happy. *adj.* Insane from confinement.

coot. *n.* A fellow; esp., and old or stupid fellow. *Colloq. One of many sl. words derog. when applied to strangers or acquaintances, but a term of intimacy among friends.*

cootie garage. One of a pair of hair puffs worn over a woman's ears. *c1920 use.*

cop. *n.* A policeman. *From the copper buttons once used on police uniforms, reinforced by the Italo-Amer. "coppo." Orig. derog., implying the speaker's superiority to law and order; now by far the most common word for "policeman." Colloq. v.t.* 1. To steal; to obtain; to deprive. *From the Yiddish "chop" = to grab.* → 2. To win; to carry off a prize. 3. To understand, perceive, comprehend; to consider. 4. To give forth with or present something, as an appeal. —*per.* *n.* 1. A policeman; esp., a tough policeman or one who is intent on enforcing the law to its fullest. *From the copper buttons worn by Eng. policemen. More of an underworld term than cop, the abbr. being less derog.* 2. An informer; a stool pigeon. 3. Time subtracted from a prison sentence because of good behavior; time off a prison sentence because the prisoner has informed on his co-criminals after the sentence was imposed. 4. A U.S. penny; one cent. *Colloq. v.i.* To work as a policeman. *v.t.* To bet against a person, card, roll of the dice, etc.

copacetic; copesetic; kopasetic; kopesetic; kopasetee; kopesetee. *adj.* Fine, excellent, all right, o.k. *From the Yiddish.*

cop a heel. To escape from prison or a policeman; to make a getaway. *Underworld use.*

cop a mope. To escape. *Underworld use.*

cop and heel. 1. An escape from prison or a policeman; a getaway. 2. A narrow escape; a close call. *Underworld use.*

cop a plea. To plead guilty to a criminal charge, thus saving the court time and money; esp. to plead guilty in order to receive a lighter sentence than if one pleads innocent, is tried, and found guilty.

cop out. 1. To be arrested; to be caught in the act of committing a crime. 2. To plead guilty.

copper a tip. To do just the opposite of what one is advised to do; to bet against a hunch or tip.

copper-hearted. *adj.* Tending to be an informer; untrustworthy.

copper-on; copper-off. A method of gambling whereby one alternately bets for and against the dice, a card, a number, etc.; also a method of betting whereby one bets several times, then does not bet, then bets again, in a definite predetermined order.

cops, on the. On the police force.

copy-cat. *n.* An imitator. *1896.*

corker. *n.* 1. Any thing or person that is exciting, colorful, excellent, remarkable, noteworthy, or the like. *c1835.* 2. An incredible story; a very funny joke or prank.

corking. *adj. & adv.* Exceedingly.

corking mat. *n.* A sleeping pad. *W.W.II USN use.*

cork opera. A minstrel show, from the burnt-cork make-up used. *c1860's.*

corkscrew. *n.* An auger.

corn. *n.* 1. Liquor, esp. corn whisky, home-made or illegally sold. 2. A state of drunkenness from too much corn whisky. 3. Money. 4. Anything overly sentimental, old-fashioned, or banal; sentimentality; banality; melodrama. —**fed.** *adj.* 1. Stout, plump; said of a girl or woman. 2. Given to or characterized by a rustic style, tastes, or ideas; unsophisticated. —**y.** *adj.* Sentimental; banal; obvious; old-fashioned or out of date; unsophisticated. *Orig. pejorative use by musicians and theatrical folk; wide teenage use after c1940; now general use, though beginning to become archaic.*

cornball; corn-ball. *n.* One who likes or perpetrates sentimentality, banality, or outdated styles; a musician or other artist whose work is vapid, sentimental, or corny. *Based on "screwball." Mainly teenage use c1943–c1953.*

corn bill = corn willie.

corn cracker. A good thing. *c1900; Dial. and archaic.*

corner = hot corner.

corner (bend), go around the. To die. *Archaic and dial.*

corn juice. Corn whisky; (inferior) whisky.

corn mule. Corn whisky; specif., home-made or bootleg or inferior corn whisky.

corn punk = punk.

corn willie; corned willie. *n.* Corned beef; also, hash made with it. *Also called "corn bill." Army use; common in W.W.II.*

corral. *v.t.* To find; to look for. *Colloq.*

cosh; kosh. *n.* A bludgeon, esp. a piece of iron pipe or a length of rubber hose filled with lead; a blackjack.

cosmo. *n.* A foreign student. *Student use.*

cosmolines, the. *n.* The field artillery; the artillery unit or units attached to an infantry group. *W.W.II use. From the cosmoline grease used in oiling and storing guns.*

cotton-picking; cotton pickin'. *adj.* Common; vulgar; damned; not valuable. *Orig. Southern use. Somewhat jocular, because it appears to be a euphem.*

cou. *n.* A girl. *From "couzie."*

couch doctor. A psychoanalyst.

cough up. 1. To pay, pay up, or pay over money. Used with or without a direct object. 2. To come forth with or present, as a confession of guilt or money owed.

countdown; count-down. *n.* The act of or an instance of counting down from a given number to zero at one-second intervals in preparation for exploding an atomic bomb or launching a missile. *Orig. c1945 atomic-bomb use; now also missile-launching use.*

count [one's] thumbs. To kill time.

count ties. To walk on a railroad trackway. *Vagabond argot.*

cousin. *n.* 1. In baseball, an easy pitcher; one who gives (certain) batters no trouble in making hits. 2. A dupe; an easy victim. 3. A close friend.

couzie; couzy. *n.* A girl.

cover. *v.i.* = cover up. *v.t.* 1. To alibi or lie for another in order that he may escape detection or punishment. 2. To protect another.

covered wagon. An aircraft carrier. *W.W.II USN use.*

cover-up. *n.* An alibi, distraction, shield, or attempt to conceal. **cover up.** *v.i.* To lie or take the blame for wrongdoing in order to allow another to escape undetected; to attempt to conceal or minimize a misdeed.

cow. *n.* 1. Milk. *Student, Armed Forces, hobo, ranch, and logger use since c1900.* 2. Cream. 3. Butter. 4. Beef in any form—steak, roast, hamburger, etc. 5. Any fat, ungraceful person. *Colloq.* —**boy.** *n.* 1. A "Western" sandwich. 2. A reckless, irresponsible man. 3. A raucous, boisterous man. 4. A king in a deck of playing cards. 5. The leader of a criminal gang or mob. *v.t.* To murder quickly, recklessly, or in a noisy, public, or sensational manner.

cowboy coffee. Black coffee without sugar.

cowboy job. A holdup staged by amateurs; a robbery staged recklessly.

cow college. A small agricultural

college; an agricultural college; any small, little-known college.

cow-hide. *n.* A baseball.

cow juice. *n.* Milk. *c1845. Still used.*

cow pilot. An airplane stewardess. *Aviator use.*

cowpoke. *n.* Cowboy. *c1885.*

cowpuncher. *n.* A cowboy. *First use c1875. Western use.*

crab. *n.* A strict, cross, or irritable person. *v.i.* 1. To complain; to nag. *Colloq.* 2. To borrow continually. 3. To complain. *v.t.* 1. To pilfer trifling articles. 2. To spoil (something belonging to another person). —s. *n.pl.* 1. [taboo]. Crab lice; a case of infestation by crab lice. → 2. A type of flea. *Hobo use.*

crack. *v.t.* 1. To open a safe by force, using either explosives or tools. → 2. To attend a social gathering uninvited; to crash the gate. → 3. Fig., to force or finally gain one's way into an occupation, social group, or the like. → 4. Fig., to solve a problem or a mystery; to reveal, explain, or comprehend. *Colloq.* 5. To mention something; to disclose something. 6. To break a banknote in making change. *v.i.* 1. To weaken or show signs of weakening under emotional strain; to lose one's emotional control, will power, or sanity. 2. To speak or talk. 3. In the card game of bridge, to double. *n.* 1. A short, often humorous, criticism; an audacious remark; a statement, esp. one that is uncomplimentary or clever; a wisecrack. 2. A try at some undertaking whether large or small. —ed. *adj.* 1. Crazy; eccentric. 2. Stupid, foolish. —erjack. *adj.* Excellent; topnotch. —ing. *adv.* Very.

crack a book. Lit., to open a book; fig., to study, to cram.

crack a smile. To smile.

crack back. To retort. crack-back. *n.* A quick or clever retort.

crack down. To take admonitory or punitive action against someone; to censure.

cracked ice = ice.

cracker barrel. 1. Fig., a place or locale where, or time when, men relax and talk philosophically. *From the actual cracker barrel, once found in all general stores, where town elders gathered, discussed local problems, and waxed philosophical.* 2. Resembling or pertaining to homely philosophy; unsophisticated, rustic; said of thought or philosophy. *Colloq.*

cracking, get. Start; start moving; begin working; begin to exert oneself. *Often in the phrase "let's get cracking."*

crack [one's] jaw. To boast.

crack up. 1. To praise. *Colloq.* 2. To wreck an airplane, automobile, or the like while operating it. *Colloq. v.i.* To lose one's emotional control, will power, or sanity; to have a crying or laughing fit. crack-up *n.* 1. An accident that badly damages or destroys an automobile, airplane, or the like; a wreck. *Colloq.* 2. An emotional or mental breakdown; a loss of control.

crack wise. 1. To speak knowingly. 2. To speak jokingly; to make a wisecrack.

cradle. *n.* A railroad gondola car.

cradle-snatcher. *n.* A person of either sex who marries, courts, or befriends a much younger person of the opposite sex. The British equiv. is "baby farmer."

cram. *v.i., v.t.* 1. To study hard, esp. for a school examination. 2. Fig., to pack information into one's mind, esp. in preparation for an examination. *c1850. Common student use, esp. college level. n.* 1. A written paper, textbook, etc. used in studying for an examination; also, a study session. 2. A student who studies hard before an examination. 3. An overly diligent student, a book worm. *adj.* Devoted to cramming. —mer. *n.* One who studies hard for an examination.

cramp [one's] style. To interfere with or hinder a person; esp. to prevent a person from expressing himself fully.

crape-hanger. *n.* **1.** A gloomy person; a killjoy. **2.** An undertaker.

crap out. 1. To lose; esp. to lose one's money or a bet. *From dicing and gambling use in the game of craps, in which a throw of 7 or 11 in attempting to make a point causes the player to lose his bet and his turn. Not common.* **2.** To evade one's duty; to become afraid, to become cowardly; to withdraw from a scheme or activity due to cowardice. **3.** To tire or become exhausted; to lose one's enthusiasm; to withdraw from a plan or excursion; specif. to become too tired to continue enjoying, contributing to, or staying at a party or social gathering. *Wide student use since c1945 and most common use.*

crash. *n.* **1.** A strong romantic infatuation; a crush. **2.** A complete flunk. *v.t.* **1.** To break into a building; to gain admission to a place by force. → **2.** To rob a place; to make a forced entry in order to rob a place. → **3.** Fig., to gain admission to, to break in; to gain admission to or acceptance in a group or field of endeavor.

crash out. To break out of prison.

crashout. *n.* A jail break.

crash project. A project or program designed to overcome an emergency; thus, one demanding immediate and intensive exertion; a project having priority over all others; a project so vital to the life of a nation or firm that no time or effort is spared to complete it successfully. *Since c1950. Orig. applied to scientific or military programs considered vital to the national defense but now widely used in clerical departments of the government and in private business.*

crash wagon. An ambulance.

crate. *n.* **1.** An antiquated or dilapidated automobile, truck, bus, airplane, or even a ship. → **2.** Any automobile, truck, bus, or airplane, or even a ship. *Very common c1938–1945.* **3.** A jail. *Vagabond argot, rarely used by others.* **4.** A coffin.

crawfish. *v.i.* To renege.

crawl. *n.* A dance.

crazy. *adj.* **1.** Satisfying one's desire for the unique; new, cool, exciting, different, and personally satisfying. *Common bop use since c1945. Usu. as a one-word comment.* → **2.** Wonderful; thrilling; satisfying. *Orig. bop and cool use. Common to teenagers since c1950.*

crazy about [someone or something]. *adj.* Crazy for; specif., in love with; having a strong liking for someone or something.

crazy-cat. *n.* A "crazy" person.

crazy for. Very eager for; in love with; attracted to; appreciative of; obsessed with. *Since c1850.*

creaker. *n.* Any old person.

cream. *v.t.* **1.** To obtain a selfish goal, cheat, take advantage of, rob, persuade, or gain dominance over another by glib talk, flattery, or the like. → **2.** To accomplish a task easily and with spectacular success; specif., to pass an examination or course of study easily and with high grades. → **3.** To defeat decisively, esp. in an athletic contest. *adj.* Easy; pleasant.

cream puff; creampuff. *n.* **1.** A weakling; a person of slight physique; a sissy. **2.** An automobile that has been driven carefully, kept in good condition from the first, and is being offered for resale.

cream-puff hitter. In baseball, a weak batter.

cream up. To carry out a task perfectly.

creep. *n.* **1.** Lit., a person who gives one "the creeps"; orig. an introvert, bore, or nonsociable person whose quiet manners and gestures seem sly or surreptitious; any odd, loathsome, or objectionable person; a drip; a wet blanket; a jerk. *Wide student use c1935–c1945. Still common.* **2.** A clandestine meeting or mission. *Some Negro use.* 3. A slow round of golf. *Caddy use.* —er. *n.* 1. A performer who comes closer and closer to a microphone during a broadcast. *Broadcasting studio use.* 2. = creep. —y. *adj.* 1. Like a creep; characteristic of a creep. 2. Cheap; inferior.

creep dive. A cheap saloon; a saloon operated by or patronized by creeps.

creep-joint. *n.* 1. A gambling business, game, or set-up that operates in a different location every night in order to avoid police raids. *Underworld use since c1930.* 2. = creep dive.

creeps, the. *n.sing.* 1. A physical, mental, or psychical sensation of fear, horror, disgust, or the like; revulsion; uneasiness. Cf. willies. 2. Delirium tremens; the heebie-jeebies.

crew. *n.* = crew cut.

crew-cut; crew cut. *n.* A style of close haircut, usu. a man's or boy's. *Since c1940. From college crewmen who have favored such haircuts for many years. Orig. pop. with students, now common. adj.* 1. In crew-cut style. 2. Collegiate; Ivy League.

crib. *n.* 1. A set of written answers used by a student to cheat at an examination. *c1860; now colloq.* 2. A student who cheats on an exam. 3. A brothel, esp. a cheap one; specif., a very small room, large enough to contain only a bed, in a brothel. 4. A nightclub; a dive. 5. A safe or vault. *Underworld use. v.t.* 1. To steal. 2. To cheat, esp. in an academic examination.

crimp. *v.t.* 1. To put a restriction on another's actions. 2. To demote. 3. To ruin a plan, idea, etc. by adding restrictions to it. —y. *adj.* Uncomfortably cold.

crip. *n.* 1. A crippled person. 2. A crippled horse. *Farm usage.* 3. In the game of pool, a ball positioned so as to be easy to take. 4. An adversary easily beaten. 5. In college, an easy course.

crip-faker. *n.* A professional beggar who pretends bodily injury to gain attention. *Tramp use.*

croak. *v.t.* To murder. *c1850. v.i.* 1. To die. 2. To flunk a school examination or course. —er. *n.* A physician; a medical doctor. *Underworld, addict, hobo, circus, etc., use.* —ing. *n.* A killing; a murder.

crock. *n.* 1. A disliked youth or man, esp. one disliked for being meticulous, superior, aloof, or selfish; specif., a successful, boasting, meticulous elderly man. 2. A worthless or disliked girl or woman. 3. A bottle of liquor. 4. A drunken person; a drunkard. *From "crocked."* 5. An animal imitator. *Radio use.* 6. A barge-like freight ship made chiefly of reinforced concrete. *1945, USN use in Pacific.* 7. A guy; a geezer. *v.t.* To hit someone over the head; to bean or conk. —ed. *adj.* Drunk.

crockery. *n.* 1. The teeth. 2. In baseball, a pitcher's arm that stops functioning.

crockie. *n.* A playing marble with a baked, glazed finish, usu. blue or brown.

crook. *v.i., v.t.* To steal.

crooked arm. A left-handed pitcher. *Baseball use.*

croon. *v.i., v.t.* 1. To sing popular songs with a soft, mellow style; to sing. 2. = sing.

croot. *n.* An Army recruit. *Some Army use.*

croppy. *n.* A corpse.

cross. *adj.* Dishonest. *n.* A double-cross. *v.t.* 1. To cheat. 2. To deny another his rights or possessions; to do something against another's wishes.

cross my heart (and hope to die). A traditional and mild oath used to affirm the truth of a statement. *Common child use.*

cross [someone's] palms. To bribe; to pay for a noncommercial service.

cross-up. *n.* = double-cross.

cross [someone] up. To mix one

up; to confuse; to lead astray; to deceive.

crow. *n.* 1. The eagle in various USN insignia. *W.W.I USN use, still common.* → 2. A USN chief or captain who wears such insignia. 3. Chicken. *W.W.II Armed Forces use.* 4. An unpopular or ugly woman or girl.

crowbait. *n.* An old, useless, mean, or ugly horse. *Western use.*

crowd. *n.* A gang, group, faction, or clique.

Crow Jimism. A strong psychological attraction to Negroes; said in ref. to whites. *Usu. used to characterize a guilt attitude arising from deep-rooted Negrophobia or the operations of a politician who courts Negro votes for personal gain. "Jim Crowism" backwards.*

crown. *v.t.* To hit a person over the head.

crow tracks. Chevrons. *Army use.*

crud. *n.* Anything inferior, worthless, ugly, or disgusting.

cruller. *n.* 1. Specif., a yeast doughnut. *From the French; colloq.* 2. A failure; specif., an unsuccessful performance or entertainment.

crumb; crum. *n.* 1. A louse; a bedbug. *Some hobo, ranch, logger, Army, and USN use since before c1900.* → 2. A dirty, slovenly, repulsive person. *Army, maritime, and hobo use. Since c1910.* 3. An untrustworthy, loathsome, or objectionable person; an insignificant, despicable person. *Since c1920; wide student use c1935–c1945.* —s. *n.pl.* Lit., a few pieces of change or silver money; a few dollars; a small amount of money. —y. *adj.* Dirty; filthy; contemptible, repulsive, disgusting. *Common use. Although "crum" for "crumb" appears so seldom as to seem illiterate, "crummy" prevails over "crumby" about 7 to 1.* 1. *n.* A train caboose. *Hobo use. From the early days when cabooses were infested with lice.*

crumb boss. *n.* A construction-camp bunkhouse janitor or porter; one who makes up beds. *Hobo and logger use.*

crumb-bum; crum-bum. *n.* Fig., a lice-ridden bum; a worthless person.

crumb house = crumb joint.

crumb joint. A flop-house infested with lice. *Hobo use.*

crumb-o; crumbo. *n.* = crumb. *One of the more common sl. words with —o suffix. Mainly newsp. columnist, theater, and gambler use.*

crumb-roll. *n.* A bed or blanket roll; a bed. *Hobo, ranch, and logger use. c1915.*

crumb the deal. To spoil a plan or plot.

crumb up. To clean clothes thoroughly, esp. by boiling, so as to rid them of lice; to clean a place. *Some W.W.I Army use; some prison use.*

crump. *v.i.* To lose consciousness from the combination of drinking and fatigue; to pass out; to crap out.

crumped out. Drunk; also, fatigued, tight, asleep.

crump out = crump.

crush. *n.* 1. An infatuation, esp. a one-sided one; a strong liking for a person, esp. one of the opposite sex; often in "to have (*or* get) a crush on someone." 2. A reception, dance, party, or other large social gathering. *Some student use since c1900.* *v.t.* To escape from prison. —er. *n.* A boy who is popular with girls and women; an attractive youth whom many girls have a crush on.

crush on someone, have a. To be infatuated or in love with someone *Esp. applied to children and early teenagers. Colloq.*

crush out. To escape from prison. *Underworld use.* **crush-out.** *n.* An escape from prison.

Crusoe = Robinson Crusoe.

crust. *n.* Gall, audacity, nerve. *c1900.* —y. *adj.* 1. Nervy; also, dirty; mean; contemptible. 2. Worthless; worn out.

crut. *n.* = crud.

crutch. *n.* An automobile. *Some Negro use.*

cry baby. *n.* One who cries frequently and with little provocation; fig., one who cannot bear criticism or reprimands.

crying jag. A period of uncontrolled crying.

crying towel. An imaginary towel freq. called for to be given one who complains, chronically or loudly, of minor defeats and ill fortune. Thus "Get out the crying towel [for another]" = once again [another] is talking too much about his minor defeats and ill fortune.

cry uncle = say uncle.

cub. *n.* A young inexperienced person. —by. *n.* A room; a home, a pad. *Some Negro use.*

cube. *n.* Lit., a three-dimensional "square"; a super "square"; one who is unbelievably innocent of current events and ideas or hopelessly ignorant of fashionable usages; an ultraconservative; a thorough bore. *Some bop and cool use since c1955, but mostly synthetic.* —s. *n.pl.* Dice.

cuckoo. *n.* An insane person; an eccentric. *Since before 1600. adj.* Crazy; irrational; eccentric. *"Coo-coo" is more common in the U.S.*

cucumber. *n.* A dollar.

cuddle-bunny. *n.* A promiscuous or delinquent girl. *Some teenage use c1940–c1950.*

cue. *v.t.* = clue.

cueball; cue-ball. *n.* An eccentric or odd person; an odd-ball. *The "cue" stands for "q" or "queer."*

cue in. To make a specif. place for, to add to, to combine with; said of parts of radio, television, and movie scripts.

cuff. *v.t.* 1. To borrow money from an individual, usu. without forewarning. 2. To charge (an expense) to; to put "on the cuff." —eroo. *adj.* Free, gratis, or, more usu., to be paid for later; on the cuff. —o. *adj.* Free of charge, gratis; nonpaying; admitted free of charge. *Since c1935.* —s. *n.pl.*

Handcuffs; a pair of handcuffs. *Colloq.*

cuff, off the. 1. Informally; extemporaneously; impromptu; unrehearsed. 2. Speaking, or giving one's opinion, advice, or confidential plan, to a person or group as a private individual rather than in one's official or business capacity.

cuff, on the. 1. On credit; on a charge account; on the installment plan; not paying but promising to pay; trusted to pay later. *Because, traditionally, the amount owed was written on the creditor's cuff.* 2. Free of charge; on a basis of no monetary payment promised or expected for goods, etc., received or consumed; done without cash remuneration for one's work. 3. Confidentially; impromptu thoughts or words, offhand.

cuffee. *n.* A Negro. *A genuine African word.*

cuke. *n.* A cucumber; a cucumber prepared for eating.

culture vulture. A person interested in or a devotee of art or intellectual concerns. *Some teenage use since c1940.*

cup of tea. Anything that or anybody whom a person likes.

cupola. *n.* The top of the human head; the brain.

cups. *n.* Sleep. *adj.* Asleep. *Some Negro use.*

cups, in [one's]. Drunk. *Fairly common.*

curbie. *n.* A waitress who serves food and drink to patrons in their automobiles parked at the curb; a carhop.

curbstone. *n.* A cigarette or cigar butt; esp. one picked up from the street; a cigarette made from the tobacco found in the butt ends of previously smoked cigarettes.

curdle. *v.t.* 1. To fail. 2. To offend; to annoy. *Lit. to curdle one's stomach.*

cure, take the. 1. Lit., to commit oneself to a hospital or sanitorium to be cured of chronic alcoholism or drug addiction. → 2. Fig., to refuse to indulge in or to refrain from participating in any pastime which one formerly enjoyed.

curry below the knee. To curry favor; to court a superior. *From "ass kisser."*

curtains. *n.sing.* Death; disaster. *From theater use when "curtain" = the lowering of the curtain in front of the stage, signifying the end of the performance.* —[for someone]. *n.pl.* Something ominously dire or final for a person; specif., death; the end, as of a career; a knockout; a prison sentence.

cush. *n.* 1. A wallet; esp. one found or stolen. *From "cushy" (money easy to obtain).* 2. A form of mush or gruel. *Borrowed from the Gullah slaves by Southern whites, the word has radiated to the more prominent connotation of anything soft or pleasurable, reinforced by "cushion."* → 3. Sex or sexual gratification. 4. Desserts; sweets. —ee; —y. *n.* Money. *adj.* 1. Easy; secure; pleasant; soft. Esp. an easy job, an easy way to earn money, a pleasant way to live, etc. *Perhaps from "cushion," but maybe from the French "couchée" or "coucher." More probably from the Anglo-Indian "khushi" (pleasant) since the British used the term before it came to the U.S. c1900.* 2. Fancy.

cushion. *n.* 1. In baseball, the bag used to mark first, second, or third base; hence the base itself. 2. Money saved for unexpected expenses, emergencies, or one's old age.

cuss. *n.* A fellow. *One of the oldest colloq. words in the U.S.; used by the colonists and still common.*

customer. *n.* A person, usu. a male; a man, guy, fellow. *Usu. preceded by an adj., e.g., "tough customer," "smooth customer."*

cut. *n.* 1. An absence from a college class; the omission of a recitation. 2. A share or percentage of profit; a commission; a share or part. 3. One's turn or try; a chance or opportunity. 4. A derisive comment; a sharp, insulting, deprecatory, critical, or reprimanding remark. *Colloq.* 5. In baseball, a swing at the ball with the bat. *adj.* 1. Diluted. 2. Shortened; censored; condensed; usu. said of books, movies, plays, a piece of music, etc. 3. Drunk. *v.t.* 1. In college, to be wilfully absent from a class or lecture. 2. To refrain from greeting an acquaintance upon meeting him; to ignore an acquaintance. 3. To share the winnings or profits. 4. To dilute a beverage, esp. whisky or another alcoholic beverage; to dilute drugs. *Colloq.* 5. To delete, shorten, or censor, as a passage of written material, esp. a book. *Universally known.* 6. To put an end to something that one is doing; to stop. *Since c1930. From "cut it out," reinforced by the order a director gives to a movie cameraman, "cut" = stop filming this sequence; cut the roll of film here and use it up to this point, while discarding the rest.* 7. To ignore, evade, or reject someone. 8. To spoil or decrease someone's pleasure, enthusiasm, or happiness. *Since c1940. Fig., to dilute, shorten, end, or reject another's happiness.* 9. To outdo another, to perform so well or be so intelligent, charming, attractive, or well dressed that one receives more attention than, or preference over, another. 10. To annoy, bother, or irk another. *v.i.* To leave; to depart for another place. *Fig., to sever oneself from a place. v.i., v.t.* To make a phonograph recording; to record. *A groove is actually cut into a record during recording.* —ter. *n.* = cutor.

cut A (a) = cut out. *Some teenage use since c1955. A euphem. for "cut ass," also a syn. for "cut out."*

cut and dried. Routine; familiar;

certain; characterized by agreement with known rules, schedules, or the like. *Colloq.*

cut and run. To leave and run away; to stop what one is doing and run away; to cut out.

cut a rug. To dance; specif., to jitterbug. *Jive use, mostly synthetic.*

cut a rusty. To show joy; to show off. *Now dial.*

cut ass [taboo] = cut out. *Some teenage use since c1955.*

cut a take. 1. To record a performance; to make a phonograph recording. → **2.** To explain something precisely. *Cool use.*

cutback. *n.* A reduction, specif. of work or production, as to a previously lower level. *Colloq.*

cut-dub. *n.* A best friend. *Reformatory use.*

cuter; kyuter. *n.* A U.S. 25-cent piece, a quarter of a dollar. *Vagabond argot, from carnival and circus use.*

cutes, the. *n.* Precocious actions or conduct.

cutie; cut(e)y. *n.* **1.** A cute person. **2.** Specif., an upstart; one who thinks himself clever. **3.** A cute or good-looking person. **4.** A smart prize-fighter. **5.** Anything that is cute or clever; a song, trick, etc. **6.** A deception. **7.** A clever, charming, but selfish or unethical person.

cutie-pie; cutie pie. *n.* A cute person; a small, alert, energetic, winsome person.

cut-in. *n.* A share; a "cut." **cut in.** *v.i.* **1.** To intercept a dancing couple; said of a male who then asks the female to dance with him. *Colloq.* **2.** To interrupt; to give unasked-for advice or opinion.

cut it off. To sleep. *Suggested by "saw wood" = to sleep.*

cut it out. An order or a plea for someone to stop what he is doing, esp. to stop annoying, bothering, teasing, or riding another. *Very common with children in 8-12-year-old age group, although common with adults.*

cut no ice. To have no effect; to make no impression. *Colloq.*

cut off [someone's] **water** = turn off [someone's] water.

cutor. *n.* A prosecuting attorney; a prosecutor.

cut out. 1. To leave, usu. to leave quickly, suddenly, secretly, or permanently; to depart. *Wide student use since c1940; some teenage and young adult use.* **2.** To refrain from; to give up; to stop.

cut-plug. *n.* An inferior horse.

cut-rate; cut rate. *adj.* Offered at less than the usual price; cheap. *Colloq.*

cutting out [paper] **dolls (dollies).** Crazy.

cut up. 1. To meet in order to divide loot, gambling winnings, or the like. *Underworld use. From "cut up the touches."* → **2.** To reminisce or gossip; to discuss. **3.** To joke; to play pranks; to misbehave. **4.** To be humorous and lively. *Colloq.* **cut-up.** *n.* **1.** A prankster; a practical joker. *Colloq. since c1890.* **2.** A jocular, pleasantly boisterous, entertaining person.

cut up [the] **touches (pipes, jackpots). 1.** Lit., to meet in order to divide loot. *Underworld use.* → **2.** To reminisce; to gossip. *Dial.*

D

D.A. 1. Stand. abbr. for district attorney. **2.** A teenage boys' hair style in which the hair is kept thick and long and combed straight back from the top and sides; strands of hair from the top and sides overlap at the back of the neck, resembling the arrangement of a duck's tailfeathers. *Common rock and roll use since c1954.*

daddy. *n.* A male lover, esp. one who supports his paramour in return for her sexual favors; one who keeps a mistress. *Clipped form of "sugar daddy." Replaced "sugar daddy" c1935. A "daddy" is usu. older than a "John."*

Daddy-o; daddy-o. *n.* An affectionate term of direct address for any male who is hip, understanding, or sympathetic, whether a father or not. *Orig. bop use c1946; now one of the most common —o words.*

daffodil. *n.* A homily, proverb, or aphorism.

daffy. *adj.* Crazy. *Colloq.* —**dill.** *n.* An insane person. *From "daffy" plus a form of "daffodil."*

daffy about. In love with; crazy about.

dagged. *adj.* Drunk.

dag-nabbed. *adj.* Darned; doggoned.

dago; Dago. *n.* **1.** An Italian; a person of Italian descent. *Sometimes derog; usu. derisive.* **2.** The Italian language. *Since c1900.*

dago red. 1. Italian red wine; any cheap red wine. *Hobo sl.; became pop. during prohibition.* **2.** Italian wine, specif. red Chianti.

dagwood. *n.* A gigantic sandwich. *From "Dagwood," a character in a synd. comic strip.*

daily double. Success in two fields of endeavor simultaneously; winning or obtaining any two different prizes, goals, or the like. *From the betting term, a combination bet on two successive races.*

daisy. *n.* **1.** Any excellent, remarkable, or admirable person or thing; a choice specimen; a honey. *Colloq. Used as early as 1750 in U.S.* **2.** Specif., a pretty girl. **3.** A grave; death. *From "pushing up daisies." adv.* Very.

daisy-cutter. *n.* **1.** In baseball, a hit ball that skims the ground; a grounder. *Still in use.* **2.** A tennis ball that skims the ground. *Still in use.* **3.** A horse that, when trotting, does not lift its feet far off the ground.

damaged. *adj.* Drunk.

dame. *n.* A woman or girl, esp. a troublesome one. *Orig. "dame" implied a young woman considered attractive but not wholly respectable by the speaker. Depending on the emphasis, it can* now mean a promiscuous woman *(prob. the most freq. use since c1940), a sexually attractive woman, an unemotional, sexless woman worker, or even an ugly old woman.*

damn; darn. *v.t.* To condemn a person or thing as without value; to judge someone or something as worthless. *Colloq. adj.* Complete, hopeless. Used to intensify a derog. statement. *Colloq. expl.* A curse or epithet of anger, disappointment, or frustration. *Not now generally considered taboo.*

damned; darned. *adj.* = damn, **darn.** *expl.* = damn, darn.

damper. *n.* **1.** That which discourages; that which reduces the joy of success, expectation, or a good time; lit., that which "dampens" one's enthusiasm, spirit, or pleasure. *Colloq.* **2.** A cash register; a drawer or compartment where money is kept, as by a store or business that has no cash register. *Circus, hobo, and underworld use since c1925.* → **3.** A bank. **4.** Fig., a treasury.

damper on, put a. To discourage; to dampen the enthusiasm of; to spoil another person's pleasure.

dance. *v.i.* To be in the power or control of another; to be forced to be subservient to another, as through threats, blackmail, or because one has a dominating boss, wife, or the like. *n.* A street fight between gangs of boys; a rumble.

dance, go into [one's]. To "tell a line."

dance-hall. *n.* **1.** A prison deathhouse; a room where condemned prisoners are put to death. **2.** An anteroom to a prison electrocution chamber; cells where condemned prisoners spend their last hours.

dance off. To die.

dance on air. To die by hanging.

dancer. *n.* A coward, as a prize fighter who spends much time "dancing" away from or evading an opponent.

dance the carpet. To appear before an official for an investigation of one's work or behavior, or, specif., to receive a reprimand, criticism, or punishment.

D and D. *n.* 1. Drunk and disorderly. *A common police charge in arrests of troublemakers.* 2. Deaf and dumb. → 3. Fig., deaf and dumb, i.e., afraid of telling what one knows or has heard; fear of fighting for one's rights. *N.Y.C. longshoreman and underworld use since c1950, because many who have complained or testified against illegal or unethical practices of the longshoremen's union have been beaten, threatened, or otherwise silenced.*

dander up, get [one's]. To make someone become angry or concerned; to become angry or concerned.

dandy. *n.* An excellent thing or person. *Since c1785. Colloq. adj.* Fine; excellent; first-rate. *Colloq. adv.* Splendidly.

dange broad. A sexually attractive Negro girl or young woman.

dangler. *n.* A trapeze performer. *Circus use.*

darby. *n.* Money.

darby cove. A blacksmith.

dark. *adj.* Closed; said of a theater, sports arena, or other place of entertainment, whether or not lighted by artificial lights. *Orig. theater use.* —**y.** *n.* A Negro. *Colloq. c1770.*

dark, in the. Uninformed; not aware of current attitudes or happenings.

dark horse. 1. An entry in a contest, such as a horse race or other sporting match, which is unknown or seems to have little chance of winning; fig., an unknown contestant for a prize, job, honor, or the like, whose chances for success are better than generally supposed. *From horse racing use.* → 2. Specif., a surprise candidate for public office in an election; one nominated without advance publicity.

dark-setting. *n.* Necking or petting in complete seclusion at night. *Prison use.*

date. *n.* 1. An engagement or appointment, esp. and usu. with one of the opposite sex. 2. A social escort or partner of the opposite sex. *v.i., v.t.* To make or have a social engagement or engagements (with one of the opposite sex). *All uses so common as to be standard.*

date bait. An attractive, popular girl. *Some teenage use since c1940. Freq. use by newsp. columnists.*

daylight (sunlight) into, let. To clarify one's thoughts or thinking on a specif. subject, to contribute facts or ideas to a specif. discussion.

daylights. *n.pl.* Consciousness; sense; life; brains or other vital organs, as "to knock the (living) daylights out of somebody."

deac. *n.* A deacon.

deacon seat. The long seat along the edge of bunks in a bunkhouse. *Hobo and woodsman use.*

dead. *v.i.* To be unable to recite in class. *College slang. adj.* 1. Exhausted; dead tired; said of a person. 2. Not working; said of a mechanism. 3. Considered and rejected; said of a plan or scheme. 4. Empty; usu. said of a beer or whisky bottle. 5. Having no chance of success; without further opportunity; said of a person. 6. Boring, dull, unexciting. 7. Completely, entirely. *In certain specific expressions, like* "dead level" = completely true or honest; "dead set against it" = completely opposed to something; "dead broke" = entirely without funds; *etc. Colloq.* —**beat; dead beat.** *n.* 1. A worthless person, specif. one who does not pay his debts; one who depends on the generosity of others; a moocher. 2. A hobo or tramp riding free on a train. *v.i.* To loaf or sponge. —**er.** *n.* A dead person.

dead as a dodo. Completely, irrevocably, and finally "dead," forgotten, or dismissed.

dead broke. Penniless; entirely without money.

dead cat. A lion, tiger, or leopard that does not perform, but is merely exhibited.

dead duck. Any person or thing that is doomed to failure, extinction, or the like, or that has died or failed; a goner.

deadfall. *n.* A night-club or all-night restaurant; a clip joint.

deadhead; dead-head. *n.* 1. A nonpaying guest or customer; a passenger who rides free, as on a train, bus, or cab; one who is a guest of the management and need not pay. 2. A train, freight car, bus, cab, or truck carrying no passengers or freight, as on a return trip to a terminal. 3. A stupid or incompetent person. *v.i.* To drive an empty taxi, as on a return trip, with no prospect of a passenger; to drive an empty truck, bus, or train; to travel empty, without passengers or freight. *Orig. railroad use.*

dead heat. A tie between two or more contestants. *Colloq. Orig. horse racing use; mainly sports use.*

dead horse. An issue, argument, or incident that does not affect or have any meaning to the present; an unfortunate incident or issue that cannot be rectified and is best forgotten; fig., something that one has used up but not yet paid for; an unpaid debt for something that no longer exists. *From traditional expression "to flog a dead horse." Since c1830. Colloq.*

dead hour. An hour during which college classes are held but during which a given student does not have a class. *Student use since c1920.*

deadlights. *n.pl.* The eyes.

deadly. *adj.* Excellent. *Jive use.*

dead man's hand. 1. In the card game of poker, a hand containing a pair of aces and a pair of eights (aces over eights). *So called because Wild Bill Hickok was reportedly holding just such a hand when Jack McCall shot him in the back at Deadwood in 1876.* → 2. Bad luck or misfortune of any kind; entering an endeavor or contest at a disadvantage.

dead marine = dead soldier.

dead one. *n.* 1. A hobo who has retired from the road; also, a stingy person. *Hobo lingo.* 2. An inefficient, dull person.

dead pan; deadpan. *n.* 1. An expressionless face; a poker face. 2. A person who keeps his face expressionless. Said specif. of an entertainer while performing. *adj.* Straight-faced; facially expressionless.

dead pigeon. One who is sure to meet death, disaster, or failure; one who has no chance to succeed or escape disaster; a goner; a dead duck.

dead president. Any U.S. banknote; a piece of paper money.

dead ringer. A duplicate; a person, animal, or thing that very closely resembles another person, animal, or thing; a double; a ringer.

dead soldier (marine). *n.* An empty bottle, esp. an empty beer or whisky bottle.

dead to rights. 1. Certain. *c1880. Colloq.* 2. Caught in the act of or irrefutably accused of an illegal, immoral, unethical, or antisocial act.

dead to the world. Sound asleep.

dead wagon. A vehicle, now usu. an automobile, used for carrying a corpse or corpses; a hearse.

dead wood; deadwood. 1. Any useless item, esp. one that is a nuisance to carry. 2. A useless person; one who does not contribute to work or festivity. 3. Specif., an unsold theater ticket or block of tickets.

deal. *n.* An unethical transaction or agreement from which both parties benefit; an unethical agreement, the trading of favors. Specif., the securing of favored

treatment by extortion or bribery. *v.i.* To be independently active in many varied businesses or
social enterprises; to be able to
make many plans and decisions;
to be in command, authority, or
control. —er. *n.* 1. Anyone who
makes a living from gambling, as
a casino employee, bookmaker,
or card sharp, whether or not an
actual dealer of cards. 2. One involved in many schemes and
plans; one with a varied and active social or business life. 3. A
professional gambler, whether actually a dealer of cards of not.

deal them off the arm. To wait
on table.

deaner. *n.* A dime [10¢]. In Eng., a
shilling.

deano. *n.* A month. *Thief use.*

dearie. *n.* One who is dear. *A vulgar endearment often used jocularly in direct address.*

Dear John. Orig. a letter to a soldier from his wife asking for a
divorce; now a letter to a male
fiancé informing him that the
engagement is broken; any letter
of dismissal from one's sweetheart. *Orig. W.W.II Armed
Forces use.*

deb. *n.* 1. A debutante. 2. A girl
member of an adolescent street
gang. *Orig. teenage use; since
c1945.*

debunk. *v.t.* To prove a lie or an
exaggeration to be false; to reduce another's stature or reputation by exposing his misdeeds.
See bunk.

decay. *n.* 1. The loss in mass of a
radioactive substance during any
specific time. 2. The loss in speed
of a guided missile or man-made
earth satellite during any specific time, owing to gravity and
friction. *Rocketry use.*

deck. *n.* 1. A pack of playing cards.
Now stand. 2. A strong or good
hand of cards. 3. The roof of a
railroad car, as a passenger car.
Still hobo and railroad use. 4. A
package of narcotics wrapped in
paper or an envelope; a portion
of a drug. *Drug addict use since*

c1920. 5. A package of cigarettes.
v.t. To knock someone down; to
floor someone with a blow of the
fist.

deck, hit the. 1. To be knocked
down. *Since c1930, common boxing use. From nautical use.* 2. To
get up out of bed; to rise. *Orig.
maritime use. Wide W.W.II
Army use.*

deck, on. 1. In baseball, next at
bat; said of a player, esp. if he is
in the area marked for batters
waiting their turn at bat. *Since
c1900; appar. from the nautical
use.* 2. Present; on hand and
ready for work, play, etc.; said
of a person. *From nautical use,
but strongly reinforced by the
baseball term.*

deck hand. *n.* A stage hand. *Theater stage hand use.*

decks awash. Drunk.

decode. *v.t.* To explain.

decrease the volume. To speak
lower. *Teenage use since c1950;
usu. a command or entreaty.*

deduck. *n.* An item or an amount
deducted from one's taxable income.

dee-dee = D and D.

deejay; DJ; D.J.; d.j. 1. = disc
jockey. 2. An F.B.I. man, operating in the Dept. of Justice.
From the initials.

deek. *n.* A detective; a dick.

deemer. *n.* 1. A dime. *Vagabond
argot, from carnival and circus
men.* 2. Any small gratuity or tip,
whether a dime or not. 3. One
who gives a small tip; a cheap-
skate. 4. Ten.

deepie. *n.* A three-dimensional
stereographic movie; a depthie.

deep-sea chef. A dishwasher. *Hobo
use.*

deep six. A grave. *Assoc. with jive
and jazz use, esp. bop and cool
use since c1946.*

dehorn. *n.* A drunkard, esp.
one who drinks bootleg whisky,
specif. one who drinks denatured
alcohol; a drunken bum.

delicatessen. *n.* 1. Bullets. 2. The
food commonly associated with
delicatessens: cold sliced meats,

smoked fish, vegetable salads, hard-crusted rye bread, dill pickles, etc.; specif., a meal consisting of these items. *Mainly N.Y.C. use.* 3. A business office. *Adman jargon.*

delish. *adj.* Delicious. *A fairly common shortening.*

delly; dellie. *n.* = delicatessen.

Demo. *n.* A member of the Democratic party.

demo. *n.* A phonograph record made for demonstration purposes, to display the talents of a singer or musician or the merits of a new song to booking agents, bands, radio stations, and the like. *From "demonstration."*

den. *n.* A house, apartment, or room.

departee. *n.* One who leaves a theater at intermission.

depthie. *n.* A three-dimensional stereographic movie; a deepie.

Derbyville. *proper n.* Louisville, Kentucky. *Because Churchill Downs, where the Kentucky Derby is run, is located there.*

derrick. *n.* 1. A successful thief, of expensive items. 2. A shoplifter. *Crook use. v.t.* To take a player out of a game before it is over. *Baseball use.*

derrière. *n.* The human rump. *From the Fr.*

desert rat. One who likes to live in the desert; esp. an old, grizzled prospector, who lives in, prospects, and loves the desert.

designer. *n.* A counterfeiter. *Crook argot.*

desk jockey. An office worker; one who works at an office desk. A term modeled on "disc jockey."

desperado. *n.* A person who borrows or gambles larger sums than he will be able to pay; one whose standard of living is sensationally more costly than his income warrants.

Detroit. *n.* A type of men's haircut in which the hair on the top of the head is cut short and the hair on the sides long.

deuce. *n.* 1. In playing cards, a two. *Colloq.* 2. In poker, a pair.

3. Two dollars. 4. A two-year prison sentence. 5. A quitter, a coward; a small-time crook; *fig.,* one not worth $2 or one who is so petty in crime that he is worthy of receiving only a two-year prison sentence. *Boy street gang use since c1940.* —r. *n.* A two-dollar bill; two dollars. *From "deuce."*

deuce of clubs. Both fists. *From the term in card playing. Reformatory use.*

deuce spot. 1. The second act of a vaudeville show. *Stage talk.* 2. The runner-up; second place in a sports contest, dog show, etc.

devil-may-care. Irresponsible; reckless. *Colloq.*

devil's dozen. Thirteen.

dews. *n.* Ten dollars.

dexie; dexy. *n.* Dexedrine; Dexedrine tablets. *Orig. drug addict use. Mainly student use, as dexies are taken to keep awake during all-night study sessions.*

D.I.; DI. *n.* A drill instructor; a noncommissioned officer in charge of recruits. *Mainly Marine Corps use.*

diamonds. *n.* The testicles.

dib. *n.* 1. Money; esp. a share, portion, or per cent of money. *From "divvy."* → 2. A dollar.

dibs. *n.pl.* Money; usu. a small amount of money.

dibs on [something]. An expression used in claiming the next use of, or chance at, something. E.g., *"Dibs on that magazine." "Dibs on going with the team." Mainly child use. From "divvy."*

dicer. *n.* 1. A stiff hat, such as a top hat, a man's sailor straw hat, etc. 2. A helmet.

dick. *n.* 1. A detective. *Criminal use until c1920. Now common.* 2. A policeman.

dicty; dickty; dictee. *adj.* 1. Stylish, high class, wealthy. → 2. Haughty, snobbish; bossy, demanding. *n.* An aristocrat; a wealthy person; a high-class person; a stylish person. *All uses Negro use. Has been some jive use.*

diddie bag. A bag for keeping valuables. A variant of standard ditty bag. *Army use.*

diddle. *v.i.* To make any nervous or idle gestures; to pick up an object and handle it idly; to idle away one's time wastefully. *v.t.* To cheat.

didie. *n.* A diaper. *Colloq.*

didie pins. A second lieutenant's gold bars. *From "didie." Some W.W.II use.*

dido. *n.* A complaint; a reprimand.

die. *v.i.* 1. In baseball, to be left on base as a baserunner at the end of a half-inning. 2. To laugh or cry uncontrollably; fig., to die of laughter. *Colloq.* 3. To experience extreme anticipation or strong desire. *Colloq.* *n.* Death.

die standing up. To fail; to flop.

diff; dif. *n.* Difference; used almost invariably in "What's the diff?" *"Diff" and "dif" appear with equal frequency.* —**er.** *n.* Difference. *Mainly dial.* —**erence.** *n.* The advantage or that which gives an advantage over an opponent, as a gun or club. —**y.** *n.* A sickbay attendant. *USN use.*

dig. *n.* 1. A hiding place for contraband; a cache. *Some underworld use.* 2. A sarcastic, contemptuous, or derogatory remark. *Colloq.* *v.i.* To study hard or diligently. *v.t.* 1. To study a subject diligently. *Some student use since c1850.* → 2. To comprehend fully, understand or appreciate something or someone; to be in rapport with someone or something. *Orig. some c1935 jive use; now associated with cool use; general jazz and hip use, fairly well known to general public. May be from the Celtic "twig" = to understand.* 3. To meet or find someone or something; to dig up. 4. To notice, see, look at, or identify someone. 5. To be present at, see, or listen to an entertainment, performance, or performer.

dig [oneself] a nod. To get a night's sleep.

dig dirt. To gossip.

digger; Digger. *n.* 1. An Australian. 2. A man; buddy; fellow countryman; pal. *From "gold-digger" in the mining sense.* 3. = gold-digger. 4. A pickpocket.

dig out. To leave quickly.

dig [someone or something] the most. To be in complete rapport with someone or something; to arrive at complete understanding or appreciation of another.

dig up. To find or meet someone or something, usu. something old-fashioned or unusual or someone disagreeable, ugly, or eccentric. *Usu. in "Where did you dig her [him, it] up?"*

dildo. *n.* A foolish, stupid person; a prick. *Common among boys between 10 and 14.*

dill; dil. *n.* = dilly.

dillion. *n.* An exceedingly large number; a zillion.

dilly. *n.* 1. Any person or thing remarkable in size, quality, appearance, or the like, as a beautiful girl, a hard-fought football game, a striking necktie, a honey, humdinger, beaut, or lulu. *Also used ironically.* 2. A best girl. *Prob. from first three letters of "delightful" plus "y."*

dilly-dally. *v.i.* To idle; to trifle; to dally. *Colloq.*

dim. *n.* 1. Evening. *Jive use.* 2. Night; nighttime. *Bop use.*

dimbox. *n.* 1. One who smooths over disagreements. 2. A taxicab.

dime a dozen, a. Cheap; plentiful; almost useless, having little or no value.

dime-note. *n.* A ten-dollar bill.

dime store = five-and-ten-cent store.

dime up. In begging: to offer a merchant ten cents for food or other goods worth considerably more, with a hard-luck story to save the dime also.

dimmer. *n.* 1. A dime. 2. An electric light. *Prison use.*

dimmo. *n.* A dime.

dim view. A lack of enthusiasm; a pessimistic attitude; a critical attitude; dislike. *Usu. in "to take a dim view of [something]."*

dim-wit. *n.* A stupid person.

dinah. *n.* 1. Dynamite. → 2. Nitroglycerine.

dine. *n.* Dynamite. —r. *n.* The caboose of a railroad train.

dinero. *n.* Money. *From Sp.*

ding. *v.i.* To beg, as on a street. *v.t.* To vote against a candidate for fraternity membership; to blackball; to veto. *Student use since c1930.* *n.* A vetoing or blackballing, as of a candidate for fraternity membership. *Student use.*

ding-a-ling. *n.* Fig., a person who acts queerly because of mental deficiency; an insane person, a screwball, an eccentric. *Lit., one who hears bells in his head.*

dingbat. *n.* 1. Money. 2. Anything suitable as a missile, such as a stone or a piece of wood. 3. A gadget, contraption, or dingus. 4. Any of various kinds of muffins, biscuits, or buns. *1895. Student use.* 5. A vagabond, beggar, or hobo. 6. A woman other than one's sister or mother.

ding-dang. *v.t.* To dang; to darn; to damn.

ding-dong. *adj.* Spirited; hard-fought; furious. —er. *n.* An aggressive go-getting vagabond. *Vagabond argot.*

dinger. *n.* 1. A tramp; a worthless person. 2. A person having a smattering of knowledge.

dingey. 1. A small locomotive; a short train; a small truck. *Hobo, railroad, and trucker use.* 2. Substandard, unregistered, or unbranded cattle. *Farm and ranch use.* 3. Eleven; the number eleven. *Used to avoid confusion with the sound of "seven." Some USN and radio use.*

ding ho(w); ding hau; ding hao. *adv.* O.K.; very good; all right; swell; everything is O.K. *From the Chinese. Orig. used by Armed Forces in Burma during W.W.II; orig. prob. "Flying Tigers" air group use.*

dingo. 1. A hobo or vagrant. *Hobo*

use. *From "ding."* 2. A small-time confidence man.

ding-swizzled. *adj.* Darned; damned.

dingus. Anything of which the correct name is unknown or forgotten; a thingamajig. *Colloq.*

dink. *n.* 1. A small and close-fitting cap worn by college freshmen; apparently from dinky = small. 2. Any hat.

dinkum. *n.* An Australian soldier.

dinky. *adj.* Small. *Very common.*

dino. *n.* A Mexican or Italian laborer, usu. a Mexican, esp. a railroad section-hand, specif. one who works with dynamite.

dip. *n.* 1. A pickpocket. *Common underworld use, universally known. Lit., one who "dips" his hand into other people's pockets.* 2. Diphtheria. *From the common pronunciation: "dip-theria."* 3. A hat. *Orig. c1910–c1920, New Eng. dial. use, esp. usu. by boys. Now some Negro use. Because one "dips" or "tips" one's hat to another on meeting.* 4. A drunkard. *From "dipsomaniac."* 5. A stupid person. *v.t.* To rob someone by picking his pockets. *adj.* Crazy; dippy.

dipper. *n.* dipper-mouth. *Usu. a nickname.* —mouth. *n.* A person with a large mouth; lit., one with a mouth the size of a dipper.

dippiness. *n.* Craziness.

dippy. *adj.* Crazy; foolish; not sensible.

dippydro. *n.* One who often changes his mind; an uncertain person.

dipso. *n.* A drunkard; an alcoholic; a dipsomaniac.

dipsy-do; dipsy-doo. *n.* 1. In baseball, a tantalizing curve. 2. One who throws a "dipsy-do" or "dipsy-doodle." 3. A fixed prize fight.

dipsy-doodle. *n.* 1. Chicanery, deception. 2. In baseball, a sharp curve pitch. To deceive or cheat.

dip the bill (beak). To drink.

dirt. *n.* 1. Gossip; obscenity; scandal. *Colloq.* 2. Specif., a novel or other entertainment abounding in sexual reference. 3. Information; the low-down. 4. Cheating. *Prize fight use*. 5. Sugar. *Convict use*. 6. Money. —**y**. *adj*. 1. Unethical, dishonest. *Colloq*. 2. Malevolent; spiteful; mean. *Colloq*. 3. Lewd; lascivious; sexually suggestive; obscene. *Colloq*. → 4. Suggesting the lewd or obscene, as by a reedy, ragged, or slurred tone in performing jazz. *Jazz use*. 5. Well supplied with money; filthy rich. 6. Radioactive; contaminated by radioactive particles or by-products. *Since c1955*. 7. Big; impressive; remarkable. *adv*. Very.

dirt, hit the. 1. In baseball, to slide for a base. 2. To jump off a still moving freight train; to get off a train. *Hobo use*. 3. To fling onself into the closest shelter or to the ground for protection from a bomb or artillery shell blast. *Wide W.W.II use*.

dirt-bag. *n*. A garbage collector. *W.W.II Armed Forces use*.

dirty linen = dirty wash.

dirty-neck. *n*. 1. A laborer; a farmer. → 2. A rustic; an immigrant.

dirty wash. Personal or family problems, esp. those that would cause gossip if made public; neighborhood scandal. *Orig. in that one's neighbors see one's dirty wash being hung out on the clothesline in the view of everyone*.

dirty work. Any dishonest or unethical act.

disc; disk. *n*. A modern phonograph record, esp. of popular or jazz music. *Orig. to distinguish the disc-shaped records from the older cylindrical records. Pop. by jive use. "Disc" now more common than "disk."*

disc jockey; disk jockey. A radio announcer who supervises a show of recorded popular music. He selects the discs, announces them, often with some comment, reads sponsors' advertisements between recordings, and tries to increase the popularity of the show by his personality. With the advent of television, many radio stations program a majority of their time to such shows of recorded popular music. *Orig. radio use; now universally known and common teenage use; colloq. since c1950*.

discomboberate; discumbobulate. *v.t*. 1. To perplex. 2. To disconcert, discomfit, confuse.

discouraged. *adj*. Drunk.

dise-drag. *n*. A freight car in a railroad train. *Vagabond argot*.

disguised. *adj*. Drunk.

dish. *n*. 1. A woman or a girl, usu. a beautiful, pretty, or sexually attractive one. *The connotation depends on the qualifying adjective. Thus, "beautiful dish," "hot dish," "dumb dish," "German dish," "old dish," etc. A prime example of a slang word relating sex and food*. 2. A thing that is exactly suited to one's tastes or abilities, as a certain book or the music of a certain composer; a preference. 3. In baseball, home plate. *v.t*. 1. To tell [something]; to disclose by talking. 2. To give or retaliate with. 3. To frustrate; cheat; set aside; shelve.

dish it out. To give out money, abuse, punishment, or the like; to hand out, dispense, inflict upon. *Lit. and fig., to attack a person violently, either physically or verbally; fig., to "dish out" or serve blows or punishment on another. Colloq*.

dish of tea. One's preference; one's environment.

dish out. 1. To give out [talk, news, abuse, information]; to dispense or issue. 2. To give, administer; to inflict [on]. 3. To pay.

dish the dirt. To gossip; to gossip with malicious intent or enjoyment.

dishwater. *n*. 1. Soup, esp. bad-tasting soup. 2. Coffee. 3. Weak tea.

dissolve. *n*. A device used to make (or an instance of making) one movie stage scene meld or blend into the next. *From the movie* *use where one scene dims or fades out as another comes into focus.*

ditch. *v.t.* 1. To abandon or run away from a person or thing. → 2. Specif., to bring down a crippled airplane on water in such a way that there will be time for the passengers to get out before the plane sinks.

dit-da artist (jockey, monkey). *n.* A short-wave radio operator. *In imitation of the sounds of a dot and a dash being transmitted.*

dive. *n.* 1. A disreputable, cheap, low-class establishment or public place, esp. a bar, dance-hall, nightclub, or the like; a place of bad repute. → 2. Specif., a place where whisky is sold illegally; a speakeasy. 3. In prizefighting, a knockout, esp. a knockdown or knockout that is feigned by pre-arrangement between the fighters.

divot. *n.* A toupee.

divvy. *v.i., v.t.* To divide or share [something, as loot]; to divide up. *Colloq. since c1890. n.* A split; a dividend; one's part or share in the profit or spoils.

divvy up. To divide spoils or profits.

Dix. *n.* A ten-dollar bill. **—ie.** *n.* 1. New Orleans. *From the "Dix" printed on ten-dollar bills issued from New Orleans.* → 2. The South. 3. Dixieland music. *adj.* Southern. **—iecrat.** *n.* A Southern Democrat, usu. an office holder or nominee, who belongs or once belonged to the Democratic party but considers local Southern loyalty, esp. to racial segregation, more important than party loyalty. *From the name of the actual "third party" that formed in 1948 but returned to the Democrats during the following Presidential election as a somewhat unified and highly vocal faction.* **—ieland.** *n.* 1. The South. 2. The style or form of jazz resembling the orig. jazz played by street bands in New Orleans c1910; recognized by a simple two-beat rhythm, ragged

syncopation, improvised ensemble passages, etc.

dizzy. *adj.* Silly; foolish.

dizzy-wizzy. *n.* Any drug in pill form.

do. *v.t.* To harm, attack, or ruin [a person].

D. O. A. Dead on arrival, the official terminology of police and hospital reports and in coroners' inquests.

do a barber. To talk a lot.

do a guy. To run away.

do black. To act as a Negro in a show. *Pitchman and vaudeville use.*

doc. *n.* 1. A doctor; specif., a physician. 2. An unknown fellow or guy; used in direct address.

dock. *v.t.* To penalize a worker part of his pay, usu. for absence or arriving late on the job. *Colloq.*

dock rat. A bum; specif., one who hangs around docks.

dock-walloper. *n.* One who idles around docks, occasionally working.

doctor. *n.* One who drugs race-horses to affect their performance.

do-dad; doodad. *n.* 1. A useless ornament. 2. A thing.

do [one, someone] dirt. To expose, inform on, or in some other manner cause another trouble; to cause another to lose status or the good opinion or good will of others; maliciously to damage another's good reputation.

dodo. *n.* 1. A stupid or inept person. *From the now extinct dodo bird [Didus ineptus], a heavy, wingless fowl once found on the island of Mauritius.* 2. An old fogy; a settled, secure, dull person. 3. A student pilot who has not yet made a solo flight. *In allusion to the dodo bird's inability to fly; orig. U.S. Air Force and Army use c1940.*

doe. *n.* At a dance, party, or gathering, a woman unaccompanied by a male escort. *Based on "stag."*

do-funny. *n.* A thingamajig. *Colloq.*

dog. *n.* **1.** A promissory note. **2.** Ostentation in dress, manner, or the like; swank; airs; often in "put on the dog." *Dial.* **3.** The sandwich made of a frankfurter on a roll. **4.** A frankfurter. *Both uses shortened from "hot dog." Colloq. since before 1900.* **5.** Something inferior; something disliked or lacking in appeal; esp. a slow-moving racehorse; merchandise that does not appeal to customers; entertainment, a performer, or performers that do not appeal to the public; an ugly or uncouth girl; or the like. **6.** A promiscuous girl; a prostitute. **7.** A college freshman; a new or inexperienced worker. **8.** An automobile inspector. **9.** A human foot. **10.** A disreputable or untrustworthy man, esp. in sexual or social matters; a cad. **11.** An ugly, unrefined, or sexually disreputable girl or woman; a boring girl or young woman who does not have the compensation of beauty. *Fairly common; wide male student and teenage use.* *adj.* Inferior; unappealing. *v.t.* To pester someone; to follow another, as to collect a debt, get information, or the like; to hound. *v.i.* **1.** Dog it = to shirk. **2.** To run away. **3.** To tell a lie. —face. *n.* **1.** A soldier, specif., an infantry private. *Prob. orig. derisive use by USN and Marines.* **2.** An ugly boy. *Some child and teenage use.* —gie. *n.* **1.** = dog, hot dog. **2.** = dogface, soldier. —ging = bulldogging.

dog, put on the. 1. To dress in one's fanciest clothes. *Archaic and dial.* **2.** = put on airs.

dog biscuit. *n.* **1.** Crackers. *Some student use.* **2.** An unattractive girl. *Some c1940 student use.*

dog days. 1. Days during which one does not feel energetic or enthusiastic; dull days; the days when a woman is menstruating. **2.** Hot, humid summer days that sap one's energy; specif., midsummer days. *So called because* anciently reckoned from the first rising of the Dog Star.

dog food. Corned-beef hash. *W.W.II USN use.*

doggone. *adj.* and *adv.* Darned.

doghouse. *n.* **1.** Any of various houselike structures more or less resembling a dog's kennel; specif., a railroad caboose, a small, temporary office shack serving a work crew, a tower on a prison wall, a bass viol, or the like. **2.** Fig., disfavor or disgrace, esp. in "to be in the doghouse."

doghouse, in the. See **doghouse, 2.**

dog it. 1. To dress up, esp. in the latest or most gaudy style; to act haughtily or in an aloof manner; to put on the dog. **2.** To make no, or but a slight, effort; to relax when one should be working hard; to fail to make one's best effort. **3.** To flee; esp. to retreat or withdraw from a social nuisance. **4.** To travel, seek entertainment, or live very cheaply, esp. by borrowing money or letting one's friends pay various bills. **5.** To avoid hard work, thought, or creating; to evade responsibility; to produce inferior work or work meeting only the minimum standard requirements.

dog kennel = doghouse.

dog-naper; dog-napper. *n.* A stealer of dogs. *From "dog" plus "kidnaper."*

do-gooder. *n.* A sincere but self-righteous worker for the welfare of others.

dog out. To dress or dress up; to tog out.

dog-robber. *n.* A baseball umpire. *Some baseball use.*

dogs. *n.pl.* The human feet; specif., a pair of human feet. *Universally known.*

dog show. Foot inspection. *W.W.II Army use.*

dog's-nose. *n.* A drink containing beer or ale mixed with gin or rum.

dog tags. The pair of metal identification tags worn by soldiers and sailors on chains about their necks. *The tags served as an identification of dead and wounded and provided various items of essential information. W.W.I and W.W.II Armed Forces use. From their resemblance to dog licenses, reinforced by "dogface."*

dog tent = pup tent.

dog up. To dress in one's best clothes.

dog-wagon. *n.* A lunch-wagon.

do-hinky. *n.* 1. A pimple or any minor skin eruption. 2. Any object; a thingamajig.

do in. To kill.

do it all. To serve a life term in prison. *Underworld and prison use.*

dokus. *n.* The human posterior. *From the Yiddish "tokus."*

doll. *n.* 1. A pretty girl or woman; esp. a pretty girl or woman whose main use in life seems to be to grace the scene rather than to make an active contribution; esp. a clear complexioned blonde, blue-eyed girl with regular features. 2. Any female, esp. a pert or saucy one. *Also the title of a pop. c1950 musical play on Broadway and a successful movie c1945, all based on the writings of Runyon.* → 3. Any attractive, sweet person; a pleasant generous person of either sex. 4. An attractive, popular boy. *Common teenage-girl use since c1940.*

dollface. *n.* A boy or youth with a good-looking, pretty, or feminine face. *Used either as a compliment or in derision.*

doll out = doll up.

doll up. To dress up; to dress and groom oneself with great care or fashionably.

dolly dancer. A soldier who receives easy duty, esp. office duty, by courting officers. *W.W.II Army use.*

dome. *n.* The head; esp. of a person.

dominos. 1. The teeth. 2. Sugar cubes pressed in the general shape of dominoes. 3. Dice.

donagher = donnicker.

done in. *adj.* Tired, exhausted, beat, bushed. *Colloq.*

done up. Tired out. *Colloq.*

donk. *n.* Whisky, esp. raw, homemade corn whisky. *Dial. Because its kick is as strong as a donkey's.*

donkey act. A stupid or foolish act; a blunder, mistake, or faux pas.

donkey's years. *sing.* A very long time. *Dial. since c1850. In allusion to the length of a donkey's ears, by elision so that the "y" of donkey makes "ears" sound like "years."*

donnicker; doniker. *n.* A toilet; a rest room, *Common underworld, carnival, and circus use.*

donnybrook. *n.* A loud, noisy argument, fight, brawl, riot, contest. *From Donnybrook Fair.*

doodad = do-dad.

doodle. *v.i.* To draw meaningless patterns or figures as a nervous gesture or idle habit while doing something else. *n.* A meaningless pattern or figure, as drawn idly.

doodle-e-squat. *n.* Money. *Carnival use.*

doohickey. *n.* 1. A pimple or other skin eruption. 2. A gadget; any small object.

doojigger. *n.* A gadget.

dookie = dukie.

doosy; doozie; doozy. *n.* Anything remarkable or unusual; something enjoyable, well liked, successful; or something humorous, confusing, or exotic.

dooteroomus. *n.* Money.

dope. *n.* 1. Any drug, esp. a narcotic such as opium or cocaine. *c1870–1920; specif. = opium. Drug addict use only. Since 1920, colloq.* 2. Any substance that acts, or is thought to act, more or less like a drug; esp. alcoholic beverages. 3. The soft drink Coca-Cola. *c1920; the original formula was supposed to contain a stimulant.* 4. Coffee. 5. A cigarette. 6. Any thick, heavy liquid, regardless of its purpose, such as sauces, cosmetics, lubricants, etc. 7. A person who acts as though drugged; hence usu. a stupid person. *Colloq.* 8. Smelling salts. 9. Information; essential, true, or direct information; data. 10. Gossip or news. 11. A prediction made from evaluating all the facts. *adj.* Stupid. *v.t.* 1. To drug. *c1880.* 2. To figure, equate, or predict from the known facts, esp. to predict a winner or result in the fields of sports or gambling. —ster. *n.* One who gathers data on past events in order to predict the result of future ones; esp. one who forecasts the results of sporting events. —y; dopy. *adj.* 1. Under the influence of a narcotic. 2. Stupid or slow, as if doped. 3. Inferior, unusual, boring, ill-planned, etc. *Said of people, objects, or actions.*

dope out. 1. To figure out a gambling or sports result from the available information and data. 2. To think or figure something out; to study available information in order to draw a conclusion, find a meaning, or plan future work.

dope sheet. Written or printed information, as a set of written instructions; esp. printed information listing the past performances of racehorses.

Dora = dumb Dora.

do-re-mi. *n.* Money. *From a pun on dough = money, plus the second and third notes of the diatonic scale.*

dorm. *n.* A dormitory; specif., a residence hall for men or women college students. *Common student use since at least 1900. adj.* Of, pertaining to, or provided by a dormitory.

dornick. *n.* A stone. *Dial.*

dose. *n.* A surfeit; esp. a surfeit of being unfairly treated or deceived.

do-se-do. *n.* A dull prize fight, which consists chiefly of prancing around the ring. *From "do-si-do," a phrase recurrent in calls for square dancing.*

doss. *v.i.* To sleep. *n.* 1. Sleep.

Tramp use. 2. A cheap, squalid lodging house; a flop house; a brothel. 3. A bed. *All meanings more common in Eng. than in U.S.; all vagabond use.* —er. *n.* A lodger or sleeper, as in a doss house.

doss house. A very cheap lodging house; a flop house; a brothel. *First two meanings more common in Eng., third meaning more common in U.S.*

do [one's] stuff. To do whatever it is one's business to do; to do as one has been doing or may be expected to do; to function in one's occupation; to work or act as one wants to.

dot. *n.* The exact time; the exact amount. *Common in the colloq.* **on the dot.** —ty. *adj.* Senile; crazy; stupid; eccentric. *c1850.*

dot, on the. Exactly on time.

do the dirty on [someone] = do [someone] dirt.

do time; do [a specific period of time]. 1. To serve a sentence in prison → 2. To spend or serve one's time, as by necessity or order.

double. *n.* 1. Any alcoholic drink containing two standard portions of whisky. 2. Two of anything; in sports, two victories on the same day. 3. In horse racing, the "daily double," the first and second races bet as and considered as one. 4. One who strongly resembles another; a ringer. 5. Specif., an actor who performs dangerous feats in the place of another actor during the filming of a movie.

double, on the. 1. At "double time," a specif. number of paces per minute according to military use. *Orig. Army use.* → 2. At a run; fast; quickly. *Often used as a command or plea to hurry.*

double back. To reverse one's direction of travel; to return to a place one has departed from comparatively recently. *Colloq.*

double-clock. *v.t.* To two-time. A fanciful variation of the colloq. two-time.

doublecross. The betraying or cheating of one's associate[s]. *Also written "XX" or "double-X."*

double-cross. *v.t.* To betray or cheat. **double-crosser.** *n.* One who double-crosses. **double-crossing.** *adj.* Betraying, cheating.

double-dealing. *n., adj.* Unethical; insincere.

double-decker. *n.* A sandwich having two layers of filling between three slices of bread or toast.

double dome. A thinker; an intellectual; a "highbrow"; a well-educated person. —**ed.** *adj.* Intellectual; having the high forehead commonly believed to indicate intelligence.

double-gaited; double gaited. *adj.* Bisexual. *An extension of the horse-pacing term.*

double-header. *n.* A customer who buys more than one of the same item at a time. *adj.* Obtaining or winning two things; successful in two ways.

double in brass. 1. To play in a circus band and perform in a circus act. *Circus talk.* 2. To do any two different kinds of work; to be able to do more than one thing well.

double-o; double O; double-oo. *v.t.* To look at, or over, carefully; to examine. *From "once-over" or the resemblance of two wide-open eyes to two consecutive o's.* *n.* 1. A close scrutiny; a once-over. *Usu. in* "the double-o." 2. A tour of inspection.

double-saw. *n.* A twenty-dollar bill or the sum of $20. *From "double sawbuck."*

double sawbuck. *n.* A twenty-dollar bill; the sum of $20.

double scrud. *n.* = scrud. *Here the "double" makes the mythical disease of "scrud" even worse.*

double shuffle. 1. The act of cheating or taking advantage of a friend. 2. A hasty and confusing interview; a brush-off. 3. Deception, trickery, intended confusion, which one has received. *Usu. in, e.g.,* "I got the double-shuffle from him." *From the "double shuffle" of card mixing or dealing by which the card manipulator can cheat his opponents.* 4. An instance of being ignored or given the cold shoulder.

double take. A quick second look or glance, usu. at a person; a sudden recognition that what was glanced over or thought of as common is actually remarkable. Specif., a second and admiring glance at an attractive woman. *Often in "do a double-take." Apparently from the photography term,* "take." *v.i.* To do a double-take.

double-trouble. *n.* Extreme trouble, difficulty, or danger. *adj.* Troublemaking.

double-X = doublecross.

dough. *n.* 1. Money; cash. *c1850. Orig. meant bribe money or money obtained unethically.* 2. An infantry soldier or other frontline soldier. *From "doughboy." Army use.*

dough-ball. *n.* 1. Any boring, unimaginative person. 2. Fishing bait made from stale bread and cinnamon.

dough-head. *n.* 1. A stupid person. 2. A baker. *Vagabond use.*

doughnut factory; doughnut foundry; doughnut house; doughnut joint. 1. A very cheap eating place; a luncheonette. 2. A place where free food is dispensed. *Hobo use.*

dough well done with cow to cover. Having bread (or toast) and butter.

do up. To beat up.

do up brown. To do thoroughly; to treat severely.

dove. A term of endearment.

dovey = lovey-dovey.

dowdy = rowdy-dowdy.

down. *v.t.* 1. To defeat another. *Colloq.* 2. To eat or drink, esp. to eat or drink rapidly or voraciously. *Colloq. adj.* 1. Depressed; melancholy; pessimistic. 2. Sickly; exhausted; defeated. 3. Toasted; served on toast. *Lunch-*

counter use in relaying an order, usu. in "a ham sandwich down." 4. Mean; tough; strong; skilled in fighting. *Teenage street-gang use since c1955. n.* In a nightclub or bar, a glass of cheap, appropriately colored liquid, as tea or a soft drink, sold to a male customer as whisky and to be drunk by a female employee of the management.

down, get. Lit. and fig., to put one's money or chips down on a gambling table in making a bet; to make a bet; to make a bet on something.

down [one's] alley = up [one's] alley.

down and dirty. *adj., adv.* Done to one's disadvantage; accomplished through trickery or deception. *From the card game of poker where "down and dirty" = the last card has been dealt, usu. face down on the table, and has not improved anyone's hand.*

down and out. Without money; unsuccessful; straitened; destitute. *Colloq.*

down-and-outer. *n.* One who is lit. or, fig. a tramp, homeless and jobless, or living in poverty, and who will probably not be able to improve his way of life or become a useful member of society; a complete and helpless failure, specif. one unable to work or lead a normal life owing to having made a major mistake or to being a drunkard.

downhill. *n.* 1. The last half of a prison term. *Underworld use since c1930.* 2. The last half of an enlistment in the Armed Forces. *W.W.II use. adj.* 1. Decreasing; becoming less valuable, healthy, or the like; worsening. 2. Easy to accomplish; pleasurable; fig., requiring no more effort than rolling down a hill.

down the hatch. A pop. toast, after which a portion of whisky is drunk in one gulp.

down the line. 1. In the district of a city that contains brothels, cheap bars, or the like. 2. To go

from one person to another, in decreasing order of their importance or authority, as in asking for a favor, seeking information, or the like.

Down Under. Australian; Australia and New Zealand.

down with it. To understand; to know; to dig. *Jive use. Older than "with it"*

down yonder. The southern U.S.

dozer. *n.* 1. A terrific blow with the fist. 2. Anything remarkable or ostentatious.

draft bait. A man or men subject to immediate conscription. *W.W.II use.*

draftee. *n.* A man conscripted for Army service. *Still in use.*

drag. *n.* 1. A town or city street, esp. the main street. *Very common.* 2. A deep inhalation or puff of tobacco smoke, esp. of cigarette smoke; the act or an instance of taking just one or a few puffs on a cigarette; to take another's lighted cigarette, puff once or a few times, and return it to the owner. *Common since c1915.* → 3. A cigarette. 4. A homosexual gathering or party in which the participants wear clothes appropriate to the opposite sex; a gathering or party of transvestites; clothing appropriate to the sex opposite that of the wearer; transvestite clothing. 5. A dancing party; a dance; a party. *Still in wide student and teenage use.* 6. A dull or boring person. *Common since c1940.* → 7. A person, thing, event, or place that is intellectually, emotionally, or aesthetically boring, tedious, tiring, or colorless. *Orig. jazz use; c1946 bop use; very common with teenagers and students.* 8. A railroad train, esp. a freight train, specif. a slow or long one; a railway freight car. *Hobo and railroad use since c1920. Because the cars "draw" on the engine or "drag" freight.* 9. A short race between two or more hot-rod cars in which the car with the greatest rate of acceleration from a standing start wins. *Orig. c1950 hotrod use; general teenage use.* **10.** A roll of money, stock certificates, or other valuables used to entice a victim in a confidence game. *adj.* Accompanied by a partner or date of the opposite sex. *Often in "come stag or drag," used in invitations to a dance or party. Student use since c1940. v.t.* **1.** To puff on or smoke a cigarette; to inhale deeply. **2.** To take or escort a girl to a dance or party; to be escorted by a youth to a dance or party. **3.** To bother or bore a person mentally or physically; to leave one with a nervous, unsatisfied feeling. *Usu. said of unsatisfying jazz music. Mainly bop and cool use since c1950. v.i.* **1.** To attend a dance or party with a partner or date rather than alone. *Since c1930.* **2.** To be unexciting, dull or boring; said of an entertainment. *Colloq.* **3.** To participate in or hold an acceleration race between two or more hot-rods. *Hot rod use since c1950.* —*ger.* *n.* A patron who asks for change when giving a tip. —*ging.* *n.* The act or an instance of drag racing. —*gy.* *adj.* **1.** Unexciting, dull, boring. *Colloq.* → **2.** Unsatisfying; nonintellectual; bothersome; emotionally or aesthetically colorless. *Cool use since c1950.*

drag [it]. To quit [a job]; to leave; to stop talking; to break off a relationship.

drag [one's] freight. To depart.

drag in. To arrive.

drag in your rope. *imp.* Be quiet; shut up.

drag out. To tell something in a long, indirect way; to make a story, book, play, or movie longer than the action or plot demands. *Colloq.* **drag-out.** *n.* A dancing party.

drag race. A race between two or more cars, usu. hot rods, to determine which can accelerate the faster. Such formal or organized races are usu. over a quarter-

mile distance on a drag strip, the competing cars starting from a complete stop. Less formal races may take place almost anywhere, including traffic-crowded streets, and begin usu. when the cars are in first or second gear and starting away from a stoplight that has turned from red to green. Such informal races are often between strangers, to show off their cars and driving ability, and from an aggressive enjoyment of being first away from a stoplight. *Hot rod use since c1945.*

dragster. *n.* A car suitable for drag racing. *Hot rod use since c1950.*

drag strip. Any straight and flat ground, road, or strip of concrete, at least a quarter of a mile long, used for drag racing. *In formal, organized drag racing, such strips are often abandoned concrete airplane runways or small air strips.*

drag-tail. *v.t.* To move or work slowly or with difficulty, as with a burden.

drag [one's] tail. 1. = drag-tail. **2.** To be depressed or melancholy.

drap. *n.* A skirt. *Teenage usage.*

drape. *n.* **1.** A suit; an ensemble of suit, shirt, tie, hat. *Jive use.* **2.** A young man wearing black, narrow-cuffed slacks, a garish shirt, a loose lapel-less jacket, and no necktie; a later, more hip version of the zoot-suiter. **3.** Any article of clothing. **4.** A dress. *Teenage use.*

drape shape. *n.* A severely draped garment, as worn by zoot-suiters. *Usu. in ref. to a zoot suit.*

draw a blank. 1. To receive nothing; to obtain a negative or no result. **2.** To forget; to be unable to remember a person, fact, etc. **3.** To be drunk. **4.** To fail to obtain another's interest or enthusiasm.

draw one. To fill a glass with draft beer; usu. as an order. *Bar use in relaying an order.*

dream bait. An attractive, personable, popular person of either sex; a desirable date. *Some student use since c1940.*

dreamboat. *n.* 1. An exceptionally attractive person who, or thing that, fulfills one's image or "dream" of a perfect specimen; an ideal person or thing. 2. Specif., an exceptionally beautiful or attractive and pleasing member of the opposite sex. 3. = dream bait. *All uses associated with young teenagers, but the word is considered corny by most young people.*

dream box. *n.* The head. *Jive use.*

dreamer. *n.* 1. A bedsheet; a cover. → 2. A bed.

dream puss = dream bait.

dream-stick. *n.* An opium pill.

dream up. To invent; to make up; to imagine; to create.

drek; dreck. *n.* 1. Any manufactured object of inferior material, design, workmanship, and overall quality; any obviously inferior product. 2. Any cheap, gaudy items of merchandise; small, cheap, useless items. *From the Yiddish "dreck" = feces.*

dress. *v.t.* To increase the attendance at an entertainment by reducing admission prices and/or issuing free tickets. *Theater use.*

dressing down. An extensive reprimand; a bawling out.

dressing out = dressing down.

drift. *n.* 1. In automobile racing, a four-wheel skid purposely executed to turn a corner or round a curve at maximum speed; a device for maintaining full speed forward while moving sideways. 2. Purport; import; meaning. *v.i.* To go away; leave; depart; get out. Also "drift away." —er. *n.* 1. A vagabond; a wanderer; a person without a steady job, occupation, or permanent address; a grifter. 2. A tramp. 3. An unimportant member of the underworld.

drift?, get the. *interrog.* An interrogatory expression meaning "Do you understand me?"

drill. *v.i., v.t.* 1. To move quickly, with force, and in a straight line; said of a bullet, baseball, car, or the like. 2. To shoot; to kill by shooting. 3. In baseball, to bat a ball.

drink. *n.* Any sizable body of water, from a small stream to an ocean; esp., however, the ocean. Often the drink.

drink, take a; take a fishing trip. In baseball, to strike out. *Baseball use.*

drink [one's] beer. To shut up or stop talking.

drip. *n.* 1. Flattery; sweet talk. *Some student use.* 2. Any person, usu. a male teenager or student, who is disliked or who is objectionable, usu. because he is a bore, introverted, overly solicitous, or is not hip to the fads, fashions, and typical behavior patterns of his age group. *Teenage and student use since c1935; most pop. c1940–c1945.* —py. *adj.* Abounding in sentimentality; corny.

drive. *n.* A stir of emotion; a thrill or kick; esp. the result of taking a portion of narcotic. *v.i.* To play jazz or swing music with great enthusiasm and vigor. *Jazz and swing use.*

drive-in. *n.* 1. A roadside restaurant equipped to serve customers food in their automobiles. *Colloq.* 2. An outdoor movie theater whose patrons watch from their automobiles. *adj.* 1. Offering customers service at their cars. Besides drive-in restaurants and movies, there are drive-in banks, cleaners, and even churches. 2. Having traveled or arrived from out of town by automobile.

drive up. *imper.* Come here.

drizzle. *n.* = drip. *Fig., a persistent or thorough drip.*

drizzle puss = drizzle, drip.

drone. *n.* An automatic, unmanned airplane, electronically controlled from an airbase or a manned plane. *Drones are used as moving targets for gunnery* or missile practice. *Air Force use since c1950.*

drool. *v.i.* 1. Fig., to drool in eagerness or anticipation; to be eager or appreciative. *Usu. in jocular "stop drooling" to one who is obviously impressed by a pretty girl, stylish dress, expensive car, or the like. Common student use c1940. Still in use.* 2. To talk nonsense; to talk vaguely or aimlessly. *c1895. n.* 1. Nonsense; foolish talk. *Since c1900; very common c1940.* 2. A boy who is not approved of; a drip. —**er.** *n.* A vague or aimless talker. Specif., a master of ceremonies, radio announcer, or other person with facility for impromptu speaking to fill in with talk when a program runs short of its allotted time or while waiting for a performer to arrive. —**y.** *n.* An attractive and popular boy. *Very popular teenage use c1940. adj.* 1. So goodlooking as to elicit expressions of admiration from the opposite sex. 2. So attractive an object as to elicit expressions of admiration; esp. applied to articles of clothing, movies, cars, etc. 3. Excellent; wonderful; heavenly.

droop. *n.* A person disliked for his languidness or stupidity. *c1940; teenage use.*

drop. *v.i.* To be arrested; to be caught in an illegal act. *v.t.* 1. To knock someone down. 2. To kill someone. 3. To catch [a thief] in possession of stolen goods. 4. To ship merchandise in small quantities to many places. 5. To supply illegal or contraband goods to a person. 6. To lose money quickly, by gambling, by making investments, or in quick business deals. *n.* 1. An ostensibly respectable place of business used as a cover for illegal business or as a hiding place for stolen goods or contraband. 2. A slum boy of unknown parentage; a homeless waif. *Harlem use.* 3. A paying passenger in a taxi.

drop a brick. To blunder; to make an embarrassing mistake.

drop [one's] cookies = shoot [one's] breakfast.

drop dead! A popular exclamation expressing emphatic refusal, scorn, dislike, or disinterest.

drop dead list. Fig., a list of people to be fired from a job, expelled from a school, excluded from a social activity, or given any type of refusal, punishment, or ostracism.

drop-in. *n.* A place frequented by a person or group, often to indulge in vice.

drop joint = drop.

dropout. *n.* 1. A withdrawal; the act or fact of withdrawing, as from school. *Colloq.* 2. The person who withdraws.

drop the boom. 1. To refuse further credit. 2. To ask a favor of someone. 3. To bawl out a person.

drop the lug on [a person]. To beg money from someone; to put the bite on [him].

drownder = goose-drownder.

drowning. *adj.* Confused; baffled; uncomprehending.

drown [one's] troubles. To forget or try to forget one's problems and troubles by becoming drunk. *Fig. to drown one's troubles in whisky.*

drug on the market, a. 1. Any item or product so plentiful as to have little value or to offer but small profit to those who sell it. → 2. Any disliked, unwanted person; a person whose presence is considered detrimental to the enjoyment of others; an average person.

drugstore cowboy. 1. A western movie extra who loafs in front of drugstores between pictures. *c1928; movie talk.* 2. A man or youth who idles around public places showing off and trying to impress the opposite sex. *The most common use. c1929; attrib. to cartoonist T. A. Dorgan.* 3. A braggart.

drug-store race. A horse race in which one or more of the horses have been drugged or given alcohol.

drum. *n.* A prison cell. *v.t.* 1. To announce; inform. 2. To try to get people enthusiastic over a product or cause; to advertise; to obtain customers or patrons. *Colloq.* 3. To sell merchandise, esp. as a traveling salesman sells to retailers. —**mer.** *n.* A traveling salesman.

drum-beater. *n.* A press agent.

drunk. *n.* 1. A drinking bout; a spree. *Colloq. since c1835.* 2. A state of intoxication. *Colloq. since 1840.* 3. An intoxicated person. *Colloq. since c1850.* 4. A habitual drunkard. *Colloq.*

drunk tank = **tank.**

dry. *n.* One who favors prohibiting the legal distilling or sale of liquor. *adj.* 1. Thirsty. *Colloq.* 2. Prohibiting or in favor of prohibiting the sale of alcoholic beverages.

dry cush. Cookies.

dry-goods. *n.* 1. A girl or woman. *Since c1865.* 2. Clothing, esp. a suit, dress, or coat. *Negro use.*

drygulch; dry-gulch. *v.t.* 1. To murder, esp. by pushing off a cliff or from a high place. *Orig. cowboy use meaning to kill sheep or cattle of rival ranches by stampeding them over a cliff or into a dry gulch.* 2. To knock unconscious; to beat up.

dry run. 1. Firing or shooting practice with blank or dummy ammunition. *Army use.* → 2. A rehearsal; any simulated action. *v.t.* To subject someone or something to a dry run.

dry up. To shut up; to stop talking. *Usu. a command or entreaty. Colloq. since c1850.*

D. T.'s *sing.* Dementia tremors; delirium tremens. *Universally known.*

dub. *n.* One who does something awkwardly; a novice; a stupid person. *Colloq. since c1885. v.t.* To insert additional material, such as background music or commentary, into a previously recorded program, sound track, or record.

ducat; ducket. *n.* 1. A ticket of admission, as to a circus, prize fight, football game, or show. *c1915 to present.* 2. A pass; a free ticket. 3. A union card or work permit. *Hobo use.* 4. A begging letter; a printed card asking for alms for a deaf and dumb beggar. *Hobo use.* 5. A dollar; money.

ducat-snatcher. *n.* A ticket taker.

duchess. *n.* 1. A girl; esp. a snobbish or aloof girl. 2. A girl who is in the know or who belongs to a jive or underworld group. 3. A female member of a street gang. *Teenage use.*

duck. *n.* 1. A dupe, a sucker. *Underworld use.* 2. A score of zero in a game. *From "duck-egg." c1900.* 3. A bed urinal. *cW.W.I to present. Common hospital use, from its ducklike shape.* 4. A partly smoked cigarette; a butt. *Perhaps from the motion used in picking one up from the ground.* 5. Any amphibious vehicle, such as a flying boat or amphibious tank. *cW.W.II.* 6. A ticket. *From "ducket."* 7. = *D.A.*, haircut. *v.t.* To evade something or someone.

duck bumps. *n.pl.* Goose pimples; goose bumps.

duck-egg. *n.* A grade or mark of zero; a score of zero, as in a game. *c1900.*

ducket = **ducat.**

duck-fit. *n.* A fit of anger. *Alluding to the loud squawking of an angry duck.*

duckie; ducky. *adj.* 1. Good-looking; attractive. 2. Fine; also often used ironically, e.g., "Isn't that just ducky?"

ducks. *n.* 1. A pair of white flannel trousers. *A perennial summer favorite of students.* 2. A lighted cigarette stub.

duck soup. 1. Any person easily overcome, convinced, or the like; one who is easy prey; a push-over. 2. Anything that is easily done; a cinch.

duck tail = D.A., haircut.

dud. *n.* 1. A shell or bomb that has been fired or thrown, but because of a faulty fuse has not exploded. *Colloq. since W.W.I. Perhaps related to "dead." →* 2. A failure; any ineffective, useless person or thing, as a worthless hand of cards, a false story, a social misfit. *adj.* Ineffective; useless.

duddy = fuddy-duddy.

dude. *n.* 1. An overdressed man. *Perhaps from or related to duds = clothes. →* 2. A man from the East or a city man vacationing on a ranch. *c1885. Western use. →* 3. A well-dressed, dapper, ladies' man. *→* 4. A bus tourist of either sex; formerly, a stagecoach tourist.

dude heaver = bouncer.

dude up. To dress like a dude; to wear one's best clothes. *Colloq. since c1890.*

Dudley = Uncle Dudley.

duds. *n.pl.* Clothes. *Colloq. Brought over by colonists from Eng.*

duff. *n.* The posterior, butt, seat.

duffer. *n.* Any elderly man who is somewhat senile, eccentric, or mischievous for his age. *Used either affectionately or critically; almost always in the phrase "old duffer."*

dugout. *n.* The refrigerator, from which it is possible to dig out food for snacks. *Teenage use.*

duke. *n.* 1. A person's hand, esp. when considered as a weapon or tool. 2. The winning decision in a prize fight. *From the winner's raising his hands over his head in victory. v.t.* 1. To hand something to a person. 2. To attempt to sell some article by handing it to one person, as a child, and asking payment from his companion, as the child's parent. *Circus and pitchman use.* 3. To shortchange a person by palming a coin that is part of the change due to him. *Circus and pitchman use.* 4. To shake hands with a person. dukie; dookie. *n.*

A lunch wrapped up at a circus cooktent to be handed out to workmen; a box lunch. —s. *n.pl.* The hands, esp. the hands as fists.

duket = ducat.

dum = rum-dum.

dumb. *adj.* 1. Stupid; foolish. *Colloq. since c1820. From Pa. Dutch, "dumm."* 2. Damn. *Colloq. since 1780. adv.* Stupidly. *v.t.* To dull the mind. —o. *n.* 1. A stupid person. 2. A stupid mistake; a boner.

dumb-bell. *n.* A stupid person. *Attributed to cartoonist T. A. Dorgan.*

dumb bunny. A somewhat stupid person; implies a shade of endearment in or toleration of the person.

dumb cluck; dumb-cluck. *n.* A dull or stupid person; one who makes many blunders or mistakes; a careless person. *Colloq.*

dumb Dora. 1. A stupid girl. 2. A man's sweetheart.

dumb-head. *n.* A stupid person. *Colloq. since c1885.*

dumbjohn. *n.* A person easily deceived or tricked; one who is not wise or worldly; an easy mark; one who is stupid; esp. one who is not hep.

dumb ox. A stupid, slow-thinking person, esp. a large, awkward one. *Colloq.*

dummy. *n.* 1. A stupid person. *Colloq.* 2. Bread. *Hobo use.*

dummy up. To refuse to reveal information or a confidence; to refuse to talk or sing; fig., to act as if one were dumb.

dump. *n.* 1. Any unattractive, cheap, shabby, or wretched house, apartment, hotel, theater, or the like; a joint. *The most common use.* 2. Any building, irrespective of the cost, state of repair, furnishings, or reputation, as a store, apartment, room, house, bunkhouse, nightclub, hotel, etc. 3. A prison. *Some underworld and prison use since c1925.* 4. A city or town. 5. A sporting contest in which one contestant or team has been bribed to lose; a fixed fight, race or game. *v.t.* 1. To bunt a baseball. 2. Purposely to lose a game or other sports contest; to play poorly in a contest because one has been bribed to do so. 3. To rid oneself of something; to reject or refuse a person.

dunk. *v.t.* 1. To dip something, usu. pastry, into a liquid, usu. a beverage. 2. To score points in a basketball game; fig., to "dump" the basketball through the basket.

dupe. *n.* A duplicate copy of something, as made from a film negative, a mimeograph or other duplicating machine, or a carbon copy of typed material.

duper = super-duper.

dust. *n.* 1. Tobacco; chewing tobacco; snuff. *Dial.* 2. The ground. 3. Powdered narcotics. *v.t.* 1. To hit or strike. 2. To spray insecticide on crops from an airplane; to spray. *Colloq.* —**er.** *n.* 1. In baseball, a pitch purposely thrown very close to the batter. 2. A woman's smock or housecoat, worn over or instead of usual clothes. *Colloq.* —**s.** *n.pl.* Brass knuckles. *From "knuckledusters." Underworld and street gang use.* —**y. Dusty.** n. = dusty butt, often as a nickname.

dust-dust. *n.* A newly promoted corporal, sergeant, or other noncommissioned officer. *In jocular allusion to the frequent brushing that they give their new chevrons. Some W.W.II use reported.*

dust 'em off. 1. To study. → 2. To talk about the past; to be required to produce facts or data that have been forgotten or filed away. *From the concept of dusting off old books.* 3. To return to a job, hobby, or sport after a long absence.

dust [one's] jacket. To beat a person up.

dust [someone] off. 1. To hit someone; to beat someone up. 2. In baseball, to pitch a ball close to the batter without hitting him, thus forcing him to move back from the plate and perhaps interfering with his ability to concentrate on the next pitch; the act of so pitching, or the pitch itself. → 3. To hit or try to hit a batter with a pitched ball.

dust [one's] pants; dust [one's] trousers. To spank a child.

dust-raiser. *n.* A farmer.

dustup. *n.* A disturbance; uproar; fuss; commotion.

dusty butt. *n.* A short person; lit., a person built so close to the ground that his butt or rump is always dusty. *Some student use.*

dutch. *v.t.* 1. Orig., to bet on each horse in a race proportionately, so that any winner will return more than the total amount bet. *The introduction of pari-mutuel totalizators made this kind of betting impossible.* → 2. To ruin something, as a plan; to ruin one's chance of successfully completing a task; to cause another to fail.

Dutch. *n.* A type of men's haircut, similar to the "Detroit." *v.t.* 1. To ruin or destroy a person's business, health, or social standing, and to do so with malice. 2. In gambling, to place a series of bets, in a mathematical relation or from knowledge of a prearranged outcome, so that the gambling house or owner of the game is ruined.

Dutch, go. To pay for one's own refreshments or entertainment when in another's company; to take part in a Dutch treat.

Dutch, in. 1. Having incurred the wrath or dislike of someone on whom one's success or happiness depends. 2. In trouble; in disfavor; in wrong.

Dutch act, the. Suicide; the act of committing suicide.

Dutch book. A small-time handbook, specif. one that will accept horseracing bets of less than one dollar. *It is assumed that such a bookmaking establishment can be "dutched" easily, but the* *other "dutch" sl. words, such as "Dutch act," "Dutch treat," and "Dutch uncle," all have some basic connotation of disaster, dislike, and cheapness, indicating that there may have been a common root.*

Dutch courage. False courage or bravery inspired or supported by intoxication. *From 17th C. Brit. sl., coined during a period of belligerency between Eng. and the Dutch.*

Dutch rub. The act of rubbing vigorously a small area of another's head, causing minor pain. *A schoolboy's trick; term common since c1910.*

Dutch treat. An instance of each of two or more persons paying his own way or for his own refreshment and entertainment; an outing or date during which each participant pays his own way. *Colloq.*

Dutch uncle. A person, usu. a man, who talks to another severely.

dynamite. *n.* 1. Part of a bet or money bet on a horse that a bookmaker bets elsewhere or transfers to another bookmaker in order to reduce possible loss. 2. Marijuana or heroin, esp. a marijuana cigarette. *Some addict use.* *v.t.* To lure customers or patrons by false or garish advertising. *adj.* Scandalous; shocking; certain to cause a scandal. *Attrib. use. Colloq.*

E

E. *n.* 1. A flag or insigne awarded during W.W.II for proficiency in helping the war effort. *A flag with an "E" on it signified that a war plant was producing quality goods rapidly for the Armed Forces; an "E" painted on the stack of a USN ship signified the efficiency of the crew; and the like.* → 2. Any award or compliment. *Some W.W.II use.*

eager beaver. One who seems overly diligent to his coworkers or acquaintances; an extremely diligent, ambitious person; esp. one who tries to impress his superiors by his diligence and eagerness to serve. *Wide student use since c1940. May be used as a compliment, but usu. is applied derisively to one who seems overly ambitious or aggressive in his work. adj.* Ambitious; industrious; eager to please.

eagle. *n.* An adept fighter pilot; a fighter pilot who has shot down many enemy planes. *Air Force use.*

eagle day. Payday. *W.W.II Armed Forces use. In ref. to the eagle appearing on U.S. banknotes and coins; also the eagle is popularly said to scream or shit on payday.*

eagle-eye. *n.* 1. Fig., one who sees or watches as well as an eagle, which is known traditionally for its keen vision. 2. A detective, esp. a detective assigned to watch for shoplifters or pickpockets.

ear. *n.* The handle of a drinking cup. *—ful. n.* News or gossip; a fairly large amount of talk.

ear, get up on [one's] = on [one's] ear.

ear, on [one's]. *Euphem. for "on one's ass." Fig., to be knocked or thrown to a sitting position.*

ear-banger. *n.* 1. One who tries to curry favor by flattery; a yes man; an apple-polisher; a handshaker. *W.W.II Armed Forces use.* 2. A braggart.

ear-bender. *n.* An overtalkative person.

ear duster. 1. In baseball, a ball pitched at or close to the batter's head. 2. A gossip; one who talks at great length to another, usually revealing confidences. 3. A piece of gossip; a piece of surprising or extremely interesting personal news.

early bright. Dawn; morning; the daytime. *Some c1935 jive use; now some bop, cool, and far out use; some teenage use since c1955.*

earn (have) [one's] wings. To prove oneself as responsible, reliable, mature, or skilled.

ears into. To eavesdrop.

easy, take it. An admonition, command, plea, or advice to another to relax, to stop worrying, to become calm and unemotional, or to enjoy life and accept it as it is. *Also often used on parting, in place of "good-by." Colloq.*

easy as pie. Very easy.

easy digging. Anything accomplished with ease; a sure success.

easy make. One easy to persuade or convince, esp. to victimize, deceive, or defeat; a customer who is receptive to a sales talk.

easy mark. A person who is easily convinced, victimized, or cheated.

Easy Street; easy street. 1. Financial independence. 2. A way of life characterized by wealth and luxury; a pleasant and successful life; successful business dealings. *Almost always in "on easy street."*

eat. *v.t.* 1. To annoy or bother a person greatly; to trouble someone to distraction; usu. in "What's eating you?" —s. *n.pl.* Food; meals. *Colloq. since c1910. Very popular on roadside restaurant signs, because it is the shortest word that can be put on a sign to advertise a restaurant.*

eat [someone] (up) (with a spoon). To consider someone as exceptionally sweet, adorable, or cute. *Usu. said of babies or children.*

eat dirt. To take severe criticism, insults, or a reprimand meekly; to grovel in front of another.

eat [someone] out. To reprimand; bawl out; chew out.

ech! interj. An expression of disgust or disinterest toward an inferior or worthless item or person. *From the Yiddish.*

echo. *n.* An underling of a politician; a close follower and popularizer of another's ideas.

Ed. *n.* A square; one who is not hip.

edge. *n.* 1. A state of mild intoxication. Usu. in "have an edge [on]." 2. A slight advantage. *Colloq.* —ed. *adj.* Drunk; having an edge [on].

edge on [someone], have an. To have an advantage over another person, esp. to have an advantage that will, lit. or fig., enable one to best another in a contest of strength. **edge on, have an.** To be drunk.

eel. *n.* A clever prisoner; a smooth guy. Esp., a criminal who is too slippery for the police to catch easily or a politician or businessman who refuses to make concrete statements of opinions.

egg. *n.* 1. A person, usu. male; a man, fellow, guy, "bird," or the like. *A neutral word which takes its sense of approval or disapproval from a modifier, as "a good egg," "a bad egg," "a dumb egg," etc. Since c1850; orig. from a concern with the edibility of actual eggs; sl. use restricted to "good egg" and "bad egg" until c1885.* 2. Something egglike in shape, specif.: a zero or nought, a baseball, the human head; etc. *Various uses since c1875.* 3. Any of several kinds of explosive missiles, esp. a bomb to be dropped from an airplane, a hand grenade or small bomb to be thrown, or a naval mine. *All these uses both W.W.I and W.W.II Armed Forces. Orig. = aerial bomb, prob. because a plane drops bombs in the manner of a hen laying an egg, rather than in ref. to the shape of the bomb. v.t. = egg on.*

egg, full as an. Very drunk.

eggbeater. *n.* 1. An airplane propeller. *W.W.II Air Force use.* 2. A helicopter. *Colloq. From the appearance and motion of its rotor blades.* 3. A woman's hair style, shoulder length or shorter, featuring a tousled, windblown, almost disheveled effect, usu. worn with a headache band. The hair behind this band is deliberately arranged to fall over the band onto the face. *Common c1958.*

egg-crate. *n.* An automobile.

egghead. *n.* 1. A bald man. 2. An intellectual; one who makes decisions intellectually rather than emotionally; one who does not participate in popular fads and diversions; a person deeply interested in cultural or scientific affairs. *Pop. during presidential campaign of 1952 when the supporters of Adlai Stevenson, Democratic candidate, were called eggheads. Thus orig. the term carried the connotation of "politically minded" and "liberal"; today its application is more general. May have originated in ref. to the high forehead of Mr. Stevenson or of the pop. image of an academician.*

egg [someone] on. To persuade or goad someone into doing something, esp. to belligerent action; to encourage; to entice; to cajole.

egg-sucker. *n.* One who seeks advancement through flattery rather than work; a "weasel."

eightball. *n.* A complete and thorough "square"; fig., an octagonal "square." *Some bop and cool use.*

eighty-eight. *n.* A piano. *From the number of keys in a full keyboard.*

eighty-six. No, nix; nothing; there is none left; we don't have the item ordered. *Common lunch-counter use; used by the cook to inform waiters that there is no more of a specific dish.*

elbow. *v.i.* To associate with as a friend; to bend elbows or rub elbows with.

elbow-bender. *n.* A convivial person.

elbow-bending. *n.* Liquor drinking.

elbow grease. Hard physical work; muscular energy, expended in any manual labor.

elevate. *v.t.* To hold up with a gun and rob; a synonym for "hold up." *v.i.* To raise one's

hands on command in a hold-up.

elevated. *adj.* Drunk.

Elizabeth club. An informal union or society of Negro household maids, cooks, and cleaning women. *It is doubtful if there has ever existed such an organization, but Southern housewives claim Elizabeth clubs meet on the members' afternoons off from work to exchange gossip about their employers, fix salary rates, and the like. Because Elizabeth is considered a typical name.*

Elk. *n.* = square, Babbitt. *From the Elks fraternal society; beat use.*

Elmer. *n.* 1. An overseer. 2. An inexperienced, stupid boy.

else = or else.

Elvis. *n.* A type of men's haircut. *Since c1955, rock-and-roll and general teenage use.*

embalmed. *adj.* Intoxicated.

embalming fluid. 1. Coffee; particularly very strong coffee. 2. Whisky.

emcee. *n.* A master of ceremonies. *A spelling of the letters in the abbr. "M.C." v.t.* To serve as master of ceremonies.

emery ball. In baseball, a curve pitched with a roughened ball.

emote. *v.i.* 1. In the theater, to act in a role which includes many emotional scenes; to act in a hyperemotional manner. *From "emotion."* → 2. To simulate any emotion; to assume an emotion or concern which one does not feel.

emoting. *n.* The act or state of displaying emotion, either by a performer in a professional capacity or by a layman who simulates an emotion that he does not feel.

end. *n.* A share, as of the spoils. *Colloq.*

end, the = most, the. The best. *Cool, far out, and beat use since c1955. Although new, "the end" is used exactly as was "sockdollager" in the 19C.*

English. *n.* 1. A twisting, spinning rotation made by a tennis ball, billiard ball, or the like, as it moves forward; the untrue bounce or carom caused by this motion. *Colloq.* 2. A type of men's haircut.

enthuse. *v.i.* To show enthusiasm. *Since c1825.*

equalizer. *n.* A pistol or other gun. *Although the word has seen underworld use, it is more common in fiction about the underworld.*

erase. *v.t.* To kill; rub out. *More often used in fiction about than by the underworld.* —r. *n.* A knockout. *Prize fight use.*

Erie = on the Erie.

Erie, on the l. Listening; eavesdropping. *Hobo and underworld use. A pun on ear and the Erie railroad line.* → 2. Not taking chances; hiding. *Underworld use.*

estate = real estate.

Ethel. *n.* An effeminate man.

eve. *n.* A rib on an airplane wing assembly. *Airplane factory and Air Force use.*

even-Steven; even-steven; even-Stephen; even-stephen. *adj.* & *adv.* Even, fair; evenly.

even with [someone], get. To wrong another, esp. to cause another a social or business loss from spite. *Colloq.*

evil. *adj.* 1. Disillusioned; disappointed; angry. *c1935 jive use. Some cool use since c1955.* 2. Wonderful; specif., thrilling, very satisfying; said of a person, act, or usu. of the playing of a piece of music, of a theatrical performance, or the like. *Pseudo cool use. Implies that, like sex, that which is really thrilling and satisfying is considered sinful by puritanical people.*

evil eye. Bad luck; lit., bad luck or misfortune as caused by an enemy or demonic person casting an evil spell.

ex; x. *n.* 1. An exclusive concession or right to sell a product. *Circus and pitchman use. From the "x" that "marks the spot," reinforced by the "x" = a signa-*ture. 2. An ex-wife or an ex-husband. *Colloq.*

exam. *n.* An examination, as a formal, written test, usu. long and authoritatively administered by a school or college; a medical, physical, or civil-service examination. *Colloq. since c1870. adj.* Concerned with or given over to an examination or examinations, as an exam question, exam paper, exam week.

excess baggage. 1. Anything or anyone not necessary, needed, or wanted; fig., that which is or could become a burden. 2. Specif., immature, outmoded, undesirable, prohibiting, or limiting ideals, beliefs, or ideas that prevent one from being objective. Fig., any intangible thing that may hinder one.

excuse. *v.t.* To request someone to depart or leave.

exec. *n.* 1. An executive officer. *USN use since c1925.* 2. Calisthenics; marching drill. *Some USN use, because an executive officer is in command. adj.* Of or by executives.

extension. *n.* Credit; specif., the maximum credit that can be extended to a customer.

extra. *n.* One who plays a minor role in a movie or play; specif., one who has no speaking part in a movie but who takes part in crowd scenes. *Colloq.* —curricular. *adj.* Unplanned; unethical; immoral; said of one's actions, usu. sexual or flirtatious actions. *From the stand. collegiate use.*

extracurricular activity. Adultery, sexual intercourse with one other than one's spouse; a girl or woman with whom one has committed adultery.

eye. *n.* 1. A private detective. *From "the eye."* 2. A television set; a television screen. *Teenage use, common since c1955.*

eye (beady eye) (fish eye), give [someone] the. To look or glance at a person, often admonitorily or sinisterly.

Eye, the; eye, the. *n.* 1. The Pinkerton National Detective Agency. *Since soon after 1850, when the agency was founded. From the watching eye pictured on the sign posted outside places of business protected by the Pinkerton Agency.* 2. A Pinkerton detective.

eyeball. *v.t.* To eye; look at; look around a place. *Harlem Negro use. Teenage and synthetic hipster use since c1950.*

eye-opener. *n.* A drink of liquor, as one taken upon rising. *c1815; still common.*

eyes, give with the. 1. = to look at; to convey a message by a glance. 2. To start; to participate; to contribute.

eyes for [something or someone], to have. To want, to desire; to admire; to work for or toward; to try to obtain.

eye-shut. A Western variant of "shut-eye."

eyes to cool it. A desire or plan to relax, withdraw from strain, work, or competition, or to take a vacation.

eyewash. *n.* Flattery; boloney.

Eytie; Eyetie. *n.* An Italian. *Common W.W.II Army use, though the term is much earlier in origin.*

F

face. *n.* A white person. *Negro use.*

face, open [one's]. To talk; lit., to open one's mouth.

fade. *v.i.* 1. To leave; go away. 2. Fig., to fade out of sight; to disappear; to depart in haste. 3. To meander; wander; stroll. *Boy use, prep school.*

fade away. To leave; disappear. *c1900. n.* In baseball, a pitch that arrives away from the batter. *Constantly used.*

faded boogie. A Negro informer.

fag. *n.* 1. A cigarette. *Some cW.W.I use, seldom heard now.* 2. A homosexual; an effeminate man; since c1940 specif., a male homosexual. *Common since c1920. It has been suggested that*

"fag" = homosexual comes from "fag" = cigarette, since cigarettes were considered effeminate by cigar and pipe smokers when they were first introduced at the end of W.W.I. Although this may have reinforced the use of the word, "fag" = a boy servant or lackey has been common Eng. schoolboy use since before 1830, and may be orig. of "fag" = homosexual. adj. Homosexual; pertaining to homosexuals.

fag along. To ride fast. *Cowboy use. Still current.*

fagin. *n.* A teacher of crime; an old malicious criminal. *From Fagin in Dickens' "Oliver Twist."*

fair-haired boy. *n.* 1. A man, not necessarily a youth, who is most favored by those in power. → 2. Specif. one who is expected to be elevated to the top position; the known replacement for a major political or business job or a sports star.

fair hell. A person who excels; one who is energetic and successful.

fair shake. 1. An honest arrangement; a fair deal; a square deal. 2. An attempt or try under the same conditions given others. *Apparently in reference to dicing. Colloq. since c1825.*

fairy. *n.* A male homosexual, usu. one who assumes the feminine role. *After "queer," "fairy" is the most common and polite word = a homosexual.*

fairy godfather. A prospective sponsor, advertiser, or financial backer. *Radio, television, and stage use.*

fairy lady. A lesbian who assumes the female role in a homosexual relationship. *West Coast use since c1950.*

fake. *v.t.* To improvise or play compatible chords or notes on a musical instrument when one does not know or has forgotten the correct notes of the composition. *Common jazz music use.*

fake it. 1. To bluff; to pretend to know or be able to do something.

→ 2. To improvise while playing music because one does not know the piece or the arrangement; to improvise, esp. to improvise a solo in a jazz performance.

fall. *n.* 1. An arrest. *Underworld use.* 2. A term in prison. *Underworld use.* 3. An unsuccessful attempt at robbery. *Underworld use. v.i.* 1. To be caught or arrested; drop. *Underworld use.* 2. To be sentenced to a term in prison. *Underworld use.* 3. To fail in an attempted robbery. *Underworld use.* 4. To be or begin to be in love with a person; to fall in love with a person.

fall apart. 1. To be overcome with desire, enthusiasm, appreciation, excitement, nervousness, or the like. *Orig. c1946 bop use.* 2. To lose one's composure; to lose one's confidence. 3. Specif., to be overwhelmed by another's presence or love. *Teenage use since c1955.*

fall down. To visit or pay a call.

fall down and go boom. 1. To fall down noisily; said esp. of a person. 2. To fail completely and publicly.

fall for. 1. To take a strong liking for [something]. *Colloq. since c1905.* 2. To fall in love with a person. 3. To be deceived, duped, or made a sucker of by some gag or trick.

fall guy. 1. An easy victim; a victim; a loser. → 2. Specif., a scapegoat; a person who is made to take the blame for another's crime, mistake, or failure.

fall money. Money set aside for various expenses involved in being arrested, such as for possible bribes, bail, and legal fees.

fall off. To lose weight. *Colloq.*

fallout. *n.* Radioactive particles distributed by an aerial nuclear explosion, falling from or floating in the atmosphere. *Colloq.*

fall out. 1. To be emotionally aroused; to be surprised; to "fall apart." *Orig. c1946 bop use; now some teenage use. Prob. reinforced by the Army command* "fall out" = dismissed. 2. To be overcome with emotion or laughter; to lose one's inhibitions in an unrestrained burst of emotion or laughter. *Fig., to fall out of one's chair, as with laughter.* 3. To die; fig., to fall out of reality and consciousness.

falsie. *n.* 1. Anything that is false or artificial. 2. Specif., a brassiere with built-in padding, to make a woman appear to have larger or more shapely breasts. 3. = falsies. 4. Any padding, as over the thighs or hips, worn by a woman to give her the appearance of having a voluptuous figure. —s. *n.pl.* Women's breast pads worn to give the appearance of having larger or more shapely breasts. *The style and the word very common c1945 to present.*

fan. *n.* 1. A devotee or enthusiastic follower, usu. of a sport or other form of entertainment. *Colloq. since before 1900.* 2. An airplane propeller. *W.W.II Air Force use.* → 3. An airplane engine. *v.t.* 1. In baseball, to cause a batter to strike out; said of a baseball pitcher. 2. To spank. 3. To search a person for money or a gun; to frisk. 4. To sweep one's hands over a man's clothing in lieu of searching him for a concealed weapon or contraband, or to determine the contents of his pockets. *v.i.* 1. In baseball, to strike out. 2. To chat or gossip; to converse; from "fan the breeze." —ner. *n.* 1. A fan dancer. 2. One who locates a wallet for a pickpocket to lift.

fancy Dan; Fancy Dan. *n.* 1. A stylishly dressed, persuasive ladies' man; a dude. *Colloq.* 2. One who looks, talks, and acts capable but who is afraid of mussing his clothes with hard work; one who is afraid of hard work. 3. In prize fighting, a clever, skilled boxer, esp. one who cannot punch or hit strongly. *Prize fight use.*

fancy pants. 1. A sissy. *Universally*

known to children. 2. An effete man; an overly fastidious man.

fandangle. *n.* 1. An ornament. 2. A mechanical gadget. *Colloq.*

faniggle = **finagle.**

fanny. *n.* The human rump.

fan the breeze. To talk; usu. to talk aimlessly; to chat.

fantods. *n.sing.* A mythical disease causing melancholy, nervousness, and depression; the willies.

fare-thee-well = **fare-you-well.**

fare-ye-well = **fare-you-well.**

fare-you-well. *n.* To a fare-you-well = to perfection; thoroughly; completely; to a finish. *Colloq. since c1885.*

far out; far-out. *adj.* 1. Descriptive of or characteristic of the most modern forms of jazz or progressive music; technically, more progressive than cool. 2. Descriptive of or characteristic of devotees of "far out" music and their behavior; intellectual. 3. Satisfying; capable of arousing enthusiasm. 4. Extremely; "gone" or far removed from reality; intent; intense; so much in rapport with, intent on, or immersed in one's work, performance, ideas, or mode or way of life that one is as if in a trance, and unaware of or removed from all extraneous things. 5. Of, by, for, or pertaining to devotees of far-out music, their fashions, fads, and attitudes. 6. Removed from standards of criticism by being unrelated to or beyond comparison with other things; intellectually, psychologically, or spiritually so cool as to be beyond comparison. *Mainly far-out use, some cool and beat use.*

fashion plate. A consistently well-dressed person of either sex, esp. one habitually dressed in the latest styles.

fast. *adj.* Amoral; suspected of riotous or unconventional behavior; hedonistic.

fast buck. Lit., a quickly or easily acquired dollar; fig., money obtained quickly or easily and often unscrupulously.

fast one. A trick; a clever swindle; a deception; an instance of double-crossing.

fast shuffle = **double shuffle.**

fast talk. Talk meant to deceive or mislead; glib talk. **—er.** *n.* One who habitually talks glibly or misleadingly; a persuasive talker; a male with more charm than sincerity.

fat. *adj.* 1. Poor, slight, slim; usu. in "a fat chance" = little or no chance. *Since c1900; orig. ironical.*

fat cat. 1. The financier of a political party campaign or politician; a provider of money for political uses. → 2. One who receives or expects special privileges. *Army and student use since W.W.II.* → 3. One who has fame, wealth, and luxuries. *v.* To receive or try to obtain special privileges.

fat-head; fathead. *n.* 1. A stupid person. *Colloq.* 2. A stupid blunder. **—ed.** *adj.* Stupid; usu. applied to persons, sometimes to actions. *Since c1750.*

Fats; Fat; Fatty; Fatso. *masc. sing.* A nickname for a fat person. *Can be affectionate, jocular, or derisive.*

faust. *adj.* Ugly; disgusting. *Cool and far out use since c1955.*

featherbed. *v.i.* To create extra and unnecessary work in order to earn more money; to demand work for unnecessary employees.

feather crew. A type of men's haircut, similar to the crew cut.

feather cut. A women's hair style with the hair shorter than shoulder length and featuring casual waves and a wind-tossed effect. *Common c1943–1946.*

feather merchant. *n.* 1. A civilian; specif., a slacker. *Armed Forces use W.W.II.* Suggested by "chicken" and perhaps by "featherbed." → 2. A Navy Reserve officer; a person who immediately receives a commission upon entering the armed services; a sailor who has an office job. *W.W.II USN use.*

feather [one's] nest; line [one's] nest. To obtain money, ethically or unethically, for oneself; to obtain money or an unfair share of money from the efforts of others; to provide for oneself with no regard to the welfare of others.

feature. *v.t.* To comprehend; to understand. *Since c1930.*

fed; Fed. *n.* Any Federal government officer.

Federal case out of [something], make a. To overemphasize the importance of something; esp. to exaggerate another's mistake or bad judgment when criticizing or reprimanding him.

fed up. *adj.* Bored; sated; disgusted. *Colloq. Since W.W.I, from Brit. sl. Orig. a version of the French "J'en ai soupé."*

feeb. *n.* A feeble-minded person; an idiot, moron, or imbecile. **—bles.** *n.pl.* A hangover; the heebie-jeebies.

feed. *n.* A meal; anything from a light lunch to an elaborate banquet, but usu. a substantial, filling, well-cooked meal. *c1820 to present. v.i.* To board; to take one's meals.

feed, off [one's]. Sick; indisposed; depressed or sad. *From the term used to ref. to a sick horse.*

feedbag; feed-bag. *n.* A meal, as dinner.

feedbag, put on the. To eat.

feedbag information = feedbox information.

feedbox information; feedbag information. Supposedly authentic advance information or a tip, esp. on a horse race; specif., a tip on a horse race that supposedly orig. from a horse owner or stable employee.

feed [one's] face. To eat a meal; to eat.

feed the kitty. To contribute to a common fund.

feel good. To be more or less drunk.

feel no pain. To be drunk.

feel out. To try to find out a person's attitude toward or opinion

of a specific subject or plan, subtly or indirectly.

feet first, go home. To die.

feeze = pheeze.

fellow traveler. 1. Specif., a follower of Communist doctrines who does not belong to the Communist Party. *Colloq.* → **2.** One who professes agreement with any idea, movement, group, or the like but does not take an active role.

fem; femme. *n.* A girl or woman; a female. *The spelling "femme" occurs four times as often as "fem"; thus orig. from Fr. "femme" = woman more important than back-clipping from "female."* *adj.* Feminine; female.

fenagle = finagle.

fence. *n.* A person or place that deals in stolen goods. *No longer common in underworld as too well known to outsiders. v.t.* To sell stolen property to or at a fence.

fence-hanger. *n.* **1.** One whose mind is not made up; one who has not made a decision. **2.** A gossip.

fetching. *adj.* Pleasing; attractive. *Since c1900; colloq.*

fever. *n.* A five-spot playing card. *A whimsical distortion of "fiver."*

F. F. V. 1. The socially elite. *From "First Families of Virginia."* **2.** A criminal or convict. *Lit., a "first family of Virginia," jocular reference to belief that Virginia was first settled as a penal colony.*

fiddle-faddle. *interj. & n.* Nonsense.

fiend; —fiend. *n.* **1.** One obsessed with or a devotee of something, esp. something evil or forbidden; specif., c1890–c1920, a cigarette smoker; c1925 a drug addict. **2.** A devotee or addict of, or enthusiast for, something indicated. *Still in use.*

fierce. *adj.* Awful; terrible; horrible; hard; intense.

fifty-six. *n.* For those who work on Saturdays and Sundays, the time off that takes the place of a week end. *Because the time is 56 hours.*

fight. *n.* A party.

fight a bottle. To drink from a bottle.

fightin' tools. Eating utensils; a table knife, fork, and spoon. *W.W.II Armed Forces use.*

figure. *v.i. & v.t.* To be expected or prophesied to be; to seem reasonable; to make sense; to stand to reason. *Sometimes the subject of "figure" appears to be in the wrong person, but then "it" or "that" is the subject. Often the passive voice is meant where active is used, e.g., "He doesn't figure to live" = "He is not figured [expected] to live."*

filbert. *n.* An enthusiast. *A variation on "nut."*

file. *n.* 1. A pickpocket. *Underworld use.* 2. A waste basket.

file seventeen. A waste-basket. *W.W.II Army use.*

file thirteen. A waste-basket. *W.W.II Armed Forces use.*

fill-in. *n.* 1. A summary; an account that fills in gaps in the hearer's or reader's knowledge. 2. A substitute worker. *Colloq.* *v.t.* 1. To summarize for someone. *Common since c1945.* 2. To work as a substitute.

filling station. A small town. *From the concept that, to one passing through, the filling station is the most important thing.*

filly. *n.* A girl or young woman.

filthy. *adj.* 1. Wealthy; having much money. Often in "filthy rich." 2. Obscene, risqué, sexy. *n.* Money. Short for "filthy lucre."

filthy lucre. Money. *Colloq. From Paul's Epistle to Titus.*

fin. *n.* 1. The human head. 2. The human arm. 3. A five-dollar bill; the sum of $5. —**if; finiff; finnif.** *n.* A five-dollar bill; the sum of $5. *From the Yiddish.*

finagle; fenagle; finigal; finnagel; faniggle. *v.t.* To contrive; to manage; to figure out a way, esp. by unethical or unusual means. —**r;** —**er.** *n.* One who contrives for others to pay or take respon-

sibility; *specif.* one who stalls until someone else pays the check.

find Rover. To work without enthusiasm or care; to relax on one's job; to make little or no effort. *Suggested by "dog it."*

fine. *adj.* Pleasing; wonderful; exciting; cool. *Wide use since c1940; now associated with bop and cool use.*

finest, the. The New York City police force; a New York City policeman. *Also used ironically.*

finger. *v.t.* 1. To point out accusingly; to point out a victim to a gunman, or a criminal to the police. 2. To inform thieves as to the location, value, etc., of potential loot. *n.* 1. A policeman. 2. A police informer. 3. Finger man. 4. An amount of liquor in a glass equal to the depth of the width of a finger. —**s.** *n.pl.* 1. A 10% share of loot. *In allusion to the ten fingers. Underworld use.* 2. A jazz piano player; often a nickname. *Synthetic use.*

finger man. A criminal who finds, obtains detailed information on, evaluates, and/or points out prospective victims or loot to thieves, holdup men, kidnapers, or killers.

finger mob. A gang of criminals working under police protection, usu. in return for informing on other gangs.

finger on [something], put [one's]. To identify, recognize, comprehend, or the like; to remember or locate in one's memory.

finger on [someone], put the. 1. To mark or point out a victim, as for killing. *Underworld use.* → 2. To identify, inform on, or make a charge against a criminal to the police. *Orig. and mainly underworld use. Fig., to point out, as with the index finger.*

finger popper. Lit., one who snaps his fingers; fig., a musician or listener who is carried away by jazz music. *Some synthetic cool use. Reinforced by "joy popper."*

finger-wringer. *n.* An actor or esp.

an actress given to overly emotional performances. *Movie use.*

finigal = finagle.

finisher. *n.* A knockout blow. *Prize fight use.*

fink. *n.* 1. A worker or private policeman hired by a factory, mine, or company to help break a strike; a scab; a company spy posing as a worker in order to report union activities. 2. A detective or policeman; a private detective or policeman. *Since c1920.* 3. An informer, squealer, or stool pigeon. *Since c1920. Underworld use.* 4. A contemptible person; an undesirable, unwanted, or unpleasant person. *Some use since c1925.* 5. Any broken, defective, or small article of merchandise, as a toy balloon; a larry. *v.i.* To inform, specif. to the police; to become cowardly or untrustworthy.

Finn = Mickey Finn.

finnagel = finagle.

fire. *v.t.* 1. To discharge an employee from his job, esp. for reasons that reflect unfavorably upon him, as incompetence, inefficiency, tardiness, or the like. *Colloq. since c1910.* → 2. To expel or dismiss someone from a place without using physical force; to request or require that someone leave. 3. To fling, hurl, or throw something, usu. a ball or missile, with the hand, esp. with force and speed. *Colloq. since c1910.*

fire, on the. Pending; under consideration.

fire-ball. *n.* An ambitious, efficient, and fast worker; a very active person.

fire blanks. To have sexual intercourse without impregnating the woman, when the couple wishes children; for a man to have sexual intercourse when he is physically unable to father a child.

firebug. *n.* An arsonist; a pyromaniac.

firecracker. *n.* A bomb; also, a torpedo. *W.W.II use.*

fired up. Angry.

fire-eater. *n.* 1. A firefighter. *Colloq.* 2. A brave or bold person, esp. one who is not afraid to argue with or criticize those in authority; one who loves an argument.

fireman. *n.* 1. In baseball, a relief pitcher. *Because such a pitcher is called into the game to stop the opposing team in the midst of a rally, i.e. "to put out the fire."* 2. A speeding motorist.

fire stick. A gun. *Teenage and adolescent hoodlum use since c1950.*

fire up. To start an engine. *Some W.W.II Air Force use; common hot rod use.*

fire-water. *n.* Liquor. *Colloq. since c1820. A common pioneer and Western term, now used jokingly.*

fireworks. *n.pl.* 1. Excitement; a spectacular display of anything fig. like fireworks. 2. Shooting; esp. artillery fire. *W.W.II Armed Forces use.*

first off. First; from the very first; at first. *Colloq. since c1880.*

first-of-May. *n.* A novice; a new or inexperienced employee. *Circus use.* *adj.* Inexperienced. *Circus use.*

first-rate. *adj.* Excellent.

fish. *n.sing.* 1. A person who is a newcomer; a novice; an inexperienced worker, a beginner. *Wide college use = "freshman" c1900; still some use. Universally known prison use = a newly arrested prisoner or one arrested for a first offense; since c1915, reinforced by "tank."* 2. A Roman Catholic. *Some derisive and jocular use since c1920, from "fish eater."* 3. A dollar. 4. A person, a fellow or guy; usu. after a modifier, esp. in "poor fish" = a pitiable or unfortunate person, or "queer fish" = an odd or eccentric person. *Since c1920.* 5. A torpedo. *W.W.II USN use. v.i.* 1. To curry favor. 2. To ask or try to get information without directly asking for it. *Colloq.* 3. To feint, esp. in boxing. *n.pl.* **1.** Dollars. **2.** Torpedoes. *W.W.II USN use.* —**eater.** *n.* A Roman Catholic. *Some derisive but mostly jocular use. Because most Roman Catholics eat fish on fast days.* —**ery.** *n.* A religious mission in a working-class neighborhood. *Hobo use.* —**skin.** *n.* A dollar bill.

fish bowl. A jail. *A variation of syn.* tank.

fish eye. An expressionless glance or a questioning stare. —**s.** Tapioca pudding. *Armed Forces, student, and prison use.*

fish-hooks. *n.pl.* The fingers.

fish horn. A saxophone. *Synthetic jazz use.*

fishing trip, take a = take a drink.

fish music = race music. An early, often slower and quieter form of rock and roll, which grew out of "race music."

fish or cut bait. A request, demand, or comment that another act, obtain a result, or bring something to a successful conclusion soon, or else stop trying and give someone else a chance to do so. *Since c1876; archaic and dial.*

fish story. An exaggerated story of one's exploits. *Colloq. since c1820.*

fishtail. *n.* **1.** A woman's dress or dress style incorporating a tight-fitting skirt that widens out, like a fish tail, at the bottom. *Popular c1955.* **2.** Automobile rear fenders that flare upward to hold the car's rear lights. *Introduced c1954 and still popular. v.i.* To swing or slide from side to side; said of a car or truck.

fish tale. A story that sounds fishy; an improbable excuse or alibi.

fish tank = tank.

fish trap = trap.

fish-wrapper. *n.* A newspaper.

fishy. *adj.* Suggestive of deception; dishonest, unethical, insincere, or untruthful words or deeds; improbable, unconvincing, or unbelievable; not quite right or

true. *Brought to U.S. by orig. Eng. colonists.*

fistful. *n.* **1.** A five-year prison sentence. *Underworld use.* **2.** A large amount of money.

fistful of money. A large amount of money; wealth.

five. *n.* Five dollars; a five-dollar bill. *Common use.* —**r.** *n.* **1.** A five-dollar bill. **2.** A five-year prison sentence. *Mainly prison use.*

five-and-dime. *n.* A 5-and-10-cent variety store. *Colloq.*

five-and-ten-cent store. *n.* A variety store or small-items department store. *Because they orig. sold only 5¢ and 10¢ items, usually "notions." Many still sell only items that cost no more than a dollar; others are actually neighborhood department stores.*

five-by-five. *adj.* Fat.

five-case note. A five-dollar bill.

five-finger. *n.* A thief.

five fingers. **1.** A five-year prison sentence. *Underworld use.* **2.** A thief. *The movie titled "Five Fingers" about a master spy and thief was very popular c1950.*

five fingers to [someone], give. To thumb one's nose at a person in derision.

five of clubs. A fist.

five-ouncers. *n.pl.* The fists; a blow with the fist. *From the five-ounce minimum weight of a boxing glove. Prize fight use.*

five-per-center; five percenter. *n.* **1.** One who influences or seeks to influence politicians or government agencies on behalf of clients or friends, often in return for a percentage of the profits made thereby. *Most common during President Harry S. Truman's administration, 1948–52, when his Republican opponents coined the phrase in making accusations of scandal in the awarding of public contracts. Still used. Because the person receives a percentage, usu. 5%, of the value of the contract awarded; reinforced by "ten per-center."* **2.** Any lawyer, businessman, or friend of politicians who possesses undue influence in public affairs.

five-spot. *n.* 1. A five-dollar bill. *Since c1895.* 2. A five-year prison sentence. 3. A playing card or billiard ball numbered 5.

fix. *v.t.* 1. To bribe a person to lose a race, contest, or the like. 2. To buy protection from the local police. *Underworld use since c1925.* 3. To give an addict an injection of narcotics, esp. heroin; to sell an addict drugs, esp. heroin. 4. To castrate an animal, esp. a cat. *Colloq.* 5. To beat up, defeat, or cause someone to fail because of malice toward him. *Colloq. v.i.* To intend; to plan. *Dial. n.* 1. A single injection of a narcotic drug, esp. heroin. *Addict use; generally known.* 2. Navigational data; the coordinates establishing a specif. location, as of a ship, airplane, or the like. 3. A stationary post, of a guard or policeman, as opposed to walking a beat. —*ed. adj.* 1. Having a result predetermined by bribery; unfair. 2. Purposely ignored or forgotten by the police or public officials owing to bribery or influence. 3. Castrated; said of an animal, esp. a cat. —*er. n.* 1. A go-between; an adjuster. → 2. A dishonest lawyer; a shyster. *Underworld and circus use.* → 3. A negotiator between criminals and officials; one who arranges for "the fix." 4. One who sells narcotics to addicts.

fix, the. *n.* 1. Bribery assuring the prearranged outcome of a sporting event; an act or instance of such bribery. 2. Bribery assuring that the police or public officials will ignore, forget, or consider lightly an illegal act or law violation; an act or instance of such bribery.

fix-up. *n.* A single dose of a narcotic. *Addict use.*

fix [someone] up. 1. To secure a date for someone. 2. To provide someone with a desired, wanted, necessary, or unique item or service. *One may be "fixed up" with a drink of whisky, a prostitute, a portion of medicine, a valuable antique, or the like, esp. a thing or service associated with illegal dealings or vice.* 3. Specif., to secure a prostitute or promiscuous woman for someone.

fix [one's] wagon. 1. To prevent another's success; to destroy another's livelihood, reputation, or expectations. → 2. To punish, to kill.

fizz job. A jet airplane. *Synthetic sl.*

fizzle. *n.* Failure. *Since c1850, colloq. v.i.* To fail. *Colloq. since c1870.*

flack; flak. *n.* 1. Publicity or advertising that is widely disseminated or repeated in the hope that some percentage of it will be heeded. *Fig. respelling of "flak."* → 2. A professional publicity worker or press agent. *Mainly theater and Madison Avenue use.*

flag. *v.t.* 1. To signal a moving vehicle, such as a train, bus, or cab, to stop. *Orig. for a station master to signal, by waving a red flag, a train to stop to pick up a passenger.* 2. To refuse or to turn a person away. 3. To hail or stop someone or gain attention, as for the purpose of talking. *n.* 1. In baseball, the pennant awarded to the best team in each league at the end of a season; the pennant awarded to the team that wins the World Series. 2. An assumed name.

flag-waver. *n.* Any aggressively or overly patriotic person; any song, book, play, or the like based on a patriotic theme.

flak. *n.* Fragments of artillery shells, esp. of those often used in antiaircraft and short range shells, constructed so as to explode with many destructive fragments. *W.W.II use.*

flake out. To lie down to rest or sleep. *W.W.II USN use.*

flamdoodle. *n.* = flapdoodle. Nonsense. *Dial.*

flame. *n.* A sweetheart; a passionately loved person. *Brought to U.S. by the Eng. colonists.*

flamethrower. *n.* A jet plane.

flange-head. *n.* A Chinese. *W.W.II Air Force use.*

flap. *n.* **1.** An air raid; an air raid alert or alarm. *W.W.II use.* **2.** A fight or row; a crisis or emergency; an alarm, a scare; an urgent conference; any loud or violent confusion or tumult; excitement. → **3.** A party, esp. a noisy, rowdy party; a brawl. *Teenage use since c1955.* → **4.** A fight between two rival neighborhood boys' street gangs, a rumble; an encounter with the police. *Boys' street gang use.* **5.** A mistake; a social error. **6.** Confusion, anxiety, disconcertion.

flap [one's] chops (jowls) (jaw) (lip). To talk, esp. idly or indiscreetly; to argue.

flapdoodle. *n.* Nonsense; foolish talk; blah, boloney.

flapjaw. *n.* **1.** Talk; chat. **2.** An over-talkative person.

flapper. *n.* **1.** The hand. *Since c1840.* **2.** The pop. female type of the 1920's, typically a young woman characterized by a cynical attitude, a frank interest in sex, a penchant for daring fashions, including short, straight dresses, no petticoats, bobbed hair, stockings rolled below the knee, etc., together with the use of bright lipstick and eye shadow, cosmetics introduced after W.W.I. *Although the article is obs., the word is still universally known and used, as often with nostalgia as with sociological objectivity.*

flaps. *n.pl.* **1.** The ailerons on the wings of an airplane. *Colloq.* **2.** The human ears.

flare up. To become angry or enraged. *Colloq.* **flareup.** *n.* In jazz, to reach a climax of intensity through the playing of repeated chords, increased tempo or volume.

flash. *n.* **1.** Thieves' argot. *Still in use.* **2.** A look; a comprehensive glance; a peek. **3.** One who has a superficial knowledge or reputation; one who has given or occasionally gives a sensational performance but who cannot be regularly depended upon to do so. *Reinforced by the expression "flash in the pan."* **4.** A display of attractive or gaudy merchandise or prizes to attract attention; valuable merchandise, ostensibly prizes, but used only for display; gaudy merchandise. *Carnival and circus use.* *v.t.* To set up a display of prizes at a gambling concession. —**y.** *adj.* Gaudy; cheap and gaudy; created or designed mainly to attract attention or to give an attractive appearance.

flash-sport. *n.* An unusually gaudily or fashionably dressed, handsome, or rakish dude or sport.

flat. *n.* **1.** A punctured or "flat" automobile tire. *Stand. since c1930.* **2.** A simple, dull, or gullible person; one who is not mentally alert. *Some use since c1925. From "flat tire."* **3.** Canvas stretched over a wooden frame and painted to resemble scenery, a wall, or other background. *Theater use.* *adj.* **1.** Without money; broke. **2.** Pertaining to or associated with any carnival gambling game, esp. one in which money, rather than merchandise, is the prize. *Carnival use.* —**foot;** **flat-foot.** *n.* A patrolman; any uniformed policeman or detective. —**footed.** *adj.* & *adv.* Unprepared; taken by surprise. *Since c1910.* —**head.** *n.* **1.** A stupid person. *Since c1885.* **2.** A policeman. **3.** A nontipping patron. —**headed.** *adj.* Stupid. —**s.** *n.pl.* **1.** Horse racing in which the horse runs and is ridden by the jockey, as opposed to harness racing in which the horse trots or paces and pulls a sulky containing the driver. *Common horse-racing use. Because a running horse appears to run flatfooted,* *placing his hoofs down flatly for traction.* 2. The human feet. 3. A type or style of woman's shoe having no or a low heel. *Colloq.* —tener. *n.* In prize fighting, a knock-out blow. *Prize fight use.* —tie; —ty. *n.* 1. A policeman. *From "flatfoot." Some c1925 use; some boy street gang use since c1950.* 2. = flat-joint.

flat broke. Entirely without funds; completely and utterly broke. *Here "flat" appears to be an adv. = entirely, somewhat redundant when used with "broke."*

flat-joint; flat point. *n.* 1. A carnival gambling or game concession or booth in which one plays for money, not prizes. *Carnival use.* → 2. A gambling or game concession. → 3. A crooked gambling or game concession. *Implying that "flat" means a wheel of chance that is weighted or not perfectly circular.*

flat out. To obtain and/or maintain maximum speed while flying a plane or driving a car; flying or driving at maximum speed. *Aviation and hot rod use.*

flattop. *n.* A USN aircraft carrier. *Colloq. during and since W.W.II. Because of its wide, flat flight deck, which serves as an airfield.*

flattop crew. A type of men's haircut, similar to the crew cut.

flea. *n.* An insignificant, annoying person.

flea-bag; fleabag; flea bag. *n.* 1. An inferior racehorse. 2. A cheap, dilapidated hotel or rooming house; a flop-house. *Lit. and fig., a place where one may become a host to fleas.* 3. Any dilapidated, dirty, or cheap public place, as a movie theater.

flea house. A cheap hotel.

flea trap. A cheap hotel.

fleece. *v.t.* To obtain money from someone by deceptive means; to cheat or swindle a person.

flesh, in the. In person.

flesh-peddler. *n.* 1. A pimp; a prostitute. 2. One who manages an entertainment that offers as its chief attraction the physical charms of young women. 3. An actors' agent; a talent salesman. *Since c1935.* 4. An employee or owner of an employment agency.

fleshpot. *n.* Lit., a brothel or entertainment where seminude girls or women may be seen; fig., a place catering to the vices or weaknesses of the flesh, as saloons, gambling houses, or the like. *Stand.*

flick. *n.* 1. A motion picture. → 2. A motion picture theater. —er. *v.i.* To faint; to pretend to faint, as from hunger, or to feign a fit in order to gain sympathy. *Hobo use.* *n.* 1. A beggar who pretends to faint or have a fit. *Hobo use.* 2. A movie. *Mainly used by newsp. columnists.* —ers. *n.sing. & pl.* A movie; the movies; the motion picture industry. *Mainly newsp. columnist use.*

flier. *n.* = flyer.

flim. *adj.* = cool. *Some cool use.*

flim-flam; flimflam. *v.t.* To trick, to deceive, to cheat or victimize. *n.* Trickery; a swindle; deception. —mer. *n.* A grafter or crook.

flimsy. *n.* 1. A sheet of thin paper. → 2. A duplicate order, often a carbon copy, written on onion skin or tissue paper; in offices, a carbon copy of invoices; in stores and restaurants, a duplicate of the employee's bill of sale, against which the cash receipts are checked; in railroading, a train order.

fling. *n.* 1. A period of irresponsible fun or enjoyment, usu. as a relief from or before one assumes responsibilities. *Usu. in "one last fling." Colloq.* 2. A try; an attempt. *Usu. in "to have a fling at."* 3. A dance; a party. *Teenage and student use.* —er. *n.* Specif., a baseball pitcher.

flip. *adj.* 1. Impudent; flippant; fresh; glib; having continuous excitement, enthusiasm, appreciation, or the like. *From "flippant."* 2. Reverse; of, on, or pertaining to the reverse or "other" side of a phonograph record; of or pertaining to the less popular song on a phonograph record containing a popular song. *n.* 1. A favor. *Teenage and student use c1940.* 2. Something that causes uproarious laughter. 3. An enthusiast; a devotee. *v.t.* 1. To catch or board a train, esp. to board a train in motion or to ride free. *Hobo and railroad use since c1920.* 2. To score a point or points in a basketball game. *Lit., to flip the ball through the basket.* 3. To cause one to laugh uproariously. *Since c1950.* 4. To make a most favorable impression on a person; to excite or shock someone; to arouse someone's enthusiasm or sense of wonder; to overwhelm. *Orig. and mainly cool use. v.i.* 1. To burst into laughter; to laugh uproariously; to flip [one's] lid. 2. To react violently; to react with enthusiasm; to have a sense of wonder and rapport with; to dig completely; to like or appreciate greatly; to be overwhelmed. *Orig. c1950 cool use; now common to most young adults.*

flip-flop. *n.* A handspring; a fluctuation; a change of direction, attitude, stature, or the like. *An instance in which a reduplication conveys a fig. meaning different from that of the basic words.*

flip [one's] lid. To show an extreme response; specif. to become violently angry; to lose one's sanity; to burst out laughing. *Specif., to laugh uproariously and without control; to go into an uncontrolled, violent rage; to like or approve of something without reservation. Orig. late bop and early cool use. Fairly common since c1948.*

flip [one's] lip. To talk; esp. to talk idly or to talk nonsense.

flipper. *n.* 1. A human hand. *Since cW.W.I.* 2. The arm. 3. A slingshot.

flip [one's] raspberry = to flip [one's] lid.

flip side. The reverse or "other" side of a phonograph record;

specif., the reverse or "other" side of a phonograph record whose major side contains a very popular song; the less popular of the two sides of a phonograph record. *Cool, rock and roll, and general teenage use. Pop. by disc jockey use.*

flip [one's] wig = flip [one's] lid.

fliv. *n.* An automobile; flivver. *v.i.* To fail or flop. *Said of a performance or performer.* —ver. *n.* 1. A hoax. → 2. A failure. 3. A small, cheap, old, dilapidated automobile. *Orig. an early model Ford, c1918. The term is now used humorously in ref. to expensive, heavy modern cars.* → 4. A small, cheap, old, or dilapidated airplane.

flix. *n.pl.* = flickers.

float. *v.i.* To be emotionally or spiritually uplifted; to be extremely relaxed, happy, optimistic, or the like; specif. because one is in love, has been complimented or rewarded, or is under the influence of drugs or alcohol. *n.* An hour or a period in which a student has no class; a free period. —er. *n.* 1. A vagrant; an itinerant worker; a skilled or nonskilled factory worker who changes jobs and union locals often. *Colloq.* → 2. A police order to leave town within 24 or 48 hours; a jail sentence suspended if the offender leaves town in a short time; often given to hobos. 3. In baseball, a slow pitched ball that appears to float in air. 4. A loan; money loaned or borrowed. *From the expression "to float a loan."* 5. A theft or fire insurance policy insuring an article or articles anywhere, no matter where the owner may travel. —ing. *adj.* 1. Drunk. 2. Under the influence of narcotics. 3. Sublimely happy.

floating crap game. A professional crap game held in a different place every day, to avoid police detection.

floating on air. Supremely happy; fig., "high" with happiness, as from praise, a just reward for one's efforts, or esp. from being accepted as a lover.

floating on [the] clouds. 1. To be sublimely happy or contented, usu. because one is in love, but often because one has been complimented or successful. **2.** To be unrealistic; to have plans beyond one's capabilities.

float one. To cash a check; to make a loan.

flock. *n.* A large number; quite a few.

floor. *v.t.* **1.** To knock someone down, as to the floor; to knock someone unconscious. → **2.** To shock or surprise someone, fig., so that one faints or is overcome with shock or surprise. *In this sense almost always used in the passive.* **3.** To drive a car at its maximum speed; lit., to hold the gas pedal of a car all the way to its maximum position, down to the floor-(boards).

floorboard. *v.i.* To go fast by keeping a car's accelerator pressed all the way down to the floorboard.

floozie; floosie; floozy; floogy; flugie; faloosie. *n.* An undisciplined, promiscuous, flirtatious, irresponsible girl or woman, esp. a cynical, calculating one who is only concerned with having a good time or living off the generosity of men; a cheap or loose girl or woman.

flop. *v.t.* To succeed by trickery or dishonesty. *v.i.* **1.** To lie down to rest or sleep; to go to bed; to sleep; to stay overnight. **2.** To fail completely; specif., to fail to gain a desired reaction from others; to fail to convince or entertain. *n.* **1.** Any trick used in successful cheating. **2.** A place to sleep; a shelter; a bed. → **3.** A night's sleep. **4.** A complete failure; any person or thing that fails, as a prize fighter, an entertainer, a play, a movie, a joke, or the like.

flophouse. *n.* A very cheap roominghouse or hotel where many men sleep on cots in one room.

flopperoo; floperoo. *n.* = flop; any spectacularly unsuccessful person or thing, esp. a stage show or movie. *Since c1930. Pop. by "Variety," the theater trade paper.*

flossy; flossie. *adj.* Overfancy, overshiny, overelegant.

flour. *n.* Face powder.

flower. *n.* A homosexual.

flu; flue. *n.* Influenza. *Since c1840. Colloq.*

flub. *v.t.* **1.** To make a blunder, error, or mistake, esp. an embarrassing one; to make a *faux pas. Very common.* **2.** To evade one's assigned duty.

flubdub; flub-dub. *n.* Awkwardness; ineptitude.

flub off; flub up = flub.

flub the dub. 1. To evade one's duty; to loaf. **2.** To think and perform inefficiently and slowly. *Both meanings common W.W.II use.* **3.** To spoil or ruin by blunders or mistakes; to ruin or fail to take advantage of one's chances for success. *Mainly boy use.*

fluff. *n.* **1.** A girl or young woman, usu. in "bit of fluff" or "piece of fluff." **2.** A slip of the tongue; a mispronunciation; momentarily forgetting what one is supposed to say or do, as caused by shyness or nervousness; specif., such a mistake made by an actor, announcer, or public speaker. **3.** A dismissal; the brush-off. **4.** Any job or task that is easy to perform. *v.t., v.i.* To make a mistake in speaking, as an actor forgetting a line or missing a cue; to make a mistake in pronunciation, or the like.

fluff, give [someone] the. To reject; to snub; to brush off a person.

fluff log. Lit. and fig., a man's small pocket notebook listing the names, addresses, and telephone numbers of accessible or available girls; a little black book. *Some W.W.II use.*

fluff off. 1. To snub, slight, or humiliate; to dismiss someone curtly. 2. To shirk or neglect one's duties or responsibilities. *W.W.II Armed Forces use.* 3. To waste time; to idle. *W.W.II use.*

fluff-off. *n.* A shirker; a blunderer.

flug = phlug.

flugie = floozie.

fluid = embalming fluid.

fluke. *n.* 1. A failure. 2. A fortuitous accident; a freak success that could not be repeated. → 3. A sham; a pretension. *v.t. & v.i.* To fail.

flukum; flookum; flookem. *n.* 1. Any of various kinds of cheap, nearly worthless, but gaudy or apparently useful merchandise, as nickel-plated cigarette lighters, silverware, cleaning fluids, potato peelers, or the like, which are attractive at first sight. *Orig. c1925 pitchman use.* 2. A powder to which water and sugar are added to make a soft drink.

flumadiddle; flummadiddle; flummerdiddle; flummydiddle. *n. & adj.* Nonsense; nonsensical. *Dial.*

flummox. *n.* A failure; said of a plan or action.

flunk. *v.t.* 1. For a teacher to give a student a failing grade. → 2. For a student to fail an examination or a course. *Colloq. since c1910.* *v.i.* 1. For a student to fail in an exam or a course. → 2. To fail in a personal or business endeavor. *Not restricted to student use. n.* A failure by a student in his studies, a course, a recitation, or an examination. → 2. A course which a student has failed; the failing grade. —ey; —ie; —y; —ee. *n.* 1. One who does menial work, such as a porter, errand boy, dish washer, waiter, or the like. 2. A young worker; an apprentice; an assistant. 3. A student who fails in his studies.

flunk out. To be dismissed from prep school or college because of failing work.

flush. *adj.* In possession of sufficient money; having much money; wealthy. *n.* A wealthy person. *v.t.* To absent oneself from a class; to cut a class. *Student use.*

flush, in a. Confused, bewildered.

flute. *n.* A suit. —r. *n.* A male homosexual.

fluzy = floozie.

fly. *n.* An alert, knowing person. *adj.* Knowing; nimble-minded; alert; saucy; fresh. —ing. *adj.* 1. Driving, moving, or working at great speed. *Colloq.* 2. Under the influence of a narcotic drug. → 3. Extremely happy; ecstatic; elated. *"Cool" use.* 4. On duty in a place removed from one's home city or district.

fly, let. 1. To begin anything, esp. a tirade or bawling out. *Fig.,* to let the words fly out at someone. 2. To spit.

fly a kite. 1. To write a letter; esp. to smuggle a letter into or out of prison. *Underworld use.* 2. To send an airmail letter, often requesting money or assistance. *Modern use, mainly underworld but gaining some popularity.*

fly a kite!, Go. Go jump in the lake! Get lost!

fly-bait. *n.* 1. A member of Phi Beta Kappa. *Used humorously or derogatorily; from "Phi Bate," a colloq. abbrev. of "Phi Beta Kappa."* 2. A corpse.

fly ball. 1. An eccentric, unusual, undesirable person. 2. A homosexual.

fly ball; fly bob; fly bull; fly cop; fly dick; fly mug. A detective, a plainclothes policeman, a policeman assigned to special duty. *"Fly cop," c1860, is the oldest and has been the most widely used term; "fly ball," "fly bob," and "fly bull" have seen wide hobo use. Note the Eng. "bob" = policeman. "Fly dick" and "fly mug" are the latest terms. All freq. with hyphen.*

fly-boy; flyboy; fly bo. *n.* 1. An aviator, esp. a glamorous, heroic, or daring aviator. *In W.W.II usu. used ironically.* 2. A U.S. Air Force pilot; any member of the Air Force. *W.W.II Armed Forces* use. *Now derog., implying snob-bishness, youth, and cautious-ness.* → 3. Any airplane pilot.

fly bull = fly ball.

fly cake. Raisin cake. *Jocular use.*

fly-chaser. *n.* In baseball, an out-fielder.

flychick. *n.* An attractive, hip girl.

fly cop = fly ball.

fly dick = fly ball.

flyer. *n.* A chance; a gamble. *Usu. in "to take a flyer at (some-thing)." Colloq.*

fly guy = fly-boy.

flying bedstead. An early, lumber-ing, but comparatively stable and steady airplane.

flying blowtorch. A jet fighter air-plane. *Synthetic sl.*

flying coffin. A glider or airplane. *W.W.II Air Force and para-trooper use.*

fly light. To miss a meal; to be hungry.

fly mug = fly ball.

fly off the handle. To lose one's temper. *Colloq.*

fly right. To be honest and useful; to be "straight"; to do the ethi-cally or socially proper thing; to live or act according to ethical standards.

fly the coop. To leave or depart, often secretly or guiltily. *Colloq. since c1910.*

fly trap. The human mouth.

fofarraw; foofooraw. *n.* 1. A loud disturbance or interruption; a commotion. *Dial.* 2. Gaudy wear-ing apparel, particularly acces-sories such as bracelets, belts, etc. 3. Ostentation; show-off; bluster. *Prob. from the Sp. "fanfaron" and Fr. "frou-frou."*

fog. *v.i.* To smoke cigarettes. *Dial.* *v.t.* 1. To kill, usu. to kill by shooting. 2. To hurl, pitch, or throw something, as a baseball, with great force and speed. *n.* Steam. —(g)y. *adj.* Confused; con-fusing, perplexing; unrealized, not specific enough. —matic. *n.* A drink of liquor. *adj.* Drunk.

fog, in a. Dazed; confused, baf-fled, perplexed. *Colloq.*

fog it in. In baseball, to pitch a fast ball; to throw hard.

fogle. *n.* A neck handkerchief.

fogy; fogey. *n.* Money received as longevity pay on completing five years of military service in peace-time or three years in wartime. *Some W.W.II Armed Forces use.*

fold. *v.i.* To go out of business owing to lack of funds; to come to an end. —ing. *n.* Money.

folding cabbage = folding money.

folding green. Money.

folding lettuce = folding money. See lettuce.

folding money. Paper banknotes, as opposed to coins; a compara-tively large amount of money; money.

Foley Square. *n.* The Federal Bureau of Investigation. *Because the main Eastern office of the FBI is located in Foley Square, lower Manhattan, N.Y.C.*

follow through. To press one's ad-vantage until success is gained; to follow one action with the next obvious one; to ascertain that something has been done prop-erly. *Colloq.* **follow-through.** *n.* A result; anything that happens after something else; the next logical action.

follow up = follow through; **fol-low-up.** *n.* A consequence or ex-pected result.

food for the squirrels. 1. A stupid or foolish person; a nut. 2. A stupid job, task, or scheme.

Fooey! *exclam.* = Phooey!

foo-foo. *n.* 1. A fool; a worthless person. *Dial. From "fofarraw."* 2. Perfume. *From "fofarraw."*

foofooraw. *n.* = fofarraw.

fool. *adj.* Foolish. *Colloq. n.* An unusually able person in any field of activity, as a dancing fool, a diving fool; an enthusiast, a buff, a fan.

fool around. 1. To do small, un-necessary, idle operations. 2. To tease. → 3. To handle an object idly, as if examining or repair-ing it. → 4. To caress one of the opposite sex in a teasing way; to make a faint, idle, or jocular attempt at seduction.

foot, give [someone] the. To kick.

football = Italian football.

footie-footie; footy-footy. *n.* Lit. and fig., = footsie.

foot in it, put [one's]. To blunder; to say or do the wrong thing; to be indiscreet or gauche. *Colloq.*

footsie. *n.* 1. Lit., the pedal equivalent of amorous hand-holding; touching, pushing, and/or more or less clumsily caressing with one's foot, as under a table, a foot or the feet of one of the opposite sex. → 2. Fig., any instance of friendly or intimate action, esp. as in courting business favors or to atone for past unacceptable behavior.

footsie-wootsie. *n.* Lit. and fig., = footsie.

footsy-footsy. *n.* = footsie.

Fooy! *exclam.* = Phooey!

foozle. *v.t.* To entangle; to blunder or bungle; to make an error. *Still in use.* *n.* 1. An old fogey; an old-fashioned, conservative person. *Since c1850. From "fossil."* → 2. An elder; a parent. *Teenage use since c1950.* 3. In sports, a bungled plan, an error. *Since c1920.*

for, go. 1. To favor enthusiastically a person or thing; to accept. 2. To fall in love with; to love.

for certain. Certain; sure.

For crying out loud! *exclam.* An expression signifying surprise, often surprise at another's stupidity.

for free. Free of charge; gratis; without compensation. *From "for nothing"; usu. applied to small items or favors, often humorously.*

for it. 1. In favor of something, as a proposal or plan. *Colloq.* 2. Expecting or prepared for punishment, chastisement, or a strong verbal reprimand.

fork-hander. *n.* In baseball, a left-handed pitcher.

fork out; fork over; fork up. To pay over or hand over. *Colloq. since c1840.*

forks. *n.* Fingers.

for real. 1. Real; existing; possible. *Often in* Are you for real? *May imply either "too good to be true" or, orig., "unbelievable." Popularized by comedian Jerry Lewis, c1950.* 2. Really.

for serious. Seriously; for a serious purpose.

for the birds. Not liked, wanted, or respected by the speaker; unacceptable to, improbable for, or corny to the speaker; fig., not for the speaker but for the birds = crazy or old people.

for the cuff. Confidential.

for the [one's] hat = under [one's] hat.

forthwith. *adv.* Immediately. *Colloq. n.* An order to be carried out immediately.

forty-eight. *n.* Week-end liberty; a 48-hour pass. *W.W. II USN use.*

fortyfive; .45. *n.* 1. A .45-caliber pistol. 2. A phonograph record, usu. of popular music, made to play on a turntable that revolves at a speed of 45 revolutions per minute.

forty-four. *n.* A prostitute. *From rhyming sl., "forty-four" = a whore.*

forty-'leven. *n.* An indefinitely large number; a great many.

forty ways for (from, to) Sunday. Every which way; in all directions, in confusion. *Still in use.*

forty winks. 1. A short sleep; a nap. *Colloq.* 2. A short time.

fossil. *n.* 1. An old fogey; an elderly person; a conservative, old-fashioned person. *From "fossil."* 2. A parent; an elder. *Teenage use since c1955. From "fossil," reinforced by "foozle."*

fotog = photog.

foul ball. 1. An inferior prize fighter. *Prize fight use since c1920.* 2. An unsuccessful, useless person; a flat tire. 3. An odd person; one having unacceptable personal, religious, or political beliefs. *Since c1945.*

fouled up; fouled-up. *adj.* In a state of confusion; confused; resulting from or a product of incompetence and blundering; ruined; spoiled.

foul-mouth. *n.* A person given to speaking obscenities and oaths. *Colloq.* **—ed.** *adj.* Given to uttering freq. obscenities. *Colloq.*

foulup; foul-up. *n.* A person who makes frequent blunders; a blunder, a mix-up. **foul up.** To ruin or spoil something; to make a mess of things; to demonstrate one's incompetence. *Wide use cW.W.II and after.*

foundry. *n.* A business office.

four and one. 1. Friday; lit. the fifth working day of the week. → 2. Pay-day. *Negro use.*

four-bagger. *n.* In baseball, a home run.

four-bit. *adj.* Costing 50¢. **four bits.** *n.* Half a dollar; 50¢. *Colloq.* Lit., two times two bits.

four-by-four. *n.* A four-wheel drive truck having four forward gear speeds. *Army and truck-driver use.*

four-eyes; four eyes. *n.* A person who wears glasses.

four-flusher; fourflusher; four flusher. *n.* One who bluffs; a pretender; esp. one who pretends to have money while living off or borrowing from others; one who does not pay his debts. *Colloq.* **—ing.** *adj.* Living off or supported by others; borrowing from others.

four hundred, the. Socially prominent people (implying also refinement and wealth); the elite. *Attrib. to Ward McAllister, New York socialite.*

four letter man. A dumb or stupid man, usu. a student. *Some student use. The four letters are "d-u-m-b." See "three letter man" for the derivation.*

four-o. *adv.* Perfect; o.k. *W.W.II USN use.*

four sheets in [to] the wind = three sheets in the wind.

four-striper. *n.* A U.S. Navy captain. *From the gold stripes worn on the sleeve. Since W.W.I.*

four-time; four-time loser. Fig., a desperate criminal. *In some states a person four times convicted of crime receives a mandatory sentence of life imprisonment. Because of the severity of the mandatory sentence, such a criminal may go to extreme and desperate lengths to avoid arrest.*

four wide ones. In baseball, a base on balls.

fox. *v.t.* To fool, outwit, or outsmart someone.

foxhole. *n.* A small individual trench or hole dug in the ground by a soldier as protection and concealment. *Wide W.W.II use.*

fox paw. A faux pas. *Still in use.*

fracture. *v.t.* 1. To cause uproarious laughter. → 2. Used ironically to cause someone to become sad, angry, or disgusted. *Usu. in "You fracture me."* 3. To evoke a strong reaction in someone; to cause someone to flip. *Some bop and cool use since c1946.*

fractured. Drunk. *Fairly common since c1940.*

'fraidy cat. One, esp. a boy or youth, who is timorous. *Common use by younger children; some adult use.*

frail. *n.* A girl or young woman.

frail eel. A pretty girl. *Harlem Negro use.*

frail job. 1. A woman, esp. a sexually attractive one, or one known to be promiscuous. 2. Sexual intercourse with a woman.

frame. *n.* 1. A human physique; a body; esp. the torso of a sexually attractive girl. 2. A pocket, pocketbook, or wallet. *Some underworld use.* 3. A heterosexual male who looks effeminate and is attractive to homosexuals. 4. In sports, a complete unit: a round of a prize fight, an inning of baseball, a quarter of a football game, etc. 5. A conspiracy against an innocent person; the act of framing someone. *v.t.* **1.** To arrest or to cause a person's arrest by means of false evidence. **2.** To put in running order. *Carnival use.*

frame-dame. *n.* A girl known only for her sex appeal, and who has little intelligence or personality. *Some teenage use since c1940.*

frame up. To victimize an innocent person by conspiracy; esp. to arrest or to cause a person's arrest by means of a faked evidence. **frame-up.** *n.* **1.** A conspiracy against an innocent person; the act of framing someone. **2.** A display of goods for sale. *Pitchman use.*

frank. *n.* A frankfurter. *Colloq.*

frantic. *adj.* **1.** Exciting; satisfying; wonderful; cool. *Wide bop use since c1946. Some cool use.* → **2.** Too emotional; motivated by or involved in the crass material pursuits of life; ruled by habit and a love of security; having middle-class values; worldly. *Beat use since c1955.*

frat. *n.* **1.** A college fraternity. *Common student use since c1900, but officially frowned upon by most national fraternities and considered unsophisticated.* **2.** A member of a fraternity. *Student use since c1900. adj.* Pertaining to a fraternity or fraternity life. *Common student use since c1900.* **—ernize.** *v.i.* **1.** To associate closely, esp. sexually, with the women of an enemy or occupied country. *Wide W.W.II Army use.* → **2.** To associate closely, esp. sexually, with any girl or woman. *Some use since c1945.*

frater. *n.* A member of a college fraternity; esp. a fellow member or fraternity brother. *From the Latin.*

frau. *n.* One's wife.

frazzled. *adj.* Drunk.

freak. *n.* A male homosexual. *Mainly jazz use.*

freckles. *n.pl.* Tobacco for rolling a cigarette. *From its appearance. W.W.II USN and Marines use.*

free = for free.

free-and-easy. *n.* A saloon.

freebie; freebee; freeby. *n.* Anything that is free of charge; anything given or performed without cost to the receiver or audience. *adj.* Free; free of charge.

free-load; free load; freeload. *v.i.* To eat, drink, be entertained, vacation, or live without charge or at another's expense. *Common since W.W.II. n.* A meal, food, whisky, or the like enjoyed at another's expense; free food or drink. **—er.** *n.* **1.** One who eats or drinks without expense to himself; a nonpaying customer or guest; one who stuffs himself with free food and drink, as at a party; one who habitually eats, drinks, or vacations at the expense of another; specif., one whose host is a business firm or an employee who has a business expense account. *Very common since W.W.II.* **2.** An open-house party; a social gathering which offers free refreshments. **—ing.** *n.* The act or an instance of eating or drinking without cost or at another's expense.

free-rider. *n.* A nonunion worker who benefits from pay scales, working conditions, privileges, or the like gained by the union workers in his factory.

free show. A look or glance, usu. at a girl's or woman's thighs or breasts, or occasionally at a nude woman, most often without the female's knowledge or consent, as when a girl or woman crosses her legs, or inadvertently forgets to close a door while disrobing. *Mainly boy and young teenager use.*

freeside. *adv.* Outside; specif. outside the walls of a penitentiary. *Prison use.*

free ticket = free transportation.

free transportation; free ticket. In baseball, a base on balls.

free-wheeling. *adj.* **1.** Spending money liberally. **2.** Unauthorized; independent; unrestricted; without concern for others.

freeze. *v.i.* 1. Lit., to remain motionless or still, in hope of not being seen. 2. Fig., to remain in the place, job, location, or the like where one is; to be satisfied with what one has. *v.t.* 1. = put the freeze on. 2. To snub.

freeze on [someone], put the. 1. = put the chill on [someone]. 2. To snub.

freight, pull [one's]. To leave; to go away. *Used since 1885. Orig. trucker and railroad use.*

French. *n.* Spoken profanity, obscenity, or oaths; profanity. *Almost always in "pardon my French" = excuse my profanity.*

French-inhale. *n. & adj.* The act of exhaling a mouthful of smoke and then inhaling it through the nose. *Considered exotic and ultrasophisticated by teenagers and students; confined to beginning smokers.*

French kiss. A passionate kiss in which the tongue of one person explores the tongue and mouth of the other. *Teenage use.*

French leave. 1. The act or an instance of leaving or departing without proper permission, esp. to leave a USN ship or Army post without authorization; to go or be awol. *Orig. W.W.I use.* 2. The act or an instance of departing secretly or without notifying one's host, friends, creditors, or the like.

French post card. Any pornographic photograph. *From the traditional tourists' story of Paris street vendors selling pornographic picture postcards and photographs openly.*

French walk. 1. = bum's rush, the. 2. Specif., ejecting a man from a place forcibly by grabbing the seat of his pants with one hand and the back of his collar with the other and thus forcing him to walk until he reaches the door.

fresh. *n.sing.* A college freshman. *Colloq. n.pl.* College freshmen; a freshman class. *Usu. preceded by "the." Colloq. adj.* 1. Fresh-

man; belonging or pertaining to college freshmen. 2. Impudent; impertinent; presumptuous; disrespectful. *Colloq. Usu. a pred. adj., sometimes an attrib. adj. →* 3. Specif., apt to try to take sexual liberties; flirtatious. *Colloq.*

fresh one. 1. A new prisoner. *Prison use.* 2. Another, newly made highball.

fried. Drunk.

fried egg. 1. The U.S. Military Academy insigne worn on the full-dress hat. *West Point use.* 2. The flag of Japan. *W.W.II use. In ref. to the red disk shown on the yellow background of the flag.*

frig. [taboo]. *v.t.* To trick or cheat someone. *Since c1925.*

frill. *n.* A girl or woman.

Frisco. *proper n.* San Francisco, California. *Colloq. A term much disapproved by San Franciscans.*

frisk. *v.t.* 1. To search a person for anything that he may have on him; specif., to pat or rub a dressed person in all places where a pocket is or wherever something might be carried or concealed. *Underworld, police, and hobo use until c1920; now universally known. One is usu. frisked by the police, as for a concealed weapon. →* 2. To search, inspect, or look over any place, as a building, an apartment, a house, or the like, to ascertain its contents or to find contraband or evidence. *n.* A search of a person or place.

Fritz. *n. A* German. *Some W.W.I use.* **fritz.** *v.t.* To put anything out of working order.

frog; Frog. *n.* A Frenchman. *Usu. derisive, if not derog., use. Prob. from "frog-eater." Orig. W.W.I Army use, adopted from British Army use; still common.*

frogman. *n.* 1. A specialist in underwater work, such as placing mines, exploring sunken ships, conducting experiments in marine biology, or the like; esp. an underwater swimmer who uses an oxygen tank strapped to his back and large rubber flippers on his feet to aid in swimming. *Since c1940.* 2. Specif., a U.S. Navy skin-diver or underwater specialist, usu. assigned to demolition. *W.W.II use.*

frogskin. *n.* A one-dollar bill.

frog-sticker. *n.* 1. A long-bladed knife; esp. a pocket knife. 2. A bayonet. *W.W.II Army use.*

from A to Z. Completely; thoroughly.

from hell to breakfast. Thoroughly; from A to Z; from one end to the other.

from hunger. Inferior; cheap; ugly; lowbrow; disliked; unwanted; corny; hammy. *Orig. assoc. with jive, swing, and jazz use c1935.*

from nothing. Nothing; not to know.

frompy = frumpy.

front. *n.* 1. The successful or respectable appearance one conveys by one's clothing, accessories, manners, possessions, or friends; esp. an assumed or calculated appearance to impress others. *Common use.* 2. A respectable, impressive-appearing, or successful person chosen to represent a group and impart to the group an appearance of respectability or success. 3. Legal or normal activities, usu. business activities, used to mask illegal activities, gambling, or the like. *v.i.* To recommend or speak favorably of a person or thing.

front and center. *imp.* A command to a person to present himself immediately; a stern way of saying "Come here."

front door. The administrative staff of a circus, as distinguished from the performers, called "the back yard." *Circus use. adj.* Respectable, honest; said of a place or business venture.

front names. The first name of a person; a given name; a Christian name.

front office. 1. The administrative or main offices of a business. →

2. Administrative officers; executives. → 3. One's husband or wife; anyone who makes final decisions. *Used humorously.* → 4. A police station. *Underworld use. adj.* Final; authoritative; formed by executives or administrators. *Usu. in "front office decision" ". . . policy," or the like. All forms and meanings since c1940. One of the sl. terms coming from big business.*

frosh. *n.sing.* A first-year student in high school, prep school, college, or university; a college freshman of either sex. *Colloq. In Germany, a student while still in the gymnasium, before entering a university, is called a "Frosch" = a frog. However, the U.S. term may merely be based on the first syllable of "freshman," with a vowel change. n.pl.* College freshmen of either sex or both sexes; a freshman class. *Colloq. adj.* Of or pertaining to freshmen. *Colloq.*

frost. *n.* 1. A failure; something, as a new book, that is coldly received. *Ascribed to F. Scott Fitzgerald.* 2. = cold shoulder.

frou-frou. *n.* Inordinately ornate dress or adornments, esp. women's *From Fr.*

frown. *n.* A drink containing Coca-Cola and lemon flavor.

frowsy. *n.* A frowzy woman.

frozen. *adj.* Frightened.

fruit. *n.* 1. A shabby, unkempt, eccentric fellow; an odd person. *Teenage and student use c1910–c1940. Still in use.* 2. A homosexual. *Since c1930. Common teenage use since c1940. The most common meaning. Kinder than "fag," "fairy," "queen."* —**y.** *adj.* 1. Eccentric; odd; nutty. *Teenage use since c1935.* 2. Homosexual. —**cake.** *n.* 1. An insane person. *From the popular phrase "nutty as* [*or "nuttier than"*] *a fruit-cake."* 2. An eccentric or unusual person.

fruit salad. Campaign ribbons, representing decorations and campaign medals, worn on the breast of the tunic by members of the Armed Forces.

frump. *n.* A dowdy woman. *Colloq.* —*y.* *adj.* Homely, dowdy, dilapidated.

fry. *v.i.*, *v.t.* 1. To put to death in the electric chair; to die in the electric chair. *Since c1930.* 2. To chastise or be chastised; to act with malice or be the recipient of malice. 3. To remove the kinks from one's hair with a hot curling iron. *Negro use.*

fu. *n.* Marijuana.

fuddy. *adj.* Untidy; disordered; inefficient; outdated. *From "fuddy-duddy."* *n.* = **fuddy-duddy.**

fuddydud = **fuddy-duddy.**

fuddy-duddy. *n.* An old-fashioned, unimaginative, conservative, and timorous person, esp. an elderly person; a senile person; a fussy, ineffectual person; an old fogy. *Since c1900.* *adj.* Ineffectual; outdated.

fudge. *v.i.*, *v.t.* To cheat a little; to hedge; to fib; to misrepresent. *n.* 1. Nonsense; bunk. 2. A polite curse word or expletive uttered when something goes wrong. *Often in* **oh fudge.**

fuff. *expl.* A reply to an obvious, unnecessary statement.

full. *n.* = **fed up.**

full-blast; full blast. *adj.* Complete; on a large scale; intense. *adv.* At or with maximum speed, efficiency, or intensity. *Colloq.*

full of beans; full of hops; full of prunes. 1. Actively foolish, mistaken, exaggerating. 2. Lively, energetic, high-spirited. *All terms have both meanings, though first meaning much more common. "Full of prunes" is prob. the oldest and most popular; "full of beans" is least popular. Note that all three foods are cheap, easy to come by, and considered laxatives.*

full of hot air. Mistaken; exaggerating; expounding false information.

full ride. With all expenses paid.

full up. 1. Completely full. 2. = **fed up.** 3. On the verge of tears; feeling strong emotional sentiments.

fungo. *n.* 1. In baseball, a practice fly ball (hit to a fielder) that the batter makes by throwing the ball up a few feet and hitting it as it falls. *Fungos are used to give fielders practice.* 2. A long, light bat used in baseball practice. → 3. Any baseball bat. 4. A mistake; a blooper. 5. Any unrewarding act. *v.i.* 1. To bat fungos. 2. To make a mistake.

fungo stick = **fungo.**

funk. *n.* A mood of idle depression.

funnies, the. *n.* A page or pages of a newspaper that contain comic strips; a funny paper. *Colloq.*

funny. *adj.* 1. Odd; eccentric; unusual; suspicious. *Colloq.* 2. Crazy. *adv.* Oddly; in an unusual manner; suspiciously. *Colloq.* *n.* A joke; a funny remark or wisecrack.

funny business. Deceit; trickery; fraud; any crooked or unethical dealings.

funny house. 1. An insane asylum. 2. A sanatorium or hospital for drug addicts or alcoholics.

furniture. *n.* A sexually attractive girl. *Usu. in "a nice little piece of furniture."*

furp. *v.i.* To go on a date; to escort a girl to a party.

fuse = **blow a fuse.**

fuss. *v.t.*, *v.i.* To visit or escort a girl; to date a girl.

fuss-budget. *n.* A fussy person; esp. an old shrew.

future. *n.* One's own fiancée or fiancé.

fuzz. *n.* A policeman or detective. *Underworld, hobo, and carnival use; hot rod use since c1950.* —*y*; —*ie.* *n.* 1. A policeman, esp. a diligent one. 2. A sure thing, a certainty, esp. in gambling, specif. in horse racing. *adv.*, *adj.* Partially drunk.

fuzzled. Drunk.

G

G. *n.* A thousand dollars.

gab. *n.* 1. Talk; gossip; gabble. 2. The mouth. *v.i.* To talk. —**ber.** *n.* A talkative person; specif., a radio commentator or critic. —**by.** *adj.* Talkative; overtalkative. —**fest.** *n.* A talk fest; a social gathering for conversation. *Colloq. since c1895.*

gaboon = goboon.

Gabriel. *n.* Any trumpet player. *Synthetic jive and jazz use.*

gadget. *n.* 1. A device, esp. a small mechanical device with which one is not familiar; any device whose proper name is not known. *Colloq. since c1925.* 2. Any useless item, such as trimming, added to a garment, automobile, or the like, solely to cause a change in appearance or style. 3. An Air Force cadet; also, an unimportant person. *Some Army Air Force use since c1945.*

gaff. *n.* = gimmick; lit. and fig., a concealed device that makes something work. *Carnival and pitchman use.* *v.t.* 1. To equip something with a gaff in order to trick, cheat, or deceive. 2. To reprimand; to bawl out. *Some USN use.* —**er.** *n.* 1. The manager of a circus. *Circus use.* 2. The chief electrician on a movie set. *Hollywood use.*

gag. *n.* 1. Almost any kind of joke or trick, whether intended to amuse or to deceive or cheat; a ruse; a funny story, practical joke, or the like. *In both theater and general use. Colloq.* 2. A trite or old excuse or alibi. *Hobo and underworld use.* 3. A prison sentence. *Some underworld use.*

gaga; ga-ga. *adj.* Lit. and fig., crazy; "crazy"; silly; irrational; having lost one's objectivity and perspective.

gage. *n.* 1. Cheap whisky. 2. Tobacco, cigarettes, cigars, or chewing tobacco. **Stick of gage** = a cigarette, either a standard cigarette or a marijuana cigarette. 3. Marijuana; a marijuana cigarette. *Narcotic addict use. adj.*

Under the influence of marijuana. —**d.** *adj.* Drunk.

gage butt; gauge butt. *n.* A marijuana cigarette. *Addict use.*

gagers. *n.pl.* The eyes.

gage up, get one's. 1. To become angry, esp. to become so angry that one takes action against the person or thing causing the anger. 2. To become emotional. 3. To become drunk.

gal. *n.* A girl or woman, esp. a young, pleasant, pert woman. *Colloq. and now widely accepted, "standard" speech.*

gall. *n.* Effrontery; impudence; conceit. *Since c1880; now colloq.*

gallaway = galways.

gallery. *n.* A porch; esp. a large porch with corner columns, as on a large house designed in the Federal style. *Southern use. Dial.*

galley-west. *adv.* Thoroughly; with great force; in confusion.

galloping dominoes. Dice. *Common usage, but somewhat synthetic.*

galways; gallaway. *n.* An ear-to-ear chin beard, as worn by a stage Irishman.

gam. *v.i. & v.t.* To boast, to show off. *Negro use. n.* 1. A discussion; a conference; a meeting or gathering which includes a discussion or much talking. —**s.** *n.pl.* The legs of a person; usu., but not invariably, the shapely legs of an attractive girl or woman. *From the Ital. "gamba" = leg.*

gamin. *n.* = pixie.

gander. *n.* A look; a glance; a visual inspection. *Usu. in* **take a gander.** *Since c1930.* 2. *v.i., v.t.* To look at or into something; to examine by looking.

gandy dancer. 1. A railroad section-hand or track laborer; one who lays railroad tracks, grades roadbeds, or digs drainage ditches. *Since c1915 hobo, railroad, and lumberjack use. From the rhythmic dancelike movements made by laborers straightening rails and smoothing gravel.* 2. A seller of novelties at a carnival. *Carnival use.*

ganef; ganof = goniff.

gangster. *n.* One who belongs to a gang. *Orig.* in ref. to politicians; now mainly in ref. to criminals. *Political use archaic by c1925; criminal use colloq. since c1925.*

gang up on [someone]. To unite against someone, as in a fight, argument, or the like. *Colloq.*

gap; jap. *v.i.* To witness a crime without taking part in it.

gaposis. *n.* A mythical disease, the symptom of which is a customary gap in one's clothing, as between buttons or when one's shirt and trousers or blouse and skirt do not properly meet. *A synthetic commercialism.*

garbage. *n.* 1. Food or meals. *Hobo and logger use.* → 2. Small pieces of food, esp. fruit or greens used to add visual appeal to a main dish or drink, such as parsley on a piece of meat or a cherry in a cocktail. 3. Worthless merchandise, trinkets; worthless or insincere talk, beliefs, or ideas; exaggerations, lies; bull.

garbage can. *n.* 1. An old, dilapidated USN destroyer. 2. In television, a microwave-relay transmitter.

garden. *n.* 1. A baseball field. *Sportswriter use.* 2. A prize-fighting arena. —**er.** *n.* In baseball, an outfielder.

gargle. *n.* A drink, as of beer.

gargle-factory. *n.* A saloon. *Synthetic.*

garrison state. *n.* A country under the complete control of a dictator or a military coalition.

gas. *n.* 1. Empty talk; bragging, exaggerated talk. → 2. Talk of any kind. 3. Gasoline. *Colloq.* 4. Denatured alcohol, ether, or any such substance that can be a substitute for liquor. *Hobo and maritime use.* 5. Anything exceptional, extremely satisfying, or successful, such as a piece of music, a person, a party, or the like. *Since c1945; orig. a Harlem Negro term; now in very common use in cool circles.* *v.i.* 1. To

converse, chat, or gossip. 2. To become intoxicated. *v.t.* 1. To impress a person as remarkable, amusing, unusual, or eccentric, in either a good or a bad way but usu. good; to amuse; to attract attention; to evoke some kind of emotional response from a person. *Orig. and mainly cool and far out use. Some general use since c1955.* 2. To deceive or cheat a person by talking. *Since c1850.* —**bag.** *n.* A braggart; a long-winded orator; anyone who talks a lot. *Since c1870.* —**sed.** *adj.* 1. Overcome with laughter; amazed; momentarily shocked or stunned by what one has seen or heard. 2. Drunk. *Common.* —**ser.** *n.* 1. A loquacious or boastful person. 2. Anything exceptional, as a piece of music, etc. → 3. Anything dull, out-dated, or corny. *Freq. use in cool circles; the antithesis of "gas."* 4. Anything that is uproariously funny, as a joke or boner. *Very common.* 5. A remarkable person or thing, in either a good or a bad sense; specif. a remarkably stupid, amusing, or eccentric person; a character; a remarkably garish, complex, useless, unusual, or corny thing; or, specif., a remarkably talented, intelligent, cool person; or a remarkably well designed, simple, satisfying thing. *Orig. c1935 jive and Negro use; cool and far out use since c1950.* *adj.* 1. Uproariously funny; amusing. 2. Remarkable; amazing; noteworthy; in either a good or bad sense. —**sy.** *adj.* Boastful; given to idle talk. *Since c1850.*

gas, a. *n.* = gasser. *Synthetic cool and far out use.*

gash. *n.* The mouth. *Some use since c1935.*

gas hound. One given to drinking denatured alcohol, ether, or other substitutes for liquor. *Hobo and maritime use.*

gas house. A beer saloon; a beer garden. *W.W.II Armed Forces use. Common.*

gas up. To make something more exciting or attractive.

gat. *n.* Any hand firearm; a revolver or pistol. *Orig. underworld and hobo use, c1910; now almost obs. with those groups and becoming somewhat archaic in general usage. Prob. from "Gatling gun."*

gate. *n.* **1.** The amount of money collected from selling tickets to spectators at a sporting event; the "gate" receipts at a sporting event. *Since c1890.* **2.** An able swing musician. *Wide swing use c1935–c1943. Prob. a shortening from "gator" or "alligator," reinforced by "swing like a gate."* **3.** An engagement or appointment, esp. an engagement or a job for a jazz musician; a gig. **4.** Any male; esp. a hep one. *Swing use.* **5.** = cat, *n.*, 4. & 5. *Some jive and swing use, c1935–c1942, often in admiration of a musician or as direct address to a fellow devotee.* *v.t.* To dismiss someone, to jilt someone. —**s.** *n.sing.* A fellow swing music enthusiast.

gate, give [someone] the. **1.** To jilt. → **2.** To discharge a person from his job.

gate, the. *n.* **1.** Dismissal from one's job. **2.** Dismissal, rejection, or the act of being jilted by one's girl friend or boy friend. *Colloq.* **3.** In baseball, a strikeout.

gate-crasher. *n.* One who, without invitation or a ticket, attends a social gathering or entertainment; an uninvited, unwelcomed guest. *Colloq.*

gatemouth. *n.* One who knows and tells everyone else's business. *Orig. Negro use.*

'gator; gator. *n.* **1.** An alligator. *Since c1840. Mainly Southern use.* **2.** = alligator; cat. *Some Negro use since c1925. Some jive use c1935-1942.*

gat up. **1.** Robbing at the point of a gun; a holdup. **2.** To arm oneself with a gat.

gauge butt = gage butt.

gauze. *n.* Unconsciousness; a daze, as from a blow. *Hollywood use.*

gay. *adj.* Homosexual (said of a person); patronized by or attractive to homosexuals (said of places or things).

gay-cat. *n.* **1.** A tramp or hobo; specif., one who is not typical or wise to the ways of hobo life, as a newcomer; a hobo willing to accept itinerant work; a hobo who is considered eccentric or unacceptable by his fellows. **2.** A criminal, esp. a young or inexperienced criminal or a youth who acts as a decoy, runner, or lookout for criminals. *Some use c1920–c1940.* **3.** Variously, an active, jovial, lusty person who enjoys life; a ladies' man; a dude; one who, with or without the help of narcotics, is never worried or troubled but who takes life as it comes without being concerned or bothered. *Assoc. with jazz use, esp. cool use. The meaning is not definite, owing to the several meanings of "gay," and "cat"; for example, it is even occasionally used to mean a homosexual jazz musician.*

gay deceivers = falsies.

gazer. *n.* A federal narcotics agent.

gazooney; gazoony. *n.* A young hobo; an inexperienced or innocent youth. *Hobo use.*

gazoozle. *v.t.* To cheat. *Whimsically formed from "bamboozle." Prob. a Runyonism.*

gedunk; g'dong. *n.* Sweets, dessert; esp. ice cream or pudding. *W.W.II USN use.*

gee. *n.* **1.** A fellow; a guy. **Front gee** = a blind used by pickpockets; **hip gee** = a guy in the know, or who can be trusted; **mob gee** = a member of a mob; **wrong gee** = man who can't be trusted. *From the first letter of "guy," reinforced by an imitated French pronunciation.* → **2.** The leader of a gang of prison or reformatory inmates; an aggressive or influential prisoner. *Underworld use.* **3.** A gallon of liquor. *Hobo use.* **4.** Money. **Hip gee** = smart money. *v.t.* To rob. *exclam.* = "Jesus!" *A very common and* *very mild euphem., based on the first syllable of "Jesus." Used absolutely to express surprise or the like.*

geed up; g'd up. *adj.* 1. Crippled; said of a person, esp. a beggar. 2. Battered; old; said of a coin. *Hobo use.* 3. Under the influence of, or elated by, drugs. *Narcotic addict use.*

geedus; geetis; geetus. *n.* Money. *c1935. Underworld use. Pitchman use.*

gee-gee. *n.* 1. A horse, esp. a race horse; specif., an inferior or no better than average race horse. *Common horseracing use.* 2. = gigi.

geek. *n.* 1. A carnival or circus performer, considered a freak, who performs sensationally disgusting acts that a normal person would not, e.g., eating or swallowing live animals. *Carnival and some circus use; fairly widely known. The geek has a low status in the carnival and is usu. considered mentally deranged or perverted.* 2. A sideshow freak, usu. spurious. *Carnival and circus use.* 3. A degenerate; one who will do anything, however disgusting, in order to satisfy or get money to satisfy degenerate desires. *Often used fig., as an insult.* 4. A drunk.

geepo. *n.* A stool pigeon.

geets. *n.pl.* Dollars; money; purchasing power; that which "gets" or buys things. *Some far-out and beat use.*

Gee whiz; Gee whizz. *exclam.* = gee! *Now often used mockingly to indicate that the surprise or its object is insignificant.*

geezed; all geezed up. 1. Drunk. 2. Under the influence of narcotics.

geezer. *n.* 1. A fellow or guy; usu. an unknown, old, and eccentric man. *Often in the phrase "old geezer." Since c1900.* 2. A drink of strong liquor. 3. An injection or inhalation of a narcotic. *Drug addict use.*

geezo. *n.* A prisoner, a convict; esp.

an old or experienced prisoner who has been in prison for a long time. *Prob. from "geezer."*

geld. *n.* = gelt.

gelt. *n.* Money. *From the German.*

general. *n.* Anyone in authority, as a boss, school principal, head of a household, or the like.

gent. *n.* Orig. a gentleman; now any man.

gents, the. *n.sing.* A public rest room for men; the john. *Because many such rest rooms have a "Gents" sign on them, to distinguish them from the "Ladies' room."*

George; george. *expl., exclam.* An expression denoting the speaker's awareness or appreciation of any extraordinary, remarkable, or attractive thing or person. *Orig. pop. by comedian Jerry Lester on his network television program. Prob. from "By George."* *adj.* Psychologically satisfying; perfect for a specific use or mood. *Associated with early bop talk, this use was pop. with several television and radio comedians, and later with teenagers. Basically, however, it must be considered as synthetic.* *n.* 1. An automatic pilot in an airplane. *Some commercial and Air Force pilot use. Prob. from the expression "Let George do it" = let someone else assume the responsibility.* 2. Anyone or anything remarkable or satisfying; anyone or anything that is "George" (adj.). *Wide fad use c1950; mainly teenage use.* 3. A theater usher. *Rock-and-roll use since c1950. adj.* Fine, good, wonderful, excellent, pleasant, enjoyable, jake, swell. *An example of how, by a synthetic, repeated, laugh-evoking use by a comedian, a word may become very common for a brief period, esp. a fad word of teenagers.*

George do it, let. Let someone else do it. *Said in avoiding responsibility. Common c1920 and during W.W.II when the term implied a lack of responsibility in helping the war effort.*

George Washington pie. Cherry pie. *Synthetic.*

geranium. *n.* An attractive person; a pretty girl.

German goiter. A protruding stomach, as from being a beer drinker. *Used humorously.*

get. For phrases beginning with "get," see under principal word of phrase.

get. *v.t.* 1. To annoy or bother someone. *Colloq.* 2. To understand or comprehend a person or an idea. 3. To return malice; to force retribution; specif., to harm, beat up, kill, or cause another trouble or failure from ill will or malice toward him. *Colloq. n.* 1. The progeny of a thoroughbred animal. *Dial.* 2. Profit; the "gate." *Lit., that money which has been received or gotten, reinforced by a mispronunciation of "gate."* 3. The route taken by robbers fleeing with loot.

getalong. *n.* One's gait; one's peculiar way of walking. *Dial.*

getaway; get-away. *n.* An escape, as from the police; the act of fleeing the scene of a crime. *Used lit. and fig. Orig. underworld and hobo use; now used fig. One makes a getaway from a person or task one wishes to avoid.* adj. Used for making a getaway.

getaway day. The last day of a horse-racing track's meeting for the season. *Common horse-racing use.*

get lost. Lit. and fig. = "go away."

getter = go-getter.

get-together. *n.* A meeting or gathering, usu. social. *Colloq.*

get-up. *n.* 1. Clothing and face make-up, esp. if either or both are stylish or extreme; a uniform or costume. *Colloq.* 2. = get up and go (under up). get up. End a jail sentence.

ghost. *n.* 1. The treasurer of a theater or theatrical company. *Theatrical slang.* 2. One who writes a book or article for pay by another who receives credit for the writing. 3. In telecasting,

a secondary image on a television screen, formed by two impulses reaching the circuitry, one the direct beam, the other a reflected beam. *v.t.* To write something, as a book, usually for pay, for another person whose name appears as author.

G. I.; GI. *adj.* 1. Of general or government issue; said of clothing and equipment issued to personnel of the Armed Forces. *Thus "G. I. shoes," "G. I. soap," "G. I. trucks," and the like. Army use since c1935; common Army use by c1940. Very wide W.W.II use.* → 2. Of, required by, assoc. with the Army or Army life. *Thus "G. I. haircut," "G. I. manners," "G. I. complaint," or the like. Abbr. for "general issue" or "government issue," but see "G. I. can" for another possible origin. Common Army use since c1942. Some W.W.II use.* 3. Done according to Army regulations; in a military manner; strict in enforcing or complying with Army regulations. *Army use since c1942.* 4. Commonplace, routine; inferior; lousy. *Army use since c1942. The above four uses were widely known in the Army during W.W.II and to civilians as well.* 5. For soldiers or veterans of W.W.II; veteran of W.W.II. *Civilian use during and after W.W.II. n.* 1. An enlisted man, a common soldier; esp. an infantry private; a soldier who is neither an officer nor a noncommissioned officer. *Orig. Army use, esp. by officers, at beginning of W.W.II.* → 2. A soldier; any soldier or member of the Army. *Wide use during and since W.W.II. The most common use.* 3. A veteran, esp. an Army veteran of W.W.II. *Common. v.t.* To scrub with brush and soap; to clean or polish or straighten. *Army use during and since W.W.II.*

G.I. can. *n.* A large iron garbage can, or can or barrel for ashes and refuse. *Some Army use since c1920. This seems to have been the earliest use of "G.I." (adj.) and to have been abbreviated from "galvanized iron" rather than from "general issue" or "government issue." If so, "galvanized iron" may be the actual root for "G.I." or at least a reinforcement for the use of "G.I."*

gidget. *n.* A gadget. *From "gadget."*

gieve. *n.* = jive. *Pronounced gieve.*

gift. *v.t.* To give; to present a gift to a person.

gift of gab. 1. The ability to talk persuasively. 2. The ability to talk, or habit of talking, fluently, fast, or often.

gig. *n.* 1. A child's pacifier or any object, as a cloth square, spoon, or the like, used as a toy; any object to which a small child is attached and with which he likes to play; any object treated by a child as a fetish; a gigi or ju-ju. *Orig. Negro slave and Southern use. From "gigi," the word is very well known to about 35% of the population, unheard of by the rest.* 2. A party, a good time; esp. an uninhibited party; occasionally but not often, an amorous session, necking party, or even a sexual orgy between a man and a woman. 3. A jam session; a jazz party or gathering; a party or gathering of jazz musicians or enthusiasts. *Orig. swing use.* 4. Specif., an engagement or job for a jazz musician or musicians, esp. a one-night engagement. 5. Something, as a jazz arrangement, that is satisfying or seems perfect. *Orig. swing use.* 6. A fishing spear; a pronged fork, as used for catching fish, frogs, and the like. 7. An unfavorable report; a demerit; a reprimand. *Army and some student use since c1940.* 8. An old car; a hot rod. *Hot rod use since c1950. From earlier "gig" = a one-horse carriage.* *v.t.* To stick, specif. with a pronged fork or gigger for catching fish,

frogs, and the like. *v.i.* To play a musical instrument, specif. in a jazz band; to participate in a jam session. *Jazz musicians' use.*

giggle smoke. A marijuana cigarette.

giggle water. Liquor.

gigi; gi-gi; gee-gee. *n.* 1. Any object, whether a toy or a common household object, cloth square, string, or the like, which a child adopts as his favorite, uses as a toy, pets, takes to bed with him, and treats as a fetish; a child's pacifier. → 2. Any object, such as a string, a pencil, or the like, with which a person habitually plays as a nervous habit. *Both meanings from the Gullah "grigri" = the doll-like image used in voodoo rituals, as the image of a person, in which pins are stuck to cast an evil spell. Orig. New Orleans creole U.S. use.*

G.I. Joe. A typical or representative soldier of W.W.II; a soldier; a G.I. *Wide W.W.II use. From "G.I." plus "Joe" = fellow.*

gil. *adj.* Insincere; phony. **—hooley.** *n.* 1. A country person; an insincere or phony person. 2. A thingamajig. 3. The skidding of a moving automobile until it faces the direction opposite from the way it has been going. *Auto racer use.*

gillion. *n.* Any very large number.

gills. *n.pl.* 1. The human mouth. 2. The lower part of the human face.

gills, blue (green) around the. 1. Nauseated; usu. nauseated for an emotional or psychological reason such as fear or disgust at an unappetizing or horrible sight. 2. Seasick, whether nauseated or not. 3. Showing the effects of having consumed too much food or alcoholic beverage, whether nauseated or not.

gilly. *n.* 1. A small circus traveling in cars. 2. A vehicle hired to transport circus or theatrical equipment.

gimmick. *n.* 1. Any trick, secret device, or gadget by which a pitchman, gambler, or the like cheats the public or stimulates business. *Orig. circus, carnival, and gambler use.* → 2. Any unusual attraction, accessory, trimming, or feature, whether useful or useless, added to legitimate merchandise, such as a car or garment, to cause a change in style and attract customers. → 3. Part of a plan or venture that can mean success or failure; the main selling point or a major flaw. 4. A selfish motive; the way in which a person hopes to benefit from a seemingly altruistic deed or plan, or from an obviously deceptive or unethical plan; one's angle.

gimmies, the. *n.* Acquisitiveness; selfishness. *From "give me."*

gimp. *n.* 1. A limp. 2. A lame or deformed person; specif., one who walks with a limp. *Orig. hobo and underworld use.* 3. Vitality; ambition. *Now dial.*

gimper. *n.* A very competent, efficient, dependable Air Force man. *U.S. Air Force use. v.i.* To limp.

gimp stick. *n.* A crutch or cane.

ginhead. *n.* A drunkard.

gink. *n.* Any man or fellow; a guy; esp. an old and eccentric or unkempt man.

gin mill; gin-mill; ginmill. *n.* 1. Any cheap saloon, bar, or nightclub; orig. a speakeasy. 2. Any kind of public drinking place, as a saloon. *Until c1920, the term had a connotation of cheap, rowdy, or dilapidated.*

ginzo; guinzo. *n.* 1. Any foreigner or foreign-born citizen. 2. Specif., an Italian or a person of Italian birth. *Prob. from "Guinea."* 3. A fellow; a guy.

gip. *n.* = gyp.

girene. *n.* = gyrene.

girl. *n.* In cards, a queen of any suit. —**ie.** *n.* A girl; esp. a chorus girl.

girl friend. A female sweetheart; a best girl. *Since c1930, so common as to be standard speech.*

girlie show. Entertainment or a

show whose main attraction is scantily clad girls. *Orig. applied to crude, somewhat illegal shows, tending toward the obscene; now used in ref. to any legitimate show featuring attractive females.*

gismo; gizmo. *n.* 1. = gadget. 2. = gimmick. 3. Any object; specif. a gadget or gimmick; usu. a device whose name one does not know. *Became common cW.W.II, may orig. have been USN use.* → 4. A person whose name one does not know; a fellow; a guy.

gitbox. *n.* A guitar. *Affected among jazz musicians.*

gits. *n.* Courage; perseverance; guts; fig., any trait that "gets" results or victories.

git up and git. *Dial.* for "get up and go."

give. For phrases beginning with "give," see under principal word of phrase.

giveaway. *n.* 1. Anything that betrays or reveals unwittingly. *Colloq.* 2. A gift, from a business concern, given to customers or patrons to increase sales or patronage or to gain publicity.

gives me a pain [someone, something]. Is disgusting, aggravating, disliked, or frustrating. *Usu. said of a person.*

gizmo = gismo.

glad eye (glad hand), give [someone] the. To greet or look at someone in a friendly, welcoming manner.

glad eye, the. A glance, look, or expression of friendliness or welcome. *Usu. in "give [someone] the glad eye."*

glad hand, the. Lit., a warm handshake; fig., a warm welcome, esp. a warm welcome or cordial reception that is overly friendly or insincere. —**er.** One who is demonstrative in his personal contacts; one who acts more friendly or more optimistic than necessary; one, as a politician, who pretends friendliness.

glad rags. 1. One's best or fanciest clothes; one's party clothes. *Com-*

mon. Since c1900. 2. Formal evening wear, men's or women's.

glahm = glom.

glamor girl; glamour girl. A professional beauty, a girl or woman known to the public as glamorous; specif., a glamorous movie actress, model, starlet, chorus girl, or the like.

glass. *n.* Sparkling imitation jewelry or gems. —**ie.** *n.* A playing marble made of glass. *Boy use.*

glasses on, have [one's]. To be haughty or formal. *Some Harlem Negro use.*

glass jaw. A prize fighter's jaw that cannot stand a hard punch. *Very common prize fight use.*

glassy eyed. Drunk.

glaum. *n.* A look or glance. *v.t.* To look at; to glance at. See glom.

Gleeps. A nondenotative exclamation used in lieu of profanity. *Some teenage use.*

glim. *n.* 1. A light, as a lamp or candle; a window, considered as a source of light. "Bring the glim" = turn on the light; "douse the glim" = turn off the light. *Introduced by Eng. colonists; prob. of Irish underworld origin.* 2. An eye. *Since c1915.* *v.t.* To look at something or someone carefully; to examine visually; to see (something). —**mers.** *n.pl.* 1. The eyes. 2. Headlights. —**s.** *n.pl.* 1. The eyes. 2. Spectacles; eye-glasses. *Since c1920; orig. hobo and underworld use.*

glim worker. One who sells plain glass eyeglasses. *Carnival and circus use.*

globes. *n.pl.* The female breasts, considered as sexually attractive. *A favorite word of story writers and semi-pornographers. Seldom spoken.*

glom; glaum; glahm. *n.* A hand, considered as a tool for grabbing, *v.t.* 1. To grab; to seize; to take hold of. → 2. To steal. *The most common meaning; orig. hobo*

and underworld use. *v.i.* To be arrested. *Lit.* = "to be grabbed by the hand of the law." —**mer.** *n.* 1. A hand, used for grabbing or stealing. *Since c1930.* → 2. One who uses his hands to grasp things, as a fruit picker.

glop. *n.* 1. Unappetizing food, specif. a thick semiviscous mixture. 2. Any semiviscous liquid. 3. Sentimentality; corn. *All uses mainly teenage since c1945.*

glow. *n.* A state of moderate intoxication. *Usu. in the phrase,* "have a glow on."

glowworm. *n.* An amateur photographer. *Synthetic.*

gluepot. *n.* A racehorse. *Fairly common.*

G-man. *n.* A garbage man. *Jocular W.W.II Army use.*

gnat's whistle, the. Anything of superior quality. *Sometimes ironically used.*

go. For phrases beginning with "go," see under principal word of phrase.

go. *n.* 1. A prize fight. *Colloq.* 2. A chance, opportunity, or try. *Always in* "to have a go at it." 3. A job; a deal; a way of life. *Thus,* "I have a very good go here." *Not common in U.S. v.i.* 1. To die. 2. To go to the bathroom; to excrete. *Euphem., common.* 3. To go on; to occur; to happen or be taking place. *v.t.* To spend or pay money. *exclam.* See go-man-go. —**er.** *n.* Anything that is going, either good or bad. *Orig. bop use. c1946; some student use since c1950.* —**ing.** *adj.* 1. Profitable; successful. *Usu. in* "a going concern," *almost always said of a small business or store.* 2. Working, performing, or talking smoothly or adroitly; in full swing. → 3. Eliciting a response; having or conveying a mood or feeling; said of a performance, piece of music, party, gathering, or remarkable person or thing. *Orig. c1946 bop use; some student use since c1950.*

go, on the. 1. Active; lit., in constant motion. → 2. Active socially; caught up in a social whirl.

go-ahead. *n.* Consent or approval to proceed.

go around together. To date the same member of the opposite sex frequently; to be known as friends.

go around with [someone]. To date the same member of the opposite sex frequently; to be a friend to a specific person.

goat. *n.* 1. A car, esp. an old or souped-up car. *Hot rod and some general teenage use since c1950.* 2. One who takes the blame for another, or for a group's or team's failure or embarrassment; the butt of a joke. *From "scapegoat."* → 3. The junior officer in an Army outfit. *W.W.II use.* 4. A racehorse, esp. an inferior racehorse. **—y.** *adj.* Awkward; ignorant. *Some Army use.*

goat, get [one's]. To annoy a person; to cause anger or frustration. *Since c1908. Became common cW.W.I; now colloq.*

gob. *n.* 1. A quantity, usu. a large amount. 2. A USN sailor, usu. an enlisted man. *Became common during W.W.I and has remained the most common word for USN sailor. Now colloq.*

gobble. *v.t.* 1. To eat rapidly and hardily. 2. In baseball, to catch a ball. **—digook; —dygook.** *n.* Talk or writing which is long, pompous, vague, involved, usually with Latinized words and much professional jargon. *So defined by the word's originator, Maury Maverick, 1944.* **—r.** [taboo]. *n.* A male homosexual, or sexual degenerate or pervert of any kind. *Prison use. In ref. to "eat."*

gobble-pipe. *n.* A saxophone. *Synthetic.*

gobo. *n.* A black screen used to decrease the light on a movie set or television stage, or to shield a movie or television camera from bright lights and glare. *Movie use since c1925.*

goboon; gobboon; gaboon. *n.* A spitton. *Since c1930.*

gob-stick. *n.* A clarinet. *Synthetic.*

go-by, give [someone or something] the. To by-pass; to ignore; to refrain or abstain from. *Since c1905, now so common as to be standard usage.*

go-cart. *n.* A car.

god-awful. *adj.* Extremely objectionable or awful. *Since c1880.*

god box. 1. An organ [musical instrument]. 2. A church.

godfer. *n.* A child; a kid. *Short form of rhyming sl. "god forbid" = kid.*

go-down. *n.* A basement apartment or room.

goff. *n.* = guff.

go-getter. *n.* An energetic, ambitious person; one who tries hard to succeed. *Very common.*

go home! = hang up, shut up.

goifa = greefa.

going, get. 1. To begin a task or project. *Colloq.* 2. = get on the ball.

going over. A physical beating or punishment.

go-juice. *n.* Gasoline. *Synthetic.*

gold braid. USN officers.

gold brick. 1. A shirker; a loafer, esp. one who makes excuses for avoiding work. *Some W.W.I use; very common during W.W.II. Still in wide use.* 2. An Army second lieutenant appointed from civilian life. *Derog. enlisted men's term, reinforced by gold bar insigne of second lieutenant.* 3. An unattractive girl; a girl who does nothing to make herself attractive. *Some W.W.II use.*

gold-brick. *v.i.* To avoid work by making excuses. *Some W.W.I use; common W.W.II use. v.t.* To swindle; cheat; take advantage of.

gold-digger. *n.* A girl or woman who befriends or becomes the lover, girl friend, or wife of a man solely for financial or material gain; a girl or woman who will associate only with wealthy men. *Very common since c1925.*

golden bantam; Golden Bantam = corn.

goldfish. *n.* Salmon; usu. canned salmon. *Common in the Army since W.W.I; in the USN cW.W.II.*

goldfish bowl. A place without privacy.

goldilocks. *n.sing.* Any pretty blonde woman or girl. *Almost always used cynically by a male to indicate rejection and imply that the woman in question is neither as innocent nor as un-worldly as Goldilocks, the hero-ine of the famous children's story.*

gold star. A prize, compliment, victory, high rating, or the like. *From the little gold paper stars for meritorious or diligent work which teachers used to give to pupils or paste on examinations.*

golf ball. A small, white, spherical firecracker, resembling a golf ball, that explodes when thrown against a hard surface, usu. a wall or pavement. *Child use since c1935.*

golf widow. A wife often left alone while her husband plays golf. *Based on "grass widow."*

go-long. *n.* A police truck used to take arrested persons to jail; a paddy wagon. *Harlem Negro use.*

go-man-go; go man go. *exclam.* An expression of encouragement to jazz musicians; an expression of enthusiasm for or rapport with jazz music or musicians. *Orig. a bop term, c1946, shouted by devotees to the musicians as they played particularly adroit solos or close-harmony passages. Now considered passé by jazz groups, but some general teenage use.*

gon = gun. A thief. *Shortened form of Yiddish "goniff" = a thief. "Cannon" = a big or im-portant thief.*

gone. *adj.* 1. Enamored; in love. 2. Under the influence of narcotics (usu.) or whisky (occasionally). *Mainly addict use.* → 3. Fig., re-moved from reality; intent; spe-cif., so much in rapport with, in-tent on, immersed in, or intense over one's work, performance, ideas, or mode or way of life that one is as if in a trance and un-aware of or removed from all extraneous things. *Orig. and mainly cool use, and applied to cool musicians and devotees in regard to cool jazz music and a cool outlook or way of life.* → 4. Capable of arousing such intense satisfaction that one forgets all else; satisfying; cool; hep. *Cool use.* 5. Old, worn, or damaged past all use or repair. *Colloq.* 6. *Orig.* cool use = eliciting a pseudo-religious cultural re-sponse; cool; intellectually excit-ing and satisfying; pleasant. *Orig. late bop and cool use. part.* = real gone. —r. *n.* A thing or per-son doomed to destruction; a dy-ing person.

gonef = goniff.

gone on. In love with. *Colloq.*

gong. *n.* An opium pipe.

gonger = gong.

goniff; gonef; gonof; gonoph; ganef; ganof. *n.* A thief; a crook; one who, though not a profes-sional thief, will take advantage of another when in a position to do so; an unethical businessman. *From the Yiddish "goniff"* = thief (*n.*), to steal (*v.*) *v.t.* To steal; to cheat; esp. applied to petty thievery.

gonk. *n. & v.t.* = conk.

gonof; gonoph. *n.* = goniff.

gonsil. *n.* = gunsel.

gonzel. *n.* = gunsel.

goo. *n.* 1. Any sticky, syrupy liquid, emulsion, or semisolid; often applied to mud, cream sauces, and oily cosmetics and hair dressings. *Common since c1900.* 2. Insincere flattery; sweet talk. *v.i.* To talk affectionately. —**by.** *n.* Prison food. *Convict use.* —**ey.** *n.* Any crisp, browned fat on cooked meat; any sugary mix-ture, such as may drip from a pie or cake while baking. *adj.* 1. Sticky, creamy, soft, viscous. *Since c1900. Usu. said of food.* 2. Sentimental, romantic, emotional, corny. *Since c1935.*

goober. *n.* A peanut. *Prob from the Gullah. Mainly Southern use, but also heard in other sections of the country.*

goober-grabber. *n.* A native of Georgia.

goober grease. 1. Butter. 2. Peanut butter.

good, make. To succeed, esp. to succeed in business. *Colloq.*

good butt. *n.* A marijuana cigarette. *Narcotic addict use.*

goodbyee; good-by-ee. *interj.* A prolonged and precious form of interj. "good-by." Analogous to "indeedy" and "all righty." Intro. from Eng. during W.W.II.

good deal. 1. A favorable business proposition or arrangement. *Colloq.* → 2. An easy or pleasant job or way of life; anything pleasurable. *Since c1940; W.W.II Armed Forces use; student use.* *adv.* Yes; o.k.; I agree.

good egg = egg.

gooder. *n.* Any person or thing held in high esteem, as a girl or a joke; a good one. *May be synthetic rustic sl., more often heard on radio and television than in real life.*

good fellow. A stupid boy; a fool. *Said condescendingly. c.1850 to present.*

Good God! *exclam.* An expression of surprise or shock.

good head. An agreeable, personable person; a nice guy. *Orig. West Coast teenager usage, c1950.*

goodie. *n.* 1. A prissy, self-righteous person; a sissy. 2. Sweets or small gifts. *c1950. Used by adults in a baby-talking voice to simulate the enthusiasm of childhood.* 3. An honest, brave person. *Usu. said humorously. Orig. used humorously to refer to the good heroes and heroines of Western cowboy movies and television shows.* —s. *n.* Any adult foods, drinks, clothing, or objects of art or culture that inspire childish enthusiasm. *Used sarcastically. Sophisticated use since c1948.*

good Joe. Any agreeable, pleasant, or generous man.

good-looker. *n.* 1. A good-looking person, esp. a woman or girl. *c1890 to present.* 2. A good-looking animal or object.

goods, the. *n.* 1. The necessary traits or resources for a given purpose. → 2. A person possessing the required traits or resources; a sincere person. → 3. The desired truth or facts. → 4. Proof of guilt. 5. Stolen merchandise; contraband.

good time. *n.* 1. Time deducted from a prisoner's sentence because of good behavior. *c1870 to present; convict use.* 2. A period of enjoying illegal or immoral acts. *Unlike the standard "good time," both words are pronounced slowly and with the same intonation.*

goody-goody. *n.* A prissy, sissified youth or man; a sissy; an effeminate youth or man. *adj.* 1. Decorous; effeminate. *Since c1885.* 2. Excessively good.

goof. *n.* 1. A stupid, eccentric, or ineffectual man. *Unlike a sap, dope, boob, or jerk, a goof is tragically stupid on all subjects at all times, and his stupidity is not due to lack of experience or innocence and is never funny. Still in freq. use, but extremely common during the 1920's when it was a popular flapper's term and during W.W.II.* 2. An insane person. 3. A narcotics addict. *Addict use.* 4. A blunder, mistake, or faux pas. *v.i.* 1. To make a mistake, blunder, or faux pas. *Orig. used by hep people; W.W.II Armed Forces use; common teenage and student use since c1950.* 2. To daydream; to give oneself up to reverie. *v.t.* To fool, josh, or kid a person. —ed. *adj.* Under the influence of a narcotic, specif. marijuana. *Addict use.* —er. *gopher. n.* = goof. —iness. *n.* The state of being goofy. —us. *n.* 1. Any small item or thingamajig. → 2. A rustic; a person easily duped; an easy mark.

c1920. Orig. carnival, circus, and underworld use. → 3. Nonartistic entertainment, gaudy styles, cheap merchandise, and the like, which is created to be sold to people with unsophisticated tastes. —y. *adj.* 1. Silly; stupid; foolish; simple-minded. 2. Infatuated with, in love with, crazy about.

goof at. To look at; to be entranced by.

goof ball. 1. Any barbiturate used as a narcotic drug by addicts. *Addict use.* 2. Marijuana; a portion of marijuana. → 3. A preparation or portion of a narcotic. → 4. A narcotics addict. → 5. A stupid awkward person; a chronic blunderer, one who makes frequent mistakes. 6. An odd person; an eccentric. 7. A tranquilizer pill; a sleeping pill. —y ball. *n.* Nembutal.

goof-butt = goofy-butt.

goof off. To idle away one's time; to refuse to work or think seriously; to evade work; to idle or loaf. *Common W.W.II Armed Forces use; some W.W.II and after civilian use, esp. among students.* **goof-off.** *n.* 1. A chronic blunderer or idler. 2. A period of rest and relaxation; a rest period.

goof up. *v.t.* To quash, kill, queer; to put out of working order. *v.i.* To blunder.

goofy-butt. *n.* A marijuana cigarette.

google. *n.* The Adam's apple; the throat. *Archaic and dial.*

googly. *adj.* Protruding or rolling.

goo-goo; gu gu. *n.* 1. [derog.] A native of a Pacific island occupied by U.S. Forces during W.W.II. 2. Crazy, insane; gaga.

goo-goo eyes. Amorous or possessive glances.

googs. *n.pl.* Eyeglasses; spectacles. *From "goggles." Pitchman use.*

gooh. *n.* A prostitute. *Underworld use, archaic; boy street gang use since c1945.*

gook. *n.* 1. Dirt, grime, sludge, sediment. *Very common.* 2. Any

viscous, semiliquid sauce or dressing. 3. [derog.] Generically, a native of the Pacific islands, Africa, Japan, China, Korea, or any European country except England; usu. a brown-skinned or Oriental non-Christian. *Wide W.W.II Army use; some Korean Army use. adj.* Foreign; made in any country except the U.S.A.

gool. *n.* 1. A goal. *Since c1840. Has been common, humorously and dial.* 2. An ill-mannered, offensive introvert. *v.t.* To elicit great applause from an audience by one's entertainment. Fig., to "knock someone for a gool."

Go on! An exclam. of incredulity or pleasure from a compliment.

goon. *n.* 1. A hoodlum; a strong man acting or employed as a thug or to commit acts of violence or intimidation. 2. A strong, stupid, unimaginative man. → 3. A boring, disliked, or silly person. *Since c1935.* → 4. An unattractive or unpopular member of the opposite sex. *Very common with teenagers and college students. Since c1935.* 5. An Army private, esp. one relegated to simple, dirty chores. *Some W.W.II Army use. In the Virgin Islands, formerly a Danish possession, native Negro workers are called "goons" or "goonies," a possible derivation.* → 6. A man; a fellow. *Usu. disparagingly or humorously. adj.* Nazi German. *Used by U.S. and Eng. prisoners of war in Ger. during W.W.II.* Thus: **goon-bread, goon-soup, goon-women, goon-box.** [a guard tower on a prisoner of war compound], **goon-soldier,** etc. —ie. *n.* A native Virgin Island Negro. *The word, as well as the island, was orig. Danish.* —y. *adj.* Odd; goonlike.

goonk. *n.* 1. Any greasy, semiviscous liquid; esp. hair tonic, lubricants, or any unappetizing, greasy food. 2. Anything unpleasant.

goon squad. A group of thugs, esp. when employed in labor disputes. *c1935.*

goop. *n.* 1. A goof; a mutt. 2. Cant, nonsense, boloney. 3. = goup.

goopher = goof.

goose. *v.t.* 1. To start a motor or a machine; to feed spurts of gasoline or power to a motor. *c1935.* → 2. To threaten, beg, cajole, or encourage another to do something faster or better. *n.* 1. The act of goosing. 2. An emergency stop of a locomotive.

goose, give [someone or something] **the.** Fig., to speed up someone or something; to ask for or create action, speed, alertness, enthusiasm, or the like; specif., to accelerate a car or other motor or engine.

gooseberry. *v.t.* To steal clothes from a clothesline. *Hobo use.*

goose bumps. Goose pimples. *Very common.*

goose-bumpy. *adj.* Frightened; having goose bumps.

goose-drownder. *n.* A heavy rainstorm. *Dial.*

goose egg. Zero, esp. in the score of a game, a grade in school, or an amount of money. *Used in school to refer to the grade of zero; used in sports to indicate that no score has been made and a zero has been posted on the scoreboard. Since c1850. Colloq. v.t.* To prevent an opposing sports team from scoring; to give a student a grade of 0%; to pay no money or leave no tip for a waiter.

go out. To lose consciousness. *Often in the phrase, "went out like a light."*

goozle. *n.* The throat. *Archaic and dial.*

gopher; gofer; gofor. *n.* 1. A young thief or hoodlum. *Since c1890.* → 2. Specif., a safe-cracker. *c1930; underworld use.* → 3. A safe, considered as an object to be robbed. *Underworld use.* 4. A dupe.

gopher ball. In baseball, a pitched or hit ball that skims low over the ground.

go places. To be successful; to have a successful career.

gorill. *n.* A hoodlum; a gorilla. *From "gorilla."*

gorilla. *n.* 1. A person with gorilla-like strength; a person known for his strength and lack of intellect. *Since c1865.* → 2. A hoodlum or thug. *Since c1930.* → 3. Specif., one hired to kill or do violence.

gorp. *v.t., v.i.* To eat greedily.

gosh-awful. *adv.* Exceedingly.

gospel-pusher. *n.* A preacher.

go-to-hell cap. An overseas cap. *Armed Forces use.*

goulash. *n.* 1. False information. *Underworld use. c1925.* → 2. An unusual hand of playing cards; a method of dealing playing cards so that all players receive unusual hands. → 3. A small restaurant or delicatessen that is a meeting place or serves as a quasi-clubroom for neighborhood criminals or for storytellers, horse-racing bettors, and card, chess, and checker players.

goulashes; goolashes. *n.pl.* Galoshes; overshoes. *A freq. mispronunciation.*

goulie. *n.* Any unfamiliar mixture of food. *From "goulash."*

goum. [derog.]. *n.* A foreigner. *From obs. "gome." = a man.*

goup. *n.* Any sticky or greasy liquid, such as a chocolate syrup.

go up (in [one's] **lines).** Specif., to forget one's lines entirely during a theatrical performance; to confuse one's lines during a theatrical performance. *Theater use since before c1920.*

gourd. *n.* The head. *Dial. since c1845.*

governor. *n.* 1. A father. 2. A superior; a manager or owner; one who governs. *Orig. carnival and circus use. c1920.*

gow. *n.* 1. Opium. *Orig. San Francisco underworld use. c1915.* → 2. Any narcotic drug. → 3. A marijuana cigarette. → 4. The effect obtained from taking a narcotic drug. 5. Drawings or photographs of pretty and provocatively posed females used on book and magazine covers, or on the outside packaging of products, in order to arrest the buyer's attention.

gowed-up; gowed up. *adj.* Under the influence of a narcotic; hopped up.

go with. To court; to date a person of the opposite sex; to keep company with; to go around with. *Colloq.*

go with, let. 1. To fire a gun. → 2. To release a verbal attack; to bawl out. 3. = fly, let.

gow job = hot rod.

go wrong. To become involved in illegal, immoral, unethical, or socially unacceptable schemes or practices.

gowster. *n.* A marijuana smoker.

grab. For phrases beginning with "grab," see under principal word of phrase.

grab, the. *n.* The main store or meeting place in a small town. *Dial. and archaic.*

grabby. *adj.* Greedy; acquisitive.

grab-joint. *n.* 1. A booth or stand that sells hamburgers, hot dogs, cotton candy, or other food, usu. at a carnival or circus. *Orig. carnival and circus use. c1935.* 2. A booth or stand that sells souvenirs. *Carnival and circus use, since c1940.*

grad. *n.* 1. A graduate of a college or university. *Colloq since c1895.* 2. A graduate student; one studying for an advanced degree. *adj.* Graduate; pursuing studies leading to an advanced degree.

graded. *adj.* Scientifically bred; thoroughbred; said of farm animals.

graft. *n.* Bribery. *Common.* —er. *n.* A faker; a confidence man; a thief.

gramps; Gramps. *n.sing.* A nickname for a grandfather; a nickname for any elderly man, old enough to be a grandfather whether he is or not.

grand. *n.sing.* 1. One thousand dollars. *Orig., c1920, underworld and sporting use. By 1930 had replaced "thou" and has been common since c1935.* → 2. A thousand. *n.pl.* 1. Thousands of dollars. *Since c1930. Much more common than "grands."* → 2. Thousands.

grand bounce. A dismissal or rejection; the bounce.

grandfather. *n.* 1. An elderly man. 2. A senior student.

grandma. *n.* 1. Any elderly woman. 2. Low gear of a motor truck.

grand slam. 1. In baseball, a home run. → 2. An instance of winning everything, defeating all competition decisively, succeeding in several fields of endeavor, or the like. —mer. A home run. *Baseball use.*

grandstander. *n.* A show-off.

grandstand play. 1. In sports, a play made to look more difficult than it is, to impress the spectators. *Since c1920.* → 2. Any action, speech, or device used to gain sympathy or admiration.

grape. *n.* 1. Wine. 2. Champagne.

grapefruit. *adj.* 1. Associated with the preseason training period of professional baseball teams. *Because such training usu. takes place in the warm citrus-fruit growing regions.* 2. Played before the baseball season officially opens. *Said of baseball games.*

grapes, the. *n.* Champagne.

grapevine. *n.* The means or route by which a rumor or unofficial information is conveyed; an informant whose name is not to be divulged.

grappo. *n.* Wine. *Orig. bums' use.*

grass. *n.* 1. Lettuce. *Since c1935.* 2. Any green salad, esp. if chopped or shredded. *Since c1940.* 3. The straight-growing hair characteristic of Caucasians. *Some Negro use.* 4. = grass weed.

grass-clipper = grass-cutter.

grass-cutter. *n.* In baseball, a ball hit hard and low to the ground. *Since c1925.*

grasshopper. *n.* An airplane that flies low, ascending and descending as the terrain demands; a plane used to dust crops.

grass weed. Marijuana. *Some addict use.*

grass widow. 1. A wife whose husband is away on an extended trip. *Since c1900. Colloq.* → 2. A divorced woman; a woman legally separated from her husband. *Colloq.*

graum. *v.i.* To worry; to fret; to complain or nag.

gravel, hit the = hit the dirt.

graveyard. *n.* = graveyard shift. *adj.* Pertaining to a graveyard shift; pertaining to late-at-night or early-morning hours.

graveyard shift. *n.* A working shift that begins at midnight or 2:00 A.M. *A factory working 24 hours a day usu. has three shifts of workers: the regular day shift of 8:00 A.M. to 4:00 P.M., the "swing shift" from 4:00 P.M. to midnight, and the "graveyard shift" from midnight to 8:00 A.M. Guards, ranchers, truck drivers, and others whose jobs necessitate employment 24 hours a day have used the term since c1915. It became very common during W.W.II when many factories were in 24-hr production. It refers, of course, to the ghost-like hour of employment.*

graveyard watch. A period of guard or watch duty from 12 midnight to 4 A.M. or 8 A.M. *Railroad and watchman use [12 midnight to 8 A.M.]. USN use [12 midnight to 4 A.M.].*

gravy. *n.* Money in excess of that expected; money in excess of that needed for necessities; money easily earned or won. *Specif., money that is obtained easily and that does not have to be spent on necessities, such as money won at gambling, money earned at easy work, unexpectedly large profits, special bonuses and allowances, and the like. Since c1920. adj.* Easy to accomplish; soft.

gravy boat = gravy train.

gravy ride. *Fig.,* a ride on or as part of a gravy train.

gravy train. 1. An opportunity to receive money easily; individual prosperity; excessive pay for easy work or no work. *Often in "to ride the gravy train." Since c1920. Orig. sporting use.* 2. A person, business, or project that pays one's way or enables one to live prosperously, even though one may not actually need money of his own. → 3. An easy job; a task that can be accomplished without exertion, esp. if connected with public life, political life. shady dealings, or the like. *Colloq.*

grayback. *n.* A louse. *Colloq. c1865 to c1910. Still some use by soldiers in the field, and hoboes.*

gray matter. Intelligence; brains. *Colloq.*

gray mule = white mule.

graze. *v.* To eat a meal. *Some student, Army, and prison use.*

grazing ticket. A meal ticket or book of meal tickets. *Some student use.*

grease. *n.* 1. Bribe money; protection money. *c1930; underworld use.* 2. Butter. *Some use since c1930; fairly common W.W.II Army use.* 3. Nitroglycerine; dynamite. *c1925; underworld use.* 4. Influence; pull. *v.t.* 1. To bribe. *Orig. intro by Brit. colonists.* 2. To eat, esp. rapidly. *c1940; some Negro use; some far out use since c1955.* —d. *adj.* Drunk. *Mainly Southern hill use.*

greasy. *adj.* 1. Addicted to applepolishing. *Some student use since c1940.* 2. Sly; unctuous; cunning. 3. Muddy, esp. muddy when the soil has absorbed all surface water and the mud has just begun to dry; slightly muddy. *Horse-racing use.*

grease-ball. *n.* 1. A dirty tramp or beggar. *Some hobo use since c1925.* 2. A hamburger stand or concession. *Circus use.* 3. An actor who uses too much make-up. *Theater use since c1930.* 4. A disliked, sly person; specif., any young man with thick, black, oily hair, a sly or unctuous look, a sheik's mannerisms, and a cynical disregard for social acceptability.

grease-burner. *n.* A cook; esp. a fry cook at a lunch counter.

grease-gun. *n.* 1. A rapid-firing, automatic pistol. *W.W.II Army and USN use.* 2. The M-3 submachine gun.

grease it in. To land an airplane smoothly. *W.W.II U.S. Air Force use.*

grease joint. 1. The cookhouse and/or eating tent of a carnival or circus. *Since c1915.* 2. Any inexpensive place where food is cooked and served, as a lunch counter, a hamburger or hotdog stand.

grease-monkey. *n.* 1. Any of various workers who lubricate machinery, esp. a garage or gasoline-station attendant who greases cars and engines. → 2. Anyone who works in a garage; esp. a mechanic.

grease-pusher. *n.* A person who makes up actors with grease paint; a make-up man. *Theater and television use.*

grease trough. A lunch counter or lunchroom.

greasy grind. A student who studies constantly; one overzealous in his studies. *c1930. The "greasy" adds further contempt to "grind."*

greasy spoon. An inferior or cheap, usu. small, restaurant or lunch counter. *Very common.*

great. *adj.* Excellent; fine; wonderful; splendid. *Still in wide use. Colloq. n.* A famous person, as an actor, a baseball or football player, a musician, etc. —s. *n.pl.* Famous people, often entertainers, athletes, artists, or writers.

greatest, the. *n.* Anyone or anything considered wonderful; the most exciting or satisfying; the best of one's or its kind; anything or anyone considered better than

anything or anyone else; the best. *Orig. bop and cool use, since c1950; now wide teenage and student use.*

great guns, go. To flourish; to succeed remarkably.

greefa; griffa; goifa; greeta. *n.* A marijuana cigarette; a reefer. *Given in order of pop. "Griffa" may be Negro usage.*

greefo; griefo; gre(a)fa; greapha. *n.* Marijuana. *Common addict use.*

Greek. *n.* 1. An Irishman. *Orig. underworld use. c1850.* 2. A Greek-letter fraternity member. *College student use.*

green. *n.* Money, esp. paper money. *Since c1920. Orig. sporting and underworld use. From "long green." An old term somewhat synthetically revived by cool and beat users.*

green deck, the. Grass.

green folding. Money in bills.

green goods. Counterfeit paper money. *Since c1890.*

greenhorn; green-horn. *n.* 1. An immigrant, usu. unassimilated and naïve. 2. A naïve or unsuspecting person.

green hornet. Any hard, military problem that must be solved in a limited time. *W.W.II use.*

greenhouse. *n.* The transparent plastic cockpit cover of an airplane.

green ice. Emeralds. *Underworld use.*

greenie. *n.* A newcomer; a greenhorn.

green light. Approval; permission to proceed; a go-ahead sign. *From the traffic signal.*

green money. Paper money; bills of various denominations.

green stuff, the. Money; paper money.

green thumb. 1. An aptitude for getting plants to grow. 2. The ability to produce a success and to make money.

greeta = greefa.

grefa = greefo.

greyhound. *n.* A fast-working butcher or salesman. *Circus use.*

grid. *n.* 1. A football playing field. *Since c1915. From "grid-iron."* 2. A motorcycle. *Some motorcycle use since c1925. adj.* Football; pertaining to football. **—iron.** *n.* A football playing field. *Common since c1900. Because the playing field was originally marked off in squares or grids, including the ten-yard stripes still used, plus lengthwise stripes indicating various playing, kicking, and passing zones. Colloq. adj.* Of or pertaining to football.

griefo = greefo.

grifa; griffa = greefa.

grift. *n.* 1. Money made dishonestly and by one's wits, esp. by swindling. 2. In general, any dishonest or unethical way of obtaining money by one's wits, such as is done by professional swindlers, gamblers, pitchmen, confidence men, and the like. *v.i.* To swindle, gamble, or make one's living dishonestly and by one's wits. *c1925, orig. carnival and circus use; assoc. with "graft."* **—er.** *n.* 1. A gambler. *Orig. a gambler who followed circuses; circus use since c1925.* → 2. A swindler, pitchman, confidence man, small-time crook, dishonest concessionaire, or the like. *Prob. older than the v. "grift."* → 3. Any vagabond or hobo. *Since c1935, by confusion with "drifter."*

grift, on the. Living, traveling, or working as a grifter.

grind. *v.i.* 1. To rotate one's pelvis, in or as in sexual intercourse; said of women. *Applied to sexual intercourse or to the strip-tease and erotic dancing.* 2. To study diligently, methodically, and for long periods of time. *Since c1850; colloq. since c1930. Student use.* 3. To spiel at a concession; to talk to a crowd in front of a sideshow about the attractions to be seen inside. *c1925, circus talk; carnival use by c1930. n.* 1. Any unpleasant, monotonous, annoying, or boring task, esp. such a task when it deprives one of freedom to do something more pleasant. *Since c1850; very common by 1900, esp. by students; colloq. by c1925.* → 2. A college course requiring a great deal of study and concentration. *c1880 to present.* → 3. A diligent, drudging, overstudious student, esp. one who ignores or does not care for the social aspects of school life. *c1890 to present; gained wide popularity by c1900. Note the word is almost always used with contempt, esp. by party-boys and wheels.* 4. The loud, colorful sales talk given by a barker to entice customers into a sideshow or to a concession; a barker's or pitchman's spiel. *Circus use, c1925; carnival use by c1930.* 5. A circus barker or sidewalk pitchman. *Circus pitchman use, c1930.* 6. The pelvic-rotation gyrations of a burlesque dancer or stripper. *Colloq. adj.* Running continuously, without intermission. *Said of a show or a theater.* **—er.** *n.* 1. A barker who talks, often continuously, in front of a sideshow about the show inside. *c1925, circus talk; carnival use by c1930.* 2. A stripper; a burlesque dancer. 3. A very large overstuffed sandwich, usu. on a long roll or short loaf of bread, split lengthwise, and containing several kinds of hot or cold meat and cheese, and sometimes even vegetables. *c1945. Often used in the South and West; the East prefers "Hero."* 4. A car, specif. an old or dilapidated car.

grind house. A theater that runs continuously, either without intermissions or for a long daily run and without closing on holidays. *Theater use. From "grind show."*

grind show. A continuously running carnival show, without intermissions. *c1930; carnival use. Some grind shows featured dancers doing bumps and grinds, but the two are not necessarily related.*

grip. *n.* A theater stagehand who shifts scenery; a stage carpenter or his helper. *Wide theater and movie use.*

gripe. *v.i.* To complain, object, or bitch, esp. to do so chronically and about routine matters. *Colloq. since c1945. v.t.* To annoy, vex, or anger someone, esp. to do so over an extended period. *Colloq. since c1945. n.* 1. A complaint; a strong objection or criticism. *Wide enough usage to be colloq.* 2. A chronic complainer; one who nags. *c1940.* —r. *n.* A chronic complainer. *Since c1935.*

gripes, the. *n.* 1. An instance or spell of complaining. 2. The habit of complaining.

gripe session. Fault-finding conversation; a bull session in which all or most of the talk is complaint. *Common to students and servicemen. c1940.*

gripes my cookies. Gripes me extremely. *Some use c1940.*

gripes my middle kidney. Gripes me extremely. *Common c1945.*

griping. *n.* The act of, or an instance of, complaining. *adj.* [attrib.] Complaining.

grit, hit the. 1. = hit the dirt. 2. To set out on a journey; to hit the road. 3. To walk or hike.

groan box. An accordion. *Though this term may have had some use among musicians c1930, it is considered very synthetic among present-day musicians. Mainly used by gossip columnists and teen-agers, who mistakenly consider it to be a hip expression.*

groaner. *n.* A singer. *A synthetic word never used by entertainers, except in reference to "The Groaner" = singer Bing Crosby.*

groceries. *n.pl.* 1. Any meal; meals. 2. Any important or necessary item, mission, or result.

grogged. *adj.* Groggy.

grog-hound. *n.* One who likes alcoholic beverages, esp. beer. *Some student use.*

grog-mill. *n.* A bar, tavern, or saloon, esp. a cheap one or one that mainly sells beer. *Based on "gin-mill."*

grollo. *n.* = growler.

grooby. *adj.* Groovy; smooth. *Jive use.*

groove, in the. 1. Speaking sensibly; thinking correctly; in the proper mood. *Some general use c1940.* 2. In top form; running or working smoothly or perfectly; in full swing. *Teenage and student use c1940–c1945.*

groovy. *adj.* 1. In a state of mind or mood conducive to playing music, esp. swing music, well; in rapport with the piece, esp. of swing music, being played. *Orig. c1935 swing use, by musicians and devotees. Some resurrected cool and far out use since c1955. From "in the groove."* → 2. Appreciative of good swing music; hep to swing music, fads, and fashions; hep. → 3. Excellent; satisfying; in keeping with one's desires or a situation.

grouch-bag. *n.* 1. A small money bag, usu. leather or canvas, often suspended by a string carried inside the clothing, containing enough money for an emergency, usu. enough money to move on to another town if one's schemes fail or if one quits a job. *c1930; circus use.* → 2. A purse. → 3. Money saved for an emergency. *c1930; some use among entertainers and grifters.*

ground biscuit. A stone of a size and shape suitable for throwing.

ground rations. Sexual intercourse. *Some Negro use.*

grouse. *v.i.* To grumble or complain. *Orig. Brit. Army sl. imported during W.W.I.*

growl. *n.* A set of notes used for cheating in an examination; a pony. *v.i.* To complain; to reprimand; to express one's bad temper or ill nature verbally. *Colloq.* —er. *n.* 1. A large pitcher or other container used to carry any liquid. 2. An electronic public-address or intercommunication system. *Orig. W.W.II USN use. In the U.S. the term has never* = a hansom cab, as it does in *Eng.*

growler-rushing. *n.* Drinking beer or other alcoholic beverages; a drinking spree. *adj.* Drinking; given to drinking cheap liquor.

grub. *n.* Food, esp. basic or filling food. *Orig. cowboy use. Now colloq. but still has a Western twang and an urgent connotation. v.i.* 1. To eat a meal. 2. To study hard.

grub out = grub.

grub-stake; grubstake. *n.* Money saved or borrowed to buy food and other necessities, and cover the expenses involved while prospecting, moving to a new region, looking for work, or starting a new business or venture of any kind. *Orig. Western use, from mining prospectors. Colloq.*

gruesome twosome. 1. Lovers; a couple who go steady. *Orig. jive talk; c1940 wide student use.* → 2. Any two associates. *"Twosome" is the root word; "gruesome" is only added for the rhyme and is not considered derog. Often used jocularly.*

grunt. *n.* 1. A bill, check, or tab for food and/or drinks. 2. Wrestling; the wrestling profession, entertainment, or sport. 3. A wrestler, esp. an inferior wrestler, or one known for grimacing, pretending to be hurt, or other emotional, crowd-pleasing devices. —**er.** *n.* A wrestler.

grunt-and-groaner. *n.* A wrestler. *Has increased pop. with the advent of televised wrestling shows incorporating excessive facial grimaces and moans from the wrestlers.*

grunt-iron. *n.* A tuba. *Synthetic use by cartoonists and newsp. columnists.*

grut. *n.* = crud. *The similarity of pronunciation may have confused the two words.*

guardhouse lawyer. *n.* 1. A soldier who, well informed or not, often quotes and discusses military law and soldiers' rights. *Orig. Army use. Since c1930.* → 2. One who

likes to advise others, freely, and authoritatively though not acquainted with the problem; one who knows little but talks much about a specific controversial subject.

gub = gob.

gubble = ubble-gubble.

guff; goff. *n.* Empty or foolish talk; chiding, exaggerated, or pompous talk, writing, or thinking; boloney. → *v.t., v.i.* To deceive, lie, or exaggerate. *Usu. in* "I'm not guffing [to] you."

guinney. *n.* A racetrack stable hand. *Horse-racing use.*

guinzo = ginzo.

gulch = drygulch.

gull. *n.* A prostitute, esp. one who follows a USN fleet or works near naval bases. *W.W.II USN use.*

gully-jumper. *n.* A farmer. *Archaic and dial.*

gully-low. *adj.* Sensuous; "dirty"; said of a style of playing jazz.

gum. *v.i.* To talk, esp. to gossip or talk needlessly. *v.t.* 1. = gum up. 2. To deceive or cheat. 3. To spoil or ruin something, esp. to spoil by interfering. *Usu. in* "gum up" *and* "gum up the works."

gum-beater. *n.* A talker; esp. a braggart or a loud, frequent talker; a blowhard.

gum-beating. *n.* 1. A chat or conversation. *Orig. Harlem jive talk.* → 2. Useless or pointless talk or discussion.

gum boot = gumshoe.

gum-foot. *n.* A policeman, esp. a plain-clothes man.

gumheel. *n.* = gumshoe. *v.i.* To work as a detective.

gummer. *n.* An old, toothless man; an old decrepit man.

gummixed up; gummoxed up. Confused, mixed up.

gummy. *adj.* Sentimental, overly emotional. *c1940. n.* 1. Glue; any sticky substance. 2. A pitchman who sells miracle glue that is reputed to join any broken item or materials. *c1930. Carnival use.*

gumshoe. *v.i., v.t.* 1. To walk quietly, to sneak, esp. to walk a beat; said of a policeman. 2. To walk in, or as if wearing, rubber-soled shoes; to walk silently and stealthily. *c1910.* → 3. To work as a police detective. *n.* A detective; any policeman. *Since c1920. adj.* Done quietly or stealthily.

gumshoe man = gumshoe.

gum up. To ruin or spoil a plan or the successful completion of a task, esp. by blundering; to blunder; to confuse a person, esp. by making a mistake.

gun. *n.* 1. A professional thief or robber; esp. a pickpocket. *Since at least c1840. From the Yiddish "gonif" or "goney" = a thief and Yiddish sl. "gonif" = to steal, both of which were taken directly into Amer. sl., reinforced by "gunsel."* → 2. A hoodlum or thug; a gunman. *From first meaning reinforced by "gun."* 3. The throttle or gas pedal of a car, truck, or plane. *Since c1925.* 4. A hypodermic needle. *Dope addict use c1935.* 5. An important person. 6. A visual examination; a look or glance. *v.t.* 1. To look at intensely; to stare at carefully; to make a complete visual inspection. *Since c1860.* 2. To shoot a person with a gun. 3. To accelerate the motor of a car, plane, or boat, specif. before releasing the brake or starting, so that the motor is warmed up and operating at maximum speed when the vehicle begins to move. *The most common verbal usage. Almost colloq.* 4. To carry something to another; to be a waiter or errand boy to another. *c1940.*

gun, give [something] the. To accelerate a car, plane, or boat to its maximum speed; to accelerate any motor or machine; to gun an engine.

gunboat. *n.* An empty one-gallon tin can. —s. *n.pl.* 1. A pair of shoes; esp. a pair of very large shoes. *Since c1885.* 2. A pair of overshoes, galoshes, or rubbers. 3. The feet; esp. large feet. *All uses somewhat humorous.*

guncel = gunsel.

guniff = goniff.

gunk. *n.* 1. Dirt in various forms; esp., oily grime; gook. → 2. Any viscous liquid or oily fluid; gook. 3. Make-up; any cosmetic. 4. Dehydrated or powdered food. *Some USN use since W.W.II.*

gun moll; gun-moll. *n.* 1. A female thief or criminal. *From "gonif" = to steal.* 2. A female accomplice of a criminal. *From the mistaken belief that the expression is from "gun," a weapon, and thus a gun moll carries a gun for her underworld paramour.*

gunpoke. *n.* A gunman; an armed robber. *A term patterned after "cowpoke."*

gunsel; gonzel; gonsil; guncel; guntzel. *n.* 1. A catamite; a young inexperienced boy, esp. a hobo, such as a catamite would desire for a companion. *Prison and hobo use since c1915. From the German "gänzel" and/or the Yiddish "gantzel" = gosling. Underworld use since c1925.* → 2. A treacherous person; a sly, sneaky person; an unethical, untrustworthy person. 3. A thief; a criminal; a member of the underworld.

gun-slinger. *n.* A gunman; a hired killer or armed robber. *Orig. an old Western term.*

gussied up. Dressed in one's best clothes.

gut. *n.* 1. The stomach. *Very common.* 2. Sausage. *In hobo lingo "punk and gut" = bread and sausage.* 3. An easy course in college; a pipe course. *v.t.* To remove all accessories, frills, or ornament from something. *Orig. hot rod use; some cool and beat use c1955.* —s. *n.sing.* Courage; perseverance; audacity. *Colloq. n.pl.* 1. The insides of a person or animal. → 2. Courage; nerve. → 3. Solid substance; forceful or meaty contents. → 4. The insides or working parts of a machine. —ter. *n.* In diving, an attempted dive in which the diver falls prone on the water instead of going in head foremost; a belly-whacker. *Dial.* —ty. *adj.* 1. = back alley. *Jazz use.* 2. Courageous.

gutbucket; gut-bucket. *n.* 1. A cheap saloon and/or gambling house where musicians could play for patrons' contributions. 2. A cheap dive or joint. *Still in use among Negroes.* 3. A sexually suggestive, dirty style of jazz, appropriate to a cheap saloon. *The orig. New Orleans hot style for playing a blues. Jazz use.*

gut-burglar. *n.* A logging-camp cook. *A term based on "belly-robber."*

gut course. In college, an easy course.

gut-hammer. *n.* A gong, usu. a suspended iron triangle used as a dinner bell for logging camps, ranches, farms, and the like.

gutter, in the. 1. Fig., as a drunken bum, who falls down drunk in the gutter. *Colloq.* 2. Without money, respect, or hope. 3. Preoccupied with the obscene or lewd. *Usu. in "to have [one's] mind in the gutter."*

gutterpup. *n.* A person of the gutter; a bum.

guy. *v.t.* To ridicule; to tease or mock. *Colloq.* *n.* 1. A boy or man; a fellow. *Orig. used without modification, often of a stranger, and implied, as it still often does, an average, pleasant fellow or "regular guy." Since c1925 sometimes takes a modifier to = an unpleasant fellow, as a "tough guy" or "wise guy." Very common since c1925.* → 2. A person of either sex. *Some use since c1930.* 3. A friend; a chum or pal.

guzzle. *v.i., v.t.* 1. To drink rapidly. *Colloq.* → 2. To drink liquor. → 3. To drink liquor constantly or in large amounts. 4. To kill, esp. by strangling to death. 5. To neck. *The last two meanings are Damon Runyon creations, n.* 1. The throat. —d. *adj.* 1. Arrested. 2. Drunk.

guzzle shop. A saloon.

gym. *n.* 1. A gymnasium. *Colloq. Refers to a gymnasium as a place of athletic significance only.* 2. Exercise taken in, games played in, or an exercise class held in, a gymnasium; specif., gymnastics.

gyp; gip; jip. *n.* 1. One who uses shrewd, unethical business methods; a swindler, a cheater. *Colloq; orig. a carnival and circus term; c1910.* → 2. A swindle, an act of cheating; an unfair transaction or decision. 3. Vim; pep. *A variation of the dial. "gimp."* 4. A female dog, esp. a racing dog. *Perhaps from the 17th c. Eng. sl. term "jip" = servant or trained animal. v.t.* To cheat or swindle. *Colloq. adj.* Dishonest. —per. *n.* A cheater, a swindler. —po; jippo. *n.* 1. Part-time, temporary work; piecework. *c1920. Hobo, itinerant laborer, and logger use.* 2. A pieceworker or itinerant worker. → 3. A small factory, logging contractor, cannery, or the like that employs a pieceworker or gives a hobo a day's work. *v.t.* To cheat; to gyp. —ster. *n.* A swindler; a gypper.

gyp artist; gyp-artist. An adroit and constant swindler or cheater.

gyp joint; gyp-joint. *n.* Any public place that overcharges, cheats, or promises its customers more than it gives them. *Common since c1935.*

gyrene. *n.* A U.S. Marine. *Also spelled "girene," "gyrine," and occas. with "j" for "g."*

gyve; jive. *n.* A marijuana cigaret; marijuana. *Since c1930.*

H

H. *n.* Heroin as used by addicts. *Addict use.*

haba haba. *interj. A command or request to hurry up or speed up. W.W.II Armed Forces use, usu. USN use in the Pacific Theater.*

habit. *n.* Addiction to a drug.

habit, off the. Cured of drug addiction; not under the influence of drugs.

hack. *n.* **1.** A taxicab. *Colloq. Orig. a horse-drawn hackney coach, the term was applied to automobiles used as taxicabs.* **2.** A persistent cough, usu. caused by nervousness or throat irritation rather than a cold. **3.** A prison guard, a prison official; a watchman. *Convict use.* → **4.** A white person. *Prison use. Negro use. In the U.S. this term never means girl, as it does in Australia.* *v.i.* **1.** To drive a taxicab as an occupation. **2.** To cough repeatedly or habitually —ie. *n.* The driver of a cab, a hack-driver. *Orig. the driver of a horse-drawn hackney cab, now applied to all cab drivers.*

hack-driver. *n.* A chief petty officer in the U.S. Navy.

had it, [one] (has, have). **1.** Emotionally or physically fatigued or exhausted, so that one is unable to respond further; defeated, esp. by fatigue caused by striving to succeed; to have failed or meet with such failure, defeat, or ill fortune that one has no further spirit, enthusiasm, courage, perserverance, or desire to succeed. → **2.** To have been given one's last chance to show one's worth or reliability, and to have failed; no longer liked, admired, or respected; no longer believed to be attractive, worthwhile, trustworthy or successful by the speaker. *Both uses common since c1940.*

hag. *n.* A homely young woman. —**gy.** *adj.* Ugly; like a hag.

haha; ha-ha. *n.* A joke; a cause of merriment. See **merry haha.**

hair, get in [one's]. To irritate, bother, or annoy a person; to get in someone's way. *Lit. = to annoy as would lice in one's hair.*

hair, in [one's]. Annoying [a person], with the implication that the annoyer is a louse.

hair bag. A person who remembers and speaks of or gossips about past intrigues, scandals, events, and the like.

hair down, let [one's]. To shed all of one's reserve, inhibitions, or dignity, usu. to act or talk very informally or intimately.

hair net = win the porcelain hair net.

hair off the dog, take. To gain experience; to grow older. *Usu. in "I've taken a little more hair off the dog." From cowboy use; lit. having branded a few more calves. Not to be confused with* **hair of the dog.**

hair of the dog. A drink of liquor. *Since c1925; from "hair of the dog that bit you."*

hair of the dog that bit [you, me, him, one, etc.]. *n.* The liquor or a drink of liquor that made one drunk or sick the previous night, or caused one's present hangover. *One tradition has it that the best cure for a hangover is a drink of the liquor that caused it.*

hairpin. *n.* **1.** A man; a person of either sex. → **2.** A woman, esp. a housewife. *Vagabond argot.* **3.** A crackpot; fig., a person with a mind bent like a hairpin; a screwball.

hairy. *adj.* **1.** Old, already known, passé; usu. said of a joke or story. *Colloq.* **2.** Unpleasant, lousy. *c1950; orig. West Coast teenager use. Increasing in pop.* *n.* A brave person. *Usu. used jocularly to indicate a man who often tells stories of his own bravery.*

half. *n.* In football, a halfback. *c1930.*

half-. *A common sl. prefix used to indicate:* **1.** Confusion. **2.** Drunkenness. *Here the "half" ceases to be a polite prefix.*

half a shake. **1.** Fig., half a second. *E.g., "I'll be ready in half a shake."* **2.** An opportunity or chance with restrictions; an unfair chance.

half-baked. *adj.* Stupid; half-witted. *Colloq. since c1915.*

half-buck. *n.* A half-dollar.

half-cocked; half cocked. *adj.* Enthusiastic or emotional about something of which one knows little; without full or proper plans, knowledge, objectivity, experience, or understanding.

half-corned. *adj.* Drunk.

half-pint. *n.* 1. A person of short stature. *Usu. used affectionately or derog.* 2. A boy. *adj.* Short of stature; small.

half-shot; half shot. *adj.* 1. Half drunk. *Since c1835; still very common.* 2. Drunk. *Since c1925.* 3. Dissipated; not in control of one's mind or muscles; suffering from dissipation or physical or emotional shock.

half-stewed. *adj.* Drunk. *Common.*

halfy. *n.* A legless man.

hall. *n.* Alcohol. *A respelling of the "-hol" of alcohol.*

halvies. *n.* Half of whatever is at hand, usu. sweets, money, or children's prizes. *Child use. To shout "Halvies!" obligates another child to give one half of his loot, purchase, or the like.*

ham. *n.* 1. An amateur worker, performer, or athlete; almost always one proficient and an amateur only in that he does a thing for the fun of it, as a hobby, rather than for money; occasionally an inexperienced or inferior worker, performer, or athlete; specif., an amateur actor or radio-telegraph operator (*colloq.*). *From "amateur" in its orig. meaning = one who does something for the love of it.* → 2. Specif., an amateur or professional actor who is affected, conceited, and who strives for attention over the other actors on the stage. → 3. A pretentious, affected person; esp. one who assumes or attempts to convey an impression of gentility not actually his; a conceited person. 4. Food; meals. *Some circus use.* *adj.* 1. Amateur. 2. Inferior. *v.i., v.t.* 1. To act a part poorly, affectedly, or obviously; to display conceit; to attempt to convey the impression that one is more important or knowledgeable than one actually is. 2. To overact; to seek attention.

ham-and-egger. *n.* Specif., an aver-

age prize fighter. *Since c1920.* **—y.** *n.* A restaurant; esp. a small restaurant or lunch counter.

hamburger. *n.* 1. A badly scarred and often beaten prize fighter. 2. A bum or tramp; anyone who is down and out. 3. An inferior racing dog; lit., one that should be ground up for food. 4. A mixture of mud and "skin-food" used as a facial treatment in beauty parlors.

hamburger heaven. Any small restaurant or lunch counter featuring hamburgers and quick meals. *Many such establishments are actually named "Hamburger Heaven," as is a chain in N.Y.C.*

hamburger out of, make. To beat up; to thrash severely.

ham-fatter. *n.* An inferior, obvious entertainer or entertainment; an actor or act whose subtlety is no greater than that of a Negro minstrel show. *Since c1880.*

ham joint. 1. A cheap restaurant. 2. A place where one can sit and relax, doing nothing.

hammer-man. *n.* A person of authority. *Some Negro use.*

ham up = ham.

hand. *n.* The clapping of hands in applause by a person or an audience. *Colloq. since c1930.*

handbasket, go to hell in a. Amateurish, small-sized (handbasket-sized) dissipation of the kind indulged in, usu. by the young, as protest against a disappointment or a frustration; driving too fast, drinking too much, and the like, for a fairly short period of time.

handbasket, in a = with knobs on.

handbook. *n.* 1. A place, other than a race-track, where horse-racing bets are made. 2. The owner or an employee of such a betting business.

handful. *n.* A five-year prison sentence. *In allusion to the five fingers. Underworld use.*

handies. *n.pl.* The act of holding hands, as by lovers.

hand it to someone. To give some-one credit for merit; to compli-ment.

handle. *n.* **1.** A person's name, nickname, or alias; the name of a person or the name he uses, whether or not his legal name. *Since c1910.* **2.** Gross profit, usu. of a sporting event, illegal ac-tivities, or short term business deal; the take. *Since c1920.* **3.** The amount of money bet on a specif. gambling or sporting event or during a specif. time with one gambling establish-ment; the receipts of a gambling establishment before the money returned to the customers as winnings is deducted.

hand-me-down. *n.* **1.** An item, usu. clothing, used by one person and then given to another; lit., clothes handed down from father to son or from an older child to a younger one. → **2.** Secondhand clothes. *adj.* Used, secondhand.

handout. *n.* **1.** A meal or a bundle of food handed out from a house to a beggar. *Hobo use since c1880.* → **2.** Old clothing handed out to a beggar. *Since c1890.* → **3.** Small sums of money given to a beggar so that he may buy food or a bed for the night. → **4.** Fig., any gift, donation, or loan, as from public funds or a founda-tion. **5.** Small brochure or other printed matter given out by peo-ple on street corners to passers-by, such as advertising matter; a broadside.

handshaker. *n.* An excessively af-fable or obsequious person; one who curries favor, as a politician trying to impress the voters or a student toadying to a professor; a flatterer and politician, rather than a worker. *Lit. and fig.,* one who goes around shaking hands with many others, esp. the in-fluential. *Often, but not always, used scornfully. Orig. military use, c1915; by 1930 had spread to college student use; now gen-eral use.*

handsome ransom. *n.* Any large sum of money. *Orig. c1935 jive and swing use; some c1940 teen-age use.*

hang. *n.* The knack. *Colloq. Usu. in "to get the hang of it." v.i.* **1.** To frequent a place; to associate with a person or persons. *Short for "hang out."* **2.** In horse-racing, to hang back, to lack re-serve speed during the last stage of a race. **3.** To wait; to await; to loaf or idle.

hang a few on; hang on a few. To drink several drinks of whisky; usu. to drink enough whisky to become at least slightly drunk.

hang around. To loiter or linger. *Colloq.*

hang it easy = Take it easy. *Some teenage use since c1950.*

hang loose = Take it easy. *A syn. for "hang it easy."*

hang one on. **1.** To hit with the fist; to land a blow on someone. *Since c1900.* **2.** To get complete-ly drunk.

hangout. *n.* Any loafing place; a recognized meeting place. *Since c1895; orig. hobo and under-world use.* **hang out.** To loaf or loiter in a recognized rendezvous, such as a bar, drugstore, or the like. *Very common.*

hang out the laundry. To drop paratroops from an airplane. *W.W.II Army Air Force use.*

hang out the wash. In baseball, to hit a line drive.

hangover. *n.* **1.** The unpleasant physiological effects occurring after drinking too much of an al-coholic beverage. *Very common since c1920.* **2.** Fat buttocks, which would lit. hang over a chair. *Used humorously and derog.*

hang up. A request or command for another to stop talking or teasing; shut up! cut it out! *From telephone usage.*

hankie; hanky. *n.* A handkerchief. *Mainly women use. Colloq.*

hanky-pank. *n.* **1.** Any of several carnival games that cost 5¢ or 10¢ to play. → **2.** A carnival barker's urgings to get customers to take a chance in such a game; a spiel. → 3. Anything cheap and gaudy; hanky-panky. *adj.* Costing 5¢ or 10¢; cheap and gaudy. —**y.** *n.* 1. Deception; anything crooked or unethical; funny business, hocus-pocus, monkey business. *Colloq.* 2. Specif., illicit sexual activity; philandering; adultery.

happenso. *n.* A happenstance. *Colloq.*

happy. *adj.* Drunk; usu. slightly drunk. *Lit., the first stage of drunkenness, when one is in a happy mood. Very common since c1920.*

happy cabbage. Money; esp. a sizable amount of money to be spent on clothes, entertainment, or other self-satisfying things.

happy money. Money earned or saved to be spent for personal enjoyment or gratification.

hard-ankle. *n.* A coal miner. *Southern hill dial.*

hard-boiled. *adj.* 1. Without sentiment; tough; mean; callous; not sentimental; cynical; unconcerned about the feelings or opinions of others. *Orig. used in W.W.I Army training camps, almost always to describe a drill officer or sergeant. May orig. have implied the stiff "boiled" collars worn by some officers as well as that one is as tough as a hard-boiled egg.* → 2. Stern, strict, exacting. *Colloq. since c1930.*

hard-boiled egg. A hard-boiled person.

hardboot. *n.* Orig. a Southern cavalryman; a Southern horseman.

hard hat. 1. A derby hat. → 2. Men who wear derby hats; specif. Eastern businessmen during the 1880's and later crooks, gamblers, and detectives. *May have orig. been a cowboy term = Easterner or absentee ranch owner.*

hard-head. *n.* 1. An uncomprehending or stupid person. 2. One who will not change his mind; one who is hard to convince and is unyielding. 3. A Southern hill

mountaineer. *Dial.* —**ed.** *adj.* Stubborn; strong-willed; practical.

hard John. A field agent of the FBI (Federal Bureau of Investigation). *Some underworld use. Reinforced by "John" Edgar Hoover, head of the Bureau.*

hard liquor. Whisky; esp. corn whisky drunk straight.

hard money. The currency of a nation that holds a high proportion of gold or silver in relation to its currency in circulation; money worth its full face value or more in purchasing power or international exchange; money that is hard to earn or borrow, but is worth its full face value or more. *A banking term that has become pop. since c1940.*

hard-nosed. *adj.* 1. Stubborn; prone to anger. *Orig. carnival sl.* 2. Homely; ugly.

hard-rocker. *n.* A prospector; a miner.

hard sell. The act or an instance of selling or advertising merchandise in an aggressive, loud, unpleasant way; an aggressive pitch. *Orig. a "Madison Avenue" term applied to television advertising.*

hardtail; **hard-tail.** *n.* An Army mule. *Army use. Orig. Southern hill dial. spread by hoboes, loggers, and mule skinners.*

hard time. 1. Trouble; difficulty; a difficult or troublesome job or position; an act, instance, or period of trouble, difficulty, or adversity; an unpleasant experience. 2. Specif., difficulty or trouble caused by another's desire, wish, personality, or whim. → 3. Specif., a sexual, romantic, or personal rebuke or refusal from one of the opposite sex. Usu. in "did she give you a hard time?" *The last two uses are the more common.* —**s.** *sing.* A period of financial adversity, either for an individual or for a community or nation; a depression.

hard top. 1. A strong-willed or hard-headed person. 2. A closed automobile with a flat roof and no upright roof supports, similar in appearance to a convertible car. *Actually a shortening for "hard-top convertible," the term signifies features introduced by the automobile industry in the post-W.W.II period.*

hard up. Much in need of something or someone, usu. either money or sexual activity.

hardware. *n.* 1. Weapons. *In use since c1865; orig. implied rifles and knives, such as could be bought in hardware and general stores, and Civil War artillery; by c1920 was limited to pistols and weapons easily concealed and was used in Southern hill regions and on ranches. From then on, the movies and detective stories so used the term to mean easily concealed weapons and associated it with underworld use, which is still the most common implication. However, with W.W.II the word again obtained its meaning of any weapons, large or small, used in individual or national defense.* 2. Jewelry, esp. identification and fraternal jewelry. *Since c1935.* → 3. Military insignia or medals. *Common during W.W.II.*

hard way, the. 1. In crap-shooting, the instance of making or attempting to make an even-numbered point by shooting two equal numbers on the dice. *Thus, "6 the hard way" is made by two 3's, as opposed to a 5 and a 1 or a 4 and a 2.* → 2. The difficult means or method for accomplishing anything; the roundabout way.

harlot's hello, a. Something that doesn't exist; nothing; zero.

harness. *n.* 1. A policeman's uniform. *Common since c1930; underworld use since c1913.* → 2. The leather jacket, boots, gloves, and cap or goggles that make up a motorcyclist's dress. *c1945, West Coast motorcyclist use. Such a harness has become the standard dress among certain nonmotorcycling teenage groups.*

harness bull. 1. A uniformed policeman; a patrolman. *Underworld, prison, and hobo use since c1915.* 2. Also used attrib. = police-like, pertaining to the police.

harness cop = harness bull.

harness dick = harness bull.

harp-polisher. *n.* A clergyman, esp. a priest.

Hart, Schaffner, and Marx. In poker, three jacks. *From the well-known firm of clothing manufacturers.*

has-been. *n.* 1. A person who formerly was successful and important; esp. an aging entertainer or athlete who is no longer in the public's favor. 2. A person who has been supplanted by a rival in love, business, or the entertainment field. 3. Any person whose personality, politics, dress, personal tastes, ideas, or the like, are outmoded; one to whom past memories are more important than the present. *Since c1900; colloq. since c1930.*

hash. *v.t.* 1. To discuss thoroughly; to hash over. 2. To make a mistake, ruin a plan, confuse an idea. *v.i.* To earn one's living or to gain free board and meals by being a waiter, esp. by being a part-time waiter in a hotel or boarding house. *n.* 1. Any cooked food; all the food served at a meal; a meal. 2. News, rumors, gossip. —**er.** *n.* 1. A waiter or waitress who serves food at a restaurant or lunch counter. *Note that a hasher may work for a better restaurant than a hash-slinger.* 2. A cook or kitchen worker. —**ery.** *n.* A small restaurant or lunch counter.

hash foundry. A cheap restaurant; a charitable institution that provides free meals to the destitute. *Hobo use.*

hash-house; hashhouse. *n.* A restaurant, lunchroom, boarding house, or the like, esp. a cheap one. *Since c1875; now colloq.*

hash mark. A military service stripe, worn diagonally or horizontally on the lower sleeve of a uniform indicating the number of years or enlistments which a serviceman has served. *The color, width, placement, and amount of service time that each stripe indicates has varied. Very common in both U.S. Army and U.S. Navy during W.W.II.*

hash over. To discuss; esp. to discuss a subject more than once; to review a discussion or plan.

hash session. A leisurely session of talking, arguing, and gossiping; a men's bull session or a women's gabfest. *Not as common as "bull session" or "gabfest."*

hash-slinger; hashslinger; hash slinger. *n.* 1. A waiter or waitress in an eating place; esp. a waitress in a cheap restaurant or lunch counter whose primary job is to deliver food from kitchen to tables or the counter, without observing the niceties of good service. *Since c1865; the implication of waitress rather than waiter and of a restaurant that specializes in cheap, quickly served food rather than in quality and service became strong c1935, with an increasing number of women workers and when Americans started to eat more meals away from their own homes.* 2. A kitchen worker, a cook, cook's helper, or the like. *Since c1900.*

hash stripe = hash mark.

hassel; hassle. *n.* A disagreement, dispute, quarrel, or argument; a struggle or fight.

hat. *n.* 1. Fig., those items of clothing that are put on and those household chores done immediately before leaving a house or office. Thus "get your hat and let's go" can mean "put on your coat, gloves, hat, and overshoes, turn off the radio, close the window, and let's leave." 2. An ineffectual railroad man, often an old employee who has no specific

duties. 3. Any of various helmets, such as a diver's helmet, or uniform caps.

hat, in [one's]. An expression of incredulity.

hat, pass the. 1. Lit., to pass a man's hat among the members of an audience or group as a means of collecting money. 2. To ask for charity; to beg.

hatch. *n.* The human mouth and forethroat, esp., but not always, when considered the receptacle for alcoholic beverages.

hatchet-man. *n.* 1. A professional gunman. *Since c1925. Successor to the oldtime "hatchet-armed killer."* 2. An aggressive, militant newspaper writer or politician's associate; one whose job is to destroy the reputation of others or to do unethical tasks for a political party, office holder, or candidate.

hatchet-thrower. *n.* A Spaniard, Puerto Rican, or Cuban. *Negro use.*

hat-rack. *n.* 1. Any skinny, old, or sickly farm animal; specif., an old horse or cow. → 2. Any skinny or sickly person; a bean pole.

haul [one's] ashes. 1. To leave or depart; to force or request someone to leave. 2. To do physical harm to another; to beat up someone.

haul in. To arrest. *Lit. = to haul the arrested person to jail.*

haul it. To run away; flee. *Harlem Negro use.*

haul off on [someone]. To hit someone hard with the fist.

haul the mail. To speed up; to make up lost time by doing something faster. *Orig. railroad and trucker use.*

hausfrau. *n.* A woman, esp. if unattractive, whose only or main interests are cleaning, washing, ironing, cooking, and other domestic duties. Used either as a compliment to or as a criticism of the woman. *From the German "Hausfrau."*

have. For phrases beginning with "have," see under principal word of phrase.

have it, let [someone]. 1. To strike someone with one's fist or a weapon; to kill a person. → 2. To accuse, criticize, rebuke, expose, or in any other way to harass a person or group severely and directly.

have-not. n. A poor person, group, region, or nation. *Colloq.*

hawk. *v.i.* To clear the throat, esp. to spit.

hay. n. 1. Marijuana. *Some addict use.* 2. A small amount of money; peanuts. Usu. in "that ain't hay." *Almost always in the negative "that ain't hay" = that's a substantial amount of money.*

hay, hit the. To go to bed; to lie down to sleep. *Common since c1910.*

hay, make. To take full advantage of one's opportunities while one can; to profit or benefit fully from one's advantage, success, or position. *From the expression "make hay while the sun shines" = work, profit, or take full advantage when conditions are favorable, because they might not always be favorable.*

hay, the. n. 1. A bed. → 2. Sleep; unconsciousness.

hay-burner. n. 1. A horse; esp. a race horse and part. a slow or cheap race horse. *Since c1915 very common race track term.* → 2. A cavalryman. *Some Army use.*

hay-eater. *n.* A white person. *Some Negro use. Not always derog.*

haymaker. n. 1. A heavy blow or swing with the fist; usu. a knockout punch in the boxing ring or elsewhere. *Orig. a boxing term. Since c1910. From "make hay" + "the hay" = sleep, unconsciousness.* → 2. Fig., any crushing or final blow with any weapon. → 3. Fig., any crushing remark, piece of news, or event. 4. Fig., any complete effort, sensational try, or last resort; often

the best song, joke, or performance of an entertainer's repertory.

hayseed. n. 1. A farmer or rustic; a hick or rube. *c1890.* → 2. Fig., rustic qualities, *adj.* Rural, rustic; resembling, suggesting, or located in or near farms, rural areas, or small towns. —er. *n.* = hayseed.

haywire. *adj.* 1. Broken, dilapidated; makeshift; flimsy; poorly constructed, operated, or equipped; jumbled or confused. *Since c1915. Farmer, rancher, and logger use; prob. from the use of the baling wire, used in a hay-baler, to mend farm implements, thus causing an association between "hay wire" and broken or dilapidated things.* 2. Crazy; in an unusual, confused manner; confused.

head. n. 1. A headache, usu. one accompanying or constituting a hangover. *Often in the phrase "to have a head." Common since c1920.* 2. The mouth. 3. Foam, usu. on the top of a glass of beer. *Colloq.* 4. One person or several esp. considered as customers or potential customers or suckers; specif., a ticket buyer or spectator. *From farm and ranch use, "head" = one of a herd of cattle.* 5. A young woman, esp. a sexually attainable woman. 6. Fig., a person, an individual. —er. *n.* 1. A head-first fall; a dive or plunge. *Colloq. since c1930.* → 2. An attempt or try; a gamble; a plunge. → 3. A failure or mistake; a fall.

head, have a. To have a hangover; to feel as if one's head is swollen and throbbing, owing to overindulgence in alcoholic beverages.

head, in above [one's]. 1. = in deep water. → 2. Certain to fail or meet with disaster. → 3. Unable to meet one's financial obligations.

head, off [one's]. Insane, out of one's mind.

head, open [one's] = open [one's] face.

head, the. *n.* A bathroom or "men's room"; esp., a toilet or urinal. *Often in "Where's the head?" c1935. Orig. USN use, because ship's toilets are often squeezed in near a bulkhead. Wide W.W.II use in both USN and USA. In Army sl. orig. = an outdoor latrine. Still the most common word for bathroom, toilet, or urinal in the Armed Forces. Has wide verbal civilian use by men.*

headache. *n.* 1. Any trouble, cause of worry or vexation. *Since c1930.* → 2. One's wife.

headache band. A women's hair accessory made of fabric, leather, or plastic, from one to three inches wide, and worn very tight across the line between the forehead and hair and over the ears, usu. with an eggbeater hair style. *Common c1925 and c1958.*

headbone. *n.* The skull, the head. *Some pop. owing to freq. use in the "Pogo" comic strip, which sometimes assumes a Southern swamp dial. Orig. from a pop. old Negro folk song.*

head hunter. The owner or boss of an executive employment agency; a business executive in charge of recruiting new personnel.

headlight. *n.* 1. A light-skinned Negro. *Some Negro use.* 2. A large diamond; a diamond ring.

head shrinker. A psychiatrist, esp. a psychoanalyst.

heads up! *imp.* A warning to get out of the way quickly, or to be careful. *Very common.*

head-up. *n.* A stupid or inattentive person.

heap. *n.* 1. Any automobile, esp. an old or ordinary one. *From "junk heap" or "scrap heap."* → 2. A motorcycle. → 3. An airplane. *Some aviator and W.W.II Air Force use. All three meanings can be derog. by others or affectionately by the owner or driver.* —s. *n.pl.* A large amount.

adj. Very much, much; many. *Colloq. since c1930.*

heart. *n.* 1. Courage; determination; stamina. *Most freq. used when speaking of the attributes of an athlete. Colloq.* 2. Kindness, sympathy, generosity. *The emotions that the ancients believed orig. in the heart rather than in the spleen or mind. Colloq.*

heart, have a. To be (more) generous, sympathetic, or understanding; to be less severe or exacting. *Usu. in the imperative, as a plea. Colloq.*

hear the birdies sing. To be unconscious. *Implies that one is dreaming of pleasant things and has ringing ears.*

hearts and flowers. 1. Sentimentality; that which is said or done for sympathy; sob stuff. *From the title of a mournful pop. song, c1910, which is conventionally played to indicate sadness or overt sentimentality. Sometimes the listener to a "hearts and flowers" story will mimic a violinist playing an imaginary violin to indicate his awareness of the sentimentality.* 2. A knockout. *Prize fight use.*

heat. *n.* 1. Trouble, usu. for criminals and usu. in the form of intense police searches or other police activity. *Underworld use, c1925.* → 2. A town, country, or area in which the police are actively looking for a criminal or are very active. *c1930.* → 3. Mob violence, the resentment of a crowd or audience due to being cheated or fooled. *c1935, carnival use.* → 4. Any trouble, esp. the anger or strict orders of a boss, superior, or friend. *Since c1940.* 5. A gun, usu. a pistol. *Underworld use, c1930.* → 6. Gunfire; usu. in "give someone the heat" = to kill by shooting. *Prison use.* 7. Drunkenness; a jag. 8. In boxing, a round. 9. In baseball, an inning. *The above two common sports usages, since c1930, are taken from the stan-*

dard racing term. —ed. *adj.* Reprimanded; chastized; punished. *Rock-and-roll use since c1955.* —er. *n.* 1. A gun; revolver or pistol. *Since c1930 widely used in the underworld and in movies and books about the underworld.* 2. A cigar.

heat artist. A drinker of canned heat. *Some hobo use.*

heat-can. *n.* A jet plane. *c1950, Air Force use.*

heat on [someone], put the. 1. To demand payment, work, or satisfaction from someone, esp. with a warning or threat; to harass; to take aggressive action against. → 2. To request or require intensified effort, as from an employee.

heat-packer. *n.* A gunman. *Lit. = one who carries trouble in the form of a gun.*

heat's on, the. A condition of being intensely sought or pursued by the police. *The best known of expressions containing "heat," this is very popular in stories and movies of crime, though no longer common with the underworld.*

heave. *v.i., v.t.* To vomit. *c1940; very pop. student and young adult use. "Heaving" is usu. associated with modern or sophisticated dissipation, worry, or a short siege of stomach virus; it is never the result of serious illness.* —r. *n.* A woman or young lady.

heave-ho. *n.* 1. The act of throwing a person out of a place; any forcible ejection of a person; the bum's rush. → 2. Fig., the act of rejecting or casting off a friend or intimate, dismissing a lover, denying another's friendship; the cold shoulder; the act of being fired, the bounce. *Both usages often in the phrase "the old heave-ho."*

heaven = nigger heaven.

heave-o = heave-ho.

heavy. *n.* 1. A hoodlum or thug; a criminal in one of the more violent phases of crime. 2. The villain in a play or movie; an actor who or a role that calls for an actor who looks or can act villainously or in a tough manner. *Theater use since c1925.* 3. A heavyweight boxer. *adj.* 1. Plentiful. 2. Hot, esp. too hot to handle or drink. *Usu. said of liquids.* 3. = hot, esp. meaning passionate, sexy, lascivious, lewd, or dangerous.

heavy, on the. Engaged in crime; working, living, or traveling as a criminal.

heavy artillery = artillery.

heavy cream. A fat girl or young woman.

heavy date. 1. An important, highly desired social engagement with one of the opposite sex; a date with one's fiancé or major love interest; usu. such dates involve heavy necking or lovemaking. *Since c1925.* → 2. One's partner on such a date. *c1925.* 3. Any important engagement.

heavy foot. A driver who presses heavily on the gas pedal of his car; a fast driver or speeder.

heavy money (sugar, dough, jack). Much money; enough money to make one important or influential.

heavy necking. Extremely passionate necking; intimate caresses and kisses often including sexual foreplay but never actual coitus, carried on passionately and during a fairly extended time.

heavy-sticker. In baseball, a hard hitter.

heavy sugar. 1. Much money; a large amount of money, esp. when assembled during a brief period or from entertainment, sports, or gambling. *Since c1920.* → 2. A wealthy person. → 3. An object, such as a diamond ring or big car, that represents much money.

hectic. *adj.* Confusing, busy, exciting. *Colloq.*

hedge; hedge off. *v.i., v.t.* To be indecisive or act indecisively;

specif., in gambling, to bet on one team, number, or entry and then to make a smaller bet on another or the other team, number, or entry, so as to recoup part of one's loss if the larger bet loses; to transfer part of a bet one has to another, to reduce possible loss.

hedgehopper. *n.* An airplane that is flying close to the ground; esp. a pilot who flies his plane close to the ground, as does a crop duster or the pilot of a military plane whose duty it is to observe an enemy's position.

heebie-jeebies. *n.* A feeling of nervousness, fright, or worry; the willies; occasionally, delirium tremens.

heebies. *n.sing.* = heebie-jeebies.

heel. *n.* 1. A contemptible, despicable scoundrel of a man; a bounder, rotter, or cad; a man who lacks gentlemanly feelings and will take advantage of attractive females and double-cross his friends. *Although most common after c1925, the word = the antithesis of a gentleman to such an old-fashioned extent that it is probably much older. Colloq.* 2. An escape from prison or the scene of a crime; a getaway. *v.t.* 1. To arm oneself; to provide arms to another. *Colloq. since c1870.* 2. To provide a person with money. 3. To seek or court; esp. to seek favor from a superior or a group; to compete for social or business status by courting the favor of special individuals or groups. *v.i.* To run away; to escape or make a getaway. —ed. *adj.* 1. Equipped. *Since c1880.* → 2. Armed; equipped with a weapon. *Since c1890.* → 3. Wealthy; equipped with much money. *Colloq. since c1930.* 4. Drunk. —er. *n.* 1. A contemptible person; a sneak. *c1925.* → 2. A sneak thief or heel.

heel-tap. *n.* A small amount of a drink remaining in a glass. *From a leather tap for a shoe heel, re-*

inforced by "heel" = end + "tap" = spigot.

heesh. *n.* Hashish. *Some dope addict and maritime use.*

hefty; heftie. *n.* A hefty or heavy man. *Colloq. adj.* Fat, heavy. *Colloq.*

heifer. *n.* A woman or girl; esp. a pretty or personable young woman. *Colloq. since c1830.*

he-ing and she-ing. Sexual intercourse; having sexual intercourse. *Jocular and dial.*

heist. *v.t.* 1. To steal, to take by robbing. 2. To hi-jack; esp. to hi-jack a shipment of alcoholic beverages. *c1920. n.* A successful hold-up, robbery, or theft; usu. an armed robbery by professional thieves. *From "hoist." Usu., in underworld use, to steal an expensive item or items; children and student use, to steal an insignificant object.* —er. hister. *n.* A hold-up man; a professional robber.

heist man. A hold-up man; a robber.

hell; Hell. *exclam. & epith.* An epithet or oath of anger, disgust, or annoyance. *adj.* Fig., unpleasant; arduous; horrible; dangerous. *Colloq. n.* 1. A bawling out; a strong verbal reprimand. *Usu. in "to catch hell" or "to get hell."* 2. A person who excels. *Some Negro and jive talker use. From "heller."*

hell, give [someone]. To bawl out; to criticize severely.

hell, go to. An expression of incredulity, anger, contempt, or rejection. *Taboo when said in anger or with emotion, but often jocular and not taboo when incredulity is implied.*

hell and gone, to. 1. Irretrievably gone, spoiled, ruined, or dissipated. 2. Very far from any given place, esp. without probability of returning or being returned.

hell-bender. *n.* A wild spree.

hell cat. An extremely spirited, reckless young woman or girl. *Colloq.*

hell-hole; hellhole. *n.* Any unpleasant place; fig., any place resembling hell.

hell of a (a time, fight, thing, scare, etc.). 1. A very bad or severe time, fight, thing, scare, etc.; exceptionally or exceedingly thorough or severe. Fig., anything unpleasant, arduous, or dangerous. *Since Colonial times.* 2. Anything insulting, audacious, bold. 3. Anything remarkable. 4. Anything confused, disorganized, or containing many blunders.

hell of a note. Anything unusual, surprising, audacious, or insulting, or the like.

Hell's bells. *An exclamation of surprise and/or anger; also used to make a following remark more emphatic.*

hell to pay. A severe punishment, penalty, or bawling out.

hell to split. Fast; at a run; lickety-split.

he-man. *n.* A strong, healthy, virile man; a man with exceptionally strong male traits and pursuits; such as broad shoulders, a rough-hewn face, deep voice, a liking for outdoor activities, a big appetite for plain food, and the like. *Colloq. adj.* Very masculine; strong; resembling, contributing to, or the result of masculine strength.

hemo-jo. *n.* A shovel or spade; work done with a shovel, such as ditch-digging; hard manual labor.

hemp; hemp, the. *n.* 1. A hangman's noose; death at the hands of the law. 2. Marijuana, esp. a marijuana cigarette. *Because marijuana comes from a hemp-like plant.*

hen. *n.* A woman; esp. a fussy old woman or a woman who likes to gossip; a termagant; a shrew. *v.i.* To gossip; to converse. *Usu. said of women. adj.* Attended by, interesting to, or composed exclusively of women.

hen-fruit. *n.* Eggs. *Since c1850. Has seen wide facetious use.*

henhouse. *n.* An Army officers' club. *Some W.W.II enlisted man use. Orig. because all the "chickens" hang out there.*

hen party. A party attended by women or girls only, usu. for the purpose of talking or gossiping.

hen-pen. *n.* A girls' school; esp. a private school for girls. *c1940; student use.*

hen tracks = chicken tracks.

hep. *adj.* Aware; informed; knowing; specif.: self-aware; aware of, informed of, wise to, and with a comprehension of and appreciation for a specif. field of endeavor, modern mode, fashion, or way of life; modern. *Always pred. and attrib. adj. use. Some student use since c1915. Common since c1935, when the word became assoc. with jive and swing use. Still considered a jazz term and fairly common with students and young adults. Since c1945 superseded by "hip," esp. in jazz and beat use.*

hep cat; hepcat. *n.* 1. A person who is hep or well informed. *Archaic.* 2. Specif., a devotee of of jive or swing music. *Mainly used by nondevotees who don't understand the real meaning of "hep" or "hepcat." Archaic.* 3. A dude, a sport; a young man who dresses fashionably and garishly, knows the latest news, witty sayings, and cynical opinions, and enjoys or pursues women, jazz, and a fast, tense, unrefined way of life. *Orig. Harlem Negro use. The most common use by hep people. Archaic since W.W.II.*

hep to the jive. Hep, esp. aware of or wise to life and its mendacity, problems, and delusions.

Herkimer Jerkimer. A fictitious, masc., personal name applied to any rustic, fool, or screwball.

Herman. *n.* A guy; a fellow.

Hero. *n.* 1. A very large, overstuffed sandwich on a long, hard-crusted roll or hard-crusted bread, sliced lengthwise and containing several kinds of cold meats and sometimes tomatoes and peppers. *Often called "Italian Hero sandwiches." These are usu. features of Ital. restaurants in the Eastern U.S. and often contain the peppers and spiced meats assoc. with Ital. cooking.* → 2. The hard-crusted Italian bread usu. used to make Hero sandwiches.

Hershey bar; hershey bar. 1. A gold stripe, worn on the sleeve, denoting six months military service overseas. *W.W.II Army use. Implying that such a stripe is a prize and worth just about as much as a candy bar.* 2. A European prostitute or woman who could be sexually possessed very cheaply. *W.W.II Army use. Food was so scarce in Europe during W.W.II that the Hershey bar, which soldiers could obtain easily, was actually a medium of exchange.*

Hey! hey! *exclam.* An exclamation of surprise, wonder, or quick anger. Often used as a greeting to show pleasant surprise at meeting a friend. *Colloq.*

Hey, Rube! A fight between circus workers and townspeople; a riot by townspeople against a circus, because they believe they have been cheated or because they dislike the attitudes and actions of the circus outsiders. *Like many circus terms, this one is also associated with carnivals.*

Hi! *exclam.* Hello. *A universal colloq. since c1920.*

hick. *n.* 1. A farmer, rustic, rube, or small-town or countrified person; an innocent; a person easily duped; a stupid, unknowing person. *Colloq. Brought to the U.S. by the orig. colonists.* → 2. A corpse or cadaver; a stiff. *Because of the fear rustics used to have that if they came alone to the city they might be waylaid and killed so their cadavers could be used for dissection by eager medical students. adj.* Rural; countrified; ignorant, unsophisticated.

hickey; hickie. *n.* A pimple; any skin blemish. *c1915. Very common oral use.*

hickory oil. A whipping.

hick town. A small, rural, and sometimes backward city, town, or village. *Colloq. since c1915.*

hide. *n.* 1. A racehorse. 2. A baseball. —**s.** *n.pl.* Drums, esp. a set of drums and traps used by a jazz musician. *Jazz use.*

hideaway; hide-away. *n.* 1. A secret refuge; a hiding place. *Colloq.* 2. A small town; a small obscure place, such as a restaurant, bar, or resort.

hide-out; hideout. A hiding place, a secret meeting or living place. *c1930. Colloq.* **hide out.** *v.i.* To hide, esp. from the police. *Colloq.*

hi fi; high fi; hi-fi. *n.* A record player (phonograph), and its components, that will reproduce the sound impressed on a phonograph record or tape recording with a high degree of fidelity, including a wide range of high and low sounds, without introducing extraneous noises. *Since c1948. adj.* 1. High-fidelity, applied to the reproduction of recorded sound. 2. Of, by, or pertaining to such a record player, its components, or accessories. *The selling and buying of hi fis have reached major proportions since c1945; there are now many devotees.*

hig = high hig.

high. *adj.* 1. Drunk. *Usu. pleasantly or happily drunk; not drunk to the point of unconsciousness. Very common.* 2. Under the influence of a narcotic drug, esp. marijuana, and esp. when the feeling is pleasant and makes one carefree and light-hearted. *Orig. addict use, c1930; now widely known.*

high as a kite = high, an emphatic form.

highball. *n.* A salute. *W.W.I and W.W.II Army use. v.i.* To go fast; to speed. *Railroad and hobo use since c1925. Some student use since c1940. v.t.* To rush something; to speed or cause something to move rapidly. *adj.* Operating under an emergency speed-up program.

high-brow; highbrow. *n.* An intellectual, well-educated, or cultured person. *A high forehead is supposed to indicate a large and good brain. Pop. since c1910; now colloq. The word has come increasingly to mean a literary person or one who appreciates the arts. adj.* 1. Intellectual, cultured, educated, literary. *Owing to recurring anti-intellectualism in the U.S., the word is sometimes used derog. or humorously.* → 2. Unreal, unrealistic. *v.t.* To impress a person with one's learning. High-brow = Highbrowville. —ed. *adj.* = high-brow.

Highbrowville. *n.* Boston, Mass. *Supposedly the home of many highbrows and a cultural center.*

high-class. *adj.* In or having good taste; refined; having good manners; honest, trustworthy.

higher than a kite. Extremely high or drunk.

higher than Gilroy's kite. Very drunk.

higher-ups. *n.pl.* Superiors, those in authority, leaders; important or influential people, esp. those who are important socially, in business, politics, or the underworld.

highfalutin. *adj.* Pompous; high class; ideal. *Since c1850.*

highgrade. *v.t.* To steal something. —r. *n.* One who appropriates another's property; a thief.

high-hat. *n.* A snob; one who acts superior; one who is conceited, aloof, or exclusive. *v.t.* To snub; to treat another superiorly or patronizingly. *v.i.* To act superior or patronizing. —ter. *n.* A snob. —ty. *adj.* Conceited; aloof; exclusive.

high hig. *n.* A snobbish, disagreeable girl.

highjack = hijack.

high jinks; hi-jinks. *n.* An uninhibited, boisterous, irresponsible good time; loud humorous fun,

often accompanying drinking; pranks.

high lonesome. A drunken spree; drunk.

high-muck. *Very derog. and angry form of "high-muckety-muck."*

high muck-a-muck; high-muckety-muck; high-muckie-muck; high-mucky-muck; high-monkey-muck. *n.* An important, pompous person; a socially prominent person. *Since c1865; used disparagingly and jocularly.*

high on [someone *or* something]. To be enthusiastic about; to like exceptionally well; to have a high opinion of.

high on the hog, eat; eat high off the hog; eat high on the joint. 1. To have the best food. 2. To prosper. 3. To live prosperously; specif., to live much more prosperously or pleasantly than formerly. *Orig. Southern use; often jocular. Because the choice cuts of meat, the more expensive ham and bacon, are taken from high up on a hog's sides.*

high pillow. An important person; a big shot.

high pitch = pitch.

highpockets. A tall man; also, a nickname for any tall man.

high roller. 1. One who gambles large sums frequently. → 2. One who spends money freely, esp. at nightclubs, entertainments, and on whisky and women; a "sport."

high sign. Any secret gesture or signal made to another person in recognition, as a warning, or the like.

high-tail. *v.t., v.i.* 1. To make a fast getaway; to leave quickly, usu. on foot. *Orig. because certain common animals, such as mustangs and rabbits, erect their tails when startled, and then flee.* → 2. To travel fast. → 3. To drive closely behind another vehicle; to follow another closely.

high-tail it = high-tail.

high-ups. *n.pl.* = higher-ups.

high, wide, and handsome. Easily,

pleasantly, and with few worries; in a carefree manner.

high-wine. *n.* A mixture of grain alcohol and Coca-Cola. *An extension of the distiller term. Hobo use.*

high yellow. A light-skinned Negro, esp. if lacking Negroid features; specif., a mulatto; esp. a sexually attractive mulatto girl or young woman. *adj.* Light complexioned and sexually attractive; said of a Negro or mulatto girl.

hijack; highjack. *v.t.* 1. To rob; specif., to rob a vehicle of its load of merchandise, as whisky. 2. To coerce or force someone to do something, as by extortion. *n.* = hijacker. —er. highjacker. *n.* A holdup man; specif., one who robs a truck, esp. a bootlegger's truck, of its merchandise.

hike. *v.t.* To alter the figures on a check, to raise the amount of money shown. *Underworld use.* *n.* An increase. *Colloq.*

hill. *n.* In baseball, the pitcher's mound.

hill, go over the. 1. To escape from prison. *Orig. by running away from a work gang.* → 2. To desert from the armed forces; to go awol. *Since c1920. Became common cW.W.II.*

hill, over the. Absent without leave; deserted. *Military use.*

hillbilly. *n.* A poor farmer who lives in the Southern hill or Ozark regions; an uneducated; unworldly rustic. *The image is of a poor, lazy, hill farmer, or member of his family, living in an isolated region in a log cabin or shack. Such a farmer may raise a small crop of corn or other vegetables, own a cow and a mule, and often possesses many chickens and children. According to pop. tradition all hillbillies carry long rifles and make moonshine whisky at their own stills. adj. Rustic; pertaining to a hillbilly.*

hill (row) of beans, a. Of little significance, importance, or bene-

fit; insignificant, inconsequential.

hind end. The rump; the rear end.

hinders. *n.pl.* A person's legs, regarded as though they were the hind legs of a quadruped.

hinge. *n.* A look or glance. *Often in "get [or take] a hinge."*

hinge, get (take) a. Look at; take a look.

hinkty; hincty. *adj.* 1. Suspicious. 2. Pompous, overbearing. → 3. A white person. *All usage Negro.* 4. Snobbish, aloof. *Mainly Negro use.*

hip. *adj.* 1. = hep. *Since before c1915. Orig. a variant of "hep," since c1945 has completely superseded "hep." Thus "hep" was assoc. with jive and swing use; "hip" is assoc. with cool, far-out, and beat use.* → 2. = cool, gone, far-out. 3. = beat. *Beat use.* —ped. *adj.* 1. Fond of; obsessed with; steeped in. 2. Informed; hep; knowledgeable; wise to —py. *n.* A person who is hip or cool. *Synthetic.* —ster. *n.* 1. One who is hip or hep; a hepster; specif., one who is hip to or gone on bop, cool, or far out music; a cool person, a member of the cool group; a devotee of bop, cool, or far out music. *Fairly common use c1945–c1955; still in use.* 2. A member of the beat generation; in the extreme, one who has removed himself from commercial, material, political, and all physical and intellectual reality, intensely believing in and protecting only his true, nonemotional, nonsocial, amoral identity; such a pure hipster has no formal or permanent contact with fellow human beings, and has only spontaneous relations with those with whom he feels in rapport. There are few pure hipsters, so that a hipster may be merely an extreme cynic, amoral, disliking permanent relationships, obsessed by the futility and mendacity of modern life, having a strong psychological death urge, or be extremely cool or gone.

hip cat; hipcat. *n.* = hipster.

hip chick. An alert, sensitive girl or young woman, esp. one cognizant of modern problems, personalities, and art, esp. of modern jazz music. *Orig. jive use, now wide student and young adult use.*

hipe = hyp.

hipper-dipper. *adj.* Superb, superduper. *n.* Superbly bad, usu. a fixed prize fight; a tank job.

hippings. *n.pl.* Anything used as bedding under a sleeper's hips. *Hobo use.*

hippo. *n.* A hippopotamus. **—ed.** *adj.* Deceived; buffaloed.

hips. *n.pl.* The unsuccessful end; "curtains."

his nibs. An important person; usu. a pompous or demanding person who is in authority; such as a police magistrate, school principal, ship's captain, or the like. *Always used with mockery.*

hissy. *n.* A fit of anger. *From "hiss." Dial.*

hit. For phrases beginning with "hit," see under principal word of phrase.

hit. *n.* **1.** A commercially, popularly, or critically successful play, movie, performance, theater or nightclub act, book, song, recording, author, performer, director, producer, composer, song writer; any notable or celebrated success. **2.** An instance of winning at gambling; a winning ticket in gambling, esp. a lottery ticket. **3.** An appointment or meeting relating to illegal business or contraband; the time, place, person, or operation from which one obtains contraband, usu. narcotic drugs; a package of drugs; an instance of injecting drugs by an addict. *Underworld and narcotic addict use. v.t.* **1.** To arrive at or reach a town or region. *Since c1885.* **2.** Fig., to attain; to arrive. → **3.** To pass an examination or a course with a very good mark.

Student use. → **4.** To attend a meeting, class, party, or event. **5.** To beg from; to accost with a request for money, food, or assistance. *Orig. hobo use. v.i.* **1.** To beg. **2.** To succeed. **3.** To win at gambling. **4.** To cause a strong reaction. *adj.* Celebratedly successful, publicly or personally successful.

hit [someone]. *v.t.* **1.** To borrow money or ask for a favor; to ask for a raise in salary; to ask for charity or beg. **2.** To present a personal or business proposition to a person. **3.** To cause a strong emotional reaction; to overwhelm or bewilder. **4.** To administer a narcotic drug to an addict.

hitch. *v.t.* To marry; to be married. *Since c1875; colloq. n.* A period of enlistment in any branch of the Armed Forces. *Colloq. Orig. Armed Forces use.* **—ed.** *adj.* Married. *Colloq. since c1860.*

hitch a ride. **1.** = hitch-hike. → **2.** To ride in the car of a friend, for convenience or to save money.

hitched, get. To be married. See hitched.

hitch-hike. *v.i., v.t.* To travel, usu. but not necessarily a long distance, by standing by the roadside and asking for rides from passing motorists. *The universally accepted method is to raise one's right arm, elbow bent, with the hand closed into a fist and the thumb extended in the direction one wishes to travel.*

hitch up. *v.t.* = hitch.

hitchy. *adj.* Nervous; frightened; trembling. *Prob. from "itchy."*

hitchy-koo. *interj.* A phrase endearingly and traditionally uttered by many adults while poking or tickling a young infant. *Also "kitchy-koo" or "kitchy-kitchy-koo."*

hitfest. *n.* A baseball game in which many hits are made and hence many runs are scored.

hit for. To start out for or toward; to head for a place.

Hi there = Hi. *Considered by the speaker as more personal and sincere than just plain "Hi."*

hit it off. 1. To be compatible; to like or love one another; to get along together. 2. To be acceptable to a group or adaptable to an occupation or situation. 3. To succeed, to bring about success.

hit it up. To play music.

Hit the road! *Exclam.* = Scram!

hit up = hit.

Hi ya; Hiya = Hi. *Shortened form of "How are you," reinforced by "Hi." Colloq.*

hizzy = tizzy.

hoary-eyed; orie-eyed; orry-eyed. *adj.* Drunk. *May be from "awry-eyed," which would explain the apparent cockney-style dropping of the "h."*

hobby. *n.* A translation, pony, trot. *Facetiously, from "hobby horse" as related to "pony."*

hock. *v.t.* To pawn something. *Since c1825; more common than "pawn." Colloq. n.* Pawn. *Since c1850; colloq.*

hock, in. 1. In a pawnshop, pawned. *Colloq.* → 2. In debt; owing money or having many unpaid bills. 3. In prison. *Since c1850; orig. underworld use.*

hockable. *adj.* Pawnable.

hockshop. *n.* A pawnshop. *c1875; colloq. since c1900.*

hocky. *n.* Lies; exaggeration; bull.

hocus-pocus. *n.* Deception; trickery; funny business; fast talk.

hoe-dig. *n.* A rural square dance; a dance. *Dial. Perh. from "hoe-down" plus "shindig."*

hoedown. *n.* 1. A rural square dance; a party or dance, esp. a lively, boisterous one. *Colloq.* → 2. A lively, loud argument; an angry discussion. → 3. Any action-filled or violent event; a lively boxing match, a brawl, a riot. → 4. A gang fight between boys of rival neighborhood gangs. *It is interesting to note that the meaning of this term has become more violent as it has moved from rural to urban use.*

hog. *n.* 1. Anyone who collects or hoards specif. items, is selfish, or takes or consumes more than his share of anything. *Usu. preceded by a noun indicating what is collected, hoarded, or consumed.* 2. A railroad engine; usu. a light, console-type engine with eight drivers and four pony trucks, used on freight trains. *Hobo and railroad use since c1915. From its comparatively high consumption of coal and water.* 3. A convict; a yard bird. *From "yardpig."* 4. A dollar; the sum of one dollar. —ger. *n.* A railroad engineer. See hog.

Hogan's brickyard. A rough, bare baseball diamond; a vacant lot used as a baseball diamond. *Baseball use.*

hog-head; hogshead. *n.* A locomotive engineer. *Since c1910; orig. Western railroad and hobo use.*

hog-jockey = hog-head.

hog-legg; hog's leg. *n.* A revolver. *Orig. Western use = a long-barreled, single-action six-shooter.*

hogshead = hog-head.

hog's leg = hog-legg.

hogwash. *n.* Insincere talk or writing; misleading arguments and discussions; lies, exaggerations; speech or writing aimed at convincing while purporting to give the facts; propaganda; boloney, bunk, garbage, etc. *Colloq.*

hog-wild. *adj.* Wildly excited; temporarily irrational owing to excitement, anger, or happiness.

hog-wrestle. *n.* Crude or vulgar dancing.

hoist. *v.t.* 1. To report freshman servants to the tutor for refusing to work. 2. To hang a person. 3. To rob a place or a person; to steal an object. *Common since c1935; orig. underworld use. The most common meaning for this word. v.i.* To steal or rob. *n.* A robbery or hold-up. —ed. *adj.* Stolen.

hoke = hokum. —y. **hoky.** *adj.*

Containing or composed of ho-kum.

hokey-pokey; hoky-poky. *n.* 1. Cheap ice cream, candy, confections, primarily made to be attractive to children. → 2. The seller of such items. → 3. Any cheap, gaudy, useless item. 4. = hokum. *adj.* Sentimental.

hokum. *n.* 1. Flattery; insincerity; nonsense, bunk, blah. *Colloq.* → 2. Any stage device used purely to please the audience; any proved song, joke, or line that is sure to elicit laughter, tears, or applause from an audience; proved but hackneyed or trite material. *Theater use.* → 3. Cheap, sugary candy; cheap souvenirs; any cheap, useless item such as is sold at carnival booths.

hokus. *n.* Any narcotic drug. *c1930; common drug-addict use.*

hold. *v.t.* To prepare or serve food or a specif. dish without its usu. condiment or side dish. *Thus "Lettuce and tomato salad, hold the mayonnaise" = lettuce and tomato salad without mayonnaise. Lunch-counter use in relaying an order. v.i.* To have narcotics for sale. *Narcotic addict use since c1945.*

hold out. To refuse to work, perform, or do one's duty unless one is paid more or given better treatment. **hold-out.** *n.* 1. An athlete, esp. a baseball player, who refuses to sign his yearly contract until he is promised a higher salary. 2. One who withholds payment or refuses to pay, usu. one who refuses to pay graft, extortion, or bribe money. 3. One who refuses to accept projected plans, sign a contract, or the like. **hold-outs.** *n.* Playing cards secretly held out of a deck, thus making certain hands impossible; cards from a deck secreted on one's person, to be used as part of one's hand at the most opportune moment.

hold the bag. 1. To be double-crossed; to be cheated out of one's share; lit., to be left hold-ing an empty bag. *Still in use.* → 2. To be left with the responsibility or blame for failure. *Colloq.*

hold the sack = hold the bag.

hold [one] up. To uphold or vouch for someone; to verify another's story.

hold-up; holdup. *n.* 1. A robbery, esp. to rob a person at the point of a gun; a stick-up. *Since c1875; almost as common as the standard "robbery." Colloq.* → 2. Fig., a sale at an exorbitant price. → 3. Fig., a request for a raise in pay, usu. supported by implying an offer of a better-paying job elsewhere. *v.i., v.t.* To rob, esp. at the point of a gun. *Now colloq. adj.* Of, pert. to, or working at hold-up. Usu. in "hold-up man."

hole. *n.* 1. Any small, dirty, crowded public place.

hole, in a. Faced with what appears to be a disastrous difficulty, an insurmountable trouble, or an unsolvable problem.

hole, in the. In debt.

hole, the. *n.* 1. The solitary confinement cell. *Common convict use.* 2. A subway. *Orig. pickpocket use.* 3. One's dwelling place, house, apartment, or room. *Usu. used facetiously.*

hole in = hole up.

hole in the (one's) head. 1. Anything that is as completely undesirable or ridiculous as having an actual hole in the head would be. *Usu. in the expression "to need [it] like a hole in the head." A very pop. expression c1948. Pop. by comedians; contains elements of Jewish wit.* 2. A mythical symptom of stupidity. *In, e.g., "He's got a hole in the (his) head."*

hole in the wall. Any small residence or place of business; often implies dislike for the place.

hole in [one's] wig = hole in the (one's) head.

hole up. 1. To hide out, as from the police; to hide or keep another person hidden. 2. To secure temporary living quarters or a place to sleep, as a hotel room. Cf. hole, hole in.

holiday. *n.* 1. A small area on a ship that has been left unpainted, owing to neglect. *Wide USN use.* → 2. A task that has been forgotten or neglected; an unfinished or unsatisfactory job. *c1935. Orig. and mainly USN use.*

holler; —**holler; holler-song.** *n.* A simple, sad song with words that are spoken or shouted. *Orig. used to give work orders to slaves, and sung in unison by slave workers. Many such songs have African origins or traits and contributed to the beginning of jazz music.* *v.i.* To inform to the police or to a superior; to squeal.

Hollywood. *adj.* 1. Gaudy; loud, flashy, sporty. *Said of objects, often said of clothing.* 2. Affected, insincere, mannered. *Said of people.*

Hollywood kiss; kiss-off. *n.* = kiss-off. *East Coast, esp. N.Y.C., use.*

Holy Joe; holy Joe. 1. A chaplain in the Armed Forces. *USN use since c1900; wide usage in all branches of the Armed Forces during W.W.II.* → 2. Any priest, minister, or clergyman. *The wide Armed Forces use during W.W.II spread the term to civilian use, where it still retains popularity.* → 3. A devout, prissy person; a pious person, esp. one whom the speaker considers sanctimonious, sissy, or corny. *adj.* Pious; sanctimonious; supercilious.

holy terror. One whose mischievous or irresponsible conduct causes worry or even terror. *Usu. said of a violently mischievous child.*

hombre. *n.* 1. A man of Spanish or Mexican ancestry. *Since c1840; orig. Southwestern use.* → 2. Any man. *Often in "bad hombre," "tough hombre," "wise hombre." Still retains a Western twang. Commonly used in books and movies about cowboys and ranchmen.*

home cooking. Satisfying; pleasing.

home free. 1. Assured of success or winning; having such a large advantage, or lead in a contest, that one is sure to succeed or win. 2. To succeed or win easily; to reach one's goal without undue expense or effort; to be sure of winning; a race horse that is leading the rest of the horses in a race by several lengths; a baseball, basketball, or football team leading an opponent by a safe number of points; a boxer who has weakened his opponent; a businessman who has overcome the main obstacles in an important deal. *All are said to be "home free," even though the race, the game, the fight, or the deal is not yet completed.*

home guard. 1. A native or permanent resident of a place; a person with a permanent home; a retired circus worker; a street beggar, as opposed to a traveling hobo. *Orig., c1910, circus and hobo use.* → 2. One who works steadily for the same employer; a nontransient worker. *Since c1920.* → 3. A married sailor. *Since c1935.*

homer. *n.* In baseball, a home run. *Since c1890; baseball colloq.* *v.i.* To hit a home run. *Baseball colloq.*

homework. *n.* Love-making, usu. necking, but sometimes coitus. *Facetiously relating to a pop. student pastime. This is a "sly" sl. word of the kind sometimes accompanied by a wink.*

homey. *n.* 1. A new arrival from one's home town. → 2. An innocent, unworldly, non-suspicious person; a hick. 3. A new arrival (to a large Northern city) from the South. *Negro use.*

homo. *n.* A homosexual of either sex. *Universally known. adj.* Of or pertaining to homosexuals or their ways.

hon. *n.* Honey; sweetheart. *A term of endearment, usu. in direct address. Colloq.* **Hon.** *adj.* Honor-

able. *When part of a title.* —ey. n.
1. One's sweetheart, fiancée, wife,
beloved. *Used for both sexes, but
most often to indicate a girl or
woman. Usu. a term of direct
address. Now standard.* → 2. Any
person who is highly regarded in
a specific field of endeavor. *Usu.
in "He's a honey of a prize fighter . . . an actor." Orig. c1920,
prize fight use.* → 3. Anything
that is highly regarded, satisfying, or well done; a dilly. *Fairly
common.* → 4. Any sweet, attractive person; any thoughtful,
kind, or gentle person. *Since
c1930.* → 5. A person who is difficult to please; a difficult problem or task. *The opposite of previous meanings, indicated by accenting or emphasizing the word
heavily in speech. v.t.* To choose;
to desire; to hozey. *Some child
use in the 6- to 10-year-old age
group.*

honest. *adj.* Truthful, fair. *Colloq. n.* A person who can be
trusted. *Colloq.*

honey barge. A garbage scow.
Some USN use.

honey-cooler. *n.* 1. A male who can
dominate or convince his sweetheart, fiancée, wife, or any attractive girl or woman of anything,
usu. by flattery or a show of affection. → 2. Flattery or affection, esp. as lavished on a sweetheart, fiancée, wife, or attractive
girl or woman in order to make
her forget anger or displeasure.
*Since c1930. Both meanings lit.
= that which "cools" or "cools
off" a "honey." Although not
common, this seems to be one of
the earliest uses of "cool" in its
modern sl. use. However, a v.
"honey-cool" does not seem to
exist.*

honey man. A kept man; a pimp.

honey wagon. 1. A garbage truck.
Most common W.W.II Army use.
2. A wagon or cart used to collect
refuse and ordure in certain prison compounds. *Army use.*

honky-tonk. *n.* 1. A cheap saloon
featuring gambling games and
dancing. 2. A cheap, small-town
theater. 3. A brothel.

honorable. *n.* An honorable discharge from the Armed Services.
W.W.II and after.

hoo-boy. *expl.* An expression of
surprise or mock surprise, con-
sternation or mock consterna-
tion, pleasure or mock pleasure,
tiredness, relief, etc. *As many
such sl. terms, can be used in
many circumstances to show an
emotional response, large or
small, when the speaker does not
wish to sound sentimental, formal, or overwhelmed. Pop. by
Walt Kelley's comic strip, "Pogo," c1950.*

hooch; hootch. *n.* 1. Whisky,
liquor; esp. inferior homemade
or cheap whisky; orig. bootleg
whisky. *Became common during
Prohibition, when = bootlegged
whisky of unknown origin; after
Prohibition = any kind of
whisky.* 2. The hoochy-cootch
dance.

hood. *n.* 1. A hoodlum, thief,
criminal, gangster; esp. one who
applies physical violence. *From
"hoodlum," although in "hood"
the long "oo" is almost always
pronounced to rhyme with
"good" rather than "mood."
Very common.* 2. [derog.] A nun.
*From the hoods worn by nuns,
plus a pun on "hood" = hoodlum. adj.* Hoodlum; criminal.

hoodang; houdang. *n.* 1. Any
jovial gathering, a party, a celebration; any period of merriment or noisy confusion. *Mainly
dial.* 2. Specif., a rural dancing
party to simple country music; a
barn dance. *Dial.*

hoodlum. *n.* A youthful ruffian;
any thug, criminal, or gangster.
*Colloq. c1920; now in stand. use.
Orig. unknown.*

hooey. *n.* Nonsense, cant; boloney,
bunk. *Usu. in "That's a lot of
hooey" and "He's full of hooey."
Sudden pop. c1925–1930 and
common ever since.*

hoof. *n.* A person's foot. *Usu. used
humorously, metaphorically, or*

emotionally. *Since c1890; the plural is "hoofs." v.i.* 1. To walk. *Since c1910.* → 2. To dance on the stage or in a nightclub. *Since c1925.* → 3. To dance socially for one's enjoyment; to dance to ballroom music. —er. *n.* A professional step dancer, clog dancer, softshoe dancer, tap dancer, or the like; a dancer on the vaudeville stage; a night club dancer or member of a dance chorus.

hoof it. 1. To walk; to travel on foot. *Usu. implies determination to reach one's destination even though the walk is long or difficult.* 2. To dance as an entertainer.

hoo ha. *interj.* A cynical and satirical expression of mock surprise, used to deflate another's unacceptable enthusiasm, innocence, or eagerness. *From a meliorative expression of genuine surprise or the state of being highly impressed. From the Yiddish sl. "hoo ha" = an exclamation indicating intense joy, excitement, surprise etc., as used by comedienne Gertrude Berg on her "Molly Goldberg" radio programs during the 1930s, 40s, and 50s.*

hook. *n.* 1. An anchor; a mudhook. *Maritime and USN use.* 2. In baseball, a curved ball pitched to a batter. → 3. A narcotic drug, esp. heroin. *By basing a word on "H," reinforced by "hook" = hypodermic needle and "hook" (v.t.).* 4. Any means of attracting customers, as a promise of a free gift, a request to radio and television listeners to send in boxtops or their names and addresses for free gifts or discounts on merchandise, or the like. *Since c1930. The last three meanings are based on "hook" = to snare, as to make or snare an addict or customer. v.t.* 1. To steal; to shoplift merchandise. *Lit., to snare something while no one is looking.* 2. To be cheated, tricked, victimized, or defeated in gambling, out of or for a large sum of money. → 3. To be forced into an unpleasant situation or difficulty, from which one cannot extract oneself gracefully. 4. To be addicted to a narcotic drug. —ed. *adj.* 1. Addicted to a narcotic drug, as marijuana, heroin. 2. Addicted to any vice, person, or cause. 3. Married. —er. *n., adj.* 1. A prostitute. *Since c1850; common until c1925.* 2. Anyone who "hooks" (snares) or hooks another, as a narcotics seller, professional gambler, etc.; one who recruits others for any purpose. 3. A drink of liquor, usu. straight whisky. 4. A warrant for arrest. *Underworld use.*

hook, get [someone] off the. To rescue a person from impending trouble, failure, or embarrassment.

hook, off the. Out of trouble; free from a specific responsibility.

hook, on the. To be tempted or ensnared; esp. to be too intrigued by, eager for, or involved in something, to withdraw from or ignore or refuse it. *Fig., to be hooked or on the hook in the same way a fish is immediately before being caught.*

hook arm. 1. The arm one uses most; the right arm of a right-handed person, the left arm of a left-handed person. → 2. In baseball, specif. a left-handed pitcher.

hook for [something or someone], go on the. 1. To go into debt or borrow money for something or someone. 2. To endanger oneself for another.

hooks. *n.pl.* The hands; the fingers.

hooky. *v.t.* To steal *n., adj.* To make oneself absent from school or a class for a one-day vacation. *Usu., "to play hooky."*

hooligan. *n.* 1. A hoodlum; a ruffian; a tough guy. *Since c1895.* → 2. A gunman. 3. The Wild West tent in a circus. *Circus use.*

hooligan Navy. The Coast Guard. *USN use.*

hoop. *n.* A finger ring. *Orig. underworld and hobo use. Colloq. since c1930. adj.* Basketball; organized for playing basketball.

hoop-a-doop; hoop-de-doop; hoopty-do. *n.* = **whoop-de-do.**

hooper-dooper; hooperdoo; hooper-doo. *adj.* Uproarious; very entertaining. *n.* 1. A humdinger; anything uproarious, entertaining, or remarkable. 2. An important person; a high muckymuck.

hoopla. *n.* 1. A boisterous, happy noise and confusion. 2. Advertising; ballyhoo. 3. Fanfare; a furor; hullabaloo; ballyhoo. *Since c1875.* 4. A carnival concession. *Orig. from the exclam., reinforced from the actual hoops thrown to win a prize.*

hoop-man. *n.* A basketball player. *Sports use. Colloq.*

hoopty-do. *n.* = **whoop-de-do.**

hoosegow; hoosegaw; hoosgow. *n.* 1. A jail. *c1920, orig. from the Sp. "husgado," first common in Army and on West Coast. Common throughout U.S. by 1935.* 2. A public rest room, outhouse, or toilet enclosure.

hoosier up. To shirk; to malinger; to plot a slowdown of work.

hootch = **hooch.**

hootenanny. *n.* 1. Fig., a shout, a hoot, a damn. *Usu. in "I don't give a hootenanny" = I don't give a damn, I don't care. Dial.* 2. = gadget; thingamajig. *Some use since c1925. Still some maritime use and dial. use.*

Hooverville. *n.* A group of makeshift shacks, usu. located on the outskirts of a town near the city dump, where unemployed workers live and scrounge for food. *After Herbert Hoover, President at the start of the Depression, which saw such shacks multiply with growing unemployment.*

hop. *n.* 1. An informal dance; a public dance; a dancing party, esp. an informal dance for students or teenagers at which only "popular" and rock-and-roll music is played. *Colloq. since*

c1755; very wide student and teenage use since c1950. 2. Opium. *Addict and underworld use; also used by general public* = any habit-forming narcotic drug. 3. A drug addict. *Addict use.* → 4. A state of confusion. → 5. A fanciful story; nonsense; lies. *Orig. may be from a "pipe dream" or "full of hops."* 6. Any journey, esp. a flight by airplane. *Colloq. v.t.* To get aboard, usu. a train. *Colloq.* —**per.** *n.* 1. A partly smoked cigarette that is long enough to be smoked again. *Some hobo and young boy use.* 2. In baseball, a ball hit so that it bounces, or rolls and bounces, on the ground. —**s.** *n.pl.* 1. Opium. *c1918.* 2. Beer.

hop-head. *n.* A narcotics addict. *Orig. addict use, now common use by the general public. From "hop."*

hopjoint. 1. A cheap saloon. *From "hops."* 2. An opium den.

hopped up; hopped-up. *adj.* 1. Under the influence of narcotics; drugged. *Orig. addict use, now some general use and almost no addict use.* → 2. Excited; enthusiastic; very alert; full of pep; nervous. 3. Emotional; emotionally upset; agitated. 4. Fig., contrived to be exciting; artificially made exciting. 5. = **souped up.**

hops, full of. Talking without knowledge of the facts; unrealistic, exaggerating, wrong, lying; fig., talking like a drunken man or a person under the influence of a narcotic.

hop-stick. *n.* An opium pipe. *Addict use.*

hop the twig. To die.

hop toad. A potent liquor, a big drink of whisky.

hop up. *v.i., v.t.* 1. To take narcotic drugs, as an addict; to drug a person. *From "hop."* → 2. To give a race horse a stimulating drug so that he will run faster than he normally would. → 3. To increase the maximum speed, acceleration, or power of an automobile by any adjustment or added engine component or device. See **hot rod.**

horn. *n.* 1. Any musical wind instrument. 2. Specif., in jazz, a trumpet. *Jazz use.* 3. The nose.

hornblowing. *n.* Aggressive advertising; advertising with a hard sell. *Advertising use.*

hornet = green hornet.

horn in. To intrude; to barge in; to butt in; to enter (anything) when one is unasked or unwanted.

hornswoggle. *v.t.* To cheat, swindle, dupe, deceive. *Since c1825.*

horny. *adj.* Carnal-minded, amative, lusty, sexually obsessed. *Colloq.*

horse. *n.* 1. A thousand dollars; the sum of $1,000. *Some circus use. Perhaps from "G" and "gee-gee."* 2. Heroin. *Wide addict use. Fairly well known to the general public.* 3. A stupid, rude, stubborn, or contemptible person. *Dial.* *v.i.* To joke, indulge in horseplay, or refuse to talk, think, or act seriously. *v.i., v.t.* To cheat; to hoax, cheat, or take advantage of someone.

horse-and-buggy. *adj.* Old-fashioned.

horse around = horse, *v.i.*

horseback. *adj.* Quick; to be done quickly; said of a task. *Fig., done while moving, as if on horseback.*

horsefeathers; horse-feathers. *n.* Bunk; boloney.

horsehide. *n.* A baseball. *Colloq.*

horse opera; horse opry. 1. A cheaply made, stereotype movie about cowboys; a Western movie. *c1928.* 2. A circus. *Circus use.* 3. = Western.

horse parlor = horse room.

horse piano. A calliope. *Circus use.*

horse room. A bookmaking establishment; a bookie.

horse's mouth, out of the. Directly from the original or most authoritative source.

horse tail. A type of women's hair style, consisting of long, straight hair drawn back toward the crown, where it is gathered and then allowed to hang free, thus resembling a horse's tail. *Orig. and still most pop. among sophisticated, artistic young women, this was the forerunner of the less severe "pony tail." Since c1950.*

hoss = horse.

hot. *adj.* 1. Moving very fast; made or modified to attain high speeds excitingly fast or speedy. 2. Lucky; competent, skilled, talented; popularly acclaimed; specif., in the midst of a series of lucky or successful actions, prone to succeed or win; specif., favored by good fortune; so lucky as to elicit excitement. *Since c1890.* 3. Angry, quick to take offense; angry and excited. *c1900–c1925; now mainly in expressions such as "hot and bothered" and "hot under the collar."* 4. Lively; vital; energetic; eliciting excitement; enthusiastic; filled with energy and activity. → 5. Passionate, sexually excited; having a strong sexual desire for a person; often in the phrase "hot for." → 6. Lascivious, lewd, sexually suggestive. → 7. Eager for; in favor of. Usu. in "hot for." 8. Exciting; specif. said of exciting jazz music played in a fast tempo and with a heavily accented beat, eliciting an emotional or physical response. *Most uses and meanings of "hot" have a connotation of physical excitement tending toward, suggesting, or at least resembling sexual excitement. Many of the uses could be grouped under the general definition of "eliciting physical excitement." This definition is basic to "hot," and includes specific physical responses such as increased pulse beat, blood pressure, and rate of certain glandular secretions, as well as the accompanying feeling of mental and psychological excitement. This concept of the specific response is important in comparing hot jazz to cool jazz.* 9. Good, fine, admirable; competent, able;

pleasing, enjoyable; charming, attractive, handsome, beautiful; popular, well liked. Often in the negative. *The negative sense always has "so" between "not" and "hot." Thus never "not hot," but always "not so hot." Common use.* 10. Stolen recently and therefore sought actively by the police. *Orig. underworld use, now fairly well known.* 11. Wanted by the police for having committed a crime; guilty and fleeing or hiding out; said of a criminal. → 12. Dangerous, scandalous, leading to possible disaster, arrest, or public reprimand. 13. Turned on; functioning; said of a microphone. 14. Radioactive. *Some use since c1950.* n. 1. A stolen item. *Some underworld use.* 2. A meal. *Mainly hobo use, some jive use. From "hot meal."* 3. = hot dog.

hot air. 1. Empty talk; nonsense; flattery; exaggeration; false promises. *Since c1870.* 2. Pompous speech; pompous and exaggerated speech.

hot baby. A girl who is passionate and sexy; a girl who lives recklessly. *Some student use since c1900.*

hotbed. n. 1. A bed or room rented to two persons, one who works during the day and sleeps in the bed at night, and one who works during the night and sleeps in the bed during the day. *Thus one gets into the bed as the other leaves, and the bed is always warm.* 2. A place, region, neighborhood, or institution that fig. produces, breeds, raises, or houses many people of a specific type. *Thus an organization controlled by followers of Communism is a hotbed of Communism. From the horticultural term.*

hot corner. 1. In baseball, third base. *Because hard, fast-moving ("hot") line drives and grounders are often hit in that direction.* 2. Any crucial place, esp. on a battlefield or politically.

hot damn! *interj.* An exclamation

of delight or joyous approval; "Hot dog!"

hot-diggety-damn! *exclam.* = hot damn!

hot diggety dog! *interj.* = hot dog!

hot diggety doggity = hot diggity dog.

hot dog; hot-dog. n. 1. A frankfurter sausage; a link of wienerwurst. *Since c1900; colloq. Said variously to be from an earlier "dachshund sausage," and from a humorous implication that the sausage is made of ground dog meat.* → 2. A frankfurter sandwich, usu. made with a split roll and served with mustard and/or pickle relish, etc. *Colloq.* adj. Of, selling, or pertaining to hot dogs or hot-dog sandwiches. **hot dog!** *exclam.* An exclamation denoting delight, enthusiasm, excitement, joyous approval, or the like. *Since c1900; colloq.*

hot foot; hotfoot. *v.i.* To go fast or hurriedly; travel rapidly; to depart in haste; to hurry; to walk rapidly; to run. *Colloq. since c1895.* n. 1. A walk; the act of walking the streets. 2. A bail-jumper; a bond-jumper. 3. The act of sticking a paper match between the sole and upper part of a man's shoe, about where his little toe ought to be, and lighting the match. *A practical or impractical joke, the object of which is to see the victim start with pain when the match burns to his shoe. Colloq.* v.t. 1. To give a hotfoot to a person. 2. Fig., to cause a person trouble.

hotfoot it. To hasten, to hurry; to run. *Since c1910, colloq.*

hot for [someone or something]. 1. Specif., wanting or desiring a person sexually; wanting or desiring an item or possession of an object. 2. Desiring a forthcoming event eagerly and openly; enthused about, ready and eager for.

hot grease. Trouble, esp. imminent or expected trouble.

hothead. n. A person easily angered or emotionally agitated; one whose anger or enthusiasm compels him to spontaneous, dangerous, or stupid actions.

hot iron = hot rod.

hot mamma = red-hot mamma.

hot number. A passionate, sexy girl or woman.

hot one. A very funny joke or prank. *Common use.*

hot pants; hot-pants. 1. A desire for sexual intercourse; a sexual passion. 2. A male obsessed with sex; a male who is always seeking sexual intercourse.

hot-poo. *adj.* Of or pertaining to a hot rock. The latest, confidential information; the latest rumor.

hot potato. Any difficult or embarrassing practical problem. *Very common.*

hot rock. 1. = hot shot. *Some W.W.II use.*

hot rod; hot-rod; hotrod. *n.* 1. A stock car, usu. an old or dilapidated roadster, stripped of all nonessential items, with its engine adjusted, modified, rebuilt, or replaced so that the car is faster and more powerful than orig. designed. *The simplest hot rod has its engine adjusted for greater maximum speed or rate of acceleration. The true hot rod is stripped of all items not contributing to speed or accelerative power, including ornaments, rear seats, and often roof, engine cover, and all paneling. Since c1950. Wide teenage and student use and interest since c1945.* 2. The driver of a hot rod; a teenage devotee and enthusiast of hot rods and drag racing. *adj.* Assoc. with or pertaining to hot rods, their teenage drivers, devotees, and enthusiasts and their dress, fashions, and fads.

hots, the. 1. Love. 2. Sexual desire.

hot seat. 1. The electric chair. 2. A witness chair in a courtroom.

hot shot; hot-shot. hotshot. *n.* 1. An important, active, successful person; a big shot; a skilled, successful person; a person who takes risks or chances in order to succeed, and who does succeed and become important; esp. a young daring person who has become a success rapidly and is self-assured and proud of his success, possibly overly confident, daring, or ambitious. *Since before 1920.* → 2. Used ironically, one who thinks he is or acts as if he were important, successful, and daring; a conceited man given to bragging about his success and daring; a smart aleck. → 3. A conceited, overconfident, overly daring, or irresponsible fighter-plane pilot. 4. The electric chair. *Some underworld use since c1925.* 5. News; a message; esp., a recent news bulletin or very recent piece of information; a news announcement. *adj.* 1. Skilled or brilliant, daring and self-confident; righteously proud of one's skill or success. 2. Conceited. 3. Skilled or competent but irresponsible.

hot-shot Charlie = hot shot; an egotist. *W.W.II use, Army Air Force.*

hotsie-totsie. *adj.* Satisfactory; pleasing; hunky-dory.

hot sketch. 1. One who is remarkably lively, colorful or the like; a card; a character. *Often used ironically.* 2. A pretty, sexy girl.

hot spot. 1. A predicament; a troublesome situation. 2. The electric chair. *Some underworld use.* 3. A popular nightclub, esp. one known for a boisterous or rowdy clientele or floor show; a nightclub featuring a lascivious floor show.

hot squat. The electric chair. *Underworld use.*

hot stuff. 1. A person of merit or quality; a superior person, an expert; a charming, dashing, reckless person. *Almost always used ironically = an audacious, conceited person. Since c1900.* 2. Sensational, exciting, violent, lascivious, or similar entertainment. 3. Stolen goods; loot 4. Hot liquid, as coffee or soup, being carried by a person, as a waitress; used as a warning to others not to cause the carrier to spill it and not to get scalded.

hot tamale. A sexy girl.

hot to go (for). Ready and eager.

hot under the collar. Angry. *Colloq.*

hot war. A war involving fighting and bloodshed, as opposed to a cold war. *Some use since c1950.*

hot water. Trouble. *Colloq.*

hot wire. News; good news.

houdang = hoodang.

hound. *n.* A college freshman. *v.t.* To pester, bother, or annoy a person. *Colloq.*

–hound. One given to a specified practice or esp. fond of a specified act, food, drink, pastime, or the like; a devotee, addict, or habitué.

hounds. *n.pl.* Feet. *exclam.* Wonderful, remarkable, "great." *adj.* Very satisfying, remarkable, wonderful, "great." *The last two meanings in teenage use since c1951.*

house. *n.* 1. Personal attention to and interest in another person; encouragement. *Freq. in "give a person a lot of house."* → 2. [Antonym of sense 1.] Inattention; lack of interest; discouragement. 3. A brothel, a whorehouse.

house, on the. Free of charge.

house around. To loaf.

house-cleaning. *n.* A reorganization of a business, government branch, etc., involving shifting and ousting of personnel.

housefrau. *n.* = hausfrau.

house moss. The tufts and whorls of dust that accumulate under beds, tables, etc., in rooms seldom cleaned.

how-de-do; how-do-you-do. *n.* A set of circumstances, a situation. *Usu. ironically in "That's a fine how-de-do."*

howl. *n.* Something fit for ridicule; a cause for laughter; a joke. *Colloq.* **–er.** *n.* A laughable mistake, esp. in something written or printed; a boner.

How's about? = How about?

hubby. *n.* A husband. *Colloq.*

hub cap. A conceited person. *Hot rod and some general teenage use since c1955.*

huddle. *n.* 1. A conference, esp. a private conference. 2. In football, a conference held by the offensive team before each play to determine what that play will be. 3. A short period of intense thought by one person before making a decision.

huff-duff. *n.* A high-frequency (radio-radar) direction finder. *W.W.II Air Force use. From the initials "H.F.D.F."*

huffy. *n.* A state of anger. *adj.* Angry, petulant. *Since c1895, now colloq.*

hugger-mugger. *adj.* Slovenly; confused; makeshift. **–y.** *n.* Deception; skull-duggery.

hulligan. *n.* A foreign performer; a foreigner.

humdinger. *n.* Something or someone very remarkable or admirable. *c1905; archaic and dial. now. adj.* Remarkable.

humdinging. *adj.* First rate.

hummer. *n.* 1. = humdinger. 2. A false arrest or false accusation. *Underworld use.* 3. Anything given free. *adj.* 1. Free. → 2. Excellent. *Perh. from "humdinger."*

hump. *n.* 1. A mountain; fig., an obstacle. *Mainly aviation use.* 2. A camel. *Circus use.*

hump, hit the. To attempt an escape from prison; to desert from the Army.

hump, over the. 1. Fig., successfully finished with or past the hardest or most dangerous part of a task. 2. At least halfway through a tedious task; serving the last half of one's work period, apprenticeship, term of military enlistment, or prison term. *Since c1930. Fig., to be coasting downhill.*

hump on, get a. Hurry; hurry up; move or act quickly. *Since c1890.*

hunch. *n., adj.* An intuitive premonition. *v.t.* To believe on the basis of a hunch. *c1905 to present, now colloq.*

hundred proof. The best; original; genuine. *From 100-proof whisky, the highest alcohol content allowed in the U.S.*

hung. *adj.* In love. *Rock-and-roll use since c1955.*

hunger = from hunger.

hung over; hung-over. *adj.* Suffering from the after effects of too much whisky; burdened with a hang-over.

hung up. *adj.* 1. = square, *adj.*; limited by old-fashioned beliefs and attitudes; incapable of being hip. 2. Delayed; detained. *Now common.* 3. Stymied by a problem; delayed in completing a task or succeeding, owing to trouble or difficulty.

hunk; Hunk. *n.* A girl or woman considered sexually.

hunk of change = piece of change.

hunk of cheese. A stupid, objectionable or disliked person.

hunks. *n.* A foreign laborer.

hunky-chunk. A sturdy, short, muscular laborer, usu. from Central Europe. *Prob. synthetic.*

hurdy-gurdy. *n.* A hand organ such as a street organ-grinder plays.

hurl. *v.t.* In baseball, to pitch a a game or an inning. —**er.** *n.* A baseball pitcher. *Baseball use.*

hush-hush. *adj.* Very secret; confidential. *n.* Secrecy.

husk. *v.i., v.t.* To undress.

hustle. *v.i., v.t.* 1. To beg. 2. To steal. *c1915.* 3. To work as a prostitute, to seek customers in order to have sexual intercourse for pay. 4. To sell something. 5. To earn or obtain money aggressively or unethically; to be active or energetic in earning money by one's wits; to seek customers or victims of a deception aggressively. 6. To hurry. *n.* 1. Any confidence game, crooked gambling game, cheating, deception, or other unethical way of earning a living or obtaining money. 2. Moving about energetically, pushing about. *Usu. in the phrase "get a hustle on," mean-*

ing "hurry." *Colloq.* 3. A quick examination; a search —**er.** *n.* A prostitute. *Fairly common.*

hustle on, get a. To hurry; to work, move, or do something faster or with more alertness. *Usu. a command or plea.*

hut. *n.* 1. A prison cell. 2. A college fraternity house. 3. The caboose of a railroad train.

hyp; hype; hipe. *n.* 1. A hypodermic needle. *c1913.* → 2. A hypodermic injection of narcotics. *c1925.* → 3. A dope peddler, a supplier of illicit narcotics. *Addict use.*

hyped-up. *adj.* Artificial, phony, as though produced by a hypodermic injection of a stimulant.

hypo. *n.* 1. Hypochondria. *Colloq. since c1900.* 2. A hypodermic needle; a hypodermic injection. *Hospital use.* → 3. A narcotics addict.

I

ice. *n.* 1. A diamond; collectively, diamonds. *Very common.* 2. A gem or jewelry set with gems. 3. Bribe money; money paid by a criminal for police and political protection; incidental profit obtained illegally or unethically. *v.t.* To assure or clinch something; to put on ice.

ice, on. 1. Sure of being won, earned, or a success, said esp. of games, situations, and business ventures. *Since c1890.* 2. In prison; not being allowed to communicate with others. 3. Waiting and ready to be called to work, perform, or play, said of people.

ice, put on. 1. To kill. 2. To postpone. 3. To assure or clinch something, as a victory.

iceberg. *n.* An unemotional person.

icebox. *n.* 1. A prison cell for solitary confinement. 2. A prison. 3. A place where performers or athletes await their turn to perform or play, such as the wings of a stage or the bull pen or dugout at a baseball park where pitchers warm up. 4. Any place noted for its cold weather. *Colloq.*

ice cream. Any of certain habit-forming narcotics in crystal form.

iceman. *n.* 1. A jewel thief. 2. A gambler, athlete, or performer who is always objective and calmly confident, esp. during times of excitement, confusion, or stress.

icky; ickie. *adj.* 1. Overly sentimental; old-fashioned; neither stylish nor striking; corny; specif., incompatible with swing music; disliked by swing music enthusiasts. *Orig. c1935 swing use; very common student use in late 1930s and early 1940s.* → 2. Preferring sentimentality or old-fashioned entertainment, dress, topics of conversation, or the like. *n.* A dull person; one who lacks worldly knowledge and a sense of humor; specif., a student who does not follow the fads and fashions of his fellow youths. *Pop. teenage use c1938–c1945.*

if bet. A bet on two or more horse races stipulating that part of the winnings from the first race will be wagered on one or more later races; if the first bet is lost, the bettor has no wager on the later races. *Horseracing use.*

iffy. *adj.* Doubtful; uncertain.

igg. *v.t.* To ignore, to refuse to take notice of. *Orig. Negro use. Jive use c1935. From "ignore."*

iggle. *v.t.* To persuade another to do one a favor. *Teenage use since c1955. Perhaps from "egg on," certainly reinforced by "the bald iggle," creature in Al Capp's synd. newsp. comic strip "Li'l Abner," which can look a person in the eye and make it impossible for the person to lie, exaggerate, or speak insincerely.*

ike; Ike. *n.* A television iconoscope.

illuminated. *adj.* Drunk. *A syn. suggested by "lit."*

immie. *n.* A kind of playing marble.

import. *n.* An out-of-town girl brought in for a college social affair, such as a fraternity house-party or dance. *College use.*

I'm sorry. An expression of one's inability or refusal to understand, comprehend, appreciate, or agree. *As an expression of refusal: colloq. As an expression of inability to comprehend, appreciate, or dig: far-out use.*

in. For phrases beginning with "in," see under principal word of phrase.

in. *n.* 1. An advantage; esp. the advantage of knowing someone in authority. *Colloq.* 2. A friend or relative in authority or who can introduce one to or influence a person in authority. *adj.* 1. Belonging to a social clique of, or accepted by, desirable, successful, or influential people; belonging to or accepted by any specific group of people; accepted or respected by a specific person. 2. Well liked by, or able to obtain a favor from, a specific person or group.

in, get. To have sexual intercourse with a female. *Lit.* "to get into the vagina."

in-and-outer. *n.* A mediocre performer or athlete, one who is sometimes successful or even brilliant but who, just as often, is a failure or gives a dull performance; a mediocre entertainment, with some entertaining and some tedious parts.

increase the volume. *imp.* Speak louder. *Teenage use since c1955. From wide teenage television listening.*

indeedy. *adv.* Indeed; certainly. *Occasionally becomes pop., as c1945, as a fad word. An emphatic form usu. following "yes" or "no." Prob. influenced by stand. "—y" added to some adjs. to form advs.*

index. *n.* The face. *Some c1935 jive, c1940 underworld, and since c1950 cool use.*

Indian hay. Marijuana.

Indian hemp. Marijuana.

indie. *n.* An independent movie exhibitor. *Movie use.* *adj.* Independent. *Some self-conscious movie use.*

info. *n.* Information. *A common "shortening."*

in for [someone], have it. To be angry at someone; to desire revenge on someone. *Colloq.*

in for it = in Dutch; for it.

inhale. *v.t.* 1. To eat, esp. a light meal or between-meal snack. → 2. To drink, esp. a soft drink or beer. *A comparatively recent teenage and student use. Perhaps an echo of narcotic addict speech.*

ink. *n.* Cheap wine. *Harlem use.* *v.t.* To sign a contract.

ink-slinger. *n.* A writer; one whose work is writing, orig. with pen and ink; specif.: an author, editor, newspaperman, or the like. *Colloq. Usu. derisive.*

inkstick. *n.* A fountain pen. *Pitchman use.*

inky-dink. *n.* A very dark complexioned Negro. *Negro use.*

in like Flyn(n) = in, *adj.*

inning. *n.* A round of boxing. *Prize fight use since c1920. From baseball.*

in one. On the strip of the stage next to the footlights; in front of the stage curtain. *Theater use.*

insect. *n.* A young, inexperienced Naval ensign. *W.W.II USN use.*

intercom. *n.* An intercommunication telephone or radio system.

in the know. Informed or aware of a specific situation or plan, esp. a confidential one; knowledgeable; sophisticated; cognizant of and alert to new ideas and the beliefs of others.

in there. 1. Trying hard; making an effort. 2. To be equal to a specific task; to be capable of succeeding or wining. 3. Satisfying. 4. In baseball, straight across the plate in the strike zone; said of a pitched ball.

intro. *n.* 1. An introduction of two people. 2. In music, an introductory passage of any kind.

v.t. To introduce. *All uses "shortenings."*

invite. *n.* An invitation. *Accented on the first syllable. Colloq.*

in wrong. To be in another's disfavor; to have made an unfavorable impression on another.

I.O.U.; IOU. *n.* A promissory note; a personal voucher containing only a date, the statement "I owe you" and the amount of a debt, and the signature of the debtor; a guarantee to pay, usu. between friends, esp. in ref. to a gambling debt. *From the words "I owe you."*

Irish confetti. Bricks, esp. when thrown in a fight.

Irisher. *n.* An Irish person; a person of Irish extraction.

Irish fan. A shovel.

Irish grape. *n.* A potato. *Jocular use. Because Ireland is assoc. with potato-growing.*

Irish nightingale. A tenor, esp. a countertenor, who sings Irish ballads with an Irish accent.

Irish pennant. A sloppy loose end, as of a sheet, rope, or blanket, that should be tucked in or straightened. *USN use.*

Irish turkey. 1. Corned beef and cabbage. *Hobo lingo.* 2. Hash. *Some Army use since c1935.*

iron. *n.* 1. A car. 2. A gun, a shooting iron. 3. A cattle brand made with a branding iron. *Western.* 4. Silver coins.

iron betsy. Any army service rifle.

iron-burner. *n.* A blacksmith. *Logger use.*

iron curtain. Fig., a curtain that prevents the free flow of communications and people to and from the Union of Soviet Socialist Republics and its allies in eastern Europe; the boundaries, frontier barriers, and restrictive policies (i.e., political censorship of news, etc.) of the U.S.S.R. *The term was first used by H. G. Wells in "The Food of the Gods," 1904 = an enforced break of communication with society by an individual. The present use, very common since c1946,* is one of the major cold war terms. *This use was orig. by Sir Vincent Troubridge, Oct. 21, 1945, in the "London Sunday Empire News," in his article "An Iron Curtain Across Europe," which described the difficulties of military government without full co-operation and exchange of information by all.*

iron hat. A derby hat.

iron horse. A military tank. *W.W.II Army use.*

iron house. A jail.

iron man. 1. A silver dollar. 2. A dollar or the sum of $1. 3. In sports, a tireless athlete; a team member who plays through a complete game, and in many games during a year. 4. A calypso musician who uses an oil drum instrument. *Since c1955.*

iron men. *pl.* Dollars; orig. and usu. dollars one wagers on horse races or other gambling events and games.

iron off. To pay.

iron out. 1. To kill, as with a shooting iron. 2. To solve one's problems or difficulties; to resolve one's differences with another. *Colloq.*

iron pony. A motorcycle.

Irving. *n.* = Melvin.

island. *n.* An oasis; a growth of trees on an otherwise treeless landscape.

iso. *n.* Solitary confinement cells. *From "isolation." Convict use.*

it; It. *adj.* Sexy; sexually attractive. *Stressed or deliberately pronounced. Usu. written within quotes.*

it [for someone], have. To be in love with someone.

Italian cut. A women's hair style, a modification of the poodle cut, being slightly longer and featuring ringlets of hair on the forehead, and over the cheekbones and ears. *Common c1952–c1955. Popularized by the actresses appearing in post-W.W.II realistic Italian movies.*

Italian football. A bomb. *Racketeer use.*

Italian Hero = Hero, sandwich.

itch. *v.i.* In pocket billiards, to fall into a pocket; said of the cue ball. *v.t.* To cause [the cue ball] to fall into a pocket, thus incurring a penalty. *n.* In pocket billiards, an instance of or the penalty for shooting the cue ball so that it falls into a pocket.

itchy. *adj.* Eager; fig., trembling with eagerness or impatience.

it girl. A girl with obvious sex appeal; a glamorous girl or woman.

it's. 1. = it's been real. 2. "It's the truth; I'm speaking honestly."

it's been = it's been real.

it's been real. 1. An expression said on leavetaking, to one's host or friends, indicating the speaker's enjoyment of the time spent together or at a social function. *Orig. from "it's been real fun"; "it's been real fine (a real fine evening or party)." By omitting the last word, the implication is that the gathering, people, and conversation have been enjoyed because they were sincere, and that the evening or good time or gathering was a real experience as opposed to a mere function.* 2. "It's been real dull, boring, stupid, insincere." *From the first use. Since the last word of the phrase is omitted, the phrase can be used to imply derision of the gathering, people, or conversation.*

it stinks. An expression of disgust toward something offensive, esp. offensive to one's sense of honesty, intelligence, aesthetic taste, or the like; specif. applied to inferior entertainment.

it to [someone], give. To beat up, chastise, or reprimand someone, usu. in anger. *Colloq.*

it with [someone], make. 1. To have sexual intercourse with someone; to establish a heterosexual or homosexual relationship with someone. *Orig. beat use, now also far-out use and the beginning of student and teenage use.* 2. To impress someone favorably; to establish rapport with someone.

ivory. *n.* 1. A billiard ball. 2. The skull. —ies. *n.pl.* 1. The teeth. 2. Dice. 3. Piano keys; a piano.

ivory dome. *n.* Any intellectual; a highly trained specialist. *c1940.*

ivory-hunter. *n.* A talent scout; esp., a baseball scout searching for talented players.

ivory-thumper. *n.* A pianist.

Ivy League. *n.* A league of football and other athletic teams representing prominent north-eastern universities (Cornell, Harvard, Yale, Princeton, Columbia, Brown, Colgate, Dartmouth, U. of Pennsylvania). **ivy-league.** *adj.* 1. Pertaining to or characteristic of the Ivy League schools and the manners and fashions cultivated by their students. *Usu.* "ivy-league," *adj., connotes a certain degree of wealth, sophistication, refinement, social prominence, and the like.* 2. Esp., representative of the modes of dress favored by students at Ivy League schools. *Generally, the term refers to conservative but youthful men's styles, currently including narrow, striped ties, button-down shirts, narrow, unpleated trousers, blazer jackets, three-button sport jackets, and the like. The ivy-league students have presumably been dressing conservatively for generations; the specif. current style evolved after W.W.II, spreading first to "Madison Avenue" and then to the country at large when several prominent clothing manufacturers adopted the style (c1955) and advertised it heavily.* 3. Conservative.

Ivy League cut = crew cut.

ixnay. *n.* = nix. *From Pig Latin.*

J

jab a vein. To use heroin as an addict. *Probably synthetic.*

jabber. *n.* A hypodermic needle. 1918. *U.S. military prison use.*

jab-off. *n.* A subcutaneous injection of a narcotic; also the effect of such an injection.

jaboney; jiboney. *n.* 1. A newly arrived foreigner; a greenhorn. 2. A tough; specif., a gangster's muscleman or bodyguard.

jack. *n.* 1. Money. *c1850 to present; orig. sporting term, very common c1920, and still in wide use.* 2. A blackjack. In gambling, esp. cards, a jack-pot. 3. Simple luxuries, such as sweets and tobacco. *Convict, student, and Armed Forces use.* 4. A locomotive; a train. **Jack.** *n.* Any man; a fellow or guy; a term of address to a person whose name is not known. *Orig. jive use.*

jack, piece of = piece of change.

jackass. *n.* A stupid person; a dullard. *Colloq.*

jack-deuce. Askew; high on one side and low on the other.

jackeroo. *n.* A cowboy. *Western use. Perhaps from Australian sl. "jackeroo" = young fellow, but more likely from Sp. "vaquero."*

jacker-upper. *n.* One who raises or increases something; specif. a price-raiser.

jacket = monkey jacket; yellow jacket.

jack out. To pull a gun.

jackpot, hit the. To succeed, usu. to a greater degree than anticipated; to succeed in a spectacular way. *Also used sarcastically to mean to fail dismally, to a greater degree than anticipated. From slot-machine gambling use.*

jackroller. *n.* A thief who robs money from persons of his victims, usu. while they are drunk. *Rather than orig. in "rolling a person for jack," the origin seems to be from "rolling" [lumber] jacks.*

jack up. To increase a price.

jag. *n.* 1. A spree, usu. a drinking party. *Colloq. and still widely used.* 2. Fig., a spree or splurge; a spell of unrestrained activity of any kind. —ged. *adj.* Drunk. *Brought to America by Eng. colonists.*

jaheemy. *n.* A movable drydock; a vehicle for elevating and shifting the position of a landing craft. Also spelled **je—, gee—,** and **—bie.** *U.S. Armed Forces use.*

jail bait. 1. Any person, as a minor criminal or esp. a female, with whom one makes an acquaintance at the risk of getting into trouble; specif., a woman of such compelling attractiveness that men will take to crime in order to furnish her wants. **2.** Specif., a sexually attractive girl who has not reached the legal age of consent. *Because having "carnal knowledge" of a minor is considered a major crime in most states.*

jail-bird. *n.* A convict; an ex-convict; a prisoner or ex-prisoner.

jake. *adj.* Satisfactory; all right; O.K.; approved of; fixed. Often used in a context of totality, as "Everything is jake." *W.W.I British army use, quickly spread to U.S. troops, now in common U.S. use. Prob. a folk ety. of "chic."* *n.* **1.** A person who is all right; one who can be trusted. **2.** Jamaica ginger extract, used as a cheap substitute for whisky.

jalop. *n.* **1.** = jollop. **2.** A jalopy.

jalopy; jaloppy. *n.* **1.** An old and/or battered automobile. **2.** Any vehicle, regardless of its condition or age.

jam. *n.* **1.** A predicament; difficulty; trouble. **2.** Small objects that are easy to steal, such as rings and watches. *Underworld use.* **3.** = jam session. *c1935 to present.* *v.t.* **1.** To play jazz music, esp. Dixieland or swing, intensely and primarily for one's own gratification; to play extemporaneously or with the enthusiasm and intensity of an extemporaneous or personal performance. **2.** In jazz, to improvise freely, usu. in an ensemble. **3.** To auction; to act as an auctioneer. *Pitchman use.* **4.** To nullify a radio broadcast by creating an interference signal on the same frequency. *adj.* **1.** Possessing the characteristics of unrestricted jazz. **2.** Lending itself to being played or being played in an intense, seemingly personal and extemporaneous manner; said of jazz music or arrangements.

jam, in a. In trouble; in a difficult, disastrous, or embarrassing position. *Colloq. From the standard verb = to be pressured into a tight place.*

jam auction; jam pitch. A pitchman's business carried on in a store; a store selling cheap souvenirs, imitation jewelry, knick-knacks, and the like.

jammed up. In trouble; in a jam.

jammy. *adj. & adv.* Extremely lucky; luckily.

jamoke; Jamoke. *n.* **1.** Coffee; esp. strong black coffee. *From "Java" and "Mocha." Vagabond, USN, and Army use.* **2.** A fellow; a guy.

jam session. Orig. an informal gathering of jazz musicians to play for their own pleasure, usu. in free and lengthy improvisations on well-known themes; later a term applied commercially to public jazz performances.

jam-up. *n.* A jam; a crowd, as of persons.

jane. *n.* **1.** A girl or young woman. *Common since c1915; sometimes capitalized.* **2.** A man's sweetheart. **3.** A (usu., but not necessarily, public) restroom, bathroom, or toilet as used by women. *The women's "john."*

jap. *v.t.* To ambush someone; to make a sneak attack or surprise assault on someone; to deceive someone. *Current teenage use.* *n.* An ambush; surprise attack.

jar-head. *n.* **1.** A mule. *Southern hill dial.* **2.** A Marine. *W.W.II use.*

jasper; Jasper. *n.* **1.** A theological student. → **2.** An exceptionally pious or meek person. **3.** A rube. **4.** A fellow; a guy.

j.a.t.o.; jato. *n.* A jet-assisted take-off. *Applied to propeller-driven military airplanes that use jet*

*boosters to achieve a quick take-
off from a short runway.*

java; Java. *n.* Coffee, whether
Java coffee or not. *Colloq. since
c1850, first common with hobos,
Army and USN men, and lum-
berjacks, now very widespread;
saw increased popularity with
W.W.I.*

jaw. *n.* A chat; a talk. *v.i.* **1.** To
talk. *c1880 to present.* → **2.** Specif., to lecture a person; to give
a long reprimand. **3.** To talk, esp.
to argue or to wrangle incon-
clusively; to gossip.

jawbone. *v.i.* **1.** To carry on sincere, rational talk that leads to
establishing financial credit or
trust. → **2.** To loan; to trust. →
v.t. **1.** To borrow; to buy on
credit. **2.** To practice-shoot a
weapon over a qualification
course; to rehearse. *W.W.II Army
use.* *n.* **1.** Financial credit; trust.
2. A loan. **3.** One who talks too
much. *adv.* On credit. **to buy
jawbone** = to buy on credit; to
buy on the installment plan.
*W.W.I and W.W.II Army use,
very common.*

jaw-breaker. *n.* **1.** A word, esp.
a long one, that is hard to pronounce. **2.** A piece of hard candy;
specif. a round piece of hard
candy with a piece of bubble
gum in the center, sold in dis-
pensing machines and, c1940,
very popular with grade-school
children.

jaw-cracker = jaw breaker.

Jax. *proper n.* Jacksonville,
Florida. *Widely used in Florida,
rarely elsewhere.*

jay. *n.* **1.** A stupid, inexperienced
person, usu. with a rural or
small-town background. *Since
c1900.* **2.** An easy victim; one who
is easy to dupe. **3.** A bank. *From
the "j" of syn. "jug." Underworld
use.*

jayhawk. *n.* An unusual or extraordinary person. *A Mid-West-
ern term.*

Jayhawker. *n.* A native of Kansas.

jaywalk. *v.i.* To walk in or across
a street in violation of traffic

rules, as to cross a street in the
middle of a block, cross an in-
tersection when the stop light
is red, and so forth. *Colloq.* **—er.**
n. One who jaywalks.

jazz. *n.* **1.** Animation; enthusiasm;
enthusiasm and a fast tempo or
rhythm; frenzy. → **2.** The only
orig. American music, traditionally known for its emotional appeal, rhythmic emphasis, and
improvisation. *This is the music
first played by small Creole and
Negro groups in and around New
Orleans in the decades before
1900. Its rhythms were based in
part on African songs, field
chants used by slaves, work
chants of railroad laborers and
prisoners, and the Spanish and
French music known to the Creoles of the region. It was first
played on battered, secondhand
instruments discarded by marching and military bands. The musicians were often self-taught,
though some were trained in traditional methods. Jazz was orig.
played for the entertainment of
and to express the feelings of the
musicians and their friends, at
parties and dances. It soon became pop. on the streets of New
Orleans, where sidewalk bands
multiplied and were quickly invited to perform inside saloons,
brothels, cabarets, etc., of the
entertainment districts, esp.
Storyville. At the same time, the
music began to absorb more elements of white American music,
esp. ragtime and the music traditionally associated with brass
bands. Once inside the brothels
of Storyville, the music became
more widely known to both local
men and out-of-town travelers.
Thus the music grew in appeal
and the musicians, now professional, could devote full time to
playing. The brothels competed
with each other for the best
musicians, thus encouraging new
musical talent, compositions, and
improvisation. Once the appeal
of the music grew and the bands*

and musicians had gained some fame, various musicians and bands began to travel, playing throughout the Delta region and taking jobs on the riverboats that plied northward on the Mississippi as far as Minneapolis. With the ending of legalized prostitution in New Orleans during W.W.I, more musicians were forced out of the South. Some moved to St. Louis and other Mississippi River towns, but in the 1920's Chicago became the chief attraction for New Orleans musicians. There they played in beer halls, restaurants, and eventually in nightclubs. In Chicago, too, many young white musicians heard and imitated the Negro players, and the first important school of white jazz emerged. From Chicago the interest in jazz quickly spread to other northern cities, esp. to New York. With the attraction of radio, recordings, and more cities to play in, more and bigger bands were formed. With larger audiences, many of whom had no rapport with the lives or feelings of the early jazz musicians, jazz lost some of its early earthy quality. Styles changed, the small New Orleans group (now often called, though improperly, "Dixieland") gave way to the larger group playing written arrangements, and in the 1930's the style known as "swing" became predominant. Pop. music, ballads, and dance tunes were incorporated in the jazz repertoire. Thus jazz has developed many styles and moods—the back alley or lowdown dirty; the slurred gutbucket; the blaring tailgate; the smooth and mellow; the swinging. The latest developments, perh. most appealing to the modern ear, are bop and cool jazz, or progressive jazz. In general, these new styles stem from Charlie Parker, the great alto saxophonist, who introduced advanced techniques, often requiring extraordinary instrumental skill and profound musical understanding. Bop is known for its long, breathless series of notes, often in high registers, and for quick changes in key and tempo; unusual rhythms, sometimes Spanish-American in orig., are used. Cool jazz orig. on the West Coast c1950 and took much of its impetus from the work of modern classical composers. The music is known for its close, intricate harmonies, its improvisations based on chord extensions, complex phrasing, etc. v.i., v.t. 1. To increase a tempo or rhythm with excitement; to increase the speed of something, to speed up; to generate excitement. It is impossible to know which of the two above meanings came first, or even if the v. uses are older than the n. uses. 2. To play jazz music or in a style similar to jazz music. Since c1900. 3. To lie, exaggerate, or attempt to generate speed for or enthusiasm about something that does not warrant it. —ed.

jazz-bo. n. A fancily dressed, hep, sharp person; a stud.

jazz it. To play jazz music, esp. to play enthusiastically.

jazz up [something]. Specif., to play any musical composition in a jazz style; fig., to enliven any activity, to make a design or presentation more colorful or appealing.

jazzy. adj. 1. Descriptive of jazz music. 2. Colorful; spirited; exciting. Orig. and still a little jazz use, basically in ref. to jazz music or playing; some general c1920 use in ref. to things or people. 3. Corny, obvious, square. The only cool use since c1950.

jeans. n. 1. A pair of trousers made of any material, esp. denim. Now standard. Prob. from the Fr. town Jean, famous for its denim cloth. 2. Specif., a pair of stiff, tight-fitting, tapered denim cowboy work pants, usu. blue, with heavily reinforced seams and slash pockets. *Very pop. with teenagers of both sexes since c1945. From c1945–c1958 the cuffless bottoms of the trouser legs were worn folded up; recently the style has been to leave the trouser bottoms unfolded; a faded, well-worn appearance is favored.*

jeasly; jeasely. *adj.* Measly; worthless.

Jebby. *n.* A Jesuit; the Jesuit order.

jeebies = heebie-jeebies.

jeep. *n.* 1. A specific bantam, squarish, open, 1¼-ton, 4-wheel-drive Army command and reconnaisance vehicle of great versatility used in W.W.II. *Early in W.W.II, and throughout the war in the U.S. Armed Forces, the word "jeep" = a small truck and what is commonly called a "jeep" was called a "peep." From the Army term "GP" [general purpose] reinforced by the noise "jeep" made by a mythical animal who could do almost anything, in E. C. Segar's comic strip, "Popeye." c1938.* 2. Generally, any car; esp. a small car. 3. A new Army recruit; a rookie. 4. A Link trainer. *W.W.II Air Corps use.* 5. A Naval escort carrier. *W.W.II USN use. v.i.* To ride or to travel in a jeep. *adj.* Small; of a size to be carried by a jeep.

jeep-jockey. *n.* A truck driver. *W.W.II Army use.*

jeeter. *n.* 1. A slovenly, ill-mannered person. *From the character Jeeter Lester in E. Caldwell's novel,* Tobacco Road. 2. A lieutenant. *W.W.II Army use.*

Jeez; jeez; Jeeze; jeeze; Jees; jees. *exclam.* 1. A mild exclamation of surprise or wonder. 2. A euphem. between the more euphem. "Gee" and the profane "Jesus." *May or may not be capitalized.*

jeezy-peezy. *exclam.* An expression of surprise or disgust.

Jeff. *n.* A boring person; a square. *Negro use.*

jell. *v.t., v.i.* 1. To close or complete a business deal or sale. 2. To materialize; to conclude.

jelly. *n.* 1. = jelly-roll. 2. An easy or enjoyable task. 3. Anything obtained free of charge. *v.i.* To loaf, esp. as a social occupation; to loiter for idle conversation.

jellybean. A term of address. *Jive talk and teenage use. c1935.*

jelly-roll. *n.* 1. A man extremely virile or obsessed with sex; a man who curries the sexual favors of women. → 2. A lover; a sweet papa or sweet mama. *Very common Negro use. Most pop. with Southern Negroes c1875–c1915, associated with and made known to white people by use in early jazz groups and lyrics; perhaps esp. by the early great jazz pianist Jelly Roll Morton. Still some Negro use.*

Jenny. *n.* 1. An airplane used in training. 2. Any airplane.

jerk. *n.* 1. A short branch railway line, a small railroad. *Prob. from "jerkwater," reinforced by the number of jolts and jerks trains make on such a railroad line.* 2. An ineffectual, foolish, or unknowingly dull youth or man, usu. applied contemptuously to one who is overfamiliar, unprepossessing, eccentric, stupid, unreasonable, selfish, or careless. *Very common. As are many other such sl. words, this can be used affectionately among friends.* 3. Any young, inexperienced worker; a rookie. 4. = Soda jerk. *adj.* Jerklike; jerkish; operated by jerks. *v.t.* To draw a gun, as from a holster or pocket. *v.i.* = jerk off. —y. *adj.* Having the characteristics of a jerk.

Jerkimer = Herkimer Jerkimer.

Jerk McGee. A jerk; a square.

jerk off. To waste time; to cause confusion; to make mistakes.

jerk-off. *n.* One who causes confusion, makes many mistakes, or wastes time; a dope.

jerk soda. To prepare and, usu., to serve sodas, ice cream dishes, and the like at a soda fountain; to work as a soda jerk.

jerk town. A small town; lit., a town known mainly as a place where trains jerk water.

jerkwater. *n.* = jerk town. *adj.* 1. Like a jerk town. *Since c1900.* 2. Unimportant; insignificant.

jerry. *n.* 1. A manual laborer. *Railroad and hobo use.* 2. A girl. *Underworld use.* 3. A small pistol that can be easily concealed. *Underworld use.* *adj.* Wise, in the know. **Get jerry** = wise up, understand.

Jerusalem Slim. Jesus Christ. *Familiar but not profane. Hobo use.*

Jesse James. Fig., anyone who cheats or misappropriates funds.

Jesus. *n.* The stuffing; insides. *Usually in "beat" or "kick" or "knock the Jesus out of [a person]."*

jet up. To work intensively, efficiently, and quickly.

jibber-jabber. *v.i.* To jabber. *n.* Jabbering.

jiboney = **jaboney.**

jiff = **jiffy.**

jiffin, jiffing. *n.* = **jiffy.**

jiffy. *n.* An indefinite but short period of time; usu. from a few seconds to a few minutes; a moment. *About 7 times out of 8, "jiffy" occurs in the phrase "in a jiffy," at the end of a sentence or clause. Maybe from "jiffin," but orig. is unknown. adv.* Quickly.

jiffy bag. 1. A small canvas or leather bag, resembling a miniature suitcase, used for carrying small articles, usu. toilet articles, while traveling. *Common W.W.II use.* 2. Several makes of cheap, heavily insulated paper bag, produced in various sizes, used for wrapping, carrying, or mailing perishable or easily damaged items.

jig; zig; jigg. *n.* A dancing party or a public dance.

jigamaree. *n.* Any new gadget. *From "jigger." Colloq. since 1820.*

jig-chaser. *n.* 1. A white person, esp. a white policeman. 2. A Southerner.

jigger. *n.* 1. An artificially made sore, usually on an arm or leg, used as an aid in begging 2. An ice-cream sundae. *Most common in Eastern prep schools and colleges.* 3. A liquor glass of 1½-ounce capacity. → 4. A drink of liquor. *v.t.* To damn. **—s! jigger!** *interj.* Look out! Run! *A warning cry, particularly that the police or one's superiors are coming. Often in "jiggers, the cops."*

jigger-man; jigger guy. *n.* A lookout. *Underworld use.*

jiggery pokery. *n.* Trickery; fakery.

jiggins; juggins. *n.* 1. A fool; a simple-minded person. *From "jughead."* → 2. A victim of a swindle.

jigs. *interj.* Beat it! *From "jiggers." Orphan home use.*

jig-swiggered. *adj.* Jiggered; darned.

jillion. *n.* A great many; an indefinitely large number.

jim. *v.t.* To spoil; to ruin; to bungle. *Underworld use.*

Jim Crow. 1. [derog.] A Negro. 2. The practice or doctrine of segregation as applied to Negroes in the U.S.; discrimination or intolerance directed toward Negroes. *v.t.* To discriminate against Negroes; to practice or enforce rules of segregation.

Jim Dandy; jim-dandy. *n.* 1. An admirable person or thing. *Colloq. since c1880.* 2. A fictional hero; the one who will solve all problems; a *deus ex machina.* *adj.* Admirable; dandy.

jim-jam. *v.i., v.t.* To jam, to jazz up. **—s.** *n.* = heebie-jeebies.

Jimmie. *n.* A car or engine built by GMC (General Motors Corp.). *From pronouncing the initials GMC rapidly. Hot-rod use since c1955.*

jingle. *n.* A phone call; a ring.

jinky board. A seesaw. *Used by children; prob. from the Gullah.*

jinx. *n.* Bad luck; a cause of bad luck; a bad luck omen. *v.t.* To cause bad luck, to put a jinx on.

jip = **gyp.**

jism. *n.* Vigor; speed; animation; excitement; pep.

jit. *n.* A nickle; 5¢. From *"jitney."* —**ney.** *n.* **1.** A car, usu. one owned by an individual, used to carry passengers along a standard route for a small fare; a private bus. **2.** A nickel; 5¢. → **3.** A small 5¢ cigar. **4.** Any unscheduled local bus, car, or limousine used as a bus. *adj.* Five-cent; cheap; improvised; inferior; miniature.

jitney bag. A coin purse; a small handbag.

jitter. *v.i.* **1.** To tremble, shake, etc. **2.** To be nervous or frightened. —**y.** *adj.* Nervous; trembling. *Colloq.*

jitterbug. *n., adj.* **1.** One who, though not a musician, enthusiastically likes or understands swing music; a swing fan. **2.** One who dances frequently to swing music. **3.** A devotee of jitterbug music and dancing; one who follows the fashions and fads of the jitterbug devotee. *v.i.* To dance, esp. to jazz or swing music and usu. in an extremely vigorous and athletic manner.

jitters, the. *n.pl.* Nervousness; fear; cowardice.

jive. *n.* **1.** Ordinary, tiresome, or misleading talk or actions; exaggerations, flattery; distraction; insincere, uncouth talk or conduct; anything that should be ignored; boloney; bull. *Orig. Negro use, and orig. perhaps alternate sp. of "gieve."* **2.** Gaudy articles, merchandise, or clothing. **3.** Fast popular music with a strongly accented two- or four-beat rhythm, as played by the pop. big swing bands c1938–c1945: fast swing music; jazz as it developed in the 1930's; swing. *By far the most common use. v.t.* To mislead with words; to deceive; to kid. *v.i.* **1.** To play or dance to jive music; to jam. *Note that all the above meanings are equated with meanings of "jazz." Thus, "jive" replaced "jazz" to some extent, c1938–c1945, linguistically as well as musically.*

2. To make sense; to equate or match two items; to match with the known facts. *Very common since c1940. Prob. from "jibe."* **3.** To talk idly or confusedly, in a jazzy rhythm and up-to-date slang. *adj.* Any person, place, group, object, or idea associated with teenagers or swing music. *c1938–c1945. One could see a jive movie with Benny Goodman, then go to a jive joint for some beer and to hear some jive records on the juke box.* **jiving.** *adj.* **1.** Playing swing adroitly or in an exciting manner. *Some swing use.* **2.** Attracting attention or showing off while playing cool or far-out music, as by blowing very high notes, playing very fast, or accenting close-harmony bass notes, while demonstrating little musicianship or comprehension of the piece, chord relationships, or arrangement. *This derisive cool and far-out use shows what these groups think of jive.*

jo. *n.* A shovel.

J.O.; j.o. = Joe, coffee.

job. *n.* **1.** Almost any item, object, procedure, machine, etc., esp. one of good quality or representing good workmanship; often an automobile or other vehicle. *Common since c1925.* **2.** Almost any person, but usu. a tough or cynical person. **3.** A crime; a criminal escapade. **4.** = snow job. *v.t.* To deceive; to frame or doublecross. *Mainly underworld use.*

job, lay down on the. To lack alertness; to shirk; to work slowly and without enthusiasm.

job pop. To inject drugs intravenously, usu. into the arm. *Narcotic addict use.*

jock. *n.* **1.** A jockey. **2.** = disc jockey.

jocker. *n.* A homosexual hobo who lives off the begging of his boy companion. *Hobo use.*

jockey. *n.* **1.** An athlete who taunts opposing players; one who "rides" another. **2.** A cab, bus, or truck driver; an airplane pilot. **3.**

A student who uses a pony. *College use.*

joe; Joe. *n.* **1.** Coffee. *Also called "j.o." "Joe" is a useful monosyllabic synonym; it apparently derives from the "j" of "Java" or perhaps the "j" and "o" of "jamoke."* **2.** A term of address; anyone whose name is unknown. → **3.** A man, esp. a friendly, pleasant one; a fellow; an egg; a guy, as "a good joe," "an ordinary joe." → **4.** A soldier. *Very common during W.W.II.* → **5.** Any American. *Used by natives of countries familiar with W.W.II U.S. soldiers.* *adj.* Informed; wise; hep. *v.t.* To inform [a person].

Joe Blow. 1. Mealtime. *Circus slang.* **2.** Any person whose name is not known. → **3.** A young male civilian. *W.W.II Armed Forces use.* → **4.** An enlisted man. *W.W.II Army use.* **5.** A musician. **6.** An average man; any man; any man at all.

Joe College. 1. A male college student, esp. a brash youth whose dress, manner, and speech suggest the social and sporting aspects of college life. *Usu. mildly derogatory.* **2.** Any callow young man whose enthusiasm for inconsequential things betrays his inexperience; a young man, not a college student who imitates the dress and manner popularly associated with college students.

Joe Doakes. Any male; a man whose name is not known; "everyman."

Joe Gish. Any midshipman. *Annapolis use.*

joepot. *n.* A coffeepot.

Joe Sad. An unpopular person. *Negro use.*

joey; Joey. *n.* A circus clown.

Joe Yale = Joe College, but with special reference to characteristics popularly associated with the old and socially prominent eastern colleges.

Joe Zilsch. Any man; a typical common man.

joggling board. 1. A swing. *Prob. from the Gullah.* **2.** A seesaw.

john; John. *n.* **1.** A toilet, esp. a public toilet for males. *Very common. Usu. not cap.* **2.** A man, esp. an average or typical man; specif. one who can be used, an easy mark. *Orig. Negro use.* **3.** An Army recruit. **4.** A man who is keeping a girl, i.e., paying her rent and expenses in return for sexual favors; a male lover; a girl's steady escort or date. → **5.** A girl's steady boy friend. *The word orig. implied sexual intimacy but does not now always have a sexual connotation.* **6.** A policeman. **7.** A law-abiding citizen. **8.** A lieutenant. *W.W.II use.* **9.** Variously: An idle young dude; a Chinese; a free spender; victim of a swindle.

John B. A hat. *From "John B. Stetson." Most common in the West.*

John B. Stetson. 1. A hat made by the John B. Stetson hat company. → **2.** Any man's hat regardless of make.

John Doe. Any man at all; the mythical average man. *From the name invented anciently to stand for the fictitious lessee in court proceedings of ejectment and thereafter used wherever a fictitious person is needed.*

John dogface; Johnny dogface. An Army recruit. *Some W.W.II use.*

John Family. A professional thief or grifter.

John Farmer. A farmer.

John Hall. Alcohol. *From "-hol" respelled and personified. Common vagabond use.*

John Hancock. One's signature. *Often in "put your John Hancock on the dotted line." From the large signature of John Hancock, prominent on the Declaration of Independence.*

John Henry = John Hancock.

John Hollowlegs. A hungry man. *Hobo use.*

John Law. The police; any law enforcement officer. *Orig. hobo and circus use.*

John L's = Long Johns.

Johnny = John.

Johnny-come-lately. *n.* A newcomer. Fig., anyone or anything that is tardy; specif., a person who joins a group after the group's success seems assured and after his support is no longer needed. *Colloq. since c1850.*

Johnny O'Brian. A boxcar. *Hobo use.*

Johnny on the spot. A person who is present and alert to his opportunities or present when needed. *Colloq. since c1895.*

John Roscoe. A gun; a roscoe.

Johnson. *n.* A tramp; a drifter. *Underworld use.*

Johnson rod. A mythical part of a locomotive, truck, car, or plane. *Jocular use, in referring to engine trouble the cause of which is unknown, and as a joke on those who are not in the know.*

join out. 1. To join; to join up. *Circus use.* 2. To get free transportation by hiring out. *Vagabond use.*

joint. *n.* 1. Almost any building, apartment, room, or sheltered area where people gather, primarily for eating, drinking, living, taking dope, lounging, conversation, dancing, listening to music, watching television, gambling, etc., but also for buying and selling. Often considered disparaging, "joint" is sometimes a neutral word for "place." A joint may mean any kind of saloon, speakeasy, nightclub, café, eating place, soda fountain, hotel, house, apartment, room, store, or any other place of business. It may be a carnival concession, a jail, a dancehall, an opium or marijuana den, a hangout, a poolroom, a garage, etc., usu. not as disreputable as a dive. Fig., any place where one person joins or may join another or others. 2. A gun. *Some teenage gang use.* 3. A marijuana cigarette. 4. A complete set of equipment necessary to inject narcotics. *Teenage narcotics addict use. Since c1955.*

joint hop. To go from one place of entertainment to another on a spree; to stop for a drink at several bars in succession. *Used almost exclusively in the phrase "to go joint hopping." Student use since c1945.*

joker. *n.* 1. Any single component of a multiple instrument that tends to negate or qualify the positive effect of the whole; e.g., a clause in a contract, an item on an agenda, a paragraph in a legislative bill the effect of which is to nullify or weaken the apparent purpose of the larger instrument. 2. That which gives one an unfair chance; that which makes a task or plan impossible or difficult to achieve. 3. A man; a fellow; a guy. *Though not derog., it often implies that the person is ineffectual.* → 4. A wiseacre; a wise guy. *Army use, cW.W.II.*

jollop. *n.* A large portion or serving, esp. of food.

jolly. *adj.* Excellent; pleasant; etc. *Colloq. adv.* Very. *In the U.S. widely regarded as a Briticism. Some jocular use.*

jolt. *n.* 1. The initial effects of an injection of drugs or a marijuana cigarette. → 2. An injection of a narcotic drug. 3. A prison sentence. *Underworld use.* 4. A drink of liquor; a shot. 5. A marijuana cigarette; an injection of heroin. *Addict use. v.i.* To take injections of heroin in the arm.

Jonah. *n.* A hipster, a rock, a cat. *Rock and roll use since c1955.*

Joneses, keep up with the. To strive not to be outdone socially or financially by one's neighbors or others regarded as one's social equals; to spend money to keep up a front.

jook. *n., adj.* = juke.

josh. *v.i.* To joke, tease, twit, banter, or kid. *n.* A joke. *Colloq. since c1895.* —**er.** *n.* One who joshes. *Colloq. since c1900.* —**ing.** *n.* Joking; teasing; kidding.

joskin. *n.* A rube; a hick.

joy-juice. *n.* Liquor.

joy knob. The steering wheel of a car, esp. a hot rod, or the stick of an airplane.

joy-popper. *n.* 1. A newcomer among narcotic, esp. marijuana, addicts. 2. One who claims to take narcotics only for an occasional thrill, as opposed to a true addict.

joy-powder. *n.* Morphine. *Orig. underworld use.*

joy rider. *n.* A nonaddict who sometimes takes a narcotic drug. *Drug-addict use.*

joy smoke. *n.* Marijuana.

joy-stick. *n.* 1. The control lever of an airplane. 2. The steering wheel on a hot rod. 3. An opium pipe.

juane. *n.* Abbr. for "marijuana," esp. a marijuana cigarette.

Judy. *n.* 1. A girl or woman. *Some W.W.I and W.W.II use. Never as common as "Jane."* 2. Used absolutely by airfield control-tower workers and pilots in radio communication with (other) pilots = "Your plane is now close enough to be seen, I see you." → 3. Used absolutely by airfield control-tower workers and pilots in radio communication with (other) pilots = "Your plane now appears on, or is locked in, my radar screen. I have located, or see, you by radar." *Both 2. and 3. common W.W.II Air Force use, and still in use.* → 4. "Exactly"; "I understand or agree." *Usu. used absolutely. Some use since W.W.II.*

jug. *n.* 1. A jail; a prison; usu. a local prison. *Since c1815; often in "in the jug."* 2. A bottle or flask of whisky. 3. A drink or shot of whisky. 4. A bank. *Underworld use.* → 5. A safe; a strongbox. *Underworld use. v.t.* To imprison [a person]. *Since c1835.*

juggins = jiggins.

jughead; jug-head. *n.* 1. A mule, esp. an Army mule. *Farm and Army use.* 2. A stupid person.

juice. *n.* 1. Liquor, esp. whisky. 2. Money used for or obtained from gambling, extortion, blackmail, or bribery, esp. a bookmaker's commission from a gambling syndicate. 3. Electricity; electric current. → 4. Gasoline; fuel. *v.t.* To milk a cow. —d. Drunk.

Juice. *n.* A stage electrician. *A nickname. Theater use.*

juice-box. *n.* 1. A car battery. 2. A junction box used for attaching electric cords. *Orig. factory and electrician use.*

juiced up. Intoxicated.

juice-joint. *n.* A soft-drink tent, stand, booth, or concession. *Carnival and circus use.*

juju; ju-ju. *n.* 1. A marijuana cigarette. 2. Any object, such as a piece of string, handkerchief, etc., with which an adult plays out of nervousness or as a habit. *Perhaps from narcotics addicts' "juju" = marijuana, implying a compulsion; perhaps an alternate form of "gee-gee."*

juke. *n.* 1. = juke house. → 2. A roadhouse, esp. a cheap one. → 3. Music, esp. the style of music played in brothels, cheap roadhouses, and the like; an early nonprofessional form of jazz music. → 4. An automatic, coin-operated record-playing machine; a juke box. *v.i.* To tour roadside bars, usu. with one of the opposite sex; to drive to one roadside bar, drink a little and perhaps dance a little, leave and go to another, and continue in this manner for an entire evening or night. *Southern use.*

juke house. A brothel.

jumbo. *adj.* Large, extra large. *P. T. Barnum bought "Jumbo," the largest elephant on record, from London's Royal Zoo in 1883; in America the animal quickly caught the public imagination and became the first major attraction of the Barnum circus.*

jump. *v.t.* 1. To attack or assault [a person]. *Colloq. since 1890.* →

2. To rob; to hold up. **3.** To pulsate or be noisy with activity, as of dancers or merrymakers. *Orig. jive talk; c1935. Most common sl. use. adj.* Pulsating with excitement; fast played or playing in quick tempo, as a jump tune, a jump band. *n.* **1.** = swing. *(music).* **2.** A jive dance; any dance or other social event; a hop. *Orig. some jive and teenage street-gang use; general teenage use by c1955.* **3.** = rumble. *Teenage street-gang use since c1955.* —y. *adj.* Nervous; frightened. *Colloq.*

jump, get the. To take a lead in a race; to have a lead or an advantage in a contest or competition.

jump all over [someone]. To berate; to criticize severely and with anger.

jump band. A musical ensemble devoted to fast swing with a powerful, accented rhythm.

jumped down [someone's] throat. To criticize severely and angrily; to berate.

jumped-up. *adj.* Hurriedly organized; improperly planned. *Colloq.*

jump off the deep end. To act quickly and without consideration; to take drastic action; to take a bold step; to go the whole hog.

jump on. To assault verbally; to reprove; to reprimand. *Colloq. since c1885.*

jumps, the = jitters, the.

jump salty. To become angry; enraged; to become malicious. *Harlem Negro use; orig. jive and teenage street-gang use. Now some general student and teenage use.*

jump smooth. To become or go honest or straight; fig., to become calm, pleasant, or friendly. *Orig. some jive use; now teenage street-gang use.*

jump the gun. To do anything prematurely. *From racing use,* *where a shot from a gun signals the official start of a race.*

jump the hurdle. To marry.

jump (dangle) up the line, take a. To journey; to move on to the next town. *Circus and vagabond use.*

June around. To be restless or aimless; to have spring fever.

jungle. *n.* **1.** A hobo camp and rendezvous, usu. a clear space in a thicket (for fuel) near a railroad (for transportation), and ideally also near water and on the outskirts of a city. **2.** A gathering place for the unemployed of a city, often near the dumping ground and usu. equipped with homemade shacks or huts for those with no other place to live. **3.** Any busy, crowded living or working district in a city; the business pursued in such an area, esp. if characterized by keen competition and a lack of ethics. —s. *n.pl.* **1.** Open country; woods. **2.** Rural districts; the sticks.

jungle buzzard. A hobo who lives in a jungle to beg from other hobos. *Hobo use.*

juniper juice. Gin. *From the flavoring.*

junk. *n.* **1.** Narcotics; a narcotic. *Since c1920. Orig. narcotics addict use; now fairly well known.* **2.** Rubbish; trash; worthless refuse. *Colloq.* **3.** Worthless talk or entertainment; cheap merchandise; dilapidated, but still useful, possessions. → **4.** Stuff; miscellaneous articles, often of practical and some monetary value. *Colloq.* —er. *n.* **1.** One addicted to any narcotic drug. *Since c1925.* → **2.** A peddler of narcotic drugs to addicts. **3.** An automobile worn beyond repair. —ie; —y. *n.* A drug addict.

junk-ball. *n.* In baseball, a pitch that is unorthodox, tricky, or anything but a straight fast ball. *adj.* Given to using such pitches; said of a pitcher.

junk heap. An old or dilapidated automobile; the implication is that it is ready for the junk yard.

K

kadigin = thingamajig.

kafooster. n. Unnecessary or confusing talk.

kale. n. Money.

kangaroo. v.t. To convict [a person] with false evidence.

kangaroo court. 1. A mock "court" held by prisoners to assess each newcomer a part of his money and tobacco. → 2. A small-town police court in which the judge levies exorbitant fines on speeding out-of-town motorists, then splits the excess money with the arresting policemen. → 3. Any local court that is harsh on vagabonds, hobos, and travelers.

kaput. n., adj. Out of working order, broken, useless; unsuccessful, without a chance of success; dead. From the Ger. W.W.II Army use.

kay. n. A knockout. Prize fight use. From the abbr. "K.O."

kaydet. n. 1. Slighting and/or humorous mispronunciation of standard "cadet." 2. Variant of sl. "cadet."

kayducer. n. A train conductor; orig. underworld use—a train conductor who would for a fee, allow known confidence men or gamblers to ply their trade among train passengers.

kayo = K.O. A spelled pronunciation of the abbr. "K.O."

keed. n. Kid. Almost always in direct address. Considered somewhat jocular.

keek. n. 1. A peeping Tom. 2. A manufacturer's spy who reports on the newest designs, research, and business details of competitors; specif. in the garment industry.

keep company. To court; to go steady; to go on dates; said of a couple often, but not necessarily, planning to marry. Colloq. since c1935.

kee-rect. adj. Correct; "What you said is very true; I am in complete agreement with what you have said." Pop. by repeated use in the synd. newsp. comic strip

"Abbie and Slats," though much earlier student use. A prime example of sl. emphasis by a louder or longer pronunciation of the first syllable of a stand. word.

keester = keister.

kef; keef; kief. n. Marijuana. Narcotic addict use.

keister; keester; keyster; kiester; kister. n. 1. The human posterior. → 2. Either of the rear pockets in a pair of pants; a pocket. Mainly pickpocket use. → 3. A suitcase, valise, satchel, handbag, grip, or case, esp. a display tray that folds up into a satchel or suitcase. Often one containing pitchman wares. → 4. A safe or strongbox.

kelly. n. A hat, esp. a derby or other stiff hat.

kelt; keltch. n. 1. A white person. Negro use. → 2. A Negro who is light-skinned enough to pass or who does pass as a white person.

keltch = kelt.

kennel. n. A house; a rented room. Vagabond use.

ken-ten. n. A lamp used to prepare opium for smoking.

Kentucky oyster. n. Any of various eatable internal organs of the pig, fried in deep fat and served as a meat course.

keptie. n. A woman provided with an apartment and otherwise supported by a man in return for her sexual favors.

kerflooie, go = go blooey.

kerflumixed. adj. Perplexed; confused.

ketchup, in the. Operating at a deficit. From "in the red."

kettle. n. A pocket watch. Underworld use.

kettle of fish. A predicament or situation, esp. a confused or unsuccessful one. Usu. in "that's a fine kettle of fish" = that situation is a mess, it's a bad predicament.

keyster = keister.

keystone. n. In baseball, second base.

keystone sack; keystone cushion. n. In baseball, second base.

key-swinger. *n.* **1.** A college student, graduate, or professor who wears one or more honorary society keys on his watchchain. → **2.** A boaster. *Both student use.*

kibitz. *v.i., v.t.* **1.** To give unwanted advice or opinions; specif. to watch a card, chess, checkers, etc., game from behind a player while offering opinions and advice on the plays to be made; to offer advice or opinions to a team, coach, or manager. *Orig. a card-playing term; common since c1935. From Hebrew "kibutzi" = a member of a group.* → **2.** To make jokes and humorous comments, often of a critical nature, while another is trying to work, perform, or discuss a serious matter; to joke, to make wisecracks. —**er.** *n.* **1.** One who kibitzes, esp. at a game, specif. a card game. **2.** A joker, a jester, a wisecracker.

kibosh = put the kibosh on.

kibosh on [someone or something], put the. To put out of action; to squelch, esp. by violent means; to beat up someone; to quash, cancel, or eliminate. *Since c1850; of Turkish orig.*

kick. *v.i.* To complain, protest, object, make a fuss. *Colloq.* *n.* **1.** A complaint; a protest; an objection. *Colloq. since c1920.* **2.** A pocket, esp. in a pair of pants. *"Keister" = "kick" =* either of the two back pockets in a pair of pants; "breech kick" = either of the two side pockets in a pair of pants; "breast kick" = an inside coat or vest pocket. *Mainly pickpocket use.* **3.** A surge of pleasurable emotion; a thrill of enjoyment or excitement; a thrill; excitement. *Orig. c1930 jive use. Widely used by jive, jazz, cool, and beat groups.* → **4.** Anything that gives one a thrill, excitement, or satisfaction, ranging from violence, narcotics, whisky, and sex through jazz, books, and art to food, dress, and sleep. → **5.** An intense, personal, usu. temporary, preference, habit, or passion; a fad. *Since c1935. Most widely used by jive, jazz, cool, and beat groups.* **6.** Power; strength; potency; a high alcoholic content. *Colloq.* **7.** A sergeant. *Army use since c1925.* **8.** A dishonorable discharge. *Some Army use since c1930.* —**er.** *n.* **1.** An objector; a complainer. **2.** A small or outboard engine used to propel a boat. *Since c1930.* **3.** Something that provides a big kick or thrill. **4.** The point of a joke; the fallacy in an argument; an item in a group that invalidates, negates, or makes worthless all the others. —**s.** *n.pl.* Excitement; pleasure; esp. amoral pleasure or excitement. *Wide bop use since c1940; also common cool and beat use.* See kick.

kick [something] around. 1. To discuss, consider, or meditate on a topic, proposal, or plan. → **2.** To think over something. **3.** To try a plan or idea on a small scale. **4.** To take advantage of one's superior strength or status in order physically to hurt, verbally abuse or insult, or dominate another; to treat someone harshly or unfairly; to take advantage of someone. *Colloq.* **5.** To go from place to place or from one job to another frequently; to have worldliness gained from a variety of esp. unsuccessful experiences.

kick back. 1. To return, esp. to return stolen goods or money to the owner. **2.** To rebate; to pay part of one's wages or profits to another in return for being given a job or an opportunity to profit. **kickback; kick-back.** *n.* **1.** Money returned unethically to a firm, purchasing agent, manager, or buyer by a seller in order to increase sales or gain favors. **2.** A rebate; part of one's wages or profits paid to another in return for a job or an opportunity to profit. → **3.** Money paid for police and political protection. *Underworld use.*

kick in. To contribute money; to pay with others; to pay one's share. 2. To die.

kick it. 1. To rid oneself of a habit, esp. narcotic addiction. *Fairly common.* 2. To play jazz, jive, or swing music with enthusiasm.

kick off. 1. To die. 2. To leave, to depart. 3. To begin anything, as a meeting or campaign. *From the football term.* kickoff. *n.* The beginning of anything, as a meeting or campaign.

kick [someone] out. 1. To dismiss or expel someone. 2. To fire someone from a job. *Colloq.* kick-out. *n.* 1. The act of dismissing. 2. A dishonorable discharge from the armed forces. *W.W.II use.*

kick over. To rob; to knock over. *Racketeer use.*

kick the bucket. To die. *Since c1785. Now widely believed to refer to the last volitional act of one who, standing on an upturned bucket, fixes around his neck a noose suspended from the ceiling. Perh. also a metaphor from the more familiar dairy accident of a cow kicking over the milk pail as the farmer finishes milking her, a serious matter on a one-cow farm.*

kick the gong around. 1. To smoke an opium pipe. *Narcotic addict use.* 2. To smoke marijuana.

kick-up. *n.* A disturbance; a commotion.

kid. *n.* 1. A child of either sex. *Colloq. since c1890.* → 2. An offspring; a young son or daughter. → 3. Any inexperienced young man or young woman. → 4. A young athlete. 5. A bomber co-pilot. *W.W.II Army Air Corps use.* 6. Humbug, kidding, a prank. *adj.* 1. Immature; innocent. 2. Younger, as used in "kid brother," "kid sister." *v.t.* To josh a person; to deceive; to make fun of a person in his presence. *Colloq. since c1900. v.i.* To speak in fun; to josh, banter,

or joke. —der. *n.* One who kids. —ding. *n.* Joshing; joking; bantering; facetious taunting. Often in "no kidding." —do. Kiddo. *n.* 1. A child or youth of either sex. *Since c1910.* 2. A person, usu. in direct address. *Familiar and jocular use.* —die; —dy. *n.* A child.

Kid, the. *n.* The co-pilot of an airplane. *Orig. Air Force use.*

kidney-buster. *n.* Any physically hard job or sport.

kid show. A circus sideshow. *Circus use.*

kid stuff. Anything childish or immature; that which presents no challenge to or interest for an intelligent adult.

kid top. The sideshow tent. *Circus use.*

kiester = keister.

kife. *v.t.* 1. To swindle. *Circus use.* 2. To steal.

kike-killer. *n.* A billy club; a kind of bludgeon.

kill. *v.t.* 1. To drink or eat all of any specified amount of liquor or food. → 2. To drink or eat the last portion. 3. To ruin; to ruin one's chances of success; to become disillusioned or hopeless about something; to defeat someone or something. 4. To entertain an audience well; to make an extremely favorable impression on a person or audience. 5. To extinguish a fire, esp. a cigarette. *n.* 1. A murder. 2. An enemy plane shot down; an enemy ship sunk. *Air Force and USN use, esp. submarine, use during W.W.II.*

killer. *n.* 1. A very well-dressed or charming person. → 2. A lady's man; a ladykiller. 3. A honey; a lulu. → 4. That which gives one a feeling of exhilaration. → 5. Specif., a marijuana cigarette.

killjoy. *n.* A gloomy person; one whose actions or remarks deprive others of pleasure; a pessimist. *Colloq. A wet blanket may decrease the pleasure of others by being dull, timorous, or pessimistic; a killjoy may do so con-*

sciously or deliberately, for logical, official, or moral reasons.

killout. *n.* Any thing or person that is remarkable or gives one a feeling of exhilaration; a kicker. *Negro use.*

kinch; kinchen; kinchin. *n.* A child.

kind. *n.* A large amount or quantity; used only in "that [or 'the'] kind of money."

king. *n.* The leader; the top-ranking person. Specif., the warden of a prison. *Underworld use. Railroad use.*

King Kong; king kong. Strong, cheap whisky or wine. *From the fictional ape "King Kong" of huge size and tremendous strength.*

king pin. The highest ranking person in a group; the leader. *Colloq.*

kings. *n.* A pack of king-sized cigarettes. *Colloq.*

King's English, the. English as spoken and written by educated, knowledgeable people; lit. the English language as spoken by the educated upper class of Great Britain.

king-size. *adj.* Big; exceptionally long. *A term popularized c1940 in ads for extra-long cigarettes. Pop. post-W.W.II.*

king snipe. *n.* The foreman of a railroad section gang; the boss of a track-laying crew. *Hobo, logger, and railroad use.*

kinker. *n.* Any circus performer. *Orig. an acrobat only. From the contortions of limbs while performing. Circus talk.*

kinky. *adj.* 1. Crooked; unfair. 2. Stolen. *n.* Anything stolen, usu. a stolen automobile. Suggested by "bent" = stolen.

kip. *n.* 1. A bed. *Mainly underworld and vagabond use.* 2. A nightwatchman; a watchman. *Underworld use. v.i.* To sleep; to go to bed. *Still current hobo use.*

kipe. *v.t.* To steal, usu. something of small value.

kiss = kiss-off.

kisser. *n.* 1. The mouth. 2. The jaw. 3. The human face. *Orig., c1850, meant mouth, by c1890 also meant the jaw or the face. Often used ambiguously so that it is impossible to distinguish if mouth, jaw, chin, cheek, or entire face is meant.*

kiss [something] goodbye. To dismiss or get rid of something; to realize that something is lost or ruined. *Colloq.*

kissing cousin. 1. A constant companion or friend, of the same or of the opposite sex, who is granted the same intimacy accorded blood relations. → 2. Specif., a close platonic friend of the opposite sex. → 3. Humorously, a member of the opposite sex with whom one is sexually familiar when the parties involved believe their intimacy is unknown. *Orig. the term implied blood relationship and still does when used in Southern hill dial. In the South during the Civil War, kissing cousins were relatives who had the same political views.* 4. A facsimile, someone or something closely resembling someone or something else.

kissing-kin. *adj.* Matching; harmonious; made of the same fabric. **kissing kin.** *n.* Those items that match; harmonious people.

kiss off. 1. To dismiss or get rid of something or someone, often rudely and curtly. 2. To dodge; to evade. 3. To kill. **kiss-off.** *n.* 1. Death. 2. A dismissal; a brush-off; the end; notice of dismissal from a job, esp. without warning. *In New York often called "the California kiss-off"; in Los Angeles often called "the New York kiss-off." Mainly advt., movie, television, and radio use.*

kiss out. To be denied or cheated out of one's share of the loot or profits.

kiss the canvas; kiss the resin. In prize fighting, to be knocked down or out.

kiss the dust. To die. *Colloq.*

kiss the resin = kiss the canvas.

kister = keister.

kit and caboodle. *n.* The entire lot of people or things.

kitchy-koo; kitchy-kitchy-koo = hitchy-koo.

kite. *n.* 1. A note or letter, esp. a smuggled one. *Underworld use.* 2. An airplane. *W.W.II Air Force use.*

kittens, have; kittens, have a litter of. To give violent expression to one's emotions, usu. anger, anxiety, fear, or excitement, occas. laughter or surprise; to throw a fit, blow one's top, or have pups.

kittle-cattle. *n.* An unreliable, undependable person or group of people.

kitty. *n.* Fig., a pot or pool of money, made up of contributions from several people; the total amount of money so available. *Orig. used in the card game of poker = the money bet.*

kiwi. *n.* An air force man, esp. an officer who cannot, does not, or does not like to fly. *From the name of the flightless bird, the kiwi.*

klupper. *n.* A slow worker; a slow-moving, slow-talking or slow-thinking person. *From Yiddish sl.: "klupper" with same meaning, from stand. Yiddish "klupper" = one who pounds a slow steady pace.*

knee-bender. *n.* A church-goer; a self-righteous person. *Underworld and hobo use.*

knee-high to a grasshopper. Hyperbolically, very short in stature because of youth. Usually in the context, "I knew you when you were just knee-high to a grasshopper."

kneesies. *n.* Under-the-table amorous play in which one touches, rubs, or bumps with one's knees the knees of a person of the opposite sex, as a sweetheart.

knob. *n.* A person's head.

knock. *n.* 1. Adverse criticism; a grudge. 2. An annoyance; a disadvantage. *v.i.* 1. To find fault; to give bad publicity. 2. To talk; to discuss. *v.t.* 1. To borrow; to lend; to ask or beg. *Negro use.* 2. To give. 3. To find fault with; to give bad publicity to.

knock a nod. To take a nap.

knock around. To idle or loaf.

knock back. To drink a glass of whisky in one gulp.

knock [someone's] block off. To hit someone very hard; to knock someone unconscious; to give someone a severe physical beating. *Usu. used in the boasting threat, "I'll knock your block off."*

knockdown. *n.* 1. An introduction to a person, job, fact, or concept. → 2. An invitation. 3. Something of highest excellence. 4. Store money stolen from a retail sale by an employee, esp. small sums taken from the cash register; specif. small sums collected from customers but never put into the cash register; graft. **knock down.** *v.t.* 1. To introduce. 2. To keep money received or collected for one's employer. *Since c1865.* 3. To earn; esp. to earn a salary, a grade in school, or a compliment. 4. To reduce the price. *Colloq.* 5. To criticize or belittle someone. 6. To drink; to kill.

knock-down-drag-out fight; knock-down, drag-out fight. *n.* A hard vicious action-filled fight.

knocked, have it. To have a specific situation under control; to be succeeding or winning at something.

knocked out. 1. Drunk. 2. Tired, exhausted. 3. Emotionally exhausted.

knocker. *n.* A detractor; a fault-finder.

knock [someone] for a loop. 1. Lit., and fig. to strike a person a terrific blow, as with the fist; to knock someone out; to make someone unconscious or drunk, said of a strong drink. 2. Fig., to make a strong, favorable impression on someone. 3. To pass a test, perform, or succeed in a spectacular way.

knock it. An order or request to stop instantly. *From "knock it off."*

knock it off. An order, command, or entreaty to stop doing something immediately, esp. talking or joking; fig., an order to knock off a smile or laugh from one's face, pay attention and become serious. *Orig. W.W.II Army use. Based on "wipe it off."*

knock off. 1. To stop work at the end of the day or to eat lunch; to take a holiday or brief rest period from work. *Since c1850.* **2.** To stop immediately whatever one is doing, esp. to stop talking, teasing, or kidding, often said as a command, order, or entreaty. *W.W.I and II Armed Forces use.* **3.** To produce, esp. by craftsmanship, writing, painting, composing, performing, or the like. → **4.** To finish, as food, drink, or work. **5.** To delete, deduct, or eliminate, as in shortening or editing. *Colloq.* **6.** To kill; to murder. → **7.** To die. **8.** To raid, as by police, to raid and confiscate; to arrest. **9.** To steal or rob; to steal or rob from. **10.** To defeat or to best another, esp. in sports. **11.** To leave or depart. → **12.** To hurry.

knock [oneself] out. 1. To elicit enthusiasm or an emotional response, esp. deep sympathy or laughter. **2.** To work excessively hard or to exhaustion. **3.** To have a good time; to exhaust oneself laughing, dancing, or the like.

knockout; knock-out. *n.* **1.** An attractive person or thing, a handsome or beautiful person or thing. **2.** An attractive item of merchandise. *adj.* First-rate.

knock out. To create; to finish a task quickly and professionally; as to write a story, type a letter, or paint a picture.

knockout drops. Chloral hydrate or some other drug put into a drink, usu. of whisky, to render the drinker unconscious. *Since c1900.*

knock over. 1. To rob a place, a bank, a store, or the like. **2.** To raid a place, as by the police; to arrest a person. **3.** To eat or drink; to dispose of by consuming. **knock-over.** *n.* A robbery.

knock (lay) them in the aisles. Lit. and fig., to overwhelm an audience with one's talent; specif., to entertain an audience with truly hilarious humor.

knock the pad = hit the hay.

knock together. To cook; to prepare [food] by cooking. *Colloq.*

knothead. *n.* An incompetent or stupid person.

know. For phrases beginning with "know," see under principal word of phrase.

know-how. *n.* Skill; practical information; knowledge of how something is done or made or operates. *Colloq.*

know-it-all. *n.* A smart aleck; a person who claims sophistication and knowledge of many things.

know [one's] onions; know [one's] stuff; know [one's] business. To be competent, capable, or qualified in one's business or field of endeavor.

knuck. *n.* A thief, esp. a pickpocket. *Underworld use since c1850.* **—er.** *and* **—sman.** *n.* A pickpocket.

knuckle. *n.* **1.** The head. **2.** Muscle; stupidity.

knuckle-buster. *n.* A crescent wrench.

knuckle-down. *n.* In playing marbles, the standard way of shooting in which the knuckles are kept down. **knuckle down.** To concentrate, become serious in one's attitude, and work hard.

knuckle-duster. In baseball, a pitched ball at the height of, or pitched close to, a batter's knuckles.

knucklehead; knuckle-head. *n.* A slow-thinking or stupid person. *Common, but most popular in Marine Corps and USN.*

knuckler. *n.* In baseball, a ball thrown from the knuckles rather than from the finger tips.

knucks. *n.pl.* Brass knuckles.

K.O. *n.* In boxing, a knockout. *v.t.* In boxing, to knock out one's opponent. *adj.* 1. Knockout, as in "It was a K.O. punch." 2. O.K.

kong. *n.* Whisky, esp. cheap or bootleg whisky. *Negro use.*

kook. *n.* An odd, eccentric, disliked person; a "drip"; a nut. *Teenage use since 1958; rapidly becoming a pop. fad word.* —y. *adj.* Crazy, nuts; odd, eccentric; having the attributes of a "drip."

kopasetic; kopesetic; kopasetec; kopesetec = copacetic.

kosh = cosh.

kosher; Kosher. *adj.* Honest; authentic; valid; ethical; fulfilling the minimum requirements of honesty or ethics. *From "kosher" = clean and acceptable, according to Jewish dietary laws. The word has been taken from Hebrew to Yiddish to Eng.*

Kriegie. *n.* An American prisoner of war in a German prisoner of war camp. *Used by Amer. Army and Air Force prisoners of war in W.W.II. From Ger. "krieg" = war + "-ie" ending.*

kyuter = cuter.

L

lab. *n.* A laboratory; a building or a room that is or contains a laboratory; a period of work done in a laboratory; also used attrib. *Very common. Orig. student use.*

labonza. *n.* 1. The posterior. 2. The pit of the stomach. *Now the most common use. Pop. c1955 by television comedian Jackie Gleason.*

lace [one's] boots. To put [someone] wise.

lace-curtain. *adj.* Well-to-do; prosperous; decent; secure.

lacy. *adj.* Effeminate; of or pert. to a homosexual.

la(h)-de-da(h); la(h)-di-da; la(h) de da(h); la(h) di dah. *n.* A sissy; a fancy pants. *adj.* Sissified; affected.

ladies' man; lady's man. A male of any age who is charming and courtly to, and grooms himself to please, the ladies; one who pursues women politely and with success.

lady. *n.* In direct address, a woman who has aroused the speaker's ill will, often expressed by sarcasm or insult. *N.Y. City use.* See old lady.

lady-killer. *n.* A ladies' man.

lag. *n.* 1. Imprisonment. 2. A convict; an ex-convict. 3. A criminal. *Underworld use.* —ger. *n.* A convict; esp. an ex-convict out on parole.

lagniappe. *n.* Lit., something given for nothing; an extra; a dividend, a tip. *A Creole usage.*

laid out. Intoxicated.

la-la. *n.* A brash, impertinent, but sympathetic person. *Usu. in "He's some la-la."*

lam. *v.i.* 1. To come or go; usu. to depart quickly; to run away, escape. 2. Specif., to elude the police. *Underworld use. v.t.* 1. To escape prison. 2. To strike or hit; to lambaste. —baste. lambast. *v.t.* To attack verbally and with vehemence; to chide severely. —ster. lammister. *n.* An escaped convict; a fugitive from the law; one who is on the lam; one who has departed after posting bail.

lam, on the. 1. In flight from the police; to be a fugitive from the law. *Underworld use since c1925.* → 2. On the move; traveling.

lamb. *n.* 1. One easily fooled, tricked, or cheated; a sucker; a mark. 2. = lambie. —ie. lambie-pie. *n.* A term of endearment; a sweetheart.

lame-brain. *n.* A stupid person. *Colloq.* —ed. *adj.* Stupid. *Colloq.*

lame duck. 1. A holder of public office who is finishing his term but has not been re-elected. *Since he will soon be out of office, his authority is somewhat impaired; thus he is "lame." Stand. polit. use.* → 2. One who cannot assume his share of responsibility; a weakling; an inefficient person. 3. A stock market speculator who has overbought; one who has taken options on stocks that he cannot afford to buy.

lame duck bill (amendment) (law). A bill, amendment, or law initiated by a lame duck legislator or legislature; a bill, amendment, or law that has little chance of being approved by a legislature or of being enforced if approved; a weak bill, amendment, or law.

lamp. *n.* A look. *v.t.* To look at someone or something; to look over. —**s.** *n.pl.* The eyes.

landsman. *n.* A countryman, a compatriot. *From the Yiddish.*

lane. *n.* A naïve prisoner; a fool.

lap. *n.* 1. A round of a prize fight. *Since c1920. From the racing term.* 2. A drink or swallow, esp. of whisky.

lard-bucket. *n.* A fat man.

lard-head. *n.* A stupid person.

large. *adv.* Boastingly, with pride. *Usu. in "to talk large." Colloq. since c1830. adj.* 1. Eventful, exciting. *Since c1895, but became very pop. c1935, esp. with jive groups, and is still common.* → 2. Well accepted; famous; popular; successful; capable of drawing large audiences; in fashion. *Usu. said of performers. Orig. theater and jazz use c1945; now common. A modern, hip variant of "big."*

large charge. 1. A thrill; lit., a big charge. 2. A very important man; a big shot. *Both uses orig. jive talk; a prime example of a jive rhyming term. In vogue with students c1945–c1950.*

larrikin. *n.* A hoodlum. *From Austral. sl.*

larry; Larry. *n.* 1. Any worthless or broken small article of merchandise, as a toy balloon, doll, souvenir, or the like. *Circus use.* 2. A shopper who does not intend to buy anything. *adj.* Worthless; bad; phony. *Circus use.*

last (long) count, take the. To die. *From prize fighting.*

lately. See **Johnny-come-lately.**

lather. *n.* An angry or excited mood; a sweat. *v.t.* To hit a baseball.

latrine rumor. *n.* An unsubstantiated, often exaggerated story or rumor. *W.W.II Army use.*

laugh. *n.* A joke; a cause or object of laughter. *Colloq.*

laugh on the other side of [one's] face. To cry; to change one's mood from happy to sad; to become a failure or be defeated after having expected or experienced success. *Colloq.*

laundry. *n.* The board of faculty members that passes on flying cadets. Such a board can "wash out" cadets. *W.W.II Army use.*

law, the. *n.* Any officer of the law; a policeman; the police; also, a prison guard, etc. *Orig. underworld use. Now colloq.*

lawn-mower. *n.* 1. In baseball, a grounder. 2. A sheep. *Western use.*

lay an egg; lay a bomb. 1. To fail; esp. to flop; to sing, act, tell a story, or perform very poorly or before an unappreciative audience. *Said of any entertainer or of a play, movie, song, or story. Orig. theater use, now common.* 2. To drop a bomb on the enemy from an airplane. *W.W.II Armed Forces use.*

lay chickie. To act as a lookout while others steal, rob, or commit an act of violence. *Since c1945, common use for teenagers and juvenile delinquents, esp. in New York.*

lay-down. *n.* 1. A failure. 2. Money paid to smoke opium in a den.

lay for [someone]. To wait for someone in order to surprise and do him physical harm, usu. to fight, hit, stab, or shoot, esp. to fight; to ambush someone.

lay low. To keep inconspicuous or hidden; said of a person. Esp., to keep hidden until another's anger has evaporated or the law has had time to forget; to curtail illegal or undesirable activities for a while.

lay off. 1. To dismiss from employment, esp. to dismiss from employment temporarily with the promise of rehiring once business gets better and more employees are again needed. *Colloq.* 2. To stop or ease one's criticizing or teasing; often used as a command or entreaty. 3. For a bookmaker, or gambler, to give part of a bet to another bookmaker, or gambler, to reduce his potential losses. **layoff; lay-off; lay off.** *n.* 1. A general dismissal of employees. 2. An unemployed actor. 3. A bet or part of a bet which one bookmaker gives to another, in order to reduce his own potential loss; money which a bookmaker bets at a racetrack, in order to reduce his own potential loss, and sometimes to reduce the odds on a specif. horse.

lay one on [a person]. To strike or hit.

lay [someone] **out.** 1. To knock a person down; to knock a person unconscious; to kill a person. 2. To reprimand; to scold.

lay [someone] **out in lavender** = **lay** [someone] **out.**

lay paper. To pass worthless checks; to pass counterfeit money.

lay them in the aisles = **knock them in the aisles.**

lead. *n.* Bullets.

lead balloon. Fig., a failure; a plan, joke, action or the like that elicits no favorable response; a flop; anything that lays an egg. *Orig. in the expression, "That [joke, performance, plan, or the like] went over like a lead balloon." Now abbr. to "That [joke, etc.] was a lead balloon." From the notion of a lead balloon that could not leave the ground. Since c1950.*

lead-footed. *adj.* Awkward; slow-thinking; stupid.

lead in [one's] **pants, to have.** To move, work, act, react, or think slowly; lit., to move as if one were weighted down. *Colloq.*

lead in [one's] **pencil, have.** To be full of energy and vitality.

lead joint. A shooting gallery. *Carnival and circus use.*

lead out, get the. To make haste; go into action; stop loafing; be alert. *A shortened form of "get the lead out of your pants." Became very common cW.W.II; the longer forms are now seldom used.*

lead-pipe cinch. Something easy; anything or anyone certain of success; a certainty. See **cinch.**

lead poison; lead poisoning. Death, of a wound, caused by shooting. *Old Western term used by underworld and by W.W.II Armed Forces.*

leaf. *n.* An Air Force or Army officer holding the rank of major. *From the insigne.*

leak. *v.i., v.t.* 1. To disclose information, esp. secret information, inadvertently or with malicious intent. 2. To let news apparently "leak" in order to make it known without making a public announcement; to release or reveal official or secret information unofficially; to start a false rumor purposely. The person who "leaks" news or secret information; the channel through which such items reach the public. *Orig. use by underworld, now most commonly refers to government officials.*

lean against; lean on. To beat up someone; to threaten to beat up someone or a member of one's family in order to get information, to persuade someone to suppress information, or to extort money; to act or be tough with someone; to coerce.

leaping heebies, the = **heebie-jeebies.**

Leaping Lena. In baseball, a fly ball hit beyond the infield but not far enough to be caught by an outfielder.

leap-tick. *n.* 1. A mattress on which clowns and acrobats leap and fall. *Circus use.* → 2. The false fat stomach of a comedian, stuffed with mattress ticking or straw.

leary. *adj.* = **leery.**

leather. *n.* 1. A pocketbook, wallet, or purse. *Underworld use.* 2. A football. 3. Boxing gloves.

leather, the. *n.* 1. A kick. 2. A hit or blow, with or without boxing gloves.

leatherneck. *n.* A U.S. Marine. *From the old custom of facing the neckband of the Marine uniform with leather. Very common.*

leave a strip. To decrease one's driving speed suddenly; to brake a car; fig., to stop a car so quickly that a strip of rubber is left on the pavement from the tires. *Hot-rod use since c1950.*

leaves. *n.pl.* 1. Lettuce. 2. Dungarees, blue jeans. *Rock-and-roll and general teenage use since c1955. From "Levis."*

Leblang. *v.i., v.t.* 1. To sell theater tickets at cut rates. *From Joe Leblang, ticket promoter. Theater use since c1930.* → 2. To reduce the admission price of a show.

lech = **letch.**

leech. *n.* 1. One who is friendly to or follows another in order to profit; one who habitually borrows; a human parasite. *v.i., v.t.* To borrow, esp. to borrow without intending to return the money or item borrowed.

leery; leary. *adj.* Wary; suspicious; doubtful. *"Leery" is about 3 times as common as "leary." Since c1850.*

left. *n.* In politics, the liberal and radical persuasion, as opposed to the "right" or conservative side.

left-foot. *n.* A Protestant. *adj.* Protestant.

left-handed. *adj.* 1. Undesirable; said of a ship. 2. Illicit; irregular; phony.

leftie; lefty. *n.* 1. A left-handed person, esp. a baseball pitcher. *This use usu. spelled "lefty." Colloq.* → 2. A shoe made for the left foot; a glove made for the left hand; a tool made for left-handed users. *Colloq.* 3. A radical, socialist, or communist, or a sympathizer with liberal or ra-

dical political philosophies; since c1945, esp. a communist or communist sympathizer. *adj.* Left-handed. *Colloq.*

leftist; Leftist. *n. & adj.* As or like a member or sympathizer of the left wing.

left-wing; left wing. *n.* The liberal and radical elements of any group, party, state, nation, etc. *Because in the Fr. republican parliament the conservative parties sit on the right of the semicircular chamber and the liberal and radical parties sit on the left. adj.* Pert. to liberal or radical views. *Since c1945, the term has usu. implied "communistic."* —**er.** *n.* A member of or sympathizer toward the left-wing.

leg. *v.i., v.t.* To depart; to run away; to travel. *Often in the phrase "leg it out of here."*

leg, pull [one's]. To make fun of a person; to kid him. *c1920 to present; colloq.*

legacy. *n.* A college fraternity member, pledge, or prospective pledge who is closely related by blood to a member of longer standing, as an older brother, father, or grandfather. *Student use since c1920.*

legal beagle. *n.* A lawyer, esp. an aggressive or astute one.

legal eagle. An extremely capable, devoted, or cunning lawyer.

legger. *n.* 1. = leg man. 2. A bootlegger.

legit. *adj.* 1. Legitimate; lawful; law-abiding; honest; authentic. 2. Concerned with the New York commercial stage, stage plays, or serious art; classical; semi-classical; other than popular. *n.* The New York stage, stage plays and shows; serious or classical art, performances, performers, or composers, writers, painters, and the like. *Orig. to distinguish the professional New York theater from traveling and nonprofessional shows, now primarily to distinguish stage plays from movie and television plays.*

legit, on the. 1. Honest; legitimate; within the law. 2. = on the level.

leg man. 1. A newspaper reporter who goes to the scene or a source of news to gather facts which may be written up by someone else. → 2. Any person who earns his living by gathering **news**, disseminating publicity, or calling on a great many clients.

leg pull. *n.* An instance of pulling [one's] leg.

leg show. Any performance or show of girls dressed or undressed so as to show their legs and bodies; a performance or show whose main appeal is mild sexual excitation.

lemo. *n.* 1. Lemonade. *Since c1900.* → 2. Lemon extract, drunk as an intoxicant. *Prison and Army use.*

lemon. *n.* 1. Something unsatisfactory, inferior, or worthless. *Colloq. since c1925.* 2. A light-skinned, attractive Negress; a mulatto. *Negro use.* 3. Any disagreeable disliked person, esp. one who does not produce, buy, or assume proper responsibility. *Each of the above uses is associated with the properties of a lemon.*

lemon, hand [someone] a. To do or give something unpleasant to a person.

Leona. *n.* A female square; a woman who nags. *Some far-out use.*

les. *n.* A lesbian. **—bine.** *n.* A lesbian. *West Coast jazz, beat, and cool use since c1955.* **—bo.** *n.* A lesbian.

letch; lech. *n.* 1. Desire; a strong liking for; a preference; a yen. 2. A lecher. *adj.* Lecherous, seductive.

let out. To discharge from one's employment; to fire. *Since c1895.*

let out; let-out. *n.* 1. A plausible way out of a predicament; an excuse for avoiding responsibility; an out. 2. A discharge; a firing.

lettuce. *n.* Money; paper money.

level. *v.i.* To be honest, truthful, or serious; to speak frankly; to tell the truth. *adj.* True; straight.

level, on the (dead). *adj.* Honest; truthful; fair; ethical; legitimate; respectable; serious; sincere. *adv.* Honestly; legitimately; truthfully; sincerely.

level with [someone] = level. To treat fairly

Levis. *n.* A pair of stiff, tight-fitting, tapered pants, usu. blue with heavily reinforced seams and slash pockets. *From the company name "Levi Strauss," the leading mfr. of such pants; this firm orig. produced and sold them to the 19C cowboy.*

liberate. *v.i., v.t.* 1. To loot; to take in looting, esp. from an unoccupied or partially destroyed building. *Wide W.W.II Army use, mainly in Europe. A jocular euphem., from the stand. term used by Allied propaganda in ref. to the reconquest of German and Italian occupied territories.* → 2. To steal, esp. to steal a small item. *Since W.W.II.* 3. To have sexual intercourse with, or take as a mistress, a girl native to an occupied country. *W.W.II Army use in Europe.*

liberty. *n.* A holiday; a vacation from work or school. *Some use since W.W.II. From the USN use.*

liberty cabbage = sauerkraut. *Some W.W.I superpatriotic use, to avoid using "sauerkraut," traditionally a German dish and word.*

liberty ship. *n.* A cargo vessel of stand. size and design, mass-produced during W.W.II to carry military personnel and supplies to overseas bases.

lick. *n.* In jazz, a break, a riff, a short phrase of improvisation introduced between phrases of the melody; sometimes a chorus of improvisation.

lick [one's] chops. 1. To wait with anticipation. *Common use.* 2. To gloat over another's misfortune.

lickety-split. *adv.* Fast; at great speed. *Since c1850.*

licorice stick. A clarinet, from its resemblance to the familiar con-fection. *Associated with swing and jazz musicians, c1935. Now considered affected usage. Some archaic jazz use; a synthetic jazz word.*

lid. *n.* 1. A hat. 2. An unskilled telegrapher. *Telegrapher and Army Signal Corps use.*

lieut. *n.* = loot.

life, not on your. *exclam.* Emphatically no. *The phrase "on your life" is never used affirmatively.*

life-boat. *n.* A pardon; a commutation of a prison or death sentence; a retrial. *Underworld use.*

lifer. *n.* A prisoner serving a life sentence. *Since c1800.*

lift. *v.t.* 1. To steal an item. *Colloq.* 2. To plagiarize. *n.* 1. A ride in a car. 2. Orig. the kick left from taking a narcotic; generally, energy, enthusiasm, power, or feeling of well-being obtained from another's encouragement, success, or a stimulant, such as whisky.

lifties. *n.pl.* Men's shoes built up inside in order to increase the wearer's apparent height.

light. *n.* A match or cigarette lighter for lighting a cigarette; the act of lighting a cigarette. *v.i.* To depart, esp. rapidly. *adj.* 1. Carrying only a light weight. → 2. Hungry; not having eaten recently; underweight. *Orig. hobo use.* → 3. Lacking or missing a required or desired item or amount; lacking a sufficient amount. → 4. Lacking a specif. sum of money; owing a specif. sum of money. 5. Sympathetic to and appreciative of progressive jazz music and off-beat art; hep. *Some far-out and beat use.*

light, out like a. 1. Unconscious for any reason, esp. from a hard blow on the head. 2. Asleep, esp. sound asleep or asleep from exhaustion.

light, the. *n.* Comprehension, understanding; the point or main conclusion to be drawn from a story, joke, or experience. *Usu. in "see the light."*

light colonel. A lieutenant colonel. *Army use.*

light-fingered. *adj.* Prone to or known to steal. *Colloq.*

lightning. *n.* Inferior whisky. *Colloq. since c1880.*

lightning rod. A jet fighter plane. *Some Air Force use.*

light of, make. 1. To dismiss airily, as a challenge, imputation, or obstacle. 2. To belittle, as another's achievement or person.

light out. To depart for another place, esp. quickly and directly; to flee. *Mainly dial.*

light piece. *n.* A silver coin; usually a quarter; a small amount of money.

lights out. Death.

like. 1. Used at the end of a sentence in place of "as," "as if," "it will be as if," etc. 2. Used before nouns, adjectives, and pred. adj., without adding to or changing the meaning of the sentence. *Thus, "It's like cold" = it is cold. Used by jazz, cool, and beat groups, esp. in New York City. Prob. to avoid making a definite, forthright statement, part of the philosophy; reinforced by Yiddish speech patterns.*

like, make. To pretend to be; to imitate; to simulate; to caricature. *Colloq.*

like crazy = like mad. Excitedly; excessively; fig., as if crazy.

like hell. An expression of incredulity, negation, or refusal. Thus "Like hell I will" = I won't.

like mad = like crazy. *Probably now the more common of the two terms.* With abandonment; with enthusiasm; without reserve, inhibitions, or dignity; quickly; completely; thoroughly. *Orig. a jive term. Now common.*

lily. *n.* 1. An effeminate male; a male homosexual. 2. = lulu; humdinger.

lily white. Innocent; *usu. in a negative phrase, as "She's not so lily white."* —*s.* 1. Bed sheets. *Usu. in "slip between the lily whites"*

= *go to bed. Negro use.* 2. The hands.

limb, out on a. Exposed; vulnerable; in danger; said of a person who has publicly championed an extreme idea, plan, procedure, etc., the failure of which may precipitate his downfall or discomfiture.

limbs. *n.pl.* Legs; esp. shapely female legs. *Colloq.*

lime-juicer. *n.* 1. An English ship. 2. A British sailor. 3. An Englishman. *Orig. W.W.I Army use. All meanings maritime use; from the ration of limes issued by the British Navy to its sailors to prevent scurvy.*

limey; limy. [derog.] *n.* = lime-juicer in all three meanings. *The most common term for "British sailor" or an "Englishman." Became common during W.W.I.*

limit, go the. To enter into sexual intercourse, as opposed to even the most intimate petting; said of a girl or a couple.

limit, the. *n.* A person, thing, or act that exceeds the usual bounds of propriety, performance, or the like, to the annoyance, exasperation, or delight of others.

limmy. *n.* A jimmy; any tool or set of tools used for house-breaking.

limp. *adj.* Drunk.

limp sock. *n.* = wet smack.

limp wrist. *adj.* Homosexual; said of male homosexuals; effeminate. *n.* A homosexual or effeminate man.

line. *n.* 1. One's usual topic and mode of conversation, esp. when persuasive; stereotyped, insincere flattery; exaggeration or attention one gives to others in order to make a good impression, ingratiate oneself, seek favor, persuade, or sell; persuasive talk; a spiel. *Very common.* 2. One's business, occupation, or craft. *Colloq.* 3. The cost of an item, the purchase price of an item. *Mainly Negro use.* 4. = lick. *v.i., v.t.* To hit a baseball, esp. to hit a line drive.

line, go down the. To take a second or third choice. *Lit. = "to go down a list of choices."*

line, in. 1. In accord with the prevailing price, quality, standards, or code. → 2. Agreeable; causing no trouble; acting as one should according to one's age and status.

line, lay (*or* put) it on the. 1. Literally, to hand over money to someone; to pay money; to pay up. 2. To speak frankly; to produce evidence or information or facts; to come across with facts.

line, out of. 1. Deviant; not in accord with established or accepted practices, modes, or attitudes. 2. Not in accord with the prevailing price, quality, standards, or code. 3. Disrespectful; troublesome, brash, impertinent.

line, the. *n.* The chorus of dancing girls performing in an act or show; lit., the line of chorus girls.

line [one's] nest = feather [one's] nest.

line one. In baseball, to hit a line drive. *Very common.*

lip. *n.* 1. Talk, esp. insolent, impudent, or impertinent talk, usu. with a negative or other context of disapproval or warning. 2. A lawyer; a mouthpiece. *Orig underworld use. v.t.* To play a musical instrument; specif., to play jazz on a brass instrument; to blow. —py. *adj.* 1. Insolent; impertinent. 2. Talkative.

lip-splitter. *n.* A jazz musician who plays a wind instrument. *Prob. synthetic.*

liquidate. *v.t.* To kill a person.

liquored up. Drunk. *Common.*

listen. *v.* To appear to be reasonable, honest, or true. —er. *n.* An ear. *Orig. boxing use.*

listen-in. *n.* The act of eavesdropping.

lit. *n.* Literature, esp. as a college course; also used attrib., as a "lit course." *Comon student use since c1900. adj.* Drunk; esp. drunk in a festive mood. *Since c1880. Very common.*

litterbug. *n.* One who litters the streets or public places. *Orig. coined for use in advts. by the New York City Dept. of Sanitation, c1947. The word has gained considerable currency, esp. in jocular use. May be based on "jitterbug."*

little. *adj., adv.* Slightly, somewhat, quite. *Colloq.*

little black book. Lit. and fig., a man's small notebook listing the name, addresses, and phone numbers of accessible or available girls; a man's address book devoted to available female companions. *Colloq.*

little go. An unimportant, unexciting, or incomplete attempt, effort, task, or performance.

little gray cells. The human brain.

Litte Joe. In crap-shooting, the point 4.

little ones out of big ones, make. To break rocks in a prison work yard; hence, to serve a prison sentence.

little school. A reformatory; a juvenile or woman's house of detention. *Underworld and hobo use.*

little shaver. A young boy. *Colloq.*

little woman, the. A wife. *Colloq. since 1880.*

lit to the gills. Drunk. *Fairly common.*

lit up like a Christmas tree. 1. Drunk. **2.** Colorfully, gaudily, showily, or flashily dressed or adorned with jewelry. **3.** Under the influence of narcotics; said of an addict. *Orig. addict use.*

litvak. *n.* A Lithuanian; one of Lithuanian extraction. *Usu. used jocularly rather than derog.*

live. *adj.* **1.** Real or potent; ready to be detonated; usu. said of ammunition. **2.** In person; staged in front of television cameras by living actors rather than filmed and then televised.

live one. *n.* A lively, exciting place or person.

Liverpool kiss. A hit on the mouth. *Some maritime use.*

Liverpool wash. A bath from the waist up. *Maritime use.*

live wire. 1. An exciting person; an active, alert, reliable person. *Since c1900.* → **2.** One who spends his money freely.

living room gig. An appearance on television, specif., of a jazz musician. *Some general jazz use.*

lizard. *n.* **1.** A racehorse, esp. an inferior one. **2.** A wallet or purse. → **3.** A dollar.

—lizard. *n.* A hound for something, a hog; one who habitually is associated with a certain act or place. *Thus a "chow lizard" is known for eating a lot, a "couch lizard" is known for necking on a couch with his girl, etc.*

lizzie; Lizzie. *n.* **1.** A cheap, dilapidated, or old automobile; orig. an early model Ford. → **2.** Any automobile.

load. *n.* Enough liquor to cause intoxication. **—ed.** *adj.* **1.** Drunk; fig., carrying a load of liquor. *One of the most common terms for "drunk." Sometimes followed by a phrase indicating extreme intoxication, as: loaded to the muzzle, loaded to the plimsoll mark, loaded to the gills.* **2.** Containing or mixed with whisky. **3.** Under the influence of heroin. **4.** Wealthy; carrying a large amount of money. *Used absolutely or in "loaded with dough" or the equiv.* **5.** Abundantly provided with anything desirable. **6.** Lit. and fig., explosive; esp. in the sense of containing elements or materials that may become dangerous, as a 'loaded' political speech or business venture. → **7.** Specif., crooked; containing or having an unfair advantage; tampered with, as dice or other gambling paraphernalia, to ensure a predetermined outcome. *From dice actually being loaded with lead or other weights to make them roll in such a way that a certain number will come up frequently.*

loaded for bear. Angry; prepared to expose or ruin someone's reputation; ready for a fight.

load off [one's] feet, take a. To sit down; to have a seat or chair; usu., "Have a seat."

load of hay. 1. A head of long hair. 2. A group of nonpaying or nontipping customers, as guests of the management at a restaurant, or people travelling, eating, or seeing shows on free passes. *Bus driver, train conductor, waiter, and theater use.*

load of this [that, something], get a. 1. To see or look at; to evaluate; to scrutinize. *Often used in the imperative.* 2. To listen; to listen carefully.

loan-out. *n.* The lending of a film actor by the company which holds his contract to another company. *Hollywood use.*

lob. *n.* 1. A sloppy, dull person; one easily duped. 2. An overzealous or overdiligent inmate or employee. 3. The act or instance of throwing an object, as a baseball, softly and gently. *v.t.* To toss lightly and easily.

lobby-gow; lobbygow. *n.* 1. One who loafs around an opium den in hopes of being offered a free pipe of opium. → 2. An opium smoker, esp. one who is also a bum. → 3. A loafer, a bum. → 4. A Chinatown tourists' guide.

lobo. *n.* A hoodlum. *Prob. from stand. "lobo" = wolf.*

lobster. *n.* A victim of a deception; one easily duped.

lock. *n.* A certainty, a cinch. *v.t.* To occupy a cell.

lock up; lockup; lock-up. *n.* 1. A prison cell. 2. A jail. 3. = lock.

loco. *adj.* Crazy; insane. *From the narcotic loco weed of the southwest plains whose leaves, when eaten by cattle, drive them insane.*

locomotive. *n.* A mass cheer, common at most schools, that begins slowly and increases in tempo, resembling the noise made by a steam locomotive in the starting up.

lollapalooza. also: **lala–, lolly–, lola–, lollo–, –oozer, –oosa, –ooser, –ouser.** *n.* Any extraordinary or excellent person or thing; a humdinger.

lollop. *n.* 1. A strong blow or hit. 2. A large portion, usu. of soft spooned food.

lonely pay. The increased wages or bonus union workers ask for to offset reduced working hours due to automation. *The term was first used in the Shell Oil and Esso plant at Cheshire, Eng., 1956, when workers asked for such an increase to compensate for losing the companionship of fellow workers who had been replaced by machines.*

loner. *n.* 1. One person by himself, as a single fare or customer; one who attends a social function by himself. → 2. A man who prefers to work, live, drink, etc., by himself, without taking others into his confidence. *Used both derog. = an eccentric or unsociable person, and compl. = one strong enough to get along without help; one who does not meddle in the affairs of others.*

lone wolf. A man who, though he may lead an active social life and have many acquaintances, does not reveal his activities, has no close friends, no confidants, and keeps himself apart from any social group.

long-arm. *v.i., v.t.* To hitch-hike. *From the gesture of extending the arm at full length to solicit a free ride from a motorist.* **long arm.** The law; a policeman.

long-arm inspection. Medical inspection of the erect penis. *Usu. Army use.*

long drink of water. A tall, thin man, esp., but not necessarily, if dull or boring.

long green. 1. Paper money. *Since c1890. Genuine money in sl., counterfeit money in argot.* 2. Money, usu. a large amount. *Since c1895.* 3. Home-grown, home-cured tobacco. *Dial.*

long-hair; longhair. *n.* **1.** An intellectual; one who likes serious books, music, theater, etc.; a person with cultivated tastes. **2.** Classical music. *Jazz musicians seldom use the word; in fact, modern musicians consider their cool and far-out music as demanding just as rigorous and serious standards as any other music.* *adj.* **1.** Appealing to or liked by intellectuals, usu. said of entertainment. → **2.** Classical; formal; usu. said of music, or of, by, for, or pertaining to classical music or classical or conservative intellectual pursuits.

long-haired. *adj.* Fig., intellectual; highbrow.

long-handle underwear. Woolen underwear with full-length sleeves and legs.

longhorn. *n.* A Texan.

longies. *n.pl.* Long underwear.

Long John. A tall, thin, lanky man. *Often used as a nickname.*

Long Johns. Long woolen underwear.

long ones. Long, woolen winter underwear

long rod. A rifle.

long shot. 1. A scene photographed from a distance; the photograph of a distant scene. **2.** A race horse with little chance to win a race and hence having high odds in the betting. → **3.** A person, scheme, or business venture with little chance of success but with potentially great returns if success should occur.

long time no see. "It's been a long time since I've seen you." *A common student and young adult greeting c1940–c1945.*

long underwear. 1. Jazz music played in a sweet, popular, or corny way. *Since c1930, orig. jive use.* → **2.** A poor jazz musician, esp. one who cannot improvise; one who has a classical musical education but does not play well enough to be entrusted with a solo chorus of jazz improvisation. → **3.** Written arrangements of music. → **4.** Classical music.

looey; looie. *n.* A lieutenant, usu. preceded by "second" or "first." *W.W.I and W.W.II use.*

loogan. *n.* **1.** = boob; sap; dope. **2.** A prize fighter. **3.** A hoodlum; a thug.

look-alike. *n.* A person whose appearance closely resembles that of another person.

look at [someone] cross-eyed. To commit the smallest fault; to do any trivial thing out of the ordinary, regardless of its wrongness or rightness; to get out of line in the slightest degree.

looker. *n.* **1.** A good-looking person of either sex. → **2.** An exceptionally attractive or beautiful girl or woman. *Colloq.* **3.** A potential customer who looks over the merchandise; one who is not able or willing to buy.

look-see. *n.* **1.** A look, esp. a visual inspection, whether cursory or protracted. *Since c1925.* → **2.** A medical license, as carried by a traveling medical-show doctor. *From freq. demands by authorities to be shown the license.* → **3.** A license to carry a gun, a soldier's pass, or any license or pass which one may have to show to the authorities. **look see.** To look; to have a look.

loon. *n.* A stupid person. **—y; ey.** *adj.* Insane; demented; fig., silly, idiotic. *n.* A lunatic, both lit. and fig. Ending "—y" about twice as common as "—ey." From "lunatic," perhaps reinforced by "loon," the bird with a cry that resembles insane laughter. Since c1900.*

loony bin; loony-bin. *n.* An insane asylum.

loop. *n.* **1.** In sports, a complete component period in a game or contest, as a "round" in boxing, an "inning" in baseball, one "hole" in golf, etc. **2.** In sports, a league of member teams, such as a baseball or football league; the towns in which the member teams of a league are located. **—ed.** *adj.* Drunk. *Very common since c1945, particularly among* college students and young adults. —er. n. 1. In baseball, a high easy hit between infield and outfield; a Texas leaguer. 2. A golf caddy. —y. adj. Stupid; slow of thought; punch-drunk.

loose. adj. 1. With a bad reputation, esp. of promiscuity; promiscuous; said of a girl or woman; lit. a girl or woman of loose morals. Colloq. 2. So skilled, adroit, charming, or intelligent that one is relaxed and at ease while performing or living; cool. Some cool, far-out, and beat use. 3. Irresponsible; fast. 4. Eccentric; nutty. 5. Having little money. 6. Unreliable; unethical. 7. Generous; free with money.

loose as a goose = loose, cool use.

loose in the bean; loose in the upper story. Crazy, lit. and fig.

loose wig = far out. Some far-out use. Fig., one has flipped one's wig a great distance.

loot. n. Money, esp. a large sum of money. Common since c1945, orig. jazz use. For fairly large amounts of money "loot" has replaced "coin."

loot; lieut; lute. n. A lieutenant. Since c1750. Some W.W.I and W.W.II use. From "lieutenant."

lorelei. n. 1. An eclectic mixture. 2. Specif. a stew, a dish of various foods cooked together.

lose [one's] wig = blow [one's] top.

lost!, get. Fig., a request or command to go away and leave the speaker alone; to stop bothering or annoying the speaker; to "drop dead."

lot. n. 1. A baseball diamond. 2. The grounds where carnivals and circuses are held. Orig. circus use. 3. The grounds and buildings where movie studios make and process films.

lot hopper. A movie extra. Hollywood use.

lot-louse. n. A person who stands around watching a circus being set up; a person who goes to a circus just to look and does not

spend money to see the various shows.

loud. adj. Garish; gaudy; in bad taste; said of persons or things. Colloq.

loudmouth. n. A person who talks loud and much; one who habitually says what is better left unsaid, tells secrets, or the like.

loud-talk. v.t. 1. To cause trouble for fellow prisoners or workers by talking loudly within earshot of a guard or superior about real or supposed violations of rules. Since c1920. Orig. prison use. 2. To flatter, to sweet-talk.

louie; Louie. n. A lieutenant in the U.S. Army. Common Army use; universally known during and since W.W.II.

lounge lizard. A ladies' man, often characterized as stingy, who calls upon girls and women but does not entertain them away from their own homes. The lounge lizard's interest is in necking.

louse. n. Any disliked person, usu. male; esp. one lacking in kindness, generosity, and ethical standards; an unethical person. Very common.

louse up. To spoil, ruin, botch, or mess up something.

lousy. adj. 1. Bad (also freq. as a pred. adj.) 2. Horrible; contemptible; despicable; extremely inferior; of poorest quality; worthless; incompetent; unpleasant; unwanted; disliked; sick.

lousy with [something]. Well provided with something, usu. money; loaded; having much or many of; overwhelmed with. From "lousy" = covered with lice.

love-bird; love bird; lovebird. n. A lover; a person who is in love; usu. in plural = a pair of lovers.

lovely. n. A lovely woman.

lover-boy. n. 1. A handsome man; a masculine idol. 2. A woman-chaser; a man who brags about his sexual exploits. Usu. jocular use.

lovey-dovey. adj. Affectionate; amorous.

low. *adj.* Sad, melancholy, depressed; physically, mentally, or emotionally exhausted.

lowbrow; low-brow. *n.* An uneducated or unintellectual person; a person who is uninterested in cultural or intellectual matters. *adj.* Pertaining to unintellectual pursuits or popular entertainment; sensational.

low-down. *adj.* **1.** Unfair; unethical; degraded; vile; low. **2.** In jazz, slow, intense, in the manner of the blues. **3.** Low-pitched and sensuous. **low-down; lowdown.** *n.* The real truth; confidential or authentic information; relevant facts; little-known intimate facts; info; dope. *Note that the syllables of the adj. are equally stressed; the noun is accented on first syllable.*

lower the boom. 1. to deliver a knockout punch. *Prize fight use.* → **2.** To chastise or punish; to attack with criticism; to treat sternly; to demand obedience. **3.** To prevent another from succeeding; to act in such a manner as to harm another's chances of success.

low fi. *n.* The opposite of hi fi. *Jocular use.*

low-life. *n.* A vile person.

LP. A "long playing" record; a phonograph record made to play at the record-player turntable speed of 33⅓ revolutions per minute, permitting a longer uninterrupted playing on a smaller record than the older standard of 78 or the intermediate 45 revolutions per minute. *Almost the only term used for this modern record; with the pop. LP records, "LP" is becoming a syn. for "record." Actually this abbr. is a patented trademark of Capitol Record Corp. Colloq. since c1945.*

L7. *n.* = square.

lube. *n.* Lubrication. *A written and spoken abbr.*

lubricated. *adj.* Drunk.

Lucifer. *n.* A safety match, as used to strike a fire.

luck, out of. Too late to obtain whatever is desired; to have no chance or opportunity for success or gratification.

lucked out. To have met with ill fortune or disaster; specif. to be killed. *Some W.W.II use; some general use.*

luck-up. To become lucky; to become successful.

lug. *n.* **1.** The face, chin, or jaw. *Prize fight use.* → **2.** Any strong but dim-witted man, esp. a prize fighter. → **3** A fellow, a guy, esp. a stupid or dull one. **4.** A request for money; money exacted by politicians or paid for police protection. *v.t.* To solicit a loan; to borrow; to extend credit. *Underworld use.*

lugger. *n.* A racehorse that bears toward or away from the inner rail, usu. toward.

lug in. To bear toward the inner rail of a race track, said of a race horse. *Horseracing term.*

lug on [someone], put the. To ask for money as a loan or gift; to put the bee on [someone].

lug out. To bear away from the inner rail of a race track, said of a race horse. *Horseracing term.*

lulu. *n.* **1.** Anything or anyone remarkable; an outstanding example of a type; anyone or anything of extraordinary size, quality, appearance, force, absurdity or the like; a humdinger; a honey; a corker; used often derisively as well as admiringly. **2.** Any item that may be listed in an official expense account and that is regarded as in lieu of money payment of part of a salary. *From "lieu."*

lumber. *n.* A baseball bat.

lumberman. *n.* A beggar with a crutch.

lummox; lummux. *n.* A clumsy, stupid youth or man, usu. of over average size.

lump. *v.t.* To accept a situation one dislikes. *n.* **1.** A package of food handed out to a beggar.

Common hobo use. 2. A dull or stupid person; a clod.

lump it. 1. A command to be quiet. 2. To give up an idea; to accept a bad situation in silence; to forego a plan of action.

lumps. *n.pl.* 1. Lit. and fig., a swelling of any part of the body caused by violence, as a beating; often in "get [one's] lumps." 2. Death caused by physical violence. 3. Fig., harsh treatment other than physical; severe criticism or questioning; exposure; rejection. *The most common use.* 4. Punishment; physical punishment.

lumps, get [one's]. To be beaten up, defeated, bawled out, or in some other way to meet with another's vengeance; to be punished or rebuffed; to fail or be caused to fail. *Often implies that the punishment, rebuff, or failure was deserved.*

lumpy. *adj.* 1. In jazz, badly played. *Cool use.* → 2. Unsuccessful; unsatisfactory. *Cool use.*

lunch-hooks. *n.pl.* 1. The hands, the fingers. *Most common c1900.*

lunger. *n.* A person afflicted with tuberculosis.

lunk. *n.* A stupid person. *From "lunkhead."*

lunk-head; lunkhead. *n.* A stupid person. *Colloq.* —ed. *adj.* Stupid.

lush. *n.* A drunkard; a heavy drinker, esp. a habitual drunkard with a job, family, and accepted place in society. *The most common use; very widespread since c1920.* adj. 1. Prosperous; flush. 2. Satisfying; exciting; modern. *Some cool and far out use since c1955. v.i., v.t.* To drink liquor. —ed. *adj.* Drunk. *Some use since c1920.*

lushed up. *adj.* Drunk.

lush-roller. *n.* A thief who victimizes drunks. *Underworld use.*

lush-worker. *n.* = lush-roller. *Underworld, mainly pickpocket, use.*

lute. *n.* = loot.

lynch. *v.i., v.t.* To kill by any method. *Mainly Negro use.*

M

M. *n.* 1. Morphine. *Wide addict use.* 2. Money. *Some far-out and beat use.*

ma. *n.* An effeminate male; usu. followed by the name of the person. *Some Negro use.*

mace. *n.* A blackjack; a club.

Mack. *n.* A masculine appellative used as a term of direct address; often used in addressing a stranger. mack. *n.* 1. A mackintosh raincoat. 2. A pimp.

mad. *adj.* 1. Angry. *Colloq.* 2. Fine; able; capable; talented; said of cool jazz musicians. 3. Impetuous; impromptu. *n.* A fit of anger.

mad about [someone or something]. To be in love with; to admire, like, or be fond of something.

madball. *n.* The glass globe used by a crystal-gazer. *Carnival use.*

made. *n.* Straightened hair, a head of straightened hair. *Negro use. v.t.* In the passive, to have been cheated, duped, or unfairly treated. *adj.* Specif., made famous, made wealthy; famous, wealthy.

made, have [something]. To be assured of success at or in something, esp. without further work or worry.

Madison Avenue. 1. Collectively, the communications and advertising businesses; the philosophies and social concepts implicit in the mass-media advertising businesses. *Because many such enterprises are located on Madison Avenue in N.Y.C.* 2. A type of men's haircut. *Orig. common among workers on Madison Avenue. adj.* Emanating from or resembling the ideas, manners, and social concepts of the large advertising agencies in N.Y.C.

mad money. 1. Money carried by a girl or woman with which to pay her own way home if she leaves her escort, usu. because of his sexual advances. → 2. Money saved by a woman against the time when she wishes to make an impetuous or impulsive purchase.

Mae West. A vestlike life preserver. *Wide W.W.II use. From its shape, which makes the wearer appear to have a large bosom, as does the entertainer Mae West.*

mag. *n.* A magazine. *A written and spoken abbr.*

magazine. *n.* A jail sentence of 6 months. *From phrase "to throw the book at" someone.*

Maggie's drawers. *n.* A red flag used on a firing range to signal a shot that has missed the target; hence a bad shot. *Army use.*

magoo. *n.* A custard pie used by actors to throw at one another in comedy scenes. *Theater use.*

maiden. *n.* A racehorse, regardless of sex, that has never won a race.

main drag. A major street in a town or city, often the most important business street; often that street of which the local populace is most proud or that street which is most attractive to visitors. *Very common. Orig. hobo use.*

main-line; main line. 1. Money. *Dial.* 2. Collectively, wealthy people, socially prominent elements in any community. *From the "main (railroad) line" leading into Philadelphia, Pa., which borders a district of wealthy homes.* 3. An easily accessible blood vessel, usu. in the arm or leg, into which narcotics can be injected. *Addict use.* 4. A prison mess hall. *Some prison use.* 5. A coaxial cable linking the stations on a television network. *v.t.* To inject a narcotic drug intravenously. *Addict use.*

mainliner. *n.* A drug addict who takes his narcotics by intravenous injection.

main queen. 1. A steady girl friend. 2. A homosexual male who takes the female role, esp. one much sought after by other homosexuals.

main squeeze. The most important or highest ranking person in a specif. organization, locality, workshop, or the like; any important person, specif. one's employer or foreman, the leader of an underworld operation, the dealer in a professional poker game, etc.

main stem = **main drag.** *Not as common as "main drag." Often implies familiarity with or affection for the town or street.*

maison joie. A brothel. *Corrupted from the Fr.*

make. *v.t.* 1. To steal something. *Since at least c1825.* 2. To rob a person or place. *Underworld use.* 3. To recognize or identify a person; to notice, discover, or see a person. *Mainly underworld use.* 4. To appoint a person to a job; to increase his rank or status; to attain success, as to be chosen by a group or to achieve a certain desirable position. *Colloq.* → 5. To attain success, fame, money, etc.; to become a success. 6. To become a business, financial, or social success in a specif. and deliberately chosen field or group; esp. to do so by being aggressive, ruthless, or taking advantage of others; to take advantage of another, to cheat, trick, or deceive another. 7. To go to or arrive at a specific place. 8. To defecate. *Adult use in talking to children.* *n.* 1. An identification; the act or instance of recognizing a person, as a criminal suspect. 2. The loot taken in a robbery. 3. = **hit.**

make a pitch. To propose something that will be in one's own favor; to request money, aid, or sympathy.

make a (the) scene. To participate or become involved or interested in or concerned with a specific activity or field of endeavor. *The specific activity or field of endeavor always precedes "scene." Thus, "I'm going to make the political scene" could mean that the speaker is going to become a candidate for office, to vote, to read a book about, or to discuss* politics. *Orig. c1955 beat use, some far out use.*

make for. To steal from.

make good. To succeed. *Colloq.*

make hay while the sun shines. To take full advantage of one's opportunity. *Orig. applied only to financial matters.*

make it. 1. To succeed, either in a specif. endeavor or in general. 2. To leave or depart hastily.

make it with [someone]. 1. To have sexual intercourse with someone. 2. To be liked, respected, or befriended by someone; to be compatible with someone. *Cool use.*

make out. 1. To fare; to get along; to succeed. *Often in "How did you make out?" = What happened?* → 2. Specif., to succeed in seducing a woman.

make-out artist. 1. A man noted for his talents in seduction. 2. One, usu. a male, who seeks to impress his superiors; a man with charm and a good line.

make something out of. To interpret as a challenge or affront. *Usu. in the expression "Do you want to make something out of it?" = Do you want to fight over it?*

make time with [someone]. 1. To date, court, or have amorous relations with another's girl friend, fiancée, or wife. → 2. To date, court, or have amorous relations with a girl or young woman. *Fairly common student use.*

make with the eyes (hands, feet, mouth, etc.). To bring the specified organ into operation. *N.B.: the term may also be used in connection with specific skills (make with the singing, dancing, etc.) or with specific instruments (make with the saw, typewriter, machine gun, etc.).*

makings; makin's. *n.pl.* The ingredients or items needed in making or doing something. *Dial.*

malarkey. *n.* Exaggerated talk; tedious talk; lies; boloney, bunk. *Colloq. since c1935.*

Mama's boy. A sissy; a boy, youth, or even man, who refuses to act independently or share responsibilities commensurate with his age and sex.

mammy boy. A mother's boy; a sissy.

man. *n.* 1. A dollar. *From "iron man."* 2. A term of direct address, to both known men and strangers, but usu. implying that the person addressed is hip and the speaker is sincere. *Perhaps from Brit. West Indies. Common since c1935, esp. among jive and cool groups.*

Man, the; man, the. *n.* 1. The law; a law enforcement officer; a private detective. Fig., Uncle Sam; specif., a federal law enforcement officer, as a U.S. treasury agent. 2. The leader of a band, esp. a jazz band or combo. *Mainly bop, cool, and far-out use; some general jazz and popular band use.*

man about town; man-about-town. A sophisticated, debonair man of any age, but usually of some wealth who is a frequenter of the better nightclubs, restaurants, bars, and entertainments, usu. with sophisticated and lovely young women.

mangy with. Covered with or full of; lousy with.

man-size; man-sized. *adj.* Large; great in amount or bulk.

map. *n.* 1. The human face. *Colloq.* 2. A check, esp. one written against a fictitious or deficient account.

maps. *n.* Sheet music. *Some cool musician use; many jazz musicians scorn those who need sheet music to prompt their playing.*

marble-dome. *n.* A stupid person.

marble orchard. A cemetery.

marfak. *n.* Butter. *From the trade name of a lubricating grease. Some Army use.*

Marge; marge. *n.* Margarine.

Mari. *n.* = Mary, 3.

marine. *n.* An empty whisky or beer bottle; a "dead marine."

mark. *n.* 1. An easy victim; a ready subject for the practices of a confidence man, thief, beggar, etc.; a sucker. *Mainly underworld, carnival, circus, and hobo use, but universally known.* 2. Among carnival workers, any outsider or member of the local community. 3. A place from which it is easy to obtain food or money by deception, thievery, or begging. *Underworld and hobo use.* 4. The amount of money taken in a robbery. *v.t.* To seek or find a person or place worth robbing. *Underworld use.*

marker. *n.* 1. A written, signed promissory note; an I.O.U. 2. A scoring point in a game.

marmalade. *n.* = malarkey.

marsh grass. Spinach. *Dial.*

martooni. *n.* A martini cocktail. *Fairly common jocular mispronunciation.*

Mary. *n.* 1. A male homosexual who plays the female role. "Mary" is the female name most commonly assumed by such homosexuals. 2. A female homosexual. 3. Marijuana; also spelled "Mari."

Mary Ann. A marijuana cigarette. *Some addict use.*

Mary Jane = Mary Ann.

Mary Warner. Marijuana.

mash. *n.* 1. Love for one of the opposite sex. → 2. A love affair. → 3. A lover, of either sex. *v.t.* To give something to another. *Negro use.* —**er.** *n.* A man who tries to force his attentions on a woman against her will. *Colloq. In the U.S. the word has never had the Eng. sl. meaning of a beau or a dandy.*

mash in. To press in the clutch pedal of a truck or hot rod. *Orig. W.W.II Army use. Some hot rod use since c1950.*

mash note. A complimentary or flattering written message of self-introduction, used as the first step in an attempt at seduction; a short love letter or note.

mask. *n.* The face.

massage. *v.t.* To beat up; to thrash.

mastermind. *n.* The planner, manager, or leader of any undertaking. *Now stand. v.i., v.t.* To plan, direct, or command; to give orders.

mat. *n.* 1. A woman; one's wife. *Some Negro use.* 2. The floor; the deck of a ship, esp. the deck of an aircraft carrier.

mat, hit the = hit the deck.

mat, on the = on the carpet. *Some student use since c1930; some W.W.II USN use.*

math. *n.* Mathematics; the study of mathematics. *Still not considered stand. by some scholars, though universally used as a written and spoken abbr.*

matie. *n.* A shipmate; any comrade.

maud. *n.* 1. A woman. *Some underworld use.* 2. An engine, esp. a steam engine.

max. *adj.* Maximum. *v.* To achieve a maximum success. *West Point use.*

mazel. *n.* Luck. *From the Yiddish "masel" = luck.*

mazoomy. *n.* = mazuma.

mazuma; mezuma; mazume. *n.* Money. *Common since c1915.*

McCoy. *adj.* 1. Genuine. 2. Neat; tidy. *Some underworld use. n.* The genuine thing. *Colloq.*

meal ticket. 1. A prize fighter in relation to his manager or agent. → 2. Any person upon whom one depends for a livelihood, as an employer, husband, etc. → 3. Any skill, instrument, talent, part of the body, etc., which provides a living for its possessor.

mean. *adj.* Orig. far out use = psychologically exciting, satisfying, and exhaustive; far out, the end, formidable, keen. *Far out and beat use, some cool use. Usu. an attrib. modifier of the direct object in a simple clause. Since c1920.*

meany; meanie. *n.* A mean, petty, or contemptible person. *Now more jocular or affectionate than derog.*

meat. *n.* 1. One who is easily defeated or influenced by another; a poor opponent in a sports contest, business venture, or the like. → **2.** A task or enterprise that is easy and pleasing; a field of endeavor for which one possesses a natural talent. **3.** The gist or meaning of a story, book, play or the like; the essential factors in a given situation; principal facts, ideas, items, etc.

meat-and-potatoes. *adj.* Basic; primary; major.

meat bag. The stomach.

meatball; meat ball. *n.* A dull, boring person; an obnoxious person; anyone regarded with disfavor, esp. one of flat or uninteresting character; a creep, a drip, a square, a wet blanket. *Fairly common W.W.II use, both by servicemen and civilians; now somewhat archaic.* *v.t.* To strike someone with the fist. *Some prison use.* —**ism.** *n.* **1.** Anti-intellectualism; the state of willing ignorance or mediocrity. **2.** A state of, or instance demonstrating, decreasing standards of integrity, ethics, intelligence, and individualism in culture, politics, education, and the like; democratic rule by an uneducated, nonthinking majority.

meat card = meal ticket.

meathead. *n.* A stupid person. —**ed.** *adj.* Stupid.

meat-hooks. *n.pl.* The hands or fists, esp. of a large, powerful man.

meat-show. *n.* A cabaret floor-show with scantily clad or unclad dancing girls.

meatwagon; meat-wagon; meat wagon. *n.* **1.** An ambulance. *Fairly common.* **2.** A hearse.

mechanic. *n.* An expert card player, esp. one skilled in dealing and shuffling unfairly; a professional card dealer in a gambling establishment; a "shark."

med. *n.* A medical student; medicine as a course of study. *A common written and spoken abbr.* —**ic.** *n.* A physician; a member of the Army Medical Corps. *Most common during and since W.W.II.* —**icine.** *n.* Information.

Dial. —**ico.** *n.* A physician. 1952: *Since c1920. Never as common as "medic" now is.*

meestle. *n.* A dog. *Dial.*

meet. *n.* **1.** An appointment; specif., an appointment to discuss or enter into illegal dealings; a hit. **2.** A sporting contest, esp. a competition in track and field sports. **3.** A jam session; a gig. *Bop, cool, and far out use. Because bop, cool, and far out musicians do not actually jam; they just "meet" together to play.*

meller. *n.* = melo.

mellow. *adj.* **1.** Mildly and pleasantly drunk. *Still fairly common.* **2.** Skillful; sincere, heart-felt; said of a jazz performance. *Orig. jive use; now some cool use.*

mellow-back. *adj.* Smartly dressed. *Some Negro use.*

melo. *n.* A movie melodrama. *Some Hollywood use.*

melon. *n.* **1.** The total profit or monetary gain from a business or enterprise, whether legal or not; the spoils. → **2.** Fame, glory, or patronage obtained by a group, esp. a political party, to be distributed among the members.

melted. *adj.* Drunk, esp. to the point of unconsciousness. *Some student use.*

melted out. 1. Having lost all one's money at gambling. **2.** Without funds; broke.

Melvin. *n.* A dull, uninformed, or obnoxious person; a profoundly objectionable person. *Sometimes used in direct address. Since c1950. Pop. by comedian Jerry Lewis.*

memo. *n.* A memorandum. *Colloq. A written and spoken abbr.*

mental job. One who is, or who is suspected of being, a neurotic, psychotic, paranoid, manic depressive, or otherwise psychologically abnormal.

merge. *v.t.* To marry. *Synthetic.*

merry-go-round. *n.* A rapid, confusing sequence of jobs, appointments, duties, or the like, usu. in the expression "to be on a merry-go-round" = to be extremely busy.

merry haha, the. Ridicule; the laugh; usu. in expression "to give someone the merry haha."

meshuga. *adj.* Crazy; eccentric. *From the Yiddish; the Yiddish feminine ending "a" is used for both sexes.*

mess. *n.* 1. A stupid person. *c1930. Still common.* 2. Pleasure; excitement; anything pleasurable or exciting; a "ball." *adj.* 1. Immoral; degenerate; ignorant. 2. Excellent; remarkable. *Some cool and beat use since c1950.* 3. An immoral person; an abnormal person. —y. *adj. & adv.* 1. Immoral; unethical. 2. Complex or confusing; said of a situation or action. 3. Bothersome.

mess around. To waste time; to idle; to work lackadaisically.

mess around with. To insult, tease, harass; to treat with ridicule, to refuse to consider seriously.

mess up. To get into or cause trouble. *Since c1915. Fairly common during and since W.W.II.*

meter-reader. *n.* The copilot of an airplane. *Mildly derog. W.W.II Air Force use.*

Mex. *n.* A Mexican. *adj.* Mexican.

Mexican breakfast. A breakfast the consuming of which amounts to smoking a cigarette and drinking a glass of water, usu. because one has no money, has a hangover, or is too tired to eat.

Mexican promotion; Mexican raise. Advancement of rank or status without any accompanying increase in income.

mezonny. *n.* Money; orig. money spent for drugs. *Addict use. From Carnes.*

mezuma = mazuma.

mezz. *n.* A marijuana cigarette. *adj.* Sincere; excellent. *Jazz use. From the jazz clarinetist Mezz Mezzrow, a musician known for his refusal to submit to commercial standards as well as for his drug addiction.*

MG. *n.* A machine-gunner. *W.W.II use.*

mib. *n.* A small playing marble.

Michigan roll. A bankroll with a genuine banknote, usu. of large denomination, around the outside and bills of smaller value, or newspaper or stage money, on the inside.

Mickey Finn; mickey finn. 1. Any strongly purgative pills, drops, or potions given to an unsuspecting person, usu. in food or drink, to force his departure or as a joke. *Since c1930. Orig. the term applied only to a laxative pill made for horses.* → 2. Any strong hypnotic or barbiturate dose administered to an unsuspecting person, usu. in an alcoholic drink, in order to render him unconscious; the drink itself.

mickey mouse; mickey-mouse; micky mouse; micky-mouse. *adj.* Sentimental, insincere, or characterized by trick effects; said of pop. dance music or the musicians who play it. *Musician use.*

Mickey Mouse (movie). A documentary or short movie vividly showing the means of prevention, the causes, development, and care of venereal diseases; a documentary or short movie vividly showing methods of hand-to-hand combat. *Wide W.W.II Army use, in ref. to such movies shown as part of soldiers' training courses.*

middle-aisle it. To marry or be married. *Synthetic.*

middy. *n.* A midshipman; a U.S. Naval Academy student. *Since c1900.*

midway. *n.* A hall; an aisle between prison cell blocks. *Some prison use.*

miff. *v.t.* To offend; to vex; to anger. —ed. *adj.* Offended, vexed, angered. *Colloq. since c1935.* —y. *adj.* = miffed; also splenetic; irascible.

mig; Mig. *n.* 1. A cheap playing marble, usu. made of clay or the cheapest china and often not perfectly round or smooth; the cheapest playing marble. *Boy use c1890–c1925. Usu. not cap. Such* *marbles have now been replaced by glass ones.* 2. Any Russian-made fighter or bomber plane. *Wide Korean War use. From the initials of the best Russian jet fighter planes used by the Communist forces. Always cap.* —s. *n.pl.* A marble.

mighty. *adv.* Very; exceedingly. *Colloq. since. c1820.*

mighty mezz, the. Marijuana; a marijuana cigarette.

mike. *n.* 1. A microphone, esp. one used in radio or television. *Since c1925. A common written and spoken abbr.* 2. A microscope. *Some student use.*

Mike and Ike. Salt and pepper shakers.

milk run. An easy military aerial mission, usu. a bombing mission —easy either because no opposition is encountered or because the distance covered is short. *W.W.II Air Force use.*

milk wagon. A police wagon or truck used to transport arrested persons to jail.

mill. *n.* 1. A prison; a guardhouse. *Fairly common Army use since W.W.I.* 2. A motor, esp. an airplane motor. *W.W.II Armed Forces use.*

millionaire. *n.* Any person whose wealth is great, or more than the speaker's.

milquetoast. *n.* Any shy, timid, or extremely gentle person. *From H. T. Webster's cartoon character Caspar Milquetoast, central figure of the comic strip. "The Timid Soul."*

Milwaukee goiter. A large midsection if attrib. to owner's propensity for beer-drinking. *Milwaukee, settled by German immigrants, is known for the quality and quantity of beer manufactured and consumed there.*

mince pies. *n.pl.* The eyes. *One of the most common underworld uses of rhyming sl.*

mingle. *n.* A dance. *Student use.*

mingy. *adj.* Mean and stingy.

minister's face; minister's head. Pig's head cooked and served at a meal. *Hobo use.*

Minnie. *proper n.* Minneapolis.

misery pipe. A bugle. *Reputedly some Army use. Prob. synthetic.*

mish-mash; mishmash; mish-mosh; mishmosh. *n.* A mixture composed of many ingredients, esp. a poorly integrated mixture; confusion; a hodgepodge. *Usu. in reference to food, such as hash, or theatrical works.*

miss. *v.t.* To fail to menstruate at the normal time.

missionary worker. An employee hired to break a strike by nonviolent means.

Mississippi marbles = African dominoes.

miss the boat. 1. To arrive too late for any occasion. → 2. To lose an opportunity; to fail, esp. to fail to understand a command, a direction, a double entendre, etc. *The most common use.*

missus, the; missis, the. *n.* One's wife. *Colloq. since c1925.*

Mister. *n.* A man, fellow, guy, used as direct address to a stranger; also, as in giving an order or reprimand to one whose name is known, to show objectivity or rejection.

Mister Big. The leader, planner, director of an underworld enterprise, esp. one whose real identity is unknown. *Also used occasionally in politics.*

Mister Charlie. A white man. *Some Negro use.*

Mister Ducrot. A term of derog. direct address to any West Point plebe.

Mister Dumbguard. *n.* = Mister Ducrot.

Mister Hawkins. A cold wind; winter; wintry weather. *Hobo use, orig. Negro use.*

Mister Right. 1. = Mister Big. *Because "Mister Big" is always right, by virtue of his power. A new term that may replace "Mister Big."* 2. A dream man; the perfect man a girl hopes to marry.

Mistofer. *n.* Mr.; Mister.

mitt; mit. *n.* 1. The human hand. *Colloq. "Mitt" is considerably more common than "mit."* 2. A boxing glove. 3. = mitt reader. 4. An arrest. *v.t.* 1. To shake hands with, as in greeting. 2. To put handcuffs on someone; to make an arrest. *v.i.* To clasp hands above the head as a signal of victory, as a boxer acknowledging a favorable decision from the ring.

mitt, the. *n.* 1. Any charitable or religious organization that gives food or lodging to hobos. *Hobo use.* 2. An arrest.

mitt camp. *n.* A fortune teller's tent. *Carnival use.*

mitten. *n.* 1. In "give [someone] the mitten" = to jilt, to reject a suitor or lover; in "get the mitten" = to be jilted. *Archaic and dial.* 2. In "get the mitten" = to be expelled from college. *Some student use.*

mitt-glommer. *n.* A hand-shaker.

mitt joint = mitt camp. *Carnival use.*

mitt reader. A palmist; a fortune teller. *Carnival and circus use since c1925.*

mitts. *n.pl.* A pair of handcuffs. *Underworld use.*

mix. *n.* The packaged and prepared (i.e., already mixed) ingredients of a cake, pie filling, or other food, usu. in such form that only liquid need be added before cooking. *Such commercially packaged goods were introduced after W.W.II and were common by 1950. Colloq. v.i.* To fight. *Orig. prize fight use.*

mixer. *n.* Water, soda, or any soft drink used to dilute whisky. *Colloq.*

mix it = mix it up.

mix it up. To fight with the fists; esp. to fight vigorously and enthusiastically.

mixologist. *n.* A bartender. *Still some jocular use.*

mix-up. *n.* A fistfight.

mo. *n.* A moment. *A common spoken abbr. but seldom written.* Usu. in "just a mo" or "half a mo."

moan, put on the. To complain.

mob. *n.* 1. An underworld gang. *Colloq.* 2. A group of men in one employ. *Colloq.* 3. A group, gathering, or class. —**ster.** *n.* A member of an underworld mob.

mockie. [derog.] *n.* A Jew.

mocky. *n.* A young mare. *Dial.*

Model-T. *adj.* Cheap; primitive; rundown.

modoc. *n.* One of the several small dummies set up to be knocked over by baseballs at a carnival tent; hence, a stupid person. *Carnival use.*

mohoska. *n.* Muscle; energy used in work. *Some maritime use.*

mojo. *n.* Any narcotic. *Addict use.*

mokers, the. *n.* Despondency; dejection; the blues. *Some use since c1955.*

mokus. *n., adj.* 1. Drunk. *Hobo use.* 2. Liquor. *Hobo use.*

molasses. *n.* A good-looking used automobile displayed to attract customers to a used-car lot. *From the traditional bait for catching flies.*

moldy fig. 1. A prude; a pedant; one whose views or tastes are old-fashioned. 2. Specif., a person who prefers traditional jazz to the progressive forms. *Orig. bop use c1946, now also cool use. Sometimes incorrectly used to = square, but specif. = a devotee of any prebop jazz form or style who cannot accept or appreciate bop or progressive jazz. adj.* Outmoded; old-fashioned.

moll. *n.* 1. A prostitute. 2. A gangster's female accomplice or sweetheart. *The most common use. Colloq. since c1930.*

moll buzzer. 1. A thief who preys on women, such as a purse snatcher. *Underworld use since c1920.* 2. A tramp who begs from women. *Hobo use since c1925.*

mollie. *n.* A state tax token. *Dial.*

Molotov cocktail. A homemade bomb, specif., one consisting of a bottle filled with gasoline or an alcohol mixture, and usu. a rag wick. *Orig. used by Russian civilians in fighting against the invading Nazi army during W.W.II. Such a bomb was supposed to have been effective in destroying tanks. Molotov was the USSR foreign minister during W.W.II.*

mom; Mom. *n.* A mother; one's mother. *Colloq.* **—ism.** *n.* The social phenomenon of widespread mother domination; matriarchism as an informal power structure supported by sentimentalism; popular mother worship. *Coined by Philip Wylie in his "Generation of Vipers" (1943), an attack on American social mores, the term and the idea have been much discussed.* **—my.** *n.* = mom. **moms; Moms.** *n.sing.* = mom.

mo-mo. *n.* A moron.

momzer; momser. *n.* 1. One who borrows frequently, or who expects much attention and many favors; a sponger. *From the Yiddish.* → 2. Any disliked person; a bastard.

Monday man. One who steals clothes from clotheslines. *Hobo and carnival use. Because Monday is the traditional washday.*

Monday morning quarterback. 1. Specif., a football devotee who, upon learning the results of the various plays of the football game played on the previous Saturday, as published in Monday morning papers, gives his detailed opinion as to what plays should have been attempted or initiated by the quarterback of his favorite team. 2. One who, after an event, gives advice or opinions on what should have been done.

money, in the. Having money, esp. a lot of it.

money-bags; moneybags. *n.sing.* A wealthy person. *Colloq.*

money smash. In baseball, a home run.

money talks. Lit., wealth is power; money buys anything. *Now a folk saying more than a sl. term.*

mongee. *n.* = mungey.

moni(c)ker; monniker; monacer;

monica. *n.* A person's name, nickname, or alias; the name by which a person wishes to be known; a name. *Colloq. Orig. hobo use, then underworld, now common. Until c1930 usu.* = *an alias or nickname, as of a hobo or criminal; after c1930 usu.* = *one's real name.*

monk. *n.* A monkey. *A written and spoken abbr., universally known.* **—ey.** *n.* 1. A man. 2. An average man; one who is not a hobo, with a carnival, or on the grift. *Hobo, carnival, and grifter use.* 3. Any of many types of employee whose costume, uniform, movements, or actions resemble a monkey; specif., a chorus girl, porter, musician in a tuxedo, bridge worker, freight handler, etc. 4. A silly, frivolous, or precocious person. *Usu. used affectionately.* 5. A term of affection freq. applied to small, mischievous boys. 6. Narcotics addiction; the drug habit. *Common addict use. v.i., v.t.* = monkey around.

monkey around. To occupy oneself aimlessly or without knowledge or confidence; to tinker with, often out of curiosity; to adjust, touch, poke at, interfere with, or play with; to loaf or idle. *Colloq.*

monkey business. 1. Any unethical, deceitful, secret, furtive, or socially objectionable conduct or dealings, something fishy; specif., cheating in gambling or business, or attempting sexual advances with one of the opposite sex. *Colloq.* → 2. Trifling or foolish conduct; monkeyshines. 3. High-spirited, good-natured pranks or teasing; frivolity.

monkey cage. A prison cell. *Some prison use.*

monkey-chaser. *n.* A drink composed of gin, sugar, water, and ice.

monkey clothes. A full-dress uniform. *Army use.*

monkey drill. Calisthenics. *W.W.II Armed Forces use, esp. USN.*

monkey-flag. *n.* The flag, insigne, or standard of an Army or Navy unit; the flag or insigne of a business firm or a social or political organization.

monkey jacket. A full-dress blouse. *Annapolis use.*

monkey meat. Inferior, tough beef. *Some Army use since W.W.I.*

monkey off, get the. To break a drug habit. *Addict use.*

monkey on [one's] back. Drug addiction, considered as a financial, physical, mental, and moral responsibility; the drug habit; lit., a strong addiction that one spends most of one's energy to support. *Common addict use, now universally known. When without drugs an addict feels weighed down and depressed, when buying drugs an addict is supporting pushers and his drug habit, thus, fig., the addict carries an extra burden; it may be a large or small monkey—some have a $100-a-day monkey.*

monkeyshines. *n.pl.* Tricks; pranks; trifling or foolish conduct. *Colloq.*

monkey suit. Almost any uniform or uniform-like suit of clothes, trousers, blouse, jacket or coat, or often cap or hat; usu. disparaging, in allusion to the fancy outfit traditionally worn in the U.S. by an organ-grinder's monkey. Specif., formal dress or dinner clothes; an Army or Navy uniform, esp. a full-dress uniform; a porter's or bellboy's uniform; the fur-lined or electrically heated suit worn by military airmen. *Colloq.*

monkey time. Daylight Saving Time. *Dial.*

Monkey Ward. *proper n.* The business firm of Montgomery Ward, a mail-order house; a Montgomery Ward store.

monniker. *n.* = **moni(c)ker.**

moocah. *n.* Marijuana. *Addict use.*

mooch. *v.i., v.t.* **1.** To beg. *Since c1880.* **2.** To steal. **3.** To borrow; to obtain gratis. **4.** To steal; to

pilfer. **5.** To beg food, money, or the like. **6.** To borrow, esp. an item of small value without intending to repay it. *Colloq. n.* **1.** A dupe; a gullible customer; a sucker. **2.** A carnival-goer; a mark. *Carnival use.* → **3.** A person who watches a pitchman but does not buy. *Carnival and pitchman use.* —**er.** *n.* **1.** One who mooches, esp. a beggar. *Since c1890; colloq.* **2.** A chronic borrower; a sponger.

moo juice. *n.* Milk. *Some lunchcounter and Army use.*

moola; moolah. *n.* Money. "*Moola*" *is prob. the most common word not in the DAE, the DOA, Merriam-Webster, the OED, Mencken, or any of their supplements. Prob. not common before c1935.*

moon. *n.* Whisky, esp. moonshine. *Since c1920.*

moonlight into, let. To shoot a person. *Lit., to make bullet holes in someone.*

moonshine. *n.* **1.** Whisky made by unlicensed, individual distillers for their own consumption or, more commonly, for illegal sale; bootleg whisky. *Because such distilling operations are traditionally conducted in rural regions by the light of the moon, to avoid detection. Orig. dial.; common since c1920.* → **2.** Any inferior, unaged, cheap whisky. → **3.** Any whisky or liquor. **4.** Nonsense; boloney. —**r.** *n.* A rustic living in any comparatively isolated section of the Southern hill area of the U.S., whether or not he makes moonshine.

moose-milk. *n.* Whisky. *Dial.*

mop. *n.* The last item or act of a sequence, the final result. *Negro use.*

mope. *v.i.* **1.** To escape; to beat it. *Hobo and prison use.* → **2.** To move along; to keep moving; to walk.

mopery. *n.* Any absurd, trivial, or imaginary offense against the law.

mop mop. Repetitious, loud, unimaginative jazz.

mop-up. *n.* Extermination. **mop up.** *v.i.* To exterminate; to finish a military or police campaign.

mop up on. To beat up; to thrash severely.

morning chow. Breakfast.

morph. *n.* 1. Morphine. 2. A hermaphrodite. **—adite.** *n.* A hermaphrodite. *Since c1890.*

mort. *n.* A girl or woman. *Underworld use since before 1800.*

mosey. *v.i.* To move along; to walk slowly or aimlessly.

mosey along = **mosey.** *Colloq.*

most, the. *n., adj.* The best; the most exciting; the most up to date. *Usu. pred. adj. Far out, beat, and some cool use.*

mostest. *n., adj.* The greatest; the best; the most. *Associated with far out use, but in some general use since the late 1940's. Usu. pred. adj.*

mother. *n.* 1. A piloted plane that electronically controls an unmanned plane or "drone." *Air Force use since c1950.* 2. An effeminate male. *Some Negro use.*

Mother Hubbard. A loose-fitting cotton smock or dress, usu. used to protect regular clothes while working. *Colloq.*

Mother Machree; Mother McCrea. An alibi; a sad story, usu. fictitious or exaggerated, told to elicit sympathy, avoid punishment, etc.; a sob story. *From the traditional Irish song of the same name.*

mott. *n.* = **mort.**

moula. *n.* = **moola.**

mound. *n.* In baseball, the pitcher's box. *Colloq.*

mountain canary. A burro.

mountain dew = **moonshine,** whisky.

mountain oysters. Sheep or hog testicles used as food.

mouse. *n.* 1. A bruise or discoloration on or near the eye, caused by a blow. *Colloq.* 2. A girl or young woman, esp. an attractive or vivacious girl; usu. a term of affection. → 3. A girl friend; a sweetheart; a fiancée; a wife. 4. A small rocket. *Some Air Force and Army use since c1955.* **—r.** *n.* A mustache. **—trap.** *v.t.* 1. In sports, to feint an opponent out of position. → 2. To fool or mislead by false promises; to entice; to cajole.

mouthful. *n.* An important, comprehensive, manifestly true, or otherwise impressive statement; used only in "You [he, she] said a mouthful!" an expression of vigorous affirmation or assent.

mouthpiece. *n.* 1. A lawyer, esp. a criminal lawyer. *Underworld use since c1910; colloq. since c1930.* → 2. A spokesman. *Colloq.*

move. *v.t.* 1. To steal or pilfer something. → 2. To transport or sell contraband or stolen goods. 3. To sell merchandise; to dispose of a stock of merchandise by selling it.

move back. *v.t.* To cost. *A variant of "set back."*

movie. *n.* A motion picture. *Although some scholars still consider this word colloq. or even sl., it has been in stand. use since c1915. At first the motion-picture industry attempted to pop. "film" or "cinema," but "movie" is now the universal term in speech and is very common in writing.* **—dom.** *n.* The motion-picture industry, considered both as an association of people and as a body of customs, attitudes, and conceptual values. *One of the most common—"dom" words, widely used by newsp. columnists and reviewers.*

movies, the. *n.pl.* 1. A motion-picture theater, as in "To go to the movies." 2. Collectively, the motion-picture industry.

moxie. *n.* 1. Courage; nerve; guts. 2. Experience; skill; shrewdness. 3. Initiative; aggressiveness.

Mr. —. Used before an item, object, or concept to personify it. *Very old Negro slave use. Still some dial. and jazz use.*

muck. *n.* 1. ≐ **high muck-a-muck.** 2. Muscle. *West Point use.* **—er.** *n.*

A laborer, esp. one who works with a shovel.

mucket. *n.* A toupee.

muckraker. *n.* One who searches out and broadcasts scandals, esp. in order to ruin another's reputation, usu. a politician's. *Colloq. Pop. and prob. coined by Theodore Roosevelt.*

muck stick. A shovel. *Hobo and dial. use since c1915.*

muck up. To make dirty; often used in passive

mud. *n.* 1. Opium before it is prepared for smoking. *Addict use.* 2. Coffee prepared to drink. *Orig. hobo use. Some lunch-counter and Army use. Universally known.* 3. Any thick, dark food, as chocolate pudding. 4. Any thick, dark liquid, as molten metal, petroleum, etc. 5. Cheap plastic figurines, souvenirs, and the like, given as prizes at a carnival concession. *Carnival use.* 6. Indistinct radio or telegraph signals. *Radio use.* 7. Vicious, derogatory talk or writing, whether true or not; "slime."

mudder. *n.* A race horse that excels when running on a muddy track.

mud-head. *n.* A Tennesseean.

mud-slinging. *n.* 1. The act of spreading malicious, vicious, derogatory statements about another, whether such statements are true or not. *Usu. political use.* 2. Gossiping.

muff. *n.* 1. A foolish fellow. 2. A duffer; a poor player. 3. In sports, an error, as a fumble. 4. A wig. *v.t.* 1. In sports, to make an error or mistake; to fail to take advantage of an opportunity; to bungle; to fumble. *Colloq.* 2. Fig., to make an error as if one were clumsy because one's hands were in a muff; to fail. *Colloq.*

mug; mugg. *n.* 1. The face. *From the 18C drinking mugs that were made to represent human faces. "Mugg" is becoming archaic and is used in approx. one in six instances.* 3. The mouth; the chin; the jaw. *Prize fight use since*

c1915. 3. A photograph of the face, esp. a photograph used for police identification. *Police and underworld use.* 4. A man; a fellow; a guy. *Common.* 5. Specif. and esp., a rough or ugly fellow. 6. A prize fighter, esp. an inferior one. *Since c1920.* 7. A criminal; a hoodlum. *Very common. v.t.* 1. To photograph a person's face, esp. a prisoner's for purposes of record and identification. *Orig. underworld use; now universally known.* 2. To attack and then rob; to garrote, beat up, or stab a victim in order to rob him. *Since c1940.* 3. To have sexual intercourse with. *Negro use. v.i.* In acting, to use exaggerated facial expressions; to overact. *Since c1925.* —*ger. n.* 1. An actor who grimaces to produce laughter. 2. A photographer who specializes in portraits. 3. A thief who first garrotes his victims; one who mugs (*v.t.*, 2d def.). *The most common use. Since c1940.*

muggle. *n.* A marijuana cigarette. *Addict use; fairly common. From "muggles."*

muggles. *n.pl.* 1. Marijuana, esp. the dried but unshredded marijuana leaves. 2. A marijuana cigarette. *Some addict use.*

mug joint. *n.* A tent, booth, or gallery in which one's photograph is taken and printed in a short time. *Carnival and circus use.*

mug shot. A photograph of a person's face.

mug up. To eat a snack.

mule. *n.* 1. An obstinate or stubborn person. *Colloq.* 2. Raw bootleg whisky, esp. moonshine. 3. A tractor. *Dial.* 4. One who acts as a delivery boy or lackey for a narcotics peddler or pusher. *Some addict use.*

mule-skinner. *n.* A mule driver. *Colloq.*

mulligan. *n.* 1. A stew made of any available meat(s) or vegetable(s). *Orig. hobo use, perhaps from "salmagundi." Often used facetiously about any stewlike food,* *however excellent.* 2. An Irishman. *Some underworld use.* → 3. A policeman.

mulligrubs, the. *n.pl.* = the blues. *Dial.*

mum. *n.* A chrysanthemum. *A common written and spoken abbr.*

mumsie; mumsy. *n.* A mother. *Often used sarcastically.*

mung(e)y; mongee. *n.* Food. *Some hobo and W.W.I Army use. An approximation of French and Italian words = to eat.*

murder. *adj.* 1. Very difficult; very painful; when used in ref. to a person, very stubborn or severe. *v.t.* To get the better of an opponent; to vanquish decisively.

murder, get away with. To do anything in flagrant violation of rules, laws, or decency.

murphy. *n.* An Irish potato. *Still in use.*

muscle. *n.* 1. Bluff; artificiality. *Some Negro use.* 2. A strong-arm man; a thug.

muscle, on the. Quarrelsome; ready or eager to fight or use force; esp. ready to commit crimes involving force or violence as opposed to skill. *Underworld use since c1925.*

muscle-head. *n.* A stupid person.

muscle in. To force one's way in; to gain by force; to encroach forcibly; to secure a share by force or threat of force. *Orig. underworld use; now very common.*

muscle out. Lit. and fig., to force out, to eject, as a person.

mush. *n.* 1. Excessive talk; boloney. *Still in use.* → 2. The mouth. *Since c1915.* → 3. The face. 4. Sentimentality; embarrassingly sentimental talk. 5. A kiss. 6. An umbrella. From "mushroom." *Pitchman use. v.i.* To earn a living by grifting or faking under cover of a legitimate occupation, such as umbrella mending. —**er.** *n.* An itinerant faker or grifter operating in the guise of an honest worker. —**ing.** *n.* Love-making. —**y.** *adj.* 1. Affectionate;

amorous. *Colloq. since c1920.* 2. Sentimental; corny.

mush-faker. *n.* An itinerant peddler, tinker, or esp. umbrella mender. *Hobo use.*

mush-head. *n.* A stupid or silly person. —**ed.** *adj.* Stupid. *Colloq.*

mush-mouth. *n.* One who talks indistinctly.

mussy. *adj.* Rumpled; disordered.

mustang. *n.* A commissioned officer who has risen from the ranks. *USN use since c1935.*

mustard. *n.* A good, alert fighter or bomber pilot. *W.W.II Army use.*

mutt; mut. *n.* A dog, esp. a mongrel. *Colloq. since c1930; usu. spelled "mut."*

muttnik. *n.* The second man-made satellite launched by Russia in 1957. *Because it contained a dog for experimental purposes.*

muttonhead. *n.* A stupid person. *Colloq.* —**ed.** *adj.* Stupid.

mutton-top. *n.* = muttonhead.

mux. *n.* Teletyping.

muzzle. *v.t.* To kiss; to spoon.

muzzler. *n.* 1. A minor criminal; a punk. *Underworld use.* 2. An obnoxious person. *Maritime use.*

myrrh. *n.* Rum. *A spelling phonetically equivalent to "mur" = "rum" spelled backward.*

N

nab. *v.t.* To catch or arrest. *Colloq. n.* A detective or policeman. *Some teenage street gang use.*

nab at. To snap at; to nip; to graze in an attempted bite.

Nada. An oath, fig. "God be my witness;" really, truthfully. *From the Zen-Buddhist state or place of nirvana.*

Nadaville. *n.* Ecstasy. Fig., completely and successfully gone or far out. *Beat and far out use. When one leaves to get far out, his ultimate destination is Nadaville.*

nag. *n.* 1. An old, small, or useless horse. → 2. A race horse, esp. an inferior one. *Colloq.*

nail. *v.t.* To capture; to arrest. *n.* A cigarette.

name. *n.* **1.** Any famous or popular performer who attracts large audiences; a big name. **2.** A famous, influential person. *adj.* Famous; of established reputation, as a name band.

Nana(w). *n.* One's grandmother. *Baby talk, prob. a childhood corruption, often carried into adult speech.*

nance. *n.* **1.** A male homosexual who assumes the feminine role. → **2.** An effeminate man; a sissy.

Nancy. *n.* A male homosexual. *Cf.* **Mary.**

nanny. *n.* A nanny goat.

nanny-goat sweat. Whisky, esp. inferior whisky or moonshine.

naps. *n.pl.* Kinky hair. *Negro use.*

nark. *n.* **1.** A person serving as a decoy; a shill; a police informer. **2.** A kibitzer.

native, go. To live in and adopt or affect the customs of a foreign country, esp. a primitive country or sea island. *Orig. USN use; W.W.II use.*

nattily. *adv.* Sprucely; neatly. *Colloq.*

natty. *adj.* Spruce; dashing; neat; stylish. *Colloq.*

natural. *n.* **1.** In craps, a first throw of 7 or 11, which wins the play. → **2.** Any thing, action, or person that is or will be obviously or overwhelmingly successful. **3.** A jail sentence of 7 years.

Nature Boy. 1. A virile man. → **2.** A man or youth who needs a haircut. *Jocular use. From the title of the c1949 pop. song.*

navigate. *v.i., v.t.* To walk; often used humorously in ref. to a person who is intoxicated.

navy chest. A protruding belly; a bay window. *USN use.*

neat. *adj.* Without being mixed with water or soda (said of whisky); straight.

nebbish; nebbisch. *n.* A drab, awkward, shy person. *From the Yiddish.*

necessary, the. Money.

neck. *v.i., v.t.* To kiss and caress intimately; to play amatively; to pet. *Since c1910. Student use at* first but considered taboo until c1920. Wide use since c1920. *v.t.* To neck with someone. —**ing.** *n.* The act or instance of amorous play.

neck, get it in the. To be refused or rebuffed; specif. to be dismissed from one's job, or by one's lover or friend.

necker's knob. A small knob attached to a car's steering wheel for easier maneuvering; it also makes it easier for the driver to drive with one hand, as when he has his arm around a girl. *Teenage use since c1950.*

necktie. *n.* A hangman's rope.

necktie party. A hanging or lynching. *Pop. by western movies; universally known.*

necktie sociable; necktie social = **necktie party.**

needle. *n.* **1.** A hypodermic needle or syringe. *Very common among doctors, nurses, dentists, drug addicts, and the general public; colloq.* → **2.** An injection from a hypodermic needle; sometimes preceded by the name of the medicine or disease involved: "penicillin needle," "polio needle," etc. *Not as common as "shot."* **3.** The stylus in the tone arm of a phonograph. *Colloq.* **4.** A joke at another's expense; a malicious insinuation or reference made to embarrass another. *Very common during and since W.W.II, esp. among students.* *v.t.* **1.** To age an alcoholic beverage artificially by introducing an electric current into it through a special needlelike rod. → **2.** To strengthen a beverage or a food with whisky, wine or spices. **3.** To make fun of, tease, belittle, or otherwise embarrass by making quasi-humorous malicious remarks; to tease or "ride" someone. *Since c1940.*

needle, on the. 1. Addicted to the use of narcotics. **2.** Under the influence of narcotics. *Both uses by narcotic addicts.*

needle, the. Provoking, sarcastic talk; critical or goading remarks.

Usu. in "give [someone] the needle." Common since c1940.

needle candy. Any narcotic taken by injection.

neighbo. *adv.* No; don't; I disagree. *Negro use.*

nellie; Nellie. *n.* An old cow. *Farm use.*

neon ribbons. Excessive pride in one's military rank and decorations. *Orig. W.W.II use; still some Air Force use.*

nerf. *v.t.* To push one car with another. *Hot-rod use since c1955. From the nerfing bar that supports the bumper on most cars.*

nerts; nertz = nuts.

nerve. *n.* 1. Audacity; impertinence. *Colloq.* → 2. Courage, guts. *Colloq. since c1930.*

nervous. *adj.* 1. Orig. cool use = eliciting a strong psychological response; wild. *Some far out, beat, and cool use, but more often used by those who assume cool talk than by actual members of the various groups.* 2. = **jazzy.**

nervous pudding. Gelatin prepared to eat. *Because it shakes.*

nervy. *adj.* Impudent. *Colloq.*

nest egg. Money saved; esp. money saved over a comparatively long period for use in one's old age.

never-get-overs. *n.pl.* A fatal illness. *Dial.*

never-was; never-wuz; never wuzzer. *n.* A person who has never succeeded; one who has never had fame or fortune. *Based on "has-been."*

New Look. A woman's hair style with the hair at ear-lobe length and featuring a soft "page boy," a left side part, and a deep wave or bangs over the right side of the forehead. *Common c1947–c1950. Created to be worn with the late Parisian designer Christian Dior's "New Look" fashions, 1947.*

New Look, the. Any revolutionary style change of clothing or any manufactured item. *From the late Parisian designer Christian Dior's "New Look" women's clothing fashions of 1947.*

newsie; newsey. *n.* A newspaper seller; a newspaper boy. *Fairly common.*

newspaper. *n.* A 30-day jail sentence. *Based on "throw the book."*

newt. *n.* A stupid person. *Some use since c1925. Maybe from "neutral" reinforced by "nut" or may imply the simplicity of the newt.*

next, get = get next to [oneself].

next off. Next; the next thing; then. *Based on "first off."*

next to [oneself], get. To realize how stupid, unacceptable, eccentric, dull, or disliked one is; to become realistic or wise; to become hip.

next to [someone], get. To become an intimate friend, associate, or confidant of someone; specif., to become sexually intimate with a girl or woman.

N.G.; n.g. No good, worthless; untrustworthy, unethical, contemptible. *From the initials for "no good."*

nibs = his nibs.

nice guy. An amiable, pleasant fellow; one who can be depended upon to be fair, understanding, and socially ethical.

nice little piece of furniture. A sexually attractive, passionate, or pert girl.

nice Nellie. A prude of either sex; one who prefers politeness to efficiency; prudish.

nicey-nice. *adj.* Overnice, affectedly nice; when applied to males, fainthearted, effeminate.

nick. *v.t.* 1. To rob. 2. To charge; to assess or tax; to demand and receive money. → 3. To withhold pay from a worker for working less than a specified time, to dock a worker.

nickel nurser. A miser; a tightwad. *Attrib. to T. A. Dorgan, cartoonist, died 1929.*

nickel up. In begging, to offer a merchant five cents for food or other goods worth considerably more.

niff. *n.* A quarrel or grudge; spite; dislike. *Dial.*

niff-naw. *n.* An argument. *Dial. From Scotch-Irish dial.*

nig. *v.i.* 1. In playing cards, to renege. *Colloq. since c1900.* → 2. To refuse to carry out a plan or do someone a favor after promising to do so. *Some use since c1930. From "renege."*

niggertoe. *n.* A Brazil nut. *Colloq. From its size, shape, and color.*

night. Good night. *Affected and jocular use.* —cap. *n.* 1. A drink one has, as to help one relax, before retiring for the night, usu. whisky, but may be tea, warm milk, or the like; the last or farewell drink of whisky one has with friends at a bar or social gathering before leaving to go home and retire for the night. *Colloq.* 2. The second of two baseball games played by the same two teams on the same day, whether actually played at night or in the late afternoon. *Baseball use. Colloq.* —**ery** = **nitery.** —**ie.** *n.* A nightgown, a nightdress. *One of the words common to children that adults use freq.*

nightingale. *n.* An informer; a squealer; one who sings; a canary.

night people. 1. People who work or live at night, sleeping during the day. → 2. Nonconformists. *Pop. by N.Y. City disc jockey and social commentator Jean Shepherd, c1956.*

night spot. A night club.

nighty-night. Good night. *Colloq. Informal and jocular use. Very much in fashion c1930 and c1950. The most freq. child's word for "good night."*

nineteenth hole, the. A drink of whisky, or period of drinking and talking about one's game, after playing golf; the bar at a golf club. *Fairly common jocular use. Because a stand. game of golf includes eighteen holes, thus, fig., the last act of the game is a drink of whisky.*

ninety-day wonder. 1. A USA or USN officer commissioned after only three months of training at an Officers' Cadet School, as distinguished from an Annapolis or West Point graduate and from an officer commissioned from the ranks after years of experience. *W.W.II use. The term was used derog. or jocularly in the Armed Forces, but occasionally with pride by the officer's family.* → 2. Any youthful-looking officer, esp. an Army second lieutenant or an Air Force officer. → 3. A member of the U.S. Army or USN Reserve mobilized and given a three months' refresher training course.

nipper. *n.* A small boy: a child. *More common in Eng. than U.S.*

nippers. *n.pl.* Handcuffs.

nit. *n.* Zero. —**wit;** **nit-wit.** *n.* A stupid person. *Colloq.*

nitery; nightery. *n.* A nightclub.

nit-picker. *n.* One who looks for and finds minor errors; a pedant.

nix. *adv.* No. "I disagree, refuse, or forbid." "Don't." *Specif.* "Don't talk about or do that now; someone is listening, watching." *Colloq. From Ger. "nichts" = nothing.* *n.* A refusal; a ban. *Popularized by the theatrical trade paper, "Variety."* *v.t.* To veto; to reject; to cancel; to avoid. *Popularized by the theatrical trade paper, "Variety"; that paper's traditional headline, "Stix nix hix pix," was a triumph of sl. usage. Often used imperatively.* *adj.* Unfavorable.

nix out. To leave; to depart.

no account. 1. Worthless; untrustworthy, irresponsible. 2. A worthless or irresponsible man.

Noah's boy. Ham, as served to be eaten. *A sl. pun, prob. synthetic.*

nob. *n.* 1. A rich, influential person. 2. A person's head.

no bargain. A person, usu. of marriageable age, who is not particularly attractive, interesting, or convivial.

nobbler. *n.* One who drugs a race horse or dog or otherwise tries to influence unethically the outcome of a sporting or gambling event. *Not as common in U.S. as in Eng.*

noble. *n.* **1.** A strike-breaker's guard. **2.** A self-righteous person; one who pretends to act from principle when actually motivated by selfish considerations.

nobody, *a.* *n.* A person without fame, notoriety, notable success, ambition, or distinction; a person whose life has no special value or meaning to society.

nobody home. An expression applied to any person thought to be stupid, feeble-minded, inattentive, etc. *Often used jocularly, and often accompanied by the gesture of tapping the person referred to on the top of the head. Since c1915.*

no-clap medal. The Good Conduct Medal. *W.W.II Army use.*

no count = no account.

nod, get the. To be chosen or approved; to be chosen over others; to be singled out for a desired job or position. *Lit.* = to get a nod of approval.

nod, the. *n.* **1.** The referee's and judge's affirmative decision. *Sports use since c1920. Usu. in "He [a prize fighter] got the nod"* = he won by the referee's or judge's decision as opposed to winning by knocking one's opponent out. → **2.** One's choice; esp. an expert's choice to win a race or sports contest, or a sport team manager's choice of a player to play in a specific game.

nod-guy. *n.* = yes-man. *Because he nods his head up and down to signify "yes."*

no dice; no-dice. **1.** No; without success; being refused or refused permission. **2.** Worthless.

noggin. *n.* The head. *Since c1890; colloq. Until c1925 primarily =* the head as an object for hitting, since then also = the head as containing the brain for thinking.

no-good; No-good. *n.* = no account. A worthless person. *Col-*

loq. adj. Worthless; almost always said of people, seldom of things. *Colloq.*

no great shakes. An unimportant or average person or group. *Usu. in "He's no great shakes"* = He's not important or outstanding. *Since c1850.*

no-hitter. *n.* A baseball game in which a team makes no hits.

noise. **1.** Chatter, nonsense, blah. *Colloq.* **2.** A gun.

no kid; no kidding. A somewhat doubting response to a statement that seems not entirely credible.

no more room. As cool or far out as a person or the playing of a piece of music can be; fig., so satisfying that there is no room for improvement. *Some far-out and beat use since c1955.*

noncom. *n.* A non-commissioned officer. *Colloq. Army use since c1930. Wide W.W.II use.*

no never mind, makes. "It makes no difference; it is not an influencing factor."

noodle. *n.* **1.** The human head, esp. as considered as a thinking organ. **2.** A stupid, unthinking, or forgetful person. *Colloq. v.i., v.t.* To think, to think over, to study.

noose is hanging, the. Everything is ready; everyone is waiting, eager, and expectant. *Some far-out and beat use since c1955.*

nope. *adv.* No. *Colloq.*

noplaceville. *adj.* Fig., a place or time suitable to squares, hence square, dull, corny. *Some cool, far-out, and beat use. Since c1955. n.* A dull or boring place or town; a small town, a jerkwater town. *Some student, teenage, and even general use.*

nose, by a. To win a contest, best an opponent, or obtain a goal by a narrow margin. *From the horse-racing use.*

nose, on the. **1.** Correct, right, on the button. **2.** Exactly on time, on the button.

nose-bag. *n.* **1.** = feedbag. **2.** Food handed out in a paper bag. *Hobo* *use.* → 3. A dinner pail or lunch box.

nose-bag, put on the = **put on the feed bag.**

nose candy. *n.* A narcotic taken by sniffing, usu. cocaine.

nose-dive. *n.* 1. The act of accepting religion at a mission revival, usu. in order to receive a free meal. *Hobo use.* 2. Lit. and fig., a sudden drop or decrease, esp. in the price of something. *Colloq.*

nose out. Lit. and fig., to win by a nose; to win, succeed, or be chosen over another in a close contest or by a small margin.

no-show. *n.* A person who fails to claim, use, or cancel his reservation, esp. on an air flight. *Since c1950. Orig. commercial airlines' use.*

no soap. Nothing doing; I don't know; No.

not all there. Lacking normal intelligence or sanity; seeming to lack intelligence or sanity owing to having an obsession or eccentric attitude.

notchery. *n.* A brothel.

not dry behind the ears. Inexperienced or unworldly, specif., because of one's youth. *Implying that one's mother has recently washed behind one's ears or has still to remind her young child to do so.*

nothing. *adj.* Insipid, colorless, dull. *As in "He's a real nothing guy," or "That's a nothing book."*

nothing, know from; don't know from nothing. To know nothing; to know nothing or little about a specific topic; esp. to know nothing, or claim to know nothing, about an embarrassing, illegal, or unethical act; to be innocent of incriminating knowledge. *Orig. c1930 New York City use; based on Yiddish speech patterns. The insertion of the "from" points to an orig. in Yiddish speech patterns. Until c1940 the double negative form was almost always used, but the initial "don't" seems to be disappearing.*

nothing doing. 1. An expression meaning emphatically No; usu. said in response to a plan or idea that fails to evoke interest and agreement. 2. An attrib. expression to signify no action, excitement, or interest (in a given place or group).

nozzle. *n.* The nose.

nudie. *n.* 1. A show or performance in which a female nude or nudes appear. 2. A nude or nearly nude female performer, esp. a dancing girl, as in a cabaret floor show.

nudnik. *n.* An obnoxious person. *From the Yiddish "nudnik"* = *a pest.*

numb. *adj.* 1. Stupid; inattentive. 2. Lit. and fig., numb with fear; afraid. —**ie.** *n.* A stupid person. *From "numb-head," reinforced by "dummy."*

numb-brained. *adj.* Stupid.

number. *n.* 1. Any person, usu. of a kind specified in a modifying word or phrase, as a "hot number," "little number," "smart number," etc.; most freq. a sexually attractive or vivacious girl. *Also used absolutely as in "back number" and "wrong number."* 2. A specific model, style, or article of merchandise, as an automobile or article of clothing. *Reinforced by the fact that many articles of merchandise have a specific manufacturer's style number.*

number, have [someone's]. To know the hidden truth about another's character, past, behavior, or motives; to have classified or identified a person.

Number One; number one; number 1. 1. Oneself. *E.g., "I've got to take care of number one first."* 2. To urinate. *Child euphem. to communicate bathroom needs.* — **boy.** 1. The one in authority, esp. the head of a business firm. → 2. A chief assistant, one's most trusted associate or employee. → 3. A yes man. 4. A movie extra who owns his own dress suit for playing in society pictures.

numbers, by the. As expected; according to the usual rules; mechanically; without enthusiasm or emotion; said of actions. *Orig. W.W.II Armed Forces use. From the army expression, which was part of an order to drilling soldiers, indicating that marching, manual of arms, or other drill would be carried out accompanied by unison counting to ensure precision.*

number two. To defecate. *Child euphem. in communicating bathroom needs.*

numb-head. *n.* A stupid or dull person. *Some student use. Not as old as "numb-headed."* —ed. *adj.* Stupid. *Colloq.*

nut. 1. A person who is insane; a stupid, foolish, or gullible person; a person of unusual habits or beliefs; a character; an eccentric; an irresponsible or humorous person. *Common since c1915. With the popular acceptance of psychology the word is being used less and less = an insane person. With the increasing conformity in American life the word is being used more and more to = an eccentric, irresponsible, or humorous personality; the word is now often applied affectionately to one who performs an unusually generous, funny, or touchingly emotional act. →* 2. A person fanatically enthusiastic about a particular activity, esp. about a sport; a fan. 3. The total expenses necessary to start or operate a business; expenses; overhead. 4. A jocular term of endearment. *adj.* Insane; stupid, foolish, gullible; mistaken, misinformed, confused; crazy; eccentric; irresponsible. **—tiness.** *n.* Craziness. **—ty;** **nuts.** *adj.* all meanings, like a nut.

nut, off [one's]. 1. Insane, crazy. *The most common of the "off one's——" = "crazy" terms.* 2. In a tantrum; irrational. 3. Mistaken.

nut factory = nut house.

nut house. *n.* An insane asylum; a prison and/or hospital for the mentally ill.

nuts! nerts! nertz! *interj.* An interjection of disgust, contempt, annoyance, or the like; a term of dislike, disbelief, scorn, or despair; an emphatic "no!" *Colloq. since c1925.*

nuts; the; nerts, the. Any excellent thing or person.

nuts about; nuts over; nuts on = crazy about; in love with; enthusiastic about.

nutty about; nutty over = nuts about.

nutty as a fruitcake. Extremely eccentric; very nutty.

nyet. *n.* A negative decision or vote; a veto. *exclam.* No. *From the Russian, often in semihumorous mockery of the Russian government's attitude in international affairs; specif. from Russia's freq. use of the veto in the United Nations. Pop. by freq. newsp. use.*

O

oat-burner. *n.* = hay-burner.

oater. *n.* A western movie; a horse opera. *Movie use.*

oats opera = horse opera. *Movie use.*

obit. *n.* An obituary, esp. as in a newspaper.

ochre; ocher; oochre. *n.* Money. *Since c1860.*

O. D. *n.,* *adj.* Olive drab; hence, an olive-drab uniform, esp. the "Class A" uniform of the Army through 1959. *Orig. Army use.* *n.* Officer of the Day. *Standard abbr. Army use.* **—'s.** *n.pl.* The enlisted man's uniform, U.S. Army, through 1959, when color changed to Army green.

oday. *n.* Money. *One of the more familiar Pig Latin words; from "dough."*

odd-ball; oddball. *n.* An eccentric, queer, or odd person; a screwball; an intensely introverted person; a creep; a nonconformist. *adj.* Eccentric; disorganized;

prone to blunder; unreliable. *Common since c1945.*

odds-on. *adj.* In gambling, having better than an even chance to win; favorite.

ofaginzy. *n.* = ofay.

ofay. *n.* A white person. *Common Negro use since c1925. It has been suggested that this may be from "foe" as said in Pig Latin.*

off. *adj.* Crazy; eccentric; loco.

off, get. In swing music, an improvised solo.

off base. Impertinent; assuming authority or intimacy which one does not have.

off-beat. *adj.* Unusual; out of the ordinary; weird; unconventional but accepted; unconventional but not unique; macabre. *Since c1935, but wide use only since c1950, often in reference to intellectuals and cool and beat nonconformists.*

off color; off-color. *adj.* Tending to be obscene, lewd, or lascivious, but hinting at or suggesting the obscene. *Usu. in ref. to a joke, song, or the like.*

office. *n.* **1.** A place; facetiously, resembling or serving as an office; any place where one does work or spends a great deal of time. **2.** A secret sign, a signal, or tip-off, as a wink, hand signal, clearing one's throat, or the like. *Primarily underworld use.*

offsteered. *adj.* Enticed away from; sidetracked.

oh fudge. An extremely mild expression of disappointment or frustration.

oh yeah. An expression of challenge, incredulity, or sarcasm. *Colloq.*

oh yes = oh yeah. *Not common.*

oil. *n.* **1.** Flattery; bunk; boloney; blah. **2.** Money, esp. graft. *v.t.* **1.** To hit, beat, or whip someone. **2.** To pay graft or bribery money; to fix the police or other public officials.

oil-burner. *n.* Any old or dilapidated vehicle, esp. a car or ship.

oil [someone's] palm. To bribe; to grease. *Colloq.*

oka; oke; okey; okay; oak. *adv.* O.K.; yes. *adj.* Good; satisfactory. *All from stand.* O.K.

okey-doke; okie doke. O.K.

okey-dokey; okie-dokie. O.K. *Since c1935.*

Okie. *n.* **1.** A migratory worker. *Orig. one of the many Oklahoma and Arkansas farmers who became migratory workers after the dust storms of the early 1930's. Since c1935.* → **2.** The family of such a migratory worker. → **3.** A resident or native of Oklahoma.

okle-dokle. O.K. *Fairly common jocular use.*

old army game, the. Any swindle; any unfair or crooked gambling game or bet.

old chap = old man. *Considered somewhat more formal, and hence affected, than other "old ——" = close friend forms of direct address.*

old goat. Any elderly, disliked person, most often a man but may be a woman; esp. an elderly person disliked for being pompous, stingy, mean, stubborn, unsympathetic to younger people, or the like. *Colloq.*

old hat. Out of style; old-fashioned.

oldie; oldy. *n.* Any old thing or person, usu. an old joke, story, song, or movie, less freq. an old man.

old lady. **1.** A wife, esp. one's own wife. *Colloq. Not considered derog. Based on the earlier "old woman."* **2.** A mother, esp. one's own mother. *Colloq. Not considered derog. Based on the older "old man." Usu. male use.*

old man. **1.** A father, esp. one's own father. *Colloq.; usu. male use.* **2.** A husband, esp. one's own husband. *Colloq. since c1895. It is interesting to note that "old man" = "father" is older than "old lady" = "mother," but "old lady" = "wife" is older than "old man" = "husband." The oldest of each of the pairs is used by men, who coin and use more sl. than women.* **3.** Old friend. *A masc. term of direct address implying affection for the man so addressed and his intellectual equality with the speaker. Because of the last connotation, the term is most often used in serious personal conversation and sometimes is considered as condescending.* 4. The captain of a ship. *Common maritime and USN use since c1850.* 5. The commanding officer of any military unit, esp. a company commander. *Army use since W.W.I.* 6. A superintendent, foreman, or boss.

old man with the whiskers = Whiskers.

old saw. 1. A homily; a folk saying; an aphorism. 2. An old joke or story.

Old Sol. The sun. *Colloq.*

old soldier = dead soldier.

old thing = old man. *Orig. one of the affectionate masculine "old ———" = "close friend" terms of direct address, esp. used by educated or sophisticated males. Occas. flippant or affected use. This is the one "old ———" = "close friend" term that is also applied to and used by females.*

oliver. *n.* The moon.

on. *adj.* 1. Aware of, wise to, or hep to something, esp. to a swindle, fake, or hoax. 2. Willing; ready to participate or accept another's participation. *prep.* Paid for by; a treat supplied by. *Colloq. since c1900.*

on [someone or something]. An expression signifying a treat paid for by the indicated person or group. *E.g., "Have a drink on me" = Let me buy you a drink; "Lunch on the company" = the company is providing lunch.*

once-over. *n.* 1. A look or glance; a visual inspection or examination, either cursory or detailed. *Usu. in "give [someone or something] the once-over." Since c1915.* 2. A quick, cursory cleaning or putting of things in order; doing a task quickly or temporarily.

once over lightly. Cursorily;

quickly; temporarily. *From the traditional phrase in ordering a shave from a barber.*

oncer. *n.* A woman who has been, or is, emotionally and sexually faithful to only one man during her life; a one-man woman.

one. *n.* 1. A specimen or instance of virtually anything, identifiable only from the context; often a blow with the fist, a pitched baseball, a tall story, an order of food, etc. *Some common examples:* "draw one" = a cup of coffee, a glass of beer; "a fast one" = a fast pitch in baseball; "a hot one" = a joke or story, often used ironically; "one with" = a hamburger with coffee or with onions; "a quick one" = a single shot of whisky. 2. One dollar; a one-dollar bill.

one-and-a-half-striper; **one-and-one-half-striper.** A Naval lieutenant, junior. *Wide USN use since c1925.*

one and only. One's sweetheart.

one-armed bandit; one-arm bandit. A slot machine. *Because the operative lever of the machine resembles an arm, and because the odds on winning are fixed against the player.*

one down. The first item has been accomplished; the first obstacle has been surmounted. *From baseball use of "one down and two to go" = one man has been put out and two more outs will retire the side.*

one for the road. A last drink; lit., the last drink before leaving a bar or a party for home. *Perhaps in allusion to the ancient tradition of the stirrup cup.*

one-horse. *adj.* Small; paltry; suitable for or typical of a small or rural community; bush-league. *Since c1850; from "one-horse town."*

one-horse town. A small or rural town; a town in which nothing exciting or noteworthy takes place; fig., a town so small as to have, or need, only one horse [before the time of automobiles]. *Colloq.*

one of the boys. An informal, popular fellow considered as a jovial companion by his male friends; a man who has similar tastes, habits, and ideas as his circle of friends.

oner. *n.* A heavy blow with the fist.

one-shot. *n.* 1. In publishing, a story, article, or the like that appears once and without a sequel. *Since c1940.* 2. Any business transaction, sports event, or the like that occurs only once. → 3. A woman who agrees to sexual intercourse once but refuses afterward. *Since c1950. adj.* Occurring only once; performed once; not part of any regular series of programs.

one-striper. *n.* 1. In the USN, an ensign, whose rank is shown by a single stripe. *USN use since c1920.* 2. In the Army a private first class, whose rank is indicated by a single stripe on his sleeve. *Some W.W. II Army use.*

one too many. Whisky sufficient to intoxicate a person; fig., that final drink that makes the difference between sobriety and intoxication.

one-track mind. A mind dominated by or limited to a single idea, subject, or point of view.

one-two. *n.* 1. A potent combination of two punches, consisting of [one] a short left jab followed immediately with [two] a hard right cross, usu. to the jaw of one's opponent. *Since c1920; orig. and mainly a prize fighting term. A traditional series of blows, it is often referred to as "the old one-two."* 2. First and second places respectively, as in a race or election.

one-two punch; one-two blow. 1. = **one-two.** 2. Fig., a hard or fast blow.

one-two-three. A series of three punches. *Based on "one-two," usu. a "one-two punch" followed by a left hook. adv.* Ably.

one-two-three-and-a-splash. A meal of meat, potato, bread, and gravy. *Dial.*

one-way guy. An honest, fair, or sincere man.

onion. *n.* 1. A stupid or boring person. *Orig. Army and USN W.W.II use.* 2. A badly planned, badly executed venture or task. 3. The head. *Orig., c1920, prize fight use.*

on the make. 1. Ambitious; usu. ruthlessly intent on, and alert to, one's own social, business, or financial advancement or profit; esp. willing or eager to do anything that will help one advance or profit; receptive toward profitable offers. *Popular since c1935.* 2. Ready or willing to take advantage of another in order to succeed. 3. To be receptive to or to encourage sexual advances from the opposite sex, usu. said of females; to make sexual advances or desire sexual intercourse with one of the opposite sex, usu. said of males; to seek or readily enter into sexual intercourse, said of both sexes.

on the rocks. 1. Stranded; without funds, esp. when one is in dire need of money; fig., stranded as a ship is when it has run aground on the rocks. 2. Served over ice cubes; said of a drink, esp. whisky. *Common use.* 3. Concluded unhappily or unsuccessfully, moving toward an unhappy or unsuccessful conclusion. *From the nautical image, fig. headed toward or having met with disaster.*

on the town. Enjoying the entertainment, sights, and excitement of a city as a tourist; specif., visiting the best, most expensive, exciting, sophisticated nightclubs, shows, restaurants, and bars; spending one's money lavishly in nightclubs, esp. in the company of a chorus girl, model, actress, or the like; to go on a spree; to paint the town (red).

oochre = ochre.

oodles. *n.pl.* A large quantity. *Since c1870; wide dial. use until c1895. Sl. since c1895, most common c1900–c1920. Still common but considered effeminate and childish.*

oof. *n.* 1. Money. *From "ooftish."* 2. Strength, power. *Some prize fight use.*

oofay. *n.* Variant of "ofay," a white person. *Negro use, orig. and usu. derisive. May be based on or reinforced by "oaf."*

ooftish; offtish. *n.* Money, esp. money available for gambling, entertainment, or business speculation. *Some New York and gambling use since c1900; by folk ety. from the Yiddish "auf tische" = on the table.*

oofus. *n.* A blundering, stupid person, an oaf. *Some c1935 Harlem Negro and jive use; some general jazz and hep use. Prob. orig. Negro use, based on "oofay," reinforced by "oaf."*

oogle. *v.i., v.t.* To ogle. *A corruption.*

ookus; ookis. *n.* Money. *Some use since c1900; Prob. from the Yiddish; may be based on "oofus," from "oof" and "ooftish."*

oomph. *n.* 1. Sex appeal. *Also wide attrib. use.* → 2. Excitement, enthusiasm.

oomph girl. A girl or young woman popularly acclaimed for her sex appeal, esp. a movie star or celebrity.

oops. *interj.* Used in surprise and as an apology on recognizing a mistake, minor accident, or slip of the tongue.

ooze. *v.i.* 1. To move forward on one's feet slowly, esp. in a sly or sneaky way. 2. To stroll or parade on a street, to saunter.

ooze out. To depart secretly; to sneak away.

O.P.; o.p. *n. possessive.* Other people's. *An abbr., usu. jocular, e.g.,* "What brand of cigarettes do you smoke?" "I smoke o.p.'s."

open. *adj.* Without police interference in gambling and vice; having a liberal attitude toward vice, gambling, and unethical practices. *Usu. in "an open town."* *v.t.* To rob; to hold up. —ing. *n.* A robbery.

opener-upper. *n.* That which opens or begins a program, as a piece of music that begins a radio program. *Mainly radio use.*

open up. 1. To begin to use all one's strength and energy in order to best an opponent, esp. in boxing; to begin a fight, to attack someone physically; to start physical violence, esp. to shoot a gun or begin firing a gun at someone. 2. To inform on another or to reveal confidential information, esp. when threatened or bribed.

operator. *n.* 1. A thief, esp. a swindler, confidence man, or pickpocket. → 2. A charming, socially adroit young man who is popular with the girls; a bold young man with a good line. → 3. A student who is prominent in school activities, often called a "Big Time Operator" or "B.T.O." 4. A dope peddler. *Narcotic addict use.* 5. One who makes a sensational first impression, often with exaggerated talk; one who can convince anyone of anything, a fast talker.

oral. *n.* An oral examination, as opposed to a written one. *Wide student use.*

oral days. *n.pl.* The "good old days" of horse racing when bettors negotiated with independent bookmakers at the track, often receiving better odds than those prevailing; horse racing before the time of the pari-mutuel totalizator machines.

orbit. *v.i., v.t.* To put a man-made object into orbit around the earth. *One of the latest examples of a noun turned into a verb.*

orc; orch = ork.

or else. Usu. used at the end of a sentence or phrase as an implied or incompleted threat of retaliation, often by violence, if one does not do as the speaker wants.

orie-eyed; orry-eyed. *adj.* = hoary-eyed.

ork; orc; orch. *n.* An orchestra; a dance band. *Popularized by the trade paper, "Variety."*

oryide. *n.* A drunkard or drunk.

oscar; Oscar. *n.* 1. A gun. *Some underworld use since c1930; prob. from "Roscoe."* 2. Any of numerous gold-plated statuettes awarded annually by the Academy of Motion Picture Arts and Sciences for professional distinction. → 3. Fig., any award, medal, or plaque. *Uses 2 and 3 are always capitalized.*

ossifer. *n.* Officer. *A common derog. mispronunciation since W.W.I. Usu. refers to an Army officer, sometimes a police officer.*

ossified. *adj.* Drunk. *Some use since c1925; often jocular.*

ostrich. *n.* One who refuses to recognize a political, economic, or personal problem or a warning of danger; one who wilfully closes his eyes to the true import of current events in any field; a know-it-all. *Some use since c1920; increasing political use since c1940. From the traditional notion that an ostrich buries his head in the sand when danger approaches.*

out. *adj.* Far-out; attractive and modern; in the latest sophisticated or hip style. *Common. Far-out and beat use. From "far-out."* *n.* 1. Out of doors. *Colloq.* 2. Any place away from one's home or business. *Thus one goes "out to lunch" or "out to a movie."*

out!, get = Go on! *An exclam. of incredulity.*

outer pasture = pasture.

outfox. *v.t.* To outwit; outsmart. *Colloq.*

out in left field. Wrong, very wrong; out of place, date, or order; unusual; obnoxious; off base.

outlaw strike. A strike by union members despite disapproval of union officials; a wildcat strike.

out-of-towner. *n.* A visitor or transient from out of town.

out on the town = on the town.

outre. *adj.* = out, far-out. *Some far-out use. From the French.*

outside chance. A remote possibility.

outside of, get. To eat. *Lit.* = "to put food inside."

out to lunch. 1. Unable to qualify socially. 2. Stupid. *Jocular imputation of brainlessness.*

oval, the. *n.* A football. *Some sports use.*

over. *prep.* When in the card game of poker one is holding two pairs, the higher pair is said to be over the lower. For example, "aces over eights" = a pair of aces and a pair of eights. *adj.* Turned, or ordered to be turned, over while being cooked; specif., fried on both sides, so that the yolk becomes hard; said of an egg. *Wide lunch-counter use in relaying an order; fairly common general use.*

over a barrel. To be in a situation in which one must compromise or admit defeat; to be in another's power.

overboard. *adv.* Extremely enthusiastic; emotionally overwrought; wholeheartedly and perhaps irrationally in favor of.

overland route. The longest route between two places; the slow way to reach one place from another, as caused by slow movement, frequent stops for talk, food, or drink, etc. *Usu. in a semi-jocular criticism to a late arrival, like "What's the matter? Did you take the overland route?"*

overland trout. Bacon. *Not common.*

overnight. *n.* 1. Any job or activity that can be planned one day and accomplished the next; a comparatively unimportant job, activity, or event; specif., a newsp. col. written one day and published the next, or a horse race for which the conditions are posted only one day in advance. 2. A short trip; lit., a journey that takes one away from home only one night. —er. *n.* = overnight.

overseas cap. A brimless, peakless envelope-like cap of cotton or wool having a cuffed, sharply creased crown, worn as part of the regulation Army uniform and adopted widely for civilian uniforms of all kinds. *Orig. Army use; colloq.*

owl. *adj.* Occurring, working, performing, or open for business at night, esp. late at night.

owner. *n.* A ship's captain; one holding a captain's rank. *Some USN use.*

ozoner. *n.* Any outdoor or open air arena, specif., a drive-in movie theater. *Since c1945.*

P

pace, off the. Behind the leader, in a race or contest.

pack. *n.* A liquor made from molasses. *Dial. Orig. New Orleans use. From Gen. Packenham, an Eng. general killed at the battle of New Orleans. v.i., v.t.* To carry (something). *Colloq.*

package. *n.* 1. An attractive, usu. small and neat, girl or young woman. 2. A large sum of money.

package (on), have a. To be drunk.

pack heat. To carry a gun on one's person.

pack in. 1. To relinquish, withdraw, or close one's interest in a business, occupation, friendship, emotional entanglement, problem, or plan; fig., to pack one's interest in a suitcase and leave. 2. To attract a large audience. *E.g., "That rodeo really packed them in." Colloq.*

pack it in. 1. To take full advantage of a favorable position; to follow up an advantage; to earn or win as much money, fame, or power as a given situation will allow. 2. To admit defeat or failure.

pack-rat. *n.* 1. A petty thief; a stranger; one who cannot be trusted. *Still some dial. use.* 2. A porter; a bellhop.

pack the mail. To run or travel fast.

pact. *n.* A contract. *Pop. by "Variety," theater trade paper, and useful to headline writers. v.t.* To sign a contract with a person or organization.

pad. *n.* 1. A couch, bed, or the like on which one reclines while smoking opium in an opium den. *Opium addict use. Very old.* → 2. Any room, apartment, or establishment where addicts gather to take narcotics. *Addict use.* → 3. A temporary bed or pallet; a bed other than one's own; a room, as a hotel room or a friend's room, in which one lives temporarily, as while traveling. *Musician's use.* → 4. One's own bed, room, apartment, or home, as opposed to temporary quarters. *Musicians' use since c1935; also some W.W.II Army use.* 5. An independent prostitute's place of business; a crib. 6. One's conception of an ideal home or way of life, either a reasonable concept or an irrational dream, such as a narcotic addict's dream; a private world in which one would like to live. *Cool and far-out use since c1950.* 7. An automobile license plate. *v.i., v.t.* To increase the length of a story, essay, book, or the like by adding material, esp. repetitious or irrelevant material. *Colloq.*

pad, hit the = hit the hay.

pad, knock the. To retire; to go to sleep.

padding. *n.* Extra material, often irrelevant or repetitious, added to an essay, book, speech, or the like to increase its length. *Colloq.*

paddle. *n.* An airplane engine. *Some Air Force use.*

pad down. 1. To sleep. 2. To search or frisk.

paddy; Paddy. *n.* An Irishman; one of Irish descent. *Prob. from the traditional Irish name Patrick and its nickname Paddy. Archaic by c1920.*

paddy wagon. *n.* 1. A police wagon used for taking arrested persons to jail. 2. Lit. and fig., any "wagon" or vehicle used to remove a person to a place of restriction, as to an insane asylum.

padre. *n.* A chaplain of any denomination. *Some W.W.I Army use; wide W.W.II Armed Forces use.*

pad room. 1. A room where opium is smoked or other narcotics are used. 2. A bedroom. *Prob. synthetic.*

pad the hoof. To tramp about. *Orig. hobo use.*

pageboy. A women's hair style consisting of shoulder-length hair in the back, slightly shorter on the sides, forming a semi-circle at the back, with the ends curled under and worn with or without a pompadour, waves, or bangs over the forehead. *Common c1935–c1943. Said to be based on the wigs worn by page boys of the English courts.*

page-one(r). *n.* 1. A front-page newspaper article. → 2. Sensational news or gossip, worthy of being put on a newspaper's front page. → 3. An entertainer, celebrity, or other person with always newsworthy name or doings.

paid in. "I am paid in" = "I have a place to sleep tonight." *Hobo use.*

pail. *n.* The stomach. *Negro use.*

pain. *n.* 1. Annoyance, vexation, irritation. *Often in "He gives me a pain." Fig., a "pain in the neck."* 2. A bothersome, tedious, or annoying person; a pain in the ass. *v.t.* To pain someone in the neck [ass].

pain in the neck. An annoying, obnoxious person; a disagreeable duty or obligation.

painted. *adj.* Registered by appearing on a radar screen. *W.W.II Air Force use.*

paint horse = pinto.

paint remover. 1. = varnish remover. 2. Inferior whisky of any kind.

paint the town (red). To go on a wild spree in a town or city; to celebrate wildly.

pair-off. *n.* The act of pairing off.

pal. *n.* A friend, usu. male but may be female, esp. one who is a close companion; a chum, buddy, side-kick. *Well over 150 years old. Prob. from the Romany. Considered insincere as a form of address.* —ly; —lie. *adj.* Friendly; intimately familiar in manner. *Since c1900. n.* A pal. *More brash than "pal."*

pal around with. To associate with as a pal.

pale. *n.* A white person. *Some Negro use.*

pale-face. *n.* 1. Whisky. 2. A circus clown.

palm. *v.t.* 1. To conceal a playing card in one's palm in order to substitute it for a card received in the deal. 2. To conceal anything from opponents in a sports or business competition.

palooka; paluka; palooker. *n.* 1. An inferior or average prize fighter. *"Joe Palooka," the title and main character of a synd. newsp. comic strip, has been the world's champion for years and is still unsophisticated and a little oafish, but the name has not become associated with champions. The orig. is uncertain.* → 2. A wrestler. *Since c1940.* → 3. Any stupid or mediocre person, esp. if big or strong. → 4. An oafish hoodlum.

palsy-walsy; palsey-walsey. *adj.* Acting as a pal or pals; friendly, intimate.

paluka. *n.* = palooka.

pam. *n.* A pamphlet. *v.i., v.t.* = pan.

pan. *n.* 1. The human face. 2. An unfavorable review or notice, usu. by a professional critic of a play, novel, or the like; adverse criticism. 3. A panorama. *Some photographer use. v.t.* To criticize adversely; to deride; to find fault with; to roast. *v.i., v.t.* 1. To move one's camera with the moving subject being photographed, so as to eliminate or reduce blur in still photography, or keep the subject in full view with a movie camera. 2. = **pan out.**

pancake. *n.* A humble Negro; an Uncle Tom. *Some Negro use.*

pancake landing. 1. A heavy, awkward fall; a flat plop, as of a pancake. → 2. Specif., in aviation, the act or instance of landing an airplane on its fusilage rather than on its wheels, done when the landing gear is damaged.

panhandle. *v.i., v.t.* To beg money from strangers in the street. *Colloq.* —*r*; **pan handler.** *n.* A beggar. *Common since c1900.*

panic. *v.t.* 1. To elicit great response, esp. applause from an audience by one's performing; to amuse or entertain well. → 2. To make a fool of oneself while trying to impress, persuade, or lie to another. *Usu. in* "You panic me" = *I consider you, your troubles, and your way of life laughable. The remark is meant to be cruel.* *v.i.* To become confused, frightened, or irrational.

panic rack. The pilot's automatic ejection seat in a jet airplane.

pan-lifter. *n.* A pot-holder. *Colloq.*

pan out. To resolve; to resolve into; to turn out; to yield favorable or unfavorable results. *Colloq. since c1930.*

pansified. *adj.* Effeminate; affected.

pansy. *n.* 1. A male homosexual, esp. one who plays the female role. → 2. An effeminate male. *adj.* Effeminate; affected.

panther. *n.* Inferior liquor, esp. gin. *From* "panther sweat."

panther sweat. Whisky, esp. when raw or inferior. *Since c1925.*

pantry. *n.* The stomach. *Mainly sports use, esp. boxing.*

pants. *n.pl.* Trousers. *Used since c1850; so common since c1920 that* "trousers" *now seems somewhat affected.*

pants rabbit. A louse. *Hobo and W.W.I Army use.*

panty-waist; pantywaist. *n.* A sissy; a frail, cowardly, effeminate boy or man. *Common since c1930.*

—**ed.** *adj.* Effeminate; cowardly. *Said of boys or men.*

pap. *n.* Money. *Now dial.*

papa. *n.* A male lover.

pape. *n.* A playing card. *Perhaps from* "paper" *on which the designs are printed, as this seems older than* "paper" = *a deck of marked playing cards.*

paper. *n.* 1. Specif., counterfeit money. 2. A pass or free ticket to a theater or circus. *v.t.* 1. To use or disseminate counterfeit money. 2. To pass worthless checks.

paper-belly. *n.* A person unable to drink liquor straight, or one who grimaces after drinking.

paper-hanger. *n.* 1. One who forges checks or passes worthless checks on a nonexistent bank account. *Orig. underworld use, c1915–c1930* = *a check forger.* → 2. One who passes counterfeit money.

paper-hanging. *n.* The act of forging or passing bad checks.

paper house. A theater or circus audience containing many persons admitted on free tickets or passes.

paper-pusher. *n.* One who passes counterfeit money. *Cf. paper.*

papoose. *n.* A nonunion worker working with union workers. *Because the nonunion worker receives the benefits won by the union workers and thus is carried* "on their back," *as a papoose is traditionally carried by its mother.*

pappy guy. An elderly man; the oldest member of a group, esp. the worker who possesses seniority in a factory or office; an old or aging man; a fatherly man.

paralyzed. *adj.* Drunk, esp. completely drunk; drunk beyond the point of action or memory. *Common since c1925.*

pard. *n.* A partner; a friend. *Colloq. since c1850. From the common pronunciation* "pardner."

park. *v.t.* To put or place someone or something in a convenient place and leave [him, her, it, or them] there for an indefinitely short or long time; to set; to lay or lay down; to hang up [as a garment]; to allow an object to remain stationary or a person to be ignored until wanted. *Common since the advent of the automobile and its parking. v.i.* To sit, sit down, or be seated and remain so for a while; to remain more or less stationary in a place.

parlay *n.* 1. In gambling, a wager on two or more events with the stipulation that the wager on the first event plus the winnings will be wagered on the second event, etc.; if the first or any subsequent bet is lost, the whole sum is lost. *Horse-racing use.* 2. An instance of parlaying. *v.i., v.t.* To understand. *From Fr. "parler" = to speak. v.t.* 1. To bet money and, upon winning, to continue betting the original stake and one's winnings; to bet money stipulating that if one wins the original stake one's winnings will automatically be bet on a subsequent wager. *Since c1890; primarily horse racing use.* → 2. Fig., to start with one item or something small and increase it into a collection or something large.

parley-voo. *v.i., v.t.* 1. To speak or understand a language. *Since W.W.I. Orig. Army use in France. From the Fr. "parlez-vous."* 2. To speak, converse, or confer; to understand.

parlor house. A brothel.

parlor pink. A mild radical; one who holds mildly liberal political opinions but takes no action to support them; a member of the bourgeois class who inclines toward radical or communistic ideas.

particular. *adj.* Excessive; special.

party. *n.* 1. A person. *Since c1925.* 2. A session of necking. *Student use since c1930.* Cf. petting party. → 3. A session of sexual intercourse, esp. a fairly extended period of sexual abandon. *Common since c1935, the most freq.*

use. v.i. To go to a party or parties; to have a good time; to drink, dance, talk, and indulge in general merrymaking. *Student use since c1945. v.t.* To entertain a person at a party or series of parties.

party boy. A young man, esp. a student, who devotes much time, thought, and effort to social activities, courting girls, and going to parties; a student who is not seriously concerned with his studies, but whose main interest in school is the social life. *Student use.*

party girl. A girl or young woman, esp. a student, who devotes much time, thought, and effort to social activities, attracting suitors, and going to parties; a student who is not seriously concerned with her studies, but whose main interest in school is the social life. *Student use. Not as common as "party boy."*

party pooper; party-pooper. *n.* The first person or couple to leave a party; fig., one who causes the end of a party or good time. *Wide student use since before c1945.*

pash. *n.* A person whom one loves or admires, esp. a celebrity who is one's idol. *Some teenager and newsp. columnist use.*

pass. *v.i., v.t.* To pretend; to counterfeit; specif., to win acceptance as a member of a dominant group, race, religion, etc., without meeting the basic requirements; said esp. of Negroes who make lives and careers as members of the white race.

pass at, make a. To make an amorous advance toward. *Colloq.*

passion pit. An out-door movie theater whose patrons view films from their cars; a drive-in movie theater. *Student use since c1940. Because such theaters give young couples an opportunity to neck in darkness and relative privacy.*

pass out. 1. To faint; to become unconscious, esp. from momentary sickness, shock, excessive drinking of alcoholic beverages, or fatigue. 2. To die; to pass away. pass-out; passout. n. 1. A distribution, as of things to people. 2. The act of losing consciousness. 3. A person who has become unconscious by drinking.

paste. v.t. 1. To defeat a sports opponent decisively. → 2. In baseball, to hit a pitched ball hard and well. 3. To put blame on another; to make a criminal charge against someone.

pasteboard; paste-board. n. 1. A ticket of admission, as to a game, prize fight, or circus. Since c1850. 2. A playing card.

pasture. n. 1. In baseball, the outfield. Since c1925. → 2. A baseball park.

pat. adj. Incapable of being improved or changed; fixed. Colloq.

pater. n. Father. Some jocular U.S. use.

patootie. n. 1. A sweetheart. 2. A girl, usu. a pretty one.

patsy. n. 1. A weak or cowardly man. 2. The person who is given the blame for any crime, esp. by others who were actually involved. 3. A dupe; a sucker; a pushover; a fall guy.

patzer. n. An inferior chess player.

paw. v.i., v.t. To caress or attempt to caress another intimately, but roughly and without invitation; to manhandle. n. A human hand.

payday, make a. To win or obtain a sum of money at a given time, other than pay for regular work; lit., to make a payday for oneself exclusive of regular earnings.

pay dirt. 1. An area of a playing field that is the scoring objective of either team; the area covered by a goal or bounded by a goal line; the goal itself. From the literal mining sense of "pay dirt." 2. Fig., any desired result, as money, a correct answer, the solution of a problem, or the like.

pay off. To murder. Some use in fiction. pay-off; payoff. n., adj. 1. Payment; specif., the payment of cash, wages, bets, bribery, or graft. Since c1925, orig. under-

world use. → 2. Fig., a final result or outcome, specif., a score in a game, a confession of guilt, the crux of a situation, and esp. the point of a story. → 3. Something unexpected or absurd. → 4. Lit., that which pays off or brings about a desired result, as a winning play in sports.

payola. n. Pay; esp. graft, blackmail, or extortion money; a payroll.

pay through the nose. To pay excessively.

pay-wing. n. A baseball pitcher's pitching arm which, fig., earns his pay.

pazaza; pazzaza. n. 1. A piazza. 2. Money.

P. C.; p. c. n. Percentage, esp. a percentage of gambling or criminal profits.

pea. n. 1. A baseball. 2. A golf ball.

peach. n. 1. A pretty, attractive, girl or woman. One of the most common of the sl. words relating to woman or sex while having a standard food meaning. → 2. An admirable or attractive man. → 3. Anything pleasing, excellent, or admirable. —y. adj. Excellent; attractive; wonderful; spectacular. Since c1900. Since c1930 primarily schoolboy use; adults more and more use the word ironically.

peachy-keen. adj. 1. Excellent; fine. More often than not, used ironically. 2. All right; fair; not good enough to warrant enthusiasm but adequate. Fairly common since c1955. This combination of two words formerly associated with youthful enthusiasm to = "just fair" or "adequate" is typical of cool usage.

peacoat. n. A heavy, hip-length, dark blue jacket, which is the official overcoat of a USN enlisted man's uniform. Orig. USN use; the style has been adopted by civilian clothiers since W.W.II.

peahead; pea-head; pea head. n. A stupid or unthinking person.

Implying that the person's brain is as small as a pea.

peanut. *adj.* Unimportant; little esteemed. *Since c1840. n.* A small or small-time person. **—s.** *n.pl.* 1. Anything, esp. a business venture, which is unimportant, insignificant, or small. → 2. A small amount of money, esp. a small profit.

peanut gallery. The top gallery or the highest rows of seats in a theater. *Since c1900.*

pearl-diver. *n.* A dish washer. *Since c1900. Fairly common jocular use. Orig. hobo use, then Army use; common Army use during W.W.II and fairly common restaurant and lunch-counter use since c1935.*

pea-shooter. *n.* 1. A rifle. 2. A pursuit or fighter pilot. *Some Air Force use since c1940.*

pea soup. 1. A thick fog. 2. A worthless person. *Some underworld use.* **—er.** *n.* = pea soup.

peat. *n.* = pete.

pebble on the beach. A person regarded as only one of a multitude. *Used only in sentences given below, esp. the second one:* "There's more than one pebble on the beach" = "There are plenty of other people I can depend on or have as friends, girl friends, or beaus." "You aren't the only pebble on the beach," *said to diminish another's self-esteem. Both uses common since c1910.*

peck. *n.* A white person. *Negro use. From "peckerwood."* **—er-wood.** *n.* A poor Southern white person, esp. a farmer; an ignorant, poor, intolerant Southerner; white trash. *Negro use, orig. dial. Southern Negro use.*

pecking order. One's comparative degree of aggressiveness, desire to dominate others, or of leadership. *Orig. used by social psychologists = the exact order of aggressiveness demonstrated by animals, esp. by fowls, in eating; thus the strongest or most aggressive eats or pecks first, the* second most aggressive eats next and so on down to the weakest, most timid animal, who eats what is left.

peckings. *n.pl.* Food. *Negro use.*

peddle out. To sell one's personal belongings, as clothing or shoes, to a secondhand store.

peddle [one's] papers. An order to go about one's business; to mind one's own business; to go away; beat it; scram.

peddler. *n.* A local or slow freight train. *Hobo use.*

pee-eye. *n.* A pimp. *From spelling the first two letters, "p" and "i."*

pee-head = peahead.

peek. *n.* In horse-racing, third place; the act of finishing in third place. *v.i.* To finish in third place.

peel. To undress; esp. to do a striptease on the stage. *Colloq.* **—er.** *n.* A strip-tease dancer, a stripper.

peel out. To leave or depart, esp. quickly or without ceremony. *Since c1955; orig. hot rod and rock and roll use.*

peep. *n.* 1. A vocal sound; a word; esp. a critical or annoying utterance. *E.g.,* "I don't want to hear a peep out of you." 2. = jeep. *Early in W.W.II, and in some cases all during the war, some units, esp. Armored Forces units, used "peep" = the quarter ton vehicle commonly called the "jeep," reserving "jeep" to designate a larger vehicle. v.i.* = peek. **—er.** *n.* A private detective. *Since c1930; most freq. found in detective-story fiction.* **—ers.** *n.pl.* The eyes. *Colloq. since c1930.*

peep show. 1. A supposedly private or surreptitious view, usu. through a hole in a wall or tent, of nude women, couples engaged in sexual intercourse, or other lewd scenes. *Once traditionally part of small carnivals and often conducted also by brothels, such shows were likely to be hoaxes, the viewer seeing little or nothing but being too embarrassed to complain.* → 2. Any burlesque show, nightclub act, or other lawful entertainment featuring chorus girls in scant attire, striptease dances, or the like.

peet. n. = pete.

peeties. n.pl. Loaded dice. *Since c1890; from "repeaters."*

peeve. n. 1. A cause of annoyance, irritation, or anger. *Often in "my pet peeve."* 2. A grudge; a mad. —d. *adj.* Annoyed; irritated; angry.

peewee. n. 1. A person of short stature. *Colloq.* → 2. Any small farm animal; often used as the name for a small or short animal. 3. A small, clear glass marble. *Schoolboy use.* **Peewee.** *prop.n.* A common nickname for a person of short stature. *Thus Peewee Reese, former Los Angeles Dodger shortstop, and Peewee Russell, distinguished jazz clarinetist.*

peg. n. A man with an artificial leg. *From "peg-leg."* v.t. 1. To classify a person, place, or thing with others of a certain type; to recognize or identify, esp. in reference to faults. 2. To taper or bind a pair of trousers toward or at the cuffs. *A style first pop. among c1935 jive enthusiasts.* —s. *n.pl.* 1. The legs. 2. Trousers. *Jive use.*

peg, on the. Under arrest, esp. when charged with a misdemeanor. *Some Army use.*

Peggy. n. A nickname for a one-legged man, esp. a beggar. *Orig. hobo use.*

peg leg. A person who wears a wooden leg. **peg-leg.** *adj.* Wearing a peg leg.

peg out. To die. *Prob. from the cribbage term.*

Pelican; pelican. n. 1. A Louisianan. 2. A cynical, tough woman. *Some underworld use.* 3. A glutton: a heavy eater. *Some C.C.C., Army, and USN use since c1935.*

pellet. n. A ball, usu. a baseball, but sometimes a football or golf ball.

pelter. n. 1. A horse, usu. an inferior or cheap one. 2. A fast horse.

pen. n. A prison of any kind, esp. a large state or federal one. *Orig. hobo use. Common by 1900. Colloq. "Pen" from "penitentiary" reinforced by "pen" = an enclosure, as for animals, and perh. by the Romany "steripen" = prison, which is also a possible orig. for "stir."*

pencil. n. [taboo] The penis.

pencil-pusher. n. Lit. and fig., one whose work is writing with a pencil, hence, an office clerk or clerical worker; a reporter, a bookkeeper, a navigator on a bomber, and the like; specif., one who works at a desk in an office in a nonexecutive capacity.

pencil-shover. n. = pencil-pusher.

penguin. n. 1. Any nonflying aviator, as an administrative officer. *Air Force use since c1925.* 2. An actor who appears in full dress as part of a crowd scene, but has no lines to speak or important action to perform. *Movie studio use.*

penman. n. 1. A forger. 2. A high school student who writes his own letter of excuse for absence and signs his parent's name to it, or who signs his own report card. *Rock and roll use, c1955.*

Pennsy. n. 1. The Pennsylvania Railroad. 2. A student, faculty member, or alumnus of the Univ. of Pennsylvania.

penny. n. A policeman. *From "cop" considered as an abbr. of "copper," from which most U.S. penny coins are made. As do most sl. words for policemen, this conveys contempt and disrespect, as well as a reduction of status to the minimum. Rock and roll and general adolescent use since c1955.*

penny ante. Involving only small sums of money; insignificant; unimportant. *From the poker term = a game in which the players ante only a penny to the pot before each hand.*

penny-dog. *v.t.* To pester someone, usu. for money or an opinion; to curry favor; to follow. *Dial.* *n.* A foreman or boss of a crew of manual laborers, esp. a foreman in a coal mine. *Dial.*

penny-pincher. *n.* A stingy or frugal person.

pen yen. *n.* Opium. *Underworld and narcotics addict use since c1920. From the Chinese, entered U.S. sl. via the West Coast, prob. San Francisco.*

peola. *n.* A very light-complexioned Negro, esp. a girl or young woman. *Negro use.*

people. *n.sing.* A person, esp. a stranger; used in direct address. *Movie use.*

Peoria. *n.* Soup, esp. a thin soup made by boiling a few scraps of vegetables or meat in a lot of water. *Hobo use since c1920. From "purée," by folk ety.*

pep. *n.* Energy, vim; enthusiasm, spirit, zest; initiative, gumption; the energy and enthusiasm that comes from health and high spirits; alertness. *Since c1915; wide sl. use during mid-1920's. Common enough since c1930 to be considered colloq. American emphasis on youth, action, and mobility makes pep a major virtue; thus many products are advertised as supplying pep. From "pepper."* *adj.* Descriptive of anything that supplies or evokes pep. *—less. adj.* Lacking pep. *Since c1925. —py. adj.* 1. Having pep; full of pep; spry; alert. → 2. Capable of starting quickly or running efficiently at high speeds; said of motors, automobiles, and airplanes. *Since c1925.*

pepper. *n.* A fast game of pitch-and-catch; infield practice; both uses by baseball players. *Since c1920. v.t.* 1. To hit a person with a series of rapid blows. *From "pepper-and-salt."* 2. To throw a baseball fast and straight. 3. To hit a baseball or golf ball sharply.

pepper-upper. *n.* Any person or thing that supplies pep, peps up, or refreshes; *Since c1940.*

pep rally. 1. A meeting, either scheduled or spontaneous, at which speakers, cheer leaders, and students try to arouse and display enthusiasm, usu. for their team in an impending sports contest. *Student use. since c1925.* → 2. A meeting to arouse enthusiasm and confidence among party workers during a political campaign; a meeting to stimulate enthusiasm among workers for their company or its product; any meeting to evoke support for a given cause, goal, or the like. *Since c1940.*

pep talk. An exhortatory harangue designed to arouse enthusiasm, as at a pep rally. *Since c1925.*

pep up. To excite, stimulate, enliven, or put pep into someone or something. *Since c1925.*

perc. *v.* = perk.

perch. *v.i., v.t.* To neck.

percolate. *v.i.* 1. To run smoothly and easily, said of automobiles and motors. *Some use since c1920.* → 2. To think or act efficiently. *Some use since c1925.*

percolator. *n.* = shake.

Percy boy. A sissy.

Percy-pants. *n.* A sissy.

perk; perc. *n.* Percolated coffee, as opposed to that boiled in a pan. *Orig. cowboy use; later hobo use. v.i.* To function well, to go smoothly; said esp. of motors, as an automobile. *Since c1925. From "percolate."*

perker-upper. *n.* = pepper-upper.

persnickety. *adj.* Fussy; fastidious; punctilious; snobbish. *Since c1890. Once dial., now colloq.*

persuader. *n.* Any weapon, usu. a revolver, but sometimes a policeman's nightstick or a knife. *Most commonly used in movies about the underworld. Some general use since c1850.*

peso. *n.* An American dollar. *Some use since c1925. From the lowest denomination of Mexican paper* *currency, which also uses the "$" sign.*

pet. *v.i., v.t.* To kiss and caress intimately or passionately; to spoon or neck. *Very common c1910–c1930. Orig. student use. Replaced "spoon" and was replaced by "neck."* **—ting.** *n.* The act or instance of passionate, intimate caressing and kissing. *In common oral use until c1930 by students, thereafter wide written and oral use by older groups.*

pete; peet; peat. *n.* A safe. *Underworld use since c1915. From "peter."*

pete-box. *n.* = pete.

pete-man. *n.* A safe-blower; a safe-cracker. *Underworld use since c1920.*

peter. *n.* 1. A trunk. 1848: criminal use. 2. Pills or injections that render one unconscious; knock-out drops.

pet peeve. An idiosyncratic dislike; a major dislike or annoyance.

petrified. *adj.* Drunk, esp. stupid or insensible as a result of intoxication.

petting party. A period or session of petting, usu. by one couple.

pez. *n.* A head of hair, mustache, or goatee. *Bop musician use since c1946.*

Pfui! *exclam.* = Phooey!

phantom. *n.* 1. A person who is on a payroll under an assumed name. → 2. A person, usu. a relative or close friend of a public official, who is paid for performing work that is not done or is unnecessary.

phedinkus. *n.* Boloney; phonus bolonus. *Prob. synthetic.*

pheeze; feeze. *v.t.* To pledge a student for membership in a fraternity or sorority.

phenagle. *v.* = finagle.

phenom. *n.* A skilled or gifted person, usu. in sports. *From "'phenomenal."*

Phi Bete. 1. The Phi Beta Kappa society. 2. A member of Phi Beta Kappa. *Both common student use.*

Phillie; Philly. *prop. n.* Philadelphia, Pennsylvania.

phiz. *n.* The face. *From "physiognomy."*

phlug; phflug; flug. *n.* A foolish old married woman. *Another Runyonism that sounds "from the Yiddish," but isn't.*

Phoebe. *n.* In crap-shooting, the point 5.

phoney; phony; fon(e)y. *adj.* Not genuine or faked; counterfeit; insincere. *Very common since c1900. The ety. is not clear. "Phoney" occurs today somewhat more commonly than "phony."* *n.* 1. A phoney thing; a fake; a counterfeit. 2. A phoney person; an insincere person; one whose words and attitudes are assumed in order to impress others; one whose outward habits do not reveal his true character.* → 3. A pompous, punctilious person; a snob; a stuffed shirt; one who pretends to be hep but isn't. *Very common since c1935. Wide student use since c1945. v.t.* To fake something. **—man.** *n.* A peddler, street vendor, or auctioneer of cheap or imitation jewelry. *Carnival, circus, and hobo use.*

phoney up. To exaggerate or lie, usu. in filling out official forms, job applications, etc.

phoniness. *n.* The quality or state of being phoney; insincerity.

phono. *n.* A phonograph.

phonus bolonus, (the). *n.* Something or someone phoney or of a quality below that represented; anything cheap, gaudy, or of inferior quality; insincere speech, exaggeration, a line; wrong or misleading advice, a bum steer. *Usu. with "the." From "phoney" plus "boloney."*

phoo! *exclam.* = Phooey!

Phooey!; Fooey!; Pfui!; Fooy!; Fuie! *exclam.* A term of contempt, distaste, or disbelief. *Common since c1930. From the Yiddish "fooy," "fooey," reinforced by the Ger. "pfui."*

photo. *n.* A photograph. *Very common colloq.*

photog; fotog. *n.* A photographer. *Common since c1930.*

piano. *n.* Spare-ribs. *From the resemblance of the bones to piano keys. Some Negro use.*

pic. *n.* A movie. *Some theater use, orig. pop. by trade paper "Variety." The plural, which is more common, is "pix."*

pick 'em up and lay 'em down. 1. To dance. 2. To run, esp. to run quickly.

picker-upper. *n.* 1. One who or that which picks up; one who picks up, or looks for, a pick-up. 2. Any food or drink that, supposedly, gives one energy or vitality; a pepper-upper.

pickle. *v.t.* To ruin or destroy; to kill; fig., to preserve by embalming. —d. *adj. usu. pred. adj.* Drunk. *Since c1900; common by c1920.*

pickle-puss. *n.* A sour-faced, disagreeable, or pessimistic person; a sour-puss.

pick-me-up. *n.* 1. A drink or snack, usu. containing sugar, caffein, or alcohol, taken in the supposition that it will provide energy or stimulation. 2. A drink of whisky, esp. as a cure for fatigue or a hangover, to restore confidence, etc. *Colloq.; common use.*

pick-up; pickup. *n.* 1. The act or instance of inviting or taking another into one's automobile for a free ride. *Since c1925; orig. student use.* → 2. A person, usu. a woman, who has accepted a social invitation from a stranger; a person, usu. a man, whose personal invitation to a stranger has been accepted; a person who has made a date by accosting or by being accosted by a stranger, usu. in the street, a bar, or other public place. *Often, but by no means always, the ultimate purpose of such invitation or acceptance is sexual intercourse. Student and Army use since c1930; increasing popularity until W.W.II when it became almost stand.* 3. An arrest by the police. 4. An im-

promptu meal; a drink, esp. of whisky, tea, coffee, or bottled soft drink. *adj.* Having met and worked together only for a specif. purpose; organized temporarily until a specif. job is accomplished. *Usu. said of musicians or athletes who are strangers but play together as a band or team for a specif. engagement or game. Orig. Negro use.* **pick up.** 1. To arrest. *Orig. underworld use, now universally used.* 2. To offer a person a free ride in an automobile; lit., to stop one's car in order to allow another to enter. *Since c1925.* → 3. To meet someone at a specified time and place before proceeding elsewhere. *Colloq.* → 4. To proffer to or to accept a social invitation from a stranger, usu. of the opposite sex. *The connotation is that of sexual activity.* 5. To be alert to or enthusiastic about; to be on the ball. → 6. To comprehend, to understand.

picnic. *n.* 1. An enjoyable or easy task, occupation, or the like; often in the negative "no picnic" = something disagreeable or difficult. → 2. Specif., a satisfying, enjoyable, easily attained experience of necking or sexual intercourse; a "ball"; specif., a prohibited, unrestricted, uninhibited good time or pleasure. *Jive, student, and W.W.II Armed Forces use.* 3. A thoroughly good time; anything enjoyable, as any entertainment or social gathering.

picture, the. *n.* A comprehensive understanding or view; a presentation of all the essential facts and relationships pertaining to the subject in hand. *E.g., the question, "Get the picture?"*

picture gallery. 1. The tattooed man in a circus side show. *Circus use.* 2. A file of photographs of known or wanted criminals kept by police departments and other law enforcement agencies.

pictures. *n.* Those playing cards which have pictures on them: kings, queens, and jacks.

pie. *n.* Any easy task; anything easy to win or earn; a weak opponent or any complex of factors that produce an easy victory, business success, or the like.

piece. *n.* 1. A share; a financial interest in any business, entertainment, or gambling project, as a stage play, a night club, a boxer, etc. 2. A gun, usu. a pistol or zip gun. *Teenage street-gang use since c1955.*

piece of change; piece of jack. An amount of money, usu. said of a pleasing amount, as "a nice piece of change."

piece [someone] off. 1. To pay another person part of one's wages in return for a job. 2. To pay a bribe. 3. To lend a small amount of money to a needy friend. *All uses orig. maritime; later underworld use.*

piece of trade. A prostitute; a promiscuous woman; a woman considered sexually.

piece up. To divide loot. *Some underworld use.*

pie-eyed. *adj.* Drunk. *Common since cW.W.I.*

pie in the sky. 1. A bourgeois heaven, concept of heaven, or earthly Utopia. *Orig. an epithet used by members of the I.W.W. (International Workers of the World) to taunt nonsympathizers, idealists, conventionally religious opponents, etc.* → 2. Heaven; Utopia. *Cynical use.*

piffle. *exclam.* Mild exclamation to signify disbelief or indifference; bunk; boloney. *n.* Drivel; nonsense; bunk.

pig. *n.* 1. Any fat, sloppy, disfavored person. *Colloq.* 2. A girl or woman having a sloppy appearance; a girl or woman with "sloppy" morals; a passionate or promiscuous woman; any girl or woman. *Common, esp. among male students.* 3. A race horse, esp. a cheap or inferior one. 4. A leather pocketbook or wallet.

From "pigskin." Orig. underworld use. —gy. *n.* A toe. *From the nursery game and rhyme.* —skin; pig-skin. *n.* A football. *Though now made of cowhide, footballs were once covered with pigskin. Since c1900; now colloq. adj.* Pertaining to football.

pigeon. *n.* 1. = stool-pigeon. 2. = mark. A victim of a swindle; one who has been duped; an innocent or naive person, one easy to dupe or take advantage of. 3. A girl or young woman. *Often used affectionately and possessively, e.g., "My pigeon." Ex. of sl. word used exclusively by men, as are most sl. words for women.*

pig-headed. *adj.* Stubborn; stubborn and uninformed or stupid. *Colloq. since c1920.*

pig-iron. *n.* Whisky, esp. inferior, home-made, or bootleg whisky. *Dial.*

pig it. To stop running or reduce one's running speed owing to fatigue or lack of wind; fig., to run as poorly as a pig.

pig-meat. *n.* 1. A girl or woman, esp. an inexperienced but sexually willing girl or an old promiscuous woman. *Orig. Negro use.* 2. An old, sickly, or often defeated person, esp. a prize fighter; fig., one ready to die.

pig salve. Lard. *Dial.*

pig's eye, in a; pig's eye, in the. Not at all; never. *Always used after an affirmative statement, to make it negative. Usu. heard as "in a pig's eye," although often written "in the pig's eye."*

pig-sticker. *n.* 1. A sword. *Student Reserve Officers Training Corps use since c1920.* 2. A children's sled, esp. an old-fashioned sled with upturned runners in the front. *Dial.*

pig sweat. 1. Beer. 2. Inferior whisky or liquor of any kind.

piker. *n.* 1. A stingy person; a miser; a small-minded person who is unwilling to assume risks. *Since c1900; now colloq.* → 2. A coward; one who accepts only easy tasks. *Since c1915.*

pile. *n.* Any large sum of money, usu. belonging to one person or agency; lit., a pile of money. *v.i.* To run rapidly, usu. in chase. —*s.* *n.pl.* A large amount of money; used either absolutely or with "of" followed by "money" or a synonym.

pile up. 1. To run aground, said of a ship. *Maritime use.* → 2. To wreck an automobile or airplane.

pile-up. *n.* An automobile accident or wreck, esp. one involving several cars in one collision.

pilfered. *adj.* Drunk. *Dial.*

pill. *n.* 1. An unlikable, obnoxious, insipid, or disagreeable person, esp. a chronic complainer or nuisance. *Early 19C Eng. sl.* = *a platitude, a cliché.* 2. A baseball. *Colloq. since c1920.* 3. An opium pellet, for smoking. 4. A Nembutal capsule. *Drug addict use.* 5. Any sedative. 6. A bomb. *Some W.W.II use.*

pillow. *n.* 1. A boxing glove. *Some prize fight use since c1900.* 2. In baseball, a base.

pillow-puncher. *n.* A maid; lit., one who makes up beds; a cabin girl.

pill pad. A place where addicts gather to take any kind of drug. *Since c1950.*

pill-peddler. *n.* 1. A physician. 2. A pharmacist or student of pharmacy.

pill-pusher. *n.* = pill-peddler. *A later term fairly common in Armed Forces during W.W.II.*

pill-roller. *n.* = pill-peddler.

pilot. *n.* 1. A manager of a sports team or athlete. 2. A jockey.

pimp. *n.* 1. A youth who does menial chores at a logging camp, ranch, or mine; a boy who carries water, washes dishes, or the like. *Since c1915. adj.* Effeminate.

pimple. *n.* 1. The human head. *Orig. prize fight use.* 2. A saddle.

pin. *v.t.* To give or accept a fraternity pin as an indication of intention to become engaged, as an indication of possessive interest, or to signify a "going

steady" relationship. *Student use since c1935.*

pin, pull the. 1. To quit a job. 2. To leave a town. 3. To leave one's wife, family, or friends. *Orig. a railroad term, "pull the pin" = to uncouple.*

pinch. *v.t.* 1. To steal, esp. to steal a small item of little value. 2. To arrest. *Said to be from Ital. sl. "pizzicane" = to pinch, to arrest, but the Eng. seems to be older.* *n.* An arrest.

pinch-gut. *n.* A miser.

pinch-hit. *v.i.* 1. In baseball, to bat as a substitute for the regularly scheduled batter, esp. at a critical point in the game. → 2. To become a substitute for any regular worker, speaker, performer, or the like; to take another's place. *v.t.* To send in a substitute batter in baseball. *E.g., "The manager pinch-hit Jones for Smith."* **pinch hit.** *n.* In baseball, a hit obtained by a batter who is pinch-hitting.

pineapple. *n.* 1. A hand grenade. *Wide W.W.I and W.W.II Army use. From its shape and also from its exterior, which is often knurled or nodulose like a pineapple to give a better grip.* 2. Any small bomb or home-made explosive device, esp. one that can be thrown by hand. *Underworld use; very common c1930.* 3. = crew cut.

pin [someone's] ears back. To defeat; to inflict physical or verbal punishment on; to administer a comeuppance.

pine overcoat. A coffin, esp. a cheap one.

pine-top. *n.* Whisky. *Dial. and obs.*

ping jockey. Any military or civilian worker whose job it is to monitor electronic equipment, especially warning or detecting equipment, that gives off audio or visual responses, as radar or sonar devices. *Orig. W.W.II USN use, applied to monitors of sonar detection devices; now applied to any human monitor or receiv-*

er of intelligence from electronic devices.

ping-wing. *n.* An injection of a narcotic, usu. into the arm, or "wing." *Narcotic addict use.*

pin-head; pinhead. *n.* A stupid person. *Colloq. since c1895.*

pink. *n.* **1.** A white person. *Negro use.* **2.** A mild political radical; esp. one sympathetic to, but not actually working for, the international Communist movement. **3.** Lit. and fig., the legal certificate of car ownership; fig., the right to drive one's car. *Thus, for traffic law violations one may lose one's "pink." Orig. and mainly hot-rod use. Because such certificates of ownership are often printed on pink paper.* **adj.** = **pinko; Pinkerton.** *n.* A member of the Pinkerton Detective Agency; the Pinkerton Detective Agency; hence any detective or plainclothesman. *The Pinkerton Agency was founded by Allan Pinkerton in 1850 and carried on by his descendants. During the Civil War it became a quasi-official intelligence organization for the Union Army. Later the firm supplied alarm systems and guards to private industry, thus incurring the wrath of hobos who had cause to fear Pinkerton guards on railway property and elsewhere. Later still the firm supplied strike-breakers to industry during the period of intense labor disputes in the first decades of the 20C; labor union and radical elements thus joined the hobo and criminal worlds in their fear and hatred of the Pinkertons.* **Pinkie.** *n.* A Pinkerton detective; any detective.* **—o.** *adj.* Radical or liberal, usu. with the connotation of harmlessness. *The meaning of the word has changed as the complexion of the radical movements in the U.S. has changed. Orig. it meant "anarchistic." Since c1945 it has been applied primarily to communist sympathizers, and in cases of heated debate it can come to* mean "communist" or "traitor." *On the other hand, it is a word often used in smear campaigns against thoroughly respectable liberal politicians.* **n.** One suspected of being a political radical, specif. a communist.

pink, in the. In good health. *Short for "in the pink of physical condition" or "in the pink of health."*

pink slip. A discharge notice; notification to a worker that he has been dismissed. *Common since c1925. From the traditional printed notice, usu. put in an employee's pay envelope.* **pinkslip.** *v.t.* To fire; to dismiss.

pink tea. 1. A formal or elaborate social affair; usu. used jocularly or slightingly. **2.** A social affair restricted to the elite of any community.

pink-toes. *n.sing.* A light-complexioned Negro girl. *Negro use.*

pinky. *n.* **1.** The little finger. *Most common on East Coast. Apparently a childhood word taken into adult vocabularly.* **2.** An attractive, light-skinned Negro girl. *Negro use.* **adj.** Pertaining to the little finger; thus the common "pinky ring" = a ring worn on the little finger.

pinochle season. The off-season in the garment industry; lit., the season when workers play pinochle instead of working. *Amer. Yiddish orig.*

pin [blame for something] on. To accuse; to impute a wrongdoing to someone.

pins. *n.pl.* The human legs. *Now colloq.*

pin-shot. *n.* An injection of a drug made with a safety pin and an eye-dropper in lieu of a hypodermic needle. *Drug addict use.*

pinto. *n.* **1.** A coffin. *Lorenzo D. Turner's "Africanisms in the Gullah Dialect" indicates that this word is of African origin, taken over from slaves by American whites. Dial.* **2.** A piebald or mottled horse. *Colloq.; orig.*

*Western use; from Sp. "pinto" =
painted.*

pin-up. *n.* A photograph or other
depiction of a pretty girl. *Although a pin-up can be a picture
of a sweetheart, the term was
most commonly used during
W.W.II to mean a publicity
photograph of a motion-picture
actress, usu. attired and posed in
such a way as to accentuate her
sexual appeal. From the custom
of pinning such photographs to
tent and barracks walls. adj.* Sexually attractive; pretty.

pin-up girl. A sexually attractive
young woman, usu. a movie star,
model, or the like.

pip. *n.* A remarkable or excellent
person or thing; a pippin. *Common since c1915. adj.* Remarkable; excellent; attractive.
—peroo. *n.* A pip or pippin.

pip, the. *n.* Annoyance jocularly
considered as a mythical disease.
From the disease of chickens.

pipe. *n.* 1. A cinch; any operation
or task easily performed. *From
"lead pipe cinch."* 2. A letter,
note, or other written message.
Circus use. 3. A business or social conversation. *Carnival pitchman use. From "stovepipe." v.t.*
1. To write a letter; to send a
message. 2. To talk; to tell; to
give information. 3. To look or
look at; to notice or observe; to
see; esp. to look at something because it is unusual or remarkable. **—s.** *n.pl.* The vocal cords,
the larynx, esp. of a singer; fig.,
any and all organs involved in
speaking, singing, or breathing.

pipe, hit the. 1. To smoke opium.
→ 2. To smoke any drug, such as
a marijuana cigarette.

pipe course. An easy course, esp.
in college.

pipe down. To stop talking; to
shut up; to discontinue any kind
of noise; often used as a command. *Orig. USN use; wide USN
sl. during W.W.I. By c1925 Army
and student use; colloq. since
c1930.*

pipe dream. Any plan, scheme,
goal, idea, or ideal that is as unrealistic as the dreams of an
opium addict after smoking an
opium pipe. *Colloq.*

pipe [someone] off. 1. To blacklist a person; to publicize the fact
that a person is unwelcome. *From
the nautical use.* 2. To complain
about someone to the police.

piss and vinegar. Energy; viva-
ciousness; mischievousness. *Not
considered taboo.*

piston. *n.* A slide trombone. *Synthetic use.*

pit boss. 1. The foreman of a mining crew. 2. Any foreman.

pitch. *n.* 1. A pitchman's or street
vendor's place of business or arrangement of wares. A "high
pitch" is one set up on a box,
wagon, automobile, or the like.
A "low pitch" is set on the
ground or pavement. *Pitchman
use.* 2. The sales talk or spiel
given by a pitchman. *Pitchman
use.* → 3. Any sales talk or speech
intended to persuade, convince,
or gain sympathy; an exaggerated story; any utterance as a
"line," intended to benefit the
speaker. 4. = pitchman. *These
meanings all were orig. pitchman, carnival, and circus use;
they became common by c1930.*
5. A preliminary, exploratory, or
speculative amorous gesture or
verbal proposition to one of
the opposite sex. 6. A specif. situation or state of affairs, or an explanation of it;
a proposition, deal, or plan of
procedure; the picture; an angle.
*From "pitch" = a sales talk or
story. Common since W.W.II. v.t.*
1. To sell gadgets, novelties, or
other small articles of merchandise on the street or at a fair
or carnival by demonstrating
one's wares and exhorting passers-by to buy; said of a pitchman. *Since c1925.* 2. To give a
party; to throw a party. *v.i.* 1.
To sell or to make one's living
by selling as a pitchman. 2. To
use a spiel or line; to attempt to

display charm. 3. To make amorous advances to one of the opposite sex. 4. To exaggerate; to speak boastingly; to shoot the bull. —man. n. 1. One who sells gadgets, novelties, or any small items of merchandise on the street or at a fair or carnival by demonstrating his wares and exhorting people to buy. *Since c1925; now colloq.* → 2. A television announcer who demonstrates a product while exhorting viewers to buy by mail. *Since c1950. In the early days of television some of these announcers were experienced pitchmen from fairs and carnivals.*

pitching, in there. 1. Making an effort. *From baseball use.* 2. Working diligently; defending one's rights; not letting oneself be defeated, insulted, or victimized.

pitch-out. n. 1. In baseball, a pitch thrown wide of the plate, enabling the catcher to receive the ball quickly and surely, usu. in order to catch a runner off base or prevent a runner from stealing a base. 2. In football, a short, quick pass over the opponent's linemen; it differs from a regular pass in that the passer throws or pushes the ball from him without cocking his arm. pitch out. To throw a pitch-out in either baseball or football.

pix. n.pl. 1. Motion pictures; the motion-picture business; the singular is pic. *Pop. by trade paper "Variety"; since c1936.* 2. Photographs, esp. the photographs used to illustrate a specif. article or feature in a newspaper or magazine; illustrations; artwork. *Wide newspaper use.*

pixie. n. An extreme, modern woman's hair style consisting of very short hair, almost as short as a man's standard haircut, worn straight and featuring ragged or zig-zag bangs. pixilated. *adj.* Bewildered; eccentric; crazy; drunk. *Since c1850; mainly dial.*

Fig., meaning prob. = affected by pixies.

pizzazz. n. Power; force; pep; aggression; audacity.

P.J.'s. n.pl. Pajamas; a pair of pajamas. *Common written and spoken abbr.*

place. n. 1. A gathering point, such as a bar, restaurant, a particular apartment, a particular house, esp. the known gathering point of the members of any specific group. 2. Second place in a race or contest. *v.i.* 1. To finish second in a race or contest. → 2. To finish well enough in a race or contest to receive a prize.

plainer. n. 1. A street beggar; a bum. *Dial.* 2. A chronic complainer. *Dial.*

plank; plank down; plank up; plank out. *v.i.,* (usu.) *v.t.* 1. To pay or put down money, esp. cash. *All forms colloq.* 2. To slam down; to place.

plank-owner. n. A sailor who has served on one ship for an exceptionally long time, esp. a sailor who has served on a ship since it was commissioned. *Some USN use.*

plant. *v.t.* 1. To bury, as a corpse; to bury or cache an object, goods, or money. *Since c1860.* 2. To hide something. *Orig. underworld use.* → 3. Specif., to secrete incriminating evidence in such a way that when it is found it will tend to cast blame on another person. 4. To land a blow, as with the fist. *n.* 1. = shill. *Since c1925.* 2. A hiding place; a hideout. *Underworld and hobo use.* → 3. A cache, usu. of stolen money or goods; anything, usu. stolen, that is hidden or stored. 4. A frameup. 5. A spy; a police spy.

plaster. n. 1. A banknote, esp. a one-dollar bill. 2. One who follows another; a tail or shadow. 3. A subpoena; a summons; a warrant for arrest. *v.t.* To mortgage, esp. a house. —ed. *adj.* Drunk. *Usu. a pred. adj. Some use since c1880; very pop. c1920–*

c1940. One of the most common words = drunk.

plate. *n.* 1. An exceptionally well- or stylishly dressed person. *From "fashion plate."* 2. An attractive woman. *A meliorative, modern form of "dish." Both meanings are fairly common.* —s. *n.pl.* The feet. *From "plates of meat" = feet, in rhyming sl.*

plater; platter. *n.* Any race horse; specif. an inferior race horse. *A plater is a race horse of any class or quality, though in modern use a horse not of the best class is implied. Orig. "plater" and pronounced with long "a."*

platter. *n.* 1. = plater. 2. A modern disc-shaped phonograph record; esp. a recording of jazz or popular music. *Some continued general use; now wide rock and roll use.* 3. In baseball, home plate. 4. A discus. *Sports use.*

play. *n.* 1. = action. → 2. Patronage, esp. at a gambling establishment. → 3. An amount of money, or the total bet during a specif. gambling session. 4. A role of leadership or authority; control of a situation. *v.t.* 1. To date; to go out with; to court. *Student use.* 2. To patronize; to do business with. —**boy.** *n.* A man of any age who is noted for an ostentatious social life, esp. one who is often seen in public with different women, usu. at expensive places of entertainment. *The term always implies wealth, education, social standing, and sophistication.*

play around. 1. To pursue a business venture or occupation without serious attitude or intent. 2. To date, court, or have sexual relations with several members of the opposite sex over a comparatively short period of time; to have sexual relations extramaritally.

play ball. 1. To begin. *From the umpire's traditional order to start a baseball game.* 2. = play ball with.

play ball with. 1. To co-operate with; to comply with; to do business with; often by way of a compromise; to be fair or honest with. 2. To appease; to give in to. *Specif., to be forced to co-operate or comply with another's request in order to receive a favor or preferred treatment, or because of blackmail or extortion.*

play catch with = play ball with.

played out. 1. Without funds; broke. *From the gambling use.* 2. Tired; exhausted. 3. No longer usable, esp. too well known to be effective, entertaining, or to elicit enthusiasm, usu. said of a type of entertainment, story, play or the like.

play for, make a. To use one's charm to impress one of the opposite sex; to court a girl; to show a romantic interest in one of the opposite sex.

play for keeps = play hard.

play games with. To deceive; to play one rival against another.

play hard. To be tough, mean, immoral, unethical, or dishonest; to do or be willing to do anything to achieve one's goal; said equally of hoodlums, prostitutes, or aggressive businessmen.

play it cool. To be deliberately, or to strive to give the impression of being, unemotional, disattached, and invulnerable; to refuse to show and attempt to feel no emotions, eagerness, enthusiasm, or interest, as a defense mechanism, so one will not be disappointed; to keep one's dignity and pride; not to commit oneself; to refuse to commit oneself. *Orig. and mainly cool, far out, and beat use. Some student, teenage, and general use since c1955.*

play the [someone]. Lit. & fig., to imitate someone, either in manner, function, or attitude; to demand the status or respect due to a social position or character other than one's own. *Thus to "play the duchess" = to act as if one were wealthy and had social status, lit. to affect the manners of a duchess; to "play the hero"*

= to act like and expect to be treated as a hero; to "play the whore" = to be sexually promiscuous or to compromise for personal gain.

play the [something]. To affect an attitude or feeling.

play the dozens. To slander one's or another's parents. *Some Negro use.*

play with = play ball with.

plead the fifth (a five). To refuse to do something; to refuse to state one's opinion, reason, or objection. *Some hip use since c1955. During c1954 several investigations were televised of the U.S. Senate's Criminal Investigation Committee and its Un-American Activities Committee. Thus for the first time the public saw and heard such investigations; many alleged criminals and communists refused to testify "on the ground that it might tend to incriminate me." Refusal to testify for this reason is granted by the Fifth Amendment to the U.S. Constitution.*

plebe. *n.* A first-year student at Annapolis or West Point. *Since c1860; the only common use since c1920.*

pledge. *v.t.* To come to an agreement with a student, binding him to join a specif. fraternity or sorority. *Common student use.* *n.* A student who has accepted an invitation to join a fraternity. *Since c1910.*

plenty. *adv.* Very; exceedingly; thoroughly.

pling. *v.i., v.t.* To beg or beg from. *Hobo use.*

plow the deep. To sleep.

pluck. *v.t.* To rob; to cheat.

plug. *n.* 1. An old worthless horse. *Since c1870.* 2. A counterfeit coin; a plugged coin. 3. An average or inferior prize fighter. *Common since c1915.* 4. A favorable statement; a recommendation; an advertisement; a blurb. *Common since c1935. v.t.* 1. To shoot someone, esp. to kill by shooting. *Since c1925.* 2. To make a favor-

able remark or recommendation about someone or something, esp. as a means of public promotion; to advertise. —ger. *n.* 1. A diligent worker or student. *Since c1900. From "plug."* 2. An enthusiast, a fan, or a spectator who freq. extols the good points of a region, idea, sport, team, etc. 3. A hired killer.

plug, pull the. 1. To dive; to submerge. *Submarine use.* → 2. To withdraw one's support. → 3. To expose another. → 4. To cause trouble.

plug hat. A top hat. *From c1870 to present.*

plug-ugly. *n.* 1. A hoodlum; a tough or ugly-looking ruffian. 2. A prize fighter. 3. A strong, ugly, uncouth man; a rowdy; a tough guy. *In use as early as 1857.*

plum. *n.* Anything, usu. a job, rank, or title, given in recognition of good work or service; esp. a political job given in recognition of service rendered during a political campaign. —my. *adj.* Pleasing, satisfying; rich and mellow.

plumb; —er. *v.t.* To ruin; to make a mistake that is impossible to correct. —ing. *n.* 1. A trumpet. *Swing musician use.* 2. The digestive tract; the bowels. *Both uses usu. humorous.*

plunging neckline. A low V-shaped neckline on a woman's dress, blouse, or the like, usu. intended to reveal part of the breast. *A style pop. c1949 and after.*

plunk; plonk. *n.* Cheap, inferior wine. *v.t.* To shoot. *Since c1890.*

plunk down = plank down. To pay money; to hand over in payment.

plunkie. *n.* A cookhouse waiter.

plush. *adj.* Stylish; luxurious; connoting wealth. Said of a place; esp. a hotel, nightclub, or the like. *From the soft textile plush. v.i.* To be wealthy; to live luxuriously; to display wealth. *n.* Places, ornaments, materials, etc., that connote wealth. —ery. *n.*

A luxurious and high-priced hotel, nightclub, etc. —y. *adj.* Sumptuous; elegant; plush. *An ex. of a sl. adj. adding a suffix that does not change its meaning.*

p. o.; P. O. *n.* The stand. abbr. for "Post Office."

pocket. *n.* 1. The place where one keeps money or valuables, whether it be actually one's pocket, purse, safe, etc. 2. A position between two objects so that one's movements are restricted. 3. An untenable situation; an unsatisfactory business or personal relationship from which one cannot extract oneself. —**book.** *n.* A pocket-sized, paperbound edition of a book, orig. sold for 25¢ or 35¢. *Colloq.*

pocket cabbage = cabbage.

pocket lettuce = lettuce.

pod. *n.* Marijuana.

pogey; pogie; pogy. *n.* 1. Any home provided by charity or government funds for the aged, disabled, etc.; a poorhouse; a government home for disabled veterans; an old-age home; a workhouse. *More recently, confused with and used for "pokey"* = *a jail.* → 2. A jail.

pogey bait; pogie bait; pogy bait; poggie bait. Candy; any kind of sweets. *W.W.I and W.W.II use, primarily by members of Armed Forces.*

poggie. *n.* An Army recruit. *Some Army use.*

point. *n.* 1. The essence; the meaning. *Pop. in "to get the point"* = *to understand. Colloq.* 2. In sports, a score.

point-head; pointy-head. *n.* 1. A hoodlum. 2. A stupid person; one who is not in the know.

poison. *n.* 1. A person, situation, or condition that bodes no good for one. 2. Any person, object, or place that seems to bring bad luck. 3. Liquor, esp. inferior liquor.

poison pen letter. An anonymous letter written to expose, intimidate, threaten, or convey obscene suggestions to the recipient; a malicious letter, often containing false information.

poke. *n.* 1. A wallet, pocket, or purse. *Underworld, carnival, pitchman, vagabond use.* → 2. A pocket. *Archaic & dial.* → 3. Money; the total amount in one's possession. *Rock and roll use since c1955.* 4. In baseball, a hit. 5. A cowboy. *From "cowpoke."* → 6. A hired hand. 7. A slow-moving, slow-talking, or slow-thinking person. *v.t.* 1. To herd, as cattle and sheep. 2. To attempt to influence; to attempt to create enthusiasm or promote action. 3. In baseball, to make a hit. *Most common present use.*

poke a tip. To give a free show or free gifts to attract a crowd. *Orig. pitchman use, later circus and carnival use.*

poke fun [at]. To tease; to chide.

poke-out. *n.* 1. Food, esp. a package of food handed out to a tramp begging at back doors. *Vagabond and tramp use.* 2. An outdoor dinner cooked over wood or charcoal; a gathering for the purpose of preparing and eating such a meal; any long hike or camping trip which includes such meals. *From association with "cowpoke" and his way of life, reinforced by "cookout," "smoke-out"; used by Boy Scouts, suburban residents, etc.*

poker face. 1. A face lacking in expression. 2. A person who does not show emotion. *Used in poker, where one tries not to reveal his hand by his facial expression.*

pokerino. *n.* 1. A game of poker played for small stakes. 2. Any small, insignificant game, business deal, or person.

pokey; poky; poogie. *n.* A jail. *adj.* Slow; small, crowded; like a jail or jail cell.

pole. *v.i., v.t.* 1. To study hard. 2. To hit a baseball very hard. 3. To take a consensus of opinion; to put to a vote. *n.* In baseball, a bat.

police. *v.t.* = police up.

police up. To clean a place or thing; to make a place or thing neat and presentable. *Army use. One can police up a barracks = scrub the floor, make the beds, etc.; police up a parade ground = pick up cigarette butts and trash, etc.; police up one's shoes = shine one's shoes. Wide W.W.II Armed Forces use and carried over into post-war civilian use to a degree.*

polish. *n.* 1. Poise, social grace. 2. Newness, freshness.

polish apples. To curry favor.

polish off. 1. To finish eating or drinking something. 2. To finish a chore; to finish or get rid of something. 3. To get rid of a person; to kill; to render unconscious.

politician. *n.* 1. Any fast, persuasive, charming talker; one with a good spiel or line. → 2. A flatterer; one who courts superiors to win favored treatment. → 3. One who, for any reason, obtains favored treatment, easy jobs, more than his share of praise or rewards, and the like.

politico. *n.* A power-hungry politician; an influential and unethical politician. *From the Ital. and Sp. c1940; was usu. used derog.; now becoming the standard abbr. for politician, losing derog. connotation.*

polluted. *adj.* Drunk. *Common.*

polly. *n.* 1. A woman who enjoys talking and gossiping; a shrew; any fat, old, unpleasant woman. 2. An echo that necessitates retaking a movie or a recording session. *From "polyphony."*

pomp. *n.* 1. Common abbr. for a pompadour. 2. A short haircut. *W.W.II use.*

ponce. *n.* 1. A pimp; a man supported by a prostitute. → 2. A man who is supported by a woman; a man whose wife works.

pond. *n.* Most commonly, the Atlantic Ocean; the Pacific Ocean; any ocean.

pony. *n.* 1. A literal translation of a foreign language text, employed without the teacher's knowledge. *Used at least as early as 1827. Very common.* → 2. Any unethical aid, list of answers, etc., used by a student in a test. → 3. Any physical or mental aid, such as a crutch, reference book, hearing aid, or list of telephone numbers. 4. A small glass for liquor or apéritifs, often bellshaped so that the contents can be more easily held, sniffed, and admired. *Since c1850.* 5. A small glass of beer; the glass itself. *Since c1885; colloq.* 6. A horse. 7. A chorus girl, burlesque dancer, etc.; esp. a small, attractive chorus girl. *Orig. theater use. From the prancing movements of such dancers. v.i., v.t.* To use a literal translation of a foreign language text without the teacher's knowledge.

pony tail. A version of the horse tail style of hair dressing, but for shorter hair. *Very pop. with adolescent girls since c1952.*

pony up. To pay. *Since c1820.*

poo = hot-poo. *interj.* A mild or jocular expression of incredulity, often used to show awareness that one is being teased. *Mainly teenage girl use. n.pl.* Feces. *Mainly child use.*

pooch. *n.* A dog. —**y.** *n.* = pooch. *adj.* Doggy; dog; dog-like.

poodle cut. A style of women's hairdressing in which the hair is cut short all around and curled, thus somewhat resembling the coat of a French poodle. *Common high style c1950–c1952; replaced by the Italian cut.*

poodle-faker. *n.* 1. A self-important newly commissioned officer. *W.W.I use.* → 2. A ladies' man; a man who is subservient to women; a gigolo. *Literally one who emulates a lap dog. In Eng., a "male date."*

poogie = pokey.

poolroom. *n.* An illegal bookmaker's place of business, wherever it is.

poo out. To fail; to make a poor showing; to disappoint.

poop. *n.* **1.** Information, esp. from an official or authentic source; data; facts. *Wide W.W.II Armed Forces use.* **2.** Excrement. *Child bathroom vocabulary.* *interj.* = poo.

pooped. *adj.* Exhausted, fatigued, etc. *Since c1930. Not now as common as "beat" or "bushed" among students and young adults.*

poo-poo. *n.* Feces. *Part of the bathroom baby-talk of very young children.* *v.i.* To defecate.

poop sheet. 1. Any official written announcement, schedule, compilation of data, or the like. *Orig. Army and student use since c1935.* → **2.** Any data sheet; a set of written detailed instructions.

poor-boy. *n.* A very large sandwich, made of a small loaf of bread or long roll cut lengthwise and filled with hot or cold meat, cheese, vegetables, and potatoes in separate sections. *The more elaborate poor-boys actually contain all the courses of a full meal, with an appetizer, such as fish, at one end and a dessert of fruit at the other. Orig. and still most common in New Orleans, but universally known since c1920.*

poor fish. Practically anybody at all; the individual person considered under the aspect of his specif. human characteristics, foibles, problems, and the like.

poor John; poor john. An average man whose fortunes are notably less than he deserves.

poor man's [something or some-one], (the or a). A less famous, less expensive, smaller, or less satisfactory version of something or someone. *The term does not necessarily imply inferiority, though it often does.*

pop. *n.* **1.** Father. From "poppa" or "papa." *Colloq. since c1830.* **2.** A pistol. **3.** A piece of popular music. **4.** A concert of popular music, esp. a concert played by a fairly large orchestra and fea-

turing a mixture of "Tin Pan Alley" songs and light classics. **5.** The common written and spoken abbr. for a popsicle, any ice or ice cream frozen on a stick and sold by street vendors or refreshment stands. *adj.* **1.** The common abbr. for "popular." → **2.** Specif., "popular" as used in music to signify commercially mass-produced sentimental songs as opposed to jazz on one hand and classical music on the other. *Thus there are pop singers, pop records, etc.* —*per.* *n.* A revolver. *Negro use.* —*s.* *n.* Popular music.

Pops; pops. *n.* A nickname or term of direct address, applied to any elderly man. *The familiarity of the term is often intended as a compliment, implying that the named person is up to date enough not to object to the jocose term. Much student and teenage use.*

pop bottle. An inferior camera or enlarger lens. *Photographer use. The term implies that the instrument in question has been made with glass of a quality only good enough to be made into a cheap bottle.*

pop [one's] cork = blow [one's] top.

Pope's nose, the. The derrière of a cooked chicken. *Jocular use.*

pop off. 1. To die. **2.** To kill. **3.** To criticize, complain, brag, rant, or state one's opinions loudly and emotionally; to talk or write volubly. *Since c1930.* **4.** To leave or depart. *A little jocular use. The term is considered affected in the U.S.* **pop-off.** *n.* **1.** An act or instance of popping off. One who pops off or complains loudly with or without cause, esp. one who does so habitually.

poppa. *n.* **1.** One's father. *Colloq.* **2.** Any elderly man. **3.** = daddy; sugar daddy; sweet papa.

pop quiz; pop test. An unexpected examination.

popskull. *n.* Powerful and inferior liquor, usu. home-made. *South-*

*ern mountain and Western
plains use.*

pop to. To come to the military
position of attention, esp. with
great abruptness.

pop-up. *n.* In baseball, a slowly
hit ball caught by the catcher or
an infielder.

porcupine. *n.* A frayed wire rope
or cable. *W.W.II USN use.*

pork-chopper. *n.* A political ap-
pointee, union official, or relative or friend of a politician,
union officer, or the like, who
receives payment for little or no
work; one who is put on a payroll as a favor or in return for
past services.

porkey; porky. *adj.* 1. Very bad;
very poor. 2. Angry.

Port Arthur tuxedo. Khaki pants
and shirt; work clothes.

port-side; portside. *adj.* Left-
handed. *From the nautical term.*
—**r.** *n.* 1. A left-handed baseball
pitcher. 2. A left-handed person.

posh. *adj.* Smart; chic; expressive
of good, or at least expensive,
taste.

possum belly. An extra storage
compartment under a railroad
car. *Hobo lingo.*

posted. *adj.* Well informed. *c1840;
now colloq.*

pot. *n.* 1. A disliked, self-righteous,
self-important person of either
sex, but esp. a woman of middle
age or over. *Since c1930. "Pot"
more often refers to a woman
than a man, thus according with
classical psychoanalytic symbol
analysis, esp. of the mother
image. When used to = a man,
may be reinforced by "pot-belly."*
→ 2. An unappealing, unkempt
girl. *Common student use since
c1935.* 3. A drunkard, esp. a
down-and-out drunkard. *Although word usu. means an unkempt tramp, it has some sophisticated use to mean a successful
man who is also a heavy drinker.*
4. Cheap, inferior, or home-made
whisky; lit., whisky that has been
made in a pot instead of in a regular distillery. 5. Marijuana, esp.

a marijuana cigarette. *Common
addict use.* 6. The total amount
of money bet at any stage in a
hand of poker, i.e., the stakes
that will be won by the winner
of the hand; the stakes in any
gambling game. *Colloq.* 7. A carburetor. *Orig. and mainly sports-
car driver and hot rod use.* 8. An
automobile engine. *Wide hot-rod
use since c1950.* 9. = **pot-belly.**
v.t. 1. To strike someone with
the fist. → 2. To hit a baseball
or golf ball.

potato. *n.* 1. The head. → 2. The
face, esp. an unattractive face. 3.
A dollar. 4. A ball, esp. a baseball.

potato-head. *n.* A stupid person.

potato-trap. *n.* The mouth. *Boxing sl.*

pot-belly. *n.* 1. A large, protruding
abdomen. 2. A man or, infreq., a
woman with a large, protruding
abdomen; a fat man.

pot boiler. A book, play, article,
or the like written merely to
earn money, i.e., to keep the
author's pot boiling; any work
of mediocre quality done by an
artist or craftsman who is capable of a better performance.

potch. *n.* A light blow with the
open hand, a slap; a spanking.
*Used only in speaking to small
children. v.t.* To slap or spank
a child lightly.

pothooks. *n.pl.* Spurs. *Cowboy use.*

pot liquor. The residue of solids
and fluids left in the bottom of
a pot after food, esp. greens and
ham, has been cooked in it.
Stand. Southern use.

pot luck. A meal composed of
odds and ends or leftovers. *Fig.,
a meal composed of whatever one
is lucky enough to find "in the
pot."*

pot out. To fail; said of an engine
in a hot-rod car. *Teenage and
hot rod use since c1950.*

potsky. *v.i.* To idle, loaf, or put-
ter; to mess around. *From the
Yiddish sl. "potske."*

pot-slinger. *n.* A cook.

pots on, have [one's]. To be potted = drunk.

potsy; pottsy; potsie. *n.* A variation of the children's game of hop scotch: a hopping game played with bean bags and squares marked upon the ground or pavement.

potted. *adj.* 1. Drunk. *Fairly common. Orig. flapper use.* 2. Under the influence of narcotics, esp. marijuana.

potted up = potted.

pottrie. *n.* A type of playing marble, usu. white and opaque, resembling china in appearance. *Prob. from "pottery."*

potty. *n.* 1. A small potlike urinal used to toilet-train children; a toilet. *Baby talk.* 2. Any toilet. *Part of the bathroom vocabulary of small children.* 3. In poker, the pot. *adj.* Slightly crazy; eccentric.

pot-walloper. *n.* 1. One who washes pots. 2. A lumber-camp cook.

pot-wrestler. *n.* A chef.

pound. *v.t.* To walk on a sidewalk or a pavement, esp. on one's beat, as a policeman making his rounds. —**er.** *n.* A policeman; lit., one who pounds a beat.

pound brass. To transmit radio messages on a hand key. *Ham radio and Army Signal Corps use.*

pound [one's] ear. To sleep.

pound the books. To study intensely. *Some student use since c1935.*

pound the pavement. To walk the streets in search of a job, either to beg from passers-by, or as a policeman walking his beat; fig., to seek employment.

pour it on. 1. To concentrate or augment one's effort; esp. to intensify one's effort in order to take advantage of an opponent's mistake. 2. To drive an automobile very fast.

pour on the coal. To drive or fly rapidly; to accelerate the speed of a car or plane; to step on the gas.

pout-out. Engine failure in a hot rod. *Hot rod and some general teenage use since c1955.*

P.O.W. A prisoner of war. *Wide W.W.II use. An abbr. that is both written and spoken.* **pow.** *n.* A prisoner of war. *W.W.II and Korean War use. Written but seldom spoken. From "P.O.W."*

powder. *n.* A drink of liquor. *v.i.* To leave; to go away. Also, to run away; to flee. *v.t.* To bat a baseball hard.

powder, take a. To depart; to run away; to leave without paying one's bill. *From the earlier "take a run-out powder."*

powder-bag. *n.* A gunner's mate. *W.W.II USN use.*

powder-puff. *n.* A cautious, shifty boxer, as opposed to a heavy hitter. *v.t.* To hit lightly.

powder [one's] puff. To go to the bathroom; to urinate. *Orig. jocular use. In ref. to traditional female excuse when withdrawing to the ladies' room, i.e., to apply make-up.*

power. *n.* An explosive.

power-house. *n.* 1. A strong, successful sports team, esp. a football team. → 2. A strong athlete, esp. a football player. → 3. Any strong, well-built male. → 4. Any group of people or objects that portend success in a game, sports, business, entertainment, etc. *The term can be applied to a hand of cards, the executives of an organization, a line of merchandise, etc.*

pow-wow. *n.* A conference; a discussion or debate. *Supposedly from an Amer. Indian word = conjurer, medicineman. Colloq.*

P.R. Public relations. *A common written and spoken abbr. Since c1940.*

prairie. *n.* 1. A poorly kept golf course. *Golfer use.* 2. A vacant lot. *Midwestern urban use. Dial.*

prang. *v.t.* 1. To crash or damage a military airplane. → 2. To bomb a target; to destroy a target by bombing from the air. *v.i.* To crash; to be shot down by antiaircraft fire; to be involved in an airplane accident. *n.* A crash landing of a military plane.

prat; pratt. *n.* The human posterior. *v.t.* To move behind someone in order to observe him without being seen or to get into a position to rob him. *Underworld use.*

prat fall; pratfall. 1. A fall on the backside or rump; said of a person. *Often used esp. of falls taken by clowns in comedy routines. Wide theater use.* 2. A defeat, a pitfall.

prat kick. A hip pocket in a pair of trousers. *Mainly underworld use.*

prayer. *n.* A chance. *Always used with a negative, as in "hasn't got a prayer."*

preem. *n.* A first showing of a movie, play, television performance, or the like. *Common theater use. Written and spoken abbr. for "première." v.i., v.t.* To appear on the stage or on television for the first time; to make a première performance. —**ie**;

preemy. *n.* A prematurely born baby. *Orig. hospital argot; now widely known.*

pregnant duck = **ruptured duck.**

prelim. *n.* 1. Any written examination, usu. lasting one class period, given during the progress of a college course, as opposed to the final examination at the end of the course. *Common student use. Usu. stressed on the first syllable.* 2. A minor professional boxing bout preceding the main fight. *Usu. stressed on the second syllable. Both abbrs. for "preliminary" are written and spoken.*

pre-med. *n.* 1. A premedical student. 2. A premedical course of study. *Common written and spoken abbr.*

prep. *n.* 1. In a prep school, a member of the first, or junior, class of students. 2. In college, an undignified upperclass student. 3. A school sports team practice. *All meanings colloq. v.i., v.t.* 1. To attend a prep school. *Wide student use.* → 2. In college, to behave like a preparatory school student; to be boisterous. *adj.* Poor; mean. *In all forms, n., v., adj., "prep" is the common abbr. for "prepare," "preparation."*

prep school; prep-school. *n.* A preparatory school; usu. a private school on the secondary level which prepares students for college. *Common student use. adj.* Characteristic of or connected with a preparatory school. *Usu. connotes social status, manners, wealth, etc. Sometimes also connotes snobbery since some prep schools are exceedingly expensive and aim expressly to prepare their students for admission to the oldest Eastern universities.*

pres; Pres = prez.

preserved. *adj.* Drunk.

presquawk. *v.t.* To inspect [a piece of work] before an official inspection. *W.W.II airplane factory use.*

press roll. In drumming, a roll that rapidly intensifies in volume.

press the bricks. To walk a police beat. *Cf. pound the pavement.*

press the flesh. To shake hands. *Rhyming jive talk.*

pretty. *adj. & adv.* 1. Slightly; considerably; quiet; "little." *As an example of the clichéd, contradictory, and pop. use of "pretty" and "little," James Thurber's humorous ". . . It [a building] was a little big and pretty ugly" will serve as a classic.* 2. = **sitting pretty.**

pretty-boy. *n.* 1. An effeminate, light-complexioned man; a dandy. *Colloq.* 2. A bouncer; a professional strong man. *c1931; circus use. An example of a sl. word taking on a humorous meaning the opposite of the orig. meaning.*

pretty ear. An ear deformed from being hit repeatedly; a cauliflower ear.

pretzel. *n.* 1. A French horn. 2. A German or one of German descent.

pretzel-bender. *n.* 1. A peculiar person; an eccentric; one who thinks in a round-about manner. 2. A wrestler. 3. A heavy drinker; one who frequents bars.

prexy; prexie. *n.* 1. The president of a college, university, or prep school. *Student use.* "*Prexie*" *now seldom used.* 2. The president of a business organization or any other organization. *Both uses almost never cap.*

prez; Prez. *n.* A nickname for a person who is outstanding in his profession. *Lester Young, renowned jazz saxophonist, was called "Prez" by his admirers.*

prick. *n.* A smug, foolish person; a knave, blackguard; a heel, a rat.

prig. *v.t.* To steal.

prince. *n.* An agreeable, generous, or noble person of either sex.

print. *v.t.* To fingerprint a person, as by the police. —**s.** *n.pl.* A set of fingerprints. *Orig. underworld use.*

private eye. A private detective.

privates. *n.pl.* The genitalia.

pro. *n.* 1. Probation. *A common written and spoken abbr.* 2. A person who is on probation, from prison, school, or on a job. 3. A professional in any field of endeavor, esp. a professional athlete, entertainer, or writer; one who is paid for his work or skill, as opposed to an amateur who performs merely for his pleasure. *A written and spoken abbr. Very common.* 4. One who is proficient, experienced, or wise; one who possesses courage, confidence. 5. A prostitute. *This is not an abbr. for "prostitute," but another abbr. for "professional." The cynical implication is that all women can be seduced, the only difference being that prostitutes are professionals. adj.* 1. Professional; of the nature of a paid worker or player, as opposed to an unpaid one. 2. Proficient. *Both meanings written and spoken abbr. of "professional."*

prof. *n.* 1. A college or university professor. 2. A teacher or master of any school. *A written and spoken abbr. for "professor."* —**essor.** *n.* 1. Anyone who wears eyeglasses. 2. An orchestra leader. *Often used jocularly.* 3. The piano player in a bar, brothel, or silent movie house; any piano player. 4. A professional gambler. 5. Any studious person; a book-lover.

prog. *n.* Food. *c1840; underworld use. Still used dial.*

progressive. *n., adj.* Jazz music based on chord progressions, rather than on a melody. The basis of cool and far out jazz music.

prom. *n.* A formal dance or dancing party, usu. one given annually by a college or univ. class or social organization; a ball traditionally held by each class in a college toward the end of the school year. *Abbr. of "promenade." Now virtually stand.*

promote. *v.t.* 1. To steal; to obtain something by cheating or chicanery. *c1915–25; underworld and vagabond use; now common sl.* → 2. To talk [someone] into making a gift or loan. → 3. To beg something [as food]; to wangle.

prom-trotter. *n.* 1. A very popular girl; esp. a female student who attends many formal dances. *Student use.* → 2. A male student who is very active in college social life; one who goes to all the dances and parties. → 3. A ladies' man.

pronto. *adv.* Quickly. *Colloq. From the Sp.*

prop. *n.* 1. A property; any article used by an actor in a play or an act, as a pistol, a book, a glass. *Theater use since 1880.* → 2. The stage crew, property man, and circus tent crew foreman. 3. An airplane propeller. *Used since W.W.I.* 4. A fist. *adj.* False; staged. *From "property."* —**er.** *adj.* Regular; first-rate. —**s.** *n.* 1. A man in charge of stage props. *Theater use since 1900.* 2. The human legs. 3. Falsies; padding worn under a brassière to give a woman the appearance of having large or shapely breasts.

pro-pack. *n.* A small kit or envelope containing a sheath, strong soap, and an astringent, for use as a protection against venereal disease. *Wide W.W.II Armed Forces use. Abbr. for "prophylactic package."*

prophylactic. *n.* A thin rubber sheath worn over the penis during sexual intercourse, usually as a contraceptive device, but legally available only "for prevention of [venereal] disease." *Not as common as "rubber."*

proposition. *v.t.* To approach a person with an offer of employment or to suggest a mutually profitable plan of action, esp. an illegal or unethical job, plan, or action; specif., to ask for sexual favors from a girl or woman, usu. in return for money or other favors to be given her.

prossie; prossy. *n.* A prostitute.

protection. *n.* Bribe money paid to the police, an individual policeman, or politicians, for allowing illegal activities to continue without interference; any money paid to protect the payer without arrest.

protection money = protection.

prowl. *v.t.* To frisk a person; to run one's hands over another's clothing, usu. in search of a gun.

prune. *n.* 1. A slow-witted person; a simpleton; one easily duped. 2. A prudish, scholarly person. → 3. An eccentric; a dreamer. 4. A man; a guy. *All meanings used since c1900.* —d. *adj.* Drunk.

pruneface. *n.* A homely or sad-looking person. Used specif. as a nickname. *Popularized by a pock-marked wrinkle-faced villain in the comic strip "Dick Tracy."*

pruno. *n.* Fermented prune juice; any fermented fruit juice.

prushun; prushon. *n.* 1. A boy tramp who begs for a mature tramp. *Obscurely from "Prus-*

sian." 2. A young homosexual who lives with tramps.

prut. *n.* Dirt, as the sweepings from a floor, deck, or the like. *exclam.* An expression of contempt, disbelief, etc.

p's and q's. Fig., one's own business, field of endeavor, or interest. Used either in "Mind your [own] p's and q's" = mind your own business, or in "He knows his p's and q's" = he knows his business well, he is skilled in his job.

psych; psyche. *n.* 1. Psychology. → 2. A course in the study of psychology. *Student use since c1900; the form "psyche" is archaic. A written and spoken abbr. v.t.* To discuss the motives of another's words or actions, usu. critically.

psycho. *n.* 1. A psychopath. *A written and spoken abbr. Seldom used in the correct psychological sense.* → 2. Any psychotic or neurotic. *The most common use.* → 3. An eccentric; a nut. *adj.* Psychopathic; unbalanced; used to describe anything from mild eccentricity to violent derangement. —**kick.** *n.* A deeply satisfying erotic response.

P.U.; p.u. 1. Phew, said on smelling a bad smell, as something rotting. *Colloq. An exaggerated pronunciation of "phew."* 2. "It stinks."

pub-crawl. *v.i.* = joint hop. *Since c1935; orig. a Briticism.*

pud. *n.* A disliked person. *College sl. c1920.*

pudding-head. *n.* A stupid but lovable person.

puddle-jumper. *n.* A small or dilapidated vehicle, esp. a public train, bus, or plane that makes short or local trips, stopping at every town.

puff. *n.* A weak or cowardly person. —**er.** *n.* The human heart.

pug. *n.* 1. A prize fighter, esp. a small-time prize fighter. *From "pugilist."* 2. Any young tough or mean man.

puka. *n.* Any small, private place, such as a pigeonhole in a desk, a safe, a purse, a small suitcase, or the like. *W.W.II USN use in Pacific. Prob. orig. Polynesian.*

puke. *n.* 1. Vomit. → 2. Fig., any object, person, or situation that is so inferior, obnoxious, ugly, or disliked that it makes one vomit.

pull. *n.* Influence; favorable standing with people of authority or influence; drag. *Colloq.* See leg-pull. *v.t.* 1. To arrest. *From "pull in."* 2. To earn; to receive. 3. To smoke a cigarette. —er. *n.* 1. A smuggler. 2. One who smokes marijuana cigarettes.

pull down. To earn, usu. a specif. sum of money, as a weekly salary.

pulleys. *n.pl.* Suspenders.

pull in. To arrest.

Pull in your ears!; Pull in your neck! 1. Look out! 2. Shut up! 3. Don't be so aggressive. Reconsider. Review the facts.

pull [it] off. 1. To accomplish or obtain, esp. something remarkable, unique, or outrageous. 2. To commit a crime.

pull [something] on [a person]. To deceive someone. *Colloq.*

pull out. To leave; depart. *Colloq. since c1880.*

pull [something] out of the fire. To save from failure or disaster, to turn a potentially disastrous situation into a successful one, to turn defeat into victory; to rescue.

pulp. *n.* 1. A magazine printed on cheap, rough, pulp paper. → 2. Any magazine devoted to sensational and ephemeral literature, for instance, cowboy and detective stories. → 3. A story or article of stereotyped design and sensational contents, usu. written for purely commercial ends. *adj.* Like or pertaining to pulp. *Colloq.*

pump; pumper. *n.* The heart.

pump, on. On credit. *Dial.*

pumpkin; pumkin; punkin. *n.* 1. The human head. 2. A small town or rural community; a rustic place; a town in the

sticks. *Carnival, circus, and theater use.* 3. A football.

pumpkin-head. *n.* A stupid person. *Colloq. since 1850.*

pumpkin-roller; punkin roller. *n.* A farmer. *Colloq. since c1905; now archaic and dial.*

punch. *n.* Force; meaning; pungency. *v.t.* 1. To fail at or to ruin something; esp. to fail a course in school. 2. To herd livestock, esp. cattle. —er. *n.* 1. A cowboy. 2. A telegraph operator. **Punchy.** *prop.n.* A nickname applied disparagingly to any person, implying that he is confused or mentally subnormal from, or as though from, blows on the head. **punchy.** *adj.* 1. = punch-drunk. 2. Forceful, emphatic, having punch.

punch-drunk. *adj.* 1. Slow or uncertain in thought or actions; not in complete control of one's thoughts and movements, esp. when due to sustained concussions in prize fighting; groggy, dizzy; fig., drunk from being punched on the head freq. → 2. Groggy, dazed, or dizzy for any reason; mentally or emotionally exhausted, esp. from a series of failures or personal misfortunes.

punch line. 1. The last line, sentence, or part of a joke that gives it meaning and humor. → 2. The last line, sentence, or part of a story, experience, or incident that gives it meaning or an unexpected ending.

punch-out. *n.* A fist fight. **punch out.** To leave, to quit, to abandon. *From an office or factory worker's punching a time card as he leaves work for the day.*

punish. *v.t.* To eat or drink copiously.

punk. *n.* 1. A petty hoodlum; one who thinks he wants to be a hoodlum but lacks real toughness and experience. 2. A young or inexperienced person. Specif. a boy tramp or child hobo; a boy, youth, or beginner; a young prisoner; any C.C.C. boy, except an official leader; a child or adolescent of either sex; a youngster. → 3. An inferior or unimportant person. Specif. a small-time criminal. 4. An inferior prize fighter, jockey, pool-player, etc. 5. A lackey; esp. a waiter or porter. 6. A man or guy; esp. a worthless man; a petty criminal. 7. Any young circus animal, specif. a baby lion or elephant. *Circus talk.* 8. Bread. *Since c1880; tramp, logger, soldier, and maritime use. May be from the Hindustani, via Brit. Army use.* 9. A liquid or salve sold as a household remedy; patent medicine. *Pitchman use. adj.* Of poor quality; bad; inferior; unwell. **—er.** *n.* A greenhorn.

punk out. To quit; to become cowardly; to turn chicken. *Orig. teenage street-gang use; some general teenage use since c1955.*

punk-pusher. *n.* The boss of hay workers in a circus. *Circus use.*

punk sergeant. A dining-room orderly. *Orig. Army use.*

pup. *n.* 1. A young, inexperienced person. 2. A wiener on a roll; a hot dog.

puppy = pup.

puppy-dog feet. In playing cards, clubs.

puppy love. Preadolescent love. *A disparaging term used by adults. Since c1830; now colloq.*

pups. *n.pl.* The feet; the dogs.

pups, have = have kittens. *Since c1900.*

pup tent. A small tent suitable for sheltering one or two persons sleeping on the ground. *Since c1900 common Army use.*

pup tents. Overshoes. *Circus use.*

purey. *n.* A kind of clear glass playing marble. *Prob. from "pure."*

purge. *n.* A newly arrived prisoner of war; a group of such prisoners. *Used by W.W.II American prisoners of war in German detention camps.*

purp. *n.* A dog or pup. *Since c1865.*

purple. *adj.* Erotic; lurid.

push. *n.* 1. A gang of neighborhood boys organized to fight other such gangs. 2. A discharge from one's job; the sack. 3. A major or sustained effort; a critical, determining, or final effort. *Usu. in "the big push." v.t.* 1. To drive a motor vehicle; specif. a truck or taxi. 2. To kill a person. 3. To approach close to a specified age. *Colloq.* 4. To sell; to encourage customers to buy or patronize; esp., to hawk merchandise from door to door. *Colloq.* → 5. Specif., to sell or distribute illicit drugs to narcotics addicts; to deal in the illegal narcotics trade. *Addict use; fairly well known.* 6. To distribute or use counterfeit money, as by a counterfeiter; to use worthless checks, as by a check forger. *Underworld use.* 7. To advertise; to publicize; to make known, esp. a product, entertainer, or the like. 8. To smuggle. *v.i.* 1. To carry an advantage too far; to be overly aggressive or enthusiastic. 2. In playing jazz, to obtain all the feeling from a musical passage; to play adroitly. *adj.* Easy. *From "pushover."* **—er.** *n.* 1. A passer of counterfeit money. *Underworld use.* 2. One who peddles, sells, or distributes illicit narcotics to addicts, esp. marijuana or heroin. *Common addict use, universally known.* **—over.** *n.* 1. A prize fighter who is easily defeated. *Prize fight use since c1915.* 2. Any person, group, or team easily defeated in a contest or easily imposed upon. *Very common.* → 3. One who is quickly receptive or responsive to persuasion, flattery, a spiel, or a line. 4. A girl or woman who is easily seduced. 5. One who is always receptive to, cannot resist, or is sentimentally attached to any specif. idea, object, or person. 6. Any easy job or task; a cinch. *All uses common since c1930.* **—y.** *adj.* Aggressive; specif., socially aggressive with an obvious or bold desire to become accepted by and part of a wealthy or socially prominent group.

push across. 1. To kill or murder. **2.** In sports, to score.

push a pen. To do clerical work in an office.

push off. 1. To go away; to beat it. **2.** To kill.

push the panic button. To demand a period of fast, efficient, and sometimes creative work; to demand that a job be done rapidly and well. *Usu. said of an employer, esp. in the advertising business, who is trying to meet a business emergency or soothe an irate client. A term assoc. with Madison Avenue.*

push up the daisies. To lie buried in one's grave. *Since c1860.*

puss. *n.* **1.** The face. *From the Irish "pus" = mouth.* **2.** A grimace; a facial expression of pain, anger, annoyance, incredulity, or the like. **3.** A disliked youth; specif., an effeminate youth.

put [something] across. 1. To make something understandable; to explain or clarify; specif., to attempt to convince by explaining; to attempt to convince or persuade. **2.** To succeed in cheating or taking advantage of another; to hoodwink; to succeed in accomplishing an unethical task.

put [someone or something] down. To reject; to criticize; to scorn. *c1955; orig. beat use, now common to far out, cool, and hip people.*

put [someone or something] down for (as). To identify or classify.

put in [one's] two cents. To contribute one's opinion or advice, esp. when not asked to.

put it on the line = lay it on the line.

put it over. 1. In baseball, to throw a strike; said of the pitcher. *Baseball use.* **2. = put over.**

put on. 1. To eat; to put on the feedbag. **2.** To act affectedly; to conduct oneself ostentatiously; to put on airs. *adj.* Affected.

put out. To feel angry, humili-

ated, offended, rejected, insulted, slighted; to be upset because of the words or actions of another.

put over. 1. = put across. 2. To make a success of; to popularize.

put [one's] papers in. 1. To apply for admission, usu. to apply for admission to a college or to enlist in the Armed Forces. *Mainly teenage use.* **2.** To resign or retire.

putter-offer. *n.* A procrastinator.

putt-putt. *n.* **1.** An outboard motor for a boat. → **2.** Any internal combustion engine of less than five cylinders; any vehicle or device with such an engine, esp. a small car or motor scooter.

put up. 1. To give someone shelter for a night; to invite or allow another to use one's room or home. *Colloq.* **2.** To wager money on the outcome of a sporting event; to present one's stakes in support of a wager.

put-up job. A prearranged affair; a frame-up. *Colloq. since c1925.*

put up or shut up. 1. Lit., back up your opinion with a money wager or be silent about it. → **2.** Fig., prove your assertion by some definite action or stop making the assertion. *Colloq. Used orig. as an invitation to wager, but now more in anger as a command to shut up.*

put up with [someone or something]. To accept or endure a person, situation, or object even though one does not want to. *Colloq.*

pygies. *n.pl.* **= P.J.'s.**

Q

Q. and A. Questions and answers.

quad. *n.* **1.** A quadrangle, as the court of a building or buildings, or a campus or part of one. **2.** A prison.

quail. *n.* A girl or young woman; esp. a sexually attractive girl or young woman. *Since c1860. From the Celtic "caile" = a girl.*

qualley-worker. *n.* An itinerant worker who makes wire coathangers, bottle-cleaners, etc. *Per-*

haps from U.S. dial. "quile," *"quarl"* = *coil, as of wire. Tramp use.*

quarterback. *v.t.* To manage a business, lead a group of people, or organize a business, group, or plan. *Since c1945; from the football term.*

queen. *n.* 1. A very generous, pleasant, remarkable, or attractive girl or woman. 2. A male homosexual who plays the female role, esp. one attractive to or pop. with homosexuals who play the male role. *v.i., v.t.* To go on a date or escort a girl. *Some student use since c1915.*

queer. *adj.* 1. Counterfeit. *Underworld use.* 2. Homosexual; perverted; degenerate; effeminate; specif., homosexual. *Common since c1925, and now so common that the stand. use is avoided; orig. hobo use.* *n.* 1. Counterfeit money. *Since c1925. Orig. and mainly underworld use.* 2. A male homosexual. *The most common, polite word in use* = *a homosexual.* 3. A homosexual of either sex. *Very common. v.t.* To put one in bad standing; to spoil or ruin something, as one's prospects or a plan, to quash, to cause hindrance or discontent. *Since c1915.*

quetch. *v.i.* To complain about insignificant things; to nag. *From the stand. Yiddish "kvetch"* = *to squeeze → Yiddish sl.* = *to whine.* —er. *n.* A chronic complainer; an annoying, bothersome person.

quetor. *n.* 1. A quarter [25¢]. 2. A tip of 25¢; also, a person who gives a tip of 25¢.

quick buck = fast buck.

quickie. *n.* 1. A single, quickly drunk drink of whisky, usu. straight whisky, as taken secretly or to bolster up one's courage. 2. A movie quickly and cheaply made. 3. A strike not sanctioned by the workers' union; a wildcat strike. 4. Anything done or made quickly, as a quick trip, a book written quickly, or the like.

quick one. A hasty drink of liquor.

quick on the draw. Quick-thinking; quick to comprehend. *The image is that of a Western gunfighter.*

quick on the uptake. Quick to comprehend, esp. relationships between people or nuances of likes and dislikes among people at a gathering.

quick-over. *n.* A hasty glance or inspection. *From "quick" plus "once-over."*

quick push. A person easy to victimize; an easy mark. *Underworld use.*

quiff. *n.* A cheap prostitute; a girl or woman who will join in sexual intercourse with but little persuasion. *Underworld use and some general use since c1925.*

quill. *v.t.* 1. To try to curry favor with a person. *More common in Eng. than in U.S.* 2. To report a cadet for a delinquency. 3. To whistle.

quim. *n.* = queen.

quint. *n.* 1. A basketball team. *From "quintet."* 2. A quintuplet.

quirley. *n.* A cigarette. *Cowboy use.*

quiz. *n.* In college, a short examination. *Colloq. since c1860.* —zee. *n.* One who is quizzed, esp. one who is a contestant on a television quiz game program. *Frequent use owing to the many television quiz shows.*

quod. *n.* 1. A prison. 2. = quad.

quote. *n.* 1. A quotation. *Colloq.* 2. A quotation mark.

R

rabbit. *n.* 1. Salad; esp. a salad composed of greens. 2. Talk. *From "rabbit-and-pork"* = *talk, in [Cockney] rhyming sl.* —foot. *n.* A prisoner who runs away from prison. *v.i.* To move quickly, to run; specif., to flee, to escape.

rabbit food. Any kind of greens, esp. lettuce; raw salad vegetable(s).

race. *adj.* Pertaining to "race" music.

race music. A simple form of jazz based on the blues, usu. with a melancholy or sometimes religious theme, a heavily accented beat, etc. *Because such music, during the 1920's and 1930's, was issued by the recording companies on records informally known as "race records," intended primarily for sale to Negroes.*

Rachel. *n.* High gear on a motor vehicle. *Army use.*

rack; rack time = sack; sack time. *USN use.*

racket. *n.* 1. Any shady or dishonest business or occupation; a swindle. → 2. Any kind of concession at a carnival or circus. *Carnival and circus sl.* 3. Any legitimate business or occupation. 4. An easy job; an enjoyable way of life. —**eer.** *n.* A person who works in a shady or unethical business; a swindler or extortionist. *v.i.* To victimize by means of a racket.

radish. *n.* A baseball. *Sportswriter use.*

raft. *n.* A large number or quantity of persons or things; a slew. *Colloq. since c1830.*

rag. *n.* 1. An article of clothing, esp. a dress. *Still used, mainly in "rags" or "glad rags."* 2. A circus tent; esp., the main tent of a circus; a "big rag." *Circus use.* 3. A semaphore flag. *USN use.* 4. Lit. and fig., a baseball championship pennant. *The above meanings refer to articles of cloth manufacture; the next three meanings refer to things made of paper.* 5. A paper dollar. *Still some use.* 6. A newspaper or magazine; esp., a newspaper or magazine for which the speaker has contempt; orig. and mainly, a newspaper. *Universally known.* 7. A playing card; esp., one which does not improve the player's hand. *Additional meanings:* 8. A simple form or style of highly syncopated music, primarily for the piano, characterized by a lively, accented tempo, the use of

breaks, and intricate figures in both treble and bass; a song written or arranged in this style; ragtime. *Strictly speaking, rag preceded jazz and was distinct from it, being mostly written music, developed by trained white musicians c1890–c1905. The style was an influence on early jazz, however, and many rags were adapted to the jazz repertory. In the public mind the two became identified, and "rag" and "ragtime" were used interchangeably with "jazz" until c1925. Since c1890.* *v.t.* To play any music in a style resembling ragtime; popularly, to play in a jazzy manner. *Since c1890. v.i.* To play a rag. —**ger.** *n.* 1. A devotee of rag or ragtime music; one who dances well to ragtime music. 2. A newspaper reporter. *Some use since c1920.* —**s.** *n.pl.* 1. Clothing, esp. new or fancy clothing. *From "rag."* 2. Paper money. —**time.** *n.* A highly syncopated style of music, esp. for the piano, characterized by a monotonous bass, a heavily accented tempo, and a melody line composed of many short, fast notes. *It is said that the word first appeared in print in 1896 on the cover of the published song, "Oh, I Don't Know, You're Not So Warm," by Bert Williams, but the word was in use among musicians before this.*

rag-chewing. *n.* Talking; conversing; esp., talking idly. *Still some use.*

raggle. *n.* An attractive girl or woman; specif. a sexually attractive young girl; one's girl friend or mistress. *Underworld use.*

rag out. To dress up in one's best, newest, or most colorful clothes. *c1865; orig. jive use.*

rag up = rag out.

rah. *interj.* Hurrah. *Since c1875.* *adj.* = rah-rah.

rah-rah. *adj.* Of or pertaining to a college; collegiate; characteristic of the spirit or feeling of college students, esp. in respect to sporting and social activities. *Always used disparagingly.*

railbird. *n.* An ardent horse-racing fan; lit., one who sits on or stands close to the railing surrounding a race track; one who times and keeps his own record of the performances of race horses for comparisons of their merits in later races. *Still in use.*

railroad. *v.t.* 1. To send a person directly to prison without proof of guilt, due process of law, or a fair trial; to send to jail by false evidence or by cheating, tricking, deceiving, or framing. 2. To force or speed up an action without due process, in disregard of regular or accepted procedures, or without the consent of others concerned; to force one's opinion or schemes upon others.

railroad tracks. An Army captain's insigne bars. *W.W.II use.*

rain cats and dogs = rain pitchforks.

rain check. 1. A ticket stub or other receipt that allows one to return to see another baseball game if the one the ticket was originally purchased for is canceled because of bad weather. *Since c1890.* 2. Any request or promise to accept an invitation at a later date.

rain pitchforks. To rain in torrents; to rain very heavily. *Colloq.*

raise Cain. To cause a disturbance; to show violent anger; to live or enjoy oneself without regard for the conventions; to raise hell. *Since c1840.*

raise hell. 1. To celebrate wildly; to enjoy oneself in a wild, boisterous manner, usually with much noise and whisky; to be drunk and boisterous. *Colloq.* 2. To criticize or castigate thoroughly and in anger.

raise sand = raise Cain. *Still some dial. use.*

rake-off. *n.* 1. Chips or money that a gambling house takes as its percentage from the money bet in a gambling game. *These chips or the money may be removed from the center of the gambling table by a croupier's rake.* → 2. A commission, percentage, share, or rebate received by a party to a transaction, esp. an illegitimate or unethical transaction. *Still used commonly.*

rake [someone] over the coals. To reprimand; to bawl out. *Colloq.*

ral; ral, the; rail; rail, the. *n.* Syphilis; a case of syphilis. *Orig. Southern use. Some Armed Forces use. Orig. "ral"; "rail" is a variant.*

rall. *n.* A consumptive. *Crook use.*

ram bam. *interj.* = wham bam.

rambling. *adj.* Fast-moving. *Esp. said of a railroad train. Vagabond argot.*

rambunctious. *adj.* Boisterous; obstreperous. *From c1835 to present.*

ramshack; ramshackle. *adj.* Dilapidated; in disorder.

R and R. 1. Lit., Rest and Rotation; a transfer or leave from a fighting military unit to a base or town removed from the fighting; a short leave or vacation given a soldier from the front lines to a rest camp or town. *Wide W.W.II and Korean Army use.* → 2. A several-day period spent in drinking, sexual activity, or general carousal. *Army use during and since W.W.II.*

rank. *v.t.* 1. To say or do anything that discloses another's guilt in a crime; to deal in innuendo. 2. To harass, annoy, or ride someone. *Since c1930; common teenage use since c1950. adj.* Ruined, spoiled; gone awry.

rank, pull. To use one's rank or business or social position, usu. in a specif. situation, to exact obedience, respect, favors, hard work, or the like; to be dictatorial or bossy. *Orig. W.W.II Armed Forces use.*

rantankerous. *adj.* Cantankerous. *c1832; colloq.*

rap. *n.* 1. A rebuke or reprimand; blame, responsibility. → 2. An instance of being identified, arrested, charged, tried, sentenced, punished, or placed in prison as a lawbreaker; the identification of a criminal; the act of charging someone with having committed a crime, or such a charge; an instance of being arrested, or an arrest; a trial; a jail sentence. *Universally known.* 3. A derogatory or highly critical remark; a complaint. *v.t.* 1. To identify, arrest, charge, try, or sentence an accused lawbreaker or criminal. 2. To kill someone. *Underworld use.* —per. *n.* A crime for which someone other than the guilty person is punished. *From "rap."*

raspberry; razzberry. *n.* 1. A sharp, harsh, contemptuous, derisive, scornful comment, criticism, or rebuke; specif., a vulgar, derisive noise made by sticking the tongue between the lips and then blowing vigorously; the bird, the Bronx cheer. *Colloq.*

rat. *n.* 1. A disliked or despised person. 2. An informer; a squealer. *The most common use. Mainly assoc. with underworld use = police informer, esp. one who informs on his friends for pay or in return for a lesser jail sentence for himself.* → 3. Any distrusted, unethical, selfish, disliked person. 4. A loose woman. *v.i.* To inform; to squeal. —ter. *n.* An informer. —ty. *adj.* Shabby.

rat cheese. Any inexpensive, nonprocessed, common yellow cheese cut on order by a grocer, esp. a large cheese; bulk cheese; store cheese.

rate. *v.i., v.t.* 1. To be entitled to something; to receive something because one is highly esteemed or well liked. 2. To be highly esteemed.

rate with [someone]. To be held in high esteem by someone; to be liked or trusted by someone.

rat-face. *n.* A sly, underhanded person.

ratherish. *adv.* Somewhat.

rat-hole. *v.t.* To store up [food, etc.] furtively.

rat on [someone]. To inform on or squeal on.

rat out. To withdraw or depart dishonorably.

rat race. 1. Any job, occupation, office, business, or way of life in which action and activity seem more important than specific results or goals. *From the traditional image of laboratory rodents being placed on a treadmill to test their energy; hence fig., a race on a treadmill.* 2. Any occupation, place, social group, or way of life in which success is based on competition and comparison of one's financial and material success with that of others, ignoring personal achievement and satisfaction. 3. Any crowded locale, scene, business, or social function of great confusion. *Orig. a euphemism implying that sanity or productive work is impossible in such a locale, scene, business, or social function.* 4. Specif., a dance or dancing party. *Student and teenage use.* 5. A full dress review. *W.W.II Army use.*

rats! *expl.* An expression of disgust.

rattle. *n.* A "deal"; treatment. *v.i.* To talk aimlessly; to gossip. Used in "to rattle on." *v.t.* To confuse; to bewilder. *Usu. used reflexively in "to get rattled."* —brain. *n.* A confused, silly, or stupid person. —brained. *adj.* Silly; stupid; prone to confusion; unable to concentrate or meditate; foolish. —d. *adj.* Confused; confused by excitement; foolish; silly. —r. *n.* A railroad train. —weed. *n.* = loco (weed). *Because the seeds in loco weed make a rattling sound. Since eating loco weed makes cattle and horses insane, "loco" = crazy and "rattle" has come to = confuse.*

rattling. *adv.* Exceedingly; extremely. *adj.* Good quality; first rate.

raunchy; ronchie. *adj.* 1. Sloppy, careless; inept, unskilled; awkward. *W.W.II Air Force use.* →

2. Dilapidated, old, worn out, used up; cheap, inferior; ugly, dirty; gaudy; corny. *Teenage use since c1950.* **3.** Drunk; drunken. *Fairly common student use.*

rave. *v.i.* **1.** To express oneself enthusiastically about a person or thing; to gush. *Colloq.* **2.** To denounce. *n.* **1.** An unfavorable criticism. **2.** A very favorable or flattering comment, usu. a review of a stage play or the like. *Note that the noun reversed its meaning c1925; the v. is still used to mean two opposite things.* **3.** A sweetheart. *adj.* Very favorable; flattering. Usu. in "rave notice."

raw. *adj.* **1.** Inexperienced, crude. **2.** Unfair, unjustified. **3.** Naked. **4.** Risqué; tending toward the obscene.

raw, in the. Naked.

raw deal. *n.* A particular instance of very unfair or harsh, malicious, or discriminating treatment of a person or persons.

rawheel. *n.* A tenderfoot.

Ray! Hurray!

razor. *v.t.* To split up loot into shares. —**back**; **razor-back.** *n.* A manual laborer; a porter; a janitor; one who does menial labor; specif., a circus roustabout or a member of a train crew. *Circus, hobo, and railroad use.*

razz. *n.* = raspberry. *From "raspberry."* *v.t.* To ridicule or express contempt or scorn for anyone; to ride someone; lit., to give someone the raspberry; to make fun of; to heckle, kid, or rib. *From "raspberry" reinforced by "razzle-dazzle."* —**berry** = raspberry. —**amatazz; razz-ma-tazz; razzmatazz.** *n.* **1.** Anything out of date; anything sentimental; anything insincere or corny. *Being replaced by "jazz."* **2.** = razzle-dazzle. Planned confusion; obvious advertising; gaudiness. *adj.* **1.** Acting, dancing, speaking, doing anything in an old-fashioned, outdated, or corny manner. **2.** = rah-rah. **3.** Dazzling. *Perhaps from the hypothetical reduplica-*

tion *"razz-tazz"* with *"-ma-"* inserted.

razzle-dazzle. *n.* **1.** Confusion, bewilderment; that which is not what it seems, that which confuses, bewilders, or deceives. *Since c1900.* **2.** Planned deception or confusion, as for a joke or in joshing or as by one sports team in order to confuse another. **3.** A business deception or swindle; an instance of cheating. **4.** Excitement; hilarity; glamor. *The above uses all stem from a basic meaning of something outwardly so dazzling that one does not see an inner deception.* **5.** A prostitute. *Some carnival use.* *adj.* Dazzling; spectacular; showy.

reach-me-down. *adj.* Ready-made; hence, cheap, without individuality or sincerity. —**s.** *n.pl.* Ready-made clothes.

read. *v.t.* **1.** To inspect clothing for lice. **2.** To inspect; to patrol; to check up on an area to be sure everything is as it should be. **3.** To ascertain, visually by lip reading, what a person is saying to another; to eavesdrop. **4.** To know a person well enough to predict his thoughts and actions. *From fig., to be able to "read [another] like a book."* **5.** To give a pilot a reading or navigational data relating to his plane's exact position. *W.W.II Air Force use.* → **6.** To locate a friendly plane on a radar scope. *When the plane is "read" or seen on the radar scope, the pilot knows he will be kept on his proper course and that any necessary assistance is nearby. W.W.II Air Force use.* **7.** To understand, comprehend, or see; to dig. *Orig. cool use; a sophisticated, intellectual syn. of "dig" since c1950. Prob. from the "reading" of sheet music, reinforced by the above Air Force uses.* —**er.** *n.* **1.** A license to do business, esp. for holding a road show or selling pitchman's merchandise. *Carnival and pitchman use.* → **2.** Money paid for a license to put on a show in a city. *Carnival and circus use.* **3.** A prescription for narcotics. *Dope addict use.* **4.** A printed circular describing a man wanted for a crime. —**ers.** *n.pl.* Marked playing cards.

read [one's] plate. 1. To say grace or give thanks at mealtime. *Southern hill use.* **2.** To eat in silence; to be forced to eat in silence as a punishment.

ready; the ready. *n.* Money, esp. cash. *From "ready cash."* *adj.* Satisfactory; perfect. *Negro and jive use.*

ready for Freddie. Ready, esp. for the unexpected, the unknown, or the unusual. *Orig. and pop. in synd. newsp. comic strip "Li'l Abner."*

real. *n.* In the game of marbles, a heavy marble with which a player shoots. *adv.* **1.** Very; really. *Colloq. since c1820.* **2.** Emphatically; extremely; definitely; sincerely; intensely; genuinely; really. *Although in use for some time, as in the familiar "real Mc-Coy," "real" became pop. as an adv. with "bop" c1946, and is freq. used by bop and cool groups, most often in "real cool," "real crazy," and "real gone." It indicates that the speaker knows or feels that the following word is genuine and is almost akin to an oath = "I swear it is . . ." Also, once a word assoc. with a specif. group gains pop. outside the group, it begins to lose or change connotation; thus, adding "real" is an attempt to qualify the word to its original group usage by members of the group that orig. used it. Although mainly bop and cool use, also some far out and beat use; often used before "fine," "most," "sheer," "weird," "wild."*

real cheese = cheese.

real estate. Dirt, such as gathers on the hands or face.

real gone. Emphatically, irrevocably, thoroughly gone. *Cool use.*

real McCoy, the. Anything or any person that is genuine, superior, dependable, or greatly liked.

ream; rim. *v.t.* To take advantage of, cheat, or swindle another.

rear. *n.* The posterior.

reat. *adj.* = reet.

Red. *n.* **1.** A nickname for a red-haired person. **2.** A Communist or one with Communist sympathies. *From the red flag used by the international Communist movement. Colloq. since c1940.* **3.** Loosely, any political radical. *adj.* Communistic; radical. **red.** *n.* A cent; 1¢. *adj.* Profitable, said of a place. *Carnival and circus use.*

red, in the. Operating a business at a deficit; losing money; in debt. *From the red ink bookkeepers use on the deficit side of the ledger.*

red ball. 1. A fast freight train. → **2.** Any express train, truck, or bus that is running on schedule and is given priority over slower vehicles.

red carpet. Lit., the red plush carpet traditionally laid out for a king to walk on; fig., elegance, extremely hospitable or preferred treatment. *Usu. in "to roll out the red carpet for [someone]." adj.* Elegant.

redeye; red-eye. 1. Thick ham gravy. *From its color. Dial.* **2.** Inferior or raw whisky; specif., bootlegged whisky; sometimes brandy, rum, or other hard liquor; cheap liquor. *c1820 to present.* **3.** Ketchup. *W.W.I and W.W.II Armed Forces use.*

red face. Fig., a state of embarrassment. —**d.** *adj.* Embarrassed.

redhead. *n.* A freshman. *From the red hats worn by freshmen in some colleges.*

red hot; red-hot. *adj.* **1.** Extremely hot. *Fig.,* something so hot that it is glowing red. **2.** Containing accounts of scandals; sensational. **3.** Lively; pleasing; peppy. **4.** Sexy. *n.* **1.** A frankfurter. **2.** A stag; a man unaccompanied by a woman.

red-hot mamma. 1. A pretty, lively, sexy, and affectionate female sweetheart. 2. Specif., a type of large, lively, and earthy female singer in vogue c1920.

red ink. Red wine.

red lead. Tomato ketchup. *c1900 to W.W.II. Maritime, soldier, vagabond, and lunch-counter use. Orig. from the color of red-lead paint, as used on ships.*

red legs. An artilleryman. *Soldier use until W.W.II.*

red-letter day. An extremely important day; a day when something very personal, important, and eagerly awaited is to happen or has happened. *Lit., a day that is printed in red on the calendar; hence, a day more important than the rest.*

red-light; redlight. *v.t.* 1. To push a person off or out of a moving railroad train; also, to kill by so doing. *Carnival and circus use.* 2. To stop one's automobile and eject a passenger so that he has to walk home under inconvenient or embarrassing circumstances.

redline. *v.t.* To delete a soldier's name from the payroll, temporarily, because of some irregularity. *Army use.*

Red Mike. A woman-hater. *Annapolis use.*

red-neck. *n.* A rustic; esp. a poor white Southern farmer. —ed. *adj.* Angry. *Rural use.*

red noise. Tomato soup; a bowl of tomato soup.

red one. A place where, or a day when, business is unusually good; good business. *Carnival and circus use. From "red-letter day."*

red paint. Ketchup.

red tape. Delay caused by duplication of work and office routine, esp. in government; petty routine. *From the red tape used to bind up official government documents.*

reefer. *n.* 1. A refrigerated railroad freight car, truck, or ship. *c1925 to present; railroad, trucker, USN, and hobo use.* → 2. A refrigerator; usu. a large commercial refrigerator. *Hobo,* *W.W.II, USN use.* 3. A marijuana cigarette. *c1930 orig. addict, prisoner, and Negro use.* → 4. One who smokes marijuana. 5. A sea apprentice.

reefer weed. Marijuana; a marijuana cigarette. *Addict use.*

reeler. *n.* A spree.

reet; reat. *adj.* 1. Satisfactory; good; correct; pleasing; right; stylish. → 2. All right; great, wonderful; extremely attractive, appealing, exciting, satisfying; hep. *Both meanings in wide jive use.*

regular. *adj.* 1. Agreeable, pleasant, friendly; fair; in the same social and economic class and with the same general intellectual level and interests as the speaker; liked by the speaker and not considered superior or inferior to him; generally liked by and acceptable to one's fellow men. *Usu. in "regular guy" or "regular fellow." Colloq. since c1920. Common since a major goal of Americans became security and social approval.* 2. Having periodic bowel movements; not constipated; specif., having a bowel movement each day. *A euphem. pop. in laxative advertisements.* 3. With the usual or average amount of cream and sugar; said of a cup of coffee. *Orig. lunch-counter use in relaying an order.*

rehash; re-hash. *v.t.* To rediscuss; to talk about the same thing over and over; to talk about the past. *Colloq. n.* A rediscussion; repeated conversation; a summary.

Remington; remington. *n.* A machine gun. *From the typewriter. Because "Remington" is a well-known brand of typewriter, and the Remington Company also manufactures weapons.*

remover = paint remover.

rent party. A party given by a person at his apartment or house in order to collect money to pay his rent. *The host thus provides a place to dance and usu. rec-*

ords and a phonograph; the "guests"—friends, neighbors, and even strangers—all contribute a small sum to the host, which he applies toward his rent. Thus the host can pay his rent and his guests can dance for much less money than if they went to a commercial ballroom. Orig. and most pop. with Harlem Negroes during c1930–c1939. The music was almost always jive or swing.

rep. n. 1. A reputation, either good or bad. 2. A representative. Since c1900. adj. Repertory. Theater use. Usu. in "rep show" or "rep company."

rep-dep = repple-depple.

repeaters. n.pl. Loaded dice. Because they repeat a specif. combination of points.

report = sugar report.

repple-depple; repple depple. n. A replacement depot where soldiers await assignment or processing. From "reple.," an abbr. of "replacement," and "deppo," a pronunciation of "depot." W.W.II Army use.

reppo depot = repple-depple.

retread. n. 1. A used automobile tire that has had new treads added to it. Colloq. → 2. A discharged or retired soldier or sailor who returns to or is recalled to active military service; specif., a W.W.I soldier who also served in W.W.II or a W.W.II soldier who left military service but was recalled for the Korean War. Army and some USN use during and since W.W.II.

Reuben. n. A rustic; a rube or hick. Orig. carnival and circus use.

rhinie. n. A first-year student in a preparatory school. Perh. from "rhino" = homesick.

rhino. n. 1. A feeling of depression or sadness. Some use since c1925; orig. USN use. 2. A rhinoceros. adj. 1. Homesick. Since c1925; orig. USN use. → 2. Melancholy; depressed, sad; discouraged. 3. Without funds; broke.

rhubarb. n. 1. A noisy argument, often accompanied by a fight, orig. and esp., on a baseball field; a controversy, dispute, quarrel, squabble, fracas, or short fight. From the custom in the theater, radio, and movies of saying the word "rhubarb" over and over again to simulate angry and menacing talk in crowd scenes. 2. A strafing mission or operation carried out by low-flying airplanes. W.W.II Air Force use. Orig. Royal Air Force use. In allusion to the low-flying pilot's close view of gardens. v.i., v.t. To strafe from a low altitude; to fly at a low altitude. W.W.II Air Force use.

rhubarbs, the. n. Small towns; rural areas; the sticks.

rib. v.t. To tease a person; to make fun of or poke fun at; to josh. n. 1. A girl or woman. Once stand. and very common; revived as very hip slang c1958. 2. A remark, prank, or gag that ribs the victim. 3. Barbecued spareribs. → 4. A piece of meat, whether actually a sparerib or rib roast or not. Specif., a portion of any kind of beef, esp. a slice of roast beef. 5. A complete dinner; hot food. c1946; bop, progressive musician, and fan use. From "spareribs," reinforced by the concept that "food sticks to the ribs."

rib-stickers. n.pl. Beans. From the phrase "to stick to one's ribs."

rib-tickler. n. A joke.

Richard; richard. n. A detective. From "dick."

Richard Roe = John Doe.

ride. v.t., v.i. 1. To cheat or take advantage of. 2. To tease or nag; persecute, harass, or annoy by continuous adverse criticism; to pick on verbally; to use sarcasm against. 3. In sports, to harass or abuse an opponent verbally in the hope of making him nervous and reducing his efficiency. 4. To go on as usual; to remain as is; to stand pat; to forget or ignore something. n. 1. An easy course of action; the easy way. 2. Anything enjoyable, esp. if free and easy to do. 3. In jazz music, an improvised passage. —r. n. 1. Specif., a cowboy. 2. Specif., a race-horse jockey.

ride, go along for the. To join in passively, usually for the fun of it, without making an active contribution.

ride, take [someone] for a. 1. To murder. *Orig. to murder in the Chicago gangster style of the 1920's, by forcing the victim to get into a car, driving him to a secluded place, and shooting him.* 2. To deceive or cheat.

rideout. *v.i., v.t.* To play the last chorus of a jazz performance in a free and abandoned, enthusiastic manner.

ride shanks' mare (pony). To walk. *Very old.*

ride the beam. To pretend innocence, as by looking at the ceiling. *W.W.II Army use.*

ridge-runner. *n.* 1. A hillbilly; a mountaineer. 2. A Southern rustic.

riding the air. Working at a great height; said of construction workers.

rif. *v.t.* To notify an employee of the termination of his employment; to can, fire, or sack a person. *From the initials of "Reduction In Force."* *n.* A dismissal from employment.

riff. *n.* 1. In jazz, an improvisation of a phrase or passage by a soloist or by several musicians playing in close harmony; a repeated figure. *Common jazz use.* → 2. An improvised or impromptu conversation; a conversation in which one improvises on events or happenings; esp. in order to create a favorable impression on the listener; a line; exaggerated, insincere talk.

riffle. *n.* In baseball, a hard swing at the ball with the bat, whether or not the ball is hit. *v.i., v.t.* To shuffle cards. *Colloq.*

riffle, make the. To succeed; to attain a specific goal. *Hobo use.*

rig. *v.t.* 1. To prearrange the outcome of something, esp. a sports contest; to throw; to fix. 2. To control the stock market by manipulating prices. *Wall Street use.* *n.* Wearing apparel; esp. eccentric or unusual clothing. *Colloq.*

right. *adj.* 1. Friendly; fair; reliable. 2. Trustworthy to a criminal group; not associated with the police; not an informer. *Underworld use.*

righteous. *adj.* 1. Terrific; perfectly satisfying; wonderful; extremely beautiful, inordinately pleasing. *The most superlative jive word. Negro and jazz use.* 2. Self-righteous, snobbish, superior. *Colloq.*

righteous moss. Hair characteristic of Caucasians. *Harlem use.*

right guy. 1. An honest, reliable, fair man. → 2. Specif., one who can be trusted by criminals not to inform to the police. *Underworld use since c1925.*

right joint. 1. A fair, reliable, trustworthy nightclub, gambling place, etc. 2. A prison, reformatory, or other institution where the inmates are treated fairly.

right money = smart money.

right off the bat. At once; initially; instantly.

right up there. Close to or almost winning or succeeding; close to being or almost famous.

righty. *n.* A right-handed person; in baseball, a right-handed pitcher.

rigid. Drunk.

rig-out. *n.* A garb; an outfit; a get-up. *Used since c1895.*

Rileyed. *adj.* Drunk.

rim-rock; rim-rack. *v.t.* To ruin another or to cause another to fail, usu. by deception.

rinctum. *v.t.* To hurt, damage, or ruin; said of a person or thing. *The "—um" = " 'em" (them), so the word is a v.i. and not truly a v.t. "Rinctum" is the form for all tenses and persons.*

rind. *n.* Money.

ring. *v.i., v.t.* To substitute one horse for another of similar appearance in a race; to put a ringer in a race. *n.* A telephone call. *Stand. since c1930.* —**er.** *n.* **1.** A person or animal having an appearance closely resembling another; specif., a race horse, illegally substituted for another in a contest, as a race; esp., a superior race horse that resembles or is made to resemble an inferior horse and is substituted for it in a race. *Horse-racing use.* → **2.** One who illegally substitutes one horse for another in a race. **3.** A double; a dead ringer. **4.** A doorbell. *Hobo use since c1925.*

ring-tail. *n.* **1.** A grouchy person. *Hobo use.*

ring-tailed snorter. A fine, strong, courageous man; a humdinger. *Since c1830.*

ring the bell. To succeed; to meet with approval or make a hit with someone. *Also, less freq., "hit the bell." From various carnival devices in which a bell rings when a player is successful. Colloq.*

ring-warm. *n.* A boxing enthusiast.

rinktum ditty = blushing bunny.

rinky-dink; rinkydink. *n.* **1.** Cheap, gaudy merchandise; junk; drek. *Orig. carnival use.* **2.** A cheap place of amusement. *Cf. honky-tonk.* **3.** A swindle; a run-around.

riot. *n.* **1.** An exceedingly successful entertainment or performance. **2.** An extremely funny or amusing person. *Colloq.*

rip. *n.* **1.** A disreputable person; a debaucher. *Colloq.* **2.** A demerit; a penalty; a fine.

ripe. *adj.* **1.** Ready, said of plans or schemes; eager, said of a person; ready and eager, esp. to be victimized. *Colloq.* **2.** Drunk.

ripple. *n.* A noncommissioned officer in the Waves. *W.W.II use.*

rise. *n.* **1.** Anger, indignation, vexation, or the like, purposely aroused in a person by an action or statement contrary to his interests, beliefs, or prejudices. *Usu. in "get a rise out of [some-*

one]." *Colloq.* **2.** A response, usu. in reply to such action.

ritz. *n.* Wealthy and aristocratic style; swank. *Usu. in "put on the ritz" or in "the ritz." The words "ritz" and "ritzy" have flourished most in nonritzy circles.* —**y.** *adj.* **1.** Swanky; elegant; luxurious; fancy; plush. **2.** Wealthy; living luxuriously and elegantly. **3.** Proud, snobbish, vain.

rivets. *n.* Money.

roach. *n.* **1.** A policeman. *Primarily Negro prison use.* **2.** A marijuana cigarette, esp. the stub of a partially smoked marijuana cigarette.

road, hit the. **1.** To travel; to move on again; lit., to enter a highway in order to hitchhike. **2.** To work as a traveling salesman.

road, the. *n.* Lit., the state of or time spent wandering or traveling, as a tourist, traveling salesman, or esp. as a vagabond or hobo.

road apples. Horse feces, as found on the highway.

road hog. An automobile driver without regard for the rights of other drivers; one who takes more than his share of the road. *Colloq.*

road-stake. *n.* Money for traveling. *Hobo argot.*

roast. *v.t.* To make fun of; to criticize adversely; to pan. *n.* An instance of criticism or bantering; a panning. *Both forms colloq.*

roasting-ear wine. Corn whisky. *Midwest use.*

Robin Hood's barn, go around. To proceed in a roundabout way. *Since c1880.*

Robinson Crusoe. **1.** To accomplish or attempt to accomplish a daring or spectacular feat without the knowledge of others. *From the character and title of the famous children's classic.* **2.** A person who prefers to work or live alone.

rob the cradle. To date or marry a person much younger than oneself. *Colloq.*

rock. *n.* **1.** Any gem, esp. a diamond. *Underworld use until c1925; now common.* **2.** A mistake; an error. *Perh. from "rockhead."* **3.** Any small hard object; esp. dominoes, ice, or ice cubes. **4.** A male teenager who is devoted to rock-and-roll music, fads, and fashions. *Teenage use since c1955.* *v.i.* **1.** To sway, jump, stomp, or swing to music, orig. and specif. jive and swing music; now also to jazz or rock-and-roll music. *Orig. jive and swing use.* → **2.** *Specif.,* to play or dance adroitly to jive or swing music; to be full of music; to be excited or satisfied, esp. by jive or swing music. *Jive and swing use c1935–c1942.* **3.** To play or dance to rock-and-roll music. *Teenage use since c1955.* *v.t.* Fig., to cause a place to resound or vibrate with the swaying, stomping, jumping, or swinging of jive, swing, jazz, or rock-and-roll devotees. *adj.* Excellent or satisfying, said of jive or swing music or dancing. *Jive and swing use c1935–c1942. From "solid."* **—s.** *n.pl.* Ice cubes; chopped ice. *Usu. in "on the rocks"* = *whisky served in a glass with ice cubes and no water or soda.*

Rock, The. *n.* **1.** Alcatraz prison. **2.** A nickname for the heavyweight boxing champion or any good boxer.

rock and roll; rock 'n' roll. **1.** A style of heavily accented, two-beat jazz evolved from "race" music. *Typically, rock and roll music is characterized by the simplest melodic line (usu. based on the blues), by elementary arrangements scored for small groups (often only rhythm and saxophone), by harsh and reedy tones (both from instrumentalists and vocalists), and by lyrics based on adolescent love problems or hillbilly themes. This has been the pop. music among adolescents since c1954, replacing love ballads and swing. First pop. by Alan Freed, N.Y.C. disc jockey, who discovered, advertised, exploited, and acted as impresario for many rock and roll pieces, performers, and concerts.* **2.** The dance or dance steps done to rock and roll music. **3.** That group of teenagers, or a teenager, who fervently likes rock and roll music; any fad or fashion associated with this large teenage group. *adj.* Of or pertaining to rock and roll music, fads, or fashions.

rock candy. A diamond; diamonds.

rock crusher. One who is or who has been in prison; the occupation of a prisoner. *Used humorously.*

rocker, off [one's]. Crazy. *Since c1930; considered the most modern of the "off one's ——" = "crazy" terms; most popular with students.*

rock-happy. *adj.* Crazy owing to living too long on a coral island.

rockhead. *n.* A stupid person. *adj.* Stupid.

rocks in [one's, the] head, have. To be lacking in mentality or sanity. *Usu. said to one who has made a ridiculous or audacious suggestion or proposal; usu. posed as a question.*

rock-slinger. *n.* A mortar operator. *W.W.II Army use.*

rocksy; roxy. *n.* A geologist. *Student use.*

rocky. *adj.* Unsteady; woozy; groggy. *Usu. from being beaten up or drinking too much.*

Rocky Mountain canary. A burro; a donkey. *Western use.*

rod. *n.* **1.** A revolver or pistol. *Underworld use until c1925; now common.* **2.** A hot rod.

rod-man. *n.* A gunman.

rods, grab a handful of. To steal a ride on a freight train; to ride the rods. *Hobo use since c1915.*

rods, hit the. To catch a free ride on a freight train; to ride the rods. *Orig. hobo use. Early hobos rode under the freight cars on the connecting rods, rather than inside or on top of boxcars.*

rods, ride the. To sneak aboard and ride a freight train, as is done by hobos.

rod up. To arm; to provide with guns.

Roger. *adv.* Yes; o.k. *Orig. W.W.II Air Force and general Armed Forces use in acknowledging radio messages, esp. in a pilot's acknowledgment of instructions relayed by radio from his base. Considerable civilian use after W.W.II.*

Rok. *n.* A South Korean. *Wide Korean War use, orig. by the Army. From the initials of "Republic of Korea."*

roll. *v.t.* 1. To rob a drunk or sleeping person, usu. a drunk. *Lit., to roll a prone victim over in order to rob him.* → 2. To rob any person, as by a hold-up, or esp. to rob a prostitute's customer when he is sleeping or has left his clothing unwatched. 3. To operate or begin operating a movie camera. *Always in "roll 'em."* *n.* Specif., a roll of banknotes; money, esp. the money one is carrying with him or a sum of money one has saved for a specif. purpose. **—back.** *n.* A reduction in the number of employees or personnel, or a reduction in wages, prices, or material on hand to a previous level. **—er.** *n.* 1. A prison guard. 2. One who robs men who are drunk.

roll bar. An iron bar or frame on an automobile which arcs over the driver or behind the driver's seat to protect him in case the car turns over. *In stand. model cars, this is incorporated as part of the body frame; in hot rod cars, which may have the frame removed, it must be added separately. Hot rod use.*

roll in. To go to bed; to turn in. *Colloq. since c1890.*

roll out. To get up. *An order to get up and get ready for the day's work. cW.W.I much more common than "roll in." Wide Army use in W.W.II.*

roll out the red carpet. To welcome someone enthusiastically and in a manner as elaborate as possible; to prepare for someone's arrival by making elaborate preparations. *Colloq.*

rollover. *n.* The last night before a prisoner's release.

roll up [one's] flaps. To stop talking. *W.W.II Army use.*

ronchie. *adj.* = raunchy.

roof, raise the. 1. To cause a loud or embarrassing disturbance, specif. in making a complaint or in expressing anger or disappointment. 2. To be loud and boisterous; to ignore conventions. 3. = blow one's top. *All uses colloq.*

rook. *v.t.* To cheat; to misrepresent or overcharge. *Lit., to take advantage of someone as if he were a newcomer.* *n.* 1. A novice. → 2. An Army recruit; a rookie.

rookery. *n.* A place frequented by hobos.

rookie; rookey; rooky. *n.* A beginner; a newcomer; an apprentice; one who is new and inexperienced in certain occupations; specif., a new, inexperienced athlete, Army recruit, or policeman. *adj.* New in one's work; beginning; esp. new as a policeman, athlete, or Army recruit.

room. *n.* 1. Specif., a room or area in a nightclub, restaurant, or hotel in which there is a small stage or cleared space for a performer to entertain patrons at surrounding tables; a nightclub; any place where a nightclub entertainer can perform. 2. = pad room.

roost. *n.* One's dwelling place.

root. *v.i.* 1. To applaud or cheer, esp. for the players in a game. *Since c1900.* → 2. To favor or show favor for the success or well-being of a person, team, or cause. *v.t.* To rob; also in "root against" and "root on." **—er.** *n.* One who encourages a person, sports team, or cause; esp. one who cheers or warmly applauds an athlete or a sports team; a fan. *Since c1895.*

root-hog-or-die. With either a complete, overwhelming success as a result of hard work or a total failure; complete acceptance, co-operation, work, and sympathy or total rejection. *Dial.*

rootin'-tootin'. *adj.* Noisy; boisterous; exciting; filled with action; exuberant.

rooty-toot (-toot). *n.* Old-fashioned music or an outdated style of playing music; corn. *Orig. musician use. interj.* An expression of derision toward something old-fashioned or corny.

rope. *n.* A cigar. *Occasional use in comic papers and by would-be wits. v.i., v.t.* To gain the confidence of a person, or pose as a friend, in order to deceive, trick, cheat, or swindle.

rope in. To deceive. *Since c1840.*

ropes, know the. 1. To be thoroughly familiar with the details of any occupation or enterprise; to be worldly and sophisticated; to know how to fend for oneself. 2. To be wise or hep, usu. in a specific field of endeavor. *Prob. from nautical use.*

Roscoe; rosco. *n.* A pistol or revolver; any gun that can be easily concealed on a person.

rosy. *adj.* Promising the best; optimistic. *Colloq.*

rot. *n.* Nonsense; boloney. —**gut.** *n.* Whisky or other liquor, esp. bootlegged or of inferior quality. *Used since earliest Colonial times. Still used in Eng.* —**ten.** *adj.* Very unpleasant; disgusting; of poorest quality; indisposed or in poor health. *Colloq.*

Rotacy = R.O.T.C., Reserve Officers' Training Corps, or a member of this Corps. *Student use.*

Rot-corps. *n.* The Reserve Officers' Training Corps.

rot-see; rotasie = Rotacy.

rough. *adj.* 1. Obscene, lewd, lascivious. 2. Dangerous; difficult; unpleasant; tough. *Wide use during and since W.W.II. n.* An automobile that has been in at least one collision. *Used-car dealer use.*

roughhouse. *n.* 1. Boisterous or rowdy behavior; brawling; a scrimmage; a scuffle; horseplay. 2. Violence. *adj.* Characterized by violence. *v.t.* To subject a person to physical violence; to strongarm. *v.i.* To brawl; to engage in horseplay, as that which puts a room in great disorder.

roughneck. *n.* 1. An ill-mannered, uncouth, rough person, esp. if burly; a rowdy; a tough guy or hard guy. 2. A working man in a circus; a circus laborer. *Circus use.*

rough stuff. 1. Physical violence, such as murder, beating, shooting, or torture. 2. Obscene literature or talk; profanity.

rough up. 1. To beat up or injure someone, esp. to intimidate that person. 2. To produce minor injuries or a mild case of shock, or shake [someone] up, as an automobile collision, football game, or the like might do.

round-heel(s); roundheel(s); round heel(s). *n.sing.* 1. An inferior prize fighter. *Some sports use since c1920. Prob. because such a fighter is knocked down frequently and spends so much time on his back that his heels become rounded, but perh. because a person with round-heeled shoes would be easy to push over.* → 2. A woman of easy virtue; a girl or woman easily persuaded to enter into sexual intercourse. —**ed.** *adj.* Easily defeated; said of a prize fighter.

roundhouse. *adj.* Lit. and fig., done with a powerful, circling, sweeping motion of the arm; usu. said of a punch, blow, swing, or the like. *n.* In baseball, a curving pitch.

round robin. A sporting contest in which several teams play each other consecutively.

round-the-bend = around the bend.

round-tripper. *n.* In baseball, a home run. *From the transportation term "round trip."*

round up. 1. To seek out and collect a group or the members of a group; specif., to arrest and bring to jail all the criminals involved in a given crime. **2.** To seek or collect all of a specif. item. **3.** To settle; to finish; to square a complaint. **round-up.** *n.* **1.** The act or an instance of so seeking, collecting, or arresting. *From the Western ranch use when cattle are so collected and brought to a central point.* **2.** A settlement of differences by violence or force.

roust. *v.t.* **1.** To arrest a person. **2.** To raid a place; said of the police.

routine. *n.* **1.** One's way of life, general attitude, personality, or philosophy; one's personal kick; that of which one is a devotee, by which one is obsessed, or which one considers as making life worthwhile. *Often in "What's his routine?" = What is he, or what kind of a person is he? Prob. from theater use where "routine" = a comedian's, singer's, etc., repertoire. Mainly cool use.* **2.** An insincere speech or conversation, esp. on a topic other than that which the listener desires or has requested; an evasion, an alibi, a line.

row = skid row.

row-dow. *n.* = rowdy-dow.

rowdy-dow(dy); rowdydow; row-de-dow(dy). *n.* A fight; a riot; a rhubarb.

royal. *adj. & adv.* Thorough(ly); complete(ly); elegant(ly). *Used as a term of emphasis, esp. before taboo words and expressions.*

rub. *n.* The gist, point, or moral of a story or conversation. *Usu. in "do you get the rub?" = do you understand?* *v.t.* To kill or murder. *From "rub out."*

rubber. *n.* **1.** A professional killer. *From "rub."* **2.** Automobile tires. *Fairly well known.*

rubber check. A check that is returned ("bounces") to the writer because there is not enough money in his checking account to cover its value.

rubber drink. *Fig.,* a drink of whisky that the imbiber cannot keep down, because he is drunk and sick to his stomach; the last drink taken before one gets sick.

rubber heel. A detective; esp. a company detective.

rubberneck wagon. A sightseeing bus.

rubber sock. 1. A timid, delicate, or cowardly person. *Hobo use.* **2.** A new USN recruit; a boot. *W.W.II USN use.*

rube; Rube. *n.* **1.** A farmer; a country man; a rustic; a hayseed. *Derisive use. Colloq. Since before 1900. From "Reuben," a traditional rural name.* → **2.** An unworldly, naïve, unsophisticated youth or man; a stupid, inexperienced, awkward person; a newcomer; an outsider; hence one easy to victimize. *Colloq. since c1900. adj.* **1.** Rustic, rural, smalltown; hick. **2.** In the manner and dress of a rustic.

rub elbows with. To become acquainted with, live among, or mingle with people of a social, intellectual, financial, or cultural level different from one's own; esp., to mingle with those thought to be one's inferiors.

rub joint. A cheap dance hall or nightclub that provides girls with whom lonely men can dance. *Because the attraction is that the male can rub against the girl with whom he is dancing; it is a common practice for the girls to wear nothing under their dresses.*

rub out. To murder a person. *Universally known as an underworld term.* **rub-out.** *n.* A murder; a killing.

ruckus. *n.* An uproar; a fight; a rowdy or boisterous celebration. *Since before c1890; dial.*

rug. *n.* A toupee. *Orig. theater use.*

rugged. *adj.* Dangerous; difficult; unpleasant; "rough." *Orig. W.W.II Army use.*

rug joint. Any elegant, expensive, lavish, ritzy nightclub, restaurant, casino, hotel, or the like.

Lit., a place with a carpet on the floor.

ruin = blue ruin.

rumble. *n.* 1. A complaint to the police; information or knowledge of a crime or criminal supplied to the police. *Underworld use.* → 2. Police interruption or interference in an illegal activity or before a crime is completed; an arrest. *Underworld use.* 3. A fight or battle, usu. prearranged, between rival teenage street gangs. *Orig. teenage street gang use. Now fairly well known, esp. in large cities. v.i.* To create a disturbance in order to distract attention from confederates while they are committing a crime or escaping. *v.t.* To see, notice, recognize, report, scare, or frustrate [someone] in an attempted robbery. *Some underworld use since c1925.*

rum-dum; rumdum; rum dum. *adj.* Drunk; stupid or shiftless, as from constant drunkenness. *Fig., "dumb" with "rum." n.* A drunkard; a person who is stupid, shiftless, or confused, as if or as from habitual drunkenness.

rum hole. A cheap, dilapidated saloon. *Since c1830.*

rummy; rummie. *n.* A drunkard. *Colloq.*

rumpot. *n.* A heavy drinker; a drunkard.

run. *n.* 1. A route followed by a vehicle. *Colloq.* 2. A ride, as in a taxi. 3. A race; esp., an automobile race. *v.t.* To drive (someone) by car.

run-around. *n.* A protracted instance of evasion, coyness, or refusal to make a decision; indecisive, evasive, or coy treatment.

run-around, give [someone] the. To stall a person; to evade, sometimes politely or without seeming to; repeatedly to postpone action on a request, as for payment or employment. *Orig. theater use.*

run a sandy on [someone]. To play a trick on; to dupe; to swindle.

run-down; rundown. *n.* 1. A summary, esp. a brief one. 2. An itemized account; a very detailed explanation.

rung up. Emotionally upset.

run-in. *n.* 1. An unfriendly encounter; an argument; a quarrel. → 2. An arrest. **run in.** To arrest someone.

run it out. To be personally and objectionably conspicuous, esp. by talking; returning too often to one topic.

running shoes, give someone his. To dismiss someone, as a suitor or an employee; to terminate a personal or business relationship, usu. in anger.

run off at the mouth. To talk too much; to shoot off one's mouth.

run of the mill. Average; common.

run-out. *n.* Any act of running away; esp. desertion; an escape; a powder.

run-out powder, take a = take a powder.

runt. *n.* 1. A very small, short person. *Colloq.* → 2. An incompetent person; a disliked, annoying person.

run-through. *n.* A rehearsal. **run through.** To rehearse; to practice.

ruptured duck. 1. The lapel pin or pocket insigne of an honorably discharged U.S. service man. *Wide W.W.II use. One wing of the eagle extends beyond the rim of the button. Called also "pregnant duck."* 2. An honorable discharge.

rush. *v.i.* To be aggressive; to try too hard; to be overly persistent. *v.t.* 1. To pay romantic attention to a girl or woman; to court; to give a girl the rush act. *Colloq. c1865 to present.* 2. To show marked attention to a student who is eligible for a fraternity or some membership. *Colloq. since c1890. n.* Acclaim; a series of frequent attentions paid a woman in courtship. —**ee.** *n.* A college student who is being rushed by and for a fraternity or sorority. *Colloq. student use.*

rush act; rush act, the. 1. The act of rushing a person. → 2. The act of courting a girl obviously and intensely, as by being extremely attentive, taking her to many parties, showering her with gifts, and the like; fig., trying to rush her into accepting one's proposal of marriage.

rush (work) the growler. To take a bucket or pail (growler) to a saloon, have it filled with beer, and carry it home; to buy a bucket of beer. *Very common before the invention of refrigerators and bottled beer. Obs.* See **growler.** → 2. To drink beer or whisky, esp. in large quantities or by the bucketful. *Hobo use.*

rust bucket. 1. An old or dilapidated USN destroyer. 2. A common, almost affectionate way of referring to any ship. *Usu. in "my rust bucket." Common W.W.II USN use. Prob. reinforced by Sp. "buque" = boat.*

rusticate. *v.t.* To punish a student by expulsion, either permanent or temporary. *Now stand.*

rustle. *n.* 1. A baby or young child given to the care of another during the day when its parents are at work or away. Traditionally such children receive little attention and less food. *Since c1880.* 2. A theft. *From the Western "rustle."*

rustpot = rust bucket.

rusty = cut a rusty.

rusty-dusty. *n.* 1. Jocularly and fig., anything not active or recently used; hence a person's rump when the speaker feels the person has been idle. 2. Specif., an old, rusty gun; a prop or toy gun. *Theater and jocular use.*

rutabaga. *n.* 1. A homely or ugly woman. 2. A dollar.

rye-sap. *n.* Rye whisky. *Some Midwestern Prohibition use.*

S

sack. *v.t.* To discharge a person from his job; to fire a person; to

expel; to dismiss. *n.* 1. A discharge or dismissal from a job; usu. in "to get the sack." *Since c1920.* 2. In baseball, a base. *Since c1925.* 3. A bag of golf clubs. *Golfer use since c1930.* 4. A bed or anything used as a bed; often preceded by "the" where "bed" would not be. *Wide W.W.II Armed Forces use. Universally known and fairly widely used since W.W.II.* → 5. Sleep. 6. A dress style or dress that fits very loosely over the shoulders, waist, and hips, and is gathered or tapered extremely near the hem line. *Common c1957–c1958 use. adj.* Sleeping; favorable for sleeping, as in "sack duty," "sack time," etc. *W.W.II Armed Forces use.*

sack, hit the = hit the hay. *Very common during and after W.W.II.*

— sacker. *n.* In baseball, one who plays the specified base. *Baseball writer and announcer use.*

sack out. 1. To sleep; to go to bed. 2. To sleep one's fill; to sleep as much as one wishes. *W.W.II Armed Forces use.*

sack time. 1. Time spent sleeping; time spent loafing or lying around. *W.W.II Armed Forces use. Common enough to have carried over into civilian use.* → 2. Bedtime; the time one usually goes to bed. *Civilian use, c1948.*

sack up. To go to bed. *W.W.II Armed Forces use.*

sad apple. A gloomy person, frequently irritable, introverted, or pessimistic; usually a person unnoticed socially; a drip.

saddle shoes. A style of white leather "oxford" shoe having a wide saddle-like brown (or, infrequently, black) leather insert over the instep. *Widely worn by students of both sexes c1940–c1950, and still fairly common.*

sad sack. 1. A disliked, noncompanionable person, specif. a maladjusted, confused, blundering, unlucky, introverted, socially undesirable boy or man. *Student*

use since c1930. → **2.** A maladjusted, confused, unlucky, down-
trodden, ill-dressed soldier; a soldier who, however well-meaning,
cannot manage to stay out of
trouble. *Pop. by comic strip,
"The Sad Sack," drawn by
George Baker for Armed Service
publications during W.W.II.
Term may be used either derog.
or sympathetically. Wide W.W.II
Army use.*

safe-cracker. *n.* One who blows
open or breaks open and robs
safes. *Colloq.*

safety. *n.* A thin rubber sheath
worn over the penis during
coitus as a contraceptive or prophylactic. *Not as common as
"rubber"; most common c1935.*

sagebrusher. *n.* A Western movie,
novel, radio play, or television
play; a horse opera.

sail. *v.i.* = sail through.

sailboats. *n.pl.* The human feet.

sail into. Lit. and fig., to assail,
to attack boldly and directly; to
criticize severely.

sailor. *n.* A ladies' man, esp. a
youth who is or believes he is attractive to the opposite sex.
*Teenage use since c1955. Indi-
cates the teenage youth's attitude
toward a man in uniform, who is
older and more romantic than
he and hence may steal a "rock's"
girl.*

sail through. To accomplish something or succeed easily, esp. easily and quickly.

Sal; Sally; Sally Ann. *n.* **1.** The
Salvation Army. *Hobo use since
c1920; orig. "Sal." from verbal
abbr. of "Salvation."* → **2.** Any
refuge where free food, shelter,
and clothing can be obtained.

salad = fruit salad.

salad days. **1.** The days, years, or
period when one was youthful
and daring; esp. when a man was
a roué or dude. **2.** One's youthful or best period of creativity,
work, enthusiasm, or vigor.

Sally; Sally Ann = Sal.

salmagundi. *n.* Any stewlike con-
coction, esp. a watery meat and

vegetable stew, the vegetables
usu. being potatoes.

salon mush. Nonjazz music; restricted jazz or semijazz music;
lit., music as played quietly and
prettily in a salon. *Synthetic;
musician use.*

saloon. *interj.* Goodby; "so long."
*c1945; sometimes used jocularly;
from mispronunciation of "so
long."*

salted down. Dead.

salt horse. Corned beef; salted
dried beef or chipped beef. *Some
use since c1850; some Army and
lunch-counter use.*

salt mines, the. A mythical place
where one is told to go or said
to be sent in punishment or isolation; a place where one is required to work very hard; hard,
tedious work. *Usu. in "back to
the salt mine(s)" = return to
work. From the idea that both
Czarist and Communist Russia
sentence prisoners, esp. political
prisoners, to manual labor in the
salt mines of Siberia.*

salty. *adj.* **1.** Audacious; daring. **2.**
Hard to accept or believe; lewd,
obscene; violent; exciting; titil-
lating. **3.** Angry; emotionally upset. *c1940.* **4.** Terrible, horrible;
fig., unpalatable. *c1940.* **5.** Smart,
neat; vivacious, alert, hep. *c1950;
these are late jive usages.*

salve. *n.* **1.** Butter. *Fairly common
W.W.I and c1915 hobo, student,
and jocular use. Some recurrence
during W.W.II.* **2.** Exaggeration;
sweet talk; a buttering-up; soft
soap. *Since c1910.* → **3.** A bribe,
usu. a small bribe of an unethical
rather than an illegal type. →
4. Money, esp. money earned
from a distasteful or boring job.
v.t. To pay; to reward; to bribe.

Sam Brown; Sam Browne. *n.* **1.**
An officer's belt, including a di-
agonal section from the right
shoulder to the left hip. → **2.**
An Army or Air Force officer.
Fairly common W.W.II use.

Sammy. *n.* Any male Jewish college student; any young Jewish
male. *From the common Ameri-*

can Jewish name "Samuel" = "Sammy"; reinforced by the Jewish college fraternity Sigma Alpha Mu, whose initials spell "Sam" and whose members are called "Sammys."

sand. *n.* **1.** Granulated sugar. *Orig. prison use; mainly prison, hobo, Army, and USN use. Since c1915.* **2.** Salt. *Mainly Army, USN, and student use. Since c1930.*

sandbag. *n.* A type of W.W.II USN life jacket that resembled a sandbag in appearance. *v.t.* To ambush and beat up a person; specif., to sneak up from behind and hit a person over the head.

sand-pounder. *n.* A USN sailor assigned to shore duty.

sandwich board. A large board or cardboard containing an advertisement and carried through the streets by a sandwich man.

sandwich man. A man who is employed to walk the streets carrying a large board or piece of cardboard on which an advertisement is printed; usu. the person wears one such board in front of him and another on his back. *Since before 1900; because the two boards resemble slices of bread; thus the man looks as though he is in a sandwich; also, most such advertisements are for lunch counters.*

sanitary. *adj.* Excellent. *Some teenage use since c1955.*

San Quentin quail. A sexually attractive girl, orig. and esp. one under the legal age of consent; jail bait. *Fig., a quail who could put a male in San Quentin prison. One of the most common examples of alliterative sl.*

sap. *n.* **1.** A stupid person; a fool; one easily taken advantage of. *Very common since c1910.* **2.** A club or blackjack; anything used as a club. *Since c1920; still retains its underworld connotation.* **3.** Whisky. *Fig., that which makes one alive, as if one's veins were running with sap. v.t.* To hit a person on the head, esp. with a

blackjack and always resulting in unconsciousness. *Since c1930.* **—py.** *n.* = saphead. *adj.* Foolish, stupid.

sap-happy. *adj.* Drunk.

saphead; sap-head. *n.* A stupid person; a blockhead; a fool. *Colloq.* **—ed.** *adj.* Stupid. *Colloq.*

sarge; Sarge. *n.* A sergeant, either an Army or police sergeant. *Colloq.*

sass. *n.* Impertinent talk; back talk. *v.t.* To speak impertinently to. *Since c1860; colloq.*

sat, pull. To receive a satisfactory mark or grade. *Student use; often in naval training courses.*

satch; Satch. *n.* **1.** Any man with a large mouth. *Often used as a nickname. Freq. applied to Negroes, whose lip and mouth structure gives the appearance of a large mouth. E.g., the distinguished jazz musician Louis Armstrong is called "Satch" or "Satchmo." From "satchel," which in turn is from "satchel mouth."* → **2.** Fig., any man who talks a lot; esp., a gossip, a politician, or the like; often used as a nickname. **—el; Satchel.** *n.* **1.** Any man with a large mouth. *Often used as a nickname. Freq. applied to Negroes, whose lip and mouth structure gives the appearance of a very large mouth; e.g., "Satchel" Paige, well-known baseball pitcher. Since c1925. From "satchel mouth."* → **2.** A musician, esp. a jazz musician who plays a wind instrument. *Since c1935. Because of the large number of Negro jazz musicians, perh. reinforced by the fact that older horn players have developed their lips and cheek muscles noticeably through constant playing.* → **3.** One who works for a bar, nightclub, or restaurant catering to Negroes or employing jazz musicians. *Mainly Southern use since c1935. v.t.* To fix, to rig. *From "in the bag."*

satchel-mouth. *n.* A large-mouthed person. *Orig. Negro use.*

sauce. *n.* Whisky, liquor.

sauce, on the. Drinking large quantities of whisky frequently; addicted to alcoholic beverages.

sausage. *n.* **1.** An inferior athlete, esp. one with rippling muscles, as a prize fighter, wrestler, or weight lifter. **2.** A prize fighter, esp. an inept prize fighter whose face is swollen, bruised, or scarred from many severe beatings in the ring. **3.** Any dull, stupid person; one who is as alert as a real sausage.

savage. *n.* **1.** An employee, esp. the most menial, lowest paid employee. **2.** A rookie policeman; a policeman who is eager to make arrests.

save it. A command or plea to another to stop talking; usu. used as a request to someone to stop telling a long story or change the topic of conversation.

savvy; savvey. *v.t.* To understand. *Since c1850.* *n.* Understanding; knowledge; worldliness, correct thinking or doing. *Since c1865; orig. Western use; colloq. adj.* Clever; intelligent; hip.

saw. *n.* **1.** An old story, joke, or saying; a cliché. **2.** A ten-dollar bill; the sum of $10. *From "sawbuck."* **3.** A landlord, esp. of a rooming house. *Negro use.*

sawbones. *n.* **1.** A surgeon. *Orig. hobo, lumberjack, USN, and Army use.* → **2.** Any physician or medical doctor.

sawbuck. *n.* **1.** A ten-dollar bill; the sum of ten dollars. *Orig. and prob. the most common use.* **2.** A twenty-dollar bill; the sum of twenty dollars.

sawdust. *n.* Sugar. *Some student use.*

sawdust-eater. *n.* A lumberjack; a sawmill worker. *Some hobo and lumberman use.*

sawdust parlor. A cheap nightclub, restaurant, bar, or the like. *Fig., a place with sawdust on the floor.*

sawed-off; sawed off. *adj.* **1.** Short of stature. *Said of a person. Since c1880.* **2.** Rejected, separated, or ostracized from one's work or by

one's friends, fellow employees, or society in general.

saw wood. **1.** To snore. **2.** To sleep. *From the resemblance of the sound of snoring to that of wood being sawed; however, this term probably orig. from comic strips, where a drawing of a saw going through a log traditionally is shown to represent both snoring and sound sleep.*

sax. *n.* A saxophone. *Universally known; common musician use, esp. jazz musician use.*

say! *interj.* **1.** A common greeting. **2.** An expression used to gain someone's attention, esp. when one is belligerent.

say a mouthful. To speak truthfully and to the point; to express an evident view or opinion. *Usu. in "you said a mouthful" = what you have said is true and wholly agreeable.*

say-so; say so. *n.* A person's word; a person's recommendation, opinion, conclusion, or the like; oral advice or permission; oral recommendation. *Since c1880; colloq.*

Says which? *interrog.* What did you say?

Says who? *interj.* A belligerent expression questioning the knowledge, opinion, or authority of another, usu. the listener.

Says you!; Sez you! *interj.* A belligerent expression questioning the opinion, knowledge, or authority of another; an expression of incredulity, esp. when the speaker does not want to believe that what he has heard is true; "says who?" *Since before c1925.*

say (cry) uncle. To give up or in; to surrender; to admit defeat. *Mainly used by boys, as when fighting.*

scab. *n.* A worker who refuses to join a union or go on strike; esp., a worker who will cross a union picket line to take the place of a striking worker. *Colloq.*

scads; skads. *n.pl.* **1.** A large quantity of money. *Since c1890.* **2.** A large quantity or number of anything. *Since c1920.*

'**scairdy cat** = 'fraidy cat.

scale. *n.* 1. A louse. *Some Army and prison use since c1910.* 2. A standard hourly or minimum hourly rate of pay for a job.

scalp doily. A toupee. *One of the more pop. jocular words for a toupee. Since c1925.*

scalper. *n.* 1. A ticket seller or agent who buys up many tickets to a pop. entertainment or sporting event and then resells them at exorbitant prices; fig., one who is not satisfied with a fair profit, but takes advantage of the public to obtain as high a price or profit as he can. *Universally known.* 2. One who obtains high odds as a bettor and then himself takes bets at lower odds, so that he will profit, win or lose, either as a bettor or as a bookmaker. *Gambling use.*

scamping. *n.* Idling while one is supposed to be working; goofing off; producing inferior work; working or talking without regard to one's fellow workers, but only to impress one's boss.

scandahoovian. *n., adj.* Scandinavian.

scandal sheet. 1. A payroll. *W.W.II Army use.* 2. A businessman's expense account. *Very common since c1945.*

Scandinoovian. *n., adj.* Scandinavian.

scare, the. *n.* Extortion; the extortion racket.

scare strap; scared strap. 1. A safety belt. *Railroad and telephone lineman use since c1900.* → 2. A safety belt on a passenger airliner.

scare up. 1. To locate and/or obtain any specific item. 2. To prepare or manufacture any specific item. *Colloq.*

scarf. *n.* Food, a meal. *Negro use. Prob. from "scoff."* *v.i., v.t.* = scoff.

scat. *n.* The fast singing of, or the gibberish or meaningless sounds often interpolated into, jazz songs; singing unintelligible sounds to the melody of a standard song. *Many old jazz and pop. singers have claimed the credit for originating scat.* *v.i.* 1. To sing scat. 2. To go fast; to drive fast. Teenage and student use. *From "scat!" the traditional sound by which one causes cats to jump up and run away.* *adj.* In or pertaining to scat.

scatter. *n.* 1. = scatter-gun. 2. A saloon; a drinking joint; a meeting place. → 3. A speakeasy; a saloon or bar that sells illegal whisky or whisky after the legal hours. → 4. An illicit or secluded meeting place; a hideout. → 5. A room, apartment, or sleeping place.

scatter-gun; scattergun; scatter gun. *n.* 1. A machine gun. *W.W.II Army use.* 2. A burp gun. *W.W.II Army use.*

scene. *n.* 1. Any locale, place, or room where cool music devotees gather to hear musicians play. *Some cool use.* → 2. Any place where cool people meet; specif., any event which a cool person attends. *Common cool, far-out, and beat use.*

schatchen. *n.* A marriage broker. *Mainly used by Jews descended from Central European parentage.*

schiz. *n.* A schizophrenic; schizophrenia. *Pronounced "skitz."* —**o.** *n.* 1. = schiz. 2. Any of the four basic types of schizophrenia. *adj.* Schizophrenic; afflicted with schizophrenia.

schlack; schlag. *adj.* = schlock.

schlemazel; schlemasel. *adj.* Illfated, ridden with bad luck; clumsy, awkward. *n.* An awkward, clumsy person. *From the Yiddish.*

schlemiel; schlemihl. *n.* An oaf, a fool, esp. a stupid, awkward, clumsy fellow; a jerk. *From the Yiddish; from "schlemazel."*

schlep. *v.t.* Drag, carry, tote, haul. *From the Yiddish.* *n.* A stupid or awkward person. —**per.** *n.* One who is always looking for a bargain; one who always has something he wishes to sell; one who expects many small favors, free merchandise, gifts, or the like. *From the Yiddish.*

schlock; schlack; schlag. *adj.* Cheaply made; of inferior material, design, and workmanship; defective; cheap and gaudy; usu. said of merchandise to be sold. *n.* Inferior, cheap, or defective merchandise. *From the Yiddish "schlock" = a curse.*

schlock joint (shop, store). A store that sells cheap, inferior merchandise, often one in which the customer and owner can bargain over prices. *From "schlock."*

schloomp; schlump; schlub. *n.* A foolish, stupid, or unknowing person; a jerk. *v.i.* To idle; to waste time; to relax. *From the Yiddish.*

schlub. *n.* = schloomp. *adj.* Second-rate; inferior. *From the Yiddish.*

schlump. *n.* = schloomp.

schmaltz. *n.* **1.** Sentiment or sentimentality exploited for commercial reasons; extreme sentimentality; corn; specif., music or a style of music that is sweet and sentimental. *Prob. the most common of the Yiddish "sch—" words used seriously or to give a jocular twist to one's speech. From the Jewish "schmaltz" = chicket fat, used for cooking, hence greasy, slick.* **2.** Hair dressing or pomade; goo, gonk. *v.t.* To do anything as if it were schmaltz or in a schmaltzy way. *Usu. in "schmaltz it up" = to make something more appealing to those who like sentimentality or corn.* —y; schmalzy. *adj.* Extremely sentimental, hackneyed, trivial, or corny.

schmear. *v.t.* **1.** To bribe; to give someone a gift or be exceedingly kind to another in order to obligate him. *From the Yiddish.* **2.** To treat someone roughly and with intended violence; to throw another to the ground. *Most freq.*

as football use = to tackle an opposing player. *n.* A bribe.

schmendrick. *n.* A completely foolish, awkward, inept person. *From the Yiddish.*

schmo(e); shmo(e). *n.* **1.** A foolish, idle person; one easily deceived, a naïve person; a goof. *As in the case of many Yiddish or Yiddish-sounding words, often used for humorous effect. "Schmo(e)" does not appear in Yiddish.* **2.** A stubborn person; a disliked person. **3.** An eccentric, a character. *Often used affectionately.*

schmoos; schmoose; schmoozl(e). *v.i.* To talk; to gossip; to discuss or converse; esp. to talk idly, pleasantly, or jocularly. *From the Yiddish "schmoose" = chat.*

schneider. *v.t.* **1.** In the card game of gin rummy, to score the winning amount of points, or win a fixed number of games, before one's opponent has scored or won any games. *Since c1940. Card player use.* → **2.** To win any game or series of games before one's opponent, or the opposing team, has scored or won a game; to shut out an opponent. *Since c1945.* → **3.** To defeat an opponent by a large margin. *n.* A tailor; a worker in the garment industry. *From the German and Yiddish = one who cuts (cloth).*

schnook. *n.* A dope, a sap; esp. one who is too meek to stand up for his rights, bargain, or defend himself from being made the butt of a joke, taking the blame, or being cheated. *From the Yiddish. Like other derisive words from the Yiddish, this is somewhat affectionate, implying that the person is more to be pitied than scorned and a realization that a person may seem foolish because he is meek, gentle, and idealistic.*

schnorrer. *n.* One who begs, chisels, or depends on the generosity of others for his living; a beggar or moocher; a chiseler; one who always attempts to bargain to obtain purchased items at a reduced price; a poor relation who expects his relatives to support him; a parasite. *From the Yiddish.*

schnozz. *n.* Lit. and fig., the nose. *From "schnozzle."* —le; **snozzle.** *n.* A nose; usu. a large nose. *From the Ger. "Schnauze" = a dog's snout or muzzle. Reinforced by the Yiddish "schnubbl" = a beak.* —ola. *n.* A nose, esp. a large one. *Since c1930 the well-known nickname for comedian Jimmy Durante, known for his large nose.*

school. *n.* A state penitentiary; a "big school."

scillion = skillion.

scissorbill; scissorsbill; scissor-bill. *n.* 1. A person whose income is not from wages, as a farm or camp owner, a coupon clipper, or one who has struck oil; a rich person. *Logger, hobo, and I.W.W. use. c1910–1930.* → 2. A worker who lacks class consciousness; one who will not join a labor union; a non-I.W.W. *I.W.W. use.* 3. A fool, victim, or sucker. *Orig. logger, hobo, and I.W.W. use, by c1930 some underworld use.* 4. A railroad detective. *Hobo use. Reinforced by "bull" and "cinder bull"; sometimes heard as "scissors bull." Orig. of the term is unknown.*

scissors bull = scissorbill.

scoff. *v.i., v.t.* 1. To eat. *Orig. maritime and hobo use; seems to have more Negro than white use. Said to have orig. in Africa.* 2. To drink. —ings. *n.pl.* Food; meals. *Hobo use.*

scollops, put on. To adopt the dress, manners, and customs of a new country, as the U.S.; said of an immigrant.

scooch; scrooch; scrouge; scrooge. *v.i.* To move by sliding or shifting one's body.

scoop. *n.* 1. Recent, official information; advance information; dope; poop. *Armed Forces and student use c1940.* 2. A single, half-sphere portion of ice-cream, as scooped out of a large container by a standard-sized, half-

spherical ice-cream spoon. *Common lunch-counter use. v.t.* To precede other newspapers in publishing a given news item.

scope; 'scope. *n.* A periscope. *Universally used by U.S. Navy; esp. submarine unofficial use. Since c1935.*

scorch. *v.i.* In baseball, to throw a ball very fast and hard. —er. *n.* 1. A critical, telling remark or speech. *Since c1840.* 2. A person given to causing excitement or a sensation. → 3. Any remarkable thing or person; a corker. 4. In baseball, a line drive. 5. Any exceptionally hot, dry day. *Colloq.*

score. *n.* 1. A victim; a mark. 2. A successful instance of robbing, cheating, swindling, gambling, or the like; loot or money obtained by robbing, cheating, swindling, or gambling. *Orig. underworld use.* → 3. The amount of cash or loot stolen, won at gambling, or obtained by cheating or swindling. 4. A stealthy meeting to transact illegal or unethical business; one who is to be met at such a meeting; a "hit." *Mainly underworld use.* 5. A share, esp. a share of loot. *Orig. c1930 underworld use.* → 6. An amount won at gambling, usu. a large amount made on one race, one game, or won from one player. → 7. Sexual intercourse, esp. as a man wins from a woman by being pleasing and convincing. 8. Narcotics as obtained from a seller; a package of narcotics for sale or newly purchased. 9. The crux of a matter, the main point, the gist of a situation. *Wide student use, c1945. v.t.* 1. To be liked or admired by another. → 2. To win sexual intercourse with a girl or woman by being agreeable and convincing. 3. To buy or obtain narcotics. 4. To be or make a success; to impress by succeeding; esp., to please an audience.

score, know the. To be fully aware of current important facts; to be alert and well informed as to realities.

Scotchman. *n.* 1. Any thrifty or miserly person. *From the traditional belief that all Scotsmen are thrifty.* 2. A golfer, regardless of his native country. *Some caddy use, because golf orig. and was first pop. in Scotland, reinforced by the caddies' belief that most golfers tip in small, miserly amounts.*

scouse. *n.* Any very cheap, often tasteless dish, such as a poor-quality stew or weak soup.

scout master; scoutmaster. *n.* 1. A major radio executive, sponsor, or advertising agency executive. *Radio studio use.* 2. An overly optimistic, idealistic, pious, or patriotic person; a moralist.

scow. *n.* 1. A large, ugly, and/or unpleasant woman. 2. A large truck.

scrag. *v.t.* 1. To hang a person. *Obs.* → 2. To kill; to murder. → 3. To put another person or firm out of business; fig., to kill. *n.* An unattractive girl. *Some teenage and student use c1940. From "hag," reinforced by Al Capp's very ugly Scragg family in his synd. comic strip, "Li'l Abner."* —**ging.** *n.* A killing; a murder.

scram. *v.i.* To depart, usu. hastily; to go away, to beat it. *Often used as a command or entreaty. Underworld, carnival, and circus use since c1900. Became common c1930 and replaced "skedaddle." Said to be from "scramble," but more prob. from Ger. sl. "schrammen" = "beat it." n.* 1. A hasty departure. *Since c1930.* 2. Any money, clothing, or items hidden and/or ready to be used for a hasty or forced departure. *Underworld and circus use.*

scram-bag. *n.* A suitcase packed in readiness for any necessary, sudden departure. *Underworld and circus use.*

scramble. 1. A race between hot-rods. *Teenage use since c1950.* 2. A teenage dance, party, or meeting. *Teenage use since c1955.* 3. An alerting of fighter planes and their ground crews defending a specif. area, for which the pilots scramble to their planes and take off in order to be ready for a possible enemy attack. *Air Force jet plane use since c1950; pop. since Korean War. v.i.* 1. To rush to one's fighter plane and prepare for an emergency air defense of a specif. area. *Air Force use since c1950; common during Korean War.* → 2. To disperse, flee, depart hastily; usu. a command. *Teenage use since c1950.*

scrambled ears. Cauliflower ears.

scrambled eggs. *sing.* The gold braid, leaves, or embroidery worn as part of a senior military officer's uniform; esp., the gold trimming on the bill of a USN or Air Force officer's dress cap. *Wide W.W.II use, may orig. have implied disrespect but usu. did not carry that implication. From the resemblance of such gold trimming to a scrambled egg.*

scram money. Money or an amount of money or cash kept available for a hasty departure.

scrape. *n.* A shave.

scrape the bottom (of the barrel); (of the pickle barrel). To be forced to rely on or choose what is considered an inferior or unreliable plan, idea, or person in a desperate attempt to succeed, as when it is impossible to use, choose, or rely on a plan, idea, or person considered more adept; to have an unusual idea or plan. *South. dial.*

scrap heap = junk heap.

scrap iron. Whisky of inferior quality; cheap liquor.

scratch. *n.* 1. Money; available cash; loose banknotes; paper money. *Since c1915. Lit., that which has to be scratched for, as a chicken scratches for food.* → 2. A loan of money; the act of borrowing money. 3. A wound, even when more than "just a scratch." 4. A horse that has been withdrawn from a race after midnight of the night before the race. 5. An unknown, insignificant, or chronically poor person, one who is to be ignored; fig., one who has been scratched off a list of friends or successful people, one who is as insignificant as an actual scratch, or one who is always scratching around for money. 6. An appointment book or pad of writing paper; a scratch pad. 7. A mention of one's name in a newspaper, esp. a favorable mention that has publicity value to an entertainer or product. *Since c1940.* → 8. An impression left by someone or something, usu. a favorable impression. *v.t.* 1. To withdraw a horse from a race after midnight of the night before the race. 2. To brush against someone or something. 3. To cause physical harm to someone. *v.i.* In sports, to make a score. *Often used in the negative: "He didn't scratch."* —er. *n.* A forger. *Since c1850; still mainly underworld use.*

scratch for [something]; scratch [something] up; scratch around for [something]. To look for an object, to try to obtain something, to hunt or seek something, esp. money or a much-wanted object; fig., to scratch in the same way a chicken does in searching for food.

scratch hit. In baseball, a hit that is almost caught, a fluke hit; a one-base hit.

scratch sheet. A small printed sheet or newspaper published daily giving the expected odds, weights, jockeys, and scratches pertaining to horses entered in races for the day.

scraunched; scronched. *adj.* Drunk.

scream. *n.* Anything or anyone that is uproariously funny, as a movie, joke, comedian, or the like. *Since c1930.* *v.i.* To move rapidly; esp. said of an airplane or car. —er. *n.* 1. A murder mystery or horror show. *Orig. c1925 radio use, now also movie and television use.* 2. A large or brightly colored advertising

plaque or banner; fig., an advertising banner that screams for attention.

screaming meemie. 1. A specific type of small Army rocket launched from a multiple rocket projector on the back of a jeep or truck. *Common Army use since late W.W.II. From the frightening noise and effect such rockets made, similar to the screaming meemies.* 2. So intense or extreme as to cause one to scream or feel effects similar to the screaming meemies.

screaming meemies, the. The delirium tremens; the jitters, the heebie-jeebies.

screech. *n.* A woman who habitually complains or criticizes; a shrew.

screeve. *n.* A movie script writer. *Some movie use.*

screw. *n. Persons:* 1. A prison guard, orig. a turnkey; a prison warden; a watchman; any law enforcement officer; usu. a prison guard. *Said to be from "screw" = key, but "screw" = guard appears to be the older use.* 2. A foolish person. 3. A key. *Still underworld use.* *v.i.* To leave or depart, esp. hastily; to scram. *v.t.* To take advantage of, to treat unfairly; to cheat, trick, or swindle. *Often used in the passive, past tense. Very common, esp. during and since W.W.II.*

screwball. *n.* 1. In baseball, a pitched curved ball that twists in and out like a corkscrew; any pitched ball that moves in an unusual or unexpected way. → 2. A very eccentric person, one with unusual ideas or beliefs; a person with antisocial beliefs; an insane person; a nut; a crackpot. *Common since c1935; prob. had an intermediate sports usage = an eccentric baseball player. Considered more tolerant than "nut" or "crackpot"; sometimes used affectionately = a close friend with a distinct personality.* → 3. A worthless, harmless person. *adj.* Eccentric, crazy; goofy; nutty.

screw-loose. *n.* A crazy or eccentric person; a nut.

screw loose, have a. To be mentally unbalanced; more or less crazy; nuts; extremely eccentric; to be a neurotic; to have an obsession. *Since c1900.*

screw-up. *n.* A chronic blunderer; one who can be expected to make a mistake or a faux pas; an awkward, inept person.

screwy. *adj.* 1. Crazy, absurd, unusual, nuts, eccentric, screwball. *Used to refer to both people and ideas since c1880.* 2. Dizzy; dazed.

scribe. *n.* 1. A letter. *Some archaic, underworld and Negro use.* 2. A writer, esp. a movie script writer or newspaper columnist. *Movie and newspaper use. v.t.* To write. *Although standard as a v.i., the word is sl. as a v.t.*

scrim. *n.* A formal or large, well-organized dance or dancing party. *Some student use since c1920. Prob. from "scrimmage," but may be related to the Brit. sl. "scrimshank" = to loaf, to relax.*

scrip. *n.* 1. A dollar bill. 2. Money.

script. *n.* 1. A prescription, almost always a forged or stolen prescription for narcotics. *Mainly drug addict use.* 2. A manuscript.

scronch. *v.i.* To dance. *Dial.*

scrooge. *v.i.* = scooch.

scrouge. *v.i.* = scooch.

scrounge. *v.t.* To borrow trifles without expecting to return them; to steal small inexpensive items; to borrow, bum, mooch. *Taken from Brit. sl. during W.W.I, grew in popularity and has become very common since c1940. n.* 1. A habitual borrower; one who is always asking for the loan of small items or small sums of money. → 2. One who asks for small items that others are about to throw away or sell. —r. *n.* = scrounge. *Since c1940. The more common form of the n.*

scrounge around. 1. To seek after a particular item or sum of money to scrounge; to seek out a person in order to scrounge from him. → 2. To loaf or idle in a specif. place or near a group of people, hoping that excitement or entertainment will be offered; to walk the streets aimlessly, or to visit a friend, in the hopes of meeting an attractive girl, of meeting someone who will offer a free drink, meal, or entertainment. → 3. To look through a group of familiar items, such as books, clothing, or to investigate the contents of an attic, basement, or closet, in hopes of finding a useful or interesting object that one has forgotten or misplaced. *All uses common since c1940. The first two uses were pop. pastimes for W.W.II soldiers. Usu. no urgency in borrowing or finding is implied; when one scrounges around one is just passing time aimlessly, hoping that something exciting or interesting will present itself.*

scroungy. *adj.* Bad; inferior; terrible; usu. as a result of being very cheap.

scrow; scrowl. *v.i.* = scram.

scrud. *n.* A mythical disease alleged to be very serious, painful, and socially objectionable. *Usu. in "you look like you got the scrud" = you look very sick. Some Army and C.C.C. use since c1935.*

scruff. *v.i.* To eke out a living; to earn just enough to buy necessary food and shelter; to live from hand to mouth. *Orig. carnival use.*

scruffing along = scruff.

scrumptious. *adj.* Excellent; wonderful. *Usu. applied to food = delicious; applied to people = well dressed, well groomed, beautiful, or handsome. Since c1820.*

scud; scut. *n.* Hard, boring, or tedious tasks; minor details that are unrewarding and time-consuming.

scuffle. *v.i.* To earn one's living by a routine, dull, legitimate job.

scunner. *n.* A dislike. *Since c1895; dial.*

scupper. *n.* A prostitute, esp. a cheap prostitute who walks the streets to solicit business. *W.W.II USN use.*

scut. *n.* **1.** A contemptible or mean person. → **2.** An inexperienced person; a newcomer, rookie, apprentice, or fraternity pledge. **3.** = scud.

scuttle. *n.* A large container, such as a water pitcher, filled with ice cubes for the convenience of whisky drinkers. *Since c1935, mainly hotel bellhop use. In order to avoid the hotel service charge for ordering whisky, many travelers carry their own and merely order such a container of ice cubes, which a bellhop delivers.*

scuttle-butt; scuttlebutt. *n.* **1.** The drinking fountain or water bucket on a ship. *Since c1840, USN use. Also Brit. Navy use.* → **2.** A rumor, a piece of gossip; a vague, unsubstantiated story; an exaggerated story; rumors, gossip; idle talk. *USN use since c1935. Because such talk is indulged in during relaxed moments around the drinking fountain. Became common during W.W.II, and is still common.*

seabee. *n.* A member of a USN construction battalion. *Wide W.W.II use. From "C.B.," initials for "Construction Battalion."*

sea dust. Salt. *Since c1925, some USN use; during W.W.II the term was used by lunch-counter waitresses.*

sea food. Whisky. *During Prohibition when the sale of whisky was forbidden, it was common to ask one's bootlegger for "sea food," meaning whisky, just in case a law-enforcement officer was listening. Thus, as criminal argot, the word was used to mislead the police or strangers. The use was so pop. that "sea food" must hold the record for an argot word universally known.*

sea-going. *adj.* Ornamented to the point of absurdity; unnecessarily large, ornamental, fancy, pompous, or dictatorial; exaggerated. Applied to manufactured objects, such as automobiles, whose basic purpose is obscured by unnecessary size, ornamentation, or added gadgets; said of people with titles of authority who are unnecessarily pompous, dictatorial, or brisk. *For emphasis the noun modified is often not the actual object or person under discussion, but is a substitute of lesser or greater rank. Thus, a "sea-going Ford" = a Cadillac or other larger, fancier car; a "sea-going alderman" = a Senator or political figure much above an alderman's rank; "sea-going beer" = any drink fancier and more expensive than beer. A relatively new sl. term; has been increasing in pop. since c1955. In the U.S. tradition of deflating, it implies that the object or person is overly equipped, as if fig. ready to undertake a long sea voyage. Orig. based on the familiar "sea-going bellhop."*

seagoing bellhop. A U.S. marine. *Orig. USN use. From the ornamentation and striped trousers of the U.S. marine dress uniform. The oldest and most common of the "seagoing" terms.*

sea gull. **1.** Chicken served at a meal; esp., canned or cold-storage chicken; occasionally turkey served at a meal. *Orig. Annapolis use c1925. Had spread to general USN and Marine use during W.W.II.* **2.** A girl or woman who follows the fleet or a specif. sailor. *W.W.II USN use. Usu. applied to wives and families but sometimes applied to casual female followers and prostitutes. Because such women follow the fleet as closely as real sea gulls do. Although sometimes implying that the women follow the sailors too closely, the term is often laudatory in that a wife who follows her sailor husband* *from port to port is considered, by some at least, as the best type of USN wife.* 3. A hearty or greedy eater. *W.W.II USN use. Because of the voracious appetite of the actual sea gull.* **seagull.** *v.i.* To travel by airplane. *W.W.II USN use.*

sea lawyer. A sailor who pretends to know more than he does, who is argumentative, free with unwanted advice, or who habitually complains. *Since before c1850, when used by Herman Melville in "White-Jacket." Wide W.W.II USN use.*

sea legs. Lit and fig., legs that are used to the pitch and roll of a ship at sea. *Usu. in "to get [one's] sea legs."*

seam squirrel. A body louse; a cootie. *Hobo and W.W.I Army use.*

search me, [you can]. I don't know. *Fig. = you can search me and won't find an answer.*

seat. *n.* The buttocks.

seat-man. *n.* A professional card dealer. *Because the dealer who works for a gambling house remains seated throughout the game while other players come and go.*

seat of [one's or someone's] pants, by the. 1. By instinct. *Mainly an aviation term = flying without instruments, and thus depending on instinct gained through experience.* 2. Succeeding by a slight margin, having succeeded when failure or disaster seemed imminent.

seaweed. *n.* Spinach. *USN use since c1925, fairly common during W.W.II.*

sec. *n.* 1. A second of time. *Very common.* 2. A secretary.

Secesh; secesh. *n.* 1. Secession, specifically the secession of the Confederate States from the Union prior to the Civil War. *c1860; obs.* → 2. A secessionist, a state or citizen of the Confederacy. *c1860; archaic. adj.* Pertaining to secession.

second fiddle. 1. Of inferior rank or standing; one who follows the ideas or policies of others. *Often in the expression "to play second fiddle."* → 2. Second choice, second best sweetheart or one who is second choice. *From the second violinist of symphony orchestras who is second best or follows the lead of the first violinist.*

second John. 1. A second lieutenant. *c1945, Army use.* 2. = **John.**

second lining. Following someone, esp. in hopes of recognition or of being invited to participate with or for him.

seconds. *n.sing.* 1. A second or subsequent portion or serving of food available to anyone who wishes to eat more. *Usu. in such phrases as "there's seconds on beans but not for meat." Colloq.* 2. A pot of coffee brewed from coffee grounds that have already been used at least once. 3. Imperfect merchandise sold at lower cost than first-quality goods; slightly damaged or soiled merchandise sold at a discount. *Very common since c1945.*

section 8. 1. A discharge from military service because one is psychologically unfit. 2. A psychopath; a neurotic; a nut. *W.W.II Armed Forces use. Orig. Section 8 of the W.W.II Armed Forces rules allowed for the discharge of psychopaths or neurotics; such a discharge paper was also called a "Section-8 discharge."*

see. *n.* A visit, esp. a visit for the purpose of inspecting and specif. an inspection of a patrolman's beat by a sergeant. *v.t.* 1. To split or give gratuities or graft. *Fig. = to see that another obtains his share of graft.* 2. In poker, to cover a bet or a raise rather than drop out of the game.

see a man about a dog, have to. The traditional and jocular excuse to leave a person, group, or room. *Thus = excuse me, I have to leave. c1920 usu. used to excuse oneself to go out and buy* *bootleg liquor. c1940 usu. as an excuse to go to the bathroom.*

seep. *n.* A special type of watertight jeep used as an amphibious vehicle by the USN. *W.W.II USN use.*

see red. To become angry or enraged. *Colloq.*

see the chaplain. To stop complaining; to shut up. *Often in the imperative. Common W.W.II Army use. Fig. = Stop telling me your troubles, because I am not interested; go and tell them to the chaplain.*

See you. *interj.* So long; good-by; I'll be seeing you soon. *Very common, esp. among students and younger people. Almost as common as "so long" or "goodbye," which increasingly are reserved for long trips and serious occasions. Much more common than the now slightly affected " 'by now."*

sell. *v.t.* To convince a person; to create enthusiasm; to convince another of the merits of an idea, object, or person; to talk convincingly.* → *v.i.* 1. To cater to the wishes of a group or audience in order to be popular or successful; to compromise one's style or ideals so as to have popular appeal. *Since c1930.* → 2. To be a popular or commercial success, usu. said of an entertainer, play, song, or the like. *Since c1935.* → 3. To have a piece of work or idea accepted by one's employer, superior, or customer. *Since c1940.* —*ing. adj.* 1. Popular, having wide appeal, highly desirable. *Usu. said of small items that are part of a fad.* 2. Personally appealing; exciting.

selling plater. A cheap or inferior racehorse, such as runs in claiming races. *Racetrack use.*

sell out. 1. To leave; to move out. → 2. To become a traitor; to compromise one's ideals or beliefs. *Colloq.* → 3. To become a coward; to leave or compromise because of fear. *Colloq.* 4. To accept a bribe; to renounce one's

principles for the sake of monetary gain. *Colloq.* **sellout; sell-out.** *n.* 1. An instance of having all tickets sold, as to a football game or a stage show. 2. Any article of merchandise that has sold out of supply.

sell out to the Yankees. 1. To have an accident; to be hospitalized. *Southern use. Dial.* 2. To move from one of the Southern states in order to take a better job in a Northern industrial town. *Negro use.*

sell [one's] saddle. To be out of funds; to be extremely poor. *Southwestern use. From the cowboy use; the cowboy's saddle was often his most prized possession, sold only in cases of extreme necessity.*

semolia. *n.* A stupid or foolish person. *Some Negro use.*

sender. *n.* 1. An expert swing or jive musician, whose playing sends one. *Orig. c1935 swing and jive use.* → 2. A swing or jive devotee; esp., an attractive, smartly dressed, hep person popular with the opposite sex. *Jive, swing, and some general Negro use until c1942.* → 3. Anything or anyone that thrills, excites, exhilarates, or arouses enthusiasm. *Some general jazz use. Almost always modified by "solid."*

send-off. *n.* 1. The act or an instance of wishing a person well on his departure or beginning of a new job, career, or the like. Often in "a royal send-off" = elaborate well-wishing or an elaborate party to celebrate a departure or new career. 2. A funeral.

send [one] to the showers. 1. In baseball, to remove a player [usu. a pitcher] in favor of another who is more effective; to eject a baseball player from a game for rudeness to the umpires. *Since c1920; because such a removed or ejected player takes a shower and changes to his street clothes.* → 2. To reject a person.

send up. To send or sentence to prison.

sensaysh. *adj.* Sensational. *Fairly common, though considered affected.*

serendipity. *n.* The faculty of finding valuable or agreeable things without actually looking for them. *Coined by Horace Walpole in 1754, after the three princes of Serendip who, in their travels, always gained by chance things they did not seek.*

serious, be. To be in love with and court one of the opposite sex. *Lit. = "serious" as opposed to dating for fun or merely because one enjoys another's company. Very common.*

serum. *n.* Any intoxicating drink, whether good whisky or merely flavored alcohol. *Usu. used humorously. W.W.II Army use.*

session. *n.* 1. Specif. = jam session. *Jazz musician use.* 2. A dance or social gathering, a jump. *Hip teenage use since c1955.*

set. *n.* A dance band's turn or time on stage during a concert or a dance.

set [someone] back. To cost someone money. *Said of a purchase or service, usu. in "How much will it set me back?" Since c1890. Very common.*

set of threads. A suit of clothing, esp. a new or stylish one as worn by a bop musician. *Orig. c1946 bop use; a variant of the older "set of drapes," which it is replacing in general jazz use.*

settle. *v.t.* 1. To imprison. *Underworld use.* 2. Specif., to take revenge on, get even with, maliciously harm, or ruin someone.

settle [someone's] hash. To refute, rebuff, or squelch; to deflate someone's enthusiasm or self-righteousness; to point out obvious flaws of character or intellect, usu. in short, telling comments.

set up. 1. To provide or give someone whisky or food, usu. by placing the items, or setting them up, on a bar, as by a bartender.

Since c1870. → 2. To treat someone to whisky, beer, or food. *Since c1890.* → 3. To treat or stake someone; to pay another's way, ranging from a movie ticket to an expensive trip or investment. → 4. To set silverware, china, and napkins on a table in preparation for a meal. 5. To weaken another so that he may be more readily overcome. → 6. Fig., to weaken another so that he may be duped or swindled; to lead another to the point of being duped. *Since c1875.* 7. To be wealthy; to be fortunate; to possess or be in a position to possess all facets of happiness.

set-up. *n.* 1. Any person easily cheated, tricked, victimized, defeated, fooled, duped, or compromised; one who is easy to convince; a gullible person. → 2. An easy task or job; that which can be done, obtained, or fulfilled easily. 3. The accouterments to a highball or a drink of whisky; a glass containing enough ice for a highball, or a glass and a container of ice, and carbonated water, ginger ale, or another mixer. *Common since c1920.* 4. An organization; the method of an organization. 5. A set of factors or circumstances. *Since c1930.* 6. A house, office, or room; the floor plan and furnishings of a room, house, or office. *Usu. in the amenity, e.g., "You have a nice set-up here." adj. Elated; encouraged. Since c1930.*

seventeener. *n.* A corpse. *Some underworld use from the Australian underworld term.*

seventy-eight; 78. *n.* A phonograph record made to play on a turntable revolving at a speed of 78 revolutions per minute, the old standard for records.

seventy-'leven. *n.* Any fairly large number, usu. under 100; many; an indeterminate number.

sewer hog. A ditch digger for a construction company or road-building firm.

sew up. To conclude, finish; to make certain of success, usu. by completing the key arrangements. *Colloq.*

sex job. 1. A female who can be easily possessed; a promiscuous woman; a nymphomaniac. → 2. A sexually attractive woman; a woman one would like to possess.

sex pot. A female who is extremely attractive sexually; a woman whose appearance and personality are sexy.

sexy. *adj.* Capable of or promising high speed and maneuverability. *Said of an experimental or new-model airplane. Mainly Air Force use.*

Sh. A hissed request or command to another to be quiet or shut up. *Colloq.*

shack. *n.* 1. A brakeman on a freight train. *There are three possible origins: from the days before automatic couplers, when brakemen "shackled" the cars together; from the brakemen's duty of "shaking" hobos awake; from the rear brakeman's position in the "shack" = caboose. Wide railroad, hobo, carnival, and circus use.* 2. Any shack, public place, town, or region where hobos meet. *Hobo use.*

shack fever. 1. Fatigue; sleepiness. *Hobo use.* 2. Fear of hopping a freight, the desire to remain out of sight, failing health, a disgust with the life of a hobo, or anything else that keeps a hobo from traveling. *Hobo use.*

shack job. 1. A promiscuous woman; a mistress, esp. a soldier's mistress; a common-law-wife. → 2. A sexual liaison of more than temporary duration. *Common since cW.W.II.*

shack man. 1. A married man. → 2. A man, esp. a soldier, who has a sexual liaison or keeps a mistress in a dwelling for which he pays the rent; a soldier who sleeps with a mistress in their room or apartment instead of sleeping in Army quarters. *Since W.W.II.*

shack rat. A soldier who shacks up. *W.W.II Army use.*

shack up; shack up with. 1. Specif., to provide living quarters for and live with, at least intermittently, one's mistress; to live with one's mistress or paramour; to have a fairly permanent sexual relationship with a woman; to have a sexual liaison of some duration with the same woman. *Orig. c1940, truck-driver and traveling salesman use. Became common with soldiers during W.W.II to mean setting up housekeeping with a local woman near an Army base. Universally known civilian use.* → 2. To spend a night or a longer period in intimacy with a woman. → 3. To occupy living quarters; to live, room, or board at a place.

shade. *n.* A receiver of stolen goods; a fence. *Because the receiver shields the thief by taking the incriminating stolen goods off his hands.*

shad-mouth. *n.* A person having a protuberant upper lip.

shadow. *n.* 1. A parasitic follower. *Colloq.* 2. A detective. *v.t.* To follow a person surreptitiously; specif., to follow a criminal or criminal suspect in order to know his whereabouts, ascertain his friends and daily routine, and the like; said of policemen and detectives. *Colloq.*

shady. *adj.* Dishonest, unethical, untrustworthy. *Colloq.*

shaft. *n.* An act or an instance of being taken advantage of, unfairly treated, deceived, tricked, cheated, or victimized; a raw deal. —**s.** *n.pl.* Attractive or sexually appealing female legs. *Since c1935.*

shag. *adj.* With a date or escort. *Usu. in "Are you going to a party stag or shag?" Fairly common student use since c1940. Some teenage use since c1955. v.i.* To depart, esp. rapidly; to run, to hurry. *v.t.* To chase something. *Almost entirely limited to use by boys between 8 and 15 years old.*

n. One's date or escort. *adj., adv.,* & *exclam.* Remarkable; wonderful(ly), very satisfying, great. *Teenage use since c1958.* —*ger. n.* A police shadow. *Lit., one who shags = chases or follows.*

shake. *n.* 1. A party to which each guest brings a small amount of money to help pay the host's rent; a rent party. 2. Lit., a shake of the dice; fig., a chance, an opportunity. *Usu. in "fair shake."* 3. The act of blackmailing; a shake-down. 4. Shakedown money; bribe money; graft. 5. A moment. *Orig. from "two shakes of a lamb's tail." v.i.* 1. To wiggle one's hips in a lascivious manner. 2. To dance. *Facetious. v.t.* To shake down someone. *Since c1920. Perhaps from the Brit. sl. "show a leg."*

shake, on the. Engaged in crime, esp. shakedowns or extortion.

shake, put [someone] on the; shake on [someone], put the. To extort money, as by torture or threat of death; to shake down. *Underworld use.*

shake, the. *n.* The act or an instance of ridding oneself of an unwanted friend or relationship; refusal or dismissal of a person. *Fig., the act of shaking oneself loose from an attachment or a follower.*

shake a leg. Hurry; make haste. *Often denotes impatience at someone's slowness.*

shake a wicked (mean) calf (hoof, leg). To dance, esp. to dance well or to like to dance.

shake-down; shakedown. *n.* 1. A search or searching of a person or place. 2. A demand for money; blackmail; extortion. **shake down.** 1. To search, esp. a person for contraband or arms. 2. To extort money by blackmail or a confidence game; to work the protection racket. *Very common. Orig. from image of shaking fruit from a tree, or perhaps of turning a person upside down and shaking money out of his pockets.*

shake it up. *imp.* Hurry; hurry up; shake a leg.

shakes, the. *n.pl.* 1. Fever or chills accompanied by trembling. *Since c1840.* 2. An attack of trembling, usu. from anxiety or as the aftermath of excessive drinking or of narcotic use; the heebie-jeebies; the willies.

shake-up. *n.* 1. A general reassignment of personnel to new tasks or locales; a general firing of old employees in order to hire new ones; a reorganization of personnel or work methods. *Since c1885. Now colloq.* 2. A mixture of two or more whiskies or liquors shaken together and drunk.

sham. *n.* 1. A policeman. *Though it is sometimes claimed this orig. in "shamrock" in ref. to Irish policeman of N.Y.C., it is claimed to be a shortening of "shamus," perhaps reinforced by stand. "sham," showing the underworld's opinion of the police.* 2. A small pillow, as used behind one's back while sitting on a couch or for decoration. *Dial.*

shambro. *n.* = shamrock, the drink. *From "shambrogue," obs. variant of "shamrock."*

shampoo. *n.* Champagne. *Some facetious use. Based on the phonetic spelling of "champagne."*

Shamrock; shamrock. *n.* 1. A person of Irish origin or descent. 2. A mixture of stout and whisky. *Traditionally a favorite of the Irish. adj.* Irish.

shamus; shammus; shamos; shommus. *n.* 1. A policeman; increasingly, a police, hotel, or private detective; also a watchman or guard. *Very common, esp. in detective fiction, since c1930. The spelling "shamus" is much more freq. than the other forms. Prob. from the Hebr. "shomus" = caretaker or synagogue watchman, reinforced by Irish proper names "Shamus" and "Seamas." The most common pronunciation rhymes with "Thomas," but the Irish of N.Y.C. pronounce it* *"shay-mus."* → 2. A police informer; a stool pigeon. 3. Anyone with minor influence or semi-official status; a political lackey. *It is interesting to note that a similar American Indian word "shaman" = medicine man had the same sl. meaning among Indians.*

shanghai. *v.t.* To abduct a man, usu. a sailor, and force him to work as a sailor on one's own ship. *Colloq.*

Shangri La. *n.* A mythical land of eternal youth and beauty; an earthly paradise; any place very well liked. *From the novel "Lost Horizon," by James Hilton.*

shank. *v.t.* To stab a person, whether in the leg or not. *Teenage street gang use since c1955.*

shanks' mare; shanks' pony. 1. The legs considered as a means of transportation. 2. Walking as opposed to riding. 3. = pot luck. *A fairly recent usage, apparently due to confusion of the orig. sl. meaning.*

shanty. *n.* 1. A shack. *Colloq.* 2. A black eye; a shiner.

shanty Irish. Poor Irish people, lit. or fig., living in shanties or shanty-towns.

shanty-town. *n.* 1. Lit., a town of shacks; a group of shacks and makeshift dwellings on the outskirts of a city, usu. populated by hobos, men out of work, and, esp. in 19C America, poor immigrant laborers. *An old term revived during Depression of the 1930's* → 2. The poorer or older residential neighborhoods of a community; a dilapidated section of town.

shape. *n.* 1. = shape-up. 2. A woman's figure, esp. when attractive. *Usu. in "She's got a shape" = she has a good figure. c1940, when a good figure meant a slim waist, fairly prominent breasts, and shapely hips and legs.*

shape in with. To associate with; to pal around with.

shape-up. *n.* The system of hiring longshoremen for a job by choosing men from a group assembled on a dock or at a union hall; the group so assembled. *The term is often, though not always, associated with the practice of paying money to the hiring boss in return for being chosen.*

shark. *n.* 1. An expert. 2. A cheater, esp. a person who uses his skill in a game to deceive his opponent, as a "pool shark" or "card shark." *The usu. method of the shark is to keep his proficiency secret until a novice has been enticed into the game or until the stakes have mounted high, then to use his superior skill to clean out his opponents.* 3. An employment agent; a hiring boss. *Hobo use.*

sharp. *n.* 1. An expert, usu. at card games or other gambling games; a shark. → 2. One skilled in forms of cheating, esp. in sleight-of-hand with playing cards; a crooked gambler; one who seeks to take, or habitually takes, advantage of others. *adj.* 1. Mentally alert; witty; quick thinking; smart; wise; in the know; hep. *Fig., having a keen mind that penetrates into problems easily; having a rapier-like wit. Reinforced by the pop. saying, "Sharp as a tack."* 2. Stylish; trim; neatly and smartly dressed; natty; specif., dressed in the latest, or in the latest hep, fashion; attractive and modern. 3. Satisfactory, satisfying; attractive or pleasing, esp. to a modern, hep person; all right, o.k. *The above two uses are assoc. with jive use, but were all common by c1935. They are in common jazz and fairly common teenage and student use. They imply an all-inclusive or complete approval of a person or thing. To older people, however, "sharp" still carries a connotation of unrefined, garish, and daring.* 4. Specif., shrewd and ambitious; aware of, alert to, and using one's intelligence only to take quick advantage of opportunities for personal gain; worldly, sophisticated, and cynical. *This shift in meaning from the first adj. use given above became most apparent during W.W.II. adv.* Stylishly; smartly; gaudily. —ie. *n.* 1. One who dances expertly to swing music; a devotee of swing. *Jitterbug use.* 2. A flashy dresser; a smartly dressed man. 3. A shrewd, alert person. 4. A cheat or swindler.

shave. *v.t.* To defeat, esp. by a small margin; to take advantage of. —r. *n.* A boy, lad, usu. in "little shaver." *Colloq.*

shave-tail. *n.* 1. A mule, esp. a young, unbroken, or untried animal. *Still some farm and lumberjack use. Dial. and archaic.* → 2. An inexperienced young man; a tenderfoot. *Still some ranch and lumberjack use. Dial. and archaic.* 3. Any second lieutenant. *Wide W.W.II Army use.*

shear; sheer. *adj.* = cool. *Some bop and cool use c1948–c1955.*

shebang. *n.* A complete residence, office, or place; a collection of all one's possessions; a collection of anything; an entire series of actions. *Usu. in "the whole shebang." Since c1870; now colloq.*

sheep-skin; sheepskin. *n.* A diploma. *Since at least 1800. From the vellum orig. used, and still occasionally used, for diplomas. Colloq.*

sheet. *n.* 1. A newspaper. From the "sheets" of paper, reinforced by hobo use of newspapers to sleep on and under. 2. *Specif.* = scratch. 3. A criminal's dossier, record, or file.

shekels. *n.pl.* Money, wealth. *Since c1870; still in use.*

shelf, on the. 1. Socially inactive; often said of a woman who has broken her engagement to be married. 2. Postponed, deferred; esp. for further study or consideration—said of a plan or project. *Business use.*

shell. *v.i., v.t.* To shell out; to pay.

shellacking. *n.* 1. A beating. 2. A

defeat; a complete failure; usu. used in sports to mean a rout or utter defeat.

shell out. To pay or contribute; to spend; to pay extortion or bribe money. *Since c1830.*

shemale. *n.* A female, esp. a disliked, distrusted woman; a bitch.

shenanigans. *n.pl.* Tricks, pranks, nonsense; petty cheating or deception. *Since c1870; may be from Irish "sionnochuigham" = I play tricks.*

she-she. *n.* A girl or young woman; a chick; orig. a sexually attractive or promiscuous girl or woman native of a Pacific Island or occupied country. *W.W.II USN and Army use. Based on pigeon Eng.*

shiever. *n.* A double-crosser.

shifter. *n.* 1. A go-between between a thief and a fence; lit., one who shifts loot from a thief to a receiver of stolen goods. *Some underworld use.* → 2. A fence. *Some underworld use.*

shiftie. *n.* An unreliable girl.

shiftie-eyed; shifty-eyed. *adj.* Sneaky; mean; untrustworthy.

shikker; shicker. *adj.* Drunk. *From the Yiddish. Some popularity since c1927.*

shikker, on the. 1. Drunk. 2. Known to be a habitual drunkard.

shill. *n.* 1. A confederate of a gambler, con man, pitchman, or auctioneer, or an employee of a gambling house, carnival, circus, or auction room, who acts as a decoy to encourage real customers to gamble, bid, purchase tickets, or the like. Pretending to be a bona fide customer, the shill places bets, makes bids, buys tickets, or pretends to be convinced by a con man, in order to start or encourage real betting, bidding, buying, or confidence. *Very common since c1925.* → 2. A card-player or gambler who is supplied with chips or money by the house so that there will always be enough players for a game. → 3. A pitchman, auctioneer, carnival barker; an advertising or public relations employee; anyone whose job it is to create business or encourage buying through personal appeals or recommendations. *c1945.* 4. A policeman's club or nightstick. *Orig. from "shillelagh." v.i.* To act or work as a shill.

shillaber. *n.* = shill. *Orig.* = *a booster or satisfied customer. Circus use. Is at least as old as, and may be the orig. of, "shill."*

shim. *n.* = square, esp. one not hep to rock and roll music. *Mainly rock and roll use since c1955, but some earlier jazz use.*

shimmy pudding. Gelatin prepared for eating.

shindig. *n.* 1. A party, gathering, or festival; any event that attracts guests or spectators. → 2. A dancing party; a dance. *Since c1925. May orig. have been a Western term ("shin" plus "dig"), but more prob. evolved from "shindy."*

shine. *n.* 1. A good recitation; a good grade. 2. Whisky; esp. bootleg whisky or moonshine. *adj.* [derog.] Negro. *v.i.* To excel; to accomplish something in a conspicuously proficient manner. *Colloq.* —r. *n.* 1. A black eye; a mouse. *Since c1900; very common.* 2. A shiny, mirrorlike area on a table top, cigarette case, ring, or the like, in which a dishonest card dealer can see the face of each card as he deals. *Gambler use.*

shine to, take a. To take a liking to. *Colloq. since c1840.*

shine up to [someone]. To curry favor.

shingle. *n.* 1. Lit. and fig., a framed certificate of a medical, law, or other professional degree; a framed certificate of any college or university degree or membership in an organization. 2. A slice of toast. *Some use since c1935.*

shinny. *n.* = shiny. *Dial. v.i., v.t.* Lit. and fig., to climb; also, to play the game of shinny; hence, to be active. *Now colloq.*

shiny; shinny. Liquor.

shirt on, keep [one's]. To be calm; not to be excited or impatient; to await [one's] turn. *In direct discourse, used chiefly in the imperative, "Keep your shirt on!" Colloq. since c1850.*

shirttail. *n.* An editorial column in a newspaper. *Newspaper use.*

shirttail kin. A distant relative, as a fourth cousin. *Mostly dial. use in Southern and Midwestern rural areas.*

shiv. *n.* 1. A knife, esp. considered as a weapon. *Orig. prob. from "shove" plus "shave." Now very common though still retaining an underworld connotation.* → 2. A razor; any object with a sharp cutting blade. *Mainly hobo use. v.t.* To cut; to stab.

shiv artist. A person who habitually uses a knife as a weapon.

shivering Liz. Gelatin dessert. *Some Army, USN, and lunch-counter use.*

shivoo; shivvoo. *n.* A party. *Some Army use since W.W.I. From Fr. "chez vous."*

shlub. *n.* = schlub.

shmeikle. *v.t.* To swindle; to con; to fast-talk. *From the Yiddish.*

shmo. *n.* = schmo.

Shmoo; shmoo. *n.* A mythical animal orig. and pop. by Al Capp in his synd. newsp. comic strip, *"Li'l Abner."* *These wonderful creatures multiply very rapidly, lay eggs, give milk, when broiled taste like steak, when fried taste like chicken, and lie down and die if one looks at them hungrily; they symbolize the richness of the earth, abundance, or a simple, good life. Reinforced by, and perh. taken from, the Yiddish "shmoo"* = profit, esp. unethical profit.

shnook. *n.* = schnook.

shocker. *n.* A shocking, horrifying, or thrilling movie, book, or story; a sensational story.

shoe. *n.* A person who is well dressed. *c1950; used by bop musicians.*

shoe-string. *n.* **1.** A small amount of money, esp. if used as working capital. *Colloq.* **2.** Wine, esp. cheap red wine. *adj.* Describing a business venture started with little capital.

shommus. *n.* = shamus.

shoo-fly; shu-fly. *interj.* A mild expression of surprise or recognition of something remarkable or unusual. *A term that has reappeared from time to time, usu. without much specif. meaning. It seems to evoke humorous images; has been used enough as a scat sound to be considered as assoc. with that form of singing.*

shoo-in. *n.* **1.** An inferior horse designated to defeat superior horses in a fixed race. *Horse-racing use.* → **2.** Any probable winner of a sporting event or contest of any kind; one favored or expected to win easily; a winner.

shook up. *adj.* **1.** Emotionally agitated, upset; shocked; lit., shaken with fear, worry, or relief. *Wide teenage use since c1955. Some general use.* **2.** Excited; enthusiastic; extremely happy, pleased, or satisfied; in love. *Wide teenage rock and roll use since c1955.*

shoot. *v.t.* **1.** To throw a baseball hard. **2.** To photograph; to take a photograph of. **3.** To pass food at the table. *v.i.* **1.** As a command = "Go ahead"; "I'm ready"; "Begin"; "Continue"; "Tell me now." *The most common use.* **2.** = shoot the breeze, shoot (the) bull. **3.** To take an intravenous injection of a narcotic drug. *Narcotic addict use.*

shoot a line. To flatter, exaggerate, or lie.

shoot [one's] breakfast (lunch, dinner, supper, cookies). To vomit. *Some student use since c1925. Fairly common.*

shoot (the) bull. **1.** To talk, gossip, chat; to lie, exaggerate, flatter, or boast.

shooting gallery. **1.** Any place where an addict or addicts can receive an injection of a narcotic drug; a pad. *Addict use.* **2.** A

gathering or party of addicts who have assembled for the purpose of taking drugs by injection. *Addict use.*

shooting iron. A pistol. *Still some Western farm and ranch use; familiar to all from cowboy movies.*

shooting match. All the persons or things concerned in a given matter; the whole shebang. *Usu. in the phrase "the whole shooting match."*

shoot off [one's] mouth (face, bazoo). To talk, esp. to talk too much and with too little regard for propriety; to disclose a confidence; to express an opinion strongly, esp. one who is insulting or enraging to others, to say what is better left unsaid; to exaggerate or brag; to talk too much, boastfully, or objectionably.

shoot-out. *n.* **1.** In the game of dice, the come-out. **2.** A gun duel.

shoot the breeze. **1.** To talk idly or gossip; to gather for the purpose of talking idly; esp., to speculate lackadaisically or relate exaggerated accounts of past events. *Wide W.W.II use, bragging, lawyering, and telling tall tales being a favorite occupation of soldiers aboard ship or confined to base.* → **2.** To speak or write windily and emptily; to speak nonsense, to lie, etc. *c1950.*

shoot the works. To go to the limit in anything whatever, as to tell all one knows about something, or to spend or gamble all one's money; to go the whole hog.

shoot [one's] wad. **1.** Lit. and fig., to chance everything on one gamble; to make a final try with all one's resources, failing which one will be defeated. *From dice player use, where one can shoot one's wad or all one's money on one throw of the dice.* → **2.** To have one's say; to speak one's piece. → **3.** To be finished or through, to have a surfeit. *All uses since c1925.*

shop. *n.* An office.

short. *n.* 1. An automobile. *c1930. Prob. orig. used in the term "hot short"* = *a stolen car, or a car stolen to be used as a getaway car by gunmen, thieves, or the like. Prob. orig. in Chicago underworld.* → 2. Any car, esp. a small foreign sports car. *v.i., v.t.* Having only a little money; not having enough money for a specif. purpose; lacking a specif. amount of money in order to be able to pay a debt or the required price of something. *adj.* 1. Lacking; missing. *Colloq.* → 2. Specif., without sufficient funds. —ie. *n.* 1. Any short person. *Used both indirectly and as a term of direct address. Colloq.* 2. Anything that is short, small, or abbreviated. → 3. A woman's short nightgown. *The style and usage have been common since c1945. adj.* Short. *Colloq.* —s. *n.pl.* Small sums of money; personal belongings.

short-arm. *n.* = short-arm inspection. *This form became common during W.W.II.*

short-arm drill = short-arm inspection.

short-arm inspection. 1. A medical inspection of the relaxed penis, usu. for signs of venereal disease. *Common Army use since c1930, the usu. expression during and since W.W.II. The "short-arm" represents the relaxed penis; the term is based on the frequent inspection of the soldier's rifle or "arm."* → 2. Any inspection of the genitals, medical or otherwise. *Some male civilian use since W.W.II.*

short-change artist. The operator of a carnival booth or circus sideshow who is skilled in cheating customers by returning to them less than their proper change. *Orig. circus use.*

short end of the stick. The least desirable lot, the worst of a transaction; an instance of being cheated, ignored, taken advantage of, or receiving unfair or unfavorable treatment. *Very common since c1940. Although the image is that of the short end as opposed to the larger quantity of the large end of a stick, which can be wielded, the etymology is more vulgar; fig., the short end is the end of a stick poked up another's rectum by the one in command of the situation, who holds the other end.*

short of hat size. Lacking in intellect; stupid.

short one. A single shot of whisky, as opposed to a double; a jigger of whisky; a quick drink.

short pint. Any extremely short person; a dwarf.

shorts, the. *n.* The "trouble" or "sickness" of being without funds.

short-sheet. *v.i., v.t.* 1. To play any practical joke. *Orig. from the common sailors' prank of folding one sheet in two to simulate both the top and bottom sheet of a bed; when the victim gets into bed, his legs are stopped short by the fold in the sheet.* 2. To give someone the short end of the stick.

short-staker. *n.* A transient or migratory worker; lit., one who works only long enough to earn a stake in order to move on. *c1920 to present.*

shortstop. *v.t.* To stop a serving plate being passed to another at the table in order to help oneself first. *n.* At meals, one who helps himself to food that is being passed to someone else.

shot. *n.* 1. A drink of straight whisky, usu. drunk in one gulp. *Very common since Prohibition. From "scot" or "sceot"* = *a portion, a tax.* 2. An injection from a hypodermic needle; a portion of a drug to be injected; often preceded by the name of the medicine or disease involved; "penicillin shot," "polio shot," etc. *Colloq.* 3. Specif., a portion of a narcotic drug or an injection of a narcotic drug taken by an addict; a fix. *Since c1930. Mainly addict use; fairly well known to* *the general public.* **4.** A photograph; a snapshot. *Colloq. since c1930.* **5.** The act or an instance of detonating an atomic device, usu. in testing atomic bombs. → **6.** The launching of a guided missile or rocket. → **7.** The range, flight, or power of a guided missile or rocket. *The above two uses, becoming common with the development of guided missiles and space flight projects c1955, return the usage to its most early sl. meaning, as it was long ago applied to catapults and bow-and-arrow warfare.* **8.** An instance or the act of ejaculation; fig., coitus or any form of sexual satisfaction enjoyed by a male. Thus "a shot downstairs (or in the front door)" = coitus; "a shot in the back door" = anal intercourse; and "a shot upstairs" = fellatio. *adj.* **1.** Drunk; half-shot. *Very common during and since Prohibition.* → **2.** Suffering from the after effects of drunkenness; afflicted with a hangover. → **3.** Sick; exhausted, tired. *Common since c1935.* → **4.** Used up, worn out, aged. *Said of objects. Common since c1930.*

shotgun. *n.* **1.** Any rapid-fire gun, esp. a machine gun. *Some W.W.II use.* **2.** Spicy, peppery sauce. **3.** A matchmaker, a marriage broker; fig., anyone who brings lovers together. *A folk ety. from the Jewish word "schatchen" = marriage broker, reinforced by "shotgun wedding."*

shotgun quiz. A short written examination given without warning. *Some student use since c1920.*

shotgun wedding. **1.** A wedding demanded by a girl's father because he knows the groom to be sexually intimate with his daughter. *Usu. used jocularly. Orig. because irate farmers were supposed to demand that the spoiler of their daughter's virginity marry the girl, and marched the groom to the preacher at gun point.* **2.** A wedding hastened or made necessary by the bride's pregnancy.

shot in the arm. **1.** A hypodermic injection of a narcotic. *Orig. narcotic addict use.* → **2.** A drink of whisky, usu. straight whisky, drunk in one swallow. *Since c1930.* → **3.** Fig., anything that gives a person new, or esp. renewed, vitality, enthusiasm, determination, or confidence, ranging from dope and whisky to a compliment or a raise in salary; anything that helps one toward success or that contributes to the successful completion of a task. *Since c1935; from "shot" = an injection of a drug.*

shout. *v.i.* **1.** To say something important or well worth listening to. *Usually in "Now you're shouting." Since c1875.* **2.** To chant a religious song with emotion; to sing a blues or spiritual in a highly rhythmic manner with key words spoken loudly and in a high voice. *n.* **1.** A religious hymn sung with much emotion and with a heavily accented rhythm; a revival meeting; an informal dance or rhythmic movement accompanying a religious sermon or spiritual. *Although accompanied by handclapping and actual shouting, the sl. "shout" probably comes from the Gullah rather than from the stand. Eng. "shout."* **2.** A slow blues as sung by a jazz singer in the traditional manner. *The above usages are assoc. with slavery and postslavery Negro congregations and singers. The Negro spiritual contributed much to the shout as used in jazz.*

shove. *v.t.* **1.** To pass counterfeit money. *Since c1850; usu. in phrase "shove the queer."* **2.** To kill. *v.i.* To depart; to leave; to go away. *Since c1870, and therefore older than "shove off."* —r. *n.* One who passes counterfeit money or forged checks.

shovel. *n.* A spoon. —er. *n.* A habitual exaggerator.

shovel, put to bed with a. Lit., so drunk that one cannot return home and go to bed by oneself, but must be assisted.

shove off. *v.i.* To leave, depart; to "shove." *v.t.* To murder.

shove out for. To set out for; to shove off for. *Since c1850.*

show. *n.* An exposure by a girl or woman of her thighs, breasts, or genitals to boys or men. *Usu. used by boys from 10 to 15 years old.* *v.i.* To appear in person; to appear on the scene; to be present.

showboat. *v.i.* To show off.

showcase. *n.* 1. An entertainment, theater, nightclub, rehearsal, or performance whose main purpose is to show the merits of the performers to an audience of prospective employers, such as theatrical producers, booking agents, directors, or the like. → 2. An audience many of whom were admitted on free tickets. *Theater use.*

showdown. *n.* 1. The act of bringing facts out into the open where the persons concerned may know of them. → 2. A meeting between two opposing people or parties to settle their disputes; a meeting between two antagonists. *adj.* Crucial, determining.

shower down. To whip a racehorse; lit., to rain blows down on the horse. *Jockey and some sportswriter use.*

shower-stick. *n.* An umbrella. *Some jocular and dial. use.*

show-off. *n.* A person given to ostentatious behavior; a braggart. *Colloq.* **show off.** To act like a show-off. *Colloq.*

show out. To brag; to show off. *Dial.*

show-shop. *n.* A theater.

show up. 1. To make a personal appearance; to arrive. *Now colloq.* 2. To expose or reveal someone; to make another person seem inefficient, ridiculous, or inferior. *Colloq.* 3. = show-up line.

show-up line. A police line-up of suspected criminals, usu. presented for possible identification by witnesses.

shrewd dude. A well-dressed, alert boy or man. *A rather artificial example of rhyming sl. attrib. to teenagers.*

shrimp. *n.* Any short person.

shuck. *v.i., v.t.* 1. To undress, esp. to take off one's clothes quickly or in the presence of another or others. 2. = fake. *Some cool and far out use.*

shuffler. *n.* 1. A worker who is out of a job. 2. A migratory worker. 3. A grifter.

shu-fly = shoo-fly.

shush; sush. *v.i.* To hush up; also, to say "Shush" to someone in order to hush him up. *Colloq.* *v.t.* To hush a person up, as by saying "Sh!" or "Hush!" *Colloq. From "sh—" plus "hush."*

shut down; shut off. *v.t.* To defeat someone, or a team, in a sporting contest. **shut-down; shut-off.** *adj.* Defeated. **shutdown.** *n.* A stoppage of work; the temporary closing of a factory.

shut-eye; shuteye. *n.* 1. Sleep. *Colloq. Common since c1920.* 2. Unconsciousness; an act or instance of losing consciousness for any reason; a pass-out.

shut of. *adj.* Rid of; finished with. *Now mainly dial.* *v.t.* To rid oneself of.

shut off = shut down.

shut out. 1. In sports, to hold an opposing team scoreless. *Since c1880.* 2. To prevent from gambling or playing, usu. by refusing to take a person's bet; usu. a pred. adj. = to be prevented from participating in a gambling play because one's wager has been placed too late. **shutout; shut-out.** *n.* A game in which one team does not score.

shutterbug. *n.* A photography enthusiast; a photographer. *The most common of the words ending in "bug."* **shutters.** *n.* The eyelids; the eyes.

shutting out = shutout.

shut [one's] trap. To stop talking; to shut up. *Brought to the colonies by Eng. settlers in 17C.*

shut up. A command or plea to another to stop talking or to talk about a different topic. *Colloq.*

shy guy. A modest or bashful boy or man.

shyster. *n.* 1. A crooked, conniving, small-time lawyer. *Always derog. Since c1885. Colloq.* → 2. Any lawyer.

sick. *v.t.* To vomit. *n.* Nausea. *Both uses colloq. adj.* 1. Lit. and fig., dangerously psychopathic; psychopathic, neurotic; needing psychiatric attention. 2. Gruesome, morbid; dwelling on the morbid. *Thus a "sick" joke is humorous because it has an unexpectedly gruesome or morbid ending. Both uses fairly common since c1955. Assoc. with earlier cool and beat use; reinforced by the sound of "sick" in "psychiatry."*

sick and tired of. Completely disgusted with; out of patience with; fed up with. *Colloq.*

side. *n.* 1. An actor's lines; a page of script for a play. *Theater use since c1925.* 2. A phonograph record; the piece of music on one side of a phonograph recording. *adj.* Other than one's job, girl friend, or the like; e.g., a "side job" is a job often part time, in addition to one's regular job. *Lit., something held or done on the side or besides something else.*

side, go over the. To leave a ship or base without a pass. *Fig. to slip over the side of a ship. A USN variant of "go over the hill."*

side, on the. *Fig.*, besides; in addition to one's main or regular job, spouse, or order. Thus one may: work part time "on the side" = to earn extra money while not occupied with one's regular job; have a lover "on the side" = in addition to one's usual or known wife, fiancée, or lover; or order a hamburger in a restaurant with beans "on the side" = in addition to the main order of the hamburger.

sidearms. *n.pl.* Salt and pepper; cream and sugar; condiments placed on the table during a meal. *Fairly common Army use during W.W.II and some Armed Forces use since c1925. Because such items supplement the meal as actual sidearms supplement heavier weapons; also reinforced by "side dishes."*

side-bar. *adj.* Auxiliary; supplementary; part-time.

side-door Pullman. A railroad box-car. *Hobo and railroad use.*

side-kick; sidekick. *n.* 1. A partner; a close friend or comrade; a pal; a buddy. *Common since c1910. A term used mostly by males.* 2. A side pocket in a garment; esp. the side pocket of a pair of trousers. *Orig. pickpocket use.*

sidetrack. *v.t.* To arrest.

sidewalks, hit the. 1. To look for employment; to go from door to door seeking a job. 2. = hit the bricks.

sidewalk superintendent. A person who passes the time by watching the construction of a new building or other construction work.

side-wheeler. *n.* 1. In baseball, a left-handed pitcher. → 2. Any left-handed person. 3. In baseball, a pitcher who delivers his pitch with a side-arm motion, as opposed to overhand. 4. A pacer; a horse that paces.

sidewinder. *n.* 1. A hard, swinging blow with the fist, esp. when the fist and arm move in an arc from the body, as opposed to a short, straight blow. *Since c1840.* → 2. A tough, rough man, prone to anger and fighting. → 3. A bodyguard; a hired thug; a gangster's side-kick.

—sie; —sy. A suffix, sometimes diminutive, usu. indicating familiarity or affection, but sometimes used whimsically.

sieve. *n.* 1. An old, dilapidated, leaky ship. *Very old maritime use.* 2. In sports, a player or team that cannot prevent opponents from scoring. 3. Any house, car, or other possession whose upkeep is high, draining money from the possessor.

signify. *v.i.* To pretend to have knowledge; to pretend to be hip, esp. when such pretentions cause one to trifle with an important matter. *Mainly Negro use.*

sign-off. *n.* The act of ending a day's broadcasting; said of radio stations. *Now also applied to television.* **sign off.** To shut up, usu. a command or entreaty to shut up. *Since c1930; orig. from the radio use.*

sign-out. *n.* The act of signing one's name upon leaving a place; also, a name so signed. *Colloq.*

sign-up. *n.* 1. Registration by signing one's name. → 2. Fig., the act of joining or giving one's support to an organization, political party, or other group.

silk. *n.* A kerchief or muffler.

silk, hit the. To make a parachute jump; to bail out of an aircraft. *Common W.W.II paratroop and Air Force use.*

silk broad. A white girl. *Some Negro use.*

silver. *n.* Small change; coins; pennies, nickels, dimes, quarters, and fifty-cent pieces.

silver Jeff. 1. A quarter; the sum of 25¢. 2. A nickel; the sum of 5¢. *Both meanings in rock-and-roll use since c1955. Because the face of Thomas Jefferson appears on modern U.S. nickels.*

silver wing. A fifty-cent piece; the sum of 50¢. *Rock-and-roll and general teenage use since c1955. Because an eagle with spreading wings appears on the U.S. silver fifty-cent piece.*

simmer down; simmer off. To become calm; to quiet down; to stop being frivolous or boisterous and prepare to think or work seriously. *Usu. as a request or a command.*

Simon Legree. 1. Any unsympathetic, unkind, or miserly person. *From the villain's name in the* very pop. novel, "Uncle Tom's Cabin." → 2. Any boss, foreman, manager, or one in authority. *Both meanings are also used jocularly.*

simpatico. *adj.* Sympathetic; understanding; specif., in rapport with the speaker, his cause, or his beliefs. *Since c1955, when several pop. songs about lovers in Italy and in Spanish-speaking countries incorporated the word.*

Simple Simon. A diamond.

sincere. *adj.* Having or deliberately creating a personality that is expertly charming and subtly ingratiating; deliberately, purposely, and subtly amiable, pleasant, and charming, in order to be accepted, liked, successful, or given preferred treatment. *Since c1940; mainly student use. A common bit of serious, albeit jocular, advice is "Whether you mean it or not, be sincere."*

sing. *v.i.* 1. To inform to the police or other officials concerning a crime or criminals; to squeal. *Orig. underworld use.* → 2. To confess; to admit one's own guilt. → 3. To give a sales talk; to make a spiel. *Orig. pitchman use.* —**er.** *n.* A squealer; a stool pigeon.

single. *n.* 1. A one-dollar bill; one dollar. 2. One who works alone, without partners. *Orig. underworld use.* 3. A nightclub or entertainment act composed of one person; a star.

single-jack. *n.* A one-legged, one-armed, or one-eyed beggar.

single-o. *adj.* 1. Unmarried; single. **sing out** = sing.

sinker. *n.* 1. A doughnut. 2. In baseball, a pitch thrown in such a manner that it dips downward in its flight as it nears the batter. *Since c1940.*

sinkers. *n.pl.* A person's feet, esp. if large. *From "boats."*

sis. *n.* 1. A sister. 2. A cowardly, weak, or effeminate boy. *c1900; colloq.* 3. Any girl or young woman. *From "sister."* —**sy; cissy.** *n.* 1. A sister. *From "sis."* 2. A cowardly, weak, or effeminate boy or man. *Colloq.* 3. Any soft drink containing carbonated water or Coca-Cola and artificial flavoring, esp. vanilla flavoring. *Onomatopoetic, from the sound of the carbonated water coming from the tap. adj.* Cowardly, effeminate, weak. *Since c1890.* —ter. *n.* Any girl or young woman. *Orig. used in exasperation or as direct address to a stranger, often implying anger, disgust, lack of sympathy, or the like.*

sissy pants. 1. An overly well-behaved boy; a sissy. 2. A squeamish person.

sit. *v.i.* To care for or watch an invalid or child other than one's own; to baby-sit. *Often in the terms "sit with [a child, invalid, or the like]" or "sit for [the parents or usu. guardian or watcher]." Since c1945 has begun to replace "baby-sit."* —ter. *n.* 1. The buttocks; usu. in the expression, "My sitter is tired [from sitting or riding]." *Colloq.* 2. One who sits with and watches over a baby, child, invalid, or the like, while the parents or usu. guardians are away temporarily; a baby-sitter.

sit-down. *n.* 1. A meal, usu. a free meal, eaten while sitting at a table, as on a back porch or the like. *Hobo use since c1850.* 2. A sit-down strike.

sit in. To join in a game (usu. of cards), conference, or the like, usu. as a substitute for a regular player or member, but sometimes as an additional member; specif., to join a jazz band and play a few pieces of music with it as a substitute or guest.

sit on [one's] hands. 1. To refrain from applauding an entertainer, act, or the like. *Theater use since c1920.* 2. To do nothing, esp. to do nothing when action is necessary.

sit tight. Lit. and fig., to wait patiently, to remain calm; to await results; to take no further action but to depend on success from actions or factors already accomplished.

sitting duck. Lit. and fig., an easy target, as for scandal or malicious action; fig., an easy mark. *Because in hunting a sitting duck is an easy traget, as compared to one flying.*

sitting in the catbird seat = sitting pretty. *Pop. by baseball announcer "Red" Barber in his c1945–c1955 radio broadcasts of the old Brooklyn Dodger baseball team games. Orig. Southern dial. use.*

sitting pretty. 1. Fig., in a favorable or commanding position; having an advantage; in command of a situation. 2. Successful; wealthy; living comfortably; safe; in an advantageous position; secure. *Common since W.W.I.*

situash. *n.* Situation.

sitzbein; sitsbein. *n.pl.* The buttocks, as used for sitting; the rump. *Lit. = "sitting bone"; from the German.*

siwash. *n.* 1. An American Indian; a hunter or prospector or the like who lives like an Indian. *Northwestern use; archaic. From Chinook jargon.* 2. A boisterous person; a person not adjusted to contemporary living. *Since c1930, some ranch and logger use.*

six bits. The sum of 75¢. *Since c1850; still most common in the West. Lit., three times two bits.*

sixer. *n.* A six-months' prison sentence. *Some underworld use.*

six-gun. *n.* A pistol; esp., a revolver or six-shooter. *Based on "six-shooter."*

six-shooter. *n.* 1. A revolver holding six cartridges. → 2. Any revolver or pistol.

six ways to (for) Sunday. In many ways, in all possible ways; thoroughly; completely. *Some use since c1840; often in "I was deceived (cheated, victimized) six ways to Sunday."*

size-up. *n.* An estimate; the act of estimating or judging.

sizzle. *v.i.* To die in the electric chair; to fry. —r. *n.* 1. Lit. and fig., anything that is or anyone who is hot or "hot" in any of their usages; anything that is or anyone who is hot, fast, exciting, sexually stimulating, or stolen. → 2. Specif., a hard blow with the fist; a knockout punch. *c1920 prize fight use.* → 3. Specif., in baseball, a fast, hard-hit, low line drive. → 4. Specif., an exciting, vivacious, sexually tempting woman. → 5. Specif., a burlesque dancer or stripper. → 6. Specif., a sensational or lurid story or scandal. → 7. Specif., a funny joke, usu. one about sex. → 8. Any extremely pop. song, book, or movie, or extremely pop. entertainer, successful athlete, or the like. → 9. Specif., an expensive item of stolen goods; a stolen car; a kidnaped person. 10. An inferior cook; esp., a logging-camp or ranch cook.

sizzling. *adj.* "Hot" in any of its usages; stolen; paid as a kidnaping ransom.

sizz-water. *n.* Carbonated water; fizz water.

skads. *n.* = scads.

skate. *v.i.* To avoid paying, to evade a creditor. *The image is of a person who skates away, reinforced by "cheap-skate."* *n.* 1. An inferior, decrepit, or useless horse. *Ranch, farm, and some racing use.* 2. A contemptible person. *Since c1890. From "cheap-skate."*

skate on thin ice. To take chances; to conduct oneself in a manner verging on the questionable or dangerous. *Colloq.*

skaty-eight. *n.* Any indeterminate large number; forty-'leven.

skee. *n.* 1. Whisky. *A respelling of "—sky" in "whisky." Mainly dial.* 2. Opium. *Some underworld use c1930.*

skeeter. *n.* A mosquito. *Colloq. since 1850; mainly dial.*

sker-ewy. *adj.* = screwy. *A prime ex. of sl. emphasis by a louder or longer pronunciation of the first syllable.*

sketch. *n.* = hot sketch.

skewgee. *adj.* Askew: said of things. *Dial.*

skid. *n.* Butter; from its resemblance in hot weather to grease. *Some use since c1920.* *v.t.* To pass food at the table. *Some student and Army use.*

skid road; skidroad. *n.* A street or district of a town containing employment agencies, eating places, gambling rooms, and brothels such as cater to or are frequented by loggers, seasonal and migratory workers, and the like; the cheap business street or section of a town. *Orig. logger use; hobo and underworld use since c1915.*

skid row; Skid Row. *n.* Any old, dilapidated street or section of a town containing very cheap bars, eating places, and flop houses where the permanently unemployed, vagrants, beggars, petty criminals, derelicts, degenerates, and, mainly unemployed alcoholics hang out. *A variant of and from "skid road." "Skid row" apparently developed some 60 years after "skid road."*

skids, the. *n.* Fig. the decline, or being on the decline, from success, fame, honesty, good reputation, or sobriety to failure, mediocrity, a life of disappointment, or a bad reputation: the decline from being, or being known as, a successful, or respected member of society to being a failure, a has-been, or a derelict. *In several idioms having to do with the decline, downfall, or ruination of a person or thing: e.g.,* "to put the skids under (to) [someone]"; "to hit the skids"; "on the skids"; "greased for the skids"; or the like. *Fairly common. May be from "skid row."*

skids under (to) [someone or something], put the. To cause someone or something to fail; to cause someone to lose enthusiasm; to ruin a plan; to cause a plan or venture to fail.

skid-top. *n.* A bald man. *Not common.*

skiffle. *n.* = rent party.

skig. *n.* A commission paid a salesman for selling hard-to-sell merchandise; a salesman who specializes in selling hard-to-sell merchandise.

skillet. *n.* A Negro. *Negro use.*

skilley. *n.* Gravy; lit., that which is washed out of the skillet. *Some prison use since c1925; in the U.S. has never = stew or porridge, as it has in Brit. sl.*

skillion; scillion. *n.* An enormous or inconceivably great number. *Often used facetiously. Colloq.*

skimmer. *n.* 1. A hat, esp. a flat-crowned straw hat with a wide brim. *Attrib. to T. A. Dorgan, cartoonist, died 1929; colloq.* 2. In baseball, a ball hit low over the playing field, so that it skims the grass; a grounder.

skin. *n.* 1. The hand as in the act of shaking hands. *In several expressions = Shake hands: e.g., "Give me some skin"; "Hand me that skin"; "Slip me some skin"; "Lay the skin on me"; and the like. Assoc. with jive use.* 2. One's life. *Colloq.* 3. A stingy person: a skinflint. 4. A horse, esp. an old or worthless horse; specif., a racehorse. 5. A pocketbook; a wallet. *Orig. underworld use; since c1925; from leather of pigskin or cowhide.* 6. A dollar bill; a dollar. 7. Any drum used in an orchestra or by a jazz musician. *Orig. and still predominantly jazz use; since c1930.* 8. A demerit; an official written reprimand. *Some W.W.II Army and Air Force use; some student use since c1945.* *v.t.* 1. To cheat; to take unwarranted advantage of. *Colloq.* 2. To defeat an opponent or opposing team decisively. —ful. *n.* Fig., containing a skin full of liquor, or having one's skin full of liquor. —ned. *adj.* Cheated, taken advantage of; having lost all or a large part of one's money to another in a gambling game or a business trans-action, usu. a dishonest one. —s. *n.pl.* 1. A set of drums. *Jazz use.* 2. Automobile tires. *Mainly hot-rod use.*

skin, get under [one's]. To irritate or annoy a person. *Lit. = to annoy as a tick would under the skin.*

skin, give me some. Shake hands; esp. to shake by extending the flat palm of one's hand and brushing a similarly extended palm. *A jive term that caught the popular imagination. Often used as a rhyming term, "Give me some skin, Flynn." Somewhat synthetic.*

skin, give [someone] some. To shake hands with someone. *Usu. in "Give me some skin" = Shake (hands), friend. c1935 jive use; some swing use; occasionally used by teenagers or, esp., writers who write about teenagers.*

skin-head. *n.* A bald man.

skinned mush. A cane. *Pitchman use. From pitchman "mush" = an umbrella, from "mushroom."*

skinner. *n.* A teamster; a driver of horses or mules. *An old Western term still in use on ranches and construction jobs.*

skip. *v.i., v.t.* To leave a place without paying one's bill or bills; to leave hastily, as a hotel or town, without paying what one owes. *n.* 1. An Army captain. *From "skipper." Some W.W.I and W.W.II Army use.* 2. A bus driver; a taxi driver. —per. *n.* 1. Captain, esp. the captain of a ship. *Colloq.* → 2. An Army captain or company commander. *Colloq.* 3. The chief police officer of a precinct.

skippy. *n.* A sissy. *Some Negro use.*

skippy strike. A workers' method of protesting working conditions by omitting or skipping part of their work or ignoring some items on which they are to work.

skirt. *n.* A girl or young woman. *Very common. Prob. of underworld orig. Some W.W.I use; very wide W.W.II use. Third in pop. to "dame" and "jane."*

skiv. *n.* = shiv.

skivvies. *n.pl.* 1. Underwear, either undershirts or underdrawers. 2. Slippers consisting of one strap across the toes and a wooden or rubber sole, usu. used in the shower or on the beach. *Some use since c1945.*

skivvy. *n.* 1. A man's cotton undershirt, esp. the type with short sleeves and a round, close-fitting neckline. *Has replaced "undershirt" in the USN; fairly common civilian use, esp. since W.W.II.* → 2. A pair of men's cotton underdrawers having three buttons or snaps down the front and with short legs.

skivvy shirt = skivvy. *Orig. USN use.*

sklonk. *n.* A boring, uninformed person; one who is not hep. *Some student use since c1945.*

skulduggery. *n.* Rascally conduct; scheming or plotting.

skull. *n.* An outstanding student, worker, or performer; an intellectual, a brain; a grind.

skull-buster. *n.* 1. In college, a very hard course. *Some use since c1920.* 2. A policeman or detective. *Some Negro use since c1930.*

skull-drag. *v.i.* 1. To study hard, *Some jive student use since c1935.* → 2. To give one's best effort; to think, work, or play with concentration. *Jive use.*

skull play. In baseball, a player's error caused by faulty judgment.

skull practice. In sports, a lecture session, often illustrated with films or blackboard diagrams, explaining a team maneuver or play, analyzing mistakes made in previous games, or detailing the weaknesses of future opponents. *Chiefly football use.*

skunk. *n.* A boy whose duty it is to wake workers in time for them to go on their shift. *Western and railroad use. Orig. the skunk was an apprentice who also lit the morning fire, carried the day's supply of water, etc. v.t.* 1. To fail to pay a debt; to welsh. 2. In sports, to defeat an opponent without allowing him to score; to shut out; to defeat decisively.

skunk [someone] out of [something]. 1. = skunk; welsh. 2. To cheat someone out of something.

sky. *n.* A uniformed policeman or prison guard. *Some, mainly Negro, underworld use since c1930; prob. from the blue uniform.*

sky-hook. *n.* A large plastic balloon used in high-altitude, cosmic-ray experiments by the U.S. Navy.

sky juice. 1. Rain. *Some jocular and student use since c1925.* → 2. Water.

skyman. *n. An aviator. Since c1920.*

sky-parlor. *n.* A garret or a room in a garret.

sky piece; skypiece. *n.* 1. A hat or cap. 2. A wig. *Since c1925.*

sky pilot. 1. A clergyman of any rank or denomination; a minister, priest, or rabbi. *Orig. hobo and Western use, some W.W.I and W.W.II use. With the importance of the Air Force in W.W.II, the "pilot" took on a more modern meaning. During W.W.II and since the term has usu. = an Armed Forces chaplain.* 2. A licensed aviation pilot.

sky scout. A chaplain. *Some W.W.II use.*

skyscraper; sky-scraper. *n.* 1. A very tall building; fig., a building so tall that it scrapes the sky. *Colloq. by c1920. Although six- or eight-story buildings with self-supporting masonry walls were called skyscrapers, technically a skyscraper now is any building supported by steel girders or other interior framework, on which the walls are "hung."* 2. In baseball, a very high fly ball or pop fly. 3. A "tall" sandwich with many layers of meat, cheese, and vegetables; any dessert with many layers of ice cream, syrup, nuts, or the like; anything tall in proportion to its width.

sky wire. 1. A radio antenna. *Radio and U.S. Army Signal Corps use.* 2. A guy wire. *Television use.*

slab. *n.* 1. A town or city. 2. In

baseball, the home plate. **3.** Bread; a slice of bread.

slack season. That season during which a specif. manufacturing, wholesale, or retail business is poor. *Thus late spring and early summer are a slack season for the overcoat business. Orig. and mainly garment worker use.*

slam. *n.* **1.** A salute. *Very little Armed Forces use, mainly police use.* **2.** An uncomplimentary or mean remark; a dig. *Since c1895; colloq.* **3.** In baseball, a hit. **4.** A drink; a slug. *From "slam" = "slug" = hit. v.t.* **1.** To make uncomplimentary or mean remarks about someone; to abuse someone verbally. *Colloq.* **2.** In baseball, to hit the ball. **3.** To strike or slap someone hard with the hand.

slam a gate. To beg food at a house. *Hobo use.*

slam-bang. *v.t.* To attack someone. *adj., adv.* **1.** Violent(ly); in an unnecessarily rough or rude manner. *Since c1890.* **2.** Thorough(ly); complete(ly); rigorous(ly). **3.** Direct(ly); straightforward(ly).

slammer. *n.* A door; an entrance way. *Jive use c1935, revived by rock and roll groups c1955. Old underworld use.*

slam off. To die.

slant. *n.* **1.** A jag; a load (of liquor). *Archaic and dial.* **2.** A look. **3.** A person's opinion or point of view. *Since c1920.*

slap. *adv.* Directly, shortly; smack; plump.

slap [one's] gums = beat [one's] gums.

slap-happy. *adj.* **1.** = punch-drunk. → **2.** Dizzy. → **3.** Exhilarated; elated; dizzy with success or joy.

slap [someone's] wrist. To chastise a person lightly; to scold a person.

slasher. *n.* An overly diligent student; a grind. *Jocular use. Because he is so serious in his studies that he may slash his throat, committing suicide, if he does*

not receive high scholastic grades. Some student use since c1950.

slat. *n.* **1.** A rib. **2.** A thin, angular woman. *Reinforced by "slut." —s. n.pl.* Ribs, esp. those of a person; often in phrases referring to laughter, as "to split, jiggle, or hold one's slats."

slathers. *n.pl.* Lots of. *Archaic and dial.*

slave. *v.i.* To work.

slave-driver. *n.* **1.** A boss, teacher, or one in authority who is disliked for overworking those under him. **2.** One's wife. *Jocular use.*

slave market. **1.** An employment office. *Orig. hobo and logger use.* **2.** In a town or city, a street or district in which employment offices are located.

slave-puncher. *n.* = slave-driver. *Some northwestern U.S. use.*

slay. *v.t.* To make a strongly favorable impression on; to win the affection or approval of, esp. by means of superior charm, humor, etc.; to "kill," esp. to cause a person to lose control of his emotions, usu. through laughter. *Very common since c1930.*

sleazy. *adj.* **1.** Dirty, grimy; filthy; old, dilapidated; in poor condition. *Wide student use.* **2.** Cheap, inferior; of cheap or inferior material, workmanship, and overall quality.

sleep. *n.* **1.** A one-year prison term. *Underworld use since c1920.* **2.** A night. —er. *n.* **1.** A night watchman. *Some underworld use since c1930.* **2.** A dull course or lecture. *Some student use.* **3.** Any entertainment or performer, or any plan, person, or item, which proves to possess greater popular appeal or wider acceptance than was anticipated; esp., a cheaply made movie that wins public acclaim despite little advertising. *Common since c1935.* **4.** In sports, esp. football, a player who maneuvers deceptively in order to take the ball without being noticed by the opponents; also, the play in which such a maneuver is used. 5. = dark horse. —ville; Sleepville. *adj.* Sleepy, asleep. *Assoc. with cool use.*

sleep with. To have sexual intercourse with.

sleeve-buttons. *n.pl.* Codfish balls. *Some use since c1880.*

sleeve on [someone], put the. 1. To arrest someone; to identify someone to the police for arrest. 2. To stop a friend on the street in order to ask for a loan of money; to ask for a contribution or for money owed.

sleighride. *n.* 1. An instance of sharing or a chance to share the wealth, power, or success of a person or pop. idea; a successful period in one's life. 2. An instance of being cheated, believing a lie, or being taken advantage of. *Almost always in the expression "taken for a sleighride."*

sleuth. *n.* A detective. *Now usu. humorous or archaic-literary.*

slew. *n.* A large number or quantity. *From the Gaelic "sluagh" = a multitude.*

slewfoot. *n.* 1. A detective or policeman. 2. In baseball, an awkward player. 3. Any clumsy person; a stumblebum.

slice. *n.* A share or interest in any profit-making enterprise; a share of loot; a piece. *Common since c1920.*

slick. *adj.* 1. Glib; smooth-talking; persuasive. 2. Clever, shrewd; adroit in business matters. 3. Smart; clever; witty. *Since c1800.* → 4. Good; swell. *Since c1830.* → 5. Crafty; wily; dishonest. *Since c1915.* → 6. Superficial; insincere; pleasant and attractive but not deeply satisfying; widely popular but vapid or merely sensational; commercially produced to win the widest possible acceptance but without concern for artistic or scientific standards. *The most common use since c1940.* n. 1. A magazine printed on glossy or coated paper; hence a magazine or book produced for sale to a wide but uncritical audience. *Colloq.* 2. A used car in good, re-

salable condition. —er. *v.t.* To outsmart dishonestly; to cheat or dupe. —um. *n.* Hair oil or hair dressing, as pomade.

slick chick. An attractive, well-dressed, hep girl. *Orig. a rhyming jive term, c1935. Became common during W.W.II. The orig. connotation was "hep," but now = merely pretty and well dressed.*

slide. *v.i.* To lose popularity or prestige. *n.* A trouser pocket. *Some underworld use.* —s. *n.pl.* Shoes. *Some c1935 jive use; some hobo use.*

slide [one's] jib. 1. To become irrational, unrealistic, or insane. 2. To be talkative; to talk too much.

sligh. *v.t.* To dismantle, as a tent. *Carnival use.*

slime. *n.* 1. Fig., the world of vice or of unrefined, amoral, unethical people and deeds. 2. A worthless, unethical, unrefined person. 3. Specif., scandalous talk or writing; unsubstantiated accusations of vice, scandal, and unethical deeds.

sling. *n.* A sling chair, usu. consisting of a (simulated) wrought iron frame over which one butterfly-shaped piece of canvas is fitted, or slung, to form a seat, back, and headrest. *A pop., inexpensive, modern style of chair often found in U.S. homes in the 1950's. v.t.* To throw. *Colloq.*

sling a nasty foot (ankle). To dance expertly.

slinger. *n.* 1. A waiter or waitress. *From "hash slinger."* 2. One who slings or throws bull; a bull-slinger.

sling hash. To work as a waiter or waitress.

sling it. To shoot the bull, throw the bull; to have a good line; to exaggerate or lie; to talk, esp. slangily or fashionably.

sling the bull. 1. To talk; to take part in a bull session. 2. To shoot the bull, throw the bull; to talk bull proficiently.

slinky. *adj.* Sensuous-looking; sinuous; said of a woman; descriptive of a woman who moves with exaggerated and deliberate hip movements. *Common since c1925.*

slip me five. An expression meaning "Shake hands." *Some use since W.W.I. The forerunner of "give me some skin."*

slipper. *v.i.* To reform and conform; said of a criminal. *Underworld use.*

slippery. *adj.* Deceitful, untrustworthy; cunning. *Colloq.*

slippy. *adj.* Quick.

slipstick. *n.* 1. A slide rule. *Student use since c1930; engineer, surveyor, and Army use since c1940.* 2. A trombone. *Early radio use; a synthetic jazz term.*

slip [one's] trolley. To become irrational, obsessive, or insane.

slip-up. *n.* An accident; a mistake; an oversight.

slob. *n.* 1. A fat or ungainly person, esp. one of unattractive or untidy appearance. 2. A hopelessly ineffectual person. → 3. An untalented, congenitally average person; any common man whose chance of happiness or success is no better than another's. *Very common since c1935.*

slop. *n.* A cheap saloon or restaurant; lit., a saloon or restaurant that serves slop. **—py.** *adj.* 1. Drunk. *Fairly common.* 2. Slovenly. *Colloq. since c1930.* **—s.** *n.pl.* Beer. *Hobo use, c1910.*

slop-chute. *n.* A saloon or tavern.

slope. *v.i.* To escape from jail. *Hobo and some underworld use.*

sloppy Joe. A long, loose-fitting pull-over sweater. *A pop. style with female students c1940, usu. worn several sizes too large.*

sloppy Joe's. Any cheap restaurant or lunch counter serving cheap food quickly. *Since c1940.*

slot. *n.* 1. A position or place. Mainly sports and gambling use. In baseball, a player may win a "slot" on the team; in horseracing, a horse may finish in the third "slot." 2. A slot machine.

slot, in the. 1. In baseball, wating to take a turn at bat; lit., in the chalked box, or slot, reserved for the next batter. 2. Ready to perform next; ready or alert to take one's turn.

slough. *v.t.* 1. To lock. *Underworld use since c1880. Also "unslough"* = *unlock.* → 2. To lock up, hence to imprison or arrest. → 3. To dismantle in preparation for moving, as tents or booths. *Circus use.* → 4. To discontinue; to close or close up, as a carnival concession or the like. 5. To disperse or dismiss, as a crowd. 6. To hit a person hard, esp. with the fist. *v.i.* To depart; to beat it. *n.* 1. An arrest; the official act of closing a carnival, saloon, or the like, usu. by withdrawing its license or permit. → 2. A policeman.

slough-foot. *v.i.* To walk slew-footedly; to walk with the toes not pointing toward one's objective.

slough up. To arrest.

slow, take it. To be careful or cautious.

slow-beat guy. An objectionable fellow; a wet smack.

slow burn. The act or an instance of becoming enraged slowly or by gradual stages, as opposed to flipping one's lid all at once. *Since c1930. From the comedian Leon Carroll, whose famous "slow burn" = a facial expression which gradually became that of intense anger, was very well known in the late 1930's.*

slow drag. A formal or boring dance. *Some teenage and student use.*

slow on the draw. Slow to comprehend or recognize; dull-witted.

slowpoke. *n.* A person who acts or moves slowly. *Colloq.*

slug. *n.* 1. A bullet. 2. A doughnut, a sinker. 3. A dollar. *Since c1875; from hobo to carnival and circus and then to theater use; now common.* 4. A drink or swallow of something, esp. whisky.

From the Gaelic "slog" = *a swallow.* 5. A blow. 6. A fellow, esp.
a disliked man. *v.t.* 1. To hit;
to fight; to battle. *Colloq.* 2. In
baseball, to hit a pitched ball
hard, esp. to do so consistently.
—ger. *n.* 1. In baseball, a player
who is consistently a good hitter,
esp. of home runs; a long-ball
hitter. 2. A boxer; a prize fighter.
Colloq. 3. An ear-to-ear chin
beard, as worn by a stage Irishman.

slug-fest. *n.* 1. A vicious or exciting prize fight. *Since c1920.* 2. A
baseball game in which many
hits and runs are scored. *Since
c1935.*

slug-nutty. *adj.* Punch-drunk;
punchy.

slug on [someone], put the. 1. To
hit, slug, or attack someone
physically. → 2. To attack someone verbally; to criticize or give
someone a bad recommendation.

sluice the worries. To drink a
large quantity of liquor.

slum. *n.* 1. Any meat-and-vege-
table stew, esp. one made of
boiled salt-beef and potatoes.
Primarily hobo and Army use.
→ 2. Rations; inferior, mass-produced food. *Prison and Army
use since c1925.* 3. Cheap merchandise, as jewelry or gilded
plaster book ends, sold at stands
or given as prizes in games of
chance or skill. *Carnival and circus use. Since c1920; in the U.S.
the word has never* = *a swindle,
as it does in Brit. sl. adj.* Cheap;
inferior and gaudy. —gudgeon. *n.*
Hash, stew, slumgullion. —gul-
lion. *n.* 1. A tasteless or poor-
tasting drink. 2. Any meat and
vegetable stew. *Orig. and primarily hobo use. More common
than "slum." Prob. from "salmagundi."* —ming. *n.* The act or an
instance of visiting a skid row or
slum area as a spectator, out of
curiosity, and to enjoy doing
something unusual that will give
one a topic of conversation later.
Usu. said of wealthy people.

slurf. *v.i., v.t.* = **slurp.**

slurp. *v.i., v.t.* To drink or eat
noisily. *Common since c1925. n.*
In jazz, a glissando. *Some jazz
use. Because the sound resembles a person slurping food.* —y.
adj. Semiliquid; said of food or
drink of such a consistency as to
cause noisy ingestion.

slush. *n.* 1. Sentiment, esp. an obvious display of sentiment. 2.
Drivel; trivial remarks; corn. *Colloq.* 3. Hash. *Some prison use.* 4.
= **slush fund,** money in a slush
fund.

slush fund. A fund or sum of
money set aside for political purposes, to use to buy influence or
votes, or to use in bribery. *Since
c1860; colloq.*

slush pump. A trombone. *Some
jazz use, mostly synthetic. Some
musician and radio use since
c1935.*

slut lamp = **bitch lamp.**

smack. *n.* 1. A hit, a slap. *Colloq.*
2. A dollar. *Hobo use.* 3. A kiss.
adv. Directly; precisely; on the
mark, sharply; suddenly. —er. *n.*
1. A dollar. *From the sound of a
silver dollar as dropped on a
counter. In Eng. sl.* = *a pound
sterling.* 2. A kiss. *interj.* 1. A
sound imitative of a hit or slap.
2. A sound imitative of a kiss.

smack down. *v.t.* 1. To reprimand
severely. 2. To cause another to
lose, or to lose, status; to get one's
comeuppance.

small. *adj.* 1. Cheap, stingy, petty.
2. Impolite, unsociable; quick to
take offense and slow to apolo-
gize.

small-arm(s) inspection = **short-
arm inspection.**

small beer. An insignificant person, plan, task, or amount; small
potatoes.

small bread. A small or insufficient amount of money. *Some
cool and far out use.*

small fry. 1. Children; a child of
either sex. *Colloq.* 2. An unimportant person or group of persons; persons lacking influence or
prestige, such as unknown entertainers, employees working on

minor jobs, petty criminals, etc. *Colloq. From the stand. "fry" = young fish.* **small-fry.** *adj.* Unimportant; minor, petty; lacking influence or prestige.

small one. Specif., a small drink of whisky. *Colloq.*

small pipe. An alto saxophone. *Synthetic jazz use.*

small pot. An unimportant person. *From "small potatoes" reinforced by "pot."*

small potatoes. 1. A small amount of money; peanuts. → 2. Any unimportant, insignificant, inconsequential, minor, or petty person, idea, attitude, object, etc.; a small business; small profit or financial gain, esp. as compared with what one expects from future endeavors. *Since c1850.*

small time. A theater or circuit of theaters in which low-salaried vaudeville acts are staged more than twice a day. *Theater use since c1915.* **small-time.** *adj.* 1. Minor, petty, unimportant; poorly paid; bush league. 2. With small ambitions or opportunities; on a small scale; lacking in importance, influence, or prestige; without fame or notoriety.

smart as paint. Very clever; very smart.

smart guy. A know-it-all, a wise guy, a wiseacre or smart aleck.

smart money. Money bet or invested by those in the know, or by influential or wealthy people who are supposedly in a position to know that their bet or investment will be profitable.

smarty. *n.* A smart-aleck, one who is overconfident of his knowledge or intellectual prowess; a wise guy. *adj., adv.* In the manner of a smart aleck.

smarty-pants. *n., n.pl.* 1. A smart aleck. → 2. A snob, esp. an intellectual snob.

smash. *n.* 1. A total failure, esp. in reciting. *Some student use c1850. Some cool and beat use c1955.* → 2. A popular success; a very successful play, movie, or the like; a hit. *adj.* Extremely successful.

Usu. in the redundant "smash hit." **—er.** *n.* Anything very large, extraordinary, or remarkable; esp., anything remarkably attractive or entertaining. **—ing.** *adj.* Wonderful, entertaining, tremendously successful or gratifying. *Although Brit., had some c1920 popularity in the U.S. and is still known and used.*

smash hit. An extremely successful, popular entertainment, esp. a play or a popular song; an extremely popular or well received entertainer or performance.

smear. *v.t.* 1. To knock out. *Prize fight use since c1920.* → 2. To defeat decisively. → 3. To murder; to rub out. 4. To destroy or attempt to destroy the good reputation of another, esp. by making false or exaggerated accusations; to degrade or slander. 5. To bribe, esp. to bribe an underling to persuade his superior to do something beneficial to the briber; to buy the influence or support of another. 6. To offer a kickback. *n.* 1. An act or instance of attacking another's reputation; an unsupported accusation; an attempt to destroy another's reputation. *All uses from or reinforced by "schmear."*

smeller. *n.* The nose.

smell the stuff. To take cocaine by sniffing.

smidgen. *n.* A small amount. *Colloq. since c1845.*

smoke. *n.* 1. A cigarette. *Very common.* 2. A cigarette, cigar, or pipeful of tobacco. *Colloq.* 3. Any substandard whisky or wine; rubbing alcohol, wood alcohol, or the like, used as a beverage, esp. denatured alcohol and water shaken together in a bottle. *v.t.* To shoot a person. *Underworld use since c1945. v.i.* To be angry; fig., to be burning with anger.

smoke-ball. *n.* In baseball, a ball pitched very fast.

smoke-eater. *n.* 1. A fireman, a firefighter. *Common since c1930.* 2.

A welder. *Some factory use since c1940.*

smoke-out. *n.* = cook-out.

smoke [something or someone] out. To find a person or obtain information, esp. when the person is hidden or the information withheld.

smoke wagon. A railroad train. *Some use since c1850.*

smooch; smooge; smouge. *v.i., v.t.* **1.** To take; to borrow, esp. to borrow an item too insignificant to return; to mooch; to steal. **2.** To kiss and caress; to pet or neck. *n.* A kiss; kissing and caressing; necking. **—er.** *n.* **1.** A habitual borrower; one who borrows or takes things without returning them; one who mooches. **2.** A man or woman, usu. of student age, who will or likes to kiss and caress; one who indulges in smooching or necking. **—ing.** *n.* Kissing; necking.

smooth. *adj.* **1.** Pleasing, personable, attractive; well and inconspicuously groomed; socially adroit, adaptable; shrewd; persuasive. *Wide student use since before 1900; usu. said of a person whom the speaker finds attractive; sometimes used in scorn of one whom the speaker finds glib and crafty.* **2.** Pleasing; excellent; esp. of, with, or having pleasing sentiment. **—ie;** **—y.** *n.* A smooth person, usu. a youth or girl whom the opposite sex finds attractive; sometimes one found to be glib or crafty; a slicker.

smooth article. A person who is smooth (in any sl. sense); a slicker.

smoudge. *n.* A rough, uncouth, unkempt person; a smoocher. *May be a further variant of "smouge" = "smooch."*

smouge = smooch.

smush. *n.* The human mouth. *From "mush" = mouth, with excrescent "s."*

snafu. *n.* A mistake, usu. large and obvious; an instance of confusion; a situation confused by a lack of intelligent direction; stupidity; any unnecessarily complex plan, action, or thinking. *Orig. Army use c1940; very wide W.W.II Armed Forces use and some postwar civilian use. adj.* Confused; snarled; haywire; completely mistaken; ruined, spoiled. *v.i., v.t.* To ruin; to make a mistake; to confuse; to goof; to foul up.

snake. *n.* **1.** One who excels in anything, esp. a diligent student. *Some student use since c1900; some c1935 jive use.* **2.** A treacherous person. *Colloq.* → **3.** A male, usu. a youth who pursues and deceives many girls. *Some student use since c1925.* **4.** A policeman. *Some teenage gang use since c1940. v.i.* To leave unobtrusively; to sneak away.

snake eyes. 1. In dice, the point of two, each die face having one spot showing. → **2.** Less commonly, the die face having two spots. *From the image of the two black spots accentuated against the white background.* **3.** Tapioca. *Army, prison, and some student use since c1935.*

snake poison. Whisky. *Archaic and dial.*

snake ranch. *n.* **1.** Any cheap, dirty saloon or bar; a joint; a dive. *Orig. maritime use.* **2.** A brothel. *Orig. maritime use.*

snap. *n.* **1.** Energy, vitality; pep. *Now mainly dial.* **2.** An easy task, course of study, examination, or the like; a cinch. *Common since c1900.* **3.** A teacher who gives an easy course. *Common student use since c1900. adj.* Easy of accomplishment; easy. **—pers.** *n.pl.* Teeth. **—py.** *adj., adv.* **1.** Quick(ly). *Usu. in "make it snappy." Colloq.* **2.** Neat(ly); smart(ly); attractive(ly).

snap [one's] cap. To become excited or flustered; to flip one's lid. *Some use since c1940; not as common as "flip one's lid."*

snap course. An easy course, esp. in college. *Wide student use since c1895.*

snap into it. To hurry up, to do something with increased energy or enthusiasm.

snap it up. To hurry.

snap out of it. To come out of an inattentive or despondent mood; to become alert or active. *Since c1920.*

snarky; snorky. *adj.* Elegant; ritzy. *Dial.*

snatch. *v.t.* 1. To arrest. 2. To kidnap; to steal. *Since c1925.* n. 1. An arrest. 2. A theft or kidnaping; the item stolen or person kidnaped. → 3. A theft, specif. of merchandise from a retail store. 4. A payroll. *Underworld use since c1940.* —er. n. 1. A policeman. *Some underworld, jive, and teenage use since c1935.* 2. A kidnaper.

snatch, the. *n.* The act or instance of kidnaping; the act or instance of stealing.

snatch on [someone or something], put the. 1. To arrest someone. 2. To kidnap someone. 3. To take, seize, or steal something.

snazzy. *adj.* 1. Stylish, in the latest fashion, modern, classy, nifty, ritzy; colorful, exciting; attractive, agreeable, pleasing. 2. Gaudy; in bad taste. *This usage increasing since c1940.*

sneaky pete; sneaky Pete. 1. Any of various illegal alcoholic beverages, ranging from home-made whisky, flavored alcohol, and fortified wine to bootlegged moonshine. *Since c1940.* 2. Cheap, raw whisky. *Some use, from confusion with the orig. meaning.* → 3. Wine, usu. a cheap red Burgundy, mixed with carbonated water and ice; any cheap wine. *Since c1945.* 4. Specif., wine, freq. or usu. muscatel, reinforced or fortified and apparently habit-forming when so prepared; distributed in pint bottles, which are called jugs, for quick, low-price sale. *Hobo use.*

sneeze. *v.t.* To kidnap; to seize and hold. *Orig. underworld use, c1920.* n. 1. A kidnaping. *Since*

c1935. 2. The act of seizing and holding, hence esp. an arrest. *Underworld use, c1925.* —r. n. A jail.

snide. *adj.* Contemptible, sneaky; underhanded, mean, low, cheap; insincere, phoney, assuming a superior attitude. *Common by c1900. Now colloq.* n. A contemptible or underhanded person. *Since c1900.*

sniffer. A handkerchief.

sniffy. *adj.* Snobbish; acting in a superior manner. *From the traditional snobbish posture of holding one's head high, with one's nose pointed upward, as if in disdain or sniffing an unpleasant odor.*

snifter. *n.* 1. A drink of whisky. 2. A large brandy glass shaped like a bowl with a stem on it. *Since c1935; colloq. So shaped to allow one to warm brandy or liqueur with the hands and thus sniff the fumes.* 3. A cocaine addict.

snipe. *n.* 1. A cigar or cigarette butt; the discarded remnant of a cigar or cigarette. *Orig. hobo use. Until cW.W.I = cigar butt; after the introduction of cigarettes term was used for either cigar or cigarette butts.* 2. A railroad track laborer. *Since c1915. Hobo, logger, and railroad use.* 3. A fireman or other member of a ship's engine-room gang. *Since c1920; some W.W.II USN use.* 4. A nonexistent animal; any mythical creature. *From the hoax of snipe hunting, in which an uninitiated person is left to watch for a "snipe," usu. at night and in a woods or field, while his supposed hunting companions, the hoaxers, leave him to discover the joke.* v.t. To steal. *Hobo and underworld use since c1915.* —r. n. 1. A thief who robs unoccupied houses, a shoplifter, a semiprofessional pickpocket. *Since c1925.* 2. A collector of cigar or cigarette butts. *Hobo use.*

sniptious. *adj.* Attractive; stylish. *Dial.*

snitch. *v.t.* To steal or take small items. *Common since c1920.* *v.i.* To inform against, betray, squeal, esp. to another's superior or teacher. *Common since c1920.* *n.* 1. An informer; a stool pigeon. 2. A theft. *In the U.S. never used in the Australian sense of "a dislike."* —er. *n.* An informer.

snitch-wise. *adv.*, *adj.* Diagonally; crosswise. *Archaic and dial.*

snizzle. *n.* A sneeze. *Some jocular use.*

snoff. *n.* A week-end girl friend, not one's steady. "Snoff" stands for "Saturday night only, friend, female." *An excellent example of synthetic sl., here based on the initials of a phrase.*

snollygoster. *n.* 1. A politician who relies on oratory rather than knowledge or ability; a politician who speaks much and does little. 2. An inept, talkative, or unethical lawyer; a shyster. *Both uses since c1860. Mainly dial.*

snooker. *v.t.* To cheat, swindle, deceive. *Always used in passive.*

snoot. *n.* The human nose. *Since c1875. Usu. used in ref. to the nose of a disliked person.* *v.t.* To treat with disdain; to snub a person. —y. *adj.* Snobbish; having a high opinion of oneself and a low opinion of others; stuck up. *Fig., with one's nose held high. Colloq.*

snoot full, have [get] a. To be under the influence of alcohol; to be drunk. *Since c1920.*

snooze. *v.i.* To sleep. *Since c1850; colloq. since c1900.* *n.* A sleep, esp. a short sleep or a nap. *Colloq. since c1900.*

snort. *n.* 1. A drink of liquor, esp. a drink of neat whisky. *Common since c1915; from "snorter."* → 2. A small piece of anything; a short distance. *Since c1935.*

snow. *n.* 1. Cocaine in any form. *Very common.* → 2. Any habitforming narcotic. 3. Deceptive, exaggerated, or flattering talk. 4. Rapidly moving white or black dots on a television screen, caused by interference or faulty recep-

tion. *Since c1945.* *v.i.* 1. To talk, usu. to repeat what one has just said. *Almost always in the expression,* "Snow again. I don't get your drift." *Some use since c1920.* 2. To exaggerate; to misrepresent or purposely confuse; to talk or write at length on a subject to a person who is uninformed in order to deceive or impress that person. —ed. *adj.* 1. Under the influence of a narcotic, esp. cocaine; doped, drugged. 2. Deceived; influenced by exaggerated, deceptive talk; influenced by a snow job. *Common since cW.W.II.*

snowball. *n.* 1. A hydrangea flower cluster. *Because of the rounded shape and usu. white tint. Colloq.* 2. Cocaine crystals. *Since c1930; addict use.* 3. = snowbird. *v.i.*, *v.t.* To grow or increase rapidly; fig., to build up as a snowball does when rolled down a slope in wet, clinging snow.

snowball chance. A very slight chance; no chance at all. *From the saying "as much chance as a snowball in hell."*

snowbird; snow bird. *n.* 1. A hobo or migratory worker temporarily working or living in the South to escape winter in the North. *Since c1920; orig. hobo use.* 2. A cocaine addict, esp. one who sniffs cocaine crystals. *Addict use.* → 3. Any narcotics addict.

snowdrop. *n.* A member of the Army's Military Police. *From the uniform, which includes white helmets, white gloves, white belts, and white puttees.*

snowed in; snowed up. 1. Doped, drugged. *Addict use since c1925.* 2. Deceived by insincere talk.

snowed under. Burdened by an excess of work or responsibilities; fig., being burdened or obscured by an abundance of anything.

snowed up = snowed in.

snow-flier. *n.* = snowbird. *Some hobo use.*

snow job. Persuasive, insincere talk or writing; usu. talk that exaggerates, deceives, or flatters for the purpose of impressing the speaker's importance or knowledge on an attractive member of the opposite sex, a new acquaintance, a business superior, or a client; a line. *Very common during and since W.W.II.*

snowshoe. *n.* A detective; a plainclothes policeman. *Reinforced by the image of large feet traditionally assoc. with policemen.*

snowstorm. *n.* **1.** A party held for the purpose of taking narcotics, esp. cocaine; a drug-induced trance. **2.** Whipped cream. *Some student use since c1925.*

snow under. To overwhelm with work, advice, or the like.

snub. *v.t.* To tie, to tie up; to make fast. *Now dial.*

snub out. To extinguish a cigarette by firmly pressing, tapping, or rubbing the lighted end against a steady surface, as the bottom of an ashtray.

snug. *n.* A small, easily concealed revolver. *Underworld use.*

snurge. *v.i.* To sneak away, esp. in order to avoid work. *Prob. synthetic.*

So? **1.** An expression showing lack of interest, rejection, refusal to comprehend, or refusal to agree with another that something is important, worthy of becoming excited about, or remarkable. *This use resembles Yiddish speech patterns and rhythms.* **2.** An interrogatory word with an exceedingly wide range of use. Usu. used in reply to a statement, it may be an expression of interest, a request for further information, a term of disbelief, etc.

soak. *v.t.* To make a person pay heavily; to overcharge; to penalize heavily, as by a jail sentence or high taxes; fig., to inflict punishment on. *n.* **1.** A drunkard; a habitual drinker. *Common since c1900; from "soaked."* → **2.** A drunken spree or binge. —ed. *adj.* Drunk. *Common since its first use, the word's popularity rises and falls every decade or so; peri-*

ods of most recent popularity include c1900 and c1920. *With the rise of many competing sl. syns. during Prohibition, the word has lost some of its oral popularity, though still universally known.*

soaker. *n.* A diaper cover, usu. a hand-knitted one; a pilch.

soak yourself, go. A rejoinder signifying disbelief or annoyance.

so-and-so. *n.* **1.** A euphem. for any of several strongly derog. epithets for a contemptible person, usu. a male. → **2.** Any male friend; a guy, a fellow. *As many curse words and epithets, this is used jocularly in greeting close friends.*

soap. *n.* **1.** Money, esp. money used for bribery. **2.** = soft soap. *Since c1930.* *v.t.* To flatter; fig., to give someone "soft soap."

soap-box. *n.* Lit. and fig., the traditional box which a public orator stands on while making a, usu. political, speech or harangue. *In such expressions as "Where's your soap-box?" = You're talking like a public orator.*

soap-grease. *n.* Money of any kind. *Some dial. use.*

soap opera. **1.** A daily dramatic serial program broadcast by radio, usu. lasting fifteen minutes each day, concerning fictitious domestic crises and troubles and often characterized by little action and much sentiment. *Because such programs are often sponsored by manufacturers of soap.* **2.** Any real situation, crisis, or burden of troubles that resembles that usu. heard on a soap opera radio program. *adj.* Like or pertaining to the situations, crises, or burden of troubles and ill fortune heard on a radio soap opera.

sob-sister; sobsister; sob sister. *n.* **1.** A woman news reporter who appeals to readers' sympathies with her accounts of pathetic happenings; a newspaper woman who reports on events of human interest, esp. one whose writing contains much sentimentality.

Since c1925. **2.** Any woman who resorts to tears, the retelling of personal sad experiences, or sentimental stories to gain attention or sympathy; any woman or man who excuses present failure on the basis of personal defeats in the past. → **3.** An actress who plays sentimental or sympathetic roles. *adj.* Sentimental. *Often used to describe sentimental plays, stories, movies, etc.*

sob story. Any very sad story, esp. a recital of personal misfortunes calculated to arouse sympathy in the listener.

sob stuff. Stories of personal sadness, esp. when used to gain sympathy or favor; sentimentality, esp. in writing or before an audience.

sock. *v.t.* **1.** To hit, as with the fist or a club. → **2.** Fig., to deliver a hard blow, as bad news, a surprise, or the like. **3.** To save money, fig., by putting it away in a sock. → **4.** To earn money, usu. said of a business, play, or the like, rather than of a person. *n.* **1.** A blow, esp. one given with the fist. → **2.** Fig., a blow, as by a concerted effort, the result of work, events, or the like. → **3.** Fig., that which is very successful with one attempt, as a knockout blow; any person or effort making a quick and spectacular success; esp. a very successful play, movie, song, entertainer, or the like; a hit. **4.** A guy, esp. one who is foolish or who can be cheated easily. *Since c1920.* **5.** In baseball, a hit. *Common since c1925.* **6.** A money receptacle, as a bag, box, safe, or the like. *Underworld use since c1930.* → **7.** Fig., a place where money is kept, as a savings account at a bank; money saved, a nest egg. → **8.** A sum of money, esp. a large sum. *adj.* Very successful financially. —**er.** *n.* A baseball player who usu. hits the ball hard; a slugger. —**eroo.** *n.* Anything of extraordinary excellence, esp. something having, fig.,

a sock, punch, or wallop; a smash hit, as a very profitable stage show, movie, or song. *More common than "socker." adj.* Hard-hitting; smashing; very successful. —**o!** *interj.* An imitative expression signifying the impact of a blow; used fig. to express the sensation of a sudden and signal success in any endeavor. *Freq. oral use.* —**o.** *n.* **1.** A punch or hard blow, esp. to the jaw. *Prize fighter use since c1925.* **2.** A great success, esp. a great financial success in the field of entertainment; a sock, a hit. *Orig. theater use; not as common as the adj. v.t.* **1.** To deliver a hard blow, esp. a punch on the jaw. *Prize fighter use.* **2.** To make a great or quick success. *Orig. theater use. adj.* Very successful, esp. successful financially. *Most common use. adv.* Very well; most profitably. *All uses prob. reinforced by "sockdollager."*

soda jerk. One, usu. a youth, who prepares and dispenses refreshments at a soda fountain. *Colloq.*

soda jerker = soda jerk.

sod widow. A widow whose husband has died, as opposed to a grass widow whose husband is merely away or divorced. *Mainly dial.*

sofa lizard. **1.** A male student who stays at home to avoid spending money for a social engagement or date. *Some student use, c1925.* → **2.** A male who does not take his girl friend to social engagements, movies, dances, or the like, preferring to visit her at her home, usu. to save the expense of taking the girl anywhere. → **3.** A male who prefers to visit a girl at home, in order to neck or pet with her in private; one who necks or pets ardently.

soft. *n.* Easy money.

soft, the. *n.* Money. *Perh. from the softness of used paper money or of "dough," or from "soft money."*

softie; softy. *n.* An excessively trusting, generous, or sentimental person; one who gives sympathy easily; a dupe, pushover, or soft touch.

soft money. 1. Paper currency. *Some use since c1860.* 2. The currency of a nation suffering from inflation; inflated currency; currency that is easy to earn or borrow but that is not worth its face value in purchasing power. *Common since c1940.*

soft-pedal. *v.t.* To de-emphasize; usu. in ref. to an opinion or intelligence that will evoke an unfavorable public response. *From the soft pedal on a piano.*

soft sell. The act or an instance of selling or advertising merchandise in a friendly, soft-spoken, indirect, self-effacing, or genteel manner. *Orig. Madison Avenue use. Often applied to television commercials.*

soft-shell. *adj.* Lenient; holding less severe beliefs; pseudo. *Thus a "soft-shell Baptist" is one with modern and moderate attitudes toward dancing, for example, which the orig. church banned; a "soft-shell egghead" is a pseudo-intellectual.*

soft soap. Flattery; flattering or sentimental talk or writing used to gain sympathy or information. *Since c1830.* **soft-soap.** *v.t., v.i.* To speak or write flattery to someone; to appeal to another's sentiment; to snow.

soft touch. 1. One who, on request, lends or gives money readily and/or generously. → 2. A person who is easily convinced, cheated, or influenced. → 3. An easy task or job; money earned at an easy task or job. *c1940.*

Sol. *n.* The sun. *Often in "old Sol," "big Sol," etc. Colloq.* **sol.** *n.* Solitary confinement in prison.

soldier. *n.* 1. An empty whisky or beer bottle. 2. A customer or fare who tips heavily. *Some use since c1935. v.i.* To fulfill one's duties, to shoulder one's responsibilities. *Prob. owing to confusion with "shoulder," reinforced by civilian concept of a soldier doing his duty.*

solid. *adj.* Great; wonderful, marvelous; exciting, eliciting one's enthusiasm; perfect, excellent. *Orig. Harlem jive use. c1935; mainly jive and swing use, widely pop. in jazz and student contexts. n.* A trusted friend. *c1920 underworld use. adv.* Surely; definitely. *Usu.* = "I agree," "You're correct in every way." *Often used as a one-word reply to a statement; mainly jive use since c1935; Orig. Harlem jive talk.*

solid, Jackson = solid. *The "Jackson" merely serves to reiterate the "solid."*

solid ivory. 1. Fig., a person's head considered as solid bone or ivory and without brains. *Often accompanied by the gesture of tapping the person in question on his head, sometimes while making a sharp hitting noise, to illustrate the point. In common use since c1900, esp. by young boys.* 2. A bonehead.

solid sender. 1. An adroit swing musician; an exciting, satisfying, well-liked piece or arrangement of swing music. *Swing use, c1935–c1942.* → 2. An attractive, sympathetic, alert, hep person, esp., but not necessarily, if a devotee of swing.

solitaire. *n.* Suicide.

solo. *v.i.* To live alone; to act independently. *Colloq.*

So long. Good-by. *Colloq. since c1850; prob. from the Arabic "salaam" and the Hebrew "sholom."*

some. *adv.* Somewhat; very; rapidly. *Since c1800; colloq. n.* A great deal. *adj.* Remarkably good or remarkably bad; may express endearment, surprise, irony, astonishment, etc. *Colloq. since c1850.*

somebody, *a. n.* An important, influential famous, notorious, notable, successful, ambitious, or distinguished individual; a person whose life has meaning or value to society.

some pumpkins. *sing.* 1. An important person or thing; an admirable person or thing. *Used only as a pred. nominative. Since c1850, has been extremely pop. Though still in use by older people, young adults prefer stronger terms.* → 2. Audacious, mischievous; clever. *Often used with an affectionate connotation, esp. by older people when talking of children. Archaic and dial.*

something. *adv.* Exceedingly. *Colloq.* *n.* An important or remarkable person or thing, a "somebody." *Often used ironically or in the negative when used for persons, as "You think you're something, don't you?" = You're disgusting or insignificant. Always = remarkable when applied to objects or events, usually in "Isn't that something?"*

something else. Greater than great; beyond description. *Some far-out use.*

something on the ball. Ability; merit.

song. *n.* 1. A confession. See sing. 2. A story of personal misfortune, an excuse, an exaggerated story or lie; any, usu. long-winded, personal recital motivated by a desire for sympathy. *From "song and dance."*

song and dance. 1. A rigmarole; nonsense, bunk. → 2. An exaggerated story or lie told to elicit sympathy; an alibi; a spiel, a snow job. *Prob. orig. theater use.*

song-bird. *n.* 1. A female vocalist. *Colloq.* 2. One who confesses, informs, or "sings." *Some underworld use.*

soogie; sujee; soujge. *n.* A mixture of soap, caustic soda, and water used for washing painted surfaces, esp. on board a ship. *Since c1900; common USN and maritime use; common W.W.I and W.W.II use. Perhaps from the Chinese "soji" but prob. from the Hindustani "suji" or "soojee," a thick mixture of* granulated wheat and water or milk, eaten as gruel, which the washing mixture somewhat resembles. *v.t.* To wash or scrub the walls, or bulkheads, of a ship. *Common USN and maritime use.*

soogie moogie; sujee-mujee. *n.* = soogie.

Sooner. *n.* A native of Australia.

sooner. *n.* Anything cheap, as clothing, or shabby, as a person; anything mongrel. *Some Negro use.*

S. O. P.; s. o. p. Standard operating procedure; the correct, official way in which something must be done. *Fairly common W.W.II Armed Forces use, and some postwar civilian use.*

sop. *n.* A habitual drunkard; an alcoholic. —**py.** *adj.* Sentimental.

soph. *n.* 1. A sophomore student. 2. Immature; childish. *Since before 1800.* *adj.* Sophomore. *Since c1780.* —**omore.** *n.* An athlete in his second year of professional competition. *adj.* Immature, unsophisticated, childish.

sore. *adj.* 1. Annoyed; irritated. *Colloq.* → 2. Angry. *Colloq.*

sore-head; sorehead. *n.* One who angers easily, or complains loudly and frequently; one who frequently feels cheated, neglected or disappointed; a person who has a grudge. *Since c1850.*

S O S; S. O. S. *n.* Lit. and fig., a distress signal; fig., a request for aid, as in finishing a task successfully or in extracting oneself from an embarrassing situation. *From the Morse Code telegraph and radio distress signal. Usu. thought to be the initials for "save our souls" or "save our ship," the letters actually represent no words, but were chosen because they are easy to transmit and understand without confusion.*

so-so. *adj.* All right, neither exceptionally good nor bad; as good as can be expected; average. Often in reply to the greeting, "How are things with you?"

So's your old man. An expression used in scornful or contemptuous reply to any remark that arouses disbelief. *Orig. West Coast use, c1915.*

soujge. *n.* = soogie.

soul kiss. A long passionate, open-mouthed kiss, during which a lover's tongue licks, caresses, or explores the tongue and mouth of the beloved.

sound. *v.t.* To taunt or insult someone, usu. a rival; to goad someone into a fight. *Teenage street-gang use since c1955.*

sound off. *v.i.* 1. To state one's name; to drill or march while counting off the procedure in unison to the rhythm of the work; to speak when ordered to do so. *W.W.II Army use.* 2. To talk, esp. to complain or expostulate at length; to list one's complaints or opinions verbally. *Wide use during and since W.W.II. Orig. Army use.* 3. To boast; to brag. *Orig. W.W.II Army use.*

soup. *n.* 1. Nitroglycerine. → 2. Dynamite. 3. Fuel used to power fast airplanes or cars; esp., a special fuel used only for powerful motors. *v.t.* = soup up.

soup, in the = in hot water. *Orig. jocular use, now common.*

soup-and-fish. *n.* A man's formal evening suit of clothes; a tuxedo.

soupbone. *n.* A baseball pitcher's pitching arm. *Since c1920.*

souped up. *adj.* 1. Containing added horsepower or a potentially greater speed or rate of acceleration than when originally manufactured; said of a car or engine. → 2. Accelerated; improved; done, presented, or performed in a faster, more exciting way than usual; made gaudy or flashy.

souper. *n.* = soupbone.

soup house. An inferior restaurant. *Orig. hobo use.*

soup job. A fast car or airplane. *Student and Air Force use.*

soup jockey. A waiter or waitress.

soup-strainer. *n.* A mustache. *Some jocular use.*

soup up. *v.t.* To increase the horsepower, speed, efficiency, or rate of acceleration of a car engine or airplane. *Universally known; wide hot-rod use since c1950.*

soupy. *adj.* Sentimental, unduly idealistic, unreal, mushy. *Said of movies, plays, books, attitudes, etc.* *n.* Mess call. *A little Army use during W.W.II.*

sour. *adj.* 1. Disagreeable; unhappy; pessimistic. *Colloq.* 2. Wrong; suspicious; unethical; illegal. *Colloq.*

sour, in. In disfavor; in trouble; to make a bad start.

sour apples. Unsuccessfully; poorly. In such expressions as, "He can't pitch for sour apples" = he pitches poorly. Used alone or in several phrases indicating incredulity or lack of faith in another's ability. *Dial. and archaic.*

sour-ball. *n.* A chronic grumbler; a pessimist.

sourdough tourist. An outdoor camper.

sour-pan. *n.* = sour-puss.

sour-puss; sourpuss; sour puss. *n.* A person who is or who looks disagreeable; one who habitually frowns or scowls and seldom smiles.

souse. *n.* A drunkard; a known habitual drunkard. *Very common since c1900.* —d. *adj.* Drunk. Used as a pred. adj. about three times as freq. as attrib. *Since c1900; very common by c1915.*

soused to the gills = soused.

southpaw; south-paw. *n.* 1. The left hand or arm of a left-handed person, esp. a baseball pitcher. → 2. A left-handed baseball player, esp. a pitcher. → 3. Any left-handed person. *adj.* Left-handed.

south with [something], go. To steal or abscond with something.

sow. *n.* 1. A nickel 2. Any young, unkempt female, esp. if promiscuous. *Some student use.*

sow-belly. *n.* Bacon or fat salt pork. *Dial. and colloq.*

So what? An expression showing lack of interest, or inability or refusal to comprehend the pertinence or enthusiasm generated by a speech, act, object, or idea.

sozzled. *adj.* Drunk. *Since c1880.*

space bandit. A press agent. *Because they try to get their clients' names in the limited space of newspaper columns. Theater use since c1940.*

spade. *v.t.* To shovel.

spades, in. Par excellence; in the extreme; doubled.

spaghetti. *n.* 1. Fire hose, esp. when lines of it lie scattered around a fire. 2. A specif. type of television antenna and antenna lead-in wire. *Since c1950.*

Spanish-walk. *v.t.* To force a person to walk by holding him, as by the coat collar and the seat of the pants, and pushing him in the desired direction, esp. out a doorway.

spank. *v.t.* To defeat, esp. in a game.

spanking new. Brand new, completely new.

spare. *n.* In bowling, the situation of having knocked down all the pins with two consecutive rolls of the ball.

spare tire. *n.* 1. Excess fatty tissue in the region of the human waist. *From the resemblance of such a roll of fat to the extra or spare tire carried in an automobile for emergency use. Jocular and euphem. use since c1925.* 2. An extra person, one whose presence is not needed or wanted, as a fifth person at a bridge game. *Since c1945.* → 3. Any dull, disliked individual; a bore.

spark. *v.i., v.t.* 1. To court. *From "spark it."* → 2. To kiss and caress; to indulge in sexual play. *Replaced "spark it" c1865; shared popularity with "spoon" c1900–c1920 and with "pet" c1920; replaced by "neck" c1935.* 3. To lead, esp. to provide inspiration, encouragement, and an example to one's co-workers or teammates.

spark it. *v.i., v.t.* = spark. *Since c1780; superseded by "spark" by c1865. Still some dial. and archaic use.*

sparkler. *n.* 1. A diamond; a diamond ring; any gem or gem-set jewelry. 2. A long, thin firecracker which, when lighted, emits a shower of silver or gold sparks for a fairly long time. *The safest and least noisy firecracker, it is preferred by parents but not by children. Children's use since c1935.*

spark-plug; spark plug. *n.* A member of a group, esp. of a sports team, who leads other members by providing inspiration, encouragement, or a good example.

sparks. *n.sing.* A ship's radio operator; often a nickname. *USN and maritime use since c1915.*

sparrowgrass. *n.* Asparagus. *By folk ety. Dial.*

speak. *n.* A cheap saloon. *v.i.* To express oneself well by any means other than speaking, esp. by playing far-out music adroitly. *Some far-out use.*

speaker. *n.* A gun. *Some Negro underworld use.*

speak [one's] piece. 1. To propose marriage. *Since c1920.* 2. To complain, to enumerate one's grievances. *Colloq.*

spear. *v.t.* To beg; to accept free drinks or food. *Some use since c1915; orig. hobo use. n.* A fork.

spec. *n.* 1. Commercial speculation. → 2. A speculator, esp. a speculator in land or in theater tickets to successful plays. 3. The spectacle that opens a circus performance; the grand entry of the circus troupe into the main tent. *Orig. circus use. v.i.* To memorize, esp. to memorize a lesson or the correct answer to a test question. *Some student use since c1935.*

special. *n.* A very large, highly spiced, all beef frankfurter; an old-fashioned, home-made style of frankfurter with an honest beef and garlic flavor, as opposed to the mild mass-produced hot dog. *Orig. by people of German and Jewish descent. This all-beef frankfurter is assoc. with kosher delicatessens.*

speck bum. A completely helpless, degenerate bum. *Hobo use since c1920.*

specs. *n.pl.* The common abbr. for "specifications" in industry and manufacturing. *Common during and since W.W.II.*

spectacular. *n.* A lavishly produced television show, usu. featuring color transmission, many famous entertainers, lasting an hour and a half or longer, and not part of a regularly scheduled program. *Television use since c1955; now generally known.*

speedball; speed-ball. *n.* **1.** A fast-working, efficient person. *Colloq.* **2.** Cheap, potent wine; a glass of such wine. *Hobo use since c1920.* **3.** An injection of a mixture of, or the mixture of, cocaine and morphine, to increase the charge or kick. *Narcotic addict use since c1930.*

speed-boy. *n.* A fast-running, agile athlete. *Sportswriter use.*

speed merchant. A fast, agile athlete.

speed-up. *n.* An act or instance of increasing speed; esp. an order for increased production in a factory or office.

speedy. *n.* **1.** A delivery boy; a messenger; often used as a nickname. **2.** A special-delivery letter or package. *Some post office and office use since c1940.* adj. Fast; immoral; dissipated; loose-living.

spell out. To explain something step by step, as one spells a word.

sphere. *n.* **1.** A baseball. *Since c1910.* **2.** A golf ball; any ball. *Since c1920.*

spic and span. **1.** A couple, as lovers, of which the male or female is Puerto Rican and the other a Negro. **2.** Mixed Puerto Rican and Negro, as a neighborhood. *From "spic" and the abbr. "Span." = Spanish, but based on the well-known phrase "spick-and-span" = new or clean, plus* the pop. trademarked detergent *"Spic and Span."*

spider. *n.* **1.** A silk worker. *Some use since c1920.* **2.** A small, round, plastic insert placed in the center hole of a phonograph record so that it will fit a smaller-diameter record-player spindle. *Used to fit 45 rpm records, with larger center holes, to narrow spindles made for LP records. Since c1945.*

spiel. *n.* **1.** An eloquent speech, talk, or story used to persuade or convince the listener; esp. such a talk that exaggerates or purposely confuses the facts; an emotional sales talk; a line, a pitch. *Common since c1900. From the Ger. "spiel" = play.* **2.** Specif., a circus barker's talk on sideshow attractions; also, a pitchman's sales talk. **3.** Specif., advertising copy to be read on the radio. *Since c1940.* —**er.** *n.* **1.** An eloquent, persuasive talker; one who gives a spiel. **2.** A circus barker; a pitchman. **3.** A radio or television announcer, esp. one who reads commercials. —**ing.** *n.* Giving a spiel.

spiffed out. Dressed up in one's best clothes. *From "spiffy."*

spifflicated. *adj.* Drunk. *Since c1920.*

spiffy. *adj.* Splendid, esp. of splendid, fashionable or colorful appearance; snazzy. *More common in Eng. than U.S. adv. Well.*

spike. *v.t.* **1.** To fortify a drink by adding an alcoholic beverage. *Since c1900; common since c1920.* **2.** = spike [someone's] gun. **3.** In baseball, to cut or injure another player with the spikes on one's playing shoes.

spiked beer. **1.** Beer that has been artificially aged, as by being subjected to an electric charge. *The most common use.* **2.** A glass of beer to which whisky has been added.

spike [someone's] gun. To stop another from reaching a goal; to spoil someone's chance for success; to deny another pleasure;

to punish. *From the sabotaging technique of driving a spike into the vent of a gun barrel, to prevent firing of the piece.*

spill. *v.t.* 1. To cause a person to fall; to throw, trip, tackle, or push another so that he falls. *Colloq.* 2. To disclose information; to confess or inform. *v.i.* 1. To talk, esp. to enumerate grievances or give one's candid opinion. → 2. To inform; to confess, to squeal or sing.

spill [one] guts. 1. To tell everything one knows. *Orig. hobo use, c1920.* 2. To inform.

spill the beans. To reveal a secret inadvertently; to spoil a plan or the like by saying the wrong thing. *Colloq. Since c1920.*

spin. *v.t.* To place a phonograph record on a record player turntable and play it.

spinach. *n.* 1. A beard. *Since c1900.* 2. Nonsense, bunk, boloney, cant, exaggeration, lies. *Often used as an epithet of scorn or abuse.*

spine. *n.* The flat board at the peak of a railroad freight car's roof, on which hobos and trainworkers walk.

spitball. *n.* = spitter.

spitbox. *n.* A spittoon.

spitter. *n.* A pitched baseball, which the pitcher has spat upon, in order to make it harder to hit; such a pitch.

spizzerinktum; spizzerinctum. *n.* Vigor; pep.

splash. *n.* 1. Water; a glass of water. 2. Water; an ocean or lake; a bath. 3. A remarkable success or newsworthy action or statement leading to fame; noteworthy success or acceptance. *Usu. in "to make a splash." v.i.* To bathe. *v.t.* To publicize someone or something widely.

splice. *v.t.* To marry.

splice the main brace. To drink whisky; to have or offer a drink of whisky.

split. *n.* 1. A small bottle of wine or beer, usu. containing six or eight ounces. *Colloq.* 2. In bowling, any pattern of pins left upright after the ball has been bowled, in which pattern two or more standing pins are separated by enough space so that they cannot be knocked down directly with one ball. *v.i.* To leave a place or gathering; fig., to split oneself off from a group or place. *Used by cool, beat, and rock-and-roll members since c1955.*

splits, the. *n.sing.* The act of lowering one's body to the ground by spreading one's legs apart, while keeping the legs and body rigid and the knees unbent.

split-up. *n.* 1. A quarrel ending with each of two persons going his own way. → 2. A divorce; the legal separation of a married couple.

split week. 1. A week in which a performer works several consecutive days in one theater or town and the rest of the week in another. *Theater use.* → 2. In the card game of poker, a straight with the middle card missing.

sponge. *n.* 1. A parasitic person; a moocher; one who lives off or takes advantage of another's generosity; a chronic borrower. *Used by Shakespeare, 1598. Colloq.* 2. A drunkard; one who frequently takes large quantities of whisky. *v.i., v.t.* To borrow, esp. without the intention of repaying. *Colloq.* —r. *n.* A parasitic person; a sponge.

spoof. *v.i., v.t.* To hoax, to tease, to kid. *n.* A hoax; an instance of teasing, a joke.

spook. *n.* 1. A quiet, introspective, introverted student, esp. one on the fringe of an intellectual group; a creep. *Wide student use. c1945.* → 2. One who, though boring and shy, tries to gain entry into a group or social set by currying favor with its members. *Some student use. v.t.* 1. To scare; to haunt; to follow, esp. in a sly, sneaky way. 2. To impart bad luck. *Student use.* —ed. *adj.* 1. Burdened with ill fortune or bad luck. *Fig., as if a ghost or spook has hexed one. Some use since* *c1935; fairly common student use c1945.* 2. Uneasy, fearful, nervous, esp. without a reason or known cause. *Fig., as if one felt an intangible presence.* —**erican.** *n.* A person of Puerto Rican and American Negro parentage. *Some N.Y.C. use since c1950. From welding "spook" and "Rican."*

spoon. *v.i.* To demonstrate affection, said of engaged or dating couples; to kiss and fondle; to neck; to pet. *c1900 very popular; now archaic and replaced by "neck" and "pet."* —**er.** *n.* One who spoons; a lover. *Archaic.* —**y.** *adj.* 1. Romantic, affectionate; displaying affection, as by spooning or petting. → 2. In love with. 3. Silly; weak.

sport. *n.* 1. A handsome, generous, carefree, wisecracking, stylishly dressed roué; an irresponsible lover of wine, women, gambling, and gaiety; one who is eager for a good time, no matter how much it costs or how many responsibilities he must ignore to have it; one obsessed with creating the impression of being carefree, generous, and having fun. 2. An agreeable, accommodating, fair person; regular fellow. —**ing.** *n.* The act or an instance of acting like a sport, of visiting bars, brothels, gambling casinos, and the like. —**y.** *adj.* Garish; flamboyant; unrestrained. *Usu. said of personalities, clothing, and/or automobiles.*

sporting house. A brothel.

spot. *n.* 1. A small portion of whisky. 2. A short sleep. 3. A restaurant, bar, nightclub, or other public place of entertainment. 4. A map. *Some c1940 underworld use.* 5. A banknote of low denomination. *But only when used in the following: "deuce-spot" or "two-spot" = a $2 bill; "five-spot" = a $5 bill; "ten-spot" = a $10 bill. The term is never used with currency of larger denominations, prob. because larger bills represent more than a "spot" of money.* 6. A

short prison sentence; "years" when preceded by a number. *Thus a one-spot = a one-year sentence; a two-spot = a two-year term in prison, and so forth.* 7. Any dangerous or difficult situation. *v.t.* 1. To put on the spot. → 2. To kill. *Underworld use.*

spot, hit the. To satisfy; esp. to satisfy the appetite or the taste; said of food or drink.

spot, on the. 1. In danger of meeting with failure, being embarrassed, or losing an opportunity to succeed. 2. Called upon to produce successful results within a short duration of time, or under some other handicap.

spotlight. *n. Fig.,* that which reveals or brings something to the attention of the public.

spots. *n.pl.* 1. Musical notes, as printed on sheet music. *Some musician use.* 2. Leopards; spotted horses. *Circus use.*

spread. *n.* 1. A newspaper. *c1850, orig. underworld use.* → 2. Specif., facing pages in an open newspaper, magazine, or book. → 3. An article or a writeup in a newspaper or magazine, esp. when favorable to a person or idea; advertising, publicity. 4. A feast or dinner. *Colloq.*

spread it on thick. To exaggerate; to flatter. *c1865 to present.*

spring. *v.t.* 1. To obtain another's release from jail; to release from jail; to pardon, to parole, or help to escape. 2. To treat a person to food or drink. 3. To do something so that it will be a surprise. *v.i.* 1. To obtain a release from jail; to escape from jail. 2. To begin working; to open for business. *Pitchman and some carnival use. n.* A loan of money. —**er.** *n.* A bondsman.

spring chicken. 1. A young inexperienced person. *Always used in "no spring chicken."* 2. A young woman. *Always used in "[she's] no spring chicken." The most common use.*

spring fever. A feeling of melancholy, inducing romantic daydreaming and reducing one's working efficiency, which young people traditionally have during the first warm days of spring; a feeling of melancholy inspired by the first days of spring, when one wishes to be wandering lazily out of doors rather than working in the material world. *Colloq.*

spring with. To introduce something new to one's friends or to the public.

sprout. *n.* A young son or daughter.

sprout wings. 1. To do a good deed. **2.** To die.

spruce; spruce up. *v.i.* To make oneself neat in appearance. *Colloq. v.t.* To clean up or make a room neat; to redecorate. *Colloq.*

spud. *n.* **1.** A spade. *Dial.* **2.** A potato. *Colloq. v.i., v.t.* To spade; to dig.

spudge around. To move or work fast; to be alert, active.

Sput; sput. *n.* = Sputnik.

Sputnik; Sputnick. *n.* A man-made earth satellite. *When Russia launched the first such satellite in Oct., 1957, U.S. newspapers quickly termed it a "Sputnik" or "Sputnik 1," from the jocular or even "cute" sound of the word, implying "sput" from "sputter" plus the diminutive "— nik." The word is actually a corruption of the Russian sl. word for the satellite and = "little fellow traveler" ("fellow traveler" in space and "fellow traveler" in communism).*

squab. *n.* A girl or young woman. *Some use since c1925.*

squad = goon squad.

squadrol. *n.* A policeman; a group of policemen. *Some underworld use.*

square. *n.* **1.** A full meal; a satisfying, filling meal. *Still common.* **2.** A person scorned because he is not in the know or, esp., not cognizant of, wise to, or aware of the modern interests, activities, groups, fashions, or fads which the speaker considers vital; one

who is or persists in being unworldly unsophisticated, naïve, old-fashioned, ignorant of current trends and interests, or unenlightened; a patron considered as a sucker; one easy to deceive, trick, or victimize because of his lack of worldly wisdom or knowledge of modern attitudes; one who accepts or believes without question all the pop. cultural, ethical, political, religious, and social rationalizations and mendacity; orig. and specif., one who is not aware of, or has no, or is probably incapable of feeling, sympathy toward or appreciation or understanding of bop and, later, cool and far-out music, or of bop, cool, far-out and beat attitudes or fashions; one who is not, and is incapable of being, hip; still later, one who has no sympathy for or understanding of teenage interests, esp. of rock-and-roll attitudes; one who accepts or likes commercial sentiment, sentimentality, and corn, esp. in music and entertainment; an uncritical spectator of entertainment and life, whose values, standards, and judgments are those popularly prevailing. *A very little and late jive use; some Negro and prison use by c1940. Orig. the meanings solidified and the word pop. as a bop use c1946, with later cool use. Now common general jazz use, and teenage and student use. One of the most widely accepted words orig. pop. by bop and cool groups. Earlier evolution from such expressions as "squarehead" and "square John." adj.* **1.** Fair; genuine, authentic; legal. *Usu. in such expressions as "square deal." Since the evolution of the second meaning, seldom applied to people.* **2.** Not hip; possessing any or all of the traits of a square; accepted, patronized, defended, liked, or believed in by squares; of, by, or for squares; pertaining to squares. **3.** Conventional, conforming; of, by, for, or pertaining to conventional people, tastes, or desires. *v.t.* To right a wrong; to make amends as for a previously accomplished illegal, unethical, or unwanted action or result; lit. and fig., to substitute or follow an unfair or disastrous deed with a fair, desirable, or successful one; to ask forgiveness for a bad or forbidden deed of someone, to calm another's anger; to re-establish one's good reputation with another.

square-head; squarehead. *n.* 1. A dull-witted, slow-thinking person. *Some student and child use since c1915.*

square John; square john. 1. A self-righteous, easily victimized person. *Some underworld use since before c1930.* 2. A self-righteous person, i.e., one who is not a drug addict. *Some addict use since c1930.* 3. An honest man; one who can be trusted; a gentleman.

square peg. A misfit.

square shooter. An honest, forthright person.

Squaresville. *n.* Conventional, conforming society. *Orig. bop use, now associated with beat use.*

square the beef. To stop or ease a complaint, as from a victim by returning his money or through influence with the police or politicians. *Orig. and mainly underworld use.*

squash. *n.* The face; usu. an ugly face or one with a displeased expression.

squat hot. Fig., to sit in the hot squat; to die in the electric chair.

squaw. *n.* 1. A wife. *Colloq.* 2. An ugly prostitute. *W.W.II USN use.*

squawk. *v.i.* 1. To complain; to find fault; to express dissatisfaction. *Colloq. since c1875.* 2. To inform. 3. To admit one's guilt, often implicating others; to squeal. *v.t.* To inspect another's work, the cleanliness of a barracks, or the like. *Some W.W.II use. n.* 1. A complaint. 2. One who complains. —er. *n.* One who

complains; a habitual complainer.

squawk box. A public address system used to make announcements; the loudspeaker of such a system. *W.W.II USN use; general orders for a ship's crew were given through a public address system.*

squeak. *n.* 1. A helper; an assistant. 2. A complaint to the police. —er. *n.* A close result; a close call.

squeal. *v.i.* To complain; to protest; to inform to the police. *Since c1900; orig. and mainly underworld use. n.* 1. Ham; pork. 2. A complaint, as to the police. —er. *n.* 1. A complainer; a faultfinder. *Since c1890.* 2. An informer.

squealer's mark. Any scar or mark on the face, as if made by criminals or hoodlums in revenge for the bearer's having squealed.

squeegee; squeegie. *n.* A jerk or goof. *Some teenage use reported.*

squeeze. *n.* 1. Extortion. 2. Graft. —r. *n.* A person who does not give gratuities; a miser.

squeeze-box. *n.* An accordion.

squeeze-gun. *n.* A pressure riveter.

squeeze on [someone], put the. To force, harass, or embarrass someone into doing something; to put the heat on [someone].

squff. *v.i.* To eat heavily; to stuff oneself with food.

squib. *n.* 1. A short, usu. one paragraph, advertisement or notice as found in newspapers, magazines, and on boxes and labels of manufactured goods. → 2. A short, often witty, paragraph or notice in a newspaper or magazine, often used to fill up space. *v.i.* To speak a small exaggeration or lie; to fib.

squire. *v.t.* To escort a girl or woman; to court a girl or woman.

squirrel. *v.i.* To weave from side to side while driving a car, esp. a hot rod. *Common hot-rod use since c1950. v.t.* 1. To cache something. 2. To climb to the top of a railroad car; to set hand brakes from the roof of a railroad car. *Railroad and hobo use. n.* **1.** Whisky. *Archaic and dial.* **2.** A psychologist; a psychiatrist; one who examines "nuts." **3.** A crazy person; an eccentric. **4.** An irrational, easily confused hot-rod driver; a novice or hesitant hot-rod driver. *Hot-rod use since c1950.* **5.** A careless or reckless driver. *Some general teenage use since c1955.* **6.** A person who would like to be accepted in a group; one who follows a group and tries to be like its members even though he does not belong and is not accepted. *Mainly teenage use, since c1955. Perh. from hot-rod v. use "squirrel" = to weave from side to side while driving, as most freq. done by a novice or incompetent driver.* —**ly.** *adj.* Crazy; eccentric.

squirt. *n.* **1.** A short man; specif., a short, insignificant man; an insignificant, unimportant person. **2.** A youth, esp. a callow, foppish, or presumptuous youth. **3.** A soda dispenser, a soda jerk. **4.** A quarter; the sum of 25¢. *Because it is an insignificant sum.* → **5.** Twenty-five dollars. **6.** A jet airplane. *c1950.*

squishy. *adj.* Sentimental; amorous.

stab. *n.* A chance; a try. *Colloq.* —**bed.** *adj.* Delayed.

stable. *n.* **1.** Several individual entertainers, prize fighters, prostitutes, or the like, serving under one manager or agent. **2.** A dilapidated, dirty room, house, or public place.

stable push. Inside information; information from influential people or people in the know. *Orig. and mainly horse-racing use.*

stache = stash.

stacked. *adj.* Having a sexually attractive body—said of a girl or woman; well built—said of people.

stack up. 1. To wreck a car; to have an accident in a car. *Mainly*

teenage use, since c1950. **2.** To emerge; to develop. *Colloq.*

stack-up. *n.* An automobile accident; a piled-up mess.

stag. *n.* **1.** A youth or man who attends a social affair without a female partner. **2.** A bachelor. **3.** A detective. *Negro use.* **4.** = stag party. *adj.* **1.** Unaccompanied by a woman or girl. → **2.** Unaccompanied by a male escort. *v.i.* To attend a social function without escorting a girl. *v.t.* To cut off trouser legs midway between the knee and the ankle, so that the trousers serve as shorts or for swimming.

stage = up-stage.

stag line. A group of stags at a dance, observing the females for possible dancing partners.

stag party. 1. A party attended by men only, often for the purpose of viewing obscene performances or movies, telling obscene jokes, and the like. **2.** Specif., such a party given in honor of a prospective bridegroom by his friends.

stairs = upstairs.

stake. *n.* **1.** A comparatively large sum of money, esp. a gift; a gift of all the necessities one requires. → **2.** An amount of money saved, borrowed, or loaned to be used to start a new business venture, or in prospecting, speculating, or gambling. **3.** All of one's money, the total assets of a person or business; the total amount of money hazarded, as in gambling or business; the total amount of money possible to win or earn in a specific venture. *Colloq. v.t.* **1.** To gamble a specif. amount on the successful outcome of something. **2.** To loan a person a sum of money to start a new business venture, or to prospect, speculate, or gamble; to loan someone money for a specif. purpose. *Colloq.* **3.** To give someone money for a specif. purpose; to treat someone to something. *Colloq.* **4.** To prepare a place as a police trap for criminals or suspects; to know or watch a place as a known criminal hangout.

stake out. To watch a suspect continuously and systematically, as by the police. **stake-out.** *n.* A police trap for criminals; a point or points from which the activities of a suspect may be observed by the police.

stall. *v.i.* 1. To delay action in order to further one's objective; to wait instead of taking action. *Colloq. since c1900.* 2. To engage in obstructive activities; to loiter or hang about without acting. 3. To walk as a pickpocket's stall. *Underworld use.* *v.t.* To put (someone) off; to distract one's attention from the main issue. *n.* 1. A pickpocket's assistant; one who diverts the victim's attention, maneuvers him into a position in which he can be readily robbed, and/or helps to conceal the work of the pickpocket. *Underworld use.* → 2. An accomplice of criminals; one who delays interference with a holdup, obstructs pursuers, or distracts attention from the crime; a lookout, esp. one who watches for the police during a crime, in order to warn his fellow criminals to flee. *Underworld use.* 3. Any delaying pretext. *Most common use.* → 4. A pretense, a false alibi. 5. A refusal. 6. A dilapidated, dirty, or cluttered room. 7. = stand. *n.*

stall; stall off. To keep away; to keep at a distance, usu. by evasion or trickery.

stanch; stanch out. *v.i.* To step out; to begin.

stand. *v.t.* 1. To treat someone to; to buy for someone. 2. To cost a specified amount of money, whether a large or small amount. *n.* 1. A robbery. 2. A store; a place of business.

standee. *n.* One who is forced to stand because there are not enough seats to accommodate everyone in a crowded theater or public place.

stand-in. *n.* 1. Orig., one who substitutes for a movie actor in order to perform dangerous or tedious parts of his work; one who knows an actor's role in a play and is ready to substitute for him when necessary. *Theater use.* 2. A substitute; one able and willing to substitute for another. **stand in.** To act as a substitute (for someone).

stand in with. To enjoy the esteem and favors of a person or group.

stand-out. *n.* 1. One whose merits, performance, or expected performance seem obviously better than others in his group; esp., one who seems sure to win a contest. 2. A very superior person or thing; anyone or anything outstanding. *Colloq.*

stand pat. 1. To keep one's original five cards in the game of draw poker, in the belief that they are good enough to win the game, rather than to attempt to better an already good combination of cards. 2. To keep a firm fixed position, opinion, or belief; to attempt to succeed or to finish a task with one's original plan, equipment, personnel, or attitude; to stand fast.

stand-up. *adj.* Not afraid but proud to state and defend one's opinions, ideas, and beliefs or the rights of others; frank and honest. *Fig., one who, like a prize fighter, is not afraid to stand up and fight.*

stand [someone] up. 1. To fail to keep an appointment, usu. a date, leaving the person standing and waiting at the appointed place; to break a date without giving advance notice. → 2. To break an engagement; to discontinue a love affair. 3. To underrate someone.

stand up for [someone]. 1. To defend another against criticism; to testify to another's honesty, sincerity, or other good qualities. 2. To act as best man for a bridegroom.

stanza. *n.* Any unit of time or action, esp. in sports: a round of a prize fight, an inning of a baseball game, a quarter of a football game.

star. *adj.* Of prime importance; first class. *Colloq. c1875 mail routes in the U.S. Far West were called "Star Routes."*

starboard. *adj.* Right-handed, as a baseball pitcher.

star boarder. A hearty eater.

starch. *n.* 1. Any adulterated drug. 2. Courage, bravery, stamina, boldness, determination. *Fig., that which is needed to give a man backbone and make him stand straight and proud.*

star-gazer. *n.* An idealist; one with idealistic but impractical ideas.

starred. *adj.* = star.

stash; stache. *v.t.* To hide something away; to store up; to save; to cache. *Colloq.; very common.* *n.* 1. A hiding place. 2. A cache. 3. A mustache.

stash away = stash.

state-o. *n.* A prison convict's uniform or clothing, provided by the state. *Common prison use.*

Stateside; stateside. *n.* The United States, considered one's home. *Fairly common W.W.II Armed Forces use; still some use.* *adj.* From, pertaining to, or resembling the United States, its products and people, or the habits, fashions, and fads of United States citizens. *W.W.II Armed Forces use.*

station. *n.* In baseball, a base.

steady. *n.* One's regular sweetheart; a girl's regular or habitual escort or the girl regularly or habitually escorted by a boy, to the exclusion of all others. *Since before c1910. Wide student use and common general use.*

steady, go. To date only one member of the opposite sex, because of a strong preference for that person's company. *Orig. "to go steady" meant that the male was seriously courting and the female accepting the courtship; since c1945, however, it has become a teenage phenomenon merely indicating a mutual crush or a de-*

sire for greater security in the social environment.

steal. *n.* 1. A theft. 2. A bargain; a low price. *Colloq.*

steam. *v.i.* To become angry.

steam, let (blow) off. To relieve one's pent-up feelings, usu. resentment, by talking to someone, usu. excitedly and at length. *From the lit. use concerning steam engines, boilers, and the like.*

steamed up. 1. Angry. 2. Eager.

steam fiddle. A calliope. *Circus use.*

steam shovel. A potato peeler. *Ironic. W.W.II Army use.*

steam up. 1. To excite; to induce excitement or enthusiasm by making a person angry or eager, by promising money, honor, or some reward. 2. To have enthusiasm; to be eager.

steel. *v.t.* To stab a person. *adj.* White; Caucasian. *Mainly Negro use.*

steen. *n., adj.* Any fairly large number; any cardinal number from 13 to 19 inclusive; umpteen.

steer. *v.i., v.t.* To solicit or direct patrons to a gambling casino, bar, brothel, con game, or the like; to act as a shill. *n.* 1. Advice or information intended as a guide; a tip. *Colloq.* 2. = steerer. —er. *n.* One who leads dupes to swindlers or gambling houses.

stem. *n.* 1. A, or usu. the, major street in a town or city. *Orig. hobo use; now associated with theatrical use.* 2. An opium pipe. *Some opium addict use.* *v.t.* To beg from strangers on the street, or stem. *Hobo use.* —s. *n.pl.* A person's legs; specif., the shapely legs of an attractive girl or woman.

step-ins. *n., n.pl.* 1. A woman's underpants. *Colloq.* 2. Men's low-cut, stringless shoes, which can be slipped on or stepped into easily. *They are similar to moccasins.* 3. Women's low-cut, non-laced shoes or slippers. *Colloq.*

step off. 1. = step off the carpet. 2. To die.

step off the carpet. To marry. *Fig.* = *to finish walking down the aisle.*

step off the deep end. 1. To rush into action without ascertaining the facts or making preparations; to become involved in something that one does not understand. 2. To die.

step on it. 1. To hurry; to hurry up. 2. To shut up.

step on the gas = step on it.

step out. 1. To go to a party or dance. 2. To go on a date.

step out on [someone]. 1. To date someone other than one's steady. 2. To be sexually unfaithful.

stepper. *n.* A student who devotes much time to social life. *Some c1940 use.*

Stetson. *n.* Any man's hat. *From the pop. manufacturer and brand.*

stew. *n.* 1. A drunkard. 2. A drinking spree. 3. Chaos; confusion; frustration. —ed. *adj.* Drunk. *Brought to America by the colonists. Universally known.*

stew-builder. *n.* A cook. *Hobo and logger use.*

stewbum. *n.* An unemployed, homeless street beggar, or hobo, who has reached this lowly position through alcoholism. *Orig. any beggar or hobo, as one who lives on stew; but the association has changed to one who is, or has too often been, stewed.*

stewed to the gills. Very drunk; completely drunk.

stick. *n.* Any fairly long, slim object that resembles a stick. *Specif:* 1. A baseball bat. *c1870.* 2. A baton. 3. A cigarette; esp. a marijuana cigarette, which is slimmer than the usu. tobacco cigarette. *Common addict use. From "stick of tea." c1900.* 4. A cane. 5. A ship's mast. 6. A clarinet. 7. A piece of dynamite. 8. A pencil; esp. a radio operator's pencil. 9. A fountain pen. *Pitchman use.* 10. The control lever of an airplane.

11. A slide rule. 12. A billiard cue. 13. A golf club. Also, any person who might carry a stick or anything resembling a stick. *Specif.:* 14. A policeman, night watchman, guard, or the like who carries a billy club or night stick. 15. Any tall, thin, ugly person. *Colloq.* 16. A dull, boring person with no interests or enthusiasms. *One who sits like a stick.* 17. In a gambling casino, an employee who rakes the money or chips from the middle of the table after each play and pushes the winners their winnings with a long rake-like stick; a croupier. → 18. = shill. *v.t.* To sell someone an inferior, useless, or overpriced object; to overcharge; to leave one's bill or debts for another to pay; to leave someone the blame or responsibility for an act. —er. *n.* A knife, used as a weapon; one who carries or uses a knife as a weapon. *Underworld use.* —ing. *adj.* = stinking. —s. *n.pl.* 1. Drumsticks used by a drummer, esp. by a jazz drummer. *General jazz use.* 2. A small town or city; a rural district; the country; the suburbs; a hick town. *Orig. vaudeville, now common.* 3. A hobo camp. 4. Legs.

stick, on the = on the ball.

stick around. To stay near a person or place; to stand by; to loiter.

stick [one's] neck out. To take a chance; to risk making a mistake; to lay oneself open to attack; to invite trouble.

stick of gage. A regular or a marijuana cigarette.

stick of tea (T). A marijuana cigarette.

stick-out. *n.* 1. = stand-out; a remarkable specimen. 2. A cinch; in sports and gambling, what looks to be a sure winner. 3. *Specif.,* horse-racing use, a horse that seems obviously superior to other horses in the same race.

stick to one's ribs. To be filling; said of hearty food. *Colloq.*

stickum. *n.* **1.** Any adhesive, such as glue. *Colloq.* **2.** Specif., hair dressing, pomade.

stick up. To rob; orig., to rob a person at gun point, forcing him to stick up his hands. **stickup; stick-up.** *n.* **1.** Armed robbery; a holdup. **2.** An armed robber; a holdup man.

stick up for [someone] = stand up for [someone], 1.

sticky. *adj.* **1.** Firm; stubborn; difficult. **2.** Sentimental; tending toward sentimentality.

sticky end of the stick, the = short end of the stick.

sticky-fingered. *adj.* **1.** Given to stealing. **2.** Miserly; holding on to money.

stiff. *adj.* **1.** Drunk. *Common use.* **2.** Formal; not relaxed or at ease. **3.** Difficult to solve or accomplish successfully; maximally extreme in content. **4.** Forged; said of a check. *Underworld use.* *n.* **1.** A corpse; a cadaver. *Common.* **2.** A drunken person. → **3.** A rough, clumsy, stupid, or overbearing man. Usu. in "big stiff." **4.** An average or common man, esp. a manual laborer, factory worker or other man employed for strength or skill rather than intelligence; a fellow, a guy. → **5.** Specif., a hobo, tramp, or vagabond. Often in combinations as "blanket stiff," "bindle stiff," "mission stiff," "railroad stiff," "jungle stiff," and the like. *Mainly hobo use.* → **6.** Specif., a migratory worker. **7.** A deadbeat or moocher, specif., a person who does not tip a taxi driver, waiter, bellhop, or the like; also, a poor tipper. **8.** A communication or official document considered as contraband; a message circulated secretly among prisoners; a letter received by a prisoner; a forged check; stolen securities. *Various underworld and prison uses since c1900.* **9.** A failure; a flop; anything or anyone that seems assured of failing or being a flop. Specif., a racehorse that will not win a race; a prize fighter who is

certain to lose a fight; a book, song, play, or movie that has little appeal and seems assured of becoming a flop. **10.** A useless person who contributes no ideas, conversation, or enthusiasm to a task or social gathering. → **11.** A contestant or team that does not try or has no chance of winning. *v.t.* **1.** To fail to tip a person; to refrain from tipping. *Waiter, porter, bellhop, and taxi driver use.* → **2.** To cheat, as a waiter, restaurant, or the like, by leaving without paying one's check. *adv.* Fig., so dull or boring as to cause sleepiness, sleep, or even death, as in "He bores me stiff." **—ener.** *n.* **1.** A knockout punch. *Prize fight use.* **2.** In sports, the deciding factor; the winning play or score. **3.** A small quantity of whisky added to a drink, usu. an alcoholic one, in order to make it stronger. **—ing.** *adj.* **= jiving.**

stiff card. A formal written invitation.

stiff-neck. *n.* A snob; a self-righteous person.

stillion. *n.* An indefinitely large number.

sting. *v.t.* To overcharge; to cheat; to steal. *n.* Money or stolen goods gained from a crime. *Underworld and Negro use.* **—er.** *n.* **1.** A railroad brakeman or watchman. *Hobo and railroad use.* **2.** An obstacle; an unresolved problem; any factor of uncertainty.

stinker. *n.* **1.** A contemptible person. *Very common since c1930.* → **2.** A term of endearment, applied usu. to children, esp. in "little stinker," and freq. to one's spouse; a mischievous but endearing person. *Since c1945. One of many sl. words used both as a term of contempt and as a term of endearment.* **3.** Anything inferior, esp. a boring or badly performed entertainment. *Very common.* **4.** A debauch; an extended social affair, as a dance or party, that continues a long time and nearly exhausts the participants. *Student use, c1950.* **—oo; stink-**

aroo. *adj.* 1. Of inferior quality; esp., boring, badly performed; usu. said of entertainment. 2. Despicable; wretched. *n.* Anything of the poorest quality, esp. an entertainment; a stinker.

stinkie; stinky. *n.* Common nickname or form of direct address for a disliked, contemptible person. *Common child use.*

stinking. *adj.* 1. Despicable; mean. *Fairly common.* 2. Very wealthy; having an abundance of money; loaded. *Fig., having so much money that one can smell it.* 3. Thoroughly drunk. 4. Exceedingly.

stinko. *adj.* 1. Drunk. 2. Smelly; odoriferous. 3. Unpleasant. 4. Of very inferior quality.

stink pot. Any disliked or scorned person. *Mainly child use.*

stir; stir, the. *n.* A jail; a prison. *Orig. and mainly underworld use, but fairly common. From the Anglo-Saxon "styr" = punishment, reinforced by the Romany "steripen" = prison, which is also a possible orig. of the syn. "pen."* *adj.* Prison; prison-like.

stir-crazy; stir-bugs; stir-daffy; stir-simple. *adj.* Dull-witted or insane as a result of long imprisonment; neurotically maladjusted to prison life; said of convicts. *"Stir-crazy" is the only well-known form; "stir-simple" has fairly common convict use.*

stir-wise. *adj.* Well informed or sophisticated, esp. about or by reason of imprisonment.

stomach. *v.t.* To accept or believe something disgusting. *Almost always in the negative, e.g., "I can't stomach that."* *n.* Courage; a lack of squeamishness.

stomach-robber. *n.* A logging-camp cook.

stomp. *n.* A jazz composition or arrangement with a heavily accented rhythm, usu. in a lively tempo and, during the swing era, repeated riffs.

stone. *adv.* Very; completely, thoroughly. *Only when used before*

certain words, e.g., "stone broke." —d. *adj.* 1. Drunk. *Wide student use since c1945.* 2. Under the influence of a narcotic. *Some addict use.* 3. Excited, enthusiastic, ecstatic, surprised, flipped; specif., aroused by a good performance of cool or far-out music. *Cool and far-out use. A pop. sophisticated word; wide young adult and student use c1945, though much older.*

stone blind. Thoroughly drunk.

stone broke. Completely penniless.

stone cold. 1. Very cold. *Said of an object, never the weather.* → 2. Dead.

stone dead. Definitely dead.

stood. Stayed. Usu. in "should have stood in bed."

stood in bed, [one] should have. An expression indicating that one is having or has had such an unsuccessful, unhappy, unrewarding experience or day that it was not worthwhile getting up.

stooge. *n.* 1. A comedian's assistant who acts stupidly or naïvely in order to be a foil for or the butt of the comedian and his jokes. → 2. An underling; esp., one who acts as a puppet for another, saying and doing what he does without question, because he is told to. *v.i.* 1. To play the part of a stooge for an entertainer. 2. To act as a stooge or puppet for another.

stool. *n.* 1. A plain-clothes policeman. 2. An informer for the police; a stool pigeon. *A sl. backclipping. v.t.* To lure. —ie; stooley = stool pigeon.

stool pigeon. An informer, usu. a police informer.

stoop. *n.* = stupe.

stoopnagel. *n.* A silly, blundering person.

stop. *n.* A receiver of stolen goods. *Underworld use; has replaced "fence" among most underworld elements.* —per. *n.* In boxing, a knockout.

store. *n.* 1. A concession. *Carnival and circus use.* 2. A business office.

store cheese. The most common yellow American cheddar cheese. *So called because such cheese used to be displayed as and sold from large blocks or wheels on the counter of every grocery store.*

storm. *n.* A fit of anger; a ruckus. **storm; storm out.** *v.i.* 1. To leave a place in anger. *E.g., "He really stormed out of here without even saying good-by."* 2. To move fast; to drive fast. *Hot-rod use since c1955.*

storm, in a. Excited; confused. *A fig. use. W.W.II Army Air Corps use.*

stove league. Baseball enthusiasts who discuss the last season until the next. *An allusion to the stove at the center of a conversational group in the once typical country store.*

stove pipe. 1. A trench mortar. *W.W.I and W.W.II use.* 2. A jet fighter airplane.

stow it. An order or request to stop doing or saying something. *USN use.*

stow the gab. To keep quiet; to shut up. *Orig. USN use.*

straight. *n.* In poker, five consecutively numbered cards, regardless of suit. *Colloq. adj.* 1. Undiluted, neat; said of liquor. 2. Honest; normal. *Depending on the context, denotes that the person referred to is not dishonest, not a drug addict, not a homosexual, and so forth. Orig. an antyn. to the stand. "crooked," reinforced by "straightforward." The uses = sexually normal and/ or not a drug addict, since c1945, and are gaining in pop.*

straight face. A face showing no expression that might reveal a joke, deception, or secret; specif., a face that does not show laughter, as might reveal a joke or hurt someone's feelings.

straight from the horse's mouth. Authentically; directly from one in the know; said of information, news, or the like.

straight from the shoulder. Honestly, frankly, and to the point.

straight goods. Truth.

straight man. A comedian's accomplice who acts as his foil; a stooge.

straight talk. Honest, sincere, succinct talk.

strap. *n.* A person, esp. a student, whose interests lie almost exclusively in athletics, to the neglect of intellectual interests. *College use.* —ped. *adj.* Penniless; without money. *Colloq. since c1860.*

strawberries. *n.pl.* Prunes. *W.W.I and II Armed Forces use, esp. USN use.*

straw boss. 1. The foreman of a crew of manual laborers. *Colloq.* → 2. Any person, esp. a foreman, who gives orders or oversees work but has no power, authority, or executive status with which to support his orders. 3. An assistant boss or foreman. *Colloq. since c1900; orig. hobo use.*

straw-cat. *n.* A harvest worker, esp. a migratory harvest worker.

straw-hat. *adj., n.* A summer theater; summer theaters, actors, or plays. *Also used attrib.*

street, put it on the. To give out information; to disclose a personal confidence or secret to many people; to let something be known.

Street, the. Variously, any of several well-known, exciting, brightly-lit streets in several major cities in the U.S. Esp., Broadway in New York City. *The connotation is always one of bright lights, excitement, and entertainment; "the Street" is always the center of the theatrical, nightclub, or gambling district of a city.*

strength. *n.* Profit, profits; specif. all possible profits, as can be realized by charging maximum prices while giving minimum value.

stretch. *n.* A prison sentence; time served in prison. *Universally* *known.* —er. *n.* 1. The neck. 2. A belt. —es. A pair of suspenders.

strib. *n.* A prison warden. *Underworld use.*

strictly. *adv.* Very well; excellently; adroitly. *Usu. in ref. to the playing of jazz.*

strictly union = corny. Swing use, said of nonswing music. *Implying that the only requirement necessary to play such music is belonging to the musicians' union, no other talent is needed, and that the musicians are fulfilling the bare minimum requirement in displaying enthusiasm or imagination.*

stride. *n.* A style of jazz piano playing in which the bass alternates between single notes on the first and third beats of the measure and chords, usu. emphasized, on the second and fourth beats of the measure. *A development from ragtime usu. assoc. with Eastern or N.Y.C. jazz and first identified with James P. Johnson.* —rs. *n.sing.* A pair of trousers. *Negro use.* —s. *n.* = striders. *Hobo, underworld, and maritime use.*

strike. *n.* 1. In bowling, the act or an instance of knocking down all the pins with one's first ball, 2. Fig., a refusal to work, play, join a gathering, or the like. *Usu. jocular; from the labor use.* *v.t.* 1. To come upon, esp. unexpectedly; to meet. *Colloq.* 2. To make an urgent appeal or request of someone; to ask someone for a job, loan of money, or the like. —r. *n.* 1. A helper; an assistant. *W.W.II USN use.* → 2. A sailor who is studying to improve his status; also, one who seeks advancement by flattery rather than by work. *W.W.II USN use.*

strike bedrock. To die.

strike·breaker. *n.* A substitute sweetheart.

string. *n.* 1. A false story. 2. A necktie.

string, on a. To have or hold in reserve; specif., to encourage the attention of one of the opposite sex after one has decided to reject that person or while one has another boy friend or girl friend.

string, pull the. In baseball, to pitch a slow ball, esp. after having pitched a fast one.

string along. To follow.

string along with [someone]. To accept another's decision, opinion, or advice; to be a disciple of; to trust, be faithful to, to agree with; to follow someone as a leader.

string band. A band composed entirely of stringed instruments.

stringbean. *n.* Any tall, thin person. *Colloq.*

string up. To hang a person. *Colloq.*

string-whanger. *n.* A guitarist. *Some jazz use.*

strip. *n.* = drag strip. —per. *n.* A striptease dancer; a burlesque or nightclub entertainer who disrobes (but usu. not completely) slowly and sensually to music; she may also, but not necessarily, dance, do bumps and grinds, or perform other erotic movements.

Strip, the = Street, the. *A newer word, sometimes, but not always, referring to a district rather than to a single street. Usu. applied to the main street containing many nightclubs, esp. in Los Angeles and Miami, and to the stretch of highway containing the luxurious class of gambling houses in Las Vegas.*

stripes. *n.pl.* 1. Tigers. *Circus use.* 2. Noncommissioned officers' rank or insignia. *W.W.II use.*

stroll. *n.* 1. A road, highway, or street. *c1935 jive use; some Negro use.* 2. Anything that is easy to do. *c1940; Negro and jazz use.*

strong. *adj.* 1. Flush with money. *Hobo use.* 2. Providing dishonest profit. *Carnival and circus use.* → 3. Costing 25¢ or more to play or bet. *Carnival use.* 4. Well liked; accepted as an equal; "large." *Theatrical use since c1955.*

strong-arm. *n.* 1. A person employed to carry out acts of violence; one who uses physical violence to obtain money or information, as a hoodlum. 2. Violence; physical force. *Since c1830.* *adj.* Done with violence or physical force. *v.i.* and *v.t.* To beat a person up; to use violence.

strong-arm man. One employed to beat up people; a hoodlum or thug who uses physical violence of any kind.

strut (do) [one's] stuff. To do well that which one is specially qualified for or noted for doing; to perform; to act.

stub. *n.* A small, stocky person; esp. a high-school or college girl.

stuck; stuck with. *adj.* 1. Having been sold an inferior or worthless item; overcharged; left to pay another's bill or debt; burdened with the undeserved or unwanted blame or responsibility for something. 2. Left with something useless or embarrassing.

stuck on. 1. Infatuated with oneself or a person of the opposite sex, usu. said of youths. 2. Greatly impressed with the merit or personality of a person.

stuck up. *adj.* Haughty; snobbish; snooty. *Colloq. since c1890.*

stud. *n.* 1. Any male; esp. a dude, sport, or roué. → 2. Any hip male. *Orig. jive use; fairly common cool use.*

student. *n.* 1. An apprentice; a novice. 2. Specif., a beginning drug addict; a drug addict who does not yet need freq. or large doses; a drug addict with a small habit. *c1936; addict use.*

stuff. *v.t.* 1. To sell misrepresented merchandise; to sell merchandise that is not genuine or that is stolen. *Underworld use until c1890.* → 2. To deceive, kid, ride, or trick a person; to make a person the butt of a joke. *n.* 1. Contraband; stolen goods. *Prob. from the 1st v.t. use, reinforced by "hot stuff." Underworld use.* → 2. Specif., bootlegged or illegal whisky.

Now in reference to "good stuff." *Since Prohibition.* 3. Specif., any narcotic, as used by an addict. *Orig. addict use.* 4. [taboo] A girl or young woman considered only sexually; tail. 5. One's stock-in-trade, as a comedian's jokes or the types of pitches mastered by a baseball pitcher.

stuff, know [one's] = know [one's] onions.

stuffed shirt; stuff shirt. 1. A pompous, pretentious bore who insists on formalities. *Always derog. use, usu. said of a man of wealth or social standing.* → 2. Any superior; any wealthy or socially prominent person.

stumble. *v.i.* 1. To make a mistake; to suffer a misfortune. → 2. To be arrested. *Underworld use.*

stumblebum. *n.* An unemployed, homeless street beggar, esp. if alcoholic, who is always or usually in a dazed condition, resembling a trance.

stump. *v.t.* To confuse, to puzzle, to nonplus. *Colloq.*

stump-jumper. *n.* A farmer. *Archaic and dial.*

stung. *adj.* 1. = stuck. 2. Cheated, esp. by a merchant; overcharged.

stunned. *adj.* Drunk.

stunner. *n.* 1. A first-rate story. 2. A striking person or thing; esp. an attractive woman.

stunning. *adj.* 1. Excellent; admirable. → 2. Striking; visually attractive. *Usu. said of women or clothes; most often used by women. Colloq.*

stupe; stoop. *n.* A stupid person, a blockhead. *Common use. From "stupid."*

stymie. *v.t.* To impede; to frustrate. *Orig. a golf term.*

sub. *n.* 1. A substitute of any kind; now specif. a substitute player on an athletic team, a member of the team whose skills or seniority does not give him priority to play but who is a team member and plays when those with more skill or seniority are resting or injured. *Colloq. Com-*

*mon sports use, which is the most
common use of this word.* 2. A
submarine. *Orig. W.W.I use; colloq. since c1920.* 3. A person with
subnormal mentality; an extremely stupid person; an imbecile, moron, or idiot. *Some use
since c1930. v.i.* To act as a substitute for another person, esp.
in a job. *v.t.* To substitute one
player of a team for another during an athletic contest, as by the
team coach or manager. —deb. *n.*
A girl younger than a debutante;
a young teenage girl. *Colloq.* —s.
n.pl. The feet. —way! *interj., n.*
A nickel or a dime tip or gratuity, as given to a food or soft
drink vendor; an expression of
thanks to the tipper, shouted by
the vendor mainly as notice to
other customers that tips are
being received and appreciated,
and notice to co-workers or a supervisor that the money is the
vendor's and is not to be put in
the management's cash register.
*Although subway fares are now
more than a nickel or dime, the
word is still use.*

suck. *v.i., v.t.* To curry favor with
people in authority. —er. *n.* 1. A
person easily deceived or
cheated; an easy victim; a dupe.
Colloq. since c1835. → 2. A fan;
one who is vulnerable to a certain type of person, business deal,
sport, or gambling game. 3. A
teacher's pet. *Student use.* 4. A
lollipop. *Child use; colloq. v.t.*
To trick someone; to make a
sucker or dupe of a person.

suck around. To hang around a
place or person with a view of
gaining preference or favors.

sucker list. 1. A list of the names
of good prospective customers,
donors, or the like. 2. A list of
people who are easily, and can
be frequently, duped, deceived,
or victimized; fig., a list of marks.

suck [someone] in. To deceive;
esp. to deceive by making false
promises.

suck up to [someone]. To curry
favor with someone by being ex-

ceptionally agreeable, or by doing menial jobs for that person.

suction. *n.* Influence; good standing with one's superiors; pull.

suction, in *a.* In love; confused,
unrealistic because of being in
love.

suds; sudds. *n.pl.* Beer. *From the
sudslike appearance of the foam.
Very common c1915 and still in
wide use.*

sugan; soogan. *n.* A quilt; a blanket. *Archaic and dial. Some hobo
use.*

sugar. *n.* 1. Money; money available to be spent for pleasures;
money easy to obtain; an abundance of money. → 2. Bribe
money. 3. Narcotics: heroin, cocaine, or morphine. 4. A sweetheart. *A term of endearment. v.t.*
To bribe.

sugar-coat; sugarcoat. *v.t.* To
make something be or seem more
agreeable than it is; esp., to relay
bad news in a gentle way, as
while emphasizing more fortunate details; to emphasize the
happier, more successful facets of
a generally unhappy or unsuccessful situation; to include a reward in a distasteful or tedious
task. —ed. *adj.* Made, or made to
seem, more pleasant; said of a
disgusting, unhappy, unsuccessful, or tedious task, duty, venture or the like.

sugar daddy. A male sweetheart
well provided with money esp.,
a wealthy, usu. elderly man who
spends money freely on girls; specif., a worldly, sophisticated man,
usu. not young and usu. wealthy,
who pays the rent and other expenses of a young woman in return for her sexual favors and
companionship.

sugar-head. *n.* Moonshine whisky.

Sugar Hill; sugar hill. *n.* 1. A district with Negro brothels; a Negro brothel. *Fig., a place where
money grows.* 2. In N.Y.C., the
wealthy neighborhood in Harlem.

sugar report. A letter from a
sweetheart, esp. from a girl to a

serviceman. *Student and W.W.II Armed Forces use; very common.*

suit, the. Lit. and fig., any Armed Forces uniform, specif. an Army uniform. *Some W.W.II use. Usu. in such phrases as "I got the suit" = I have been drafted into the Army; or "I'm going to put on the suit" = I'm going to enlist in the Armed Forces.*

suitcase. *n.* A drum. *Swing musician use.*

sujee. *n.* = soogie.

sum-up. *n.* A summary. *Colloq.*

Sunday. *adj. and adv. When used in combination with certain words:* 1. Best, most effective, perfect. *As in "Sunday clothes." Fig., saved for a special day.* 2. Amateurish; part time. *As in "Sunday driver."*

Sunday clothes. One's best clothes; new or dressy clothing. *Fig., clothes saved for Sunday churchgoing and social functions. Now archaic and dial.*

Sunday driver. A poor automobile driver; one who drives uncertainly and erratically. *Fig., one who drives very seldom, only on Sundays.*

Sunday pitch. A powerful throw; usu. in baseball, but also any pitch.

Sunday punch. A hard, effective blow with the fist; any powerful attack.

Sunday run. A long distance. *Fig., a long trip between towns in which one has to work and, therefore, a trip taken on a Sunday, when one cannot work. Circus and traveling salesman use.*

Sunday soldier. An Army reservist who is not on active duty. *c1945.*

Sunday thinker. A self-proclaimed visionary; an impractical person; an eccentric.

sun-downer. *n.* A strict disciplinarian; a martinet.

sun-fisher. *n.* A twisting, bucking horse.

sunny. *adj.* Happy, pleasant. *Colloq.*

sunny side up. Fried on one side only, so that the yolk remains soft; said of an egg. *Because the yolk is round and yellow, like the sun, and lies on top of an egg fried in this manner. Orig. lunchcounter use in relaying an order; now common.*

super. *n.* 1. A superintendent, esp. a worker's overseer. → 2. Esp., a combined superintendent, watchman, and janitor of an apartment house or small office building. *adj.* Wonderful; marvelous; very pleasing. *Young teenage girl use since c1935.*

super-duper. **sooper-dooper.** *adj.* Colossal; exceedingly large and remarkable; remarkable, esp. for its size or scope.

sure. *adv.* Yes; certainly; surely; I shall. *Freq. used as a one-word reply. Colloq.*

sure-fire. *adj.* Unfailing; certain of winning applause. *Colloq.*

sure thing. 1. A certainty; a standout. *Colloq. since c1850.* 2. Yes; certainly; surely; I shall. *Colloq. since c1890.*

sush. *v.t.* = shush.

swab. *n.* A merchant sailor. —**bie**; **swabby.** *n.* A sailor. *Usu. used in direct address.*

swag. *n.* 1. Stolen money or goods; loot. 2. Any article or articles forbidden to prisoners; contraband articles.

swagger. *adj.* Stylish.

swak; SWAK; S.W.A.K. *adj.* Sealed with a kiss. *Written on the back of love letters; fairly common teenage and young student use; from the initials.*

swallow. *v.t.* 1. To believe or accept something false, deceiving, or leading to being tricked, cheated, or taken advantage of. *From the expression "to swallow it hook, line, and sinker."* 2. To believe or accept something. *Often used in the negative, as a refusal to believe or accept something, e.g., "I can't swallow that."*

swallow the anchor. To go ashore permanently; to get a shore job; to leave the USN.

swallow [or eat] the Bible. To lie; to swear falsely. *Archaic and dial.*

swamper. *n.* 1. A truck driver's helper. → 2. A porter.

swamp-root. *n.* Whisky. *Archaic and dial.*

swan. *v.i.* To leave a position for some trivial reason and without authorization.

swank. *adj.* Stylish, elegant, ritzy. *n.* Stylishness; smartness. *v.i.* To display stylishness in an ostentatious way. —s. *n.* Best clothes; dressy clothing. —y. *adj.* 1. Stylish, esp. in an ostentatious way. → 2. Cultured; luxurious.

swat. *v.t.* To hit or to hit at; usu., to hit or to hit at a person lightly or to hit or hit at a small object, such as a baseball. —s. *n.pl.* = brushes.

swat flies. 1. To beg money from people standing at curbstones or store windows. *Hobo use.* → 2. To do one's job or to do anything in a leisurely manner.

swat-stick. *n.* A baseball bat.

swazzled. *adj.* Drunk.

sweat. *v.t.* 1. = sweat it out. 2. To give the third degree to someone. *v.i.* 1. = sweat it out. 2. Fig., to work hard at something; to concentrate consciously on performing, comprehending, speaking, or being hip; to strive for a conscious goal. *This is a key word in cool, far out, and beat use. An underlying principle of these groups is that whatever one does, achieves, or believes should come naturally, from natural talent or understanding. Thus one should be relaxed, at ease, cool, loose, natural, or even beat. If one isn't these things, one can't and shouldn't strive for them, because either you are or you aren't. To sweat means that one has no natural talent at, understanding of, or feeling for these things. n. The third degree. Some underworld use.*

sweater girl. 1. A movie actress or model known primarily for her sexually attractive physique, spe-cif. for large, shapely, prominently displayed breasts. *Sweater girls and prominent breasts were much in vogue during the early 1940's.* → 2. Any girl or young woman with attractive, shapely breasts; any girl or young woman who, esp. habitually, wears tight-fitting sweaters or other clothing that emphasizes her breasts.

sweat it. To be bothered or annoyed by something; to sweat it out. *Rock-and-roll use since c1955.*

sweat it out; sweat [something]; sweat out. 1. To wait (for something) anxiously and helplessly; to hope for and expect something (to happen) when one has no control over the matter; to wait (one's turn) impatiently or in dread. 2. To question a person in a rough or embarrassing way; to obtain information from a person by intimidation or torture; to give the third degree to someone.

sweatshop. *n.* A dilapidated factory employing unskilled labor, often newly arrived immigrants, for long hours at low pay. *Colloq.*

Swede; swede. *n.* 1. A blunderer. 2. A piece of clumsy work.

sweep. *n.* The act or an instance of one athlete or team winning a tournament without losing an individual game or contest. *v.t.* To win a tournament without losing a game or contest. *v.i.* To flee, esp. from danger or potential discovery. *Some underworld use c1930.*

sweepswinger. *n.* One who rows as a crew member of a racing shell. *Student use.*

sweet. *adj.* 1. Easy and lucrative; said of a job or business. 2. Hospitable; pleasant and homelike. 3. Esp., hip or sympathetic to and appreciative of progressive jazz and its players or off-beat art.

sweeten up. 1. To flatter, cajole, or court a person, in order that the person will like or favor one; specif., to talk or act sweetly to one's lover or superior, usu. to regain one's good standing after anger or an argument or a preparation for asking a favor. 2. = sugar-coat.

sweetened (up) = sugar-coated; made happier.

sweetheart. n. 1. A pleasing person. 2. Anything excellent; a honey. v.t. To court, to squire or escort to social functions; to act as a sweetheart.

sweetie. n. A sweetheart; used as a general term of endearment as well as in reference to one's beloved.

sweetie-pie. n. 1. A sweetheart; used most often in direct address. *Now considered corny by young people.* 2. An attractive, pleasing, personable, pert girl. *Some student use c1930–c1940.*

sweet mama. A female lover. *The image is of a dark-complexioned or plump girl or woman, not necessarily young, who is extremely sensuous and generous to her lover. Assoc. with Negro use.*

sweet man. A male lover. *The image is of a dude or sport, who is extremely sensuous and generous to his lover. Assoc. with Negro use.*

sweet on [someone]. In love with, infatuated with; in love with and hoping to be courted or accepted by someone. *Colloq.*

sweet papa. A combination of "sugar daddy" and "sweet man" in one person.

sweet pea. 1. A sweetheart of either sex. 2. One easily duped; a sucker.

sweet potato. An ocarina.

sweets. n.sing. Sweetheart; a term of endearment for one's sweetheart; always in direct address. *Some use since c1930.* n.pl. Sweet potatoes, usu. roasted or mashed, served at a meal. *Most often in the combination "ham and sweets."*

sweet-talk. v.i., v.t. To persuade, or gain an advantage or personal goal, by flattery and glib talk; to sweeten up a person, esp. one of the opposite sex. n. Talk intended to sweeten up or persuade a person, esp. one of the opposite sex; a line.

swell. n. A stylishly dressed person, usu. male; a dandy, dude, or sport; a genteel or refined person; a wealthy, socially prominent person, esp. if somewhat of a dandy or sport. *Colloq.; becoming archaic.* adj. Pleasing; excellent; grand; fine; elegant; stylish; wonderful; enjoyable; friendly; hospitable. *Colloq. since c1880; gained present pop. c1920.* adv. Excellently; pleasingly; elegantly; wonderfully; enjoyably; stylishly; hospitably.

swelled head = swellhead.

swellhead. n. 1. An egotistic or conceited person. *Colloq. since c1850.* 2. Conceit.

swift. adj. Dissolute; fast. n. Speed.

swig. n. A swallow, gulp, or mouthful, esp. of whisky.

swindle. n. Any business transaction, task, or job; a deal.

swindle sheet. An account ledger kept by a traveling salesman or business executive, listing the business expenses incurred and paid out of his own funds, so that he may be reimbursed by the business firm; an expense account. *Fairly common since W.W.II. Orig. so called because exaggerating the cost of, or adding extra, items allows the salesman or executive to make a profit.*

swindle stick = cheat stick.

swing. v.i., v.t. 1. To create or play swing music adroitly or in an exciting or satisfying way; to play a piece of music in the style of swing. → 2. Satisfactorily composed, arranged, or adroitly played in swing; said of a piece of music. *Can be considered as a v.t. as such a piece of music seems to create itself and continue on its own momentum.* → 3. To seem to be created or grow out of its own natural or inherent design, form, or rhythm; to satisfy or be so perfect, for a given time, place, feeling, or mood, that a thing seems to have grown from the time, place, feeling, or mood; to grow naturally or develop from its own momentum; said orig. of swing music, later of any art, entertainment, or the like. → 4. To attract, excite, satisfy, completely envelop; to be hep, in rapport with, swing music, or with anything or anyone; to demonstrate complete understanding of or appreciation for swing; to be hep, in the groove, or with it. *Can be considered as v.t., as a thing or person that actually swings the speaker, with excitement, or seems to swing or create itself. Orig. swing use, c1935–c1942. One of the most common swing words, later some general jazz, and esp. cool, use. Also fairly well known to the general public.* n. 1. A style or form of music that evolved in jazz during the early 1930's and which became the most pop. music, esp. for dancing, among students, teenagers, and young adults c1935–c1942. *Swing is usu. played by large bands; both pop. love ballads and stand. jazz tunes make up the swing repertory. Swing died at the advent of W.W.II. Its now older audience lost interest; sophisticated Ivy League youth turned to bop and cool, seeming to prefer the more complex nondance music played by small groups; and teenagers were first commercially subjected to and then completely captured by rock and roll.* 2. Collectively, the devotees of swing music; the fashions, fads, moods, and attitudes assoc. with devotees of swing c1935–c1942. 3. A rest period or time off from work, as a worker's lunch period or a ten-minute rest period. 4. = swing shift. —ing. adj. Hip; in rapport with modern attitudes; satisfying, exciting or pleasing to a modern, hip person; on the ball. *Orig. swing use; some resurrected cool and far-out use.*

swing, in full. Performing or working smoothly or perfectly; performing without strain; at maximum efficiency or speed.

swinging gate. An adroitly playing swing musician completely involved and in rapport with the piece being played and the rest of the performers.

swing like a (rusty) gate. 1. In baseball, to swing or strike wildly at a pitched ball. 2. To play swing music well; to swing. *Swing use.*

swing room. A room set aside in a factory in which the workers may eat, smoke, or relax.

swing shift. A work period or shift between the standard day and night shifts, usu. beginning in the afternoon and ending in the evening, but sometimes beginning in the early morning and ending in the afternoon; a work crew or group of workers who work during these hours.

swipe. v.t. 1. To steal a small object, usu. one that can be concealed in the hand; to take without asking permission. 2. To appropriate another's idea, sweetheart, or the like. n. 1. A hard sweeping blow, as with the hand or a bludgeon. 2. A racing stable worker who rubs down horses.

swish. n. A male homosexual, esp. one with obviously feminine traits. *Fairly well known. From the effeminate hip motion made while walking. Perh. reinforced by the Brit. sl. "swish" = fancy, which is known in the U.S.* v.t. Acting, walking, or gesturing as a homosexual; making effeminate gestures.

switch. v.i. To give information; to inform, as to the police. n. A knife, whether a switchblade or not. —blade. n. A pocket knife with its long blade concealed in the handle; on pressing a button the blade springs out. *Assoc. with teenage hoodlums and street*

gangs. *Common since c1945.*
—eroo. *n.* A switch or reversal of
position; a substitution of one
thing for another; an old story,
idea, game, or the like with a
new ending. *One of the most
common "—eroo" words.*

switch-hitter. *n.* 1. In baseball, an
ambidextrous batter who bats
left-handed against a right-
handed pitcher and right-handed
against a left-handed pitcher.
Colloq. → 2. One who does two
things well; a versatile person.
→ 3. A bisexual person.

switch hog. A railroad yardmaster.

swivel. *n.* A look; a turning of the
head to get a better look.

swivet, in a. Hurried; anxious;
nervous; fidgety. *Since c1890.
Dial.*

swobble. *v.i., v.t.* To gulp one's
food; to eat hurriedly. *Negro
use.*

swoony. *n.* An attractive boy. *adj.*
Attractive. *Teenage use, c1940.
More often in movies and stories
about teenagers than used by
teenagers.*

swutty = sweetie.

sync. *n.* An act or instance of syn-
chronizing; the synchronization
of a movie sound track with the
action on the film, of a flash gun
with a camera shutter, or of the
audio and visual components of
a television set. *v.t.* To synchro-
nize one thing with another.

syringe. *n.* 1. A trombone. *Synthetic sl.* 2. A vaginal douche
taken as a birth control measure.

T

T. *n.* = tea.

tab. *n.* 1. A bill, an unpaid bill;
the total amount of money owed
on a bill. *Colloq.* → 2. A hand-
written acknowledgment of a
debt, endorsed by the debtor at
the time and place of incurrence;
an IOU.

table = under the table.

tab-lifter. *n.* A night-club customer.

T-bone. *n.* A Model T Ford automobile; any early model Ford

automobile. *Teenage hot rod use
since c1950.*

tack. *n.* 1. An adviser in a boys'
school; a school dean. 2. The
saddle and all other equipment
used by a jockey in racing.
—head. *n.* A stupid person. —y.
adj. 1. Not quite respectable.
*Orig. U.S. and Sp. use in New
Orleans.* → 2. Shabby; dilapidated. 3. Untidy, neglected; unrefined, vulgar. *n.* 1. A neglected,
ill-kept, or inferior horse. *Since
c1835; dial.* 2. An untidy, neglected, or sloppy person. *Dial.*

tack hammer. A large sledge hammer used for driving tent stakes.
*Ironic comparison to an actual
tack hammer.*

tad. *n.* A boy; a child. *Archaic and
dial.*

tag. *n.* 1. A person's name; a name.
2. = dog tag; an identification
tag. 3. A letter smuggled out of
prison. *Underworld use.* 4. A warrant for arrest. 5. An automobile
license plate. *v.t.* To arrest.

tail. *n.* 1. The human posterior;
the buttocks. *Since before c1895.*
→ 2. Fig., a person's trail. → 3.
A person, as a detective, who
trails or follows and observes another's actions; a shadow. *v.t.* To
follow or trail a person, as a detective might follow a suspect or
a robber, an intended victim. —s.
n.pl. 1. Full dress; a man's formal suit with a long-tailed coat.
2. A tuxedo. *Colloq.*

**tail, have [someone or something]
by the.** To be in command or
control of a situation; to be assured of success.

tail bone. The rump; the buttocks. *Usu. jocular use. Made
somewhat more pop. by its freq.
use in Walt Kelly's synd. newsp.
comic strip "Pogo."*

tail-gate. *n., adj.* A style of playing jazz which is supposed to resemble the style of the early New
Orleans musicians. *The term is
supposed to have originated in
the practice of New Orleans jazz
bands that played in horse-drawn
wagons during street parades and*

political rallies; the tail-gate was left down to make room for the slide trombone. Thus the word is assoc. with jazz in general and specif. with a style of playing the trombone, and refers broadly to a spirited, intense, hot manner of performance.

tailor-made. *adj.* 1. Made in a factory, according to standard specifications. 2. Fitting one's expectations and abilities; just right. *n.* 1. A suit of factory-made clothes. 2. A plainclothes policeman or detective.

take. *n.* Gross profit, esp. of a short term business venture, speculation, entertainment, sporting event, gambling casino, or the like; *lit.*, the money taken in. *v.t.* To rob, cheat, or swindle a person, esp. out of a comparatively large sum of money; to deceive or trick a person; to "stick" a person.

take a gander. Take a look at; look over.

take five. To take a five-minute or a short rest period from work or, esp., from a theatrical rehearsal; to take a five-minute break.

take it (on the chin). 1. To withstand punishment or abuse; to bear up under attack, strain, or hard work. *Most common in prize fight use.* 2. = buy, to agree.

take it big. To express any marked emotional response, such as surprise, fear, or pain; to exaggerate one's sentiments.

take it in. 1. To take time off from walking a beat. *Said of a patrolman.* 2. To see and do everything that a specific locale or job has to offer; to comprehend.

take it on. To eat, esp. to eat voraciously or large quantities.

take off. 1. To take a short vacation from work. *Colloq.* 2. To leave or depart, specif. in order to go to, or visit, another place. 3. To give oneself an injection of a narcotic drug. *Some addict use.*

take on. 1. To make a fuss about something. *Colloq.* 2. To put on airs. *Colloq.*

take (someone, something) on. To accept a challenge; to fight someone; to accept a difficult or unrewarding task.

take-out. *n.* 1. Prepared food, sold by a restaurant, that the patron takes out to eat elsewhere, as at home or at an office. 2. A percentage of the gross profits; one's share of money, esp. profits or loot.

take [someone] to the cleaners. *Lit.* and *fig.*, to take all of another's money, specif. by deception or cheating; often passive use usu. = to have lost all one's money, esp. at gambling.

talk [one's] ear off. To talk a great deal; to bore a person by talking too much.

talker = barker. *"Talker," and not "barker," is in wide carnival and circus use.*

talkie. *n.* 1. A movie with a sound track. *Very common c1928–35.* 2. A portable two-way radio telephone used by the Armed Forces in W.W.II.

talk-talk. *n.* Talk, esp. idle gossip.

talk through [one's] hat. To talk nonsense; to lie. *Colloq. since c1885.*

talk turkey. To talk plainly and frankly; to discuss the facts. *Colloq. since c1920.*

tangle. *v.i.* To fight. *Colloq.*

tank. *n.* 1. A small town. 2. A jail or cell; specif. a cell for prisoners awaiting investigation, trial, or the like. "Drunk tank" = cell where drunks are kept to sober up. "Fish tank." = cell where suspects or new prisoners are kept. 3. The stomach. 4. A locomotive. *adj.* Fixed. *Said of a prize fight.* —*ed. adj.* Drunk. *Colloq. since c1920.*

tank, go in the. To allow oneself to lose a prize fight; to throw a fight. *Suggested by "take a dive."*

tank act = tank fight.

tanked up = tanked.

tank fight. A prize fight in which one fighter is paid or bribed to lose, as by his opponent or gamblers; a fixed prize fight; one in which a fighter takes a dive.

tank job = tank fight.

tank town. A small town; a town too small to have a railroad station, but having a railroad water tank, if little else.

tank up. To drink one's fill of liquor; to drink a great deal of liquor.

tap. *v.t.* To borrow, or attempt to borrow, money from someone.

tap out. *v.i.* To lose all one's money, specif. gambling; to lose one's money; to become broke.

tapped out. Broke.

tar. *n.* 1. A sailor. *Colloq.* 2. The insides; the stuffing. Usu. in "beat [*or* knock] the tar out of [someone]." 3. Opium.

tar bucket. A military full-dress hat. *Orig. West Point use.*

Target A. The Pentagon Building in Washington, D.C. *Jocular use. In ref. to an atomic attack against the U.S. in any future war.*

tarp. *n.* 1. A tarpaulin. → 2. Specif., a special piece of tarpaulin or canvas used to fit over the seat of a roofless sports car, as protection from rain. *Sports car owner use since c1950.*

tart. *n.* A prostitute; any promiscuous girl or woman. *Colloq., becoming archaic.*

taste. *n.* A small portion or sample of anything. *Colloq.*

ta-ta. *interj.* Good-by. *Some use since c1895. Usu. jocular, as it is assoc. with Eng. use and is considered an affectation.*

tattler. *n.* 1. A night watchman. 2. An alarm clock.

taw. *n.* Enough money to finance an enterprise; a stake.

tawny. *adj.* Most excellent. *Teenage use.*

TD. *n.* In football, a touchdown. *Colloq.*

t'd off. *adj.* = tee'd off.

tea; T. *n.* 1. Marijuana. 2. A marijuana cigarette. 3. Any of certain stimulants illegally given to a racehorse to make it run faster.

teaed up. Under the influence of or high on marijuana.

tea-hound. *n.* 1. A ladies' man; a man who devotes much of his time to parties. → 2. A sissy. *College use.*

tea pad. Any place where marijuana addicts gather to smoke tea.

tea party. A party or gathering of addicts for the purpose of smoking marijuana. *Some addict use.*

tear. *n.* 1. A spree; a bender. *Note pronunciation "tare."* 2. A pearl. *Note pronunciation "teer."*

tear-jerker. *n.* Something that is created or designed to elicit sadness or tears; specif. an entertainment, as a play or song, full of sadness and sentiment, whose main appeal is that it gives one a good cry; an actor or speaker able to elicit sympathy from his audience.

tear off. To have, to obtain; to create, to perform; usu. but not always implies haste stemming from desire, eagerness, or lack of time. *Fairly freq. in "tear off some sleep" = to sleep while one is able to or has the time; sometimes in "tear off a piece of music" = to play the piece of music; less freq. in various other expressions.*

teaser. *n.* A girl or woman who seems to invite a male's attention and favors, but who does not return them when given.

tea-stick. *n.* A marijuana cigarette. *Some addict use.*

tech. *n.* A school of technology; a technical institute. *Often in the names of schools, e.g., Georgia Tech.*

Tee Dee. *n.* = TD.

tee'd off; teed off; t'd off. *adj.* Angry; fed up; disgusted. *From "tee-off."*

teed up. Drunk.

teen. *n.* Teenager. **—ager; teen-ager.** *n.* An adolescent; a person between the ages of 13 and 19, but specif. a high-school student between the ages of 15 and 19. *Colloq. since c1930; stand. since c1945. The U.S. is the only country having a word for members of this age group, and is the only country considering this age group as a separate entity whose influence, fads, and fashions are worthy of discussion apart from the adult world.* —er. *n.* Teenager.

tee off (on [someone]). 1. In baseball, to make many hits in a game, or off a specif. pitcher of the opposing team; in prize fighting, to hit one's opponent with many hard blows. *From the golf term.* → 2. To reprimand or criticize a person severely.

telegraph. *v.t.* To make known one's intention by an unintentional, involuntary gesture or word; specif., in boxing, to signal unintentionally the blow that one intends to deliver next, as by a glance or twitch in the arm.

telephone number (bit). A prison sentence of more than 20 years but less than life. *Underworld use. From the high numbers.*

tell a green (blue) man. Tell me the truth; inform me; make me hip. *Some jazz use.*

tell off. 1. To tip a person off; to inform him in advance of some impending occurrence. 2. To reprimand; rebuke; bawl out. *Most common and widely popular meaning. Colloq.*

tell [someone] where to get off. To reprimand or rebuke strongly; usu. to tell a person that he is not as important as he believes.

ten. *n.* A ten-dollar bill; the sum of $10.

ten, take. To take a ten-minute rest period from work, or esp., from a theatrical rehearsal; to take a ten-minute break from marching [Army use], from a rehearsal [theater use], or any job.

ten-carat. *adj.* Big; remarkable, as an atypical specimen or example of something, usu. something bad; thorough.

ten-minute man. A go-getter; a fast talker; *Orig. hobo use.*

tenner. *n.* 1. A ten-dollar bill. 2. A ten-year prison sentence. *Mainly prison use.*

tenor = whisky tenor.

ten-percenter. *n.* 1. An actor's, performer's, writer's, etc., agent, whose commission is 10% of the money earned by his clients. *Mainly theater use.* 2. One who receives 10% of the loot, profit, or transaction. *Now usu. a politically influential person who obtains political favors or public contracts for his clients, and receives a percentage of the cash value of the favor or contract.*

ten-spot. *n.* 1. A 10-dollar bill; the sum of $10. 2. A 10-year prison sentence.

ten-vee; 10-V. *n., adj.* The worst, the lowest; of the lowest rank. *In analogy with "1-A" = the best.*

terrible. *adj.* Wonderful; great; the best; the most. *Some far-out use.*

terrific. *adj.* 1. Wonderful, marvelous; beautiful; remarkable; large; when used as a pred. adj. or attrib. adj. 2. Very much of a, complete; skilled; experienced; used only to emphasize the following noun. *Thus a "terrific bore," "a terrific actor," etc.*

terror = holy terror.

Texan border, the; Texas border, the. The United States border with Mexico, actually the Mexican border.

Texas leaguer. In baseball, a hit falling between the infield and the outfield.

thank-you-(ye-)ma'am. A bump or hole in the road, such as causes riders to bounce up and down. *Since at least 1895.*

that ain't hay. "That's a lot of money." Always used after a specific sum of money, as "He makes $30,000 a year, and that ain't hay."

that kills it. Fig., "That destroys the mood, takes away my enthusiasm, or pleasure; that causes me to reject, refuse, or refrain; that ruins or spoils it; that guarantees failure." *Since c1945. Now fairly common.*

that's all she wrote; that's what she wrote. Fig., "That's all there is, that's all; this is the conclusion; it's finished." *During and since W.W.II. Orig. and lit., ref. to a soldier's last letter from his sweetheart, terminating the relationship.*

that's the (my) boy. Fig., an expression of encouragement or pride. *As of a father pointing with pride and saying, "That's my boy who did that."*

that's the way the ball bounces. Fig., "That's fate, the fortunes of life, the way things happen." *Said in resignation or commiseration. Orig. very wide Korean War Army use.*

that's what she wrote = **that's all she wrote.**

that way. In love. *Usu. in "They are that way about each other." c1940.*

the — *article* **1.** Often prefixed to a surname to give the effect of a nickname or to imply that the person has an extremely individual personality or talent and is considered a natural force of nature. *Some far-out and beat use. Student use since c1920; also freq. theater and jazz use, esp. cool use. Thus "the Monk"* = *Thelonius Monk, well-known jazz pianist and composer.* **2.** Sometimes prefixed to a place or locale name, often to a shortened or abbreviated form of the name, to indicate one's sophistication and that one is hip and familiar and accepted there. *Thus "the Village"* = *N.Y.C.'s Greenwich Village section; "the Quarter"* = *New Orleans' French Quarter section; "the Chez"* = *the Chez Paree nightclub in Chicago; etc.* **3.** Used before specif. words, as indicated in the entries in this dictionary, to form specif. n. expressions or to confine a noun's meaning to one specif. unalterable sl. use. *In such in-*

stances "the" is used to indicate the sl. meaning; if "a" were used the word would have its stand. meaning. Thus "the man" = a law enforcement officer, whereas, of course, "a man" is just two stand. words from a sentence.

there. *adj.* Competent; skilled; capable of performing, or performing, remarkably well. *E.g., "When it comes to painting a house (playing football, telling a joke, being generous, etc.) he's right there." Since c1925.*

there you go. **1.** Fig., "Now you're talking sense, telling the truth, comprehending it fully, learning the knack of it"; "You're right, I agree, that's a good idea." *Orig. c1935 jive use; mainly general jazz use; some student and teenage use.* → **2.** Fig., "I know you can do it, keep trying, you'll succeed, I have the utmost confidence in your ability." *Some Korean War Army use; now some civilian use.*

thick. *adj.* **1.** Slow-thinking. *Colloq.* **2.** Incredible; seemingly exaggerated or a lie.

thin. *adj.* **1.** Broke; out of funds. *Hobo and carnival use.* **2.** Unsubstantiated. *n.* A dime. *From "thin dime."* **—ly.** *n.* A runner or other track athlete. *From the physical thinness of such athletes, reinforced by their being thinly clad.*

thin dime. A dime; the sum of ten cents. *Always used to emphasize the low price of a product or ticket of admission or to underline the poverty or need of one who, lit. or fig., has only a dime. Thus "thin dime" is used by carnival barkers in their spiel, "For only the cost of a thin dime, buy a ticket and see the tattooed lady. . . ." and by poverty-stricken persons, as in "I have only a thin dime to my name."*

thinga(ma)jig;   thing(um)abob; thingumadoo(d)(le);   thingama-doger;   thingamadudg(eon); thingumbob;   thing(ma)nanny. *n.* Used to indicate any item of which the speaker does not know or has momentarily forgotten the name; esp., used to ref. to any, usu. a small, new, or unfamiliar device, mechanical part, gadget, tool, or ornament; a thing. Such *"omnibus" words are in general use. The oldest is "thingumbob," in use since at least 1750.*

things and stuff. Very well dressed; very witty. *Negro use.*

thin in the upper crust. Deficient or defective in mentality.

think-box. *n.* The brain.

thinker. *n.* The brain; the mind.

think-piece. *n.* A thoughtful or provocative piece of journalistic writing, as opposed to a factual news account.

think-tank. *n.* = think-box.

thin man = thin one. *Rock-and-roll use since c1955.*

thin one. A dime. *From "thin dime." Orig. hobo use; assoc. with jive use. Because a dime is the thinnest U.S. coin.*

third = third degree.

third degree. Prolonged questioning and/or rough handling of a person, as by police, in order to obtain information or to force a confession of guilt.

third lieutenant. 1. One who has completed officer's training, but has not been commissioned. *Fig. = one below a second lieutenant.* 2. A sergeant. *W.W.II Army use.*

third party. Any new, completely American, completely political party other than the Republican and Democratic parties. *From time to time such parties are formed, usu. by dissatisfied factions of one of the two major parties. Generally speaking, the Socialist Party is not new enough nor the Communist Party sufficiently American to be called third parties; other organizations, such as the Vegetarian Party, are not completely political; but such parties as the Progressive, the Greenback, and the Socialist Party of 1908–12 were true third parties.*

third rail. 1. Any of various strong alcoholic drinks. *From comparing the potency of a drink to the shock gotten from the electrically charged third rail of an electric railroad.* 2. An honest person who cannot be bribed. *From "touch" = bribe; one cannot touch an electrically charged third rail.*

third sex, the. Homosexuals. *Now the only common meaning.*

third wheel. A useless or unwanted person; one who contributes nothing or is even a detriment to the successful completion of a task or to the enjoyment of a good time, party, or social gathering.

thirteen. *n. A word used as a warning that one's employer is nearby. From the belief that 13 is unlucky.*

thirty; 30. *n.* 1. Orig. used as the last word to signify the end of a telegraph message; hence the end of a newspaper correspondent's dispatch; later, used to signify the end of a newspaper article, then a radio newscaster's broadcast. *Well known.* → 2. Good-by.

thirty-day wonder. A second lieutenant; one who has become an officer by completing a 30-day officers' training course. *Used ironically. W.W.I and W.W.II use.*

thirty-three. *n.* A phonograph record made to be played on a turntable that revolves at 33⅓ revolutions per minute.

thou. *n.* A thousand dollars. *Mainly theater, gambling, and underworld use.*

thousand-miler. *n.* A dark-blue shirt, esp. a dark-blue work shirt. *Because it shows less wear and dirt, hence lasts a long time and can be laundered less freq. than others.*

thousand on a plate. Beans; a plate of beans.

threads. *n.pl.* Clothes, esp. a suit of clothes. *Orig. c1935 jive use; fairly common general jazz and hipster use.*

three-dollar bill. 1. An odd or eccentric person; specif., a person who claims to be what he is not or tries to assume the identity of another. *Because there is no such thing as a U.S. three-dollar bill. From the expression "as phoney as a three-dolar bill."* → 2. Specif., a homosexual; a sexual pervert.

three-letter man. An effeminate man; specif., a homosexual. *The three letters are "f-a-g" = fag. A pun on the collegiate term "three-letter man" = a student athlete. Reinforced by "three-dollar bill." Some student use since c1935.*

three-sheet. n. An advertising circular or handbill; esp., a theater or circus advertising poster.

three sheets in [or to] the wind. Drunk.

three-striper. n. 1. A USN commander. *USN use.* 2. A sergeant. *Army use.*

three-time. v.t. To combine in a trio to fight someone or to beat him up.

thriller-diller = chiller-diller.

through the line = across the board. *Horse-racing use.*

through the mill. 1. Long and hard practical experience in any field. E.g., "He has been through the mill." 2. To have been frustrated, defeated; to meet with obstacles. *Colloq.*

throw. n. The cost per unit or cost per portion of an item; any single-unit price; the unit by which something is sold, as a glassful, a bottle, a ticket, an hour's lesson, a pair of shoes, or the like. *Fig., each time the customer throws down his money. Reinforced by crap-shooting term = each throw of, and hence each bet on, the dice.* v.t. 1. To hold or give a social affair, as a dance, luncheon, or party. 2. To lose, or play so as to lose, any sports contest in return for a bribe. —away. n. 1. A ticket of admission sold at a reduced price. 2. An advertising circular; a handbill. → 3.

A cheap magazine. 4. A short, quickly said joke or witticism, as used by a comedian between his major jokes; an incidental joke or witticism. *Orig. vaudeville use.* → 5. A line in a play or movie which the actor purposely understates or slurs, in order to add realism to the speech. *Theater use.*

throw a fit. To have an extreme emotional reaction, esp. of anger.

throw down on. To draw a gun on someone.

throw [one's] feet. To get food or money by begging; to look for temporary work.

throw in the sponge (towel). To concede defeat; to surrender. *From prize fighting use; a manager whose prize fighter is being badly beaten signifies that he wants to stop the fight, and concede defeat, by actually throwing a towel or sponge into the ring—two items readily at hand since they are used to sponge and dry perspiration off the fighter between rounds.*

throw lead. To shoot or shoot at.

throw leather. To box with gloves.

throw-money. n. Small change, such as a tip.

throw-out. n. A professional beggar who feigns injury to gain sympathy. *Hobo use.*

throw the book at [someone]. 1. To sentence a guilty person to the maximum term of imprisonment. *Orig. underworld use. From the image of a judge sentencing a criminal to every penalty found in books of law.* → 2. To penalize, punish, reprimand, or criticize a person severely. *Fairly common since c1950.*

throw the bull = shoot (the) bull. To talk nonsense or bull.

throw the hooks. 1. = throw [one's] feet. 2. *Specif.*, to beg on the street by extending one's hand for a hand-out.

throw the hooks into. To cheat; to get the better of someone through deceit.

thrush. n. A singer.

thumb. *v.t.* 1. In baseball, to hit the ball over the infield with the bat handle. 2. To hitch-hike.

thumb, on the. Hitch-hiking.

thumb a ride = thumb, hitch-hike.

thumbprint. *n.* An individual's personality as reflected in his work, plans, or deeds.

thumb-pusher. *n.* A hitch-hiker.

Thunderbird! *interj.* 1. An expression of excitement or of a feeling of power, exultation, enthusiasm, or ecstasy. *Used absolutely.* → 2. An expression of recognition, or appreciation, as of a sexually attractive girl, of music, or of a fellow dude, sport, or hipster. *Used absolutely.* 3. "Great!"; "I feel full of vigor and enthusiasm." *In the jive-like rhyming answer to the greeting: "What's the (good) word?" "Thunderbird!" Harlem Negro, mainly hipster, use. From the trade name of a cheap and supposedly potent wine, "Thunderbird," highly advertised in N.Y.C.'s Harlem, orig. in the Spring of 1957. Reinforced by the Ford Motor Co.'s "Thunderbird" model sports car.*

thusly. *adv.* Thus. *Now common serious use. Because many adverbs have the "—ly" ending.*

tick. *n.* Credit.

tick, full as a. Very drunk.

tick, hit the = hit the hay. *A sl. variation reinforced by being a rhyming term. Some Southern and Western use.*

tick, on. On credit. *Mainly dial. More common in Eng. than U.S.*

ticker. *n.* 1. A watch. *Pitchman use.* 2. Courage; stamina. 3. The heart. *Colloq.*

ticket. *n.* 1. A playing card. 2. Official papers showing that one has been paroled from prison or has served all of one's prison sentence. → 3. Official papers discharging one from military service; a discharge from military service. *Some W.W.II use.*

ticket, the. *n.* The very thing; the exact thing called for or needed. *In the pleased "That's the ticket"* = *That's what I meant or wanted.*

tickled pink. Exceedingly pleased. *Colloq.*

tickler. *n.* 1. A small portion of anything. 2. A mustache.

tickle the ivories. To play the piano.

tiddly. *adj.* Drunk. *From rhyming sl. "tiddly-wink"* = *a drink.*

tie a (the) can to (on). 1. To dismiss a person from service; to sever relations; to can. 2. To eliminate or get rid of something.

tied. *adj.* Married.

tied up. 1. Busy; having no free time. 2. Finished.

tie-in. *n.* A connection; a relationship. *Colloq.*

tie-in deal. *n.* A business deal whereby one must also buy or hire a less desirable item or person in order to obtain the desired item or person.

tie into. *v.t.* To attack; to approach or do something with fury, speed, or enthusiasm.

tie it off. To quit work for the day; to let something remain as it is. *Orig. maritime use.*

tie it up. To finish a job.

tie off. To stop talking; shut up.

tie on. To eat.

tie one on. To get drunk; to go on a drunken spree. *Very common.*

ties, hit the. To travel by walking along a railroad track.

tiger. *n.* 1. Fig., a strong, virile man easily aroused to anger or passion; a good fighter and/or a "sweet" man. *Freq. a nickname, esp. of prize fighters, or given to "sweet" men by their lovers. The most common use.* 2. In poker, the lowest hand a player can hold. *Orig. from faro use, or fig., because the player must bluff if he is going to win, and thus has "a tiger by the tail," that is, he can be hurt financially.* → 3. An obsession; that vice, talent, or idea which a man must dominate in order to succeed. 4. Faro. *Since c1845.*

tiger eye; tiger's eye = **tiger sweat.** *Perh. reinforced by the faro term.*

tiger meat. Beef. *Synthetic sl.*

tiger sweat; Tigersweat. 1. Cheap, raw whisky; esp., unaged, bootleg whisky. 2. Beer. *W.W.II Armed Forces use.*

tight. *adj.* 1. Stingy, parsimonious. *Colloq. From "tight-fisted," reinforced by "tightwad."* 2. Drunk. *Colloq. since c1840. Prob. one of the most common of the sl. words = drunk. Also often used in expressions such as "tight as a tick."* 3. Friendly, exceedingly compatible; intimate, in rapport with; said of two people, as co-workers, friends, or lovers. *Most common orig. as c1946 bop and now as cool use. Some student and teenage use since c1950.*

tight as a tick (drum, lord, owl, goat, mink, brassière, ten-day drunk, etc.). Very tight, completely drunk.

tight money = hard money.

tight spot. Lit. and fig., an unfruitful, embarrassing, disastrous, or dangerous situation from which one will have difficulty extracting oneself or succeeding; a situation in which one needs assistance, luck, or all one's ingenuity to extract oneself or succeed; a potentially disastrous situation.

tightwad. *n.* A miser; one who has money and does not readily part with any of it. *From the tightly folded wad of money. adj.* Stingy, miserly.

timber. *interj.* Fig., an expression of success or achievement; also used jocularly when a person drops or breaks something. *From "timber!" as shouted by loggers, in warning and jubilation, when a tree is felled. n.* One who sells lead pencils on the street; often a street beggar. *Hobo and street beggar use.* —s. *n.pl.* Human bones, esp. the ribs. *From the shipbuilders' term. Used chiefly in the stock expression, "Shiver me timbers!" a common saying of fictional buccaneers.*

time, have [oneself] a. To have a good time; to enjoy oneself.

time of day, not give [someone] the. To ignore someone; fig., to dislike or distrust someone so much that one would not tell that person the correct time if he asked. *Always used in the negative. Colloq.*

tin. *n.* 1. A policeman's badge. → 2. A policeman or detective. *Some underworld use.*

tin can. *n.* 1. A depth charge. *Fairly common USN use.* 2. Any naval warship; usu. a destroyer; esp. an old destroyer; a submarine chaser. *Orig. humorous ref. to armor plating and because the destroyer was smallest fleet ship in use during W.W.II. Very common W.W.II use.*

tin cow; tinned cow. Canned milk. *Hobo use as early as c1930. Some W.W.II Armed Forces use, but not as common as the use in war novels and movies.*

tin fish. A torpedo. *Common W.W.II USN use.*

tin-horn. *n.* A small-time gambler; a cheap, flashy person.

tinkle. *n.* A phone call. *v.i.* To urinate. *Common usage by small children; humorously used by adults.*

tinkle-box. *n.* A piano. *Synthetic jazz use.*

tin Lizzie; tin lizzie. 1. An early automobile, esp. a Ford. *c1917.* → 2. Any cheap or dilapidated car, truck, or airplane.

Tin Pan Alley. Fig., the place where popular songs are written, published, and made into commercial successes; popular music; pertaining to or in the style of a popular song, esp. in the style of songs pop. c1925. *Lit., Tin Pan Alley is the offices, buildings, and rooms located roughly between 48th and 52nd Sts. on 7th Avenue in N.Y. City's Times Square area. Here many composers, arrangers, music publishing companies, and recording* *studio agents have business offices.*

tinpot. *adj.* Inferior; small time.

tin star. A private detective.

tip. *n.* 1. A small audience or crowd of prospective customers gathered around a pitchman or in front of a carnival sideshow, in response to the spiel or ballyhoo. *Pitchman and carnival use.* → 2. The spiel or ballyhoo made by a pitchman or carnival barker. → 3. Advice, esp. short, succinct advice that can be stated in a sentence or two; information, a fact. → 4. Esp., advance information supposedly from those in the know, as on the expected outcome of a horse-race or sporting event. *v.t.* To inform someone; to tip someone off.

tip [one's, the] elbow = bend [one's, the] elbow.

tip [one's] mitt. To disclose or inadvertently reveal a secret, motive, plan, or the like.

tip off. To warn of something impending; to put someone wise; to inform, to forewarn; also, to point out a victim to a crook. **tip-off.** *n.* A forewarning; a clue; a hint.

tip over. To rob or loot, as by criminals; to raid, as by the police.

tip-top. *adj.* Excellent. *Since before 1900.*

tired. *adj.* Dull, boring; unimaginative; specif., out of fashion, reminiscent or repetitive of things previously seen or heard. *Said of entertainments.*

tire patch. A hotcake; a pancake. *W.W.II Army use. Prob. synthetic sl.*

tissue. *n.* A carbon copy, as of a letter, railroad way-bill, or the like; an original or a carbon copy on thin paper.

tit. *n.* Lit., teat or nipple; fig. used in the plural to = noticeable nipples on shapely, protruding female breasts, as of a sweater girl. *Universally used. Applied to both animal teats and human teats. "Teat" is now no longer* ever used in referring to women; women have tits or nipples, animals have teats.

titty-boo. *n.* 1. A wild, undisciplined, young girl. 2. A female juvenile delinquent. 3. A young female prisoner, usu. convicted for nonprofessional, nonviolent crime, such as dope addiction, vandalism, sexual misconduct, etc.

tizzy. *n.* A fit or period of nervousness, anxiety, or confusion. *Dial.*

TKO. *n.* In prize fighting, a technical knockout, resulting from one fighter's having been so injured that he is declared unable to continue the fight, even though he has not actually been knocked out. *Colloq. v.t.* 1. To score a TKO against an opponent. → 2. Fig., to defeat; to show to be wrong.

TL; tl. *n.* A compliment; esp. a compliment given to a person because one has received a compliment from that person; specif. a compliment relayed from the giver to the person complimented by an intermediary, as when the giver is shy or embarrassed by having made the compliment. *From the archaic and dial. "trade last."*

tlac. *n.* Money. *From the Spanish and Mexican "tlaco" = a Spanish coin once worth 1/8 of a "real." Dial.*

toad. *n.* A toady; a contemptible youth. *c1940; teen use.* —*v. v.i.* To attempt to gain familiarity or favor with one's superiors by flattery or extreme subservience. *n.* One who acts as a lackey to his superiors.

toady up = toady.

together, go. To keep company in courtship. *Said of an unmarried couple. Also "go around together." Colloq.*

togs. Clothes; clothing. *Colloq.*

toke. *v.i., v.t.* To smoke or take a drag on a cigarette, usu. but not necessarily a marijuana cigarette. *n.* A drag of (or on) a cigarette, usu. but not necessarily a marijuana cigarette. *Some addict use, even less general use. Lit., a token or sample of a cigarette or smoke.*

tokus; tokis; tuckus. The posterior.

tomato. *n.* 1. A very attractive girl or young woman. *Since c1920. The word implies "luscious" = desirable or "ripe" = with a mature, sexually attractive body. Universally known. Not respectful, but like "dame" or "doll" implies no disrespect.* 2. An inferior prize fighter. *Some prize fight use.*

tomato can. A town constable's or policeman's badge of office. *Hobo use.*

tomboy. *n.* A girl, usu. between eight and 15 years old, who enjoys or excels at boys' sports and interests and who has as yet developed little if any feminine interest in clothes or grooming. *Very common.*

tomcat; tom-cat. *v.i., v.t.* Orig., to dress up in one's best clothes, as a dude or sport, and walk the street, visit public bars, nightclubs, and the like in search of a female; to seek a female, esp. a promiscuous one; esp., to dress in one's best clothes, visit a girl or young woman, and mix boasting and sweet talk in an attempt to persuade her to enter into sexual activity. *Negro and dial. use. n.* A woman-chaser.

Tom, Dick, and Harry. *Fig.,* just any youth or man (men) regardless of worth; a nobody, nobodies. *Usu. in the expression "every Tom, Dick, and Harry."*

tomgirl = tomboy. *From confusion with the older term.*

tommy; Tommy. *n.* 1. A girl; a tomboy. 2. A British soldier. *Very Common W.W.I use.* 3. = Tommy gun. *Underworld and W.W.II use.* → 4. A machine gunner.

Tommy Atkins. A British soldier. *"Tommy Atkins" is the British equivalent of our "John Doe" or wartime "G.I. Joe." The full term was used early in W.W.I,* but was quickly shortened to "Tommy."

Tommy gun; tommy gun. *Orig. and specif.,* a Thompson submachine gun; *fig.,* any automatic, portable, machine gun. *Orig. underworld use.*

Tom show. *Specif.,* a performance of the melodrama *Uncle Tom's Cabin;* any melodrama; a theatrical troupe specializing in performing *Uncle Tom's Cabin* and/or similar melodramas. *Mainly theater use.*

tong. *n.* A fraternity house. *From the Chinese. Some West Coast college use.*

tongue. *n.* A lawyer; a mouthpiece.

tonk. *n.* = honky-tonk.

ton of bricks, hit like a. To impress in the extreme; to stun; to awe.

tony. *adj.* 1. In, of, or respresenting the best society or latest fashion. → 2. Assuming the manners, speech, or dress of the best society; conceited; arrogant; egotistical. *Most pop. among Negroes.* 3. Stylish; swanky; high-toned; snobbish. *Colloq. since c1880. n.* Socially prominent people.

Toodle-oo. *interj.* Good-by. *Considered Eng. or an affected use. Thus seldom seen in print, but has fairly common serious use among middle-aged women. Jocular use by males.*

took. *adj.* = stuck.

tool. *n.* A pickpocket; one who in a mob of pickpockets actually does the removing of the victim's wallet from his pocket; the chief of a mob of pickpockets. *Common underworld use since at least c1920.* 3. One easily victimized or deceived; a stupid person. *Fig., one who can be used, as a tool, by others. v.t.* To drive an automobile, esp. speedily and with confidence or skill. —s. *n.pl.* Table utensils; a knife, fork, and spoon. *Since c1900. Lit., eating tools.*

tool-box. *n.* A small railroad depot. *Hobo use.*

too much. 1. Beyond logical criticism or comprehension, in either a good or bad sense; ridiculously good or bad. *Fairly common c1935 jive use; fairly well known general use since c1940.* → 2. = **far out;** so intellectually, psychologically, or spiritually removed from standards of criticism, by being unrelated or beyond comparison, that one is awed. *Far-out use since c1955.*

toot, on a. On a spree, esp. a drunken spree; carousing. *Since c1860.*

toothpick. *n.* 1. Any large, long object as a tree-trunk, steel beam, or the like. *Typical sl. understatement.* 2. A pocket-knife, esp. a knife with a spring blade; a switch-blade. *Since c1850. Mainly teenage street-gang use since c1935.*

tootle. *v.i., v.t.* To play a musical instrument, esp. a wind instrument.

too too. *adj.* Excessively polite, stylish, or affected.

tootsies. *n.pl.* The feet.

tootsy; tootsie. *n.* A person's foot. *Baby talk and jocular use. From "tootsies."*

toot the ringer. To ring a doorbell. *Hobo use.*

top. *v.t.* 1. To hang a person. 2. To kill; to bump off. *Underworld use.* 3. To do something better, to perform better, to tell a funnier joke, or to surpass or prove oneself better than another in any way. *Colloq.* *n.* A tent used in a circus or carnival. *Common carnival and circus use. adj.* Best; most competent; having the best reputation; known as a leader. *Colloq.* —**per.** *n.* 1. A man's top hat. *Colloq.* 2. A joke, wisecrack, or gag that is funnier than a previous one told by another. *Orig. comedian use.* 3. A memorable remark or statement to which there can be no answer; a statement so audacious, scandalous, true, wise, or fitting that

nothing more can be said on the subject. See **top.** —**ping.** *n.* Dessert; any bakery goods, esp. cake, pie, or pastry. —*s. n.pl.* 1. Loaded dice. 2. The best of anything, either people or things. *adj.* Of highest quality; wonderful; rated highest.

top dog. 1. In the most desirable position; most important; best; most competent; most desired; having the best reputation for success. 2. The chief, leader, boss, etc.; the person in authority.

top-drawer. *adj.* Most important; known only to high-ranking officials; said of military plans or secrets.

top eliminator. An athlete, entry, or contestant with the best chance to win a contest. *Hot-rod and some general teenage use. From hot-rod use. In some drag races only two hot rods are raced against each other at a time; the loser is eliminated and the winner races another car, until the top eliminator or the only car left is the winner.*

Top Kick; top kick; top-kick. 1. An Army first sergeant. *Common use since cW.W.I.* → 2. One in authority; a boss.

top notch. The best of anything; of greatest excellence. *Colloq. since c1830.*

top story. The head.

torch. *n.* 1. A pistol. *Some underworld use since c1925.* 3. Fig., a torch carried by a rejected or unrequited lover; the memory or pain of a rejected or unrequited love. *Usu. in the expression "to carry the torch for (someone)."* → 3. = **torch song.** *Theater use.* 4. An arsonist; a professional incendiary; a firebug. 5. A cigar. —**y.** *adj.* In love with someone who does not return the love; fig., smoldering with unrequited love.

torch song. A pop., sad song about lost or unrequited love.

torpedo. *n.* 1. An assassin, a hired murderer or gunman, esp. if from out of town and imported to commit a murder; any hoodlum or gangster who thrives on violence. *Orig. underworld use.* 2. An enormous sandwich made from an entire small loaf of hard-crusted bread, the top and bottom halves spread with butter and mayonnaise and filled with a variety of meats, cheeses, vegetables, and relishes. *From its shape.*

torpedo juice. Any raw, inferior homemade alcoholic beverage, esp. as made under adverse conditions and from whatever ingredients one can find. *During W.W.II Armed Forces personnel would occasionally find themselves in a position or locale which gave no access to whisky or other alcoholic beverages. Those who felt a desire for some often used much ingenuity to concoct an alcoholic beverage from the ingredients at hand. The orig. of this term is from a typical recipe, based on pure grain alcohol as drained from a Navy torpedo.*

toss. *v.t.* To give, hold, have, or put on a social party, dance, luncheon, or the like.

toss [one's] cookies. To vomit. *Very much in fashion, esp. with students, since c1945.*

toss in the sponge (towel) = throw in the sponge (towel).

toss it in. To surrender; to stop trying; to concede failure. From "throw (toss) in the towel (sponge)."

toss it (something) off. 1. To accomplish something quickly or with little effort; specif., to drink a shot of whisky quickly, to write a book or play easily, to sing a song without effort, or the like. 2. To fail to consider another's warning, advice, insult, or compliment.

tote. *v.t.* To total. *n.* An electronic totalizator. *Horse-racing use.*

touch. *n.* 1. The act or an instance of asking for a loan of money from a friend; a loan or gift of money obtained by request or

begging. *Since c1920.* 2. Bribe money; a bribe.

tough. *adj.* 1. Conscientious; diligent; persistent. 2. Fig., impossible to surpass; the best; the greatest; the most. *Some far-out use. adv.* Roughly; harshly. —**ie.** *n.* 1. A tough hoodlum; a tough guy. 2. A hard or difficult question to answer or problem to solve. 3. A game or contest difficult to win; an opponent difficult to defeat.

tough buck. Fig., money earned at hard or strenuous work; hard work, a difficult way to earn money.

tour. *n.* One's working day or working shift of eight hours. *Fig., one's daily "tour of duty."* —**ist.** *n.* 1. One easy to cheat or victimize; a victim, a mark. 2. A lazy worker.

tout. *n.* Specif., one who frequents race tracks to sell tips to bettors; one who sells horse-racing information or acts as an advisor to bettors. *v.i.* To give or sell tips or advice on horse races.

town, go to. 1. To succeed; to perform successfully or well. 2. To respond, perform, plan, work, talk, play, or love without restraint, qualification, or inhibition.

town, on the. 1. Having a good time by enjoying a city's night clubs, theaters, and bars; enjoying all the entertainment a town can offer, esp. in one spree and without being concerned about the cost. 2. Receiving financial help from government, either city or state; living on public relief money.

town, out of. In prison. *Some underworld use.*

townie; towney. *n.* 1. Specif., in a town in which a college or university is located, a resident of the town, as opposed to a student. *Still in student use.* 2. A resident of a town in which a carnival or circus is performing, as opposed to a member of the carnival or circus; a carnival or circus spectator. *Carnival and* circus use. *Both uses often derisive.*

tracks. *n.pl.* An Army or Air Force captain's insigne bars. *Some W.W.II use.*

trade-last; trade-lassie; trade-melass. *n.* A compliment given for one received. *Since c1890; archaic since c1930. The orig. of "T.L."*

trailer. *n.* A short film shown after a full-length movie, as a preview of a forthcoming movie, a travelog, or the like. *Movie use since c1925.*

train with. To associate with.

tramp. *n.* A promiscuous girl or woman, regardless of social class, marital status, or intelligence. *Thus a tramp can be the cheapest prostitute or a refined married society woman who can't resist her.* *Colloq.*

tranquilize. *v.t.* To subdue a violent person, as a mental patient. *Pop. by the tranquilizer pills taken to calm one's nerves.*

trap; fish (talk, clam, fly, potato, kissing) trap. *n.* 1. A person's mouth, specif. considered as an organ of speech. *The expression "to shut [one's] trap" has been cited as early as 1776.* 2. A joint, esp. a nightclub. —**s.** *n.pl.* Clothes.

trial balloon. A small-scale test made in preparation for a larger endeavor; specif., a testing of public opinion in a limited area to discover how it will respond in a larger area.

trick. *n.* 1. A prostitute's customer; a prostitute's "sale" or business transaction. 2. A prison term. *Convict use since c1915.* 3. The act or an instance of committing a crime; a caper, a robbery. *Underworld use since c1925.*

trigger. *n.* A gunman; a trigger man. *Some underworld use since c1935.* *v.t.* 1. To motivate; to cause something to happen; to initiate or activate. *Colloq.* 2. To commit, manage, engineer, or take a prominent part in an armed robbery.

trigger man. An assassin; a gunman for a criminal mob; a bodyguard. *Underworld use since c1925.*

trill. *v.* To stroll, esp. to strut. *Some Negro use.*

trim. *v.t.* To defeat an opponent or opposing team, as in a game, esp. to defeat by a narrow margin.

trip. *n.* An arrest; specif. a prison sentence. *Some prison use since c1930. Fig., a trip to prison.*

tripe. *n.* 1. Untruthful, exaggerated, or insincere talk. 2. An aesthetically insignificant or vulgar thing. 3. A tripod upon which a peddler sets his display case. 4. Entrails; innards; specif., the lining of the stomach. *Now dial.* 5. Inferior or worthless stuff; esp., worthless speech or writing; boloney, lies, exaggeration.

trom. *n.* A trombone.

trots. *n.pl.* Harness races, whether actually trotting or pacing races; harness racing. *Horse-racing use.* *n.sing.* Diarrhea.

trotters. *n.pl.* = trots.

troupe. *n.* Any criminal or violent gang or mob, as of pickpockets or a teenage street gang. —**r.** *n.* 1. Anyone who travels with a circus. *Colloq.* 2. An experienced actor. *Colloq.*

trout. *n.* = cold fish.

truck. *v.t.* To haul, to carry. *Colloq.* *v.i.* To jitterbug.

trumped-up; trumped up. *adj.* Made up, imagined; hence, false.

trump up. To make up something out of one's imagination, as a lie or alibi; to make something out of makeshift ingredients or parts, by using one's ingenuity; to use one's imagination or ingenuity to make or create something.

try-on. *n., v.t.* = try-out.

try-out. *n.* The act or an instance of giving a person or thing a test or trial, under actual or simulated working conditions, to determine fitness, skill, usefulness, or workability. *Since c1910.* *v.t.* 1. To give a person or thing a test or trial under actual or simulated working conditions, in order to determine fitness, skill, usefulness, or workability. 2. To submit oneself to a test or trial of one's skill, fitness, or ability, often in competition with others, before a prospective employer in order to secure a job or, specif., in order to earn a part or role in a theatrical production or place on an athletic team. *Colloq.*

tub. *n.* 1. = bucket, a ship or vehicle. 2. Specif. = bathtub. 3. Any 16-ounce beer glass; a beer stein. *Dial.* 4. = tub of lard. —by. *n.* A fat person; often as a nickname or in direct address. *Affectionate or jocular use, never derisive.* —s. *n.* Drums; a set of drums.

tub, in the. In bankruptcy.

tub-of-guts. *n.* = tub of lard.

tub of lard. A fat person; esp., a person so fat that he is flabby and ugly; specif., a disliked or obnoxious fat person.

tuckus = tokus.

tumble. *v.i.* To understand, to recognize; to become or be wise to. *n.* An introduction; a sign of recognition or awareness of another's existence. *Usu. in "to give someone a tumble."*

tummy. *n.* The stomach; the abdomen. *From "stomach." Said to be a 19C and Victorian euphem. Used as baby talk and jocularly more than in serious speech. Colloq.*

tune up. To get into the proper physical or mechanical condition for a contest or task, as by exercise, practice, or making mechanical adjustments; an exercise or practice session, as part of one's conditioning for a contest or task; a warm-up.

turf. *n.* The neighborhood, or city blocks, controlled by a teenage street gang; a teenage street gang's territory, which is defended against the encroachment of other gangs.

turf, on the. 1. Engaged in prostitution. → 2. Without funds; having little money; being in such dire need of money that one lit. or fig. considers prostitution to obtain funds.

Turk; turk. *n.* 1. A strong man; a large, strong, energetic, overbearing man; a man quickly aroused to anger; a stubborn man, one hard to deal with. *Orig. applied mainly to and used by the Irish and people of Irish descent. Now fairly common; often a nickname given to a prize fighter. From the Gaelic "torc" = a wild boar.* 2. A sexual degenerate; specif., an active pederast. *Because this form of perversion was once thought to be prevalent among Turks.* 3. A turkey.

turkey. *n.* 1. Any of various cheap meats, meat dishes, fish or fowl, regarded as inferior to turkey, esp. bacon, hash, or canned tuna fish; specif., chicken. *Some jocular use at the table.* 2. An inferior entertainment, esp. a stage play that is exceptionally dull, badly written and produced, and a financial failure; a flop. *Since before c1930. The most common use.* → 3. Any worthless, useless, unsuitable thing. → 4. An ineffective, incompetent, objectionable or disliked person. *Some student use since before c1945.* → 5. = square. *Some bop, cool, and even teenage use.*

turkey on [one's] back, have a. = monkey on [one's] back.

turkey-shoot. *n.* An easy task; a task that is easy to perform successfully; now specif., an airplane attack that is highly destructive of enemy aircraft. *Very old; because turkeys are slow to show fear and hence are easy to get close to. Specif., war use, some W.W.II USN and Air Force use.*

turn. *v.t.* To earn or solicit money; to accomplish a task for money. *Thus a waiter is said "to turn a tip" = to have worked for or received a tip for his services.*

turn blue (green) = drop dead.

Pop. c1948 by actress-comedienne Judy Holliday.

Turner. *n.* A German; a person of German ancestry. *From the German immigrant fraternal and athletic society called "The Turners."*

turn in. To go to bed; to go to sleep. *Colloq.*

turnip. *n.* A pocket watch. *Underworld and dial. use since c1885.*

turn off. To rob a place successfully. *Some underworld use.*

turn off [someone's] water. To stop a person from talking, esp. from boasting or exaggerating, as by a direct refutation or a witty or insulting remark; to prevent another from beginning a project or from succeeding, esp. when his project or success is undesirable or unwarranted; esp., to prevent a person from achieving an advantage, reputation or success that is unearned.

turn on. To begin smoking a marijuana cigarette; to smoke a marijuana cigarette; to take a narcotic or to be under the influence of a narcotic. *Narcotic addict use.*

turn on the heat. To strive for or pursue anything vigorously; to use all one's talent, skill, or influence to succeed; to become exciting; to strive to arouse another's passion; to search diligently for a criminal; to make it hard for a criminal to escape; to intimidate a person; to begin shooting a gun. *Many various meanings based on "heat" and "hot."*

turn-out; turnout. *n.* 1. A crowd or audience, esp. a large one; spectators, guests. *Colloq. Fig.,* those who have turned out to see or be present at an entertainment, spectacle, or gathering. 2. The acquittal of an arrested person. *Underworld use.* 3. A suit of clothes.

turnover. *n.* 1. The number or percentage of people or items replaced during a specif. time. *Thus the turnover of a factory's* employees may be 20% a year, the turnover for a specif. table in a restaurant may be two customers per hour, or a merchant may hace a turnover of his entire stock twice a year. 2. The night before one's release from prison.

turn the tip. The accomplishment of the talker or spieler, after he has collected a "tip" or crowd by means of his bally, in turning or directing its attention to the product he has for sale.

turn turtle. *v.i., v.t.* 1. Lit., to turn or be turned upside down; fig., to be helpless or defenseless. 2. To retreat or turn back when necessary; to become cowardly, to turn chicken.

turn [someone] up. To turn a person over to the police; to inform to the police, as to who committed a crime or where the criminals are hiding.

turn up [one's] toes (to the daisies). To die.

turtle. *n.* An armored car, as used to deliver money to or from a bank. *Some underworld use.*

turtle doves. A pair of lovers.

tush. *n.* A light complexioned Negro; a mulatto. *Negro use. adj.* 1. Belligerent, malicious; dangerous. 2. Belonging to high society; wealthy, sophisticated, and influential; ritzy. *Some Negro use.* —**eroon(y).** *n.* Money. *Some Negro and jive use. Reinforced by "tush," but prob. of an earlier orig.*

tux. *n.* A tuxedo; a man's formal evening dress suit; sometimes a man's formal afternoon, dining, or evening ensemble consisting of a white or black formal dinner jacket, black trousers with satin seam stripe, and a black bow tie. *Colloq.*

tuxedo. *n.* A straitjacket, as used to restrain a violent prisoner or mental patient.

tuxedo junction. A public place catering to swing devotees; any place, as a dance hall, record store, or lunch-counter, where swing fans gather. *c1940 swing use.*

tweeter. *n.* A small paper-cone loud-speaker that vibrates electromagnetically to reproduce high frequencies without distortion, used in addition to other speakers in a high-fidelity phonograph or sound-reproducing system. *Common hi-fi use since c1950.*

twelve-hour leggings. Puttees, esp. as worn by timekeepers and foremen. *Contemptuous use by laborers and hobos.*

twenty. *n.* A twenty-dollar bill; the sum of $20.

twerp; twirp. *n.* A person of either sex but esp. a male who is or is thought to be peculiar, insignificant, objectionable, weird, or the like. *Wide teenage and student use c1930–c1945. Still some use, now mostly adult use.*

twiddle. *v.i.* To chat; to converse idly.

twig. *n.* A tree. *v.t.* To punish. *Fig., to punish a child or youth by using the rod.*

twin pots. 1. Dual carburetors installed in a car. → **2.** A car with dual carburetors. *Hot-rod use since c1950.*

twirl. *v.i., v.t.* In baseball, to pitch, *n.* A duplicate or skeleton key. *Mainly underworld use.*

twirp. *n.* = twerp.

twist. *n.* A girl or young woman. *From rhyming sl. "twist and twirl" = girl.* —*ed.* *adj.* A little abnormal, mentally or emotionally; showing some neurotic or psychopathologic symptoms; at best, confused, at the worst, "sick." —*er. n.* **1.** A tornado. *Fairly common dial. use.* **1.** A raid by the police.

two-a-day. *n.* = big time. Vaudeville use. *Because the more important theaters in large cities had two complete vaudeville performances a day.*

two-and-a(one)-half-striper. *n.* A Naval lieutenant commander. *USN use.*

two-bit. *adj.* **1.** Lit., worth twenty-five cents. → **2.** Cheap, inferior, insignificant; small-time; tinhorn.

two bits. A quarter; the sum of 25¢. *Colloq.*

two cents' (worth), [one's]. One's opinion, advice, or remark.

twofer. *n.* **1.** A cigar that sells at the price of "two for 5¢"; a cheap cigar. **2.** A ticket, usu. theater, that admits two for the price of one. *Both uses from "two for . . ."*

two shakes (of a lamb's tail). Fig., a minute, a second; a very short time. *E.g., "I'll be there in two shakes."*

two-spot. *n.* A two-dollar bill.

two-striper. *n.* A Naval lieutenant, senior grade. *USN use.*

two-time. *v.t.* To double-cross someone, esp. in affairs of the heart; specif., to deceive one's sweetheart or spouse by being unfaithful. *Colloq.*

two-time loser. 1. A person who has been convicted and sent to prison twice. *In some states a third conviction for a major crime carries a mandatory sentence of life imprisonment.* **2.** A twice-divorced person. *Usu. jocular use.*

typewriter. *n.* A machine gun; specif., an automatic, portable machine gun. *Some Army use since W.W.I. Underworld use since c1920. Specif. W.W.II Army use = a .30 caliber machine gun.*

tzuris. *n.sing.* Ill fortune, esp. chronic ill fortune or bad luck; problems. *From the Yiddish "tzuris" (plural) = troubles, specif. problems.*

U

ubble-gubble. *n.* Meaningless talk; gibberish.

ugly. *adj.* Mean; despicable; said of a person or act.

umbay. *n.* A bum. *From Pig Latin.*

ump. *n.* An umpire. *Baseball use since c1910. v.i.* To act as an umpire.

umpchay. *n.* A chump. a sucker; a dupe. *From Pig Latin.*

umpire. *n.* A legal or labor relations mediator.

umpteen; umteen. *n., adj.* Any large indeterminate number; used to suggest quantity too great to count.

umpteenth; umteenth. *adj.* Any large indeterminate ordinal number.

umpty. *n., adj.* Any unspecified number ending in "—ty" from 20 to 90 inclusive.

umpty-umpth. *adj.* Any unspecified ordinal number from the 24th to the 99th inclusive.

unc. *n.* 1. Uncle. 2. = uncle, all meanings.

uncle. *n.* 1. A pawnbroker. → 2. A receiver of stolen goods; a fence. *Underworld use.* 3. Any elderly male Negro. *Since before the Civil War.* 4. A Federal law enforcement agent, esp. a narcotics agent. *Underworld and narcotic addict use. From "Uncle Sam."*

Uncle Dudley. I; myself; me. *Dial.*

Uncle Sam. 1. The United States of America; the government, power, or authority of the United States. *From the bewhiskered symbol of the United States.* 2. A federal law-enforcement agent or agency. *Underworld use.*

Uncle Tom. [derog.] A sycophantic Negro; a meek or ambitious Negro who defers to, and curries the favor of, white people, either for personal gain, from habit, or usu. in an attempt to appease whites who are anti-Negro in feeling; a Negro who casts himself as inferior to white people. *Orig. Negro use. From the chief character in Harriet Beecher Stowe's "Uncle Tom's Cabin."* *v.i., v.t.* To act servilely toward whites; said of a Negro.

Uncle Whiskers. *n.* = Whiskers.

uncool. *adj.* Not cool; square; hyper-emotional, obnoxious, loud, rude, uncouth. *Fairly common cool use.*

under, get out from. 1. To recoup one's gambling losses; to recoup one's business losses; to pay off one's debts. 2. To extract oneself from a failing, embarrassing, or unpleasant enterprise, job, or relationship.

under [one's] belt. Successfully accomplished; as part of one's experience; to one's credit. *Colloq.*

undergrad. *n.* 1. An undergraduate student in college. 2. A university course for undergraduate students.

under [one's] hat. *adj.* Secret; confidential; often in "keep it under your hat."

underpinnings. *n.pl.* The human legs. *Since c1850.*

under the table. *adj.* 1. Drunk. *Colloq.* 2. Involving illegal or unethical payment or bribery. *From notion of bribe money passed under the table.*

undies. *n.pl.* Underwear, specif. women's underpants.

unfrocked. *adj.* Dismissed or barred from a professional society or pursuit; without recognition or status, esp. stripped of recognition as by a professional society, union, or governing body. *Usu. jocular use.*

ungepotch(ket, ed). *adj.* Accomplished in spite of many blunders or much confusion; untidy, sloppy, nonprofessional, makeshift. *From the Yiddish.*

unhep. *adj.* Not hep; square.

unhipped. *adj.* = unhep. *Jive use since c1935.*

unkjay. *n.* = junkie. *From Pig Latin.*

unmentionables. *n.pl.* 1. Underclothing. *Now jocular use only.* 2. Specif., women's underpants and brassières.

un poco. A little; a small quantity or portion. *From the Sp.*

unrooster. *v.t.* To tame a horse to work after he has wintered on the range. *Southwestern cowboy use.*

unshoed. *adj.* Dressed cheaply or in bad taste. *Some student use since c1950.*

unslough. *v.t.* **1.** To extract a watch from a vest or pants pocket, as by a pickpocket. *Underworld use.* → **2.** Fig., to separate a person and his money or valuables; to steal; to win or take by cheating or chicanery.

unwell. *adj.* Menstruating. *An old and familiar euphem. Colloq.*

up. *adj.* Fried on one side so that the yolk remains soft; said of an egg. *Orig. lunch-counter use.*

up [one's] alley. To be entirely within one's capabilities or interest; to be one's natural task.

Up anchor! *imp.* Get out! *Orig. Annapolis use, c1925. Still some USN use.*

up-and-down. *n.* A look or regard; a visual inspection, usu. of a person.

up and go, get. Ambition and vitality; energy, enthusiasm, gumption. *Usu. complimentary and used in the phrase,* "He has a lot of get up and go."

up and up. Honest; trustworthy; fair-minded.

up and up, on the; on the up-and-up. *adj.* Honest; fair; legitimate; sincere; permissible; on the level. *adv.* Honestly; legitimately; sincerely.

up a tree. In a dilemma; caught in a predicament. *Since c1825. From the notion of a person chased up a tree by a wild animal.*

up-beat; upbeat. *n.* **1.** The first note or beat of a musical composition; lit., the first note played when the conductor raises his baton. → **2.** The first note or notes of a musical theme whenever they are repeated within a single composition. → **3.** A familiar, well-liked passage in music. *adj.* Entertaining rather than dramatic; familiar, colorful, fast-moving; happy; said of movies, books, plays, etc. *Common since c1940.*

up-chuck; upchuck. *v.i., v.t.* To vomit. *Since c1925. Orig. student use. Considered a smart and sophisticated term c1935, esp. when* applied to sickness that had been induced by overdrinking.

update. *v.t.* To furnish with up-to-date information. *adj.* Up to date.

uplift. *n.* A brassière or style of brassière that lifts a woman's breasts so severely that they protrude and become prominent. *An item and style very popular c1940–c1948 and necessary to the sweater girl. During this period prominent and shapely breasts were considered most desirable and sexually attractive.*

upper story. The brain; head. *Common since c1910.*

uppity. *adj.* Snobbish, aloof; having a superior manner; presumptuous. *Colloq.*

up-stage; upstage. *v.t.* **1.** To steal the attention of the audience from another actor, as by standing upstage or in front of him. *Old theater use; very common.* → **2.** To ignore or snub a person; to treat another coldly. *Since c1910. adj.* Aloof, snobbish; vain; fig., affecting the manner of a theatrical star.

upstairs. *n., adv.* In the head, brain, or mind.

up stakes. To leave a place, esp. to leave town hurriedly. *Since c1840. Possibly from circus use:* "stakes" = tent stakes; *or perhaps from old Western use:* "stakes" = money, accumulated possessions, bindle.

up sticks = **up stakes.**

upsweep. *n.* A women's hairdressing style in which the hair is brushed upward toward the crown.

up the creek. Out of luck; in a predicament; in trouble, in difficulty; close to failure or ruin. *Very common, esp. among students.*

up there. Heaven.

up the river. In prison. *Orig. underworld use; pop. since c1935. From Sing Sing prison, which is up the Hudson river from New York City.*

up to here; up to there. 1. Lit., filled with food; full, capable of eating no more. *Often accompanied by a gesture of pointing to the throat or chin, implying that the stomach is full to that level.* → 2. Fig., surfeited with another's talk, actions, etc.; bored, disgusted, fed up.

up to (the) snuff (mustard). Equal to the usu. or desired quality or standard.

up to the gills. Drunk; full of liquor.

use [one's] bean = use [one's] head.

used-to-be. *n.* = has-been. *Colloq.*

use [one's] head. To think; to take thought. *Colloq.*

user. *n.* A narcotics addict.

use the needle. To have a narcotic addiction; to be a drug addict.

ush. *v.i.* To work as an usher. *Since c1890.*

ut. *adj.* Extreme, esp. in ref. to the manners of the socially elite or to the affections of a social climber. *From "utter(ly)."*

utmost, the = most, the. *Some cool use.*

V

vacation. *n.* A prison sentence.

vag. *n.* 1. A vagrant, a tramp; a jobless person; often defined legally by municipal courts as a person without a permanent job, without a permanent home address, and with less than a specific amount of money (usu. $15) in his possession. *The word is derog., connoting a petty criminal or an incompetent.* 2. Vagrancy; a charge of vagrancy. *v.t.* To arrest a person for vagrancy; to sentence a person convicted of vagrancy.

valentine. *n.* A written warning to an employee who has done poor work; a notification of dismissal from a job.

vamose; vamoose. *v.t.* To leave a place, town, or region. *v.t.* To depart, esp. to depart quickly; to flee; to beat it. *Both uses colloq.*

vanilla. *interj.* An expression of disbelief. *Usu. jocular, used when the suspected lie or exaggeration is of no great consequence.* *n.* Unfounded talk, rumors; lies or exaggeration; bull.

varnish remover. *n.* 1. Strong coffee. 2. Whisky, esp. inferior, cheap, or home-made whisky.

varsity. *n., adj.* A univ., college, or student team or group, usu. an athletic team. *Colloq. From a Brit. pronunciation of "university." In U.S. the word never = university.*

vaude. *n.* Vaudeville. *Since at least 1915.*

V.D.; VD. *n.* Venereal disease; a case of venereal disease, esp. syphilis. *Common since W.W.II when the Armed Forces used the abbr. in educational anti-venereal-disease campaigns among servicemen.*

veeno. *n.* = vino.

veep. *n., adj.* A vice-president. *First pop. applied to U.S. Vice-President Alben Barkley. From the stand. abbr. "V.P."*

vehicle. *n.* A rocket; esp. a rocket, or part of a rocket, used to carry instruments, another rocket, or explosives to a great height. *Since c1952.*

vein. *n.* A double bass, esp. when used to play modern jazz. *Some far-out use.*

velvet. *n.* Net profit; money in excess of that expected; winnings; hence any money.

verbal diarrhea. A mythical disease which causes one to talk too much.

vessel-man. *n.* A pot washer. *W.W.II USN use. Prob. synthetic.*

vestibule. *n.* The rump, the buttocks. *Jocular use.*

vet. *n.* 1. An experienced professional athlete or worker; a person who is thoroughly competent in a specific line of endeavor. 2. The stand. abbr. for "veterinarian" or "veterinary." 3. A veteran of the Armed Forces; an ex-soldier. *Since W.W.I, but pop.*

only since W.W.II. adj. Experienced; thoroughly competent as the result of long employment in a specific vocation.

V-girl. *n.* **1.** A girl or young woman who dispenses sexual favors in the professed cause of patriotism, esp. one in frequent contact with soldiers, sailors, etc., through being employed on an Armed Forces post or in a nearby establishment; a woman who accords sexual favors to servicemen through being impressed by the glamor of uniforms or service ratings; a nonprofessional prostitute catering to servicemen. *Common W.W.II use. From abbr. of "Victory girl."* → **2.** A girl or young woman who has or is suspected of having a venereal disease. *W.W.II Armed Forces use. Reinforced by the "V" of "V.D."*

vibes. *n.* The vibraphone or vibraharp. *Jazz use.*

vic. *n.* A convict; a con. *Orig. and primarily still prison and underworld use.*

Victory girl = **V-girl.**

viggerish; vigorish. *n.* The money or percentage of money paid, lost, won, or earned in illegal dealings; specif. the rate of interest paid on money borrowed from a loan shark, the betting percentage in favor of a gambling house, or a share in the proceeds of a criminal enterprise.

vinblink. *n.* = **vinegar blink.**

vinegar blink. White wine, esp. cheap or inferior white wine. *Some hobo and vino use. Orig. W.W.I Army use as a corruption of the Fr. "vin blanc."*

vines. *n.pl.* Clothing, esp. smart or hip clothes. *Some far-out use; prison use c1930.*

vino; veeno; wino. *n.* Wine, esp. cheap or inferior wine and usu. red wine. *Orig. hobo and some West Coast use since c1925, from the Sp. Not common until reinforced by W.W.II Army use among troops stationed in Italy, but now very common.*

V.I.P.; vip. *n.* A big shot, a person of importance, usu. an Army officer, business executive, politician, or visiting dignitary. *Orig. W.W.II Army use. From the initials for "Very Important Person." The separate initials more common than the word in both speech and writing.*

viper. *n.* A person who lives for or by narcotics, esp. marijuana; a marijuana addict; a marijuana pusher. *Narcotic addict use since c1935.*

virgin coke. *n.* A glass of Coca-Cola with cherry-flavored syrup added. *Some lunch-counter and student use.*

visiting fireman. An influential or free-spending out-of-town visitor, often a member of a group holding a convention. *Colloq.*

vocals, give with (the). To sing [songs].

vulcanized. *adj.* Drunk. *Some use since c1925.*

W

wack; whack. *n.* One who is wacky; an extreme eccentric; a screwball, a nut.

wacky; whacky. *adj.* Eccentric; nutty; crazy.

wad. *n.* Lit., a roll or wad of paper money; money, esp. a lot of it or all that one has.

waffle-iron. *n.* A grating in a sidewalk.

wag [one's] chin. To talk.

wagon. *n.* = **paddy wagon.**

wagon, off the. Having resumed the use of alcoholic beverages after a period of abstinence.

wagon, on the. Not drinking alcoholic beverages, either for a short or a long period. *Also used in various expressions, as "go on the wagon," "climb on the wagon," "hop on the wagon," "put [someone] on the wagon." Also, contrariwise, "fall off the wagon"* = to resume one's drinking. *These "wagon" idioms have long been universally popular.*

wahoo. *n.* A yahoo; a rustic; a simp or yap.

Wahoo. *n.* Hawaii. *Orig. USN use from Oahu Island, the part of Hawaii best known to USN sailors and to tourists.*

wail. *v.i.* 1. To play any musical instrument or style of jazz intensely and adroitly. *Some general jazz use since c1930, esp. applied to the blues, but not pop. until c1950, then by cool and far-out use.* → 2. To be exciting and satisfying; to do anything well. *Far out use.* 3. To depart quickly; to flee. *Beat use.*

wait up. When walking or running, to stop and wait for someone to catch up.

wake-up. *n.* The last day of a prison sentence. *Some prison use.*

walk. *v.i.* To play jazz music, or to play it well, esp. in an ensemble; said of a band or a section of a band. *Far-out use since c1955. Possibly related to old jazz associations with "cakewalk."*

walk-around. *n.* A comedy routine performed by a circus clown while walking around the ring of the circus tent. *Circus use since c1915.*

walk-away; walkaway. *n.* 1. Change left behind absentmindedly by a purchaser, esp. a ticket purchaser. *Orig. circus use.* → 2. Money acquired by a ticket seller by short-changing the public. *Carnival use.* 3. An athletic contest that is certain to be won by one player or team because of inequality in the skill or prowess of the opponents; a cinch.

walkie-talkie. *n.* A small, portable radio-telephone. *Such instruments were in wide use in U.S. Army during W.W.II and have since been adopted in many commercial undertakings. Very common sl. term; now almost stand.*

walking dandruff. *n.* Lice; cooties.

walking papers. 1. A dismissal, whether written or not; a discharge. *Colloq.* 2. Dismissal or rejection by one's sweetheart or a friend.

walk-on. *n.* In a play or movie, a nonspeaking actor or part. *Theater use, universally known.*

walk out. To court a girl; lit., to take a girl out for a walk, both for amusement and privacy. *Rural use.* **walk-out; walkout.** *n.* A strike by union employees against an employer. *Colloq.*

walkover; walk-over. *n.* An easy victory. *Colloq.*

walk [someone] Spanish. To force someone to leave, usu. from a public place, by lifting him by his coat or shirt collar to a walking position and propelling him toward the door.

walk-up. *n.* 1. A room or apartment higher than the main floor and reached by stairs only. 2. An elevatorless residential building of at least two floors.

wall, go over the. To escape from prison.

wall-eyed. *adj.* Drunk. *From stand. meaning = strabismic.*

wall-flower; wallflower. *n.* 1. A person, usu. a girl or woman, who is not popular or who is shy; lit., one who attends a dance but does not take part and sits by the wall watching the others. *Colloq. since c1910.*

wallop. *n.* In baseball, a hit. *v.t.* To hit a baseball hard; sometimes to hit anything with force.

walrus. *n.* 1. A short, fat person. *Some use since c1925.* → 2. An awkward person; specif., one who cannot swim; also specif., one who does not know how to dance. *Some student use since c1935.*

waltz. *n.* A round of boxing; a "stanza." *Sportswriter use. v.i.* In boxing, to spar lightly, to clinch, to fight unaggressively; said of both boxers in a match.

wampum. *n.* Money. *Orig. a folk etymology for the Indian word for money.*

wangle. *v.t.* To obtain something by bartering; to acquire something by devious means, deceit, or influence.

wanted. *adj.* Sought for arrest by the police; used absolutely. *Colloq.*

wapsed down. *adj.* 1. Knocked down or ruined by a storm; said of crops. *Rural use. Dial.* → 2. Drunk. *Rural use. Dial.*

war club. A baseball bat. *Synthetic.*

ward heeler. The lowest-ranking official of a political organization; a political worker who canvasses a city ward or district for his party during an election campaign. *Colloq.*

war horse; warhorse. *n.* Generally, a veteran; one who, though old, is still active or enthusiastic, usu. in ref. to a specif. job, goal, vocation, etc. *Colloq.*

warm [someone's] ear. To talk to a person, esp. volubly or excitedly.

warmer-upper. *n.* Something that warms a person, as clothing or, more usu., a drink of liquor or hot coffee, tea, or cocoa.

warm up. To get into the proper physical condition for a contest or task; an exercise or practice session, as part of one's conditioning for performing a task or in a contest. *Colloq.*

warm wise. To become informed, or to become aware of the facts or conditions; to become hip.

war paint. Cosmetics; specif., lipstick, powder, and rouge. *Orig. jocular use, now almost stand.*

wash. *n.* A chaser, as of water or beer, following a drink of liquor. **—er.** *n.* A saloon or tavern.

wash-out; washout. *n.* 1. A failure; a fiasco; a misfit; a bankrupt; applied to either persons or enterprises. *Taken into U.S. sl. from Brit. sl. during W.W.I.* → 2. A person who is a failure in a social or sporting context; a wallflower. *Since c1920; most common student use c1925.* → 3. A student pilot, esp. in the Air Force, who has been expelled or eliminated from flight training, usu. owing to failure in a course or examination. *Universally*

known *W.W.II Air Force use.*

wash out. 1. To fail; to be rejected; to lose or be beaten in a sports or other contest. → 2. Specif., to fail or be eliminated in a course of flight training. *Since c1935; common W.W.II Air Force use.* 3. To kill someone, either deliberately or accidentally.

washtub-weeper. *n.* = soap opera.

wash up. 1. To bring a piece of work to a successful or favorable completion. *From the notion of a worker washing his hands at the end of a day's work.* 2. To finish something, as a job, a career, a friendship, etc. 3. To lose a chance of success; to fail; to nullify or cancel; to become obsolete or unfashionable. *Usu. in the passive, as "to be all washed up."*

waste. *v.t.* To defeat completely; to beat up thoroughly; lit. and fig., to lay waste, to destroy. *Orig. teenage street-gang use; general teenage use since c1955.* **—d.** *adj.* 1. To be a narcotics addict. *Narcotics addict and cool use.* 2. Without funds; broke. *Cool and beat use since c1950, rock-and-roll use since c1955.*

water, in deep. In difficulty or trouble; faced with a problem which one is probably not experienced, intelligent, or aggressive enough to surmount; in difficulty or trouble or faced with a problem for which one is not prepared. *From the image of a swimmer in deep water (above his head) and unable to reach shore.*

water, in hot. In trouble, esp. in trouble from having incurred the wrath of those in authority. *Fig., in a pot just boiling with trouble.*

waterboy. *n.* One who courts his superiors, esp. one who is willing to take on menial tasks in the hope of winning favor; a yesman or ass-kisser.

wax. *v.t.* 1. To excel; to overcome. *Colloq. since c1850.* 2. To make a phonograph record; to record for the making of a phonograph record. *A recording technician can wax an orchestra or musician; the orchestra or musician is waxing a piece of music. Common since c1925.* n. A phonograph record. *Orig. radio and musician use, c1925.*

wax, put on. To record phonographically; to wax.

way, in a big. Enthusiastically; to a great extent.

way-out. 1. In progressive jazz, descriptive of the state of a musician who loses consciousness of everything except the development of his improvisation, esp. when his playing is based on extremely complex chord progressions; far gone. *Assoc. with advanced jazz of the late 1940's and 1950's.* 2. Descriptive of the manners, dress, etc., associated with avant-garde jazz musicians and their followers. 3. Excellent, extremely satisfying, esp. in the sense of being individualistic, creative, unusual, unsentimental. *Replacing the earlier hep and cool.* 4. Removed from reality; under the influence of narcotics. *All meanings have evolved since c1955; the last meaning indicates that the term has already begun to degenerate as it has passed from the small clique of musicians with whom it originated to their followers and thence to the general public.*

weak sister. An undependable or cowardly person. *Usu. in reference to a man; colloq. since c1860.*

wearies, the. *n.pl.* A feeling of weariness and despair; a melancholy feeling; a subdued form of the heebie-jeebies.

Weary Willie. A tramp or hobo.

weasel. *n.* 1. An informer. *Prison and underworld use since c1920.* → 2. A sneak; one who courts superiors; an inferior man. *Usu. applied to small, thin males, the word retains its physical connotation; since c1925.* 3. A small amphibious truck used by the

U.S. Navy in W.W.II. *v.i.* To inform. *Prison and underworld use since c1925.*

weasel out. To withdraw from a group or from the obligations imposed by the group; to renege on a promise, usu. for cowardly or selfish reasons. *Colloq.*

weather, under the. 1. Suffering the aftereffects of having been drunk or having consumed too much whisky the night before; suffering from a hangover. *Common use.* → 2. Drunk. *Colloq. since c1930.* Fairly common. 3. Menstruating; suffering from dysmenorrhea.

web. *n.* A radio or television broadcasting network. *Radio use since c1930.*

wee. *v.i.* = wee-wee.

weed. *n.* 1. Tobacco. *Since at least 1600.* 2. A cigarette. *Common since c1920.* 3. A marijuana cigarette. *Addict use since c1930.* *v.t.* 1. To give or hand over something. 2. To remove money, usu. from a stolen wallet or the like. *Orig. pickpocket use.* —**head.** *n.* A marijuana addict. —**ing.** *n.* Petty thievery. —**s.** *n.pl.* 1. A suit of clothes, esp. a new and gaudy suit which the wearer considers dapper. *Orig. jive use. Possibly related to stand.* weeds as in "widow's weeds." 2. Clothing of any kind.

weed, the. *n.* Marijuana. *Since c1925. Narcotic addict use.*

weed off. To remove money from a rool of banknotes; to "weed" a purse.

weeds, the. *n.pl.* A hobo camp; a jungle. *Hobo use.*

weed tea. Marijuana.

weed to. To give money, esp. to one's moneyless friends.

weenchy. *adj.* Tiny; teeny-weeny. *Dial. use since c1900.*

weenie; weeney; weinie; wienie; wiener; weener. *n.* 1. A wienerwurst or frankfurter; a hot-dog. *Colloq.* 2. That which threatens success; anything that may cause failure or disappointment; the kicker, the catch. *Since c1925.*

May have orig. in vaudeville or the movie industry, perh. in ref. to the large bladders used by comics to hit one another over the head in slapstick comedies. Such bladders are the descendants of the mock phallus wielded by ancient Greek comedians. 3. The act or result of being cheated or taken advantage of; losing or not obtaining what one has expected to gain; the short end of the stick. *Usu. in "I got the wienie." In this context the word definitely has a phallic meaning. Very common since c1940.* 4. A disliked person; a jerk. *Another term that seems to relate sex and food, and sex and deceit.*

weeper. *n.* A movie, play, book, or song that makes the audience cry; a tear-jerker.

weepie; weepy. *n.* = weeper.

weeps. *n.pl.* Tears.

weeps, put on the. To cry.

wee-wee. *v.i.* To urinate. *Used euphem. by adults in talking to small children; one of the first words many children learn. Used jocularly in adult conversation.* *n.* Urine.

weirdie; weirdy. *n.* A weird, eccentric, or unusual person, object, work of art, or the like. *Very common since c1950, now part of every young person's vocabulary. The word applies equally well to introverts, geniuses, homosexuals, abstract painters and their products, bird watchers, etc., and may be applied to any nonconformist.*

welch. *v.i.* = welsh.

well-fixed; well fixed. *adj.* Wealthy, well-to-do. *Colloq.*

well-heeled; well heeled. *adj.* 1. Wealthy. 2. Armed; carrying weapons.

well oiled; well-oiled. *adj.* Drunk. *Fairly common since c1920. The "well" does not necessarily imply any greater degree of drunkenness than "oiled" alone. This more emphatic form is now more common than the plain "oiled."*

welsh; welch. *v.i.* To fail to keep a promise or meet an obligation; esp. to fail to pay a gambling debt. *Colloq.* *n.* An instance of welshing. —**er.** *n.* One who welshes; one who loses a bet but does not pay it.

wench. *n.* Any girl; specif. an attractive or vivacious girl. *Although a very old word, "wench" is so archaic that its widespread revival among young people marks it as sl.*

West Coast. 1. The musicians, credos, arrangements, characteristics, fashions, and fads associated with the highly intellectual, cool jazz music developed on the West Coast in the late 1940's. *Jazz use.* 2. New, unusual, and satisfying. *Briefly popular c1950 when the West Coast (progressive or cool) school of independent jazz musicians excited jazz circles with their revolutionary forms and style.*

western; Western. *n.* 1. Any historical or pseudohistorical book, play, or movie about the early history and development of the Western U.S. *Colloq.* 2. Eggs fried or scrambled with chopped ham, onions, and green peppers, served either as an omelette or as the filling for a sandwich. *Colloq.*

wet. *adj.* 1. Specif. describing the state of an infant whose diaper is wet with urine. 2. Describing itinerant workers who have entered the U.S. illegally, usu. applied to Mexican immigrants. *v.i., v.t.* To urinate. Said of children and pets. *Colloq. euphem. and baby talk.* *n.* One who favors the legal manufacture and sale of alcoholic beverages.

wetback; wet back. *n.* An immigrant who has entered the country illegally, esp. a Mexican itinerant worker in the southwestern U.S. *Orig. because most such Mexicans swim the Rio Grande river. Most such illegal immigrants enter to work as migratory workers during the harvest sea-*

son to earn wages higher than those paid in Mexico; they return to Mexico at the end of the season.

wet behind the ears. Innocent, inexperienced, uninitiated, unsophisticated. *Prob. in allusion to new-born animals or human infants not yet altogether dry.*

wet blanket. One who habitually deters or discourages others from having fun; one whose presence prevents others from having fun or enjoying a party or social gathering; one who emphasizes dangers and problems, thus lessening the high spirits or enthusiasm of others; a person, esp. a prude, who subverts the gaiety or levity of a gathering; a pessimist.

wet [one's] **goozle** (throat, whistle). To drink whisky.

wet-head. *n.* An unsophisticated, inexperienced, or uninitiated person; a youth; a rustic.

wet hen. A disagreeable person; a termagant or shrew; a wet blanket.

wet hen, mad as a. Extremely angry.

wet-nose. *n.* An inexperienced person; a yokel; a youth.

wet smack. A disliked person, esp. a bore, a kill-joy, or a wet blanket.

wet sock. 1. A jerk; a dull, dreary person. 2. A limp, flaccid handshake.

whack. *n.* 1. A try; a chance; an opportunity. *Colloq.* 2. A hit, a punch, a thrust. → 3. In baseball, a hit. *v.t.* 1. To hit or punch. 2. To chop with a knife or cleaver. —ed. —y. *adj.* = wacky.

whack, on. On minimum rations. *Maritime use.*

whack, out of. Out of order; not functioning properly. *Colloq.*

whack out. To lose all one's money at gambling.

whack up. To divide or cut into even shares; to distribute loot or gambling winnings.

whacky Willies. Those members of an audience who applaud by cheering and whistling.

whale. *n.* Any large or fat person. *adj.* Large; gross; excellent. *Used esp. in phrase "a whale of a [person or thing]." Since c1900.* —r. *n.* A very large person or animal. *Colloq.*

wham. *v.t.* To hit; to whack.

wham-bam. *adj., adv.* Quick(ly) and rough(ly); displaying more energy and enthusiasm than finesse.

whammo!; whamo! *interj., n.* Indicating force, shock, violence, or surprise; a sudden, violent blow.

whammy. *n.* 1. The evil eye. *Pop. by Al Capp, cartoonist, who created "Eagle Eye Feegle," a character who could put people into a trance by looking at them; his stare with one eye is called the "whammy," but in emergencies he uses both eyes, i.e., the "double whammy." From comic strip "Li'l Abner."* 2. *Fig.,* a burden, a threat of failure, a jinx, bad luck.

whammy on [someone or something], **put the.** 1. *Lit. and fig.,* to render someone unconscious or motionless; to make something useless; to overpower someone, or overrule a plan. *Pop. by Al Capp's comic strip character "Eagle Eye Feegle."* → 2. To wish someone ill fortune; to criticize someone or something, esp. by predicting failure.

whang. *v.i., v.t.* To shoot, fire, blaze, bang.

whatchamacallit = thingamajig. *Prob. the most common of the omnibus terms.*

What cooks? = What's cooking?

What do you say? A conventional greeting that needs no reply. *Common since c1920. Prob. orig. in western U.S. Usu. slurred rapidly and accented on last word to distinguish it from a true question.*

what-for. *n.* A beating, a thrashing; a bawling out; any punishment.

What gives? 1. A common greeting. 2. "What's happening?" "What did I do to make you say or do that?" 3. = What's new? *Perhaps a lit. translation of the Ger. "was ist los?"*

what it takes. 1. Ability, strength, courage, any quality needed for a particular task; e.g., "He has what it takes." *Colloq.* 2. Money. *Fairly common c1920.* 3. Sex appeal. *The most common meaning since c1940.*

What say? = What do you say?

What's cooking? 1. A common greeting = "What's new with you?" "What news is there?" as of mutual friends and interests. 2. "What's going on here?" "What's happening or being planned?" *Orig. jive and swing use. Very common c1938–c1945, esp. student and Army use. Still in use.*

what'sit(s) = thingamajig. *A more modern word.*

What's new? A common greeting requiring no answer.

What's up? "What's happening or being planned?" "What's going on here?"

What's with [something]. A query meaning, "What's happened to [something]?" "What are the facts or your opinion about [something]?" "How do you explain [something]?" *Prob. orig. by Yiddish-speaking Americans.*

What's with you?; What's the matter with you?; How are things with you?; How about you? Common greetings = "How are you?" *The speech pattern indicates that these phrases prob. orig. among Yiddish-speaking people.*

What the hell(?). 1. Emphatically what? 2. An interj. indicating anger, surprise, disappointment, etc. 3. What's the difference? Why? What's the use? I don't care.

what-you-may-call-it; whatchamacallit. n. = thingamajig. *Colloq.*

whatzis. n. Any object whose name is not known or remembered; a gadget. *A corruption of "What's this?"*

wheats. *n.pl.* Wheatcakes; pancakes.

wheel. n. 1. An important or popular person; a leader. → 2. A person in authority. *v.i., v.t.* To drive a vehicle at high speed. *Since c1940.* —er. n. 1. A motorcyclist, esp. a motorcycle policeman. 2. = big wheel, wheel. —s. *n.pl.* A car. *Hot-rod use since c1950; some general teenage use since c1955.*

wheel and deal. To act independently, without restrictions or supervision; specif., to act independently, dynamically, and often ruthlessly or unethically, in business or social affairs.

wheeler-dealer. n. Fig., one who wheels and deals; an adroit, quick-witted, scheming person; a person with many business or social interests.

wheel-man. n. A skillful driver, esp. one who drives criminals away from a robbery; the driver of a get-away car.

wheels, on. 1. Emphatically; definitely; with enthusiasm. *E.g., "Will I come to the party? I'll be there on wheels."* 2. = with knobs on. *A modern hep variant. Some student, teenage, and young adult use since c1940.*

wheep. n. A small glass of beer; a beer chaser.

wheeze. n. An old, familiar joke; a chestnut.

wherewithal, the. n. Money.

whiff. *v.i.* In baseball, to strike at a pitched ball and miss. *Since c1920. v.i., v.t.* To strike out. n. In baseball and golf, an unsuccessful attempt to hit the ball.

whiffer. n. A flute, esp. as used in progressive jazz. *Prob. synthetic.*

whiffle-board. n. A pinball machine. *Some use since c1935.*

whimsy-whamsy. n. A whim; capriciousness.

whing-ding. n. = wing-ding.

whipped-up; whipped up. adj. Exhausted, beat. *Some far out use since c1955.*

whippersnapper. *n.* A slight, unimportant but pretentious person.

whip the dog. To shirk one's duty. *Maritime use.*

whip through [a specif. task]. To complete quickly and easily; to dash off.

whip up. 1. To form a plan or create or make something quickly. *Most often used in ref. to cooking, as to whip up a cake.* 2. To speak or write in order to incite others to action, esp. violence; to elicit strong emotions, to attempt to create enthusiasm or strong feelings; esp. to create anger in a person or group against a person, idea, or contemplated action.

whirly-bird; whirlybird; whirly bird. *n., adj.* A helicopter.

whiskers. *n.pl.* 1. The jaw, chin, or cheeks. *Primarily prize fighter use. Since c1920.* 2. Any elderly man, whether whiskered or not. *Colloq.* 3. Seniority, esp. union seniority in a trade. *Since c1925.* 4. Artificial eyelashes. 5. = Whiskers.

Whiskers; Mr. (Uncle) Whiskers; the old man with the whiskers. *n.* The U.S. government, or any of its law-enforcement officers, such as an internal revenue man, a narcotics agent, an FBI agent, or the like. *Common underworld use since c1930. From the whiskers on the cartoon figure of Uncle Sam.*

whisky tenor. A husky tenor voice, as if made husky from too much drinking; a falsetto voice, a voice that is being forced to sound like a tenor's.

whispering campaign. A concerted effort to discredit a person or agency by originating malicious or false rumors.

whistle bait. An attractive woman. *Very common c1945. From the custom of whistling to signify approval of a woman's appearance.*

whistle jerk. An Army corporal. *Some W.W.II use. Because drill commands were sometimes given by whistle signals.*

whistle-punk. *n.* = whistle jerk.

whistler. *n.* 1. A police car. *Some underworld use since c1930.* 2. A police informer. *Underworld and police use since c1935.*

whistle stop. A very small town. *Lit. and fig., a town so small that a train does not regularly receive passengers there.*

white. *adj.* Ethical, honest, fair; faithful, dependable, decent; friendly, regular. *Since c1860. adv.* Fairly. *Since c1900. n.* 1. Gin, esp. bootlegged or cheap gin. *Some use since c1920.* 2. Any white wine. *Colloq.* 3. White bread. 4. Vanilla ice cream. 5. Any of various thick white sauces and syrups, such as cream sauce, marshmallow syrup, and the like. 6. Cocaine. *Since c1945. From "white stuff."*

white bread = bread.

white collar. Of or pert. to office work and workers, mainly clerical. *Colloq.*

white cow. 1. A vanilla milk shake. *Since c1930.* 2. A vanilla ice cream soda, made with both vanilla syrup and vanilla ice cream. *Since c1950.*

white-face. *n.* A circus clown. *Circus use.*

white-haired boy; white-headed boy = fair-haired boy.

white hope. 1. A white prize fighter who may be good enough to win a championship. *Prize fighter use since c1910 in ref. to a white boxer able to beat Negro Jack Johnson.* 2. Anyone, esp. a politician, athlete, or entertainer, whose accomplishments may bring fame or respect to his native town or country, his ethnic group, his school, etc.

white horse = white mule. *Dial.*

white hot. Wanted by the police for having committed a major crime.

whitehouse; white house. *n.* Vanilla ice cream with cherries in it or on it. *In ref. to legend of*

George Washington and the cherry tree.

white lightning. Cheap, inferior, homemade, or bootleg whisky, usu. uncolored corn whisky. *Mainly Southern use.*

white line. Flavored or diluted grain alcohol drunk as liquor; bootleg or homemade whisky. *Orig. hobo use.*

white meat. 1. Any easy task; anything that can be acquired easily or with pleasure. *Because the white meat of a fowl is considered the choice part of eating.* 2. Any white woman whose time or presence is for hire for legitimate purposes, usu. an actress or singer. *Since c1935. Mainly theater use.*

white mule. Diluted or flavored grain alcohol used as liquor; cheap or bootleg whisky. *Common since c1920. Orig. Southern use. From the kick of the drink, presumably like a mule's.*

white one. A shirt of any color.

white sidewall; white sidewall haircut. A haircut so short on the sides that the scalp shows through.

white slave. Any young woman who has been kidnaped and forced to enter prostitution by an organized criminal group. —**er.** A criminal organizer of trade in prostitution.

white stuff. 1. Cocaine. *Since c1920; mainly underworld use.* 2. Alcohol used in making bootleg whisky. *c1920.* 3. = snow. 4. Morphine. *Narcotic addict use.*

white trash. A poor Southern white farmer or laborer; the class of poor Southern whites generically considered. *adj.* Descriptive of poverty and ignorance among Southern white rural folk. *Colloq.*

whitewash. *n.* 1. In sports, a defeat in which the losing team is scoreless. *Since c1860.* 2. Fig., an instance of whitewashing, i.e., covering up or glossing over a misdeed; esp. used in politics to refer to an opinion, report, or public statement intended to excuse a misdeed or exonerate an unethical or inefficient person. *v.t.* 1. To defeat an opponent utterly. 2. To conceal in public the bad record of a prominent figure, esp. a politician; to proclaim the innocence of a person who is really guilty; to influence public opinion favorably in the case of a reprehensible action.

white-wing. *n.* A man, often white-coated, who works as a street-sweeper.

whiz. *n.* 1. A short written examination given in a school class; a quiz. 2. Any person who is remarkably proficient, intelligent, talented, industrious, or successful in a specif. field; an expert, a shark, a go-getter. *Common since at least c1900. From "wizard," reinforced by "whiz" = to go fast.* 3. A remarkable specimen of anything. 4. Any member of a mob of professional pickpockets, usu. excluding the star member who actually removes the wallet or money from the victim's pocket. *Since c1920.* 5. Energy, vigor, pep, vim, zing. *v.i., v.t.* 1. To pick pockets. *Some underworld use.* 2. To drive an automobile rapidly or recklessly.

whiz-bang. *n.* 1. A mixture of morphine and cocaine, or an injection of this mixture. *Drug addict use since c1930. Because the effect is sudden and explosive.* 2. = whiz. 3. Anything remarkable. 4. A joke, esp. a hilarious one.

whodunit. *n.* A work of prose fiction in which the narrative is based on the solution of a problem posed by the discovery of a crime, usu. a murder; a detective story or murder mystery; any movie, play, book, radio script, or the like based on such a story. *As for the coining of the word, whodunit remains a mystery. From the illit. "Who done it?"*

whole-hog. *adv.* Completely; thoroughly.

whole hog, go the. Thoroughly, completely; to go the limit; to take a bold step. *Since c1830.*

whomp. *v.t.* To defeat decisively. *From "whop" = whip.*

whomp up. To create, construct, or imagine; to cook up, whip up.

whoop-de-do; hoopty-doo; hoop-de-doo. *n.* Exuberance; noisy confusion; celebration; a lavish display of emotions or material wealth; advertising, ballyhoo.

whoop-de-doodle. *n., adj.* Ballyhoo; inflated, insincere praise; whoop-de-do.

whoopee water. Liquor or wine, esp. champagne.

whooper-dooper. *n.* A spree; a spell of merrymaking. *Since c1930. adj.* Excellent.

whop. *v.t.* **1.** To strike a blow, as with the fist. *Dial. Imitative of the sound of a blow.* **2.** To beat or defeat another, lit. or fig. *Reinforced by corrupting "to whip."* *n.* **1.** A blow, as with the fist. **2.** A fall. *Dial.* —**per.** *n.* **1.** Anything large or outsized. *Colloq.* **2.** A lie or exaggeration, esp. a story obviously falsified for humorous effect. *Colloq.*

whore. *n.* **1.** Any man or woman who compromises his beliefs or talents for personal advantage. **2.** Any person who changes lovers, jobs, friends, ideals, beliefs, etc., frequently, esp. for personal gain or comfort.

whorehouse. *adj.* In a sensuous or gaudy manner as befitting a brothel.

whose its = thingamajig. *A more modern word.*

whozis. *n.* **1.** Any person or object whose name is unknown or forgotten. → **2.** Any gadget. *From "Who is this?"*

whump. *v.t.* **1.** To defeat by a large margin. **2.** To attack; to strike a telling blow against. *Used both lit. and fig.*

why, sure. Certainly; surely.

wicked. *adj.* Excellent in any way; potent, strong, capable; "fierce," keen, "mean." *Often used as an attrib. modifier of the direct object in a simple clause. Orig. cool use = intellectually or psychologically so satisfying that one becomes exhausted; cool.*

wicker. *v.t.* To throw into a (wicker) wastebasket; to discard. *Prob. synthetic.*

wick-willie. *n.* A jet plane pilot. *Some Air Force use since c1950.*

widdie. *n.* In card-playing, a widow, or spare hand.

wide open. 1. Without protection or defense; lit., open to assault, failure, disappointment, etc. *Colloq.* **2.** Unrestricted by police or other authority; freely given over to all manner of illegal activity; said of a city, district, region, etc.

wide place in the road. A small town. *Since c1935. Orig. Western and truck driver use.*

widget. *n.* **1.** A gadget. *Since c1920.* → **2.** Any useless device attached to an automobile, to a garment, or the like, in order to cause a change in style; trimming. *Orig. New York City garment district use.*

widow. *n.* **1.** Any extra or spare item that exists by itself. Thus, in publishing, a widow is a short line that appears at the top of a page; in cards, a widow is an extra hand or kitty. **2.** A woman whose husband is alive but often away from home. *Often preceded by a word that indicates the husband's reason for being away, as "golf widow."*

widow-maker. *n.* **1.** Anything, such as a specif. task or machine, that endangers a workman. *Thus in logging a widow-maker is a dangerous hanging limb or dead tree; in mining it is a diamond drill.* **2.** A gunman. *Not common.*

wiener. *n.* **1.** = weenie. *Short for "wienerwurst." Stand. use. This is the most common use of the word.* **2.** = weenie, in all sl. senses.

wienie. *n.* = weenie.

wif = wiff.

371

win

wife. *n.* One's best girl friend; one's steady. *Some student use since c1920.*

wiff; wif. *n.* 1. A wife. 2. A glance, look, or cursory examination. *v.i.* In baseball, to strike out.

wig. *n.* 1. A head of hair. *Colloq.* 2. One's head, brain, or mentality. *Jive use since c1935; often used in jive expressions, e.g., "don't blow your wig," etc.* 3. An intellectual; a studious person. *Student use since c1940.* 4. A progressive jazz musician. *Cool and far out use since c1955.* 5. A white person. *Negro use; in ref. to the long straight hair of the white race. v.i.* To talk, esp. to talk idly or foolishly. *Jive use since c1935. v.t.* 1. To annoy someone; to be a nuisance. *Jive use since c1935.* 2. To play cool or way out jazz music. *Cool use since c1955.* 3. To experience ecstasy from listening to music. 4. To experience ecstasy from any cause; to be well satisfied with someone or something; to be in rapport with someone; to dig something. *Cool uses.*

wiggle. *v.i.* To dance. *n.* A dance.

wiggle [move] [hustle] [hump] on, get a. Hurry up. *All in use c1900 to present; "get a wiggle on" and "get a move on" are much more common than other variants.*

wiggle-waggle. *v.i.* 1. To sway. *Western use since c1860.* 2. To gossip; lit., to move one's tongue back and forth rapidly.

wild. *adj.* 1. Very eager or enthusiastic. *Usu. in "wild about" or "wild over." Since c1920.* 2. Exciting and satisfying; unusual and satisfying. *Orig. cool, jive use; far out use.*

wild about [someone]. In love with, attracted to, infatuated with someone or something. *Colloq. since c1920.*

wildcat. *v.i.* To work secretly or with a secret plan or goal in order to gain an advantage; specif., to prospect for oil or minerals secretly on another's property in order to buy the property at a low price if valuable discoveries are made. *adj.* 1. Spirited; active, energetic; fun-loving and independent beyond the bounds of social approval; usu. said of a girl or young woman. *Colloq.* 2. Secret; unknown to or unsanctioned by the person most concerned; said of an oil well or mine discovered on someone else's property; done by an individual or small group without the support of or in opposition to a larger or parent group; unsanctioned, illegal, unlicensed. Thus a wildcat bus is an unlicensed bus, a wildcat strike is one not openly sanctioned by the workers' union, and a wildcat oil well is one drilled for speculative purposes, often on land which is not owned or leased by the driller. *Since c1930. n.* 1. A person who is easily angered or aroused. *Colloq.* 2. An unofficial strike by union workers.

wild mare's milk. Whisky. *Some jocular Western use.*

willie; Willie. *n.* 1. Beef, esp. canned or preserved beef. *Primarily Army use, since W.W.I.* 2. A male homosexual. *Some use since c1930.*

willies, the; Willies, the. *n.pl.* Nervousness; fear; nervous uneasiness or discomfort, esp. when due to uncertainty, fear, or the aftermath of too much drinking; the creeps, the jim-jams. *Common since c1895. Since c1940 has been partially replaced by "the jitters" and "the heebie jeebies."*

willy-boy; Willy-boy. *n.* A sissy.

willy-nilly. *adj., adv.* Unplanned, unorganized; haphazard(ly); uncertain(ly); occasionally.

Wimpy; wimpy. *n.* A hamburger sandwich. *From the hamburger-ophagous "Wimpy," a character in the comic strip "Popeye the Sailor."*

wim-wams. *n.pl.* = heebie-jeebies.

win. *n.* A victory, esp. in sports. *Common colloq. since c1900. pret., past part. Sports and gambling use.*

Winchell. *n.* A sound-recording worker. *From Walter Winchell, a radio broadcaster who wears earphones during his broadcast, as does such a worker.*

Winchester. *n.* A rifle, regardless of the manufacturer. *Since c1870; from the name of the famous arms manufacturing company.*

wind. *n.* The air.

wind, give [someone] the. 1. To discard or jilt a suitor with great suddenness. **2.** To dismiss or fire someone precipitately. **3.** To brake a moving vehicle suddenly and sharply.

windbag. *n.* A talkative or garrulous person; esp. one who talks pompously. *Colloq. Often refers to an old person or a politician.*

wind-box; wind box. *n.* An organ or accordion.

winder-upper. *n.* A song or other musical piece played last on a radio program; the piece that winds up a program. *Common radio use since c1930.*

winding = **wind-ding.**

wind-jammer. *n.* **1.** An Army bugler. *Some Army use.* **2.** A musician in a circus band. *Circus use since c1930.*

window, out the. 1. Lost; forfeited; destroyed; gone out of one's possession; said of the goods, fame, career, etc., of one who has lost everything, usu. at one sweep. **2.** Sold out as soon as put on display; said of merchandise.

windows. *n.pl.* Eyeglasses.

wind pudding. Nothing to eat. *Usu. in phrase "to live on wind pudding"* = to have nothing to eat and no means of getting anything. *Hobo use.*

wind up. To bring something to a conclusion; to complete a task or assignment successfully. *Colloq.*

wind-wagon. *n.* An airplane. *Prob. synthetic.*

windy. *adj.* Talkative; boastful. *Colloq. n.* A talkative person; esp. one who lies or exaggerates. *Since c1930.*

wineeo. *n.* = wino.

wing; whing. *n.* An arm, esp. a baseball pitcher's pitching arm. *Mainly sports and jocular use. Since c1920 v.t.* To wound, hit, or nick with a gunshot, not necessarily in the arm. *Common during and since the Civil War.* —*s. n.pl.* Cocaine. *From its effect. Some West Coast use since c1920.*

wing-ding; wingding; whing-ding; whingding. *n.* **1.** A fit, esp. an epileptic fit; a fit induced by drugs; a faked fit used to gain sympathy. *Orig. hobo, prison, and drug addict use. Since c1920.* → **2.** A violent fit of anger, frustration, or nervousness; a loud emotional outburst. *Since c1935.* **3.** A ruckus; any noisy or exciting incident; a commotion, esp. a noisy celebration or argument. *The most common use. Since c1940.* **4.** A gadget; a dingus; a doodad. *adj.* Boisterous, noisy, exciting; uninhibited.

wing-dinger. *n.* **1.** One who has or fakes a fit. **2.** An uninhibited, boisterous celebration or celebrator. **3.** Anything remarkable.

Wingy. *prop. n.* A nickname often applied to a one-armed man, esp. a beggar.

winkus. *n.* A wink, sign, or spoken code word, given as approval, warning, or the like. *From "wink" plus Latin ending "—us."*

wino. *n.* **1.** A grape picker; a vineyard worker. *Some hobo use.* **2.** A habitual wine drunkard, esp. a jobless alcoholic who favors cheap wine because it gives the most kick for a little money. *Since c1920.* → **3.** Any drunkard.

win out. To win; esp. to succeed as a result of perseverance and against odds. *Since c1890; colloq.*

win [one's] spurs. To be accepted as an experienced and trustworthy worker and person; to become a professional; to prove by an action or series of actions that one is experienced enough to be considered no longer a novice. *From the cowboy use.*

win the porcelain hairnet; win the fur-lined bathtub; win the tinfoil doorknob; win the cast-iron overshoes; win the barbwire garter; win the solid gold chamber pot. Phrases used ironically on the occasion of a remarkable action by someone else; fig., to win a strikingly useless prize for doing something well, to perform a useless action in a superior manner.

wipe. *n.* 1. A handkerchief. 2. One who washes or wipes cars or dishes; thus "car-wipe," "dish-wipe," etc.

wipe it off. 1. An order to stop smiling or joking, to concentrate on the business at hand and be serious; fig., to wipe a smile off one's face. *A common W.W.II Army order, by sergeants getting soldiers ready for inspection or marching. Some civilian use since W.W.II.* → 2. A command to be serious and pay attention; an order to stop all frivolous activity and merriment. *Wide W.W.II Army and USN use.* 3. To forget and forgive; to make retribution. *Fig., to wipe the slate clean.*

wipe off. To destroy; lit. and fig., to wipe someone or something off the map.

wipe out. To kill or murder; to eradicate a person or a group. *Underworld use since c1925, pop. in fiction and the movies; some W.W.II use. Colloq.*

wiper. *n.* A gunman; a hired killer. *Underworld use since c1930. From "wipe out."*

wire. *n.* 1. A pickpocket; that member of a gang of pickpockets who does the actual stealing. *Common underworld use since c1920.* 2. A lackey, esp. one who helps a prisoner communicate with his friends outside prison. *Prison use c1925.* 3. A warning, as of impending arrest; also, information; advice. 4. A telegram. *Colloq.*

wire city. A jail; a wire enclosure around a prison stockade, esp.

an Army guardhouse or prisoner-of-war stockade. *Some Army use.*

wire-puller. *n.* A person who uses influence, stratagems, or the influence of others in order to obtain a desired result; specif., one who obtains a desired result by political influence; an "operator."

wires, pull. To use influence or pull to obtain favors.

wiry. *adj.* Artful. *Some c1950 student use.*

wise. *adj.* Informed; alert; on the inside; cognizant of the true course of events even if it is not immediately apparent; hip. *v.t.* To wise [someone] up; to inform someone of pertinent facts or information.

wise, get. 1. To be or become impertinent, impudent, or fresh. 2. = get next to [someone]. 3. = get next to [oneself].

wise, put [someone]. 1. To inform someone of another's personal attitude, feelings, or ideas; to warn, caution, or advise someone. 2. To inform someone of a group attitude, basic concept, or point of view, esp. in order generally to enlighten the person, or make the person more alert, receptive, or hip. *Fairly common student and young adult use. In both uses, the person put wise is considered of inferior intellect, experience, or sensitivity to the speaker.* 3. = wise up.

wise apple = wise guy.

wisecrack; wise-crack. *n.* A bright, smart, witty, or sarcastic remark; an impertinence; a joke, esp. when it emphasizes another's shortcomings. *The late columnist O. O. McIntyre attrib. this coinage to comedian Chic Sale. Since c1920. v.i.* To utter a wisecrack.

wisecracker; wise cracker. *n.* One who wisecracks; a joker.

wise guy. 1. A person, usu. a male, who is aware of contemporary happenings; one who is hep; most freq. used ironically. *Since c1910.* → 2. A person who thinks he knows everything, a smart aleck; one who says everything he thinks, one who gives advice and criticism freely; a trouble-maker. *Since c1910, common since c1925.* 3. An egoistic extro-vert, often with a cynical and superficial philosophy of life, who delights in offering sarcas-tic suggestions and making jokes at the expense of the pride of others.

wise hombre = wise guy. *Some Western use, but esp. in Western fiction.*

wise up. To become informed, to see the point of something; to give someone information that is of personal benefit to him; to tip someone off; to warn a person of the real consequences of his ac-tions, utterances, etc.

wish book. A mail order catalogue. *Since c1930; jocular and rural use.*

wishy-washy. *adj.* Vacillating, fal-tering, weak. *Colloq.*

witch. *n.* Any girl or young wom-an. *Colloq. since c1925; mainly student use.*

with [something], give. To give or give out something.

with a bang. Very successfully; with popular acceptance.

with it. 1. Officially connected with or employed by a carnival or cir-cus. *Carnival and circus use since c1930.* 2. Appreciative of and sympathetic to jazz; in rapport with, esp. jive or swing; hep. 3. Alert, spirited, wise, hip. 4. Aware and appreciative of the manner, speech, and fads used by cool or far out musicians and their adherents; hip to the jazz, esp. cool, genre. *Cool use since c1950; beat use.*

with it, get. To get on the ball; to get going; to get busy.

with knobs (bells, tits) on. Defi-nitely, emphatically; with enthu-siasm and in the proper mood, dress, and condition. *Often in "I'll be there with knobs on," in accepting an invitation. Since at*

least *c1935. Usu. follows an ac-cusation or oath.*

with tits on = with knobs on.

wizard. *n.* A person who excels at a specif. function, usu. intellec-tual or mechanical; a whiz. *Col-loq.*

wolf. *n.* 1. A male homosexual se-ducer; an aggressive male homo-sexual. *Prison and hobo use.* → 2. A youth or man who habitual-ly pursues women; a sexually ag-gressive male; a seducer or would-be seducer; a youth or man who appropriates the girl friends or wives of others; a ladies' man; a man with a psy-chological need to prove his mas-culinity or potency by seduction or attempted seduction of a great many women. *This use evolved c1930 and was stand. by c1945. Great student popularity by c1940 and wide W.W.II use. Orig. containing derog. overtones of "seducer," it now is considered complimentary by youths who wish to be known as ladies' men, and is often used jocularly. Thus the meaning of the word, prob. along with pop. conceptions of morality, changed during W.W.II. v.i., v.t.* 1. To appropri-ate another's girl friend or boy friend. 2. To be, or act as, a heterosexual wolf.

wolf whistle. A whistle to show awareness of, approval of, and sometimes an invitation to a sex-ually attractive woman. *The wolf whistle is commonly a brief ris-ing note followed immediately by a longer descending note. Most common during W.W.II.*

woman-chaser. *n.* A ladies' man; a libertine.

womp. *v.t.* To beat or defeat an-other person or team severely. *n.* In television, a glare from some white object, as a shirt front, within range of the camera lens; a "bloom." *Television use since c1945.*

wood; wood, the. *n.* The actual bar in a nightclub or saloon.

wood butcher. 1. In the U.S. Navy, a carpenter's mate. *W.W.I and II use.* 2. A poor golf player. *Some golf use since c1935.*

wooden coat = wooden overcoat.

wooden-head. *n.* A stupid person, a blockhead. *Colloq.*

wooden kimona; wooden kimono = wooden overcoat. *Some underworld and fictional use since c1930.*

wooden overcoat. A coffin. *Some use since c1860.*

woodfish. *n.pl.* Mushrooms. *Dial.*

wood-head. *n.* A lumberjack. *Hobo use.*

woodpile; wood-pile. *n.* A xylophone or marimba. *Some radio use since c1935; jazz usage.*

wood-pusher. *n.* An inferior chess player.

wood-pussy. *n.* A polecat. *Dial.*

wood-shed. *n.* A rehearsal for a radio program, esp. an arduous rehearsal. *Radio use since c1935. v.i., v.t.* To work, practice, or play alone; to seek quiet or solitude. *From the archaic and rural image of the woodshed as the place where a boy could retire to smoke or otherwise occupy himself without detection.*

woof. *v.i.* To talk foolishly or aimlessly. *Usu. used in the negative = to talk sense or to the point. Orig. jive use, from the sound of a dog's barking, c1935; mainly student use, though common in Armed Forces during W.W.II. v.t.* To eat rapidly. *Always in "to woof one's food." Colloq.* —**er.** *n.* 1. A breathy singer; a singer whose breathing can be heard through a microphone. *Radio use.* 2. A small paper-cone speaker that vibrates electromagnetically to reproduce low frequencies without distortion, used in addition to other speakers in a high-fidelity phonograph or sound-reproducing system. *Common hi-fi enthusiast use since c1950.*

woofled. *adj.* Drunk.

wool. *n.* The hair on any human head. —**lies;** —**ies.** *n.pl.* 1. = willies. 2. Wool underwear, esp.

men's woolen underwear with long sleeves and legs. *Since this item is considered old-fashioned and rustic by most youths and city dwellers, the word is most often used in a jocular way.* —**ly;** —**y.** *n.* A sheep.

wool over [one's] eyes, pull the. To deceive a person. *Colloq. since c1900.*

woozily. *adv.* In a woozy manner.

woozy; wuzzy. *adj.* 1. Mentally befogged, dazed; confused. *Common since c1890.* 2. Drunk. 3. Psychologically uncomfortable; affected by eeriness or weirdness. *Since c1930.* 4. Dizzy, faint. *Colloq.*

workout. *n.* 1. A beating. *Underworld and prison use.* 2. A task, game, or exercise that tests endurance; a task that leaves one exhausted.

work over. To beat someone, usu. in order to gain information or in retaliation; to rough up someone.

works, gum up the. To ruin something, as a job or chance of success or making a good impression; to fail to take full advantage of one's opportunity; to commit a *faux pas.*

works, the. *n.* 1. Everything available; the complete operation available as part of a service; a complete account. *Common since c1930.* 2. A killing, beating, roughing up.

work the growler = rush the growler.

work the stem. To beg on the streets. *Hobo use.*

world, out of this. Perfect; extremely beautiful, moving, etc.; wonderful; too good to be true; extremely happy; heavenly.

world-beater. *n.* A champion. *Colloq.*

worm. *n.* A disliked, untrustworthy fellow; a cad, a deceiver. *Colloq. v.i.* To study. *Some jive use since c1935.* —**s.** *n.pl.* Macaroni or spaghetti. *Some student and Armed Forces use since c1925.*

worm out of. To retreat or withdraw from a difficult situation; to renege on a promise or obligation; fig., to crawl or sneak away from a problem or distasteful duty.

worry, I [one] should. "I don't care." "I have no reason for alarm or concern." "I am not concerned." *Colloq.*

worry wart. One who worries excessively and unnecessarily; a brooder; an introvert.

wow. *n.* 1. Any remarkable and exciting person or thing; often used as a one-word comment showing awareness of or appreciation of a remarkable thing or person, esp. a sexually attractive girl. *Since c1925.* → 2. A sensational or striking success, usu. said of popular entertainment or entertainers. *Common since c1935; orig. a theater term.* 3. A slow, wavering tone resulting from imperfect sound reproducing equipment, as a phonograph turntable that revolves unevenly. *Used by high-fidelity enthusiasts since c1950. v.t.* To elicit enthusiastic approval, esp. from an audience. *Since c1925.*

wowser. *n.* A formal person; a killjoy; a stuffed shirt. *From the Australian sl. use, where orig., c1890, a "wowser" = a prohibitionist or a missionary.*

wrap it up. 1. To conclude any task or operation successfully. 2. To strike the winning blow, fig., in a contest or competition.

wrap-up. *n.* 1. Any item sold to the customer before he sees it, esp. items purchased by mail, by sending in money to radio and television advertisers, and the like. *Advertising, radio, and television use since c1950.* → 2. Fig., any easy task; anything at which one's success is assured; a certainty, a sure thing, a cinch; said of a task or sports contest. → 3. Fig., a packaging; a presentation of several things as though packaged. 4. A conclusion, an ending; a summary and conclusion.

wreck. *n.* 1. A dilapidated vehicle, as an automobile. → 2. A person who is fatigued, indisposed, dissipated, or the like. *Colloq. since c1930. v.t.* 1. To change a banknote into coins of equivalent value. → 2. To spend an amount of money quickly, esp. for a good time.

wringer, put [someone] through the. 1. To try someone severely; to subject someone to an exhausting period of questioning. 2. = put the heat on [someone].

wrinkle. *n.* 1. Style or fashion. *Usu. in phrase, "the latest wrinkle."* 2. An ingenious or unusual idea, method, or approach to a problem. *Usu. in "That's a new wrinkle."*

wrinkle-rod. *n.* A crankshaft. *Factory use since c1940. Now hot-rod use.*

wrist-slapper. *n.* An effeminate or affected youth or man; a goody-goody.

writ. *n.* A written examination. *West Point use.*

write-in. *adj.* Written on a ballot at the time of voting; said of a candidate's name that does not appear on the prepared ballot.

write-up. *n.* A written account or article, as in a newspaper, esp. a written account or review of a product, celebrity, entertainment, or the like.

wrong. *adj.* 1. Contrary to the underworld code. *Criminal use since c1925.* 2. Not trustworthy; dishonest; habitually or congenitally criminal. *n.* An informer. *Some underworld use.*

wrong number. 1. A mistaken idea or concept. 2. A psychopath; a dangerous person. 3. A dishonest or untrustworthy person. *All meanings from the stand. phrase for a wrong connection on a telephone circuit.*

wrong side of [the] bed, get up on the. To be in a bad mood or in bad temper; to be peevish or fretful. *Usu. in "You must have got up on the wrong side of bed this morning."*

wuzzy. *adj.* 1. Mean; contrary. *Dial. since c1875.* 2. Confused; faint; woozy.

X

X. *n.* 1. A signature. *Colloq. From the ancient custom of allowing illiterates to sign documents with a cross, thus signifying their obligation under God to carry out the terms of the agreement; the cross eventually degenerated into an "x."* 2. The common written symbol for a kiss, usu. put at the bottom of a letter. *Colloq.* 3. An unknown person, esp. one who wishes to conceal his identity; a criminal boss; Mr. Big. **x.** *n.* 1. Any unknown quantity. *A stand. math. symbol.* → 2. Any unknown or untried factor that may influence the outcome of a business venture, sports contest, or the like.

x-factor. *n.* = x.

x marks the spot. A common expression meaning, fig., "That is where it is" or "That is the place where something is located, even though not actually marked with an 'x.'"

x out. 1. Lit., to delete words from a written contract by typing "x's" over them; to erase or delete any material from a written document. 2. To cancel, to nullify.

XX = double-cross.

Y

yack = yak.

yackety-yak; yakitty-yak. *n.* Useless, voluble talk; stupid chatter; gab. *v.i.* To talk too much; to talk loudly, volubly, or stupidly.

yaffle. *v.t.* To steal. *Dial. and some maritime use.*

yak; yack; yock; yuk; yuck. *n.* 1. A friend or pal, esp. one who can be depended upon or used. *Some underworld use.* 2. A stupid or innocent person; a dope; a rustic. *Since c1920; made somewhat pop. by the comedian Fred Allen.* 3. A watch. *Some underworld use.* 4. A laugh, esp. a deep, long

laugh; more esp. a laugh produced in an audience by a professional entertainer. 5. A joke, esp. a very funny joke. *v.i., v.t.* 1. To talk; to chat, gossip, or banter. *Usu. "yak," often reduplicated.* 2. To laugh.

yammer. *v.i.* To talk vociferously; to complain, whine, nag, etc. *n.* Talk, esp. idle or nagging talk.

yan. *n.* = **yannigan.** —**nigan.** *n.* A professional baseball player; esp. a young inexperienced athlete who has just joined a team; a crude or uncouth baseball player. *Baseball use.*

Yank. *n.* 1. A citizen of the U.S. *From the now stand. "Yankee."* 2. A United States soldier. *Orig. W.W.I use from Brit. sl.* yank. *v.t.* 1. To arrest. 2. To relieve a person of his duties because he has failed to produce satisfactory results.

yap. *n.* 1. The victim of a criminal undertaking, esp. a pickpocket's victim. *Some underworld use since c1920.* 2. The mouth, considered only as the organ of speech. *The most common use. Since c1900.* 3. A request; a complaint. *v.i.* 1. To talk, esp. to talk idly or without thought; to nag; to gossip. 2. To complain; to protest.

Yarborough. *n.* In card games, a worthless or losing hand.

yard. *n.* A $1,000 bill; the sum of $1,000. *Underworld use since c1930, replacing original meaning ($100).*

yard bird; yardbird. *n.* 1. In the Army, a raw recruit; a rookie. *Army use. Because recruits are confined to camp during their basic training.* 2. A soldier, sailor, or marine who freq. is punished for violations of regulations, such punishment usu. being confinement to camp and assignment to duty of cleaning the parade ground or yard; a soldier assigned to manual labor or menial chores. *Armed Forces use.* 3. An infantryman; any soldier. *Some newsp. use.* 4. A prisoner, a convict. *The great jazz musician Charlie "Yardbird" Parker was nicknamed when he served a prison sentence for narcotics addiction; later the name was shortened to "The Bird" and many references to it occur in cool and bop usage during the late 1940's and early 1950's; cf., for instance, the many jazz compositions entitled "Ornithology" or variants thereof and the famous N.Y.C. nightclub called "Birdland." The most common use. Because most prisons are built around yards where prisoners exercise.*

yard bull. 1. A railroad guard or detective assigned to duty in a freight yard. 2. A prison guard.

yard dog. A mean or uncouth person.

yard hack = yard bull. *Some prison use.*

yard patrol. 1. The prisoners in a jail; a prisoner in a jail; a yard bird. 2. The police who patrol a jail; a prison guard.

yardpig. = yard bird.

yatata yatata. *n.* Monotonous talk; idle chatter. *v.i.* To talk idly and at length.

yatter. *n.* Talk; chatter. *v.i.* To talk loquaciously or inanely.

yea big; yea high. 1. This big, or this high, accompanied with the spreading of the hands to indicate the size; very large or high, overwhelmingly large or tall. 2. Not very big or high. *A sophisticated fad phrase since c1955.*

yeah. *adv.* Yes.

year. *n.* A banknote; a dollar. Thus "5 years" = a $5 bill or five dollars. *Orig. underworld use.* —ling. *n.* At West Point, one who has begun his second year of studies.

yegg. *n.* 1. A safe-blower, orig. an itinerant one. *Orig. hobo, then underworld, use; now in common use but shunned by underworld. Said to be from John Yegg, traditionally the first safecracker to employ nitroglycerine.* 2. Any thief who travels as a ho-

bo, using the freights. *Hobo use.* 3. Any thief.

Yehuda. *n.* A Jew. *From the Arabic "yahudi" = Jew. The plural is "Yehudim." Not derog.; used almost exclusively by Jews.*

yellow. *adj.* Cowardly. *Since c1850. Colloq. n.* Cowardice. —ness. *n.* Cowardice.

yellow-bellied. *adj.* Cowardly. *Most common among adolescents and young students.*

yellow-belly. *n.* A coward.

yellow dog. An inferior or worthless person or thing. *Some use since c1900.*

yellow dog contract. A contract required by employers of prospective employees forbidding them to join a union.

yellow girl. A mulatto girl or woman; a light-skinned Negress, esp. if sexually attractive. *Since c1865; both Negro and white use.*

yellow jacket. A Nembutal (trade mark) capsule. *Orig. narcotic addict use.*

yen. *n.* A strong craving, yearning, or desire; a habit. *Orig. West Coast and hobo use. From the Chinese word for opium. v.i.* To desire; to crave. *Perhaps reinforced by stand. "yearn."*

yenems. *n.* Another's possession freely offered; freq. used jocularly in reference to cigarettes: "My brand of cigarettes is yenems" = whatever brand someone offers me. *Transliterated Yiddish.*

yen-hok; yen-hook. *n.* The implement used in preparing opium for smoking and putting it into the pipe. *Opium addict use.*

yen-shee. *n.* 1. Opium, as used by addicts; orig. the cake or opium "dottle" at the bottom of a smoked opium pipe. *Opium addict use; universally known. From the Chinese word for opium.* → 2. Heroin. *Some addict use.*

yentz. *v.t.* To cheat; to fleece. *From the Yiddish.* —er. *n.* A cheater; one who cannot be trusted.

yen-yen. *n.* A strong craving for narcotic drugs; lit., a "yen" for "yen-shee" or another drug. *Some addict use.*

yep. *adv.* Yes. *Colloq. since c1840.*

yesca. *n.* Marijuana, as taken by addicts. *Addict use.*

yes-girl. *n.* A sexually compliant young woman.

yes-man. *n.* An employee whose main fuction is to endorse his superior's decisions and opinions; an acquiescent subordinate; an ass-kisser. *Orig. c1925 prob. in Hollywood where the term was early used to mean an assistant director.*

yesterday, today, and forever. Hash. *Lunch-counter use, usu. jocular. Implies that one pot of hash is maintained, to which each day's leftovers are added ad infinitum.*

yet. *adv.* 1. Sometimes used after a gerund that is preceded by "still"; a redundant use which adds emphasis, immediacy, or impatience to the sentence. Thus "He's still sleeping yet." 2. = already.

yippie. *n.* A yard or harbor patrol craft. *W.W.II USN use. From the initials "Y.P."*

yock. *n.* = yak.

yodeler. *n.* 1. In baseball, a third-base coach. *Some baseball use. Because the third-base coach shouts instructions to baserunners.* 2. An informer; a criminal who gives information to the police.

yok. *n.* 1. A laugh, esp. a long, loud laugh. 2. A joke, esp. a very funny joke. *v.i.* To laugh, esp. to laugh loud and long.

yoot. *n.* A teenage hoodlum; a member of a teenage street gang; a juvenile delinquent. *Synthetic. From a corruption of "youth," perhaps with the "oo" of "hood" or "zoot suit."*

you bet. Sure(ly); certainly; an expression of affirmation. *Colloq. since c1870.*

you bet you = you bet.

You can say that again = You said it.

you-know-what. *n.* Anything so obvious from the context that it need not be named; specif., money or sex.

young. *adj.* Small. *Used often to qualify a hyperbole.* —ster. *n.* A second-year cadet at the U.S. Naval Academy.

young horse. Roast beef. *Some prison, student, and Army use.*

Your mother wears Army boots! An exclam. of derision. *Orig. a strong W.W.II term of derision; now mainly jocular.*

yours (his, hers, etc.), get. To get punished; to be found out; to fail. *Usu. implying that the punishment or failure will be deserved.*

yours truly. I; me; the speaker or writer.

You said it. Emphatically yes; "I agree with you"; "You are right."

yo-yo. *n.* A compromising person; one whose political opinions and ideas change as necessary for personal gain; a free-loader. *From the toy that winds and unwinds in a vacillating manner.*

yuck; yuk = yak.

yuk-yuk. *n.* Empty, idle, or stupid talk.

yum; yum-yum. *exclam.* An expression signifying delight, usu. in ref. to a specif. sensory perception, as of taste, smell, etc. yum-yum. *n.* 1. Food. *Baby talk.* 2. Sweets. *Used by young children.* —my. *adj.* 1. Delicious. *Orig. baby talk, in vogue c1930 and again c1955.* → 2. Good, satisfactory, pleasing, attractive. *Mainly schoolgirl use.*

Z

zap. *v.t.* To kill.

zazoo. *n.* A fellow; a guy.

zazzle. *n.* Sex appeal, esp. in an exaggerated degree. *Orig. Negro use.*

Zelda. *n.* A female square. *Some cool and beat use since c1950.*

Zen hipster. *n.* A hipster or esp. a member of the beat generation who adheres to Zen Buddhism.

zero hour. 1. The exact time at which a planned action begins, usu. in ref. to military operations. *W.W.II use.* → **2.** An appointed, dangerous, or critical time.

Zex! *interj.* = Cheese it!

ziggetty! *exclam.* = hot damn!

zig-zig. *n.* Sexual intercourse. *One of several reduplications = coitus that were fairly common with W.W.II Armed Forces, usu. from folk etymologies of native terms in occupied territories.* *v.i.* To have sexual intercourse.

zillion. *n.* An exceedingly large indeterminate number; a larger number than can be imagined. **—aire.** *n.* One who has a zillion dollars; a person whose wealth is of mythical proportions.

zing. *n.* Vitality, zest, animation; pep. *Since W.W.I.* *adj.* Chic; attractive; appealing. **—y.** *adj.* Having zing; full of energy or ambition. *Mainly adolescent use.*

zip. *n.* **1.** Vitality; vim; energy; zing. *Colloq.* **2.** Syrup; molasses. *Dial.* **3.** Sugar. *Dial.* *v.i., v.t.* To shut up. *From "zip(per) your lip."* **—po.** *n.* Zip; zing; vim. *adj.* Having zip; peppy; snappy. **—py.** *adj.* Peppy.

zip fuel. Any high-energy jet airplane fuel.

zip gun. A homemade or makeshift gun, usu. consisting of a metal pipe for a barrel, a wooden stock, and some spring or elastic material to actuate a firing pin. *Wide use by teenage street gangs.*

zombie. *n.* **1.** A weird looking person; a person exhibiting eccentric behavior; emphatically a character. *From the traditional "zombie" = a walking corpse. Student use since c1940.* → **2.** An unpopular, disliked person. *Student use, most common c1940–c1950.* **3.** A putatively strong alcoholic mixed drink.

zool. *n.* Anything attractive, well made, or satisfying. *Rock and roll use since c1945.* **—ie; zooly.** *adj.* Excellent; satisfying. *Rock and roll use since c1955.* **—ix.** *n.* Syrup. *Dial.*

zoom. *v.i., v.t.* To get something without paying for it. *adj.* Free; gratis.

zoot. *n.* A dude.

zoot snoot. 1. A large nose; a person who has a large nose. **2.** An overly curious person; a gossip or snoop.

zowie. *n.* Zest; energy; *joie de vivre.*

zuch. *n.* An informer; a stool pigeon. *Underworld use since c1940.*

Supplement of New Words
by Stuart Berg Flexner
An asterisk (*) placed after a
word indicates the appearance of
that word in the original text.

A

A-bone. *n.* A Model A Ford. *Hot-rod use since c1950.*

ace*. *n.* 1. A hole-in-one. *Golf use.* 2. A single, unaccompanied customer, esp. in a restaurant; a table for one, in a restaurant. 3. The academic grade A. *Some student use.* 4. A very close friend; buddy; pal. *Orig. teen-age street-gang use.* *v.t.* To do something perfectly; to accomplish something without errors or mistakes.

acid. *n.* = LSD. *Habitual users' and student use.*

acid head; acidhead. A habitual user of LSD.

affirm. *adj.* Affirmative. *n.* An affirmation: an affirmative reply. *Orig. U.S. Air Force use in Vietnam.*

aggressive. *adj.* Very good; wonderful. *Some cool and student use.*

amp*. *n.* 1. An amplifier, as of a high-fidelity phonograph. 2. An ampoule of a drug. *Mainly addict use.*

angel*. *n.* 1. A misleading image on a radar screen, usually in vague white shadows, and often caused by bird flights, unusual atmospheric conditions, or faults in the radar's electronic circuitry. *Armed Forces use.* 2. A helicopter, esp. one flying near an aircraft carrier to rescue pilots who may crash into the sea during takeoff or landing. *Orig. Navy use in the Vietnam war.*

animal*. *n.* An athlete. *Some student use.*

Anzac. *n.* An Australian or New Zealand soldier; any Australian or New Zealander. *Since W.W.I; an acronym of "Australian and New Zealand Army Corps." Colloq.*

A-OK; A-Okay; A-O.K. *adj.* Favorable; perfect. *adv.* Perfectly suitable, agreeable, congenial, very fine; better than just O.K. *From "A-1"* plus "O.K." Orig. aerospace use, pop. by use in the televised launching of the flight of Alan B. Shepard, Jr., in 1961 as well as by the other first seven U.S. astronauts, to signify that all electronic circuits were functioning properly in a spaceship and that it was ready for launching.*

ape*. *adj.* Frenzied; uncontrolled; wild. *Common student use.*

ARVN; Arvn. *n.* The Army of the Republic of Vietnam; one of its soldiers. *An acronym pronounced to rhyme with "Marvin." Armed Forces use in Vietnam war.*

ASP. *n.* = WASP.

Aunt Jane. A sycophantic Negro woman; a female "Uncle Tom."*

Aunt Jemima = Aunt Jane.

B

baby-sitter*. *n.* A destroyer, esp. one accompanying an aircraft carrier. *Navy use in Vietnam war.*

back off*. To be ejected from or asked to leave a public place, such as a bar.

bad news*. 1. Any unfortunate or unpleasant situation or event. 2. A depressing or undesirable person.

bad talk. Pessimistic comments. *Negro and some Southern use.*

bag*. *n.* 1. One's disposition or recurring mood, behavior pattern, or way of life; that niche to which one has assigned oneself; that which one currently is or feels. *Thus a person can be known for frequently having "angry bags" or "sad bags," may be in a "jazz bag" or "the cool bag" or a musi-*

cian may be in or play in the "blues bag." *Orig. jazz use to designate the school of jazz to which a musician belonged.* 2. One's special or current interest, obsession, talent, enthusiasm, or liking; one's vocation, hobby, habit, or vice; that which one prefers above all else; one's "kick."* *Jazz, beat, student, and teenage use.* 3. An environment or social milieu; a clique or group. *Orig. Negro use; now common beat and student use.* 4. A portion or addict's supply of narcotics, often wrapped in a paper or small envelope. *Addict use. Orig. a grain of heroin or an amount of heroin costing $5 or less. Is replacing "deck."* *The usual quantities or sizes of "bags" are: "trey" = $3 worth (esp. cocaine and heroin); "nickel bag" = $5 worth (esp. marijuana, cocaine, or heroin); "dime bag" = $10 worth (esp. marijuana, cocaine, or heroin); "half load" = fifteen $3 "bags" (esp. cocaine and heroin); and "bundle" = twenty-five $5 "bags" (esp. cocaine and heroin). Prices indicate the cost to the addict.* v.i. To pursue one's own pleasure or gratification above all else; to do as one pleases; to indulge in a vice, such as drug addiction; to act amorally. *Mainly Negro use.* v.t. 1. To be absent from; quit. 2. To resign oneself to a loss, failure, etc.; to fail, ruin, lose, or be defeated at or by something. *Student use since c1960.* —ged. *adj.* Drunk. —gies. *n.pl.* A pair of loose-fitting boxer-type men's swimming trunks. *Surfer use.*

baldy; baldie*. *n.* A worn automobile tire having little or no tread left.

bamboo curtain = iron curtain,* as applied to the Chinese People's Republic.

bandit. *n.* Any enemy.

banger. *n.* A cylinder in an automobile engine. *Always preceded by a number. Hot-rod use.*

barber chair. The adjustable seat, equipped with many electronic circuits, breathing apparatus, etc., used by an astronaut in a spacecraft. *Aerospace use.*

barn. *n.* Any summer theater in a rural district, whether an actual barn, an impromptu theater, or a well-equipped legitimate theater.

barry. *n.* A baritone saxophone. *Some musician use; from "baritone."*

basket. *n.* A bribe given to a hiring boss to assure oneself of being hired. *Orig. Italian-American use.*

beach bunny. An attractive girl who may or may not surf, but spends much time with surfers. *Surfer use.*

beads, the. *n.* Fate; destiny.

bear*. *n.* A difficult course. *Some student use.*

beatle. *n.* = beetle. (defs. 1, 2)*.

beatsville. *n.* The state or condition of being beat.

beerbust; beerburst. *n.* A beer party.

belly stand; belly platform = bally stand.

bevels. *n.pl.* A pair of crooked dice with some of the edges beveled to influence the roll.

bi. *n., adj.* Bisexual.

Big*. *adj.* An admiring or affectionate epithet used with proper names in direct address, generally among males. *Widespread student use.*

big bloke = bloke.

big wienie = top dog*. *Some hot-rod and student use.*

binders. *n.pl.* The brakes on an automobile. *Some police, hot-rod, and student use.*

bird*. *n.* 1. Any airplane. 2. A girl friend, steady date, or fiancée. *Orig. Negro use, some student use since c1962.*

birdfarm. *n.* An aircraft carrier. *Navy use in Vietnam war.*

birk. *n.* A stupid or slow-thinking person. *Some teenage use.*

bitch. *n.* 1. A pleasant or remarkable thing or event. *Often used* *as an expression of approval: "That's a bitch!" = "That's fine!"* 2. A male homosexual, esp. one who is viciously gossipy, sarcastic, etc. —ing. *adj.* Excellent; very good; fine.

black money = skim. *Gambling use.*

blackshoe. *n.* Any member of the crew of an aircraft carrier whose duty is concerned with sailing and servicing the carrier; a sailor on an aircraft carrier, rather than a member of the air crew. *Navy use.*

blade*. *n.* A knife considered as a weapon, esp. a "switchblade."* *Orig. Negro and teenage streetgang use.*

blast*. *v.t.* To use or take narcotics. *Addict use.* *v.i.* To accelerate, drive very fast, or pass another car.

bloke*. *n.* Cocaine. *Addict use.*

blood brother. 1. A fellow member of one's racial, religious, national, ethnic, or social group. 2. A fellow Negro. *Negro use only; the most common use since c1962.*

blow*. *n.* An inhalation of heroin or cocaine. *Addict use.* —er. *n.* A supercharger for an automobile engine. *Hot-rod use.* —n. *adj.* (of a car engine) equipped with or using a supercharger. *Hot-rod use.*

blow a fix. To lose part or all of an injected narcotic by missing the vein, the drug being thus diffused in the tissues. *Addict use.*

blow [one's] cool. 1. To lose one's composure; to release pent-up feelings, esp. by shouting, weeping, laughing, etc. 2. To become flustered, esp. in a social situation; to become excited or angry.

blow [one's] mind. 1. To lose one's composure; lose control of oneself; esp. to express strong feelings or emotions or to release pent-up feelings; specif. to scream or shout in joy, anger, fear, etc. 2. To be deeply and emotionally stirred or impressed; to be overwhelmed with feeling; esp. to be overwhelmed by a sin-

cere statement, loving gesture, musical performance, etc. *Jazz, Negro, beat, and student use.*

bluebird. *n.* A policeman. *Some Negro use.*

bluecoat. *n.* A policeman.

bod. *n.* A person; fig., a body. *Orig. Brit. use. Now some U.S. student use.*

Bogners. *n.pl.* A pair of ski pants. *From the trade name "Bogner's," makers of ski clothing.*

bogue*. *adj.* In need of narcotics; suffering from a craving for narcotics. *Addict use.*

boiler room. *n.* = bucket-shop*. *Orig. stock market use.*

bolter. *v.i.* Of an airplane, to miss the arresting cables while attempting to land on an aircraft carrier. *Navy use in Vietnam war.*

bomb*. *n.* Anything that causes or is a sudden success or failure. *Thus a "bomb" may be either a home-run or a strike-out in baseball, and in the entertainment world an instantaneously successful song, play, performance, etc., or one that is a complete failure.* *v.t.* 1. To do something extremely well, as to write a good examination. 2. To do something very poorly; usu., to fail an examination. *Mainly student use.* —ed. *adj.* Drunk. *Common student use.*

bombita. *n.* Any amphetamine pill or capsule used by addicts. *From the Sp. = "little bomb." Addict use.*

bongoed. *adj.* Drunk.

boob*. *n.* A mistake; blunder.

boob tube. A television set.

boonie; booney. *n.* Any remote, unpopulated area; "boondocks." *From boondocks*. Usu. in the expression "the boonies."*

boot*. *v.i., v.t.* To inject a narcotic gradually into a vein, by drawing blood mixed with the drug repeatedly back into the syringe, and discharging the mixture again into the vein, to heighten the drug's initial effect. *Addict use.* *n.* A Negro. *Negro use.* —s. A shoeshine boy.

boss. *n.* Anyone or anything thought to be the most wonderful, exciting, or best in a specific field of endeavor. *adj.* 1. Major; best; best known. *Usu. applied to an entertainer or professional athlete to indicate his superiority in his field.* 2. Excellent, wonderful, fine. *Orig. Negro and jazz musician use; teenage use since c1960.*

bosshead. *n.* The boss, foreman, or head of a project or work detail.

bottle, the*. Prostitution, esp. male prostitution.

bottom-end. *n.* The crankshaft, main bearings, and connecting rod bearings of an automobile engine. *Hot-rod use.*

bottoms. *n.pl.* A pair of shoes; shoes. *Some jazz use; replaced by* "ends."

box*. *n.* An unfeeling, stupid person; a "square."* *Some hipster use since c1960; an extension of* "square." *—ed. adj.* Drunk. *Common student use.*

box office. Having great popular appeal; predictably successful (said of actors, directors, writers, plays, films, etc.). *Theatrical use.*

boy*. *n.* Heroin. *Addict use.*

breastworks. *n.pl.* The female breasts considered as sexual objects.

brew. *n.* Beer; a glass, bottle, or can of beer.

brickyard. *n.* The Indianapolis, Ind., Speedway. *Automobile racing use.*

bright*. *n.* A light-complexioned Negro or a mulatto. *Negro use.*

bringdown; bring down*. *n.* A critical or cutting remark; that which depresses one or deflates one's ego.

bring [someone] down. To depress; sadden. *Common jazz use since c1958, student use since c1960.*

bring up. To vomit; specif. to vomit food or drink that has disagreed with one.

brodie; Brodie*. A flop, complete fiasco, or failure.

brother*. *n.* A male Negro; a "blood brother." *Negro use only.*

brown-bagger. *n.* A married man, esp. a white-collar worker. *Fig., one who carries his lunch to work in a brown paper bag.*

brutal. *adj.* Very good, exceptional, great. *Mainly student use.*

buckwheater. *n.* A beginner, novice, or greenhorn. *Mainly lumberjack use.*

buddy-buddy*. *adj.* Very friendly.

buddy store. A military tanker, refueling ship or plane, or a fuel supply base. *Air Force and Navy use in Vietnam.*

buff*. *adj.* Naked.

bug*. *n.* 1. A joker in a deck of playing cards; any wild card in a poker game. 2. A girl. *Student use.* 3. A small, two-man vehicle designed for exploration of the lunar surface. *Aerospace use.*

bugger*; booger; boogie. *n.* A piece of solidified mucus picked or blown from the nose. *Colloq.*

buggy whip. 1. A long radio antenna on an automobile. 2. A transmitter antenna on a police car.

bughouse*. *adj.* Insane; crazy.

bull horn. An electronic megaphone, loudspeaker, or public-address system, esp. as used aboard a ship to relay orders from officers to enlisted men on or below decks. *Orig. W.W.II Navy use.*

bumper. *n.* The coupling mechanism on a railroad car. *Railroad and hobo use.*

bundle*. *n.* Twenty-five $5 packets of a narcotic, esp. twenty-five "nickel bags" of marijuana or cocaine. *Addict use.*

bunk*. *v.t.* To be absent from, quit, or leave something.

bunny*; bunnie. *n.* 1. Any girl, esp. a pert, attractive one. 2. A girl who may or may not surf, ski, etc. but who associates closely with men who do; esp. a feminine and sexually submissive girl who attaches herself to a particular sport, hobby, field of interest, etc., not only because she finds the men active in it exciting but also in order to express her identity with a group and a way of life which the activity symbolizes. *Used in combinations indicating in the first word the particular activity, as "beach bunny" or "surf bunny" = a girl who spends much time with surfers, "ski bunny" or "snow bunny" = a girl who spends much time with skiers, "jazz bunny" = a girl who spends much time with jazz musicians or enthusiasts, etc.* 3. A lay-up shot in basketball.

burn*. *v.t.* 1. To cook or heat food. 2. To perform well; to act quickly or efficiently. *Negro use.* 3. To borrow; to beg. *Some hipster use.*

burn rubber. To leave; esp. to leave rapidly. *From the image of rubber tires burning from a quick acceleration. Since c1955.*

bush*. *n.* Marijuana; "grass." *Some addict use.*

bust a cap. To take a narcotic, esp. heroin.

butter and egg man* = angel. (def. 2).*

butterhead; butter head. *n.* 1. A Negro who degrades his race, or embarrasses his race or other Negroes. *Negro use only.* 2. Any stupid, rude, or unsophisticated person. *Student use since c1962.*

button*. *n.* 1. A small amount. *Orig. a Mafia word; now common underworld use.* 2. A policeman's badge. *Police use.*

C

cake. *n.* A person. *Used in phrases such as "he's a sad cake," or "she's a wild piece of cake." Some Negro use.*

California tilt. An automobile having its front end lower than its rear end; an automobile whose hood slopes downward toward the front; the style or actual downward slope of such an automobile. *Usually found on cars assembled or modified by their owners. Hot-rod and car-buff use.*

campfire boy. An opium addict. *Reoccurring nonce use.*

camp it up. 1. To behave effeminately; to exhibit obvious effeminate gestures, speech, mannerisms, etc.; to display homosexual characteristics blatantly. 2. To take part in a wild party or similar social gathering, esp. of homosexuals. *Homosexual use since c1945.*

cancer stick. A cigarette. *Some facetious use since c1956.*

candy. *n.* 1. Hashish. *Addict use.* 2. A sugar cube of LSD; LSD. *Habitual users' use. From the earlier use = cocaine.*

canvas back. 1. A hobo. 2. A rural youth newly arrived in the city. *Fig., anyone who carries his possessions in a gunny sack on his back. Reinforced by the image of a migratory duck.*

cap*. *v.t., v.i.* 1. To open or use a capsule of narcotics. 2. To buy narcotics; "cop." *Addict use.* *n.* A capsule of LSD. *From the older addict use = a capsule of heroin. "Caps" vary in size from the large type common in the East to the smaller, more concentrated capsules common on the West Coast, and variously called "West Coast caps," "Tijuana caps," "Mexican caps," "Frisco caps," etc. Habitual users' and student use.*

Castro. *n.* A beard; esp. a full beard. *Some student use since c1960, after the Cuban leader Fidel Castro and his original rebel forces, who grew beards while fighting guerrilla warfare.*

Cat. *n.* A Cadillac car. *Mainly Negro use. From "Caddy."**

catch a rail = take gas. *Surfer use.*

chaff. *n.* Insolent, exaggerated, or senseless talk.

chalk talk. *n.* 1. An informal intellectual discussion, as between a professor and his students. 2. Any lecture or discussion of an analytic nature; specif. a briefing at which a football coach draws chalk diagrams on a blackboard to illustrate individual plays, or a talk, by a mathematician or physicist, illustrated by written formulae on a blackboard. *From the chalk-writing image.*

charge account. 1. Access to bond money needed for posting as bail. 2. Any person or organization that may be called upon to post bail bond. *Some prostitute and Negro use.*

charger. *n.* A driver, esp. of a hot rod. *Some hot-rod use.*

Charley Goon. A policeman. *Some Negro use.*

Charlie*. *n.* 1. The Viet Cong or any Viet Cong soldier; "Victor Charlie," the "V.C." → 2. Any enemy. *Armed Forces use in Vietnam. The abbr. "V.C." was lengthened to the communication phrase "Victor Charlie" and then shortened to "Charlie."* —s. *n.pl.* C-rations. *Army use. From the communications symbol "Charlie"* = C.

Charlie Nebs. A policeman. *Some Negro use.*

chaser. *n.* A prison guard. *Convict use.*

cheaters*. *n.pl.* 1. = falsies*. 2. Any padding worn by a woman to improve her figure, as over the thighs, buttocks, etc.

cheat sheet. A set of written answers used by a student to cheat during an examination; a "pony"* or "crib."*

cheese*. *n.* An attractive girl or young woman. *From "cheesecake."* Some student use.* adj. Traitorous; cowardly; "chicken."* *Some teenage use.*

cher. *adj.* Personable; attractive; knowledgeable about currently popular fashions, tastes, trends, etc. *From the French "cher"* = dear. *Teenage use.*

chi-chi; chichi*. *n.* Anything sexually stimulating; a sexually attractive woman. *From "chisai chichi," a corruption of the Japanese for "little breasts." Some post-W.W.II and more Korean War Armed Forces use.*

chicken switch; chicken button. 1. A switch or button that destroys a malfunctioning rocket in flight. → 2. A switch or button that an astronaut can use to cause his capsule to be ejected from a malfunctioning rocket. → 3. A switch that a pilot can use to cause his seat or his cockpit to be ejected from a jet plane in an emergency. *From chicken** = afraid.

chicklet. *n.* A girl; "chick."*

chili. *adj.* Mexican; Mexican style. *Most commonly in the combinations "chili whore"* = Mexican prostitute, *"chili food"* = Mexican-style food, *"chili boots"* = Mexican-style, high-heeled, hand-tooled boots.

chili-bowl*. A slovenly, dirty person, a stupid or embarrassing person.

chill*. *n.* A beer; a glass, bottle, or can of cold beer. *Some student use.*

chintzy*. *adj.* Stingy, cheap.

chippy*. *v.i., v.t.* To take narcotics only for an occasional thrill or to show that one is "hip."* *Said of nonaddicts, "students,"* and "joy-poppers."* Addict use.*

choi oy. An interjection of disgust, dismay, disappointment, etc. *Army use in Vietnam. From the Vietnamese.*

chop*. *n.* Food. —ped. *adj.* Of a car, having the chassis lowered or the fenders removed or both; of a motorcycle, having the front brake and fender removed, the wheel fork extended forward, and the handlebars raised. *Hot-rod and motorcycle use.* —per. *n.* A "chopped" car or motorcycle. *Hot-rod and motorcycle use.* —s. *n.* 1. Musical ability or technique. *Some jazz use; an extension of "chops"** = the mouth; the lips. → 2. Talent, skill, or technique; esp. a seemingly inborn ability to succeed at some specific type of endeavor. *Orig. theatrical use; became more pop. far-out use c1962.*

schnozz(le) (nose)
(Germ + Yiddish).

klupper (slow person)
landsman (compatriot)
yentz (cheat)
goniff (thief) (steal)

_____

klutz
kvetch

kibitz (H)
kosher (H → y → E)

schlemazel   (written ē bad luck)

schlemiel, schlemihl   (oaf, fool)

schlep (carry ; stupid person)

schlock, schlack, schlag (cheap
        + gaudy [curses]),

schloomp, schlump, schlub
        (a jerk)

schmaltz (corny music).
        [chicken fat].

schmear (bribe)

schmendrick (inept person)

schmoos(e), schmoozl(e)
        (gossip)

schneider (tailor [one
        who cuts])

schnook (dope)

schnorrer (moocher)

Christmas tree*. The control panel in a submarine. *W.W.II Navy use.*

church key. A bottle or can opener, esp. as used to open a container of beer.

chuzpa; chutzpa; hutzpa. *n.* Impudence, gall; impudent talk. *From the Yiddish.*

ciao. *interj.* 1. Good-bye. 2. Hello. *From the It. Very common among students and young adults since c1955.*

citizen. *n.* A person who belongs to a more prosaic, conservative group than one's own; a "square."* *Thus, to a Negro a white may be a "citizen," to a convict an honest man who has never been in jail is a "citizen," etc.*

clam*. *n.* A sour or wrong note. *Jazz use.*

clank. *v.i.* = clank up. —ed. *adj.* Tired; exhausted; depressed or despondent. *Some student use since c1960.*

clank up; clank. To cease to function through fear, anxiety, nervousness, etc. *Some student use.*

clean on. To beat up; to defeat in a fight. *From the colloq. "clean up on."*

click*. *n.* A kilometer. *Armed Forces use.*

close*. *adj.* Very satisfying; wonderful; "far out."* *Some jazz, beat, and student use since c1960, from the jazz use of "close"* (def. 3) of the 1950s.*

clutch*. *n.* An unpleasant, cheap, or despicable person. *v.i.* = clutch up. —ed. *adj.* Nervous; tense. —y. *adj.* 1. Tending to become tense, nervous, anxious, etc. 2. Nerve-wracking; difficult; dangerous.

clutch up. *v.i.* To get nervous; to cease to function through fear, anxiety, nervousness, etc.

clyde. *n.* = square*. (def. 2).

cobbler. *n.* 1. A forger of passports. *Some recent Central Intelligence Agency and underworld use.* → 2. A forger; one who engraves, prints, or distributes counter-feit money, bonds, etc. *Underworld use.*

cockamainie; cockamamie. *adj.* Absurd, quixotic, crazy, unusual.

Company, the. *n.* The Central Intelligence Agency, the Federal Bureau of Investigation, or a metropolitan police force. *Orig. Central Intelligence Agency use; now some underworld use. May have orig. from the abbreviation CIA = Central Intelligence Agency, which abbreviation stands for "Company" ("Compañía") in Sp.*

coño. *interj.* = damn, hell. *From the Sp.*

contract. *n.* An assignment, order, or obligation; esp. a major or dangerous job, as the paid killing of another. *Underworld use.*

cook*. *v.t.* To dissolve a narcotic in water over a flame before injecting it. *Addict use.* —er. *n.* A small container, as a bottle top, used for heating and dissolving a drug with water prior to injection. *Addict use.*

cool*. *n.* A state of mind characterized by detachment, disdain for emotional involvement, and a distant and reserved rather than enthusiastic attitude toward persons and ideas: composure. *This noun use was the last use of the word "cool" by the cool groups that flourished in the mid-1950s, the mood and groups dissolving c1965.* *v.t.* To ignore; to be aloof from, unconcerned with, or disdainful of a person, idea, belief, statement, etc. *v.i.* To die.

coonjin; coongin; *v.t.* To work, think, or try hard at anything; to be forced or tricked into working or making a profit for another. *The image of hard work is due to the weight of a cotton bale: 500 pounds. Some Southern Negro use.*

cop*. *v.i., v.t.* To obtain or buy narcotics. *Addict use.*

cop out*. 1. To renege or withdraw from involvement in some action, plan, task, etc.; to cease to be actively engaged in an endeavor; to evade a question or an issue; to break a promise. 2. To compromise or abandon one's ideals, principles, etc.

corazon. *n.* Courage; manliness. *From the Sp. = heart, often in the phrase "puro corazon" = all heart. Teenage street-gang use, pop. by Puerto Rican youth.*

corn-pone. *adj.* Southern; esp. with a Southern accent or attitudes.

cotton. *n.* 1. Amphetamine in any form; specif. cotton saturated with Benzedrine and inhaled by an addict. 2. Anything saturated with a drug that can be inhaled. *Addict use.*

cotton curtain. The South; "Dixie."* *Formed by humorous analogy with "iron curtain."* Some Negro and jazz use.*

cotton freak. A drug addict who inhales his drug. *Orig. one who inhaled Benzedrine from a piece of cotton saturated with it. Addict use.*

cowabunga! *interj.* An exhortative or victorious cry used by surfers while riding waves. *Surfers use.*

cowboy*. *n.* A reckless driver.

cow peeler. A cowboy. *Some Western use since c1880.*

crack*. *v.t.* To open, as with a bottle opener or can opener.

crack on [something or someone]. To prove something or convince someone of; to present facts, arguments, or evidence to support one's idea, belief, or statement. *Some Negro and jazz use.*

crash*. *v.i.* To pass out drunk. *Student use.* —ed. *adj.* Drunk.

cream*. *v.t.* To beat up, severely injure, or kill.

creeps, the*. *n.* The feeling of discomfort, esp. itching, caused by low pressure, as in a submarine or in a space capsule.

crib*. *n.* A room, apartment, or other living quarters; a "pad."* *"Crib" is replacing "pad"* in Negro, jazz, beat and student use. The connotation is that of a small, cramped room ("crib,"*

def. 3) rather than a baby's bed. Obs. since it was underworld use c1890, this is a prime example of a word becoming pop. with one subgroup long after it has become obs. with another.

Crow Jim. Strong antiwhite prejudice among Negroes. *A reverse form of Jim Crow* (def. 2). Orig. Negro jazz musician use.*

cruise. *v.i., v.t.* 1. To walk, drive a car, ride a motorcycle, etc., slowly through a particular area in order to survey the general activity, social prospects, etc., esp. in search of a sex partner; to move about in a place, usually a crowded or public place, party, etc., in search of a sex partner; to look for a "pick-up." 2. To make a subtle, tentative, usually unspoken sexual approach to someone.

cube*. *n.* A sugar cube containing LSD. *Habitual users' and student use.*

curse, the. *n.* Menstruation; the days of a period during which a woman menstruates.

curve killer. A superior student; one who gets very high grades. *Student use, deriving from the practice of grading "on the curve."*

cut*. *v.t.* To share; to live in, pay for, share the responsibility of, etc., with another or others. *n.* A phonograph recording or a recording session.

D

D. A dollar.

daddy*. *n.* The most respected performer in a field; a person whose work or personality is so unique and successful that others seek to imitate him.

dash. *n.* The dashboard of an automobile. *Colloq.*

deadhead*. *adj.* Empty or unused, as a truck, train, or cargo ship, factory or warehouse, a telephone or telegraph line, a radio frequency or television channel, etc.

deadneck. *n.* A stupid person; a "jerk."* *Fig.*, one who is "dead" from the neck up.

deck*. *n.* Three grains of heroin; an amount of heroin worth $5 or more. *Addict use.*

deuce*. *n.* A powerful or good-looking hot rod, specif. a 1932 Ford. *Hot-rod use since c1940.*

deuce it. 1. To come second in order; esp., in vaudeville, to work as the second act on the bill, usu. assigned to one of the least known or least interesting acts. 2. To do something as a two-some; to become engaged; to date a member of the opposite sex.

diddly. *adj.* Worthless, silly, medi-ocre, insignificant. *Some student use.*

diddlybop. *v.i.* 1. To waste time; pass the time in idle chatter. → 2. To do anything pleasant, en-tertaining, or exciting. *n.* A diver-sion; any social gathering, enter-tainment, etc., whether to pass the time idly or to enjoy one-self doing something exciting. *Some student use.*

dime. *n.* A ten-year prison sen-tence. *Some underworld use.*

dime bag. Ten dollars' worth of a drug, as a half-ounce of mari-juana. *Addict and student use.*

dinch. *v.t.* To extinguish a ciga-rette.

dingy-dingy. *adj.* Crazy; "nuts."* *Armed Forces use in Korea.*

dip*. *n.* A slovenly or untidy per-son. *Some teenage use.*

dirty dozens. Long, jivelike, usual-ly rhyming phrases in response and answer, usually disparaging, obscene, etc. *Negro and teenage street-gang use.*

disappear. *v.i.* To be murdered, esp. in such a way that no trace of the crime or the body is found. *Underworld use.*

dish. *v.i.* To gossip; chat.

dispatchers. *n.pl.* A pair of dice that are loaded or in some other way crooked.

ditty bop; ditty bob. *n.* A stupid,

crude, or unsophisticated Negro; a "butterhead." *Negro use only.*

DMT. Dimethyltryptamine, a hal-lucinogen similar to LSD but having an effect usually lasting less than an hour.

dodge. *n.* An illegal or unethical way of earning a living; racket; profession or calling.

dog*. *n.* The academic grade D. *Some student use.*

dog collar*. A collar having the opening at the back, as worn by priests.

doghouse*. *n.* A bulge or rounded extension on the surface of a rocket or missile for containing scientific instruments. *Aerospace use.*

dolce vita; Dolce Vita. 1. A dec-adent way of life. → 2. An easy, sophisticated, fun-filled life; a way of life characterized by wealth, leisure, a sophisticated social milieu, exciting amuse-ments and parties, etc.; sophisti-cated enjoyment and excitement. → 3. Wealthy, sophisticated, and exciting. *From the Italian (lit., "sweet life"); orig. from the title and subject of Federico Fellini's film "La Dolce Vita."*

dolly. *n.* = doll*. (defs. 1, 2).

donar; donah. *n.* A girl, esp. one's steady girl or fiancée, or a girl attached to a teenage street gang. *Prob. from the It. "donna" = lady. In Brit. Cockney use since c1900 and in U.S. street-gang use since c1955.*

donkey roast. A large, elaborate, festive, or noisy party, celebra-tion, etc.

doo. *n.* = do-dad*.

doolie. *n.* A first-year cadet at the U.S. Air Force Academy. *Air Force use.*

doublet. *n.* Any fake or imitation item sold as genuine; specif., glass sold as a precious stone. *Orig. glass with a thin layer of dia-mond pasted on top so it would pass the scratch test.*

doublet stone = doublet.

dove*. *n.* A person who advocates peace or a nonbelligerent national policy. *The most recent use refers to a person advocating negotiating in Vietnam, withdrawing U.S. troops, or keeping the Vietnam war to the smallest possible scale. The dove of peace is a common metaphor and art symbol. Colloq.*

down*. *adj.* 1. Sympathetic and "hip;"* "cool"* and understanding; in rapport with oneself. 2. Excellent; appealing to or satisfying one's deeper emotions. 3. Ready, prepared; spontaneous or uninhibited. *Mainly Negro and teenage use.*

down home. 1. The South; "Dixie"*; Southern. *Some Negro use, often sarcastic.* → 2. Southern racial prejudice; white Southern traditions and culture. *Some Negro use.* 3. Resembling or approximating the early New Orleans style of jazz.

DPT. Dipropylphyptamine, a hallucinogen similar to LSD but having an effect lasting only for an hour or two and considered somewhat safer.

drag*. *n.* Transvestite clothing. *adj.* Of, pertaining to, or wearing transvestite clothing, esp. female dress, jewelry, and cosmetics as worn by transvestite male homosexuals. *Used either in combination, as in "drag-queen," or as a modifier, as in "drag party." v.i.* To dress as a transvestite. *Orig. homosexual use. Now commonly known.*

drag party. A party given by and for transvestites, almost always male homosexuals, who may attend in the dress of the opposite sex; any party for homosexuals.

drag-queen. 1. A male homosexual who frequently dresses or is esp. fond of dressing as a woman. 2. A male homosexual who blatantly affects female gestures, speech patterns, etc.

driver. *n.* An airplane pilot. *Navy and Air Force use, esp. in the Vietnam war.*

drug. *v.t.* To depress, bother, or bore: "bug,"* "drag"*; to make [someone] unhappy. *n.* = drag.* (def. 7).

drum. *n.* Eardrum.

dubok. *n.* An ostensibly respectable person or place of business used to transact illegal business or to hide stolen goods or contraband; a "drop."* *A cold-war word taken from the Russian = oak tree, first used by the Central Intelligence Agency and now spreading to the underworld.*

duke*. *v.i.* 1. To fight with the fist. *Orig. Negro use; then teenage gang use.* 2. To be involved in any kind of action, to argue, to "party,"* etc. *Negro use.*

dullsville. *n.* Fig., the place from which all dull things emanate; the epitome of dullness. *Thus: "This party is dullsville"* or *"This party is from dullsville"* = "This party is very dull." *Cool use. adj.* Dullest; most "square."*

dump*. *v.t.* To kill.

dynamite*. *n.* Heroin of good quality. *Addict use.*

dypso. *n.* A dipsomaniac; an alcoholic.

E

eagle*. *n.* The academic grade E. *Some student use.*

ease on; ease out. To leave; to depart. *Some student use.*

egads button; egads switch = chicken switch.

eggbeater*. *n.* An outboard motor.

eighty-six*. *v.t.* Lit. and fig., to reject or disqualify a person; to ignore, insult, or tease someone; to eject someone from a place or group, esp. from a bar, against his will.

elephant ears. Large, thick metal discs added to a missile's outer shell to reinforce it, to distribute the heat caused by friction in flight, and to stabilize the flight orbit. *Aerospace use.*

ends. *n.pl.* A pair of shoes; shoes. *Jazz musician use.*

endsville. *n.* = the end;* the most*. *adj.* Fine, most exciting, most satisfying. *Orig. cool and* *beat use. Has replaced the earlier "endville."*

evergreen. *n.* An old favorite, such as a song.

evil*. *adj.* Spiteful, gossipy, sarcastic, "bitchy."* *Orig. homosexual use.*

exhibeseh. *n.* = exhibición.

exhibición. *n.* A lewd performance of sexual acts, presented before an audience, involving either live actors or a film. *From the Sp. = exhibition.*

F

fab. *adj.* Very thrilling or satisfying; excellent, great, wonderful. *From "fabulous." Common student and teenage use since c1963.*

face*. *n.* 1. A celebrity; a well-known person. *Orig. show-business use.* 2. A person. *Some hipster and student use.*

fack. *v.i.* To tell the truth; to speak facts. *Negro use.*

fade*. *n.* 1. A white person. 2. A Negro who prefers white sexual partners, white friends, or white attitudes. *Negro use only.*

fake off. To idle or shirk; "goof off."*

fake [someone] out. To bluff or deceive; to mislead intentionally.

fall in (up, by, out) = fall down.*

fall off the roof. To begin a menstrual period. *Common since c1925.*

fall out*. To go to sleep.

fanny-dipper. An ordinary swimmer, as opposed to a surfer. *Surfing use.*

farmisht. *adj.* Lit. and fig., mixed up; in a state of conflicting emotions; emotionally ambiguous. *From the Yiddish.*

fat city. An excellent condition, state, or mood. *Student and teenage use.*

feel a draft. 1. To sense a feeling of racial prejudice against oneself. *Negro use; orig. pop. by jazz musician Lester Young.* 2. To sense a lack of welcome or a feeling of dislike or rejection eman-

ating from another. *Both uses from the image of "cold."*

fink out. 1. To withdraw from or refuse to support a project, activity, scheme, etc. 2. To become untrustworthy.

fish*. *n.* A heterosexual woman. *Lesbian use.*

five pointer. 1. A superior student. 2. A high grade received on a test or for an academic course. *From the five-pointed gold star assoc. with excellence, formerly pasted by teachers on superior papers and report cards, reinforced by stand. and slang "star." Student use.*

flack out. 1. To fall asleep; to become unconscious, as from drunkenness or from lack of oxygen in an airplane or while scuba or skin diving, etc. 2. To be tired or despondent. 3. To die. *Orig. cool and beat use.*

flag*. *v.i., v.t.* To fail an examination or course. *Some college student use.*

flag it. To flunk an examination or course in school. *Some college student use.*

flake. *adj.* Uninhibited, imaginative; having a colorful, highly individual personality. *Orig. and mainly baseball use.* *n.* A colorful, highly individual personality or style; a "screwball"* or eccentric personality or style. —y; *flaky. adj.* Colorful; eccentric.

flake off. Go away; "beat it."* *Student and teenage use.*

flake out*. 1. To leave; to depart. *Jazz musician use.* 2. To fail. 3. A complete failure; flop.

flash*. *adj.* Excellent, wonderful, great. *Some teenage use. Orig. from the Brit. sl. meaning. v.i.* To vomit. *Some student use. n.* 1. The sensation experienced by a person soon after heroin has been injected into a mainline blood vessel. *Addict use.* 2. A thrill, a feeling of excitement or pleasure; "buzz."* *Some cool and student use.*

flash rider. A professional bronco-buster; one who breaks and trains wild horses. *Orig. c1870 cowboy use.*

flathead*. *n.* An L-head or side-valve engine. *Hot-rod use.*

flat-out. *adj.* Complete, utter, total.

flats*. *n.pl.* A pair of crooked dice having flat, beveled edges; crooked dice. *Some gambler use.*

flavor. *n.* A sexually attractive woman. *Some Negro use.*

flight. *n.* = trip. *LSD users' and student use.*

flit. *n.* A male homosexual; a male exhibiting female mannerisms. **—ty.** *adj.* Homosexual; effeminate. *Considered less derog. than "queer"* because the connotation is more often of effeminate mannerisms than of sexual acts.*

floss. *n.* Spun sugar; cotton candy. *Carnival and circus use.*

fluff*. *v.t.* To criticize severely or harshly. *Some jazz use.*

flush*. *v.t.* To ignore, reject, or dismiss someone, usually socially. *v.i.* To flunk an examination or course in school. *Student use.*

flush it. To flunk an examination or course in school. *Common student use.*

Foggy Bottom. The U.S. State Department. *In ref. to the main State Department offices, located near the Potomac River on a section of land called "Foggy Bottom," the imagery being humorously transferred to the State Department.*

forked-eight. A V8 engine or a car having such an engine; a "bent eight."* *Hot-rod use.*

forwards. *n.pl.* Pills containing amphetamine or its derivatives. *Addict use.*

four pointer. 1. A grade of A on an examination or for a course of study. → 2. A superior student. *Because in many colleges and universities a grade of A is worth four points toward graduation. Student use.*

fox. *n.* An energetic, attractive, desirable girl, esp. one having a happy and alert personality. *Orig. Negro use. Pop. into white*

use during 1963 by heavyweight boxer Cassius Clay.

frat*. *n.* A male student who accepts middle-class norms of conduct and dress; a typical "square"* student. *Student and teenage use.*

friendly. *n.* A member, ship, airplane, etc., of one's own or an ally's armed forces; villagers or guerrillas friendly to one's own side during a war. *Some W.W.II and Korean War Armed Forces use; very common Armed Forces use in Vietnam.*

fringes. *n.pl.* Fringe benefits; any benefits or remunerations, other than salary, granted to employees, such as bonuses, paid vacations, paid holidays, pensions, employer-paid insurance and medical plans, etc. *Labor union use since c1960.*

frit. *n.* A homosexual.

frog*. *n.* 1. An unpleasant, cheap, or despicable person. 2. An introverted, boring, or old-fashioned person; a "drip"* or "square."* *Student and teenage use.*

front-end. *adj.* On or pertaining to that portion of a midway which is near the main entrance. *Carnival and circus use.*

fun and games. 1. A good time, as a party; a pleasant experience. → 2. Necking, foreplay, or sexual intercourse. 3. A difficult, annoying, or embarrassing task. *Used facetiously.*

funk. *v.i.* 1. To fail, esp. to fail an examination; "flunk."* 2. To be thrown into a panic. *Orig. Brit. use.* *n.* A style of jazz reflecting elements of Negro culture, such as spirituals, African rhythms, etc. *In vogue with some Negro jazz musicians since c1957, partly in order to maintain something that white musicians had not appropriated.* **—iness.** *n.* The melancholy, pensive, or bittersweet mood associated with the blues. **—y.** *adj.* 1. Old-fashioned; *specif.,* playing jazz in its older New Orleans style, emphasizing rhythm and uncomplicated breaks. *Orig. Negro use.* 2. Sad or depressing, as jazz music played slowly, in a low register, or in a minor key; melancholy, pensive, or bittersweet, like the mood produced by the blues. *Jazz and Negro use.* 3. Emotional; without restraint, form, or goal. 4. Inferior or obnoxious, said of a person, performance, or manufactured object. *Mainly Negro use.*

funsie; funsey. *n.* Any task that is difficult, requires special effort, or that leaves one exhausted. *Teenage and student ironic use.*

G

gaff*. *v.t.* To cheat someone; spec., to short-change a customer and pocket the money, or to withhold for oneself money from the sale of a ticket of admission that should be put in the cashbox. *Orig. and mainly carnival use.*

gaffer. *n.* One's father.

gago. *n.* A non-Gypsy. *Gypsy use.*

gangster*. *n.* A marijuana cigarette. *Addict use.*

garbage down. To eat; "chow down."* *Orig. W.W.II Navy use; now Navy and some student use.*

gavar. *n.* The art or technique of picking pockets. *Gypsy use.*

G.B.; g.b. = goof ball*. (def. 1). *Addict use.*

gear. *adj.* Excellent, wonderful, great. *Popular teenage use since c1960.* *n.* Something spectacular, exciting, or entertaining. *Teenage use.*

george* *v.t.* To lure or invite into sexual activity.

geronimo! *interj.* Used to express surprise, pleasure, or triumphant achievement. *From the cry used by W.W.II paratroopers upon jumping (after the name of the Indian chief). Since c1945 it has replaced "eureka!" among students and young people.*

get [one's] back up. To become angry; to sulk.

get [one's] jollies = get [one's] kicks.

get [one's] kicks. To do that which is personally satisfying, amusing, or thrilling; to indulge in one's preferred vice, form of entertainment, habit, or relaxation.

get off. 1. To obtain relief or pleasure by obtaining or injecting a dose of narcotics. *Addict use.* 2. To drop formally out of a college or university but to remain on campus or in the vicinity taking advantage of some aspects of the academic community. *Student use.*

Gibson Girl. A hand-cranked emergency radio transmitter. *Orig. and mainly W.W.II Armed Forces use.*

gidget*. *n.* A pert, attractive young woman.

gig*. *n.* Any job, as in an office, factory, etc., esp. a dull, menial, or temporary job while awaiting more exciting or satisfying work. *Orig. jazz musician use; cool, beat, and student use since c1960.*

gin. *n.* A street fight or "rumble."* *Some Negro and teenage gang use.*

ginger-peachy. *adj.* Fine and admirable in a conventional or sentimental way; "peachy-keen."* *Often used ironically, as criticism, in order to show the speaker's sophisticated superiority to the person, object, or idea referred to. One of several arch. terms thus use.*

gink*. *n.* A dull, ineffectual, or insignificant person; a "jerk."*

girl*. *n.* 1. A male homosexual. *Homosexual use.* 2. Cocaine. *Addict use.*

glazed. *adj.* Drunk. *Orig. jazz use; now student use.*

glitch. *n.* Any mechanical defect, malfunction, problem, or emergency. *Orig. aerospace use.*

go*. *adj.* 1. Favorable; O.K.; ready to begin. *From use by the orig. seven U.S. astronauts to signify that a spacecraft was functioning properly and ready to be launched. Has replaced "A-OK."* 2. = swinging.*

go ape. 1. To lose emotional or mental control; to behave irrationally. 2. To exhibit enthusiasm; to become excited, frenzied or wild. *Common student use.*

google-eye. *n.* = redeye*. (def. 2).

gold. *n.* money. *Some jazz and student use.* —**en.** *adj.* 1. Easy to accomplish, excel at, or make a high grade in. *Student use.* 2. Lucky; having good luck, talent, easy tasks or assignments; sure of success; certain to obtain fame, wealth, a high rank, or a desired goal. 3. Fine; superb; excellent.

goma. *n.* Crude opium. *Addict use.*

gomer; gomar. *n.* A first-year or naive Air Force Cadet. *Air Force use.*

gonif*. *n.* A homosexual.

Go-No Go; Go-No-Go. Pertaining to that moment in a missile launching when the operation must either be canceled or allowed to continue toward completion without the possibility of cancellation. *Aerospace use.*

gook*. *adj.* Cheap, flashy, inferior. —**y.** *adj.* Sticky, messy, or greasy.

Gooney Bird. The DC-3 airplane; "the three." *Airplane pilots' use.*

goopus. *n.* A stupid, undesirable person; a "square,"* a "goof."* *Some adolescent and teenage use.*

go to bed with = sleep with.*

go up*. To become high on narcotics; be under the influence of a drug. *Addict and student use.*

grab*. *v.t.* To cause a strong emotional response in; to interest, startle; to obsess. —**ber.** *n.* Any extremely interesting, provocative, or startling comment, person, piece of news, book, movie, play, or performance; that which interests, stirs, or obsesses someone.

grass*. *n.* Marijuana. *Hipster and student use since c1960. Replacing "pot"* as the most common sl. word for "marijuana."*

grayhound. *v.i.* To run, esp. in escape or pursuit.

greatsie; greatsy = ginger-peachy.

green, the. *n.* The unbroken forward part of a wave. *Surfer use.*

gremlin. *n.* 1. A beginner or person past the beginning stage, but not yet of expert caliber. 2. A person (usu. a girl) who hangs out with surfers but does not surf; a "beach bunny." 3. Any annoying troublemaker, parasite, or hanger-on. *An extension of the orig. use in the Armed Forces during W.W.II, from the Air Force use = an invisible imp who caused malfunctions, problems, or confusion. Pop. c1950s through surfer use; now common, esp. in student and Armed Forces use.*

gremmie. *n.* = gremlin. *Mainly student and Armed Forces use.*

grinder*. *n.* A parade ground or drill field. *Marine Corps use.*

gripe [one's] back, *etc.* To annoy one greatly. *The expression always concludes with ref. to a real or imaginary part of the body, as if the annoyance caused physical pain. Taboo parts of the body are most commonly named, then those parts most easily hurt, as the extremities. Expressions containing taboo parts of the body are taboo.*

grit. *v.i.* To eat. *n.* Food. *Some Negro use.*

groaty; grotty. *adj.* Slovenly; ugly. *Teenage use.* From "grotesque."

groove*. *n.* 1. Any habit, preference, or habitually exciting or satisfying activity; one's "kick"* or "bag." 2. Anything that is considered exciting, satisfying, fashionable, or "hip."*

grunge; grunch. *n.* A dull or boring person. *adj.* 1. Very ugly or slovenly. 2. Dull or boring. *Mainly teenage use.*

grunt*. *v.i.* To defecate. *Used euphem. by adults in speaking to small children; also some adult use.* *n.* An Army infantryman, soldier. *Orig. Marine Corps use in Vietnam.*

guilty big. Undergoing or in need of psychiatric treatment.

gun*. *n.* A long, heavy surfboard *Surfer use.*

gung-ho. *adj.* 1. Innocently and uncritically enthusiastic, optimistic, patriotic, zealous, devoted, or eager; childishly believing; having unrestrained enthusiasm; fanatic. 2. Lacking sophistication; appealing to noncritical judgment; emotional. *Orig. W.W.II use, from the Chinese "keng ho" = awe-inspiring (lit. "more fiery"). Now almost always used with a connotation of disapprobation which it did not orig. carry in W.W.II.*

guru. *n.* A psychiatrist. *From Sanskrit = venerable one, via India, spiritual leader or teacher. Orig. humorous use.*

gutty*. *adj.* 1. Eliciting an emotional response; strongly evocative or emotional. 2. Essential; basic; appealing to or arising from a basic emotion, feeling, motivation, etc. 3. Powerful; capable of great force or high speed; having a powerful engine. *Automotive and hot-rod use.*

gypsy. *n.* 1. A taxicab operating without a taxi license. 2. A trucker who owns and drives his own truck and obtains freight wherever possible.

H

hack around. To do nothing in particular; to wander about; to idle. *Student and teenage use.*

hacked. *adj.* Annoyed. *Some jazz use.*

hairy*. *adj.* Difficult to cope with; dangerous, treacherous, tortuous; difficult; exciting; challenging. *Said of an assignment, task, situation, etc.; of a place, such as a battlefield, racetrack, etc.: of people; and of objects.*

half load. Fifteen $3 packets, or "bags," of a narcotic, esp. cocaine or heroin. *Addict use.*

hame. *n.* An unpleasant job, esp. a menial task or a job in which one cannot make the best use of one's talent; "gig." *Jazz use.*

hang up*; hang-up. *n.* 1. A mental block; a psychological disturbance or problem. 2. The cause of a psychological disturbance; that which one is obsessed by or extremely emotional about; a special enthusiasm or interest; that person, thing, idea, etc., on which a person is "hung up." 3. An annoyance, bother, hindrance, encumbrance; anything that or anyone who is burdensome, annoying, bothersome, or irritating.

hard-hat. A full-time Viet Cong soldier, as opposed to a guerrilla or reservist. *Armed forces use in Vietnam.*

hash*. *n.* 1. Hashish. *Addict and student use.* → 2. Marijuana or any other narcotic. *Some addict and beat use since c1960.* *adj.* Wonderful; "cool"*; "swinging." *Beat use since c1963.*

hauler. *n.* A very fast car, esp. a hot rod. *Hot-rod use.*

have a thing about. To be obsessed with; to have a strong liking or dislike for; to be devoted to or hate.

hawk*. *n.* A person who advocates a war or a belligerent national policy. *Orig. from John C. Calhoun's "War Hawks" political party of 1812, revived in modern use during the Cuban missile crisis of 1961 and common in ref. to those seeking escalation of the Vietnam war. Colloq.*

head*. *n.* 1. A ship's toilet or bathroom. *From "bulkhead." Orig. maritime use. Colloq.* → 2. Any toilet or bathroom. *Common since W.W.II.* 3. A narcotics addict or habitual user of a nonaddictive drug. *Also used in combinations with specific drugs, as "acid head."*

heavy*. *adj.* Crooked, illegal. *n.* A large wave, esp. one excellent for surfing. *Surfer use.*

heel. *v.t.* To serve as an apprentice, esp. said of a student serving as an apprentice in a campus activity, such as on the student newspaper; to work at a campus job in return for free room and board in a dormitory or for part of one's tuition. *The object of the* *v.t.* is always the occupation or place of work; thus a student "heels the newspaper," "heels the campus cafeteria," etc. *n.* An apprentice worker; often a student or a worker who does menial jobs.

hen*. *n.* A young woman; a "chick."*

high-hat*. *n.* = sock. *Some musician use.*

Hill, the. 1. Capitol Hill in Washington, D.C.; site of the U.S. Capitol, where Congress meets. → 2. Congress, or its acts, rules, and opinions. *Colloq.*

hit*. *v.t.* 1. To deal a card to a player, esp. an extra card which the player requests, as in draw poker. 2. To serve a drink to someone, usu. an alcoholic drink; esp. to serve someone a second portion, to refill someone's glass. 3. To beg or borrow from. 4. To murder. *Underworld use.* *n.* A premeditated murder; a planned murder. *Underworld use.*

hitch*. *v.i.*, *v.t.* = hitch-hike*. *n.* A ride, usually as a result of hitch-hiking, but not necessarily.

hit on. To try to sell someone something, often a useless, defective, or overpriced item; to annoy by soliciting, arguing, flirting, etc.; to attempt to force one's attention, ideas, or merchandise on another; to pester.

hit the bricks. To walk out of a plant, factory, etc., on strike.

hit the panic button = push the panic button.

Hoagy. *n.* = Hero*.

hocky*; hooky; hookey. Any unappetizing food; food having an unappetizing appearance.

ho-dad; hodad; ho dad; ho-daddy. *n.* 1. A boastful but amateurish person; a wise guy; an objectionable, unpopular person who pretends to be "hip,"* knowledgeable, or expert. 2. A person not active in a sport, hobby, field of interest, etc., who spends much time with those who are active, enjoying a false feeling of excitement and belonging. 3. A person

who gets no fun from life, esp. a dedicated white-collar worker; a stuffy "square."* *Orig. surfer use; now common sports and student use.*

hog*. *n.* 1. A locomotive engineer. *Some railroad use. A shortened form of "hog-head,"* from "hog"* = a locomotive.* 2. A Harley-Davidson motorcycle. *Motorcycle use.* 3. A large car, esp. a Cadillac.

hog, on the. Without money, broke. *Some hobo use.*

hold*. *v.i.* To have narcotics in one's possession. *Addict use.*

home plate. The airfield, landing strip, or aircraft carrier on which an airplane or crew is based and to which the plane returns after successful flights. *Mainly Air Force use, since c1960.*

honcho. *n.* The boss; the man in charge of any work or detail; a leader or organizer. *v.t.* To boss, lead, or organize. *Orig. Armed Forces use in Korea; now common Armed Forces use.*

hooch*. *n.* 1. A Korean house, room, or esp. a shack, inhabited by a prostitute. *Armed Forces use in Korea.* 2. A typical Vietnamese village hut of woven straw, branches, leaves, corrugated tin, etc. *Armed Forces use in Vietnam.* → 3. An American barracks, esp. a quonset-style barracks in South Vietnam. *Armed Forces use in Vietnam. From the Japanese "uchi" = a house.*

hook*. *v.t.* To grab, find, or locate.

hopsan. *n.* A taxi. *Armed forces use in Korea.*

horses. *n.pl.* A pair of dishonest or loaded dice; specif. mismatched dice that can produce only specific combinations.

hospital. *n.* A jail. *Central Intelligence Agency use; some recent underworld use.*

hot dogger. *n.* A skilled surfer, esp. one who performs stunts or tricks while surfing. *Surfer use.*

hot shot*. *n.* A narcotic injection that is fatal because of an impurity in it or because poison has been added to it. *Addict use.*

hot walker. A groom who walks a racehorse to cool it down after a race or workout. *Horserace use.*

Hound, the. A Greyhound bus. *Orig. trucker use; now some motorcycle, jazz, Negro, and student use.*

hound dog. A man who thinks of little else but sex; a womanchaser. *Southern hill use, but pop. by rock-and-roll singers, esp. Elvis Presley in his pop. song "Hound Dog," c1958.*

hubba-hubba; huba-huba. *adv.* Quickly; on the double. *Some Armed Forces use since W.W.II.*

Huey. *n.* The helicopter, Utility, Model 1-B. *Army and Air Force use, esp. in Vietnam.*

huffer. *n.* A supercharger for an automobile; "blower." *Some hotrod use.*

hummy. *adj.* Content; happy; esp. content or happy because one is innocent and not aware of danger, expense, or possible disappointment. *adv.* Happily, contentedly; with innocent expectation. *Negro use.*

hump*. *n.* A worthless or insignificant person.

hung*. *adj.* 1. Annoyed; peeved. 2. Tired; exhausted. *Some jazz use.* 3. = hung over*.

hung up (on)*. Obsessed (with); frustrated or stymied by; unable to live, act, think or function normally (because of); esp. extremely emotional about, fond of, or devoted to.

hurt. *v.i.* To be in dire straits of one sort or another; to be in trouble. *v.t.* To kill; to wound seriously or beat up badly. *Teenage street-gang use.*

hutzpa. *n.* = chuzpa.

I

ice*. *v.i.* To become or remain silent. *v.t.* 1. To ignore or pay no attention to. 2. To kill. *Underworld use. adj.* Good; very fine;

great. *Prob. from "cool"** *(def. 4)* = *satisfying.*

idiot board. A cue card; a large card held up out of the range of a television camera to prompt performing actors. *Television use c1945–1960.*

idiot box. A television set.

idiot girl. A girl who works in a television studio and holds cue cards for the performers. *Television use c1945–1960.*

ill. *adj.* Arrested on suspicion or for questioning; jailed. *Underworld and Central Intelligence Agency use.*

in front. In advance; paid or requiring payment in advance. *Orig. underworld and theatrical use.*

in orbit = way-out*. *(def. 3). Mainly teenage use.*

J

jack around. To waste time; to fool around; to engage in horseplay. *Some student use.*

jag house. A brothel of male prostitutes catering to male homosexuals.

jam*. *adj.* Heterosexual. *Homosexual use.*

jank. *v.i.* To change altitude and direction simultaneously so as to avoid anti-aircraft fire. *Air Force use, orig. in Vietnam.*

jazz*. *n.* 1. Lit. and fig., ornamentation; trimmings; anything added to improve the appearance of something. 2. The usual, expected argument, story idea, plan, etc.; routine insincerity; middle-class mendacity. *Esp. in the expression "and all that jazz," which is used to* = "et cetera."

J.B. = Stetson*. *Some railroad and hobo use.*

Jersey green. A type of marijuana. *Addict and student use.*

jink. *v.i.* To dodge enemy planes, anti-aircraft fire, etc., by following a zigzag course. *Air Force use, orig. in Vietnam.*

jock*. *n.* 1. An athletic supporter; a jockstrap. 2. An athlete, esp. a college athlete. *Common student* use. From "jockstrap" and the slang "jockstrap."

jockstrap. *v.i.* To travel widely and make a meager living in the lower brackets of the sporting world; esp. to make one's living in small towns as a prize fighter or wrestler.

Jodie; jodie. *n.* A civilian male; one who has been rejected by or deferred from the draft. *W.W.II Army use.*

Joe Storch = Joe Zilch*.

Johnny Reb = Rebel.

Johnny Trots = trots*. (diarrhea).

jollies. *n.pl.* Thrills or excitement; "kicks."*

josan. *n.* A girl friend. *Armed Forces use in Korea.*

jug*. *n.* A carburetor. *Some hotrod use.* —**s.** *n.pl.* The female breasts considered as sexual objects.

juice*. *n.* = pop. *v.t.* To excite, encourage, inspire; to enliven; to increase one's confidence in.

juice dealer. An underworld usurer; a racketeer who loans money at exorbitant interest to gamblers who have lost; an underworld boss who loans money at illegally high rates of interest to gamblers, gambling casinos, bookies, etc., so that they can pay winners or expand their businesses.

juicehead. *n.* A heavy drinker.

juice man. An underworld money and loan collector; specif. a hoodlum employed to collect a gambling debt or loan by intimidation or to beat up or kill one who does not pay.

jumping. *adj.* Of a place, gathering, etc., pulsating with excitement and activity. *Orig. jive use.*

junked up = hopped up*.

K

katusa. *n.* **1.** A Korean soldier attached to the U.S. Army. *An acronym for "Korean attached to U.S. Army."* **2.** Any South Korean soldier. *Armed Forces use in Korea.*

key. *n.* A typical Ivy League student; one who assumes the dress, manners, attitudes, etc., associated with the typical Ivy League student. *Has replaced "white shoe" since c1955. Prob. from the image of a fraternity key or pin.*

kick down. To shift to a lower gear. *Mainly truck drivers' use; some automobile racing and sports car use.*

kicks*. *n.pl.* Shoes. *Jazz use.*

kimble. *v.i.* To try hard to be liked, popular, etc. *Some student use, mainly synthetic.*

Kitty. *n.* A Cadillac car. *Mainly Negro use. From "Caddy" via "Cat."*

klepto. *n.* A kleptomaniac.

klutz. *n.* A stupid, worthless person. *From the Yiddish* (Ger. *Klotz* = lump, block).

knock*. *v.t.* To have under control; to be assured of having solved a problem or having gained a desired result; esp., in student use, to be certain of passing an examination or a course. *Since c1955.* —**er.** *n.* An important, prominent, or influential person, or one who talks and acts as if his words and views are important and influential.

kook*. *n.* A beginning or inexperienced surfer. *Some surfer use.*

kvetch. *v.i.* To complain, whine, be overly concerned with the negative. *n.* A person who complains or whines habitually. *From the Yiddish.*

L

lame. *adj.* Not in the know; naive; unaware of current fashions, attitudes, interests, etc., but not completely out of touch with them and hence capable of learning; somewhat "square."* *Some hipster use since c1960.*

large for. *adj.* Enthusiastic about; having a liking or strong desire for.

later. *interj.* Good-bye. *Shortened form of "See you later, (Alligator)." Some jive, jazz, and student use.*

lay a batch. In driving or racing a car, to leave black rubber marks during acceleration. *Hot-rod use.*

lay rubber. In driving or racing a car, to spin the wheels on the pavement, as in making a fast start, skidding, etc. *Automobile racing and hot-rod use.*

least, the. *n.* The worst. *adj.* Worthless or dull; "square."* *Some jazz use.*

leather. *adj.* Of or pertaining to sadists and masochists, whether heterosexual or homosexual; affecting leather jackets, boots, chain bracelets, etc., signifying that one is a sadist or masochist; sadistic or masochistic.

left-handed*. *adj.* Homosexual.

leg*. *n.* An Army infantryman. *Facetious and derog. paratrooper use, esp. in Vietnam.*

lez = les*.

lightfooted. *adj.* Homosexual. *Fairly common since c1955.*

like fun = like hell*. *Colloq.*

little Michael; little Mike = Mickey Finn*.

loid. *v.t.* 1. To unlock a door with a celluloid strip, as a burglar. *From "celluloid." Underworld use; the method and the word are replacing "jimmy."* 2. To rob a building or an apartment.

long hitter. A heavy drinker.

low-belly strippers. Marked playing cards. *Gambler use.*

lox. *n.* Liquid oxygen, esp. as used as a rocket fuel. *From combining the first letters of the words, reinforced by the stand. "lox" = smoked salmon. Early rocket and aerospace use.*

LSD; LSD-25. Lysergic acid diethylamid (D-lysergic acid diethylamide tartrate). *A potent but nonaddictive hallucinogenic drug. It is tasteless, odorless, colorless, and water-soluble. The initials are taken from the original Ger. name "Lyserg-Säure-Diaethylamid." The drug was created in 1938 by Dr. Albert Hofmann of the Sandoz Research Laboratories in Basel, Switzerland, on the 2nd day of the 5th month (May 2), hence the medical code name "LSD-25." Commonly known since c1962 when addicts, students, and others seeking new experiences began to use it by swallowing it in capsules or in small sugar cubes, 100 micrograms being the average beginner's dose, 300 micrograms the average dose of a habitual user. It causes hallucinations, illusions, and euphoria, initially accompanied by slight nausea, dilation of the pupils, etc., that last from four to eight hours. For several hours after this psychedelic period the user alternates between the hallucinogenic state and reality, followed by a period of fatigue and tension that may last up to 24 hours. About 5% of those who try LSD, prob. latent schizophrenics, suffer prolonged, severe, and dangerous psychotic reactions.*

lunch; lunchie; lunchy. *adj.* Stupid; inadequate.

M

macaroni. *n.* Any long, thin, flexible item that fig. resembles macaroni, specif. long, thin copper rods, various types of flexible tubing, radio antennas, etc.

macht nichts = mox nix.

mackman. *n.* A pimp; a "mack."*

maggot. *n.* A cigarette butt.

make it*. To be satisfied; to be true to one's personal inner needs and values.

make like. To imitate; to pretend to be; to act in a manner resembling someone or something. *For example, "Make like Einstein." = "Act intelligently" or "Be smart."*

make out*. To neck heavily or passionately.

make the scene*. To arrive, appear or be at a particular place or gathering.

Man, the*. *n.* 1. Anyone in authority; anyone to whom respect is due; one's employer. → 2. Anyone to whom obedience is owed or granted through fear; specif.

the police, a drug addict's peddler, an underworld vice boss, etc. → 3. Any person who sells narcotics: a "pusher"* or "connection."* *Addict use.* 4. A white man, esp. one in a position of authority, as a policeman, employer, etc.; white people, the white race; the white establishment, society, or culture, etc. *An extension of "the Man"* = the law. Negro use only.*

manhole cover. Any large, round, flat object, esp. a pancake, but also a plate, phonograph record, etc.

marge*. *n.* A female homosexual who takes the passive, female role. *Lesbian use.*

maricon. *n.* A male homosexual. *From the Sp.; often used as an interj. having a force equivalent to that of "bastard."**

mask*. *n.* Large wrap-around sun glasses as worn by hot rodders, traffic policeman, etc. *Some teenage and police use.*

Mau Mau. A Negro who belongs to or supports one of the more militant Negro nationalist organizations, esp. the Black Muslims. *From the name of the African terrorist organization that fought against the white government of Kenya during the 1950s before that country obtained its independence. Negro use.*

meat*. *n.* 1. A strong but stupid person; one whose physical deeds overshadow his mental powers; esp. a professional or college athlete. *Student use.* 2. A male considered as a sexual object; homosexual gratification. *Homosexual use.* 3. The amount of tread on an automobile tire. *Orig. automobile racing and teenage use.*

megillah. *n.* 1. Something considered as a whole, esp. a tedious, lengthy, excessively detailed speech, account, explanation, etc. 2. The complete details. *Usually in the expression "the whole megillah." From the Hebrew "megillah" = scroll, "The Megillah" = The Book of Esther.*

member. *n.* A fellow Negro. *Negro use only.*

mensch. *n.* Lit. and fig., a very manly man who is also sincere, affectionate, and agreeable; a sweet and masculine man. *From the Yiddish.*

Mexican red. A type of marijuana. *Addict and student use.*

Mickey Mouse; mickey mouse*. 1. Cheap, shoddy, or inferior; unfair, confused, or senseless; mean or "lousy."* 2. Simple; easy; childlike. 3. Foolish; inconsequential. *Mainly student use.* 4. An easy task; specif. an easy course in college, one that is of slight educational value and almost impossible to fail; "crib,"* "gut,"* "pipe."* *Student use.* 5. Action, behavior, etc., that is unnecessary, cowardly, confused, etc.; a mistake. *Mainly Armed Forces use.*

mince. *n.* A person who is considered unfashionable or not in touch with currently popular modes of dress, behavior, etc.; a bore; a "drip."* *Teenage use.*

mintie. *adj.* Homosexual, exhibiting or affecting mannerisms of the opposite sex; "gay"* or "queer."* *n.* A homosexual, esp. an aggressive or masculine lesbian. *Orig. homosexual use.*

mishugah; mishoogeh. *adj.* Mad, "nuts,"* crazy; witless. *From the Yiddish.*

Mister Tom. A Negro who seeks or has achieved middle-class white values or assimilation into white society or culture. *Negro use.*

mola. *n.* A homosexual.

monkey dish. A small serving dish or bowl, as a salad bowl, a bowl for peanuts, etc.

mono. *n.* Mononucleosis. *Widespread student use.*

moonlight. *v.i.* To work at a second, often part-time, job in order to supplement the salary from one's regular job. *Because the second job is often done in the evening after the usual day's* *work. Pop. during and since W.W.II.*

moonman. *n.* An astronaut who journeys to, explores, or lives on, the moon.

moose. *n.* A prostitute. *Armed Forces use in Korea. From the Japanese "musume" = girl.*

mope*. *n.* A fool; a stupid person.

mossback. *n.* An unsophisticated person; "hick"* or "hayseed."*

mother*. *n.* **1.** The social leader, spokesman, or most attractive member of a group of homosexuals. → **2.** Any homosexual or effeminate man. *Almost always used derisively, even by homosexuals themselves.* **3.** The leader, the most necessary member, or the one who gives others a sense of security in any illegal or immoral relationship; specif. one who peddles narcotics, a pimp, a madam of a brothel, one who carries a gun in a gang fight, etc. *These slang degenerations of the stand. "mother" used to show a psychologically dependent relationship have become fairly common in subgroup use since c1955.* **4.** A fine, interesting, or remarkable event, object, or person.

mox nix. It doesn't matter; it doesn't make any difference; it's not important. *Corruption of Ger. "es macht nichts." Post-W.W.II Army use in Ger., some civilian use since c1950.*

MTA. A medical-technical assistant. *Specif. a medical student, intern, or orderly in charge of clinic or hospital supplies when a registered doctor is not on duty, as at night; hence any nonofficial who is responsible for or has access to drugs. Addict and prison use.*

mui. *n.* A talisman or charm, as a devil's head, a tiny snake, etc. *Gypsy use.*

murphy*. *n.* Any confidence game in which the victim is left with a sealed envelope which he expects to contain a list of prostitutes, places to obtain narcotics, sure-thing stock-market or racing tips, or his share of money from an unethical or get-rich-quick scheme, etc., but which contains newspaper, scrap paper, or blank paper instead. *v.t.* To fleece a victim by such a confidence game.

N

narcos. *n.* Agents of the police narcotics squad; a narcotics detective. *Addict use. From "narcotics squad," reinforced by "nark."*

nash. *v.i., v.t.* To eat snacks; nibble. *n.* A snack; a little something eaten between meals. —**er.** *n.* A person who snacks frequently. *From the Yiddish.*

neat*. *adj.* Adroit; "keen,"* "swell."* *Although assoc. with the 1920's and said strongly as if it were sl., this is one of the stand. meanings of the word.*

nerd; nurd. *n.* A contemptible, undesirable, or unpleasant person, esp. one who is not in the know; a "square."* *Teenage use.*

nickel. *n.* A five-year prison sentence. *Some underworld use.*

nickel bag. Five dollars' worth of a drug, as a quarter-ounce of marijuana. *Addict use.*

nigger-pot. *n.* = moonshine*. (def. 1). *Some Southern use.*

nitro. *n.* **1.** Nitroglycerin, esp. as used in blowing open a safe. *Commonly used in crime movies and books.* **2.** Nitromethane, esp. as used as a fuel additive for automobiles. *Hot-rod and racing use.*

nitty-gritty. *n.* The basics or essentials of any situation, predicament, action, etc., esp. the hard, unvarnished facts, "brass tacks," or harsh realities. *Negro use.*

nod. *n.* A comatose state experienced by an addict after an injection of narcotics. *Addict use.*

nose cone. The ultimate; anything sensational or remarkable. *Because the nose cone of a space rocket is as "far out"* as one can get. Some teenage use c1961.*

no sweat. No problem; with no

difficulty; easily. *Usu. as a reply to a question or to a statement expressing doubt.*

nowhere. *adj.* Dull, "square,"* not "hip."* *Orig. cool and far-out use.*

nuke. *n.* Any nuclear weapon.

Number One*; **number one.** Very good; best. *Orig. Armed Forces use in Korea.*

number ten. Very bad; the worst. *Orig. Armed Forces use in Korea.*

nurd = nerd.

O

O.D.* *n.* An overdose of a narcotic. *Addict use.*

oil spot. In the war in Vietnam, a village or area, esp. one that has just been captured or pacified, used as a center from which to spread civilian and military influence farther into the hostile area. *Armed Forces use in Vietnam.*

old Joe. *n.* Any venereal disease, esp. syphilis or gonorrhea.

one-eye. *n.* 1. = hillbilly*. *Because family inbreeding, as in isolated areas, is popularly believed to make the eyes of children of each succeeding generation grow closer together. Arch. and rural use.* → 2. A stupid person; a mentally defective person, as a moron. 3. An automobile driving with only one headlight. *Some police use.*

one thou; one thousand. The worst; even worse than "number 10." *Orig. Armed Forces use in Vietnam.*

on the make. 1. To be available for sexual intercourse; promiscuous. → 2. To be willing to say or do anything in order to attain success, fame, money, etc.; ambitious and immoral. → 3. Habitually dishonest, said of an opportunist.

on the rims. With the absolute minimum amount of money necessary; on the borderline of poverty; cheaply, as cheaply as possible. *Thus one may live, travel, or operate a business "on the rims." The image is that of an automobile without the luxury of tires.*

ouch. *n.* A wound; or injury.

out*. *adj.* 1. Not modern, popular, or in accord with modern tastes, fads, or trends. *Colloq.* 2. Uninformed; not "hip"*; "square."*

out of it. 1. With little or no chance to win or succeed; not considered capable of succeeding; not worthy of regard or respect. 2. Elated, happy, 3. Not concerned with mundane things, as when under the influence of a drug, obsession, all-consuming idea, etc.; in a state of euphoria. 4. Not "with it"*; stupid; "square."*

out of sight = way-out*. *Jazz, cool, and student use. An extension of "far out."*

P

P; pee; pea*. Any of various basic units of foreign currency beginning with the letter "p," esp. the Mexican peso or the Vietnamese piaster.

paddy*; **patty.** *n.* 1. A worthless or lazy person. *Orig. hobo use.* 2. A white person, esp. one despised. *Negro use only.*

pad out. To go to sleep. *Some beat and student use since the 1950s when "pad"* (def. 4) gained currency.*

Panamanian red = Mexican red.

paper*. *v.t.* To distribute many free tickets or passes to a theater, auditorium, etc. in order to ensure a large audience. *Theatrical use.*

pasty; pastie. *n.* One of a pair of small circular pieces of adhesive material, often decorated with sequins, etc., applied to the nipples by a burlesque performer, exotic dancer, etc. in order to satisfy laws banning the display of bare breasts, or as a gesture of propriety. *Burlesque and theatrical use.*

pay dues. 1. Fig., to put in a period of apprenticeship, as holding a series of menial jobs while working one's way toward a specific goal. **2.** To have to work hard, lose money, suffer, or in some other way find oneself paying the penalty for past mistakes, work hastily done, or for entering into ill-considered relationships or bad habits. *Thus, a convict is "paying dues," as is a drug addict who is trying to break his addiction, as is a student who is suffering over a lost girl or retaking a course he failed to pass.*

payola. *n.* Bribery money paid by recording companies, singers, etc., to disc jockeys for promoting and playing their records so they will become popular. *Common in the music industry since the 1930s.*

pecks. *n.pl.* Food. *Teenage gang and addict use. Prob. derives from "peckings"* = *food; orig. Negro use.*

penetrate. *v.t.* To break and enter; to break into or enter a room, apartment, building, etc., secretly and without permission. *Some Central Intelligence Agency and underworld use.*

pep pill. Any amphetamine pill.

Philadelphia bank roll. A roll of $1 bills with a $10 or $20 bill wrapped around the outside.

pick. *n.* A phonograph.

piddle. *v.i.* To piss. *Colloq.*

piece*. *n.* An ounce of heroin or other narcotic. *Addict use.*

piece of cake. Any task or duty that is easy to perform. *Orig. Brit. use.*

pigeon*. *n.* A counterfeit, void, or useless bill, ticket, or pass that is used, sold, or cashed as if it were good; esp. a losing ticket on a race, lottery, etc., that is sold or cashed as a winning ticket.

pin*. *v.t.* **1.** To pursue a member of the opposite sex in hopes of romance and/or sex. **2.** To understand another person, and that person's motive, thoroughly; to be able to predict what another person will say, do, or think, esp. for the purpose of

taking countermeasures. **3.** To know, recognize; to look at, survey. —**ned.** *adj.* Constricted (said of the pupils of the eyes).

pincers. *n.pl.* The eyes. *Some student use since c1964, esp. among young teenagers. Pop. by the Brit. singing group the Beatles.*

pipe*. *n.* **1.** A telephone. **2.** The part of a wave that is fastest, where the water rolls over and downward. *Surfer use.*

piss poor. Very poor, wrong, or weak; disgustingly poor, bad, inefficient, etc. *Like "piss and vinegar,"* this a "piss" expression usually considered not taboo.*

pix*. *n.* A homosexual.

pizzazz. *n.* **1.** Any item or trimming designed mainly to attract attention or give a gaudy appearance; specif. chromium strips, oversized grills and headlights, etc., that give automobiles a sporty or new look. **2.** Loud, colorful, aggressive advertising or salesmanship. *adj.* Sporty; flashy; esp. used to refer to automobiles having unnecessary gadgets reminiscent of true sport or racing cars, such as bucket seats, manual four-speed gearshifts, etc.

plasma. *n.* Rocket fuel. *Aerospace use.*

play on down. To go from one place to another. *Jazz and beat use.*

plonk. *n.* A boring or socially awkward person.

pluck*. *n.* = plunk*.

plug. *n.* An advertisement or favorable statement, specif. one that is received free of charge. *Orig. advertising and show business use; now common.* —**ged.** *adj.* Angry. *Most common c1935.* —**ola.** *n.* **1.** Compensation given television performers, producers, writers, etc., for mentioning a manufacturer's product in the course of a program. *Payment may be in cash but is usually in kind, the person receiving the car, or refrigerator, etc., mentioned. Orig. television use, now also applied to movie directors,* *newspaper writers, etc.; coined by analogy with the more pop. "payola."* 2. The free advertisement or favorable comment or review itself; a "plug."

pogey*; pogie; pogy. *n.* 1. Free food, as given out by a charity; food or food packages as sent by parents or friends to a student, soldier, or prisoner away from home, esp. sweets. 2. A homosexual. *Because gifts of food or sweets may be used to tempt another into a homosexual relationship.*

point*. *n.* A hypodermic needle; "spike." *Addict use.*

pop*. *n.* Nitromethane or any other fuel additive for automobiles and hot rods. *Automobile racing and hot-rod use. v.i.* To take narcotics or a shot of narcotics by injection. *Addict use.*

popout. *n.* A mass-produced surfboard. *Surfer use.*

potato digger. An undesirable person; a "square."*

pothead. *n.* A marijuana user. *From "pot"* = "marijuana." *Addict use.*

poundcake. *n.* A beautiful or desirable girl. *From "pound"* + "cake."

pro*. *n.* A prophylactic for the prevention of venereal disease. *Orig. W.W.II Armed Forces use.*

prosty; prostie. *n.* A prostitute; "prossie."*

prune*. *v.t.* To out-accelerate another driver in a drag race. *Hotrod use.*

pseud. *n.* A fake or phoney person or thing. *From the prefix "pseudo."*

psych out. 1. To lose control through fear; to lose one's nerve. 2. To understand someone; to discover someone's deeper psychological motivations.

pucker. *n.* Fear.

pud*. *n.* An easy course; a "snap."* *Some student use.*

pudding. *n.* Money. *Some student use since c1964, esp. among young teenagers. Pop. by the Brit. singing group the Beatles.*

puff*. *n.* Lit. and fig. a free advertisement; a favorable mention of a product or brand name in a news report; a favorable mention of a business firm or individual; a "squib."* *v.t.* To extol or praise highly, esp. an article for sale.

pull a train. Of a girl, to have sexual intercourse with several males consecutively. *Orig. West Coast motorcycle club (Hell's Angels) use; now some student use.*

push the panic button*. To become momentarily immobilized through fear, anxiety, nervousness, etc.; to become panicky, unnerved, or irrational.

pussycat. *n.* An agreeable or sweet person of either sex; "doll."* *Sometimes used as a term of endearment in direct address. Orig. theatrical use.*

pussy whipped. Henpecked; dominated by one's wife or girl friend.

put-on*. *n.* A person who fakes good taste, class, or being "hip."*

put [someone] on. To tease, make fun of, or play for a fool; to misrepresent something to; to convince someone that something fake is real. *One of the most common slang expressions to gain currency since c1956. Orig. jazz, student, and swinger use.*

putz. *n.* = prick*. *From the Yiddish.*

PX. 1. Post Exchange, a government-owned store, similar to a department store, located on a military base and selling articles to military personnel at prices generally lower than retail prices elsewhere. 2. Standardized; common. *Some Army use.* —ies. *n.pl.* = falsies*. *Armed Forces use, orig. in Korea, because such American items can only be obtained in a "PX."*

Q

quad*. *n.* Any automobile having four headlights. —s. *n.pl.* A set of four headlights on an automobile.

qualm. *v.t.* To bother or disturb. *Some student use.*

queer for. To have an inordinate or uncontrollable liking for something, ranging from a type of work to music, clothes, hobbies, food, etc. *Not taboo, orig. used without any homosexual implication though now occasionally used with humorous or ironic homosexual connotation.*

quick. *adj., adv.* Tight; snugly.

quit it. To die. *Some Negro use.*

R

rack*. *n.* = pad*; crib. *Some jazz, beat, and student use.* —ed. *adj.* Under control; mastered; sure of success or of the desired result; confident of passing an examination or course. *From the billiard image of racking up winning points.*

racket*. *n.* A party or social gathering, esp. a rough or drunken one.

rag top; rag-top. *n.* An automobile with a convertible top; a "chopped top."

rain. *v.i.* To complain. *Orig. Negro use.*

raked. *adj.* Of a modified car or hot rod, having the front end lower than the rear end. *Hot-rod use.*

R and R* = rock and roll*.

rat*. *v.i.* To wander; to idle or loaf.

rat fink. A treacherous, despicable, or unpleasant person. *Pop. by theatrical use.*

ream [someone] out = chew out.

Reb = Rebel.

Rebel. *n.* A white Southerner. *Commonly used among non-Southerners as a jocular epithet. Orig. derog; from the Civil War's "Johnny Rebel"* = Confederate soldier. *Colloq.*

ricky-tick. *adj.* 1. Pertaining to the jumpy popular music of the 1920s; ragtime. 2. Old-fashioned; out-of-date.

ride*. *n.* 1. A horse race. 2. An automobile race. 3. = trip. *LSD users and student use.*

rif*. *n.* A demotion. *v.t.* To demote.

rigor. *n.* Lack of enthusiasm; coldness in attitude; an unwillingness to perform. *From "rigor mortis" and punning on "vigor." In theatrical use before c1960 but more common thereafter, with the pronunciation "riguh" in imitation of President John F. Kennedy's pronunciation and frequent use of the word "vigor," in his Boston accent.*

roach*. *n.* An unattractive or unpopular girl. *Student use.*

rock*. *v.t.* To surprise; shock; stun.

roll in the hay. Sexual intercourse. *Usu. humorous use because of its rustic connotation.*

romp. *v.t.* 1. To smash or break something. → 2. To fight or quarrel with someone. *n.* A fight. *From the Sp. reflexive verb "romper(se)"* = to break. *Orig. N.Y.C. teenage street-gang use, introduced by Puerto Rican youths.*

rooty. *adj.* Sexually aroused or passionate; "horny"*; rutty.

rosewood. *n.* A policeman's nightstick; a "billy."* *Orig. underworld argot, now mainly Negro use.*

rough trade. *n.* A tough or sadistic homosexual, as one who affects meanness, wears boots, etc.; a male homosexual who prefers anal intercourse for sadistic reasons; a male prostitute who caters to such homosexuals. *Orig. homosexual use.*

round-eye. *n.* An Occidental woman, as opposed to an Oriental. *Armed Forces use in Japan and Korea.*

rug merchant. A spy. *Humorous ref. to the fact that spies often pose as foreign traders. Cold war use since c1960.*

run on the rims = on the rims.

S

S.A. 1. Sex appeal. *Applied most often to women, but can be applied to men. Often used to de-*

scribe movie stars, celebrities, etc., but also used in ordinary conversation about people one knows. 2. Santa Anita racetrack. 3. San Antonio, Texas.

Sam; sam. adj. Having sex appeal and magnetism, usu. said of a male. n. Masculine sex appeal and magnetism; a male with sex appeal and magnetism. Student use.

—san. One in charge. Orig. Armed Forces use in Korea. This suffix is used to follow an English or pidgin word to = the top one or boss. Thus "Mama-san" = boss mother, the madam of a brothel; "Papa-san" = the man in charge, etc.

sandbag*. v.i., v.t. To win a race; drive very fast. Hot-rod use.

S and M. Lit., sadism and masochism; a sadist and a masochist; any sexual pervert; sexual perversions of any sort. Orig. homosexual use; some general use since c1962.

sao. n. A repulsive, disagreeable, dishonest, or stupid person. Armed Forces use in Vietnam. From the Vietnamese.

savage*. adj. The very best, excellent, superlative. Student use.

scam. n. A swindle, esp. a dishonest carnival concession or game of chance. Carnival use. v.t. To swindle; to rob or cheat, usu. of a small sum of money.

schatzi; schanzi. n. A German girl friend; a German prostitute. From Ger. "schatz" = treasure, diminutive = sweetheart. Post-W.W.II Army use from soldiers stationed in Germany.

schlang. n. = prick*. From the Yiddish.

schmuck. n. = prick*. From the Yiddish.

schtoonk. n. A contemptible person; "stinker."* From the Yiddish.

scobe. n. A Negro. Negro use.

screech*. n. Cheap, inferior whisky, esp. homemade or bootlegged; "rotgut."*

scrub. v.t. 1. Fig., to wash away a score or mark; to tie, eliminate, or eradicate an opponent's score. Colloq. 2. To cancel or stop, usually referring to a sports contest or a missile-launching operation; to ignore or forget a person, deed, or idea; to fire an employee; to cancel a planned action; to postpone an activity; to eliminate a plan from consideration. Fig., to wash something out of existence, similar to the image of "wiping a slate clean."

scrub club. Any group, factory, office, scientific or business project, etc., that has proved inefficient or had many failures.

scuffle*. n. = scruff*. In the transition from carnival to general theatrical use "scruff" has become "scuffle."

send-up. n. A parody; an instance of mocking, teasing, or pulling someone's leg; an instance of "putting on" someone.

set*. n. A small party or social gathering; a personal conversation; a good time shared with good friends. Some jazz, beat, and Negro use.

shades. n.pl. A pair of sunglasses; sunglasses. Orig. bop musician use c1948–c1955; now mainly beat and student use.

shaft*. v.t. To take advantage of; to victimize; to deceive.

shank*. n. A knife.

shaved. adj. Of a car, having the ornamentation and unnecessary hardware removed. Hot-rod use.

sheep-dip. n. Cheap, inferior liquor.

sheik. v.t. To tease; to deceive in a joking way.

shirt; shirty. adj. Excellent, great, wonderful. Some student use.

shmeck; shmack; smack. n. Heroin. Addict use.

shoe*. n. 1. A plainclothes policeman or a detective. From "gumshoe."* Mainly underworld use. 2. A forged passport. Some recent Central Intelligence Agency and underworld use. 3. An automo-

bile tire. *Orig. racing driver and mechanic's use.*

shook. *adj.* = shook up*.

shoot [someone] down. 1. To ruin someone's chance to win or succeed. 2. To deflate someone's ego; to put someone to shame, as by pointing out a lie, exaggeration, or character flaw. 3. To defeat, outdo, or best. *Mainly student use.*

short. *v.t.* To inhale heroin or cocaine in crystal form. *Addict use.*

shot. *n.* One's habit, hobby, or vice; one's penchant, "kick,"* or "bag." *Since c1960.*

showboat*. *v.t.* To take advantage of one's superior rank; to bully or exact patronage from an inferior.

shrink. *n.* = head shrinker*. *Orig. Calif. use c1960.*

shtick. *n.* 1. A special talent, attainment, or ability; a typical trait or characteristic. 2. A part, detail, item, etc., that is attractive and appealing and has its own individuality and essence; a "bit."* 3. That which attracts, appeals, elicits a response, etc.; "gimmick."* *From the Yiddish.*

shuffle. *v.i.* To fight; to have a "rumble."* *Teenage street-gang use.*

sick*. *adj.* To be in need of an injection of narcotics. *Addict use.* *n.* The extreme physical discomfort and craving felt by a drug addict in need of a drug. *Addict use.*

side*. *n.* A single band on a long-playing record.

sister. *n.* A female Negro. *Negro use only.*

sit fat. To be in a powerful, successful, or commanding position.

sitzfleisch. *n.* Perseverance. *Based on Ger. and lit.* = *sitting flesh or buttocks, used only fig. to* = *the patience to sit in one place until a problem is solved.*

siwash*. *v.t.* 1. To blacklist. 2. To prohibit someone from buying liquor. *Orig. Chinook jargon,* from "Siwash" = "American Indian." *Northwestern use.*

skag. *n.* Someone or something foolish, undesirable, repulsive, dull, or insignificant. *Teenage use.*

ski bunny. An attractive girl who may or may not ski, but spends much time with skiers. *Some skier use.*

skim. *n.* Income, usually gross winnings, that is not reported by a gambling casino to state or federal revenue collectors. *From the image of skimming the cream off whole milk. Gambling use.*

skim board. A round or oval disc used in riding shallow water or a spent wave on the slope of a beach. *Surfing use.*

skin*. *n.* 1. An automobile or truck tire, esp. one with a worn-out or smooth tread. *Orig. truck-driver and hot-rod use.* 2. A person; "head"* (def. 4). *v.t.* To disarm a person or a military device. *Armed Forces, underworld, and police use.* —**ned.** *adj.* Unarmed, said of a person who habitually carries a weapon, or esp. of a military vehicle whose guns, rocket launchers, etc., have been removed to increase its speed for reconnaissance missions. *Armed Forces, underworld, and police use.* —**ny.** *n.* Information; inside or authentic information; the facts; the "poop."* *Mainly student use.*

skin-head*. *n.* 1. A man with a shaved head or a closely cropped head of hair. → 2. A Marine recruit.

skin house. A burlesque theater or a movie theater showing burlesque movies.

skinny-dip. *v.i.* To swim in the nude.

skin pop. To take an intramuscular injection of narcotics, as opposed to an injection taken directly into a vein. *Addict use.*

skunk*. *n.* Any unidentified and possibly hostile object seen on a radar screen. *Navy use.*

slam*; slammer. *n.* Jail; a jail. *Some Negro and beat use.*

slat*. *n.* A ski. *Skier use.*

slice*. *v.t.* To cheat, as by overcharging.

slick*. *n.* An automobile tire with but little tread left; a wide, smooth-tread tire, esp. as used in hot-rod races.

slim. *n.* A tobacco cigarette; a "straight" or "square." *Some jazz musician use.*

smack* = shmeck.

small change = small potatoes*.

smashing*. *n.* Kissing or "necking." *Teenage use.*

smoke*. *n.* Lies, big talk, exaggeration, or flattery.

snake*. *n.* An unpleasant, cheap, or despicable person. *v.t.* To get into trouble. *Usu. in the expression "to get snaked." Some Negro use.*

snap*. *v.i.* To laugh; to mock or tease. *Some Negro and beat use.*

snipe*. *n.* Any member of an aircraft carrier who services and maintains the airplanes. *Navy use.*

snort*. *v.i., v.t.* To take a narcotic by inhaling or smoking. *Addict use.*

snow bunny = ski bunny. *Some skier use.*

snuff. *v.t.* To kill someone; fig., to snuff out another's life.

sobe. *adj.* Sober. *Some student use since c1960.*

sock*. *n.* A drummer's set of double cymbals operated by a foot pedal, as used in dance and jazz bands. *Musician use.*

socked in. *adj.* Of an airport, unable to allow landings because of fog, rain, snow, etc.

sop*. *v.i.* To drink, esp. to drink beer or liquor. *From such older phrases as "sopping it up" = to drink large quantities of beer or liquor.*

soul. *adj.* 1. Negro; pertaining to or having the essence of things, feelings, moods, etc., that are considered to be basically Negro; esp. having or expressing authentic sensitivity, emotional sincer-

ity, a feeling of "the blues,"* etc., which status-seeking, commercialized, puritanical white Americans do not have. *Orig. Negro use; wide jazz and musician use; now common.* 2. Not segregated; welcoming, catering to, or friendly to Negroes. *Negro use only. n.* Profound and authentic sensitivity, feeling, or sincerity.

soul brother. A male Negro; a "blood brother." *Negro use only.*

Soul City. Harlem. *Negro use.*

soul food. 1. Food that is generally associated with the South, as black-eyed peas, hominy grits, ham hocks, etc. 2. Anything sincerely, profoundly, and personally satisfying, ranging from sex and love to music. *Still mainly Negro use.*

soul music. Modern jazz that is based upon or emphasizes blues or Negro gospel music.

soul sister. A female Negro. *Negro use only.*

Soulville = Soul City. *Negro and jazz use.*

soup*. *n.* Foam formed by a breaker; the froth or foamy part of a wave. *Surfer use.*

spider*. *n.* A skillet, esp. an iron skillet as used by hunters, hikers, etc.

spike*. *n.* A hypodermic needle or syringe, esp. a homemade one used by a narcotics addict. *Addict use.*

splay. *n.* Marijuana. *Some addict use.*

splib. *n.* A Negro. *Negro use.*

split*. *v.t.* To hit someone, esp. to knock a person out with one's fists or a weapon.

spooked*. *adj.* Annoyed; bothered. *Some jazz and beat use.*

spoon*. *n.* The nose-to-tail bow or curve in a surfboard. *Surfer use.*

springbutt. *n.* An overly diligent or enthused person; an "eager beaver."

square*. *n.* 1. A regular, tobacco cigarette, esp. as opposed to a marijuana cigarette; a "straight" or "slim." *An extension of "square"* = not "hip."* Orig.*

addict use. Some Negro, hip, and student use since c1960. → 2. A person who does not use or approve of others using drugs, esp. marijuana. *Addict and student use.*

squat. *n.* = zot.

stack. *n.* An exhaust pipe on an automobile. *Usu. in the expression "twin stacks" = a dual exhaust, as orig. on some European and sports cars.*

stallion. *n.* = stud*.

stand tall. To be ready for an inspection; to be prepared; to have things under control. *Army use.*

stick*. *n.* 1. A ski; a ski pole. *Skier use.* 2. A surfboard. *Some surfer use.* 3. A manual gearshift on an automobile, attached to the floorboards. —*s.* *n.pl.* A pair or set of various sporting equipment, as golf clubs, fishing rods, etc.

stink with. To have an abundance of.

stone*. *adj.* Attractive, fine, desirable. *Negro use.*

storch. *n.* 1. An ordinary man; a guy. 2. = mark*.

straight*. *adj.* Having taken an injection of a narcotic and thus able to go about one's business, esp. said of a drug addict after his first injection in the morning. *Addict use.* *n.* A regular tobacco cigarette, esp. as opposed to one containing marijuana; a "square." *Orig. addict use; now some jazz, beat, and student use.*

straighten [someone]. *v.t.* 1. To obtain a narcotic for or administer a narcotic to. *Addict use.* → 2. To help; aid. *Some beat and student use.*

Street,* the. *n.* 1. The world outside of prison; normal free life or society. *Some underworld use.* 2. Society or the world as a place of violence, immorality, cruelty, etc. *Mainly Negro use.*

stretch out. To play a musical instrument without restraint; to become completely uninhibited; to express one's emotions intensely and without restraint. *Jazz musician use. Lit., to play "riffs"**

or improvise after the orig. harmonic statement in jazz, to leave the written bars of harmony and stretch one's own imagination and technique in improvising on it.

string out. To use or be addicted to narcotics; to be "high"* on a drug. *Addict and student use.*

strung out. 1. Disturbed, worried, concerned; involved with psychological problems. *Some Negro use.* 2. Sick and disturbed or thin, weak, and nervous from a lack of or long use of narcotics. *Addict and student use.*

sub*; subby. *n.* = Hero*. *Because the long sandwich with tapering ends resembles a submarine's shape.*

submarine watching = necking*. *Some student use. Pop. by rock-and-roll announcer Murray the K.*

suck*. *n.* Special influence or favor which has been purposefully curried. *Usually found in the phrases, "to get suck" or "to have suck."*

sunshades. *n.pl.* A pair of sunglasses; sunglasses; "shades." *Neither as old nor as common as "shades."*

surf bunny = beach bunny. *Surfer use.*

swave. *adj.* Fine, wonderful, splendid. *Teenage and student use.*

sweet tooth. Addiction to narcotics. *Some addict use, based on the standard meaning = a craving or extreme liking for sweets.*

swing*. *n.* A short or hurried journey that includes several stops or visits in one region of a country or continent. *Now usu. applied to travelers who use jet airplanes to hasten their trips. Colloq.* *v.i.* 1. To belong; to run with a gang. *Teenage street-gang use.* 2. To follow, cultivate, be in rapport with, or embody currently fashionable attitudes and tastes; to be a member of a vanguard that is considered socially and culturally stylish, sophisticated, etc. 3. To be active and exciting. —er. n. 1. A person who inhabits a socially fashionable world and whose taste in dress, music, entertainment and places of entertainment, resorts, etc., reflects what is considered modern, stylish, youthful, and sophisticated. *A new and very pop. use, and an American type since c1961.* 2. Any person who cultivates or who is representative of, or a leader in, what is considered fashionable, sophisticated, etc., within a given social framework. —ing. *adj.* Fashionably lively; tasteful, sophisticated, modern; avant-garde; following, representing, or embodying whatever is currently considered most sophisticated, exciting, etc.

swipe*. n. Any homemade alcoholic beverage, esp. raw, inferior whisky or wine.

switch on. 1. = turn on. 2. To be part of the modern scene; to be "hip"* to enjoy modern fads, music, etc.

T

tach. *n.* Tachometer.

tailgate; tail-gate*. *v.i.* To drive a motor vehicle too closely behind the vehicle in front.

take a leak. To urinate. *Very common.*

take gas. To lose control of one's surfboard while riding a wave and fall into the water. *Surfer use.*

take [someone's] mind. To disturb someone, to upset someone psychologically; to obsess someone. *Mainly Negro and beat use.*

take off*. n. To rob. *Underworld and police use.*

tap*. n. The act of, or a device for, secretly listening to or, esp., recording the telephone conversations of others. *v.t.* To listen to or record a telephone conversation secretly or to do so to a specific telephone, address, or person. *From the earlier "wiretap."*

taste*. n. 1. A share or percentage of profits. *Theatrical use.* 2. Any

alcoholic drink. *Usu. as offered by a host as "would you like a taste?" or in ordering from a bartender, "Give me a taste of bourbon."*

teenybop; teenybopper. n. A stereotyped teenage rock-and-roll enthusiast; a teenager considered as an annoying, insignificant, undesirable boring burden. *Orig. Negro use.*

ten cents = dime bag. *Addict use.*

that's the way the cookie crumbles = that's the way the ball bounces*. *The most pop. of many variations, all beginning with "that's the way—" followed by a mundane or humorous action such as: "—the bread rises," "—the doughnut rolls," "—the fish fry," "—the ink spills," "—the owls hoot," "—the pill breaks," "—the stars shine," "—the wine spills." The last words are often created on the spur of the moment as nonce expressions and may contain images taken from popular sayings, jokes, etc.*

Three, the. The DC-3 airplane; the "Gooney Bird." *Mainly airplane pilot use.*

thud. n. 1. An airplane crash; esp. the act or an instance of being shot down by an enemy aircraft or by anti-aircraft fire. *Orig. Air Force use in Vietnam.* 2. An F-105 Thunderchief jet fighter plane. *Air Force use in Vietnam. So called because of their record of being shot down in the Vietnam war.*

ticked off = tee'd off*.

tick [someone] off. To annoy; to make angry. *Usu. in the passive.*

tip*. *v.i., v.t.* To be sexually unfaithful to one's spouse or current lover; to "cheat." n. An attractive, pert girl; a "chick"; "fox." *Orig. Negro and jazz use; now becoming beat and student use.*

tish. *v.t.* Lit. and fig., to pad something with tissue paper; specif. to wrap bills of large denomination around a tissue-paper core so that one appears to have more money than one actually has; gen. used to imply any physical exaggeration, as to make an automobile look longer than it is by adding large bumpers, for a woman to wear a padded brassiere, etc. *Orig. and mainly carnival use.*

t. o.'d = tee'd off*.

Tom. *n.* = Uncle Tom*. *Negro use.*

ton. *n.* Specif., a speed of 100 miles per hour; any high speed. *Orig. motorcycle racing use = an average speed of 100 m.p.h. during a race or over a measured course. Some teenage and automobile racing use since c1960.*

tool*. *n.* A diligent, overstudious student; a "grind."* *Student use.*

touchdown. *n.* The landing of an airplane, lit. and fig. the moment the wheels touch the runway.

touristas, the; turistas, the. *n.* Diarrhea. *This post-W.W.II term is replacing "G.I.s" as more Americans travel abroad as tourists. Based on Sp. word formation; prob. first used by tourists returning from Mexico. Changes in water, food, altitude, and time zones often upset travelers' stomachs, and the term need not imply a serious illness or contact with tainted food or drink.*

tracks*. *n.pl.* Scars or marks on the arm or leg caused by repeated puncturing with hypodermic injections. *Addict use.*

trade. *n.* A man or woman considered sexually, esp. in a commercial sense; a "piece."* *Orig prostitute and homosexual use.*

trank; tranx. *n.* A tranquilizer, a pill or capsule containing a tranquilizer.

tref; treff; trif; triff. *n.* A clandestine meeting to transact illegal business, such as to plan a robbery, distribute illegal drugs or weapons, etc. *From the Ger. "das Treffen" = meeting. Not used in the underworld until after W.W.II. Prob. orig. came to*

U.S. *Central Intelligence Agency from German spies and thence spread to the underworld.*

trey. A $3 packet of a narcotic, esp. a $3 "bag" of cocaine. *Addict use.*

trif; triff = tref.

trip*. *n.* 1. An instance of being under the influence of a drug, esp. LSD. *Addict, habitual users', and student use.* 2. Any activity, outing, period of time, or way of life. *Some beat and student use since c1965.*

tube. *n.* The inside curve of a wave. *Surfer use.*

tube, the. *n.* 1. Television considered as a medium. 2. A television set. *Orig. teenager use c1955; increasing use since c1960. From the cathode-ray oscilloscope "tube" that is the basis, and forms the screen, of television receivers.*

tube it. To flunk an examination or course in school. *Student use.*

tuff. *adj.* 1. = tough*. (def. 2). *Very pop. student and teenage use since c1962.* → 2. Good-looking, energetic, and popular. *Student and teenage use.*

tullies, the. *n.pl.* Remote or rural areas. *From "tule" or "tule land" = Southwestern regions covered with tule bulrushes.*

tuned in. 1. Skillful; expert; aware of problems and solutions in one's work. 2. Aware; knowing; in rapport with modern attitudes, fads, etc. *Teenage and synthetic use; one of many words "squares"* consider "hip."**

turn [someone] off. To bore; depress.

turn [someone] on. 1. To introduce; to arouse someone's curiosity or interest in something. 2. To supply someone with something, as a drink, cigarette, advice, etc. 3. To become or get "high"* on narcotics. → 4. To arouse or excite sexually; to be sexually appealing to someone. 5. To excite, stimulate, or thrill someone; to cause to become interested, enthused, alert, happy, etc. *One of* *the most common sl. expressions to gain pop. since c1960. Orig. addict, jazz, and student use; now common.*

turn out* = pull a train, esp. for the first time.

twink. *n.* An effeminate male; a homosexual; a "queer."*

twisted*. *adj.* High on narcotics. *Addict use.*

U

unflappable. *adj.* Calm and clear-thinking; lit., so competent and calm that one cannot become confused or make a mistake in an emergency. *Orig. Air Force use. The opposite term "flappable" has never existed.*

unglued. *adj.* 1. frantic, out of control, disorganized, wild. 2. insane, crazy.

unreal. *adj.* Unbelievably wonderful; great; excellent. *Cool, beat, and student use.*

unscrewed. *adj.* = unglued.

unzip. *v.t.* 1. To overcome someone's defenses; to break down resistance. 2. To solve a problem, find a solution for; to organize or accomplish successfully. —ped. *adj.* = unglued.

up*. *adj.* Under the influence of a narcotic; "high."* *Addict and student use.*

upstairs*. *n.* The inside of a freight car, where a lucky hobo might ride instead of below the car. *Hobo use.*

up tight. 1. Thoroughly known, remembered, or familiar, as a piece of music to be played by a jazz musician or the information necessary to pass an exam or course in school. *Orig. jazz use; now student use.* → 2. = hip*; with it*. *Beat and student use.* 3. O.K.; fine; everything is great. *Some cool and student use.* 4. In or pertaining to the Madison Avenue or Ivy League style of dress, esp. button-down shirts, vests, etc. *Some jazz and Negro use.* 5. tense; "hung up." *Mainly student use.*

urb. *n.* A large city, esp. a sophisticated, modern city where "hip"* people and "swingers" may find culture, excitement, jazz nightclubs, discotheques, bohemian neighborhoods, etc., as San Francisco, New York, London, etc. *Some use by "swingers," musicians, and beat people. From "urban."*

use. *v.i.* To be a drug addict; take narcotics or a dose of narcotics. *Addict use.*

V

V.C. 1. The Viet Cong or one of its soldiers, guerrillas, or supporters in South Vietnam. *Orig. Armed Forces use in Vietnam.* 2. A stupid, inept, or irresponsible soldier. *Armed Forces use in Vietnam.*

vette. *n.* A Corvette automobile. *Mainly hot-rod use.*

Victor Charlie = V.C. (def. 1). *Armed Forces use in Vietnam. From the communications symbols "Victor"* = V *and "Charlie"* = C.

Vietnik. *n.* One who demonstrates against America's involvement in or escalation of the Vietnam war, esp. a student, or "beatnik."* *Usu. derog.; most common in pro-Vietnam war tabloid newspapers. Based on "beatnik,"* and reinforced by being made to rhyme with it.*

W

walk heavy. 1. To be important; to be in a position to command or intimidate others. 2. To have or assume an appearance of importance or superiority. *Orig. Negro use.*

walk wide. To be careful; to be on one's guard. *Now mainly Negro and some beat use.*

WASP; wasp. *n.* A white Anglo-Saxon Prostestant; specif. a member of the dominant American middle class who is descended from the earlier northern European settlers of the country, as opposed to one belonging to a racial or religious minority or someone of more recent immigrant stock. *Used derog., usu. to refer to an average, noncreative, noncritical American who enjoys traditional American values, beliefs, fashions, entertainment, etc., unquestioningly. adj.* Of, pertaining to, or suitable for WASPs.

wax. *v.t.* 1. To beat up, injure severely, or kill. 2. To defeat decisively, as in a sports contest, military operation, etc.; "zap." —**ing.** *n.* A beating. *Underworld, police, and some Armed Forces use.*

wear a hat. To have a girl friend; to be married; fig., to be or become respectable. *Arch. except in theatrical use.*

weathercock. *v.i.* Of an airplane or missile, to tend to turn in the direction of the wind. *Aerospace and Air Force use.*

weejuns. *n.pl.* Moccasin-style loafers (shoes). *From the trademark. Teenage use.*

weight. *n.* 1. Influence. *Some underworld use.* 2. An ounce of marijuana or heroin. *Addict use.*

weirdo. *n.* = weirdie*.

whale; **Whale.** *n.* The A-3 Sky warrior, a twin-jet military airplane used to refuel other airplanes in flight. *Air Force use.*

wheels-up. *n.* The departure of an airplane from a runway, the take-off of an airplane. *Orig. and still in pilot use* = *the retraction of the wheels into the body of the airplane after it is airborne.*

whip out. To perform a prescribed greeting or stance, usu. from respect. *Orig.* = *to shake hands; at military schools* = *to stand at attention, present arms, etc.*

whipsaw. *v.t.* 1. To defeat an opponent easily. 2. To beat up another person badly. 3. To accomplish any task easily or rapidly.

white*. *adj.* Not good, lacking in feeling. *Orig. Negro jazz use.*

Whitey; **whitey.** *n.* A white person; white men, the white race; the white establishment, culture, society, etc. *Now the most common urban Negro sl. word for white man.*

wig*. *n.* A thrilling or satisfying experience, a "ball."* *Some jazz use.* *adj.* Excellent, wonderful, great. *Teenage use.*

wigged out. 1. Removed from reality. 2. Very high from the influence of narcotics. *Addict use.*

wig out. To react with unrestrained enthusiasm and appreciation; to be excited, aroused, or thrilled; to "flip"* or "dig"* completely. *Orig. jazz, Negro, and cool use; now some teenage use.*

Willie Fudd. The WF-2 propeller-driven airplane, designed and used as a flying radar center. *Navy use in Vietnam.*

wimp. *n.* An introverted, boring, overly solicitous person; a meek, passive person; one who is out of touch with current ideas, trends, fads, etc.; a "drip"* or "mince." *Some teenage and student use.*

wing it. 1. To leave; depart. 2. To start; get going. *Cool and student use.*

wipe*. *v.t.* To defeat or trounce an opponent.

wipe out*. To lose control of one's surfboard while riding a wave and fall into the water. *Used in the active voice, as in "I wiped out." Surfer use.* —**ed out.** 1. Conforming, dull; "square."* *Some beat use.* 2. Drunk. *Student use.*

wiretap. *n., v.t.* = tap.

woke. *adj.* = hip*. *Negro use.*

working girl. A prostitute. *Orig. prostitute use.*

works*. *n.pl.* The paraphernalia used to prepare and inject a drug: an eyedropper, hypodermic needle, and "cooker." *Addict use.*

workshoe. *adj.* Rugged, solid, long-lasting, dependable.

wuzzy*. *n.* A girl. *Some teenage use, via British rock-and-roll use, from the French "oiseau"* = *bird.*

Y

yard*. *v.i.* To have sexual relations with someone other than one's spouse or current lover; to be unfaithful; to "cheat."*

yenta. *n.* A talkative or gossipy woman. *From the Yiddish.*

yold. *n.* A gullible person, a dupe. *From the Yiddish.*

yo-yo*; yoyo. *n.* 1. A stupid, incompetent, or undesirable person; a "jerk."* *Orig. teenage and student use.* 2. A gullible person; a dupe.

Z

zap*. *v.t.* 1. To shoot someone. *Underworld, teenage street-gang, and Armed Forces use.* → 2. To defeat decisively, as in a sports contest, a military operation, etc.

zero cool. Very "cool"*; as "cool" as possible. *Synthetic jazz, cool, beat, and student use.*

zilch. *n.* A completely dull, ineffectual, unattractive, or insignificant person.

zip*. *n.* A score of zero; no score.

zoftig. *adj.* Plump in a sexually attractive or pleasing way, said of a woman. *From the Yiddish.*

zonked. *adj.* Drunk; dead drunk. *Student use.*

zoo. *n.* Any jungle or jungle area. *Army and Marine use in Vietnam.*

zot. *n.* A grade or a score of zero; "zip." *Student use.*

Dictionary of
Foreign Phrases and
Abbreviations
by Kevin Guinagh

For the first time, an intelligent reader's guide
to the most used expressions in Latin, French, Spanish,
Italian, German, Greek, Portuguese, etc.
Indispensable for crossword puzzlers.

75159/75¢
